Gardens of Court and Country

PUBLISHED FOR THE PAUL MELLON CENTRE FOR STUDIES IN BRITISH ART BY
YALE UNIVERSITY PRESS · NEW HAVEN AND LONDON

David Jacques

GARDENS OF
Court AND *Country*

ENGLISH DESIGN · 1630–1730

Designed by Emily Lees
Printed in China

Library of Congress Cataloging-in-Publication Data

Names: Jacques, David, 1948–
Title: Gardens of court and country : English design 1630–1730 / David Jacques.
Description: New Haven : Yale University Press, 2016.
Identifiers: LCCN 2015044970 | ISBN 9780300222012 (cl : alk. paper)
Subjects: LCSH: Formal gardens – Great Britain – Design – History – 17th century.
Classification: LCC SB466.G7 J334 2016 | DDC 712.0941 – dc23
LC record available at https://lccn.loc.gov/2015044970

A catalogue record for this book is available from the British Library

Half-title page: Anon, engraving of the rewards of husbandry, from Castell 1728, 55.
Reproduced by kind permission of John Harris.
Frontispiece: Leonard Knyff, a view of Hampton Court from the east (detail), *c.*1702. RCIN 404760.
Royal Collection Trust / © Her Majesty Queen Elizabeth II 2014.
Image on p. viii: Stoke Edith hanging: linen canvas embroidered with silk and wool, with some details
in appliqué (detail), 1710s. Victoria and Albert Museum, T.568-1996. © V&A Images.

Contents

Acknowledgements

Following the garden exhibition at the Victoria and Albert Museum in 1979 John Harris was invited by Batsford's to write a book on formal gardens. That never came to fruition, but he has made many discoveries and acute observations in his career, and has been unfailingly helpful and informative to me over many years. Indeed, he made over a very useful collection of photographs of formal gardens whilst the picture research for this book was underway.

In 1993, when I left English Heritage, I decided to reawaken a PhD that I was supposed to have been doing at the Courtauld Institute with John Newman as my supervisor. He allowed me considerable leeway, and intervened at appropriate moments, steering me to completion in 1999. I chose Tom Williamson as external examiner because I knew of his important work in East Anglia; he at least would understand that garden history starts by looking at particular places in detail, and he has been a friend before and since.

My professional life in historical research, producing surveys and/or management plans for Hampton Court, Chiswick House, Gray's Inn, Marble Hill, Compton Verney Hall, Stonyhurst Hall, Burton Constable Hall, Boughton House, Wotton House, Kenilworth Castle, and many other places, and my time at English Heritage, when I dealt with numerous examples of former formal gardens, brought me into contact with colleagues, historians, owners and their advisors. Walking the ground and exchanges of information with them have proved immensely valuable in understanding specific important gardens.

Similarly, my time teaching at the University of York and the Architectural Association involved booking lecturers, teaching my own coursework, and involving myself in student projects and theses, giving many opportunities to discuss points regarding formal gardens and correspond afterwards. My thanks go out to this community of generous-minded enthusiasts, including the students who unearthed much valuable material. But particular thanks are due to my erstwhile colleagues, Peter Goodchild, Jan Woudstra and the late Ted Fawcett, with whom I have shared research, illumation and discoveries on formal gardens over the years in both academic and professional spheres. Peter Goodchild has unstintingly shared work on Chiswick House, Holme Lacy House and elsewhere. Likewise, Jan Woudstra was a valuable colleague at Travers Morgan Planning on Chiswick House, the Privy Garden at Hampton Court and the Historic Royal Palaces Garden Strategy Group, and we have often swapped thoughts on Stainborough Hall, Chatsworth House, Squerryes Court and other places.

Others to thank over many years of often intermittent information gathering include Bill Brogden on Switzer, Peter Hayden who encouraged an early interest in Patshull and Ingestre, Judith Oppenheimer on Castle Howard, John Phibbs on many places and theories, Leo Godlewski on Shireoaks, Harriet Jordan as a colleague at English Heritage, Susan Cambell as an inspiration on Herriard and early kitchen gardens, Chris Taylor for his advice when on the English Heritage Gardens Committee in the late 1980s and up to the present, Brian Dix on the archaeology of the gardens at Kirby Hall and Hampton Court, Fiona Cowell for sending me the Gisburn plan, Edward Martin for sharing his researches on canals, Jennifer Meir on Farnborough Hall, Simon Thurley, Terry Gough and Susanne Groom as colleagues at Hampton Court, Richard Stone for getting me involved in Boughton House and Wotton House, Katherine Myers concerning the archives for Cannons, her thoughts on picturesque vision and her interpretation of Castell, and Sally O'Halloran whose thesis on gardeners it has been a pleasure to examine.

Collecting illustrations for a book like this is hard work, especially now that all one's old photography has been made redundant by digitisation. Many people have been helpful, but some have been generous too, amongst whom have been the Duke of Beaufort, Lord Braybrooke, Lord Astor, Charles Berkeley of Berkeley Castle, Elisabeth Prideaux-Brune of Prideaux Place, Charles and Mairie Wynne-Eyton of Tower, Gill Weston of the Melbourne Estate Office, Christine Hiskey of the Holkham Estates, Peter Goodchild, Min Wood over Hackwood, and Simon Scott of Northampton, whose own endeavours have resulted in *The Follies of Boughton Park Revisited* (Scott Publications: Northampton, 2011). Mrs Margaret Grace of the Beaconsfield and District Historical Society responded patiently to enquiries over several months.

In 2010 I was given a 'curatorial scholarship' at the Yale Center for British Art in New Haven, which gave me six weeks of delightful studenthood. The astonishing collection there, coupled with the helpful attitude of all staff that I met, gave me the valuable opportunity to inspect and consider the images of formal gardens in paint, print and pencil. My wife, Karen, and I treasured that short time insulated from all other pressures.

There are countless other librarians and archivists to whom I owe a debt, from early days in the Staffordshire and Surrey record offices over forty years ago, and to which my bulging files attest. Hence, many people may find traces of their conversations, advice, and information in this book, but the mixing and mingling of my thoughts has been the work of several decades and I hope that my informants and colleagues will forgive me if I have omitted a specific mention.

I should add a word on the approach to endnotes in this book. The research behind the thesis which has underpinned many of my observations on style included 300 histories of individual gardens, each headed by a list of owners, supported by a list of all known relevant sources, and divided into the principal overlays. Dates and designers were fed into a database, which had over 100 fields for possible garden elements. The number-crunching identified the decades during which such-and-such an element was commonly seen. Many of the statements in the text below derive from this analysis, but citing sources in full would result in it drowning in its own supporting evidence. If it seems that sources on particular gardens are cited sparingly it is for this reason, not because they are undervalued. I will gladly answer any reader's enquiries about the evidence for any statement made.

Finally, my greatest debt is to friends and family from whom I have selfishly withheld time and attention in pursuit of my own passions.

Note on the Text

Areas are given in acres. Rods (4 to the acre) and perches (40 to the rod) are also mentioned. 1 acre = 0.405 hectare.

Money is in pounds, shillings and pence, or *librae*, *solidi* and *denarii*, abbreviated to £ s d.

Dates are generally those in use prior to the reform of the calendar in 1754, after which the year started on 1 January rather than on 25 March. The convention of giving both years for the overlap period – for example, 28 January 1733/4 – was widely used in early Georgian times and has been followed here.

Place names are generally those used at the time for the place in question. Several have since changed; for example, referring to a house (not just a lodge) within a park as '[name] Park' was increasingly common from the late seventeenth century – for example, Moor Park and Bramham Park. See the section 'Parks and status' in Chapter Four.

Counties are given as the historic counties as they existed before local government reorganisation in 1888.

Some words for landscape elements had a more precise meaning than they do today, and when the more usual archaic spelling is used it is deliberate, e.g. 'visto' and 'bason', rather than 'vista' and 'basin'.

Prologue

Formal Gardens as a Topic

One modern garden historian has observed that 'Despite recent studies of the Italian influence on English gardens from 1660 to 1750 and several publications on the gardens of William and Mary, a comprehensive work on formal traditions in Britain after 1660 awaits its author'.[1] Indeed, while there are books on Capability Brown and Victorian gardens a-plenty, this period in English garden history has seldom been satisfactorily tackled as a whole. It has been my ambition for many years to remedy this, which has encouraged me to research the motives of the garden-makers, to explore several aspects of the period, including physical components such as *compartiments*, bowling greens and deer parks, as well as the style of formal gardens, and to ruminate on several of the major designs of the period, all of which themes have found their place in this book.

CR

The literature on gardens designed between 1630 and 1730

Older English garden histories skimmed lightly over the gardens of the period from 1630 to 1730, being content to show a few engravings by Leonard Knyff and Johannes Kip and share a few facts on the nurserymen George London and Henry Wise. English design history of the period has been treated largely as if it were homogeneous, without development, and essentially derivative and uninteresting. This is still the approach when English gardens are discussed in an international context. When histories of Western gardens have come to be written, the sixteenth century belongs to Italy, the seventeenth to France and the eighteenth to the 'English Garden'. English gardens of the seventeenth century are given no more regard than Italian gardens of the eighteenth.

The mid-twentieth century was a time of intense interest in the origins of the 'English landscape garden', a term unknown in the eighteenth century, when the irregular garden was described as 'natural', 'English' or 'modern'. Humphry Repton referred to 'landscape gardening', and the term 'the Landscape Garden' was first coined in about 1805. It was seized upon by Nikolaus Pevsner, who liked to think that garden design was a branch of the Picturesque movement, even though there is no evidence of this before the 1770s. When historians mentioned earlier, formal, gardens it was often in order to contrast them to ensuing naturalistic forms. This has led to aspects that were important in their time to be overlooked in favour of those that could be compared, usually unfavourably, to the later and more glorious period.

WHIGS AND ANTIQUARIES

One reason why gardens of the period 1630 to 1730 have been neglected is because formal gardens have, it seems, suffered from the distortions of polemicists from the outset of the 'natural taste' in the eighteenth century. In 1753 the novelist Francis Coventry identified William Kent as the reformer who rescued the nation from 'Dutch absurdity'.[2] The wit and poet Richard Owen Cambridge agreed, writing in 1755 that the Dutch taste 'for more than half a century deformed the face of nature in this country'.[3] This *post-hoc* invention of derogatory epithets such as 'Dutch' did not reflect the way that formal gardens were seen when they were made.[4] Cambridge, together with his fellow Whigs Horace Walpole and the poet William Mason, were promoting a narrative of garden history to accord with their preferred version of historical progress, with Kent's genius prevailing from the early 1730s. Walpole's essay 'On Modern Gardening', written in 1770, gave a detailed and seemingly plausible account of the overthrow of regular gardens by a style that followed the forms of landscape painting, and has been influential ever since.[5]

By the 1780s certain antiquaries, unconstrained by this Whig ideology, were no longer censorious of the taste of the previous century, and were appreciative in antiquarian and often picturesque terms of the ancient gardens remaining. They regretted

that concrete facts about them were hard to elicit. In 1782 Daines Barrington, a Chester circuit judge, delivered an account of the history of gardens to the Society of Antiquaries.[6] He assembled a number of literary references, including an essay from the 1710s by the garden writer Stephen Switzer, 'The History of Gardening'.[7] Barrington surmised that in Charles II's reign, 'probably many of what were then called improvements, might have been imitated from those of Lewis the Fourteenth'. William of Orange 'introduced or gave a vogue to clipt yews, with magnificent gates, and rails of iron'. He remarked on the gates at Leeswood Hall, Flintshire, a place which, he thought, was 'laid out by Switzer in Bridgeman's first style' (fig. 1).

Samuel Felton, another antiquary, published a compendium of miscellaneous writings on gardens, including short bibliographies under various headings.[8] He later wrote that he had 'formed a plan of publishing views of some secluded, curious old mansions, such as those not generally known to the public'.[9] Subsequently he lost interest – and indeed his notes – and it was the Picturesque movement rather than antiquarianism that kept the interest in formal gardens alive.

HISTORICISTS AND HISTORIANS

By the end of the eighteenth century the style of Lancelot 'Capability' Brown came under attack from promoters of the Picturesque, and garden designers were returning to terraces and then to parterres and avenues. Writers on taste sought some guidance on the earlier style that had displayed these elements. Repton, when first asked, made a simple division between the ancient, or formal, style that he associated with 'André le Nôtre' (the eighteenth-century and modern spelling of Le Nostre), and modern, or natural, gardening.[10] He himself devised a garden in 'the ancient formal style', with arcades after an illustration in John James's *Theory and Practice of Gardening*, first published in 1712 (fig. 2). However, in reply to an enquiry a few years later, he crafted his answer in terms of supposed national styles. The French was 'only a corruption of the Italian style, and was never generally adopted in England'.[11] He surmised that it was followed, at William's accession, by the

1   The White Gates, Leeswood Hall, Flintshire, a watercolour of c.1790, possibly by Thomas Pennant. In 1782 the antiquary Daines Barrington drew attention to the old gardens at Leeswood, stating that they had been designed by Stephen Switzer.

2   Humphry Repton's design for a garden at White Lodge, Richmond Park, 1816. The proposal for a garden on land enclosed from the park 'boldly reverting to the ancient formal style' with *treillage* arches would have been surprising at the time, but in retrospect was an early symptom of the reintroduction of formal gardens.

'Dutch style', lasting for half a century, to be superseded by the 'English style' when Brown destroyed the Dutch style in order 'to restore the ground to its original shape'.

For his *Encyclopaedia of Gardening* (1822), John Claudius Loudon amassed material from John Evelyn's *Diary*,[12] Switzer, Daines Barrington, articles in *Archaeologia*, and miscellaneous other sources.[13] Felton reappeared with his *Gleanings on Gardens, Chiefly Respecting those of the Ancient Style in England* (1829). This made use of all previous compilations, the Knyff and Kip views, Daniel Defoe's *Tours* from the 1720s onwards, and the *Letters of Mr Alexander Pope, and Several of His Friends* (1737), and included chapters on conventual gardens, garden burial and cottage gardens. Although Loudon's and Felton's approach was mostly additive rather than analytical, Loudon adopted Repton's first argument, that a powerful impulse was given to ancient gardening 'in the time of Charles II, by the introduction of the splendid style of Le Nôtre; it changed again, with the introduction of the modern style during the reign of George II'.[14] Loudon seems to have dated the demise of the ancient style to around 1730.

The largest published garden bibliography at the time was in *A History of English Gardening* (1829) by George Johnson, a horticultural journalist. Despite all his learning, however, his treatment of 'the period 1558–1714' (or Queen Elizabeth to Queen Anne inclusive) relied heavily on previous authors. Being interested principally in horticulture, he omitted to mention Joseph Addison or Pope, although he enthused over Switzer. From June 1850, as editor of the weekly *Cottage Gardener*, he published a series of sixty biographical sketches on gardeners. Of these, twenty-four were writers from before 1660, twelve were published between 1660 and 1735, sixteen were from the period 1735 to 1800, and six after

1800. This was a composition that reflected Johnson's interest in early writers on gardening. Likewise, Alicia Amherst's *A History of Gardening in England* (1895) had thirteen chapters, and she did not leave Queen Elizabeth behind until Chapter Nine.

Walpole's essay was republished in 1826, a further reason why there were few authors during the High Victorian period with a good word for the grand formal gardens of England. William Carew Hazlitt, still waving a flag for Walpole in 1887, including his criticism of the craze for clipping associated with London and Wise, wrote:

> The free growth of the box, the yew, and the holly was sacrificed to the mania for the quaint and grotesque in art, and from the occasional survivals of this bastard style one gets some imperfect conception of what it must have been, when it was in its full glory.[15]

Amherst's treatment of formal gardens was hardly more sympathetic. Centring her attention upon kitchen and flower gardens, she barely introduced the huge ornamental layouts of that time. Following Repton and Loudon, she noted French influence, and the involvement of Le Nostre in certain English gardens was vaguely asserted.[16] Curiously, despite the disregard of England's own Baroque gardens, the French Baroque was at this time accepted by some owners as the acme of taste.

THE ARTS AND CRAFTS PERSPECTIVE

A new appreciation of the design and craftsmanship of the formal garden was given impetus with *The Formal Garden in England* (1892), by a pair of architects, Reginald Blomfield and Inigo Thomas. Blomfield, who wrote the text, saw his mission as being to re-establish sound architectural principles in garden design, such as unity between house and garden. He made no bones about his approach: 'This book has been written entirely from the stand-point of the designer'.[17] To his mind, control of garden design needed to be wrested away from the horticulturalists and landscape gardeners.

Blomfield's version of the history of formal gardens concluded that: 'Garden design (of the seventeenth century) took its place in

GATE PIERS: CANONS ASHBY: NORTHANTS

3 Gate piers at Canons Ashby House, Northamptonshire. Inigo Thomas's illustration of a garden gate of about 1710 for Reginald Blomfield's *The Formal Garden in England* (1892) emphasises its craftsmanship in stone and timber.

the great art of architecture, with the result of that well-ordered harmony which was characteristic of the house and garden in England down to the middle of the eighteenth century.' Le Nostre had 'carried the art of garden design to the highest point of development it has ever reached'.[18] Blomfield attributed the demise of formal gardens to the excesses during William of Orange's reign: 'Over-elaboration, incapacity for self-expression, these were the vices which wrecked the formal garden, and opened the way for every kind of imposture'.[19] He found much to detest about the destroyer, Lancelot Brown.

If garden style was to be reformed in Blomfield's own day, garden architects needed a vocabulary and a library of design motifs with which to work. He made sketches or photographs of miscellaneous extant architectural detail which could be turned

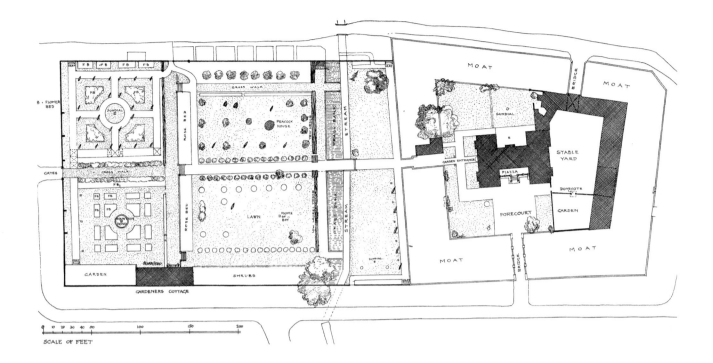

SCALE OF FEET

into ink drawings by Thomas (fig. 3), and thereby serve as a library of visual images of how ancient gardens had achieved taste and beauty. Blomfield also gleaned information on details of construction from garden literature, starting with earlier authors, such as Thomas Hill and Gervase Markham, but also Leonard Meager, John Worlidge and James's *Theory and Practice of Gardening*. He scrutinised the prints by Knyff and Kip and those in topographical works, such as county histories.

Meanwhile, John Dando Sedding's influential *Garden-Craft Old and New* (1891) showed that Blomfield had caught the mood of the time, though ensuing surveys were less overtly polemic. Inigo Triggs's *Formal Gardens in England and Scotland* (1902) included 'historical and descriptive accounts' of 47 places, high-quality photographs of 92 of them and plans of 42 (fig. 4).[20] Gertrude Jekyll

prepared *Some English Gardens* (1904), beautifully illustrated by reproductions of watercolours by George Elgood. Then *The Gardens of England* was published by *The Studio* in three volumes between 1907 and 1911, illustrated by a few Elgood watercolours and copious photographs.[21] Above all, *Country Life* appeared from 1897, almost invariably with an article upon some country house and its garden. Jekyll was an early contributor. After a few years there were enough garden articles for a collection to be issued as *Gardens Old and New*. A few years after that, *Country Life* published Jekyll's *Garden Ornament* (1918), a massive compendium of formal garden detail.

ART HISTORIANS' SEARCH FOR GENIUS

The natural, or 'English', style, which had been eclipsed by the reawakened passion for the formal garden in the nineteenth century, underwent a fresh rehabilitation in the mid-twentieth century at the hands of Nikolaus Pevsner and the garden historian Frank Clark, who preferred the epithet 'the landscape garden'. Both had vested interests in the consequences of their historical assessments. Clark was seeking a rationale for the choice of motifs applicable to Modernist landscapes, and hoped to learn from the

---

4 Groombridge Place, 1902, one of a number of survey plans by Inigo Triggs. Groombridge Place had been rebuilt within its old moat, against the advice of John Evelyn; its gardens rose up the bank to the north and a visto continued through a gate.

process by which the landscape garden had emerged. Pevsner was trying to draw historical parallels between the Whiggery and Palladianism of the Earl of Shaftesbury's and Addison's day, and the Socialism and Modernism of his own.

Clark and Pevsner sought validation through certain key texts, and their studies of the gardens themselves were cursory. The first stirrings of irregularity in garden design could, by selective use of the literature, be pushed back to Addison writing in *The Spectator* or Pope in *The Guardian*, both in the early 1710s, or even John Milton writing in the previous century. The problem for historians comparing theory with practice has been that the first modest irregular gardens, at Chiswick, Claremont and Stowe, all associated with Kent, were not started until 1733 (see fig. 257).[22] A convincing reconciliation of these dates was needed.

The problematic twenty-year period between Addison and Kent happened to be one of the most glorious episodes in English garden history, as will be seen in this book, but Clark and Pevsner downplayed it, choosing to characterise it as one of confusion or 'transition'. Clark accepted that Addison 'was not so successful as a practitioner', but to him Pope was 'one of the founders of the landscape movement', along with Bridgeman and Kent.[23] Pevsner, for his part, considered that the landscape garden was created 'between 1710 and 1730', and examined Sir William Temple's use of the term 'sharawadgi' in 1685,[24] and writings on 'natural' gardening by Shaftesbury, Addison, Pope, Switzer and Batty Langley.[25]

In editing an article by Clark on Chiswick, Pevsner admitted 'to what a small extent the early landscapists with their formal axial development (Sphinx avenues, etc.) round the house really departed from the orthodoxies of the Grand Manner' (see fig. 292), and that even the wriggling lines of walks in the wilderness were determinedly irregular, rather than natural (see fig. 196).[26] A term was required that would describe the 'transitional' state between formality and naturalism. Pevsner found what he was looking for in the title of Fiske Kimball's *The Creation of the Rococo* (1943).[27] Seeking to demonstrate an example of the Rococo, Pevsner, evidently no great geomorphologist, selected a print that showed a stream meandering through a meadow (fig. 5), which he described

5 Detail of a bird's-eye view of Miserden Park, Gloucestershire, from the south-east by Johannes Kip, 1712; he evidently enjoyed the meanders of the River Frome in the valley below the 1620s house and garden. In 1944 Nikolaus Pevsner drew attention to this feature, as he considered the meanders to be a landscape improvement, Rococo in style.

as 'clearly a recent improvement – and decidedly Rococo in its elaborately asymmetrical twists'.

The horticultural journalist Miles Hadfield included a chapter entitled 'France Triumphant 1660–1719', in his *Gardening in Britain* (1960). The odd date of 1719 was to allow the next chapter, 'The Landskip 1720–1780', to start in 1720, the median date that Clark and Pevsner had proposed as the start date for the landscape garden.[28] For 50 years gardening authors, overawed by Pevsner, would try to fit their findings to his overarching interpretation.[29]

This was not inevitable, as three books from the 1950s had worked outwards from detailed studies of places and people rather than inwards from some grand theory: Dorothy Stroud's

Capability Brown (1950), Laurence Whistler's *The Imagination of Sir John Vanbrugh and his Fellow Artists* (1954) and David Green's *Gardener to Queen Anne: Henry Wise (1653–1738) and the Formal Garden* (1956). Incorporating actual field evidence, their work might have served as a corrective.

Green, who had access to material at Blenheim Palace and other country houses, assembled a wide collection of biographical oddments from previous histories of gardening, material in the possession of Wise's descendants and the records of the Office of Works. From these he derived the first substantial biography of any garden designer working in the formal manner. Green seems to have accepted that there might have been a 'transitional' stage between formality and naturalism, but placed Wise firmly in the French-style mould of formal gardeners:

> He was by no means, like Bridgeman and Switzer, typical of the transition (from formal to landscape). He was the last of the great formalists and his gardens reflected nothing of the awkwardness of the Hanoverians but everything of that stately orderliness which imparted a sheen of grace and tranquillity to the tempestuous reign of Anne.[30]

Stroud's biography of Brown came about through working for Christopher Hussey while she was at *Country Life*. When in his twenties, Hussey had precociously written *The Picturesque* (1927), in which he referred to Pope's view of poetry and painting being gardening's sister arts. Many years of visiting country houses led to books on eighteenth-century architecture. He had also enjoyed the great landscapes of the eighteenth century when they were still in their maturity, and initially intended a book on extant eighteenth-century gardens. In the event, *English Gardens and Landscapes, 1700–1750* (1967) covered only the first half of the century, whilst Stroud's books on Brown and afterwards Repton dealt with the second half.

Hussey chose not to dissent from Clark's and Pevsner's analysis in his more theoretical introductory chapters, whilst his 'descriptive chapters' on places formed an impressive assemblage of scholarship on a number of individual gardens. He was fully cognisant that gardens in the first half of the eighteenth century were overwhelmingly formal, even if looser than the walled gardens of the seventeenth century. Hussey declined to adopt 'Rococo' for the 'transitional' garden, and proposed to call it the 'Early or Formal Landscape', meaning that gardens in his period began to embrace the countryside.[31]

Whistler made use both of Green's researches and of Vanbrugh's published letters.[32] He was particularly interested in determining the respective contributions of the clients, architects and gardeners to garden design. Bridgeman began to emerge as a major figure in the period, though in the tradition of formal gardens, not as a founder of the landscape garden. This conclusion was passed over by Peter Willis, who undertook a PhD under Pevsner's supervision, and was anxious to reveal Bridgeman as 'the unsung pioneer of the establishment of *le jardin anglais*'.[33]

On the other hand, a doctoral student under the supervision of Clark at Edinburgh in the 1970s, William Brogden, returned to Whistler's viewpoint and ventured that the problematic twenty years were not, in fact, a period of 'transitional' or 'proto-landscape' gardens, but a phase within the formal garden tradition: 'it is interesting to consider whether early eighteenth-century essays in garden design and theory were in opposition to the formal style or conscious attempts in it'.[34] In his thesis, Brogden pointed out that Addison admired the French tradition in extensive design, and that the principles of grandeur propounded by James's *Theory and Practice* (1712) accorded with Addison's view.[35] Because Switzer was principally known for his writings rather than his actual designs, Brogden examined both closely, providing a clear explanation of 'rural gardening' that fitted the field evidence neatly.

LITERARY HISTORIANS

The leadership of English garden history passed around this time from art historians to literary historians. They took over the quest to explain the origin of the landscape garden, with arguments that were not art historical, but poetic and psychological. Maren-Sophie Røstvig's two-volume *The Happy Man: Studies in the Metamorphosis of a Classical Ideal* (1954 and 1958), an early example, explained the sentiments of retirement in the seventeenth century. An anthology of literature's relationships with landscape gardening was provided by a professor of English, Edward Malins, as *English Landscaping and Literature, 1660–1840* (1966). A decade later, Peter Willis joined a lecturer in English literature, John Dixon Hunt, to produce *The Genius of the Place: The English Landscape Garden 1620–1820* (1975), another valuable anthology. The origins of the landscape garden continued to dominate discussion, and the very title indicated that all literature during the period chosen was judged in this light. Up till 1714 it was a 'Prelude', and from 1714 until 1750, starting with Addison and Switzer, it was 'the Early Landscape Garden'.

In the 1980s discussion had reverted to national styles and their influence elsewhere. Whereas Hadfield had argued for French influence on seventeenth-century English gardens, Hunt's *Garden and Grove: The Italian Renaissance Garden in the English Imagination, 1600–1750* (1986) made the case for Italian influence. The tercentenary of the accession of William III and the 'Glorious Revolution' gave an opportunity to juxtapose Dutch and English garden traditions. Hunt, with Erik de Jong, organised a special issue of the *Journal of Garden History* in 1988, 'The Anglo-Dutch Garden in the Age of William and Mary'.

Architectural historians meanwhile continued to make valuable discoveries and place important material in the public realm. Foremost amongst them was John Harris, who could draw upon his superlative personal collection of historic architectural publications, and also from the drawings collection of the Royal Institute of British Architects, of which he was then curator. Harris was among the several researchers who contributed to *The Gardens of William and Mary* (1988). The present author, one of the editors, brought out new material respecting the royal palaces, in particular Hampton Court. Other architectural historians made contributions through other channels, notably Gervase Jackson-Stops through the National Trust, and Marcus Binney through *Country Life*.

Two literary and garden-making personalities attracted much attention in the late twentieth century. First, the publication of Alexander Pope's *Correspondence* in 1956 came at a time when scholars were seeking to add flesh to the post-war account of the emergence of the landscape garden. After a lengthy period of ges-

tation several academic works were published, notably by American historians, including Morris Brownell's *Alexander Pope and the Arts of Georgian England*, in 1978, and Peter Martin's *Pursuing Innocent Pleasures: The Gardening World of Alexander Pope* in 1984. Both wished to see Pope as a leader of taste in garden design.

The second personality was John Evelyn. A quarter-century-long ambition of transcribing his *magnum opus*, 'Elysium Britannicum', came to fruition in 2001. The transfer of the Evelyn papers to the British Library in 1995 triggered Frances Harris and Michael Hunter's *John Evelyn and his Milieu* in 2003. Evelyn as a gardener was a topic pursued by the garden historian Mark Laird, providing materials for a chapter in his *A Natural History of English Gardening* (2015). In 2012 proposals for development on the site of Evelyn's house and garden at Sayes Court, London, leading to a successful campaign to save much of what was left, brought Evelyn further notice.

HETEROGENEOUS WRITINGS

Into the 1980s the standard account for most garden history readers remained Miles Hadfield's 1960 book, updated as *A History of British Gardening* (1979). Christopher Thacker, having been the historian who brought English Heritage's *Register of Parks and Gardens of Special Historic Interest in England* to fruition in 1988, wrote *The Genius of Gardening* in 1994, in which he devoted about 45 pages to the period between the Civil War and the start of the landscape garden. There have been no substantial attempts to provide such an overview since.

A by-product of the increasing sophistication of garden restorations in the 1990s, discussed below, was evidence of the details and planting of gardens of various dates. Plant lists in John Harvey's *Early Nurserymen* (1974) had provided a foundation for the research on planting, which bore fruit in, for example, an article he wrote for *Garden History* with Mark Laird in 1993, '"A Cloth of Tissue of Divers Colours": The English Flower Border, 1660–1735'. The garden historian Jan Woudstra continued research on this period as a result of his work on re-creating historical planting design for the restoration of the Privy Garden at Hampton Court in 1994–5

6 The Privy Garden, Hampton Court, 2007: one of the *plates-bandes*, with a yew and other smaller evergreens flanked by flowers and a low box edge in the style of the 1690s, designed by Jan Woudstra as part of the restoration of the garden in 1995.

(fig. 6), whereas Laird's attention was drawn to the planting of the English garden.

Other writing on formal gardens in the 1990s was stimulated by events. Harris's *The Palladian Revival: Lord Burlington, His Villa and Garden at Chiswick* of 1994 accompanied an important exhibition in Montreal and London, and *The King's Privy Garden at Hampton Court Palace 1689–1995*, edited by Simon Thurley, celebrated the opening of the restored garden in 1995. Mavis Batey's *Alexander Pope: The Poet and the Landscape* was supportive of the collaborative venture in 1994 by the public bodies concerned in formulating the Thames Landscape Strategy, whilst Christopher Ridgway and Robert Williams's *Sir John Vanbrugh and Landscape Architecture in Baroque England 1690–1730* (2000) was the proceedings of a conference.

In the 2000s an interest in the geometry that underlay the design of parks was explored. John Phibbs, a very experienced landscape surveyor, at first considered the regular ('metric') spacing of trees in avenues planted by the seventeenth-century gardener Moses Cook and others. However, as *pattes d'oie*, star-points and diagonals to prominent features in the landscape became common, the designer's skill became more a matter of the angles between vistos. As the vistos widened out over time, pleasing perspectives, rather than pinhole views, were sought. Phibbs called this 'projective' geometry. He thought that the geometry of angles continued into eighteenth-century park design, and was even continued by Lancelot Brown.[36] A few years later there was an attempt to interpret the park and garden design associated with Vanbrugh as the result of natural features being matched up to the principles of Classical geometry, principally 'the Vitruvian man'.[37] It was proposed that hidden axes explained the positioning of such features as temples.

An implication of 'projective geometry' was that parks were becoming viewed as scenes. This was likewise an implied outcome of a new 'Theory of Vision' being promulgated in the early eighteenth century by the cleric and philosopher George Berkeley. He argued that we learn to see the world three-dimensionally through tactile experience, but what we in fact see through the retina is depthless, akin to the picture plane of a perspective drawing. This theory was related to garden and park design by Katherine Myers, who argued that the traditional assumption that gardens were two-dimensional designs in plan was supplanted by the painter's way of looking, that is in snapshot scenes.[38] She offered this as the reason, for example, for topographical artists abandoning the bird's-eye view for ground-level viewpoints from the late 1720s (see Chapter 1), and remarked that Kent and Southcote employed painterly techniques. It may be noted that Berkeley was a friend of Pope's at the time when the latter was beginning to lay out his garden at Twickenham, though the connections have not yet been explored.

Meanwhile, a few major studies on well-defined topics stood out. *Royal Landscape: The Gardens and Parks of Windsor* (1997) by the Royal Librarian Jane Roberts is a magnificent record of just one designed landscape (though the largest in England), whilst *The London Square:*

Gardens in the Midst of Town (2012) by Todd Longstaffe-Gowan provided an in-depth account of that subject. Susan Weber's monumental *William Kent* (2013), which accompanied an exhibition at
Bard College in New York and at the Victoria and Albert Museum
in London, spanned the full breadth of his activities, not just his
gardens, in remarkable detail. The essence of gardening, manipu-
lating the ecology of gardens whilst contending with the vagaries
of the weather and other natural disasters, has been the subject of
Laird's highly informative *A Natural History of Gardening 1650–1800*
(2015). Although this range of topics amply demonstrates some of
the scope of English garden history, there has until now been no
work that embraces them and sets them within an overall narrative
of formal gardens between 1630 and 1730.

Surveys, extensive and intensive

By contrast to paintings and prints depicting gardens (a tradition that will be discussed in Chapter One), the manuscripts and
archives relating to gardens' creation and care have been much
less accessible, for the most part resting in muniment rooms for
over 200 years, and only comparatively recently being opened up
and studied. These archives may consist of account books, contracts, designers' plans, estate surveys, correspondence, journals
and property deeds. They may be royal records, in which case
they migrated in the nineteenth century to the Public Record
Office (now The National Archives). They could be the records
of the major landowners kept in their muniment rooms or estate
offices, or at their solicitors', and often deposited in county record
offices at some point in the twentieth century. Or they could be
records of institutions, including the Church, the universities and
the Inns of Court, which often are still with the libraries of the
bodies concerned.

PUBLISHED AND UNPUBLISHED

Accounts of formal gardens were included in tourist literature,
chiefly by John Macky and Daniel Defoe, and there is often some

mention in the county histories. However, it was soon realised
that some manuscripts were of such importance for historical
studies that they should be published, and the Society of Antiquaries was active in this. The Parliamentary surveys of royal
property from 1649 were printed in the society's journal, *Archaeologia*, in 1789 as was, a few years later, and a century after it was
written, an account of London's gardens by John Gibson. The
early histories of formal gardens by Loudon and others drew on
a limited range of material, and *Archaeologia* was one of the few
means to expand it.

With the greater interest in historical sources in the early nineteenth century, other texts from the seventeenth and early eighteenth centuries were brought to publication, many having useful
passages relating to gardens. Hence John Aubrey's notes on Wiltshire, made in 1685, were published in 1847, and Charles Hatton's
letters of the 1690s concerning horticultural exploits at Hampton
Court and Kirby were edited for the Camden Society in 1878.

Published notes and journals by early British tourists generally related to foreign travel. Likewise, there were the journals of
foreigners in England, such as Samuel de Sorbière's *Relation d'un
voyage* (1664), and Béat Louis de Muralt's *Letters* (1726).[39] Several
tourists' journals remained amongst family papers at home and
abroad. In the nineteenth century, some of the more interesting
ones were dusted off. Evelyn's *Diary*, which included his notes of
a tour in 1656, and other papers appeared in 1818. The 1820s saw
the publication of the journal of Count Lorenzo Magalotti, an
attendant of the Grand Duke of Tuscany on a diplomatic mission
in 1669. Celia Fiennes's journeys mostly of the 1690s came out in
1888, and John Loveday's tours of 1729–47 in 1890.[40]

By these various means, and although not, of course, to any
coordinated plan, material relevant to the history of the formal
garden was gradually being put into the public domain. Right at
the end of the nineteenth century some historians complemented
previous material with their own archival research. Ernest Law,
the historian of Hampton Court, delved into the archives of the
Office of Works in the Public Record Office around 1880, and
in the process revealed much factual material about the gardens
of Henry VIII and subsequent monarchs. Then during the 1890s

Alicia Amherst researched medieval manuscripts, which led to her *A History of Gardening in England*. Meanwhile, the Historical Manuscripts Commission was steadily cataloguing the archives of major country houses, and its publications contained many useful transcripts.

These same archives filtered into the county record offices in the middle of the twentieth century. The first such office was established for Bedfordshire in 1913, and 40 years later all but eight counties had one, and acquisition and cataloguing was in full spate. The steady rise of architectural history through the twentieth century caused historians to search private libraries, and those of the Oxford and Cambridge colleges and the learned societies. Much material was published in *Architectural History*, including the drawings made by Edmund Prideaux on his tours of 1716 and 1727, edited by John Harris. Other drawings by Samuel Buck, intended for a county history of Yorkshire, but abandoned, was published late in the twentieth century, as were Peter Tillemans's drawings for Northamptonshire noted above.

Some unpublished drafts of garden books made it into print. Sir Thomas Hanmer's 'Garden Book' of 1659 was printed in 1933, partly due to the influence of Eleanour Sinclair Rohde, the well-known writer on herbals. The surviving parts of John Evelyn's 'Elysium Britannicum', begun about 1657 and still being added to in 1702, were published in 2001.

The great volume of garden history research since about 1970 has thus had the benefit of topographical paintings, estate maps, estate records, diaries, oral histories, aerial photographs, archives and sale particulars. Publication has included much material on formal gardens. While the scope for publishing further important manuscript material is now probably diminishing, researchers have merely taken the first skim from the vast store of archive available.

The tools of research have meanwhile been changing. In the past a major challenge was to discover the relevant sources which may be scattered through many county record offices and libraries, and the chief aid was printed or typewritten indexes and catalogues. Today, one looks to the power of the internet for the initial search for one's sources, and finds that some archivists will have helpfully listed the contents of The National Archives and the county record offices online, and, if one is in luck, a brief description of items may be provided. There thus remains great scope for filling in the details, garden by garden, and for making lists of the works of named designers. Access to archives has thus grown to be immeasurably greater than it was for nineteenth-century historians.

SURVEYS

Local historians, archaeologists, professional landscape surveyors and landscape practices writing management plans have, since 1980, revolutionised garden history 'from the bottom up' by providing histories of thousands of individual gardens across Britain. In the process they have shown that much of the art historians' schema about original geniuses and their influence needs drastic revision.

Field archaeology has revealed much lost or unappreciated detail, and often could be correlated with archival findings. Even small gardens have been revealed to have a complex history of overlays and survival of older elements. The examination of several strands of information together allows designers' plans to be interpreted and bird's-eye views tested for accuracy. John Harris noted in 1981 that 'The old ideas about garden development are now under attack because all of a sudden plans, accounts, and descriptions of gardens are emerging from archives.'[41] He himself, through *The Artist and the Country House*, put on display a wealth of topographical images to reveal in full colour many of the pre-1735 gardens.

The greatest spur to research into individual gardens was systematic historical survey, both extensive and intensive. Extensive surveys have been called for by planners and conservationists seeking to identify the gardens that should be protected from building development and highway proposals. The first United Kingdom list of parks and gardens was produced by the International Council on Monuments and Sites (ICOMOS) UK in 1978. The Garden History Society then started compiling lists at county level, and when English Heritage was formed in 1984 these

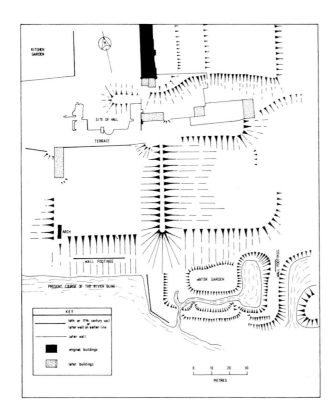

KITCHEN
GARDEN

SITE OF HALL

TERRACE

ARCH

WALL FOOTINGS

WALL FOOTINGS

PRESENT COURSE OF THE RIVER BURE

WATER GARDEN

KEY

16th or 17th century wall
or
later wall on earlier line

later wall

original buildings

later buildings

0   10   20   30

METRES

7   A field survey of Oxnead Hall, Norfolk, 1988. This earthworks plan demonstrates how such surveys can reveal the presence of former garden elements.

were taken over and developed by Dr Christopher Thacker into the *Register of Parks and Gardens of Special Historic Interest in England*. The English *Register* was thoroughly updated in the late 1990s, and a survey of Welsh gardens, promoted by Cadw (the Welsh government's historic environmental service) and ICOMOS, was completed in 2002. Meanwhile many county-wide surveys were conducted by county councils, garden trusts and academics (fig. 7). In 2002 Timothy Mowl began the publication of a series of books on the gardens of the English counties.

The National Trust carried out the first intensive historical survey of any garden in the UK, at Osterley House in 1979, and has undertaken many others since. In 1981 the Department of the Environment initiated the Royal Parks Historical Survey,

the largest component of which covered Hampton Court and Bushy Park.[42] This gave the opportunity to delve deeply into the records of the Office of Works. Restoration studies on Chiswick House, Painshill, Castle Bromwich Hall and other places followed through the 1980s. Probably the most intensive historical survey undertaken anywhere in Europe to date was that in the Privy Garden at Hampton Court in 1994.[43]

I was the first to be appointed Inspector of Historic Parks and Gardens at English Heritage with responsibility for maintaining of the *Register*, but within a month I took up the task of organising replanting in parks and gardens in the aftermath of the Great Storm of October 1987 and another in January 1990. The storms were both a disaster and an opportunity; from early 1988 English Heritage began offering grants to owners whose parks and gardens had been damaged, but this was conditional upon restoration schemes being prepared. These had to be based on historical surveys. By this means about a third of the 1,200 sites on the Register were subjected to historical survey by landscape consultants, throwing up much information across the southern half of England. The requirement to prepare historical surveys for historic parks and gardens was adopted by the Countryside Commission when they started Countryside Stewardship in historic parkland in 1992 and by the Heritage Lottery Fund through its Urban Parks Programme a few years later.

These extensive and intensive surveys have produced much information on formal gardens, and their findings have questioned old assumptions and raised new questions. Tom Williamson has had much to say on the 'new garden history', as he called it. His local studies perspective was evident when he declared his standpoint that 'the history of designed landscapes . . . cannot be divorced from the wider history of society'.[44] He concluded that:

the design of parks and gardens . . . cannot be read as a simple concrete expression of ideas formulated in high cultural texts . . . Parks and gardens in eighteenth-century England were not simple artefacts, but complex environments, moulded by all aspects of the culture, attitudes, and activities of the class that owned them.[45]

8   Oxnead Hall, Norfolk, 1809, an engraving by John Smith of a conjectural view by John Adey Repton of Oxnead as it would have appeared in the seventeenth century. Repton had observed the remaining walls and buildings and postulated a parterre design; the fountain survived, as it went to Blickling at the sale of Oxnead in 1742. This was one of the first attempts at the reconstruction on paper of a relict formal garden.

9   View of Holme Lacy House, Herefordshire, drawn and engraved by Thomas Ravenhill for the *European Magazine*, 1786. In 1788 the Revd Stebbing Shaw remarked that 'the gardens to the south front are all in King William's style of fortifications, surrounded by yew hedges, cut in a variety of forms, according to the taste of that time'. He was right as far as the side terraces with outgrown clipped yews were concerned, but the shaped slopes below would have been from the 1720s.

With these thoughts he raised questions about whether garden history should be about the intellectual life of the past, or the commonplace, and whether only those few gardens in the forefront of fashion should be the subject of serious study, or the far greater number of gardens belonging to the squire and parson.

ARCHAEOLOGICAL FIELDWORK

Earthworks were evident to antiquaries of the late eighteenth century. Daines Barrington observed those of the Maastricht Garden at Windsor (see fig. 83), and admired several of the ancient features at Hampton Court, including the arbour in the Fountain Garden, the Pearce and Cibber urns, the Tijou screens along the Pavilion Terrace, the wilderness with its maze, 'perhaps

the only such garden device now remaining, after the devastations of Messrs. Kent and Brown', and the eight-acre kitchen garden (see frontispiece). In the 1800s John Adey Repton, after visiting his uncle's farm in Norfolk and 'upon carefully tracing out the foundation some years ago, and collecting various information from the old inhabitants, who are now no longer living, I have attempted, in this view, to restore Oxnead-Hall to its original state'. The sketch showed how he imagined the mansion and its terraced gardens might have looked (fig. 8).[46]

Doubtless many other antiquarian-minded visitors observed relict gardens on the ground (fig. 9). However, it was not till 1926 that the plan of one was published.[47] Work in Cambridgeshire in the 1960s by Christopher Taylor of the Royal Commission on the Historical Monuments of England (RCHME) began to identify several more, and his work from the 1970s in Northamptonshire attracted attention to many famous 'lost' gardens (see fig. 110).[48] Taylor, who published a booklet, *Garden Archaeology*, in 1983, and his colleague Paul Everson established that archaeological technique was as applicable to gardens as it was to such topics as monastic houses and deserted villages.

Although most sites identified by Taylor were pre-1640, typically having been abandoned at the Civil War, several gardens made in the period 1640–1730 were studied by him and others at the RCHME, including Boughton House, Eastbury, Oxnead, Greenwich Palace, Risby, Stowe (in Kilkhampton, Cornwall) and Wanstead. Other archaeologists contributed along the lines set by Taylor and Everson.[49] By the end of the twentieth century a significant body of fieldwork had been achieved by the RCHME (merged in 1999 with English Heritage, which continued similar work, published as its 'Landscape Investigation Reports') and the Royal Commission on the Ancient and Historical Monuments of Wales.

The interpretation of standing trees was an even newer aspect to field archaeology. John Phibbs, whose first landscape study, on Wimpole, Cambridgeshire, started in 1979, showed how the growth of the trees could reveal evidence of past management, and how assemblages of surviving trees, or even their stumps, could be interpreted as hedgerows, groves or avenues. Phibbs went on to survey Painshill, Surrey, and many other sites of all dates. The dating of standing trees was also investigated by the present author, following a survey of 10,000 trees at Hampton Court in 1982.

Excavation of gardens had disappointed till 1985, when the first of a series of successful exercises was carried out, all in the context of restoration. Examples were Gilpin's flower garden at Audley End, Essex; a town garden at No. 4, The Circus, Bath; the walled garden at Castle Bromwich Hall, Warwickshire; a formal layout at Painswick House, Gloucestershire; and the grounds at Chiswick House, London.[50] The most spectacular exercise was the excavation of the Privy Garden at Hampton Court (see fig. 135) by Brian Dix and his team from Northamptonshire Archaeology in 1994.[51] Resistivity, magnetometry and other non-destructive techniques likewise offered useful information on buried wall foundations, pipework and fountains, and the positions of beds.

The approach of this book

With formal gardens becoming an established topic in archaeology, and with the huge mass of research amongst archives and with topographical paintings, the factual basis for considering the whole period of this book, the 1630s till the 1730s, was in place. What was left to do was analysis of the evidence for stylistic change and investigation of the background to it. Perhaps now the formal garden period can be better understood and appreciated, it can be recognised as one of the glorious episodes in English and Welsh garden history.

THE DEFINITION OF 'FORMAL'

The term 'formal' is usually taken to denote the period's 'regular', 'symmetric', 'geometric' or 'ancient' gardens, in contradistinction to the 'irregular', 'natural' or 'modern' gardens that have been generally referred to as 'landscape gardens' or 'landscape parks'. Strictly speaking, the landscape garden, with its predictable vocabulary of sloping lawns, winding walks and shrub banks, is formal too. Walpole used the term 'formal', however, as did Blomfield, after some 'question-begging'.[52] In his 1986 history of French Renaissance gardens, Kenneth Woodbridge also chose to use 'formal', partly because of its double meaning.[53] It was widely accepted as applying to gardens where the straight line predominates, but it also meant 'ceremonious', which suited seventeenth-century gardens as venues for formal occasions. 'Formal', if not perfect, at least has some rationale, and is widely understood.

Several historians have identified the two decades, 1713 to 1733, as a time when gardens and plantations were made on a grand scale, but incorporated meandering walks and water, and were merged with the countryside by the demolition of walls and the use of ha-has. Switzer styled it 'rural and extensive gardening'.

Walpole referred to Bridgeman's 'simple yet still formal style'.[54] To Pevsner's 'Rococo', and Hussey's 'Early or Formal Landscape', can be added John Harris's 'arti-natural style'.[55] The landscape historian Tom Williamson has called it 'Late Geometric'.[56] Although the twenty-year period in question certainly had quite a different notion of garden style to the late seventeenth century, it can nevertheless still be included as a 'formal' period in contradistinction to the self-consciously 'rural', or naturalistic, forms of the landscape garden that followed.

THE WRITING OF GARDEN HISTORY

At the opening of this century the historiography of garden history was under examination.[57] This provided an opportunity to consider garden history as a subject. Indeed, one question that arose was whether garden history has sufficient weight to be considered a subject in itself. It still struggles to establish itself in academe, and its professors by necessity nuture it under the cover of more established fields. Others, pursuing academic fashion, write on gardens in the light of postmodernism, Marxist interpretations, gender politics or some other perspective, all essentially seeking to underpin a modern agenda, with relevance to the subject a secondary consideration.

John Dixon Hunt asserted that garden history is a subject in itself, and proposed some guidelines for how to construct it.[58] The many fine works on the seventeenth-century gardens of other countries suggest that this approach is entirely valid. For example, two books on Dutch gardens, *Courtly Gardens in Holland 1600–1650* (2001) by Vanessa Bezemer Sellers and *Nature and Art: Dutch Garden and Landscape Architecture, 1650–1740* (2000) by Erik de Jong, have undeniably advanced Dutch garden history as a subject. The cursory treatment of English garden design of this period in histories of European or even English gardens does not negate the point.

Hunt also pointed to the affinity that garden history has with many other subjects. Very true: just as fine gardens were expressions of the aspirations, wishes, dreams and ideologies of their owners, and their making was influenced by many practical and design factors, and impressed others in many diverse ways, an unusual number of other historical subjects converge on the history of gardens.[59] The subject thus has much in common with the study of cultural landscapes and environmental history, both of which have attracted much attention since 1990. These too lie at the confluence of art and science, and are integrative in character.

Hence this book seeks to narrate the phenomenon of garden-making in our period: what, where, by whom, why, when and how much? At the same time it touches on politics, religion, taste, men's fashion, cuisine, transport, 'undertakers', attitudes to flowers, husbandry, plant introduction and many other topics where these illuminate the story.

Writers who see garden history from some narrow perspective surely miss the greater part of the subject. Yet there have been writers on garden history who have claimed to find a new, or more correct, way in which the subject should be approached. One author asserted that 'Garden History has been abducted by the art historians', adding that 'This book is an attempt to get it back for the social historian'.[60] Another author, in being critical of (as he saw it) the myopic contribution from literary studies, argued that 'real garden history' cannot be written till the hundreds of gardens out there have been walked.[61] However, there need be no disobliging words if everyone recognises the contribution of others. Garden history embraces very many aspects; indeed, this is the joy and reward of studying the subject.

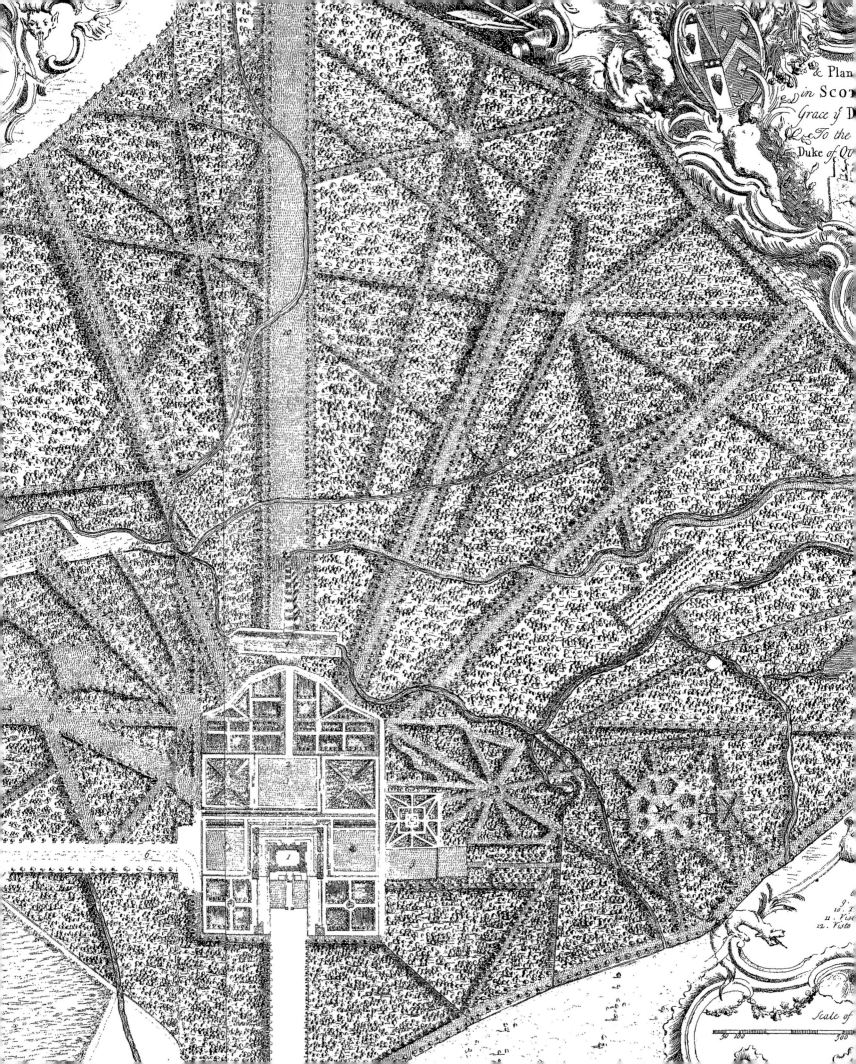

& Plan

in Scot

Grace ij D

To the

Duke of Qu

9.

10. T

11. Vist

12. Visto

Scale of

50 100   300

1

The Phenomenon of Formal Gardens

The visual record of the highest-ranking formal gardens, such as those drawn by Leonard Knyff and engraved by Johannes Kip, is a source of continued wonderment. The wholesale erasure of these gardens during the mid- and late eighteenth century, usually in favour of naturalistic parkland, means that the modern world can catch only glimpses of a very different tradition, and some writers have even doubted whether they existed as illustrated. However, modern documentary and archaeological research leaves no doubt that they did, and indeed existed in great numbers. This chapter will examine the evidence for their number, distribution and size, and draw out some of the general issues common to gardens in this period.

♏

The number of élite formal gardens

Research for this book was in part generated for my doctoral thesis, which dealt with the period 1660–1735.[1] The 300 or more country seats studied included all the major gardens in England and Wales of the period, plus some contemporary town houses, squares, colleges and hospitals, and samples in Scotland, Ireland and the American colonies.[2] The great majority of these seats belonged to royalty and the nobility, who generally set the pace as far as fashion was concerned, though lesser numbers belonged to baronets and moneyed men, such as lawyers, bankers and plantation owners.

The extent of garden- and park-making during the period of this book, the 1630s to the 1730s, has to be seen as a display of social, political and economic pre-eminence by the kingdom's landed élite, and part of the phenomenon of the country house.

Foreign tourists noticed that the greatest houses and gardens were the country seats: 'Everyone agrees, Sir, that the finest houses in the kingdom are to be found outside London and in the English countryside', wrote the French tourist Pierre-Jacques Fougeroux in 1728.[3] Almost all the politically powerful had fine gardens, and men of less elevated origins who were raised to greater heights took immense pains to acquire them.

One study of the six centuries of parliamentary history from around 1300 identified an 'élite' of about a thousand English families that dominated politics over the period.[4] At its core was a largely indestructible group of under 150 families who might be termed the 'magnates'. One of the most striking facts about them even today is that 85% have been settled at their seats for over 300 years, and half for over 500 years. Meanwhile, half of the wider élite had little more than a century of importance, but then declined or disappeared. Such numbers were reflected in garden-making: when the Worshipful Company of Gardeners sought to extend its influence in 1701, it estimated that there were ten garden designers, 150 noblemen's gardeners and 400 gentlemen's gardeners working in England and Wales.[5]

Eldest sons succeeded to titles, and they were expected to assume the responsibility of head of the family. Younger sons found themselves a profession, whereas the women were urged to find a role in the domestic sphere. As gardens and parks reflected the status of the family as a whole, the makers of gardens in the period were mainly heads of families, whilst the womenfolk were by tradition prominent in the flower and physic garden. However, sometimes women would find themselves *de facto* head of the family. Hence a tradesman's widow could pick up his business, and when the head of a landed family was detained elsewhere, say because of a position as a governor, ambassador, or in the royal household – or was a prisoner in the Tower of London – his wife or sister could step in to administer the family property. This was seen, for example, in the making of the garden at Melbourne Hall, Derbyshire (see fig. 146), where Thomas Coke, Vice-Chamberlain to Queen Anne, relied heavily on his sister Betsy to manage the changes.

℞

The rises and falls in garden-making

In the first three decades of the seventeenth century garden-making by the powerful was innovative and frenetic. However, the worsening relations between the Court and Parliament, depredations of war, sequestrations (appropriation of revenues) and loss of confidence during and after the Civil War (from 1642 to Charles I's beheading in 1649) and Interregnum (from 1649 to Charles II's restoration in 1660) suppressed further thoughts of high-status gardens. Furthermore, Parliament confiscated and sold the parks and gardens of the bishops and then the monarch, and this led to tree-felling, disparkment and other acts of dismemberment. The new rulers of the Interregnum constructed a mere handful of significant gardens, notwithstanding a considerable literature on estate improvement and fruit gardening by Puritan authors.

As the state of affairs for the nobility and gentry eased from the late 1650s, and after the Restoration, the urge to make fine gardens was reawakened. Charles II himself, at St James's, Hampton Court and Greenwich palaces, his relatives and the ministers of his 'cabal', were able to take advantage of their positions at the centre of government to fund ideas derived from their sojourns in Continental Europe.[6] Those of the nobility who were rewarded for their loyalty were quickly able to recover lost estates and were anxious to re-establish themselves at Court. Other landowners had to concentrate on repairing their houses and estates, but a number of commercial men began to make gardens in the 1670s, such as Sir John Lewys (factor of the East India Company) of Ledston Hall, Yorkshire, Sir William Blackett (coal mine owner) of the New House, Newcastle, and Josiah Child (banker) at Wanstead House, Essex (see fig. 105).

Towards the very end of Charles II's reign, the pace of garden-making was picking up significantly, and this continued during the reign of James II (1685–8). The political upheaval of the Glorious Revolution (1688–9) and the drain on the public purse in funding the Nine Years' War (1688–97) hardly dampened the pace, which reached a peak in the reign of William III (1689–1702). The War of the Spanish Succession (1702–13), however, led to further taxes and high interest rates, and as disposable income was thereby eroded garden-making dipped in much of Queen Anne's reign.

Released from wartime exigencies, English commerce, for the first time leading Europe, flourished exceedingly in the reign of George I (1714–27). A period of stability and peace under Sir Robert Walpole's ministry created the conditions for the country to realise its inherent propensity for building and garden-making in the 1720s.[7] A significant proportion of the money for new gardens was from banking and the law. After this new peak, garden-making declined somewhat in the following decade.

Geographical distribution

The 300 seats mentioned above often had more than one 'overlay', or phase of garden-making. Six hundred overlays were identified in my thesis, 17% concentrated in just two counties, Middlesex and Surrey, reflecting not only the landowning gentry in these counties, such as the Evelyns of Wotton House, Surrey, but, closer to London, the numbers of politicians and merchants who desired residences and villas out of the Great Smoke but within an easy distance of it. The Thames Valley and the healthy higher ground in Wimbledon and Richmond proved particular draws. Garden-making in Kent, at 5%, was somewhat boosted by this out-of-town phenomenon. In addition, there were royal palaces, the London squares, and institutions such as Gray's Inn and Chelsea Hospital.

Another great concentration was in Yorkshire, at 9%, though this is partly because of the sheer size of the county. Other counties well stocked with wealthy landowners were Berkshire, Buckinghamshire, Essex, Gloucestershire, Hampshire, Hertfordshire, Northamptonshire, Nottinghamshire, Oxfordshire and Wiltshire. Counties with few high-status gardens tended to be in Wales, the Marches and the north-west, including Herefordshire, Shropshire, Worcestershire, Staffordshire and Lancashire, and the wilder outlying counties in the North, Cumberland, Westmorland and Northumberland. Welsh garden-making at the time was not markedly distinct from English practice, though an interesting aspect is that much of it was funded by revenues from minerals.

10 'A Plan of yᵉ Garden & Plantation', Drumlanrig Castle, by John Rocque, 1739. This was the seat of the Duke of Queensberry. Its spectacular gardens were first made in the 1690s, but in the 1730s the third Duke grassed the extravagant parterres and Sir John Clerk of Penicuik designed a cascade on axis with about nine falls; attention had turned to the ornamentation of the park, with its innumerable vistos.

The distribution of garden-making in Scotland and Ireland mirrored, on a smaller scale, that in England. In Scotland, the castles of the great clan chiefs, such as Drumlanrig (fig. 10), Inveraray, Taymouth and Castle Kennedy, were scattered over a wide area, but there was a concentration of places newly built for the financial and legal élite within easy reach of Edinburgh. Similarly, in Ireland the strongholds of great landowning families, such as Antrim Castle, Dromoland, Kilkenny Castle and Lismore Castle, were spread out, but several new high-status gardens were made within about 30 miles of Dublin, the island's political, legal and financial focus.

Size of gardens

For gardens, in the 1680s Sir William Temple thought that 'from four or five acres to seven or eight Acres, is as much as any Gentleman need design'.[8] The walled area at Albury, Surrey, created in 1667 and containing house, courts, canal and gardens, was thus unusually large at 23 acres (see fig. 27). The largest of all enclosed gardens at the death of William III were those at Hampton Court. Having been 27 acres in 1689, William had increased them to 46 acres by 1696. After Queen Anne had added further areas they were 58 acres by 1710 (see frontispiece). For comparison, Kensington Gardens was then a mere seventeen acres. Melbourne had 30 acres at this time, mostly an ornamental plantation (see fig. 146)

In George I's reign layouts embraced increasing areas of plantation outside the walls, and sizes leaped up. Although Stephen Switzer thought that 'I would never advise above twenty Acres of Ground in the innermost parts of the largest Gardens, let the Exterior be what they will, to appear, if possible, two or three hundred'.[9] This kind of talk was viewed with alarm by lesser owners, such as the Revd John Laurence, who wrote that: 'I could never be of the Opinion of a certain Noble Person, who spake very contemptibly of his own Garden, to one that admir'd it; *Alas!* (says he) *This is a small inconsiderable Place, of only Thirty Acres; whereas my Lord ----- has above Fourscore.*'[10]

At this date the garden wall was being razed and new plantations merged in with the pleasure gardens, giving extended or 'prolated' gardens, some reaching over 100 acres. The Duke of Montagu laid out extensive gardens at Boughton House, Northamptonshire, from 1694 till his death in 1709. The second Duke then added further wilderness areas in about 1712, after which the design reached 100 acres, perhaps the first to do so (see fig. 217). Colen Campbell wrote in 1725 that the gardens 'were formed by the late Duke, and improved by his present Grace, with so many Additions, that they are esteemed now, the largest in England'.[11]

However, after 1714 Cannons, at Edgware, Middlesex, was a new contender (see fig. 150). According to a survey of 1729, it had 28 acres within its iron palisade, and another 63 acres of plantations and physic garden, and 11 acres of kitchen garden, melon ground and orchard, making 102 acres.[12] Meanwhile, Wanstead House was claiming 101 acres.[13] The gardens at Stowe House, Buckinghamshire, would have been more typical of middling to large grounds in the late 1710s, being 28 acres, including the new plantations (see fig. 216).

In the 1720s middling layouts of twenty acres were quite usual. Marble Hill, in Middlesex, for example, was this size in 1725 (see fig. 203). Meanwhile, the sizes of the larger places were still shooting up. That at Stowe continued to increase, more than doubling in size when the Home Park was taken in about 1725, and gaining 40 acres more to the east, making over 100 acres in 1733 (see fig. 257). The distinction of being the largest pleasure garden belonged to Kensington Gardens in 1727 after it ballooned to 170 acres when George I added 114 acres of Hyde Park for his paddocks for exotic animals (see fig. 210).

Parks

Very many of the greater houses of the period were within or close to medieval deer parks. These were not necessarily wholly grazed, as parks often included significant areas set aside for woodland and other uses, but their primary purpose was for hunting. John Aubrey looked back from Restoration times to a golden age of hunting in Charles I's day: 'It was the right hon. Philip Earle of Pembroke, that was the great Hunter. It was in his Lordship's time a serene calme of Peace, that Hunting was at its greatest Heighth that ever was in this Nation'.[14] Hunting and banqueting outdoors continued as major social occasions till the years leading up to the Civil War. Hunting gave participants the chance of some hard riding, with the opportunity for much useful social intercourse. The giving of haunches of venison was a tradition that indicated one's status and obliged one's friends with a commodity that could not be bought.

Parks are included in this book, in part because they were the essential setting to so many of the top seats, but also because they too became the object of embellishment. At first this was mostly confined to avenue planting, then to woods and belts, but increasingly the gates and lodges at the forecourt moved to the park entrance, and the parterres, groves and basons of the garden became grander and looser as they migrated out into the park as lawns, plantations and lakes. The period covered by this book is sometimes regarded as a fallow period of emparkment, between the park-making of Tudor times, and the neo-classical park of the late eighteenth century. There was indeed a crisis for parks in Civil War and Interregnum times, but the association between parks and high status was strong enough for parks to be re-established at the Restoration, and for fresh emparkment to continue. Indeed the early eighteenth century was one of the busiest times for emparkment ever.

Estimating the actual number of parks at any moment in history is fraught with difficulty. Knyff and Kip's views of 71 royal palaces and 'principal seats of the Nobility and Gentry of Great Britain' published in 1707 provide a top-slice. Several were in city locations, so the 40 shown with deer parks was a high proportion. To take one medium-sized county as an example, Staffordshire had one royal forest – Needwood – with its accompanying parks, but not one of the county's major seats was in Knyff and Kip. However, five lists of deer parks over the period 1610 to 1768 give a longer-term picture, revealing that Staffordshire as a whole had about 30 deer parks.[15] Once matters had stabilised following the Restoration, emparkments and disparkments balanced each other out and the county retained that number of deer parks over the next century. If this pattern was repeated across England (Wales's more modest parks had their own history), the number of parks would have remained fairly constant through the seventeenth and into the early eighteenth centuries, in the high hundreds, with a brief hiccup during the rule of Parliament.

SIZE OF PARKS

The largest parks were mostly medieval in origin, the greatest of all being the Great Park at Windsor (see fig. 145). This was measured at 3,377 acres in 1662 but land was added during the early eighteenth century, making it 4,494 acres by 1750.[16] Other massive medieval parks included that at Woodstock, Oxfordshire, at 2,120

acres,[17] better known as Blenheim after being given to the Duke of Marlborough, and the Earl of Lindsay's Grimsthorpe Park, Lincolnshire, at about 2,350 acres.

Other medieval or Tudor parks much admired for their extent and incorporating planting of the 1660–1735 period included Bushy Park (1,080 acres), and Hampton Court Park (600; see fig. 90), both in Middlesex; Cobham, Surrey (692; see fig. 130); Cornbury, Oxfordshire (655); Duncombe, Yorkshire (730); Euston, Suffolk (over 700); Heythrop, Oxfordshire (780); Knole, Kent (998); Osterley, Middlesex (588); Studley Royal, Yorkshire (785); Tottenham, Wiltshire (with large parts of Savernake Forest, 1,413; see fig. 278); and Uppark, Sussex (892).[18] The typical non-royal park originating in Elizabethan times was much smaller in extent – in the region of 100 to 150 acres.[19]

Some large parks were made prior to the Civil War, the largest by the Duke of Buckingham at Burley-on-the-Hill, Rutland, and New Hall, Essex. Charles I's New Park at Richmond, formed in 1637, was 2,355 acres. Emparkment by the nobility and gentry also continued into the seventeenth century, though it is noticeable that most of these parks were in the range of 50 to 100 acres, minnows compared to the expansive parks of the far-off past.

Some of the most grandiose schemes of emparkment since early medieval times were seen between 1710 and 1735. Lord Bathurst joined his park at Cirencester House, Gloucestershire, to Oakley Wood, eventually achieving the expansive modern Cirencester Park at 2,600 acres (fig. 11). Between 1700 and 1730 the Earl of Carlisle reordered the moorland around Castle Howard, Yorkshire, to 1,841 acres of designed grounds and park (see fig. 197). Sir Robert Walpole's megalomaniac park-making at Houghton, Norfolk, in the 1720s and 1730s resulted in a park and gardens of about 1,810 acres (see fig. 289), and the dukes of Bedford kept enlarging their park at Woburn Abbey, Bedfordshire, from 645 to 1,565 acres in a few years leading up to 1738 (see figs 40 and 288). There were also some middling park and garden schemes, such as Combe Bank, Kent (170 acres), Painshill, Surrey (217), Rokeby (188; see fig. 283) and Stainborough (420; see fig. 260), both in Yorkshire.

By this time, owners were not just adding ornamental plantations, but were also thinking in terms of ornamenting whole parks

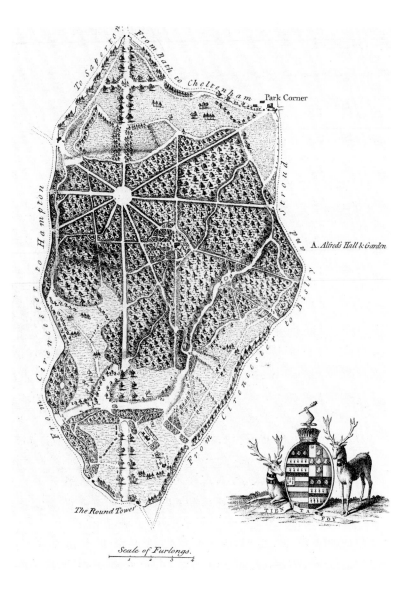

sometimes 4, 5 or 600 Acres, all appear as if it was a Garden'.[20] His vision was not far wrong for some great estates with outer plantations, such as Castle Howard and Bramham Park, Yorkshire (see fig. 188). Such new forms of extensive layout, with the *ferme ornée* and afterwards the neo-classical park, began to make raw figures for area less meaningful. As the century progressed, boasting about size frequently took the form of estimating the park's circumference.

The advance of fashion

A traveller from beyond Europe would have noticed a shared European tradition in garden-making in the formal garden period. There were variations, of course. England did develop some stylistic preferences of its own for religious-cum-political reasons, and across Europe differences may often be seen, responding to the imperatives of topography, climate and cultural landscape patterns. Superficially each country's gardens differed slightly from those of other countries, but these differences should not be allowed to mask a broad uniformity of design norms. For example, Dutch gardens should not be thought to be in a different tradition to the Italian or the French merely because they specialised in high palisades and canals; these were rational responses to local conditions.[21]

The school of garden history to which Frank Clark and Nikolaus Pevsner belonged, and after them the literary historians, discussed in the Prologue, emphasised the contribution of original geniuses envisioning new garden styles, and played 'the influence game' of suggesting inspiration from such individuals specifically, or foreign national styles generally. Much has been made by some authors of supposed Italian, French and Dutch influences on English garden style in the formal gardens period. There are always difficulties in pinpointing the characteristics that especially denote national styles, but even if some are identified, they rarely transfer in an unambiguous fashion. When foreign gardeners were imported to England their designs tended to be adapted to suit the owner's preferences and the local conditions. In his surveys of East

11   Oakley Park, Cirencester House, Gloucestershire, 1779. This is the earliest plan of Oakley Park (north is to the right). It shows the park 60 years after Lord Bathurst had commenced his vast planting scheme around a ten-pointed star, including many vistas aligned on churches, which was connected to the house by avenues and platoons through Cirencester Park to the east; Alfred's Hall was buried deep in the woods.

with avenue systems, woods, belts and lakes, thus expanding the designed area in another great leap. Switzer had envisioned this, writing in terms of the 'whole adjoyning Estate of 1, 2, 3, nay

Anglian gardens Tom Williamson found few, perhaps no, direct international influences, and reflected that clear or pure examples of French or Dutch gardening in England should not be expected. He considered that classifications into Italian, Dutch, French and English styles were little help in practice.[22]

The theory of original geniuses deserves even more scepticism when one considers the normal process of design. Decisions on garden layout were primarily the responsibility of the owner, sometimes advised by an architect, though there were only a few, such as Vanbrugh, who could speak to owners as social near-equals, and were in a position to influence their thoughts substantially.[23] Gardeners were by training and instinct practical men, even such eminent ones as George London and Henry Wise. An owner's demands would be interpreted by the executant gardener as best he could, though with the advance of pleasure gardens into the eighteenth century some gardeners had skills and knowledge enough to devise substantial portions of new garden layouts.[24]

Lord Arlington, the host of a debauched house party in 1671 at Euston Hall with Charles II and his new mistress, Louise de Kérouaille, plus 200 other guests, took one of them, John Evelyn, out into the park to discuss tree planting. Evelyn discovered several years later that he had been listened to.[25] Moses Cook recalled an occasion at Cassiobury, Hertfordshire, in 1675 when the owner, the Earl of Essex, was discussing the pruning of trees with Sir Samuel Morland and Hugh May.[26] William III took a close interest in the Privy Garden at Hampton Court, ordering designs, patterns and a wooden model in March or April 1701.[27] The screens by Jean Tijou were erected for a visit in June by William and his entourage, whereupon it was decided that the whole garden should be lowered again for a better view of the river (see fig. 16). Meanwhile the name of the designer of the parterre went unrecorded.

Such glimpses of the design process at work in late seventeenth-century gardens suggest a picture of negotiated, sometimes trial-and-error, decision-making. Ideas for design improvements would have been generated within social circles of owners, or in competition with others, and might have had eclectic origins: gardens admired at home or abroad, the study of prints and books, or suggestions from a valued acquaintance, architect, engineer or undertaker.[28] Furthermore, all ideas would have been mediated by agricultural, sporting, topographical, financial, legal and other considerations. Changes did not arise simply through some genius being at work.

As an examination of fashionable garden-making, this book does not attempt to describe the general state of all pleasure gardens in England and Wales in this period. That could certainly be done, by studying a much more inclusive sample, which would include gardens belonging to knights, squires, parsons and merchants.[29] A common observation or rather supposition is the time lag between the advent of a particular fashion in leading circles and its adoption by those less keen or less able to keep up to date. At any moment there might be a range of styles represented in a county's gardens – indeed, one can point to impecunious squires' houses retaining their formal gardens right through the period of the 'modern' garden. However, that in itself does not indicate divergent aspirations, merely an incapacity to achieve them.

To what degree fashionable new design might vary regionally within a country as tightly knit politically as England is a moot point. The idea of design innovation 'spreading' from London doesn't bear scrutiny, since virtually the whole social and political élite congregated in London during Parliamentary sessions, and as it dispersed ideas could be spread simultaneously to all parts of the country. The observable differences are most obviously a result of whether the garden was in town or country, but were also a product of local conditions, such the prevailing land ownership, topography and building materials. However, travel, tourism and publicity all contributed to a dissemination of ideas and design.

PUBLICITY AND TOURISM

It was quite common to travel up to twenty miles for a dinner engagement, but you would probably meet other persons of your own standing from the other end of the county only during the annual assizes in the county town. One way to increase your circle somewhat would be to engage in horse racing, or to attend fox hunts. Nevertheless, apart from your geographically close social circle it might be that other gentlemen in the county, and even more so the magnates (who might have their estates distributed through more than one county) would seldom have the chance of visiting your home.

Owners therefore sought to advertise their achievements in print. When Edmund Gibson, editor of a new edition of Camden's *Britannia*, invited contributions in the early 1690s the opportunity to advertise the magnificence of a county's seats was seized. One contribution affirmed that the Duke of Beaufort's Badminton was 'so adorn'd with stately additions to the house, large parks, neat and spacious gardens, variety of fountains, walks, avenues, Paddocks, and other contrivances for recreation and pleasure; as to make it justly esteem'd one of the most complete seats in the kingdom'.[30] Meanwhile, the Earl of Exeter's Burghley House 'for terrasses, conduits, fish-ponds, fountains, &c . . . may vie with the best in England'.[31] The number and nature of such claims were typically so hyperbolic that the editor had to warn his writers that often 'such and such a building should only be call'd *Stately*, and the *Gardens* and *Walks*, *neat* and *curious*; after they have roundly affirm'd both *to be the best in the Kingdom*'.[32]

Another route to publication, discussed below, was to pay for a print, which could then be distributed to a wider public. Robert Plot wanted to keep the cost of his *Staffordshire* (1686) down, and seems to have thought it not unreasonable to ask the owners to pay for the artist and engraver themselves. The plates were then 'gratefully dedicated' to the individuals whose properties were displayed (see fig. 51). The plate belonged to the publisher, who could at any time arrange for another edition.

Owners with remarkable gardens could increasingly expect to be visited. William Harper, chaplain to Lord Cholmondeley, noted in 1732 that: 'whenever we hear any remarkable Seat very much commended, the first Question generally ask'd is, What *Gardens* has it?'.[33] It is clear from the first tourist accounts of Britain published, by John Macky from 1714 and Daniel Defoe from 1724, that access to famous gardens was taken for granted if you presented yourself in a respectable manner. Indeed, the number of tourists at Cannons and Wanstead became somewhat burdensome. Defoe, on visiting the latter, was informed that 'it has been the general diversion of the citizens to go out to see

them, till the crowds grew too great, and his lordship was obliged to restrain his servants from shewing them except on one or two days in a week only'.[34]

Visits further from London encountered the appalling provincial roads at the time. When Evelyn made a tour of England in 1656 in order to see the finest gardens, he had to do so on horseback, and so did Celia Fiennes, who visited many parts of England in William III's reign, supposedly side-saddle. However, touring became less of an ordeal with the maps and guides by John Ogilby from the 1670s, and afterwards the improved roads necessary for stage coaches. Well-connected tourists like Fiennes would rely upon family networks for accommodation. Tourists without such connections were reliant on inns that were springing up along the stage-coach routes. Other journal keepers besides Fiennes included John Gibson, who described his visits to London gardens in 1691,[35] Sir John Percival, who recorded his 'A Journey Thrô Severall Countys of England' in 1701, and Ralph Thoresby in 1710.

In 1727 Sir John Clerk made an extended tour of English country houses when he planning alterations to his seat at Penicuik, near Edinburgh.[36] He travelled via Studley Royal and Bramham to London. He then spent some months visiting from London, taking in Wilton House, Ham House, Wanstead, Hampton Court, Kensington, Chiswick, and the home of the former Secretary of State for Scotland, James Johnston, at Twickenham. Other visitor descriptions can be found for Richmond Gardens, Pope's garden in Twickenham, Gobions and others too numerous to mention. In many cases no journal was produced, but evidence may be found in the accounts. Thanks to his minutely kept account book, we know that John Campbell, Viscount Glenorchy, visited Cliveden, Hampton Court, Windsor Castle, Castle Howard, Wentworth Woodhouse and Chatsworth in 1734 in order to furnish his mind with examples of what he might accomplish at his Staffordshire and Perthshire seats.[37]

After the War of Spanish Succession came to a peace in 1713, foreigners could be tourists once more. A Frenchman in 1728 travelled in an organised party in a wide anti-clockwise loop via Wanstead, Newmarket, Wimpole, Boughton, Oxford, Wilton and

Hampton Court.[38] Prints of houses and gardens by the Frenchman John Rocque had titles in both English and French, surely an indication of the tourist market of the 1730s.

PAINTERS AND ENGRAVERS

The record of parks and gardens seen in paintings and prints has been the principal reminder of them since they were at their height. English topographical art was not at first by the English, though. Northern Europe had a fine tradition of painting and engraving long before England developed its native talent. As a consequence, most depictions of English gardens until well into the eighteenth century were by draughtsmen and engravers from the Low Countries, and to a lesser extent from France and Germany.

The patrons that drew in these foreign artists were interested in topographical art as a form of advertisement. The royal and aristocratic desire to record the great places, often in multiple versions, was catered for at the Restoration principally by Hendrik Danckerts and Thomas Wijck up till 1675, and by Jacob Knyff, Johannes Vorstermans and Jan Siberechts thereafter, the last till the turn of the century (fig. 12). Often the paintings of country houses were actually hung in his lordship's town house so that others might see without yet having visited. So we find Evelyn taking the Duke of Norfolk to the Earl of Sunderland's residence in London to view Vorstermans' 'View or *Landscip* of my Lords palace &c: at Althorp'.[39]

---

12 *Greenwich Park* by Johannes Vorstermans, c.1672. This view from the south-east shows the recent planting in the park, the observatory to the left and the partially rebuilt palace to the right. Several versions of this painting are known, suggesting that they were for presentation to Charles II's friends.

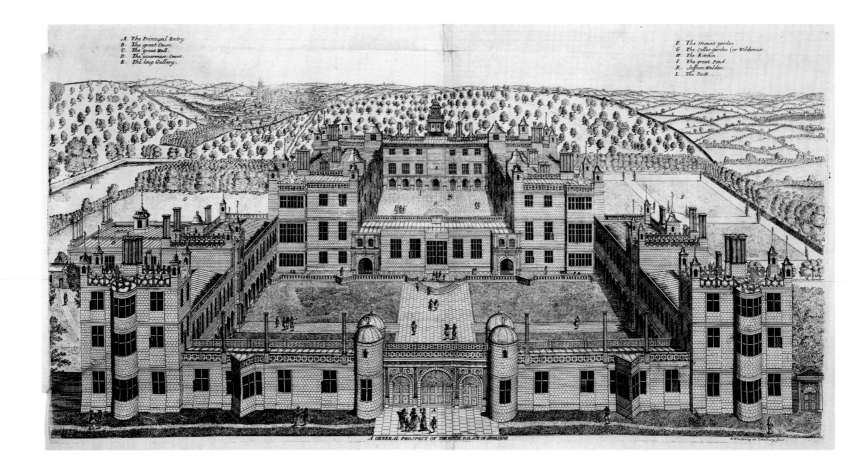

The tradition of painted views of important houses thus continued, but from the 1670s sets of engraved views were made for presentation to family and friends, and later on to tourists. Examples were Henry Winstanley's set of Audley End of 1676 (fig. 13), Robert Thacker's set commemorating the Greenwich Observatory in the same year (see fig. 67), his 1680s set of Longford Castle, Wiltshire (fig. 14), and Kip's of Wanstead in about 1713 (see fig. 105). Engraving for books was a long-standing trade, given an impetus by the new empirical science emanating espe-

cially from Oxford as county histories came to be published – the word 'history' being used in the sense of a description. Wenceslaus Hollar produced a few plates for William Dugdale's *Warwickshire* (1656) (fig. 15) and Elias Ashmole's *Order of the Garter* (1659). Aubrey made drawings intended to be engraved for his projected histories of Surrey and Wiltshire. David Loggan's *Oxonia Illustrata* (1675) and *Cantabrigia Illustrata* (1690) had views of the university college gardens. Michael Burghers provided views for Plot's *Staffordshire* (1686; see figs 32, 59, 106 and 114), and John Drapentier engraved views taken by others for Sir Henry Chauncy's *Hertfordshire* (1700; see figs 19, 31 and 55).

Jacob Knyff's brother Leonard carried on in the tradition of painting country houses from about 1690, but towards the end of that decade conceived a project to record a hundred of the country's chief seats in engravings by Kip. Either Knyff or his printseller placed an advertisement in *The Post Boy* that set out the terms

13   *A General Prospect of the Royal Palace at Audlyene*, by Henry Winstanley, *c.*1676, from a presentation set of prints of Audley End. The plain Mount Garden was so-called because it was surrounded by a treed terrace. Such sets of engraved views were made for presentation to family and friends, and later on for tourists.

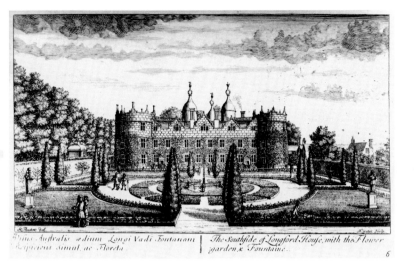

14 *The Southside of Longford House with the Flower Garden &
Fountaine*, one of a set of views of Longford Castle, Wiltshire, by Robert
Thacker engraved by Nicholas Yeates, c.1680. The house is Elizabethan,
built as a triangle; the south front opens onto a balustraded terrace
overlooking the *parterre à l'Angloise* recently made by Lord Coleraine,
who commissioned the views. Cypresses stand at the corners and figures
in the grass.

15 'The Prospect of Compton House from the Grounds, on the South-
East Side Thereof', from William Dugdale's *Antiquities of Warwickshire
Illustrated* (1656). This engraving of Compton Verney Hall by Wenceslaus
Hollar is an early example of an illustration of a country house in a county
history.

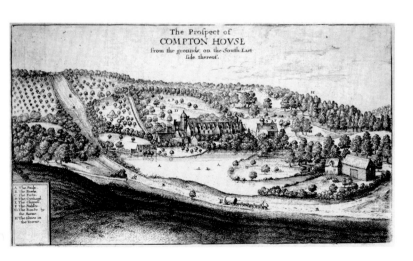

for owners, who would become 'subscribers'. They would pay £10
and receive two copies of every print; other copies would be sold
through the printseller at two shillings each.[40] In some cases, subscribers could dictate other terms: in 1698 the Duke of Newcastle
wanted three of his seats depicted, and wanted 400 prints of each,
for which he would pay £12 when Knyff had completed the print
studies, and another £8 when the prints were delivered. Later, in
January 1702/3, Knyff remarked of Prince George of Denmark
(consort to Queen Anne) that: 'I have done a great many of
Hampton Court and Windsor for his Highness which are not yet
engraved. I not being payd for them.' (fig. 16). It seems that the fee
would have to cover all costs and expenses. Thirty years later, after
Thomas Badeslade – an Englishman – had put in a bill for his
print of Boughton Park, Northamptonshire (see fig. 230; not to be
confused with Boughton House), the owner, the Earl of Strafford,
wished to abate it on the basis that he had paid for Badeslade's
board and lodging.[41]

The first engravings were under way in 1697 but the project
slowed to a halt in 1703 after 71 places had been recorded. No
doubt being impressed by the popularity of the prints in the
county histories, Knyff's publisher afterwards gathered the prints
into *Britannia Illustrata* (1707) (see figs 20, 29, etc.). Kip went on to
take the views and make the engravings for Sir Robert Atkyns's
Glocestershire (1712) (see figs 5, 118, 159 and 173), and, with Badeslade
as the artist, for Dr John Harris's *Kent* (1719) (see figs 176, 193 and
206). By this time prints had become the normal means to depict
country houses and their gardens (fig. 17). The third volume of
Colen Campbell's *Vitruvius Britannicus*, published after a long delay
in 1725, contained many engravings by Hendrik (or Henry) Hulsbergh of gardens after drawings by or borrowed by Campbell (see
figs 136, 204, etc.).

Peter Tillemans produced several oil paintings of country
houses in the 1720s, and made print studies for an abortive county
history of Northamptonshire, though his style of depiction had
changed somewhat.[42] Whereas the views in oil prior to 1700 were
highly detailed, allowing a count of the flowerpots for example,
the alternative was of views from closer to the ground level, giving
a more atmospheric impression of the setting of house and garden

16   Leonard Knyff's bird's-eye study of Hampton Court from the south, 1702. This was referred to in correspondence in 1702, but was never engraved. It shows the gardens as completed by William III, including the Privy Garden in the foreground, and his expanded Banqueting House and new greenhouse to the west, and prior to any changes by Queen Anne; annotations indicate the surfaces.

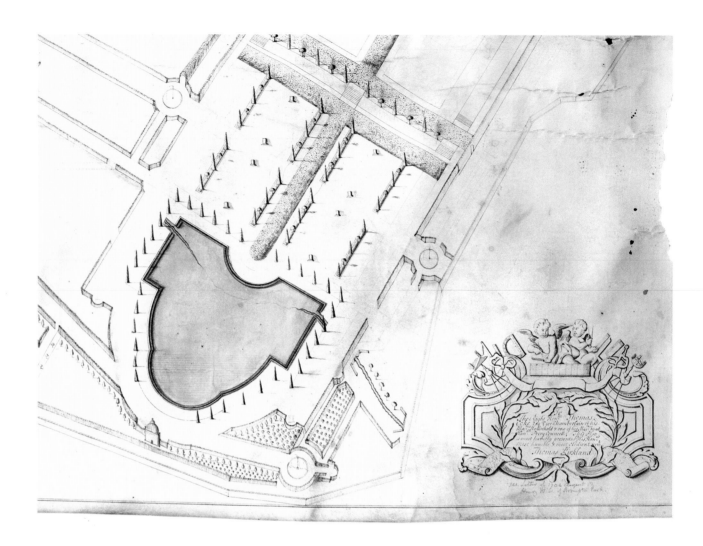

17 Melbourne Hall, from an incomplete study for a print, 'Melbourne House and Gardens', by Thomas Kirkland, c.1722. Such studies were intended for engraving and publication – hence the impressive cartouche dedicated to the owner.

(fig. 18). This style became common with Tillemans and with John Wootton (an Englishman) in the 1740s. Also taking a similar viewpoint were the series of views at Chiswick House painted around 1729 by Andreas Rysbrack for Lord Burlington (see figs 199 and 245), followed by another set, by Jacques Rigaud, in 1734 (see fig. 239). Charles Bridgeman sought out Rigaud to produce pen and ink drawings of Stowe, intended for engraving and the tourist market (see figs 215, 222 and 269). These were eventually ready for sale by his widow in 1740.[43]

Rocque's series of engraved plans, often enlivened with vignettes, give some idea of the importance of tourism to the print trade. He started with Wanstead (1735) and followed this with Hampton Court (1736), Richmond Gardens (1736), Chiswick (1736), Dalton Hall, Yorkshire (1737), Esher Place, Surrey (1737), Oatlands House, Surrey (1737), Wrest Park, Bedfordshire (1737), Claremont, Surrey (1738), Windsor Castle (1738) and others. Those completed by 1739 were included in a fourth volume of *Vitruvius Britannicus*.[44] Although Rocque engraved maps of places outside the Home Counties, Wilton House for instance, these were few by comparison, suggesting that most tourism took place

within an easy reach of London. Meanwhile Badeslade produced drawings of Kiveton, Boughton Park, Belvoir, Stainborough, Exton, Southill, Belton, Chirk Castle, Mount Edgcumbe and elsewhere in the north and west, in his case from the traditional bird's-eye viewpoint.

It remains to answer queries on the reliability of all these prints and paintings as evidence of actual gardens. As with all forms of evidence, a particular image's content and its context need interpretation. There are cases of garden areas being added as if they existed, there can be confusion between plans for and maps of estates, naïve paintings frequently have poor perspective, and there may be other reasons why an image won't be a photographic representation. However, owners were proud of what they achieved,

and to have falsified it deliberately would have defeated the object. In the course of minutely examining hundreds of images, I have generally found a high degree of correspondence between their content and other evidence, such as archives.

---

18   Bifrons in Patrixbourne in Kent, attributed to Jan van der Vaardt, c.1690. The owner is riding out north up Bifrons Hill with his hounds for some fox hunting. The gardens are typical of Restoration times, being a set of walled compartments with gateways, that at the end of the garden providing a visto, although, untypically, the parterre has acquired figures. This is an early example of a viewpoint close to the ground level, giving a more painterly impression of the house and garden than a bird's-eye view.

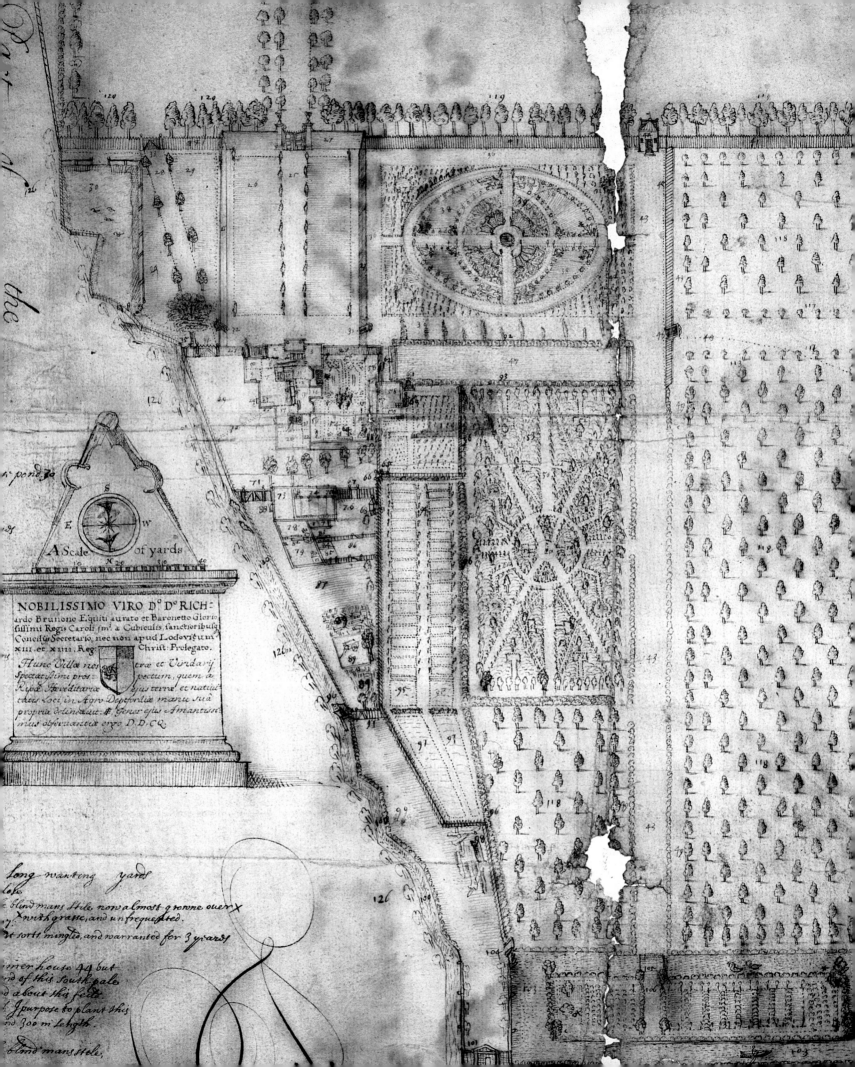

S
E · W
N

A Scale of yards

10   20   30   40

NOBILISSIMO VIRO D° D° RICH-
ardo Brunono Equiti aurato et Baronetto Glorio-
siſſimi Regis Caroli (m?) a Cubiculis, ſanctioribuſq;
Conciliis Secretario, nec non apud Lodovicum
XIII et XIIII Reg: Chriſt: Prolegato.

Hunc Villæ noſtræ et Viridarij
Spectatiſſimi pros-   pectum, quem a
Ripâ hæreditaria   ejus terræ, et natali-
tiis loci, in Agro Deptforia manu ſuâ
propria delineavit. # Gener ejus Amantiſſi-
mus obſervantiæ ergo D.D.CQ.

long wanting yards

lofe

blind mans ſtile now almoſt growne over
with graſſe, and unfrequented.

ſorts mingled, and warranted for 3 yards

mer houſe 44 but
of this South pale
about this feild
I purpose to plant this
300 in length.

blind mans ſtile,

2

Profit and Pleasure

THE PURPOSES OF GARDENS

Periods of English architectural and garden history are often separated by the Civil War of the 1640s, and in terms of the legacy of great gardens the sale and dismemberment of royal and episcopal property, and sequestration of the royalists, do seem to mark the end of an era. Yet in terms of style in garden-making a change-point can be detected slightly earlier. This coincided with another particular and significant change: one in constitutional history. Charles I's reluctant acceptance of the Petition of Right in 1628 meant that no person could be compelled to provide a gift, loan or tax without an Act of Parliament. Parliament thus had the veto on any taxation. It was a crucial moment in Charles's lengthy struggle with the increasingly assertive House of Commons, and an issue that served to polarise the nation. Although the Church of England dominated religious affairs, the nonconforming Puritans rose in influence, and the 1630s saw their first great emigration to

Massachusetts and other colonies, where they could live as their consciences dictated.

In garden-making as in other matters the qualities of simplicity and utility reflected the increasingly Puritanical national ethics. Courtly gardens aside, this tendency of English gardens of the middle of the seventeenth century contrasted with the desire for showy flamboyance in the gardens of the French Court, making them closer in spirit, if not necessarily in look, to the Dutch Classical style, sharing its emphasis on symmetry, proportion and harmony. If France could be said to be discovering how the Baroque translated into gardens, owners in the Low Countries and England adhered more to rational Renaissance principles. This chapter examines the pleasures and purposes of English gardens and parks in this period, and several of the more important religious and philosophical aspects of their design.

Attitudes to display

Some Puritans regarded long hair as a vanity and cut their hair off at the collar (hence 'Roundheads'). Puritan divines preached sermons on the sinfulness of fine dress. Quakers, for long afterwards, were remembered for their 'plain dress' of simple colours and style, a self-conscious statement of their modesty and freedom from the dictates of fashion. When, in the next century, the Earl of Orkney jokingly wrote to his brother about his grass parterre at Cliveden that 'I call it a Quaker parter for it is very plain', he was referring to such eschewals of display.[1] The extravagant clothing at European Courts up to the early 1630s, with high-topped Spanish leather boots, breeches becoming softer and longer, and exaggerated ornamentation with ruffles and ribbons, was recognised as excessive. In the 1630s Charles I and his courtiers – 150 years before Beau Brummell – were to be seen in black doublets and knee-breeches and this dress continued in fashion for another decade.[2] It was not cheap: black dye was expensive, and the material was high-quality silk, often figured, and fringed with costly braid and lace. Young men might hanker for French-inspired fashions but black suits were sober yet graceful, and readily adopted amongst politicians and older men in a Protestant country.

So too in gardens. French parterres were being ornamented by *broderie* designs, named after their counterparts in embroidery, in sprigs and flourishes in boxwork. The English were not ignorant of 'trayles', as *broderie* was termed, but they held little appeal. Admiration was bestowed upon a well-conceived layout and simplicity and utility in the detail. The embellishments of Jacobean gardens had included balustrades, flowerpots, interlacing knots, figures (sculpture), sundials, obelisks, arbours, galleries, figurative topiary, mounts, terraces, summerhouses, mazes, cherry gardens, water gardens and treed walks. These elements and types of garden virtually disappeared from English garden-making in the middle third of the seventeenth century (fig. 19).

The Puritans were ideologically committed to improved husbandry, some being active in improving techniques and others in promoting orchards. Their unease at showy display even extended to the use of flowers for decoration. On the one hand, they were one of God's fine creations, but on the other they hinted at unnecessary luxury and heathenism, and when used in church on feast days or at funerals their very gorgeousness were a distraction from the word and worship of God.[3] In his book *Paradisi in sole* (1629), discussed below, John Parkinson, though a committed Protestant, elided such considerations by emphasising the usefulness of flowers, both in physick and in delight. After all, had not Adam been placed in Paradise, where flowers provided both nourishment and pleasure to the senses?

Puritans also abhorred garden sculptures as a form of graven image, expressly forbidden, they thought, in the Second Commandment. Charles I's brass figures of Venus and Cleopatra, and marble ones of Adonis and Apollo were taken to Hampton Court as the residence of Oliver Cromwell as Protector in 1651, and were placed in the Privy Garden for his pleasure (see fig. 133).[4] Before long, Mrs Mary Netheway addressed a letter to him, beseeching him to destroy them. Her letter (put into modern spelling) reads:

> This one thing I desire of you, to demolish those monsters which are set up as ornaments in Privy Gardens, for whilst they stand, though you see no evil in them, yet there is much evil in it, for whilst the groves and altars of the idols, remained untaken away in Jerusalem, the wrath of God continued against Israel.[5]

Charles I had assembled sculpture in the garden of St James's Palace, encouraged by the Earl of Arundel's fine collection of Antique pieces at Arundel House in the Strand. In 1651 the Council of State ordered that some of the St James's statues should be left unsold because of their rarity and the likelihood that they would be of little value in a sale.[6] The Surveyor of the Works was to make a selection of these statues and to arrange their removal to Whitehall Palace, where they would be set up in the Privy Garden there. This aroused the ire of a Quaker cook, who in 1659 rushed into the garden with a large blacksmith's hammer: 'Hee brake there those goodly statues of brass and marble which, report said, they were the neatlest made and the best workmanshipp in Europe; in half an houers time did above

BALLS

19   Balls Park, *c.*1685, in John Drapentier's engraving in Henry Chauncy's *Hertfordshire*, showing the gardens much as they had been made in about 1640. A dummy double avenue is aligned with the forecourt gate with ball finials, leading to a walk to semicircular steps up onto a terrace with flowerpots in front of the house. The best garden, to the left, has an expensive statue at its centre but is otherwise very plain. House, garden and yard are contained within a rectangle with turrets at the corners.

£500 worth of hurt.'[7] The offender's bail was paid by richer sympathisers.

Most of the élite were repelled by these excesses by the Puritans. Gradually through the 1650s persons of quality, Parliamentarians and Royalists alike, returned to their French tailors. However, some deeper habits of thought were not to be reversed, and propriety, proportion and simplicity had been engrained into the national consciousness. These concerns, which saw the Royal Society founded to promote science, and Classical architecture become the accepted taste of the Commonwealth and Restoration periods, also underlay the preference for plain gardens based on rational geometry and utility. Although in due course fashion brought in sculpture and fine flower borders in the 1680s, the undercurrent in favour of plainness explains why the English never took to *parterres de broderie* in any great numbers, and was to lead to the plain parterres and lawns of the reign of George I.

The pleasures of gardens

Sir William Temple considered that once a man had satisfied his basic needs he would turn to 'the Pleasures of the Senses' in embellishing the scenes he chooses to live in:

> the most exquisite delights of Sense are pursued, in the Contrivance and Plantations of Gardens; which, with Fruits, Flowers, Shades, Fountains, and the Musick of Birds that frequent such happy places, seem to furnish all the pleasures of the several Senses, and with the greatest, or at least the most natural Perfections.[8]

The nature of garden embellishment would be a reflection of an owner's personality and beliefs. A Puritan would exhibit his well-tended fruit trees, a gentleman florist his curious blooms, and the aristocrat his lordly mansion and expensive statues. As to the 'delights of sense', the age-old signals of a flourishing garden, chiefly water, the colour of the flowers, and green or evergreen foliage, continued to be amongst the measures, as the following hints and snippets show.

WATER AND FOLIAGE

John Worlidge, perhaps remembering pre-Civil War fountains, thought that they 'are Principal Ornaments in a Garden'.[9] He considered that 'a Garden cannot ever be said to be complete, nor in its full splendour and beauty, without this Element of Water'.

John Evelyn admired the situation of Ham House 'at the banks of the Sweetest River in the World' (see fig. 81).[10] He also observed in 1675 that Althorp House was 'placed in a pretty open bottome very finely watered' (fig. 20).[11]

As to plants, André Mollet described the particular pleasure derived from Nature's bounty seen in their parts and their variety, 'which yield us so much delight in the variety of their Enamel, Colours, pleasant Odors, that there is not one of our senses which finds not it self charmed by them'.[12] Gardening, he wrote, concentrated and heightened these effects for monarchs as well as everyone else:

> when Art helps this good Mother, and disposes all these Vegetable Productions . . . It then appears in a regularity, which . . . contributes to the delights of the greatest Monarchs, and Mighty Princes . . . after the toilsomness of Political Studys, and the weighty affairs of State, then Walking under some shady covertures, and in Garden-Allies . . .

Sir Francis Bacon, who believed in the restoration of the world from decay since the Fall, was gratified by the appearance of health and renewal. The great enemy was degeneration, such as 'flies and frogs', 'slime or mud' and 'mossiness or putrefaction'. Evelyn agreed, advising against sycamore trees because their leaves turned to mucilage.[13]

Bacon would have had a 'green' in his ideal garden 'because nothing is more Pleasant to the Eye then Greene Grasse kept finely shorne'.[14] Parkinson noted a few grasses 'which I thinke fit to be planted in this Garden . . . for the excellent beauty that is in them above many other plants'.[15] His clear favourite was the 'lesser feather-grass' (otherwise 'bent', *Agrostis tenuis*), which was of 'a fresh greene colour in Summer'. In about 1670 Sir Roger Pratt advised that a house was best set in grassland, 'for so the surface of the earth being always green, will accordingly be pleasant, whereas arable is never so, but whilst the corn is upon it'.[16]

A fresh green colour was appreciated too in trees. Parkinson admired the lime tree (*Tilia cordata*).[17] Evelyn remarked on the 'glossie and polish'd verdure which is exceedingly delightful' of the hornbeam (*Carpinus betulus*), and the ability of beech (*Fagus syl-*

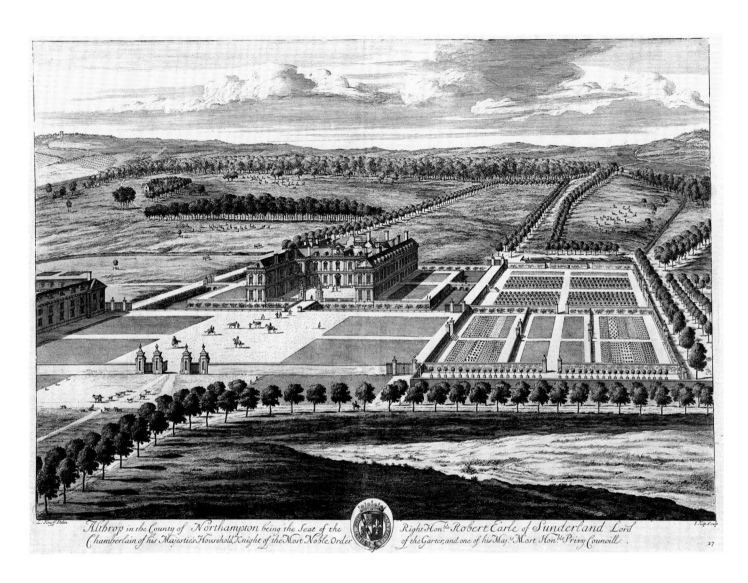

Althrop in the County of Northampton being the Seat of the Right Honble Robert Earle of Sunderland Lord Chamberlain of his Majesties Household, Knight of the Most Noble Order of the Garter, and one of his Majts Most Honble Privy Councill.

vatica) trees to make 'noble Shades with their well furnish'd and glistering leaves'.[18] The lime tree was also admirable for its 'conick or pyramidal Form' and its sweet scent. Worlidge preferred the

plane tree (*Platanus orientalis*) because it grows large and the leaves are broad and of pleasant colour – 'In truth, the World doth not yield a more beautiful Tree for shade than the Plane'.[19]

Evergreen foliage, somewhat rare in Britain, was much prized. Evelyn was particularly proud of his evergreen hedge of holly at Sayes Court: 'Is there under *heaven* a more glorious and refreshing object of the kind, than an impregnable *Hedge* . . . which I can shew in my poor *Gardens* at any time of the year, glitt'ring with its armed and vernish'd *leaves*?'[20] Worlidge expanded on such 'transcendent' pleasures that 'the Owner of a Complete Garden with its Magnificent Ornaments, its Stately Groves, and infinite variety of never dying Objects of Delight every day enjoys'.[21]

20   Althorp House, Northamptonshire, by Knyff and Kip, 1697. This view shows Althorp while still the seat of the second Earl of Sunderland, who had remodelled the house and gardens in 1666–8. The whole layout was rationally planned as a set of squares; there was no parterre, but the fruit garden was ornamental. Sunderland appears to have added the orangery at bottom right. A double avenue framed the approach and a park lawn was defined at the rear.

Good prospect was strongly admired. Charles II remarked that Mount Edgcumbe, with its spectacular views of Plymouth Sound, 'was the pleasantest Seat in the World' (fig. 21).[22] Evelyn thought that Burley-on-the-Hill (see fig. 38) was 'worthily reckon'd amongst the noblest seates in England, situate on the brow of an hill, built à la modern neere a Park Waled in, & a fine Wood at the descent'.[23] In 1701 Sir John Percival liked Hinchingbrook House, Huntingdonshire, which 'stands upon rising ground, & commands Severall good Prospects'.[24] He observed that Burghley House 'Stands in the middle of a large Park upon a rising ground, by which it commands a Prospect not only of Stanford but many vilages & Gentlemans houses' (see fig. 91). Percival's most profound admiration was reserved for Haigh Hall near Wigan, from which thirteen counties could supposedly be seen, 'besides the Ile of man'.[25]

Pratt wished that such scenes would be diversified: 'as here pasture, there arable, here wood, there water, here high ground there lower, the view yet clear, and uninterrupted, the horizon made by some pleasant hills'.[26] At his own home at Ryston, Norfolk, Pratt removed a hedgerow 'because it much hinders ye prospect of ye howse towards the Hill and ye most graceful Wood upon it'. Objects such as castles, great houses and jagged hills were incorporated into topographical paintings. Hence Vorsterman's view of Althorp showed the ruins of Holdenby House on the horizon.[27]

The tradition of viewing mounts continued at New College, Oxford, where the fellows decided in 1642 to enlarge theirs to a square rising through three 'lifts' (terraces) to a height of 50 feet. The work was completed after the Civil War, in 1648.[28] It gave students and fellows opportunity to exercise in the limited space of the college garden while providing a view in towards knots and out over Magdalen College meadows. Castle mottes could be appropriated for similar purposes. The impressive mound at Marlborough Castle was cut with a spiral walk prior to the Civil War, and was known to all who travelled the Bath road (fig. 22).[29] Warwick Castle's motte was similarly shaped, and in the 1680s the antiquary John Aubrey knew of plans for another near Hamstead

21 A sketch of Mount Edgcumbe, Cornwall (on the far right), by Edmund Prideaux, from across the Tamar estuary, *c.*1727. Charles II said it was 'the pleasantest Seat in the World' for its views.

Marshall, Berkshire, 'which is a hill like Silbury Hill on which Captain William Wynde designs to make a screw-walk, as at the keep of the Castle of Marlborough, at the Lord Seymour's'.[30]

Several owners constructed cupolas atop their houses, principally to show off the views to their visitors. Celia Fiennes admired one at Coleshill House, Berkshire, a house by Pratt: 'This gives you a great prospect of gardens, grounds, woods that appertaine to the Seate, as well as a sight of the Country at a distance'.[31] She also climbed up to 'a large Cupelow' at Newby Hall, Yorkshire, in 1699 whence 'you may see a greate way round the Country'.[32] Near London, Arlington House was given one whence one could admire St James's Park (fig. 23).

TAKING THE AIR

From Tudor times riding and the constitutional walk had been seen as health-giving pastimes. Disease, it was thought, was carried in the air. Expelling bad vapours from the lungs by vigor-

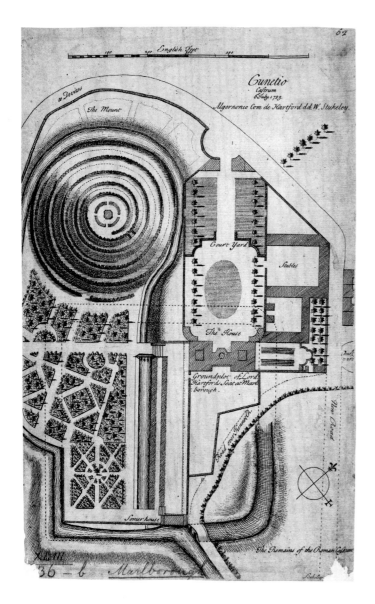

22 An engraved plan of Marlborough Castle, Wiltshire, by William Stukeley, 1723. The spiral path up the prehistoric mound (reused as a medieval castle motte) was seen by John Evelyn in 1654, and the wilderness was later designed to be seen from its summit.

23 A 1680s etching by an unknown hand of Arlington House, Westminster, from St James's Park. When the house was rebuilt after a fire in 1674 the park wall was replaced to the east of the house by an iron grille, which was probably aligned with the lime avenue south of the walk used for the game of pell-mell, and the house was given a cupola to enjoy a wider view; meanwhile, the entrance remained to the south of the house, on the road to Chelsea.

ous exertion kept one healthy. Charles II was a firm adherent of the constitutional, defending the English weather on the grounds that he could be out walking most days of the year, 'and this He thought He could be in *England*, more than in any Country he knew of in *Europe*'.[33]

Worlidge nominated 'good Air' amongst the 'best Ornaments of the Seat': 'It is not the least part of the pleasures of a Garden, to walk and refresh your self either with your friends or Acquaintance'.[34] Evelyn was persuaded to help John Rose get *The English Vineyard* (1666) to print having encountered him 'one day refresh-

ing my self in the garden at Essex-house'.[35] In July 1666 Samuel Pepys was in St James's Park, where he joined Hugh May, the Comptroller of the Office of Works.[36] As they walked, Pepys listened to the other's views: 'Our business here being ayre, the best form of garden was in plain grass and gravel.'

Pepys often walked in gardens. He was in Gray's Inn Walks by himself on the Lord's Day, 30 June 1661, 'seeing the fine ladies walk there', and was a frequent visitor thereafter. Their adjacency to the City of London and the other Inns of Court ensured their popularity, which was attested by references by visitors and the number of times that the Inn's Pension (governing council) made regulations to control their use.[37] The layout had remained substantially as created by Bacon between 1598 and 1609. Appreciation of the Walks' good air was no doubt all the stronger following the ravages of the plague in 1665. Worlidge was one of the authors who

remarked on its views.[38] That from the terrace northwards towards Highgate contributed much to the place's attractions and was jealously safeguarded. In 1711 Addison wrote of his fictional friend, Sir Roger de Coverley, in *The Spectator*: 'I was no sooner come into Gray's-Inn Walks, but I heard my Friend upon the Terrace hemming twice or thrice to himself with great Vigour, for he loves to clear his Pipes in good Air (to make use of his own Phrase).'[39]

24   A sketch, possibly by Hendrick Danckerts, of Charles II walking in St James's Park with his dogs and entourage, c.1670. The Banqueting House and the Whitehall steps are in the background, and the recently staked trees and canal can be seen to the right.

The principal walking place in London, however, was St James's Park (fig. 24). Opportunities to meet friends, personages, even the King, informally was part of the attraction; another was the variety of things to see. There was a pell-mell alley in St James's Fields before the Civil War. In this game players would give the ball a mighty strike with a long-handled mallet. Cockleshells were beaten into loam as the running surface, and side boards were erected for safety, as onlookers would be numerous. Because this course was partly built upon during the Commonwealth, Charles II had a new pell-mell course constructed in St James's Park at the Restoration (see fig. 71).[40]

Charles kept a herd of cattle in the park, handy for the making of syllabub. He also established a decoy, contrived by a Shadrack

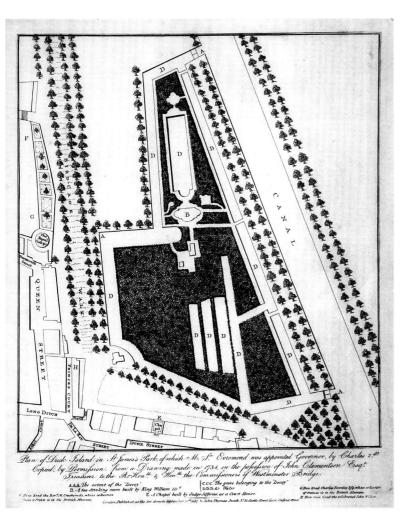

Plan of Duck Island in St James's Park, of which M.r S.r Evremond was appointed Governor, by Charles 2.d
Copied by Permission from a Drawing made in 1734, in the possession of John Clementson Esq.r
Treasurer to the R.t Hon.ble & Hon.ble the Commissioners of Westminster Bridge.

AAA The extent of the 'Decoy'
B A tea-drinking room built by King William III.d
CCC The grove belonging to the Decoy
DDD.&c Water
E A Chapel built by Judge Jefferies as a Court House.
F Here lived the Rev.d M. Crachrode, whose collection
G Here lived Charles Townley Esq. whose collection of statuas is in the British Museum
H Here once lived the celebrated John Wilkes

London Published as the Act directs Septem.r 1.st 1807 by John Thomas Smith, N.º 31 Castle Street East, Oxford Street.

him much curiosity.[42] At Windsor Little Park, the new lodge built in 1675 was given a canal that served as another menagerie for water fowl.

Some gardens and courtyards were lined with wire cages in order to keep pheasants and other birds of brilliant plumage. Charles I had such a 'volery' (aviary) garden in Whitehall Palace, which lasted, in name at least, till 1663.[43] Pheasants were ordered up to Chatsworth in 1658 and an ambitious birdhouse and yard were created there in 1697.[44] The Duchess of Lauderdale turned one of her bedrooms at Ham House into an aviary in the 1670s, presumably for small songbirds in cages; it is still known as the Volery Room.[45] A volery garden was made alongside the banqueting house at Hampton Court in 1701/2.[46] In the eighteenth century several collections of pheasants or waterfowl were incorporated into gardens.

BOWLING

The moist English climate is conducive to good grass. The game of bowls had been popular since the Middle Ages, and became associated with taverns frequented by gamesters and prostitutes. It was seen as diverting yeomen from practising archery and was thus subject to a succession of restrictive statutes: an Act of 1541 banned the playing of bowls outside a person's own garden or orchard with a penalty of 6s 8d. Accordingly, a yeoman, John Snelson of Croxton, Staffordshire, was fined in 1599 when he was found playing unlawful games, namely 'English Bowles against the form of the statute in this case published and provided'.[47] An exception was made for those with lands of the yearly value of £100, who might obtain licences to play on their own greens.

However, it was a losing battle to enforce the restrictions, as John Stow explained in 1598 in writing about London's suburbs.[48] Any spare ground was likely to be purloined for bowling and gaming, as had formerly happened at Northumberland House in Aldgate, though 'so many Bowling Alleys, and other houses for unlawful gaming have been raised in other parts of the City & suburbs, that this [place] is left and forsaken by the Gamesters'. Grub Street was one of these: it had been the area for bowyers,

Hilens, in 1661 (fig. 25).[41] Although designed for the conventional purpose of trapping ducks in nets, Charles was soon keeping exotic birds there, as is seen by a payment 'to William Thawsell for Fish for the Cormorant the xij.th of March 1661'. There were other payments for oats and hempseed. Charles paid for 'six leggs for the Crane', presumably wooden replacements for a wounded bird. Evelyn, visiting in 1665, noticed a pelican, which caused

25   *Plan of Duck Island in St James's Park*, an engraving of 1807 from a drawing made in 1734. Having been designed as a decoy in the 1660s, the island soon accommodated Charles II's collection of water birds.

fletchers, and bow-string makers, but was in Stow's time 'giving place to a number of bowling-alleys and dicing-houses, which in all places are increased, and too much frequented'.[49]

It had long been a custom in England that sports and games were played on Sunday afternoons, though the Puritans saw this as a violation of the Fourth Commandment, which prescribed that the Sabbath should be holy and no manner of work should take place on it. Its interpretation had become a point of contention with the gentry, and James I attempted to adjudicate by issuing a proclamation in 1617 called 'The Book of Sports', which forbade bowls on Sundays. Many places of public entertainment were already based around greens, and as the craze spread, private greens were made in the gardens of gentleman enthusiasts. William Lawson remarked in 1618 that in his ideal garden 'it shall be a pleasure to have a Bowling Alley . . . to stretch your armes'.[50] Gray's Inn had already made a green in 1609 immediately outside the garden wall.[51] The master of Magdalen College, Oxford, no doubt attempting to divert his charges away from worse temptations, had a bowling green made within the grounds of the college about 1630.[52]

Around 1610 Prince Henry installed a bowling green in the north-east corner of St James's Park, called 'The Spring Garden', and in 1631 the keeper for both was mentioned in a grant. Members of the Court, and increasingly gentlemen with no connection to it, already walked in the park. As the door into the Spring Garden was just next to the park's Tiltyard Gate, it had by 1635 become enough of a public resort, serving food and drink, and witnessing scandalous behaviour, for an attempt to close it.[53] In 1647 it was closed on Sundays and public fast days. Evelyn found this so in 1654: '*Cromwell* and his partisans having shut up, and seiz'd on Spring Garden, which 'til now had ben the usual rendezvous for the Ladys & Gallants'.[54]

Instead, Evelyn was entertained at the Mulberry Garden, a four-acre walled garden at the west end of St James's Park in which James I had attempted to establish silk growing, and which was added to the gardens of Goring House (later Arlington House) in the 1630s. Confiscated and disposed of by Parliament in 1645, it opened shortly after as 'the onely place of refreshment about the Towne for persons of the best quality'. The Spring Garden itself could not reopen, as it had been divided up for building plots in the 1650s, but the Restoration in 1660 was an opportunity for a 'New Spring Garden', a former market garden just across the river at Vauxhall, which became instantly popular.[55] The Mulberry Garden served its last mulberry pie in about 1670, when it was reincorporated into the gardens of Goring House, its gambling and whoring having already removed to the New Spring Garden.

Bowling greens continued to be the main attraction for many places of entertainment, especially for the lower orders. Around 1650 the gardens of Marylebone Manor House, including its bowling green, were detached from it and made accessible through the Rose of Normandie tavern, later being known as 'Marylebone Gardens'. A green on Putney Heath, operated between 1690 and 1750, and became perhaps the most noted in the neighbourhood of London. However, interest in bowling amongst the gentry was to wane by George I's reign. According to Sir John Cullum, a Suffolk antiquary, 'S[r] Thomas Hanmer, the Speaker, who died in 1746, had a very fine bowling green, contiguous to his house at Mildenhall; and was perhaps one of the last gentlemen of any fashion in the county, that amused themselves with that diversion.'[56]

Paradisus terrestris

Sir Francis Bacon argued for observation, experiment and the compilation of natural histories. By the end of the seventeenth century most scientists, however religious, were preferring knowledge induced from scientific inquiry over explanations from the Bible, or Greek or Roman texts. However, in the early part of the century many older beliefs or ways of seeing the world had coexisted with the discoveries in astronomy, microscopy, chemistry and other sciences. Experimental science took some false turns – witness the supposed philosophical qualities of caves, which led to a brief interest in them in gardens. Those who believed in the restorative power of prayer and hard work achieved more solid gains in husbandry, estate improvement and fruit growing. Although with culinary rather than religious connotation, kitchen gardens were to improve and multiply at the hands of practical gardeners.

SCIENCE AND RELIGION

Beliefs, such as communication with angels, had sometimes arisen from biblical passages. Scientific discovery itself was thought to be knowledge handed down from God through this medium. The title page to Parkinson's *Paradisus Terrestris* (1629) showed such angels and Jehovah's blessings shining through the clouds. Evelyn likewise told the Norwich physician Thomas Browne that 'caves, grotts, mounts, and irregular ornaments of gardens do contribute to contemplative and philosophicall enthusiasm . . . and prepare them for converse with good angells'.[57] Believing in astrology, Evelyn also thought that the moon's motion controlled the circulation of sap in trees. He took care that his planting was carried out at the most propitious phase of the moon. Browne had in the same year published *The Garden of Cyrus*, which explored the mystic qualities of the number five, as seen in quincunx plantations.

Medical theory was becoming dominated by the followers of Paracelsus, who had proposed chemical therapies, which progressively supplanted herbalism. Parkinson's *Theatrum Botanicum* (1640) was to be the last great English herbal. The science of botany was emerging, and classifications stemming from observing the plants themselves, rather than their uses, were now required. An early attempt, supported by Browne, was a broad classification by the degree of the plant's woodiness, into: '*Arbor, frutex, suffrutex, herba* and that fifth which comprehendeth the *fungi* and *tubera*'.[58]

Parkinson's earlier book (*Paradisi in Sole, Paradisus Terrestris* in full) was a pun on his own name (Park-in-sun), and also alluded to the popular conception of the 'Garden of Pleasure' as an earthly paradise. In this book he gave the first comprehensive account in English of the pleasure garden with details of all those plants that were worthy, by virtue of their beauty, to be planted in it. Parkinson made it clear, as did Dutch writers, that the creation of an earthly paradise was to him an act of devotion to God and His works.[59] He expressed the Protestant view that the earth's abundance had been provided for Man by a generous Maker. Upon Adam's transgression, mankind forfeited Paradise and succeeding generations lost Adam's perfect knowledge. Furthermore, the Earth itself was in a constant state of degradation. Protestants believed that this slide into decay and barbarity could be reversed only through unremitting physical toil in a garden, a form of devotion, as the remaking of the Garden of Eden on Earth should go hand in hand with the reform of Man's spiritual state.

PHILOSOPHERS' GARDENS

Bacon promoted the idea of caves in gardens as an aid to philosophical reflection. His *New Atlantis* (1627) described a fictional country that had reached an almost perfect state. The 'father of Solomon's House' revealed some of the 'preparations and instruments' that laid the foundations of knowledge:

> We have large and deepe *Caves* of several Depths: The deepest are sunke 600 Fathome: And some of them are digged and made under great Hills and Mountaines: for *Prolongation of Life*, in some Hermits that choose to live ther, well accommodated of all things necessarie, and indeed live very long; By whom also we learne many things.[60]

Bacon's physician, Dr William Harvey, who discovered the circulation of blood, formed caves in his own garden, perhaps in the 1630s: 'He had a house heretofore at Combe, in Surrey, a good aire and prospect, where he had Caves made in the Earth in which in Summer time he delighted to meditate.'[61] Harvey was also physician to the Earl of Arundel, who made caves at Albury in about 1635 'wherein he delighted to sit and discourse' – Arundel narrowly escaped death when his collapsed. One of Arundel's sons, Charles Howard, must have started on his garden at the Deepdene, Dorking, Surrey, in 1655 or before, for that year Evelyn 'went to Darking, to see Mr. Charles Howard's Amphitheatre Garden . . . he shew'd us divers rare plants; Caves, an Elaboratory' (fig. 26).[62] Evelyn kept a 'private garden' at his home at Sayes Court, in which, under a pigeon-house, he too had an 'Elaboratorie'.

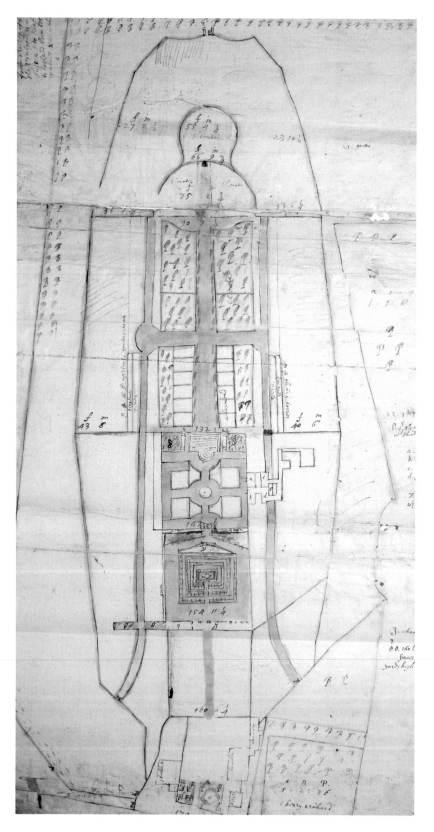

John Aubrey described the caves of Howard, the 'Christian philosopher', in 1673:

In the hill on the left hand, being sandy ground is a cave digged thirty six paces long, four broad, and five yards high; and at about two thirds of the hill (where the crook, or bowing, is) he hath dug another subterranean walk or passage, to be pierced through the hill; through which as through a tube you have the vista over all the south part of Surrey and Sussex to the sea . . . on the West side of the garden is a little building which is . . . divided into a laboratory and a neat oratory, by Mr. Howard . . . In short, it is an epitome of Paradise, and the Garden of Eden seems well imitated here . . .[63]

Charles Howard's older brother Henry was part of the group that set up the Royal Society in 1661, and, as administrator for their father, had taken possession of Albury during the 1650s. Henry was not able to establish himself at Court but was easily persuaded that he was a patron of the arts and sciences of a high order. He or Evelyn thus may have seen him as being a successor to Nicolas-Claude Fabri de Peiresc, a great virtuoso and promoter of scientific inquiry in the reign of Louis XIII. Evelyn had himself already been cast in that mould as the translation into English of Peiresc's biography in 1657 was dedicated by the translator to him for his own 'Peireskian Vertues'.[64]

Evelyn thus knew of Peiresc's chateau, Boisgency (modern Belgentier), near Toulon, which had a garden on which the superintendant of the French Royal gardens, Jacques Boyceau de la Barauderie, had advised.[65] It had a lengthy upper terrace with orchards and large vegetable quarters falling to a broad canal. Apart from the house at Albury being at the base of the hill, rather than the top, its situation thus had a topographical affinity with Boisgency, which could be furthered by design. Eve-

26   John Aubrey's manuscript map of the Deepdene, Surrey, 1673, showing his parterres and orchards, as well as the caves dug into the hills to either side and cherry orchard bottom right. North is at the bottom.

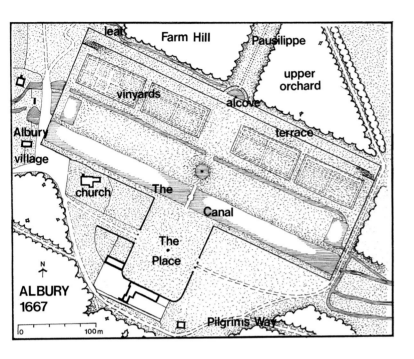

Farm Hill — leat — Pausilippe — upper orchard — vinyards — alcove — Albury village — terrace — church — The Canal — The Place — N — ALBURY 1667 — Pilgrims Way — 0 — 100m

27   A reconstruction by the author of the garden at Albury Place, Surrey, as made according to Evelyn's ideas, 1667. The ground rose from a canalised millpool through vineyards to an impressive terrace and alcove, where a tunnel ('Pausilippe') was dug through the soft sandstone of the hill.

lyn's suggestions for Albury in 1667 was a replanting of the vine-yard on the south-facing slope, enclosing it with walls, creating a canal from the millpond and forming a quarter-mile terrace by the top wall from which the whole of the garden, the house and much of the park could be seen (fig. 27). He designed a tunnel through the hill from the upper terrace in imitation of the tunnel near Virgil's tomb near Naples, hence creating a *locus* of great philosophical power.[66]

Another facet of the philosophical garden was the idea of *ver perpetuum* (perpetual spring). Bacon had proposed that 'there ought to be gardens for all the months in a year', including hollies, ivy, bays, junipers, cypresses, yews and other evergreens in the garden for the winter months, 'that you may have *Ver Perpetuum* as the Place affords'.[67] Other authors agreed. Thomas Browne stated that 'the

verdant state of things is the Symbole of the Resurrection'.[68] Sir Thomas Hanmer, grandfather of the Sir Thomas mentioned above, gave a catalogue of 'GREENS which are such plants whose VERDURE is PERPETUAL, being never wholly uncloth'd of their sweet or beautiful Leaves and therefore much esteem'd by us'.[69]

One of Evelyn's aims at Sayes Court appears to have been to gain the practical knowledge to bring *ver perpetuum* into reality. One of the chapters in the abortive 'Elysium Britannicum' was to have been 'Of verdures, Perennial-greenes, and perpetuall Springs'. Not only did he plant a holly hedge of magnificent proportions, seven feet high and 160 feet long, along his mount or terrace, but he carried out many experiments on 'greens' in the 1650s. He argued in favour of yew (that it was not poisonous and was very 'tonsile' (suitable for clipping)) and later claimed that he had brought it into general use in parterres.[70] He also recommended the bay tree (*Laurus nobilis*), juniper (*Juniperus communis*) and laurel (*Prunus laurocerasus*).[71]

Pierre Morin of Paris had acquired alaternus (*Rhamnus alaternus*) from Provence and was selling it as an alternative to phillyrea (*Phillyrea angustifolia*). Evelyn begged his father-in-law to send some from Paris, and by 1658 he was able to boast that 'I might glory to have been the first propagator in England'.[72] By 1664 he was recommending that 20-foot-high hedges were possible with phillyrea, which kept its branches right down to the ground. He recommended the Italian cypress (*Cupressus sempervirens*), if 'shorn into a conique or pyramidal form', and claimed great popularity already:

the Cypress-tree was, but within a few years past, reputed so tender, and nice a Plant, that it was cultivated with the greatest care, and to be found only amongst the Curious; whereas we see it now, in every Garden, rising to as goodly a bulk and stature, as most which you shall find even in Italy it self . . .[73]

He had 'neer a thousand' growing in his garden in 1664.

At this time, when cabinets of curiosities were being assembled, rare or alternate forms of plants were curious and collectable. Sir Thomas Hanmer mentioned variegated holly and phillyrea in 1659.[74] Worlidge, welcoming such plants as lightening ever-

28 Golden holly (*Ilex acquifolium* 'Aureamarginata') at Hampton Court, propagated from early eighteenth-century hollies in the Privy Garden that were removed when this garden was restored.

green plantations, noted gilded sports of laurel, phillyrea, box and rosemary, but thought that the 'most excellent of all which gilded plants is the Holly whose Bark as well as Leaf is variegated with a bright yellow' (fig. 28).[75]

HUSBANDRY AND IMPROVEMENT

Those who believed in the new Protestant order paid much attention to husbandry. Their literature on the subject was voluminous, and always claimed to be of utility to the nation. The central figure was Samuel Hartlib, who provided information and encouragement to a large number of correspondents, and whose *His Legacy* (1651) was perhaps the most famous of his group's publications.

The title page to Ralph Austen's *A Treatise of Fruit-Trees* (1653) showed a figure representing 'Profits' shaking hands with another,

'Pleasures'. Improvement 'as well for Pleasure as Profit' was the theme of John Smith, an officer of the Royal Forests in the reign of Charles II.[76] He envisaged on his estate of 200 acres

> several Orchards and Gardens, with Fruit, Flowers and Herbs both for Food and Physick, variety of Fowl, Bees, Silk-worms, Bucks, Does, Hares, and other Creatures . . . Also Fish-ponds and Streams of water stored with many kinds of Fish, and stocked with Decoy-Ducks; And the Use and Vertues of all the Plants in this Garden of Pleasure.

Indeed, he considered such an estate would have been a 'little Theatre of Nature', and a 'pleasant Land, Garden, or Paradise'. A walk through arable land, for example, would have enabled the reader to 'behold God's blessing by the great increase of Corn'.[77] The estate had become an ideal, delighting the senses and demonstrating God's benevolence. Smith summed up: 'although this be not the Paradise we read of, yet it does much resemble the same . . . a thousand pleasant Delights are attendant in this Pleasant Land'.[78] Slightly later a Scottish gardener, John Reid, published an idealised plan of an estate, organised into a huge octagon.[79]

Travellers were invited to admire the productivity of a seat, for example its fruit, or the game in the park. Sir John Percival was to notice that the gardens at Newby Hall 'afford much fruit', and in the house was a picture 'of an Ox wch Sr Edward Blacket had kill'd in 1692 wch weigh^d 146 Stone & odd pounds'.[80] Sir Richard Allen's gardens at Somerleyton, Suffolk, were out of order, but his otherwise happy situation was remarked upon:

> This Gentleman . . . has a large Park in which are Deer, Sheep, & Oxen for he kills his own meat. Besides this he has a Warren, Dove house, Fish Ponds, Decoys, & all manner of game within half a mile of it . . . he can see Norwich Spire wch is 18 miles distant, on the other Side he can see the Sea . . . so that Sr Richard has all conveniencys either for the Eye or mouth.

Fruit trees were the subject of a disproportionate number of the Puritan publications. The supposition that, before the Fall, Adam and Eve had eaten only fruit and nuts may have spurred on arborists to conduct practical experiments. Certainly, the works on orchards by Austen and John Beale were a great advance over the earlier manuals of Thomas Tusser and Gervase Markham. The most respected treatises were French, or sometimes Dutch, however.[81] If French, the answer could be one of a number of translations by Evelyn.

A general shortage of timber for ship building, iron foundries and other uses led to the encouragement of planting. In *The English Improver Improved* (third impression, 1653), Walter Blith, a Parliamentary captain, and agent for the sequestration of Royalist land, included a chapter on how to plant trees in 'a New Plantation . . . in such a way as shall raise as much in twenty yeares growth, as usually and naturally growth in forty or fiftie years'.[82] As a landed gentleman himself, he saw that planting had an ornamental dimension, anticipating Evelyn, Moses Cook and other later authors on planting. He thought that wooded blocks of 10, 20 or 30 acres set out as squares, triangles or ovals 'as thy Phantasie leads thee' would suit.[83] Inside, there should be a circle at which vistos would intersect. This arrangement would be useful when removing timber, but 'as well as for walks for thy recreation'. Walks could be carried onwards as rides through such woods.

Blith also advised that 'several Groves or Plumps of Trees may be Erected about any Manour, House or Place', both for the production of timber and 'for delight and pleasure'.[84] A 'plump' describes an unordered cluster or tuft of objects. A number of tree plumps, or clumps, in this pure sense, can be seen in the Knyff and Kip view of the ancient park at Stansted House, Sussex (fig. 29). During the seventeenth century the term was employed for small, usually circular, nurseries outside garden walls. Evelyn described how to obtain elm suckers, which 'you may . . . plant in the *Ulmarium*, or place design'd for them; and which if it be in *plumps . . .* or in *Hedge-rows*, it will be the better'.[85]

Evelyn's own garden was at Sayes Court, Deptford, belonging to his father-in-law (fig. 30). He had purchased a copy of *Paradisus Terrestris*, made contact with the leaders of the scientific community in Oxford, and bought the Puritans' books on husbandry as they were published. Concerned to be useful himself, he carried out many experiments from 1651 to improve skills in the seminary and the nursery. For most of the 1650s he was a keen exper-

29 Bird's-eye view from the west of Stansted House, Sussex, by Knyff and Kip, *c*.1700. There are 'plumps' (or clumps) in this ancient parkland, owned by Lord Scarborough, as well as a belt. Both house and garden date from the 1680s. In general plan the garden is similar to places associated with Robert Hooke.

imenter, intending his results for *Elysium Britannicum*, a book that he never managed to get to press. The fame of Evelyn's experiments spread. Before long, in 1656, he was showing his garden to the Marquess of Argyll, Lord Lothian '& some other Scotch noblemen all strangers to me'.[86] A stream of increasingly eminent notables followed, including Charles II in 1663.

Evelyn was thus well-placed to write *Sylva* (1664), and became the acknowledged expert on trees when it was published. This book, in its several editions in Evelyn's lifetime, was the standard work on tree planting and remained so for over a century. He later gave warm approval to Cook's *The Manner of Raising, Ordering, and Improving Forrest-trees* (1676).[87] Yet such books were only modestly successful in their professed aim of accelerating planting. Likewise, Austen's works were unsuccessful in changing laws and setting up academies. These books on improvement were acquired by many

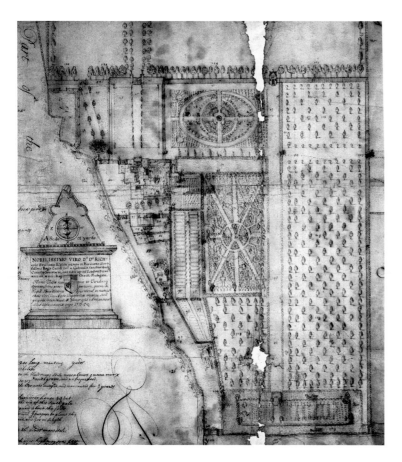

30 Evelyn's plan of his gardens at Sayes Court, 1653. The approach was by a short avenue leading to gates and a forecourt. East of the forecourt was his oval parterre and east of the house was his 'grove', both after French models. They were divided by a terrace. Further east were orchards.

landowners, and whilst they may not have inspired owners as much as the authors had hoped, they did prepare the ground for the practical improvements in husbandry and tree planting in the late seventeenth century.

FRUIT AND KITCHEN GARDENING

Fruit was losing its connotations with medicinal purging as it became possible to eat it raw and enjoy its culinary uses. The fruit garden, as opposed to the common orchard, could be regarded as a 'garden of delight'.[88] The beauty of a fruit tree in blossom was one obvious delight, and several early seventeenth-century fruit gardens were referred to as 'cherry gardens' (see fig. 26). Such a garden might also include other attractive or interesting plants, and the commoner sorts of flowers. Another pleasure was to show off the latest and best varieties.

The practice of training fruit trees against walls was established by Carolean times and soon every available surface was used. The walls were heightened to twelve or more feet, giving scope for training apples and pears, and they were provided with borders of at least three feet, sufficient to nourish the roots but also to allow easy picking. These higher walls also afforded protection against wind and helped to trap the heat of the sun.

The number of varieties available was astonishing. Parkinson in 1629 listed 48 apples, 54 pears, 53 plums, 29 cherries and 19 peaches, besides a handful of apricots and nectarines.[89] He and various later authors up to 1670 mentioned in total 100 varieties of apple, 109 of pear, 68 of plum, 42 of cherry, 66 of peach, 15 of nectarine and 10 of apricot. After 1660, the bulk of newly described fruit trees were apple, pear and peach, many being imported from France and the Low Countries. It is clear why Sir William Temple thought that 'gardening had grown into such Vogue, and to have been so mightily improved in three or four and twenty years of His Majesty's Reign, that perhaps few Countries are before us, either in the Elegance of our Gardens, or in the number of our Plants.'[90]

Earth walls were best for absorbing the sun's rays and hastening the ripening of the fruit, with the branches pinned by means of wooden pegs. Much better for training was a brick wall, which could accept nails. Worst was a stone wall, which was slow to heat up and difficult to nail into. Arborists soon discovered which aspects suited particular trees: peaches and apricots were usually planted against the warmest, south-facing, walls, whilst cherries thrived on north-facing walls. Rea and others advised that more ornamental forms of wall fruit could be planted in the flower garden, such as double-flowered varieties of peach, cherry or pomegranate.

At first, the training of fruit trees against walls was unsophisticated, but standards improved with experience and the reading of French manuals. Sir Henry Capel imported several varieties of fruit tree to his garden at Kew, noted by Moses Cook in 1676, and admired by Evelyn in 1678 for its 'choice fruit'.[91] 'Here is an incomparable Collection of the choicest fruits', enthused Evelyn about Cook's efforts at Cassiobury, Essex, in 1680, and in 1688 at Sir William Temple's at Sheen, in Surrey, he noted that 'the wall Fruite-trees are most exquisitely nailed and applied, far better than in my life I had ever noted'.[92]

'The kitchen garden' was a term used by Parkinson, but separate walled areas devoted to pot-herbs were uncommon at country seats before the Civil War. A significant number were then made from the 1650s. Whilst the Puritan authors encouraged the better growing of pot-herbs as well as fruit, and some even argued for a purely vegetarian diet, those who first made separate walled kitchen gardens were those who had travelled to France and Italy. They would be inclined to the use of forks at table and to embrace the new French *haut cuisine* instead of the famous preference of English squires and parsons for roast beef, pies and tarts.

The most popular books on *cuisine* were Pierre François de la Varenne's *Le Cuisinier François* (1651), and Nicolas de Bonnefons's *Le Jardinier Français* (1651), which Evelyn Englished, and *Les Délices de la Campagne* (1654). De la Varenne emphasised the natural flavours of foods and smaller, lighter, but more numerous, dishes, such as individual pastries and turnovers. His recipes included baked pears and baked Jerusalem artichokes. De Bonnefons encouraged cooks to use the freshest and simplest ingredients from their gardens, and believed that flavours should never be diluted; so, for example, a pea soup should capture the essence of peas. Much food, both meat and vegetable, was traditionally preserved by salt or vinegar, but this new *cuisine* led to a rage, headed by Louis XIV himself, for the freshest peas, fine fruit and young tender leaves. Many more varieties of fruit than ever before began to be cultivated, and asparagus, artichokes, and spinach became much sought after.

'Saletts' now came in several forms: fresh leaves (lettuce, cress, chickory, purslane, tarragon, saxifrage, garden cress, watercress, lamb's lettuce and pimpernel, for example, and flowers as well as herbs) with vinaigrette (vinegar, oil, salt and spices), pickled salads (cucumbers, asparagus, cabbage, and other vegetables, packed in vinegar, salt and spices), composed salads (chopped greens with salted meats), boiled salads (warm vegetables dressed in vinegar and spices), and fruit salads (lemon and pomegranate in syrup). As a rule, the greater the variety of ingredients, the more Nature's bounty was enjoyed. Any gourmet aristocrat at his country seat would thus perceive that his cook required the support of a specialised kitchen quarter.

The cook might also desire an ice house for making ice creams, whilst cold drinks were much in vogue in France and then in England. Charles II built a 'snow-house and an ice-house' in Green Park at the Restoration and followed this with one at Windsor, appointing a Simon Manselli as Yeoman Keeper of Ice and Snow in 1665. Ice houses were often found in parks where there was a convenient body of water, but were ideally placed in reach of the kitchen.

Early kitchen gardens were set out in the traditional way with railed or hedged square quarters. The hedges could be of soft fruit, or rails could support either soft fruit or apples trained laterally. In time, locks on the garden doors lessened the need for railing as security, but some method of drawing the attention of visitors away from the broken ground, untidy rows of pot-herbs and manuring was desirable. The borders around the quarters might thus retain their soft fruit hedges, or perhaps be planted with the new 'dwarf' fruit trees. These were smaller trees more suited to gardens than orchards. By mid-century, dwarfing rooting stocks, such as Paradise and Doucin for apples, and quince for pears, were becoming available from France and the Low Countries. The Mollets used dwarfs in the Royal Garden at St James's (see figs 66a and b). André elsewhere advised 'high Palissados' so that the 'deformity' of kitchen quarters might be hidden: 'For we do not allow that the Garden of Pleasure should admit common herbs; nor yet of Fruit-trees, except they be planted as Wall-fruit'.[93] In fact, by this time any garden wall commonly supported wall-fruit as in the fruit garden.

Having discussed the pleasures of gardens and matters of gardening in the mid-seventeenth-century garden, it is now time to turn to their design.

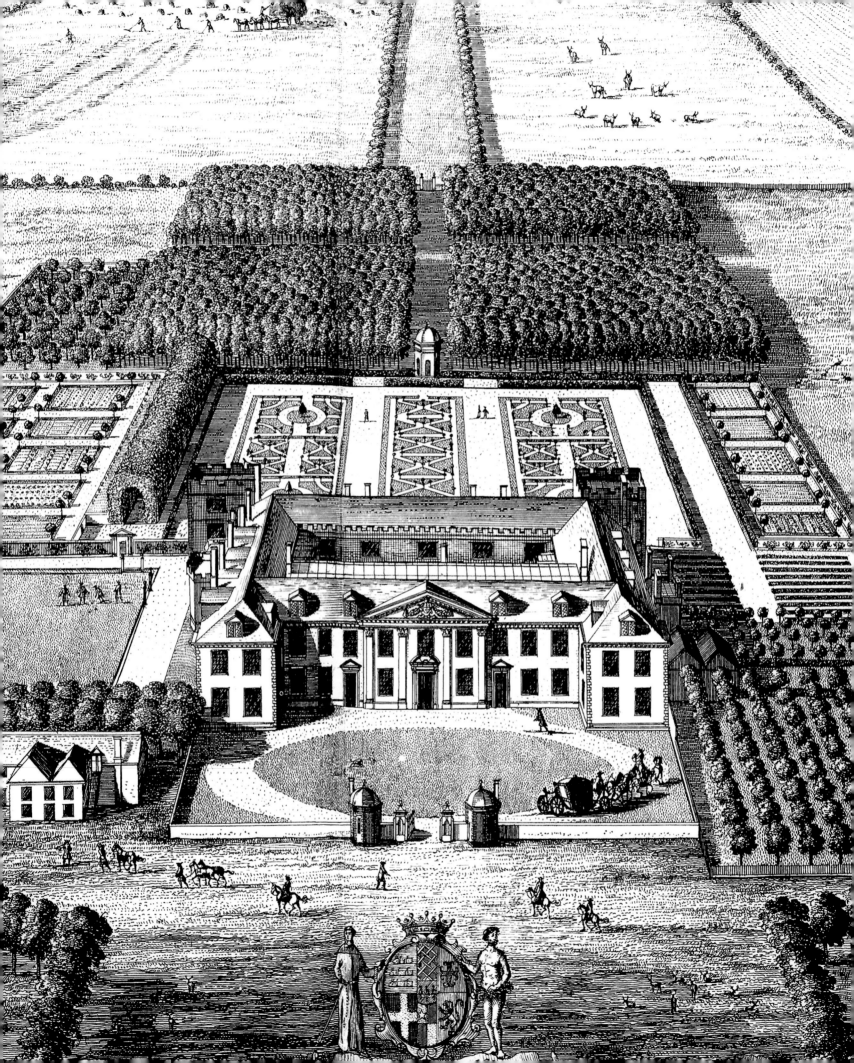

3

English Garden Design

1630–1680

The previous chapter considered the political and cultural background to the national tradition in garden-making from 1630 to about 1680. The attempts by English monarchs to rival royal examples abroad have also to be judged in an international, diplomatic, context. The wider background influenced the style and look of non-royal gardens through Parliamentarian times, the Commonwealth and after the return to royal rule, until about 1680. Throughout the political turmoil of this half-century there were only minor alterations in the conventions governing the making of fine gardens. The principal aspects of garden design were its adherence to fashionable qualities in denoting its owner's standing, its response to such issues as prospect, aspect, shelter and soil, and the disposition of the garden's several walled gardens into a well-planned whole.

Theory and practice on situation

The owner, architect and gardener each had their respective responsibilities in devising fine gardens. The development of Italian principles in the English context led, for example, to the differentiation of garden areas. At the same time, another Italian feature, the end-terrace, was having to give way as a new fashion for a principal axis advanced. Advice on situation originating in the sweltering heat of the Mediterranean summer needed to be radically recast for the temperate latitudes of England.

THE OWNER'S RESPONSIBILITY

Just as a gentry owner was expected to have, or to acquire, some architectural knowledge prior to building a house, his accomplishments should likewise include the devising and enclosing

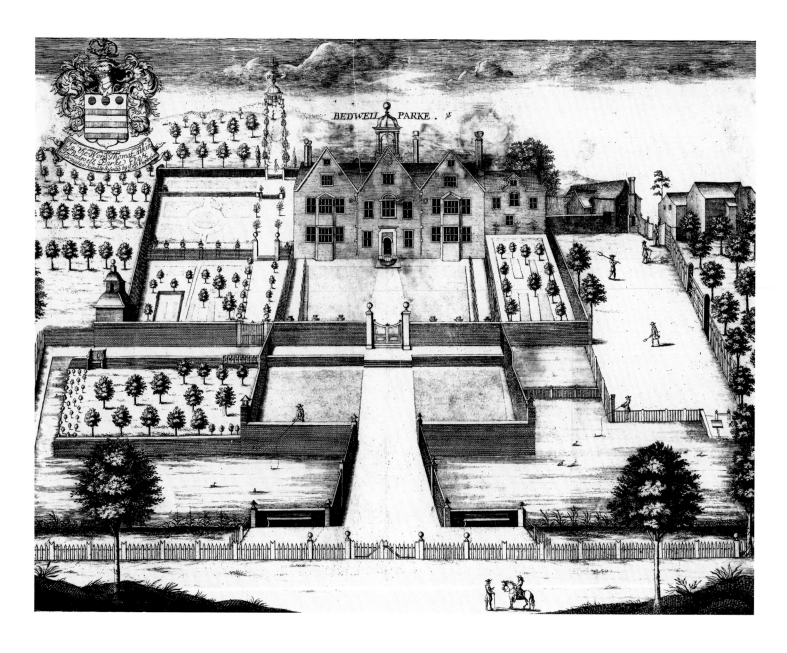

BEDWELL PARKE.

31 Thomas Atkins's garden at Bedwell Park, *c.*1685, from Henry Chauncy's *The Historical Antiquities of Hertfordshire* (1700). This illustrates the many odd assemblages of gardens found at the time: the moat was probably from an earlier house, which, with its gardens, were improved, probably by Thomas's mother and stepfather in the 1650s. Thomas's own contribution appears to have been some flower pots and the walk up the rising ground in the park to a summerhouse topped by a weather vane.

of fields, farmyards and garden grounds. John Parkinson trusted that gardens would be commensurate with the owner's standing: 'Gentlemen of the better sort and quality, will provide such a parcel of ground to bee laid out for their Garden, and in such convenient manner, as may be fit and answerable to the degree they hold.'[1]

An owner would need the skills of a gardener to choose the best ground and to convert it into a polished garden. Gardeners were practical men who would realise the owner's desires on the ground by adapting suitable designs seen elsewhere. Often, one suspects, the instructions were as unspecific as to make a kitchen garden, parterre or wilderness larger than a rival's. It had always been like that for gardeners. Owners might, depending on their interests, become 'curious' as florists or in tree planting. Sir Thomas Hanmer and John Evelyn were examples, and John Rea encouraged others, especially in flower gardening:

> Fair Houses are more frequent than fine Gardens; the first effected by Artificers onely, the latter requiring more skill in the Owner: few Gardens being found well furnished out of the hands of an affectionate Florist . . . I shall now proceed to inform all such as desire to be Florists, how they may do as I have done, make their own Gardens themselves, assisted onely by ordinary Labourers . . .[2]

This still left some matters on which written guidance to the owner and his gardener might be welcome, these being how to choose a site for a new house and devise a general plan for the courts and gardens, having taken into account aspect, prospect, soil and shelter. Also, there was the question of the layout and contrivance of the form of enclosure, any earth-shaping, ponds, terrace walls and steps.

On such matters the agricultural writer John Worlidge unhelpfully advised that there could be no rules: 'Every Builder may better please himself in the shape and contrivance of his Garden better than any other can do for him'.[3] Where money was scarce, and did not allow for radical redesign, succeeding generations might simply add new garden areas. Strange and awkward juxtapositions, as depicted in Sir Henry Chauncy's *Hertfordshire* (1700), could be the testimony to this (fig. 31).

The greater owners could afford better, and often consulted people experienced in such matters or even enlisted their practical help. The gentry would have lacked such ready assistance, and texts relating to Italy were often not helpful, even if famous and authoritative. Advice was needed that was applicable to the colder English climate. Notwithstanding Worlidge's pessimism, there were several garden writers to whom they could turn. Gervase Markham, William Lawson, John Parkinson, John Rea and Worl-

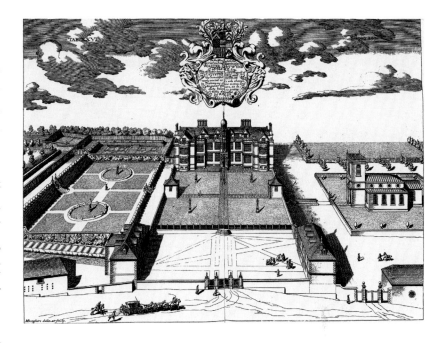

32 'S.S.E. Prospect of Ingestre Hall, and the Beautiful Church Newly Erected at his Sole Charge' by Michael Burghers, 1686. This planned layout was a rare scheme by Wren. The rising terraces to the west answered the church across the forecourt; a wooden palisade, rather than a wall, formed the southern enclosure to the forecourt.

idge himself all addressed their own countrymen who were building or improving their country residences.

Among the architects who took an interest in planning gardens was Sir Christopher Wren. He designed a new church for Walter Chetwynd at Ingestre in about 1672, and the view in Plot's *Staffordshire* showed that the churchyard was part of a comprehensively planned arrangement of forecourts, gardens and service yards around the house (fig. 32). About 1686 Wren wrote to Sir William Fermour at Easton Neston, Northamptonshire, about the garden walls not being too high because of 'the Libertie of a prospect towards Towcester from the great Garden & also that from the windowes of your parlour may looke over them'. He advised Sir William to make a trial with a board 'till you are your selfe satisfied what highth the walls may be not to prejudice your prospect'. The great bulk of such help and advice must have gone unrecorded or has not survived, and 'general plans' for gardens are unknown till the end of the century. Nevertheless, an increasing sophistication in the planning of gardens, at least the superior ones, became apparent in the second half of the century.[4]

DIFFERENTIATION

Gradually during Jacobean times English gardens followed contemporary Continental trends in the differentiation of uses through the garden. The increasing specialisation of coronary (or flower) gardening, fruit gardening and kitchen gardening had meant at first differentiation within a garden. By Carolean times the differentiation had come to mean separate walled gardens. Parkinson divided his notional 'Paradisus Terrestris' into 'The Garden of Pleasant Flowers', 'The Kitchen Garden' and 'The Orchard'. Rea described his perfect arrangement of a flower garden, fruit garden, kitchen garden and grove, the first three being separate walled areas.[5] Evelyn differentiated the parterre, coronary, medicinal, and olitory gardens, and the orchard.[6]

Gardens could contain a single plot, railed in to keep off the unwanted, and an alley around. There would then be narrow borders between the alley and the wall, suitable for florist flowers and fruit trees. If the walled area was larger, the traditional division was into four fenced or hedged *compartiments*, or quarters. This form, with alleys round about and athwart, had been the norm in Italy and France from the early sixteenth century, and had become general in England from Elizabethan times.[7]

Garden areas could always be enclosed with tall hedges, but walls of typically nine feet, or more later on, were preferred because of the microclimate and security they afforded. Traditionally, communication with other yards or gardens was through doorways. Corner turrets had been incorporated into the walls of several Jacobean gardens, and this produced such pretty architecture that owners and architects seemed reluctant to quit the custom altogether. They were not infrequently constructed after the Restoration, despite new ways of obtaining views out.

'ITALIAN' GARDENS

Italy had gained its reputation as the seat of inspiration as the style and detail of its gardens swept across Europe in the late sixteenth century. Most were square in plan and were overlooked both from the upper storeys of the house and a terrace on the far side of the garden, under which there might be a grotto with running water that afterwards served the garden. In England, homage to Italian gardens continued to the mid-seventeenth century. John Raymond wrote in the 1640s that: 'For their Gardens, I dare confidently avow all Christendom affords none so voluptuous, as those within the Walls and Territory of Rome'.[8] John Ray, travelling there in 1662, considered that what he saw 'excel the orchards, gardens and walks of any Prince in Christendom that I have seen'.[9]

When Evelyn was seeking support for his 'Elysium Britannicum' in 1659, the academics in Oxford considered that:

> it would be very likely to bee most acceptable to oʳ english nobility and gentry: many of whom wee know have esteemed it a sufficient recompense for the paines of cost of a journy not only to Sᵗ. Jermins in France but of yᵉ travaile over yᵉ greatest part of Italy that they have thereby understood yᵉ beauty gallantry and state of such workes as Mʳ.. Evelyn is by us supposed to describe in this his Elysium . . .[10]

Saint-Germain-en-Laye was particularly famous for its terraces descending below the Château Neuf. Jacques Boyceau had worked here: perhaps it is no coincidence that, as at Boisgency, the slopes below the garden had been replanted as orchards (fig. 33).

Evelyn recalled Italian practice in explaining that viewing terraces, or 'mounts' would best be situated towards the remoter parts, 'as from whence to take a universall prospect not onely of the Gardens, but of the whole Contry'.[11] His brother George shaped a hill behind his family home, Wotton, Surrey, into a mount in 1651, and a cousin devised a grotto behind an Ionic portico let into this hill (fig. 34). Evelyn's still clear memory of Italian gardens gave rise to some parallels – for example, the Duke of Buckingham's arcade at Cliveden reminded Evelyn of 'Frascati', presumably the nymphaeum behind the Villa Aldobrandini.[12]

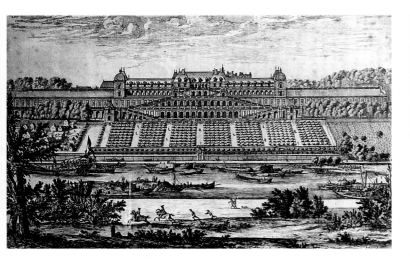

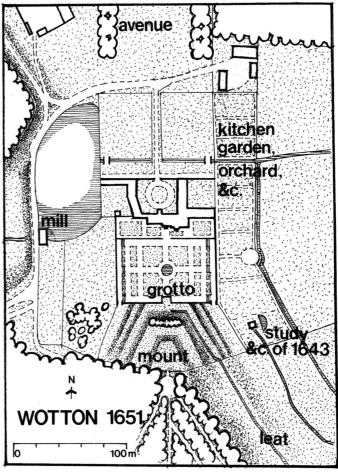

33 This view of the Château Neuf at Saint Germain-en-Laye by Israël Silvestre shows the palace in the mid-seventeenth century, hardly changed since Henri IV had the elaborate terracing formed from 1595. Queen Henrietta Maria and Charles II lived here during the Protectorate, and James II after 1689.

34 A reconstruction by the author of Wotton House, Surrey, as it appeared in 1651, when George Evelyn shaped the mount, built the grotto and formed the grass plats and *jet d'eau*; the kitchen garden was a simple addition alongside.

Several Carolean mounts remained in Restoration times, often with grottoes under. John Worlidge admired the 1630s mount at Wilton especially (fig. 35). He described such structures, with a breast wall (retaining wall) on the outside, and either a grass slope or breast wall on the inside, being raised 'at the farthest distance from your house . . . for the advantage of the Air and pleasure of the Eye'.[13] A small number of terraces continued to be made at the ends of the walled enclosure. Even as late as the mid-1670s the Earl of Arlington raised a terrace along the western perimeter of his new gardens at Arlington House.[14] Despite this and a few other late examples, the fashion for viewing terraces had subsided as a new generation of owners sought instead to see their house's axis continue through the garden and into the countryside beyond, as described below (fig. 36).

John Aubrey, the antiquary, fantasised about redesigning his family home at Easton Pierce, Wiltshire, in 1669, incorporating Italian-style terraces.[15] He remained loyal to the Italian tradition well after the time that the reputation of the French garden had become supreme, and it is revealing to see what he thought 'Italian' meant. He referred in 1686 to the mount and grotto at Wilton as 'Italian'. In 1691, after visiting the house at Chelsea that had once belonged to Sir John Danvers, he asserted that there had once been a fashion for Italian gardens in England.[16] Danvers had 'first taught us the way of Italian gardens', by which Aubrey seems to have meant Danvers's Italian-inspired mount-cum-grotto of the 1620s at the further end. He was also struck by the oval bowling green lined by cypress trees, which may have been an added ingredient that made the garden particularly Italian to Aubrey (fig. 37).[17]

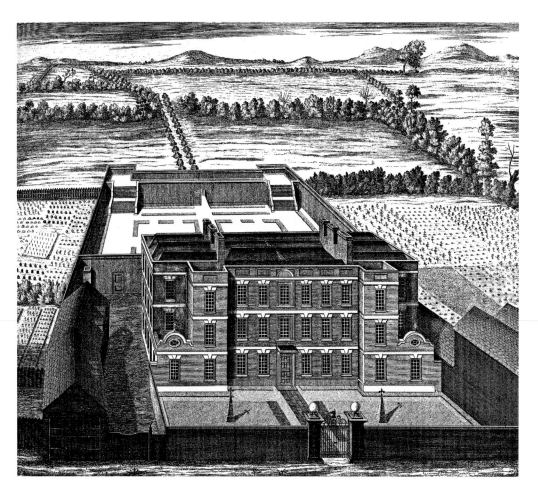

35 This pen and wash view of Wilton House in 1669 by Lorenzo Magalotti, an Italian visitor, shows the mount and gladiator in place. The elaborate gardens by Isaac de Caus had been swept away by 1654 in favour of grass plats, probably associated with John Webb's work on the house from 1650.

36 Montague House, Wokingham, in the 1730s, when it was owned by Colonel Henry Williamson, drawn by G. Williamson and engraved by James Smith. The mount in the garden, probably erected by Henry Montague in about 1660, was an attempt to reconcile the recently fashionable mount with an axial arrangement by substituting an arch giving onto a walk across a field for the usual grotto. The colonel added the shaped clipped greens to the forecourt, and the iron gate bears his arms and wyvern crest.

In his *L'Idea dell'architettura universale* (1615) Vincenzo Scamozzi advised that approaches to palaces should be lined with trees to focus attention on the principal façade and end in a semicircular parade large enough for coaches to turn.[18] The Duke of Buckingham had been the first in England to take up Scamozzi's advice, and in 1621 had planted a mile-long great walk at New Hall with a half-round at the house front. He also planted a double walk, though without a parade termination, at Burley-on-the-Hill (fig. 38). In England a new term was invented when Evelyn started using the word 'avenue' in the 1650s,[19] which he defined as 'the principal Walk to the Front of the House or Seat'.[20]

An early and spectacular example of what Scamozzi had in mind, set out and planted about 1620, was to be found at the Prince of Orange's palace of Honselaarsdijk, near The Hague.[21]

37   'A Draught of Sʳ John Danvers Garden at Chelsey . . .' by John Aubrey, 1691. North is at the top. The house, off to the south, was fronted by small trees and shrubs; beyond was an oval bowling green surrounded by cypresses; statuary flanked the four entrances. Between summerhouses at the northern end of the garden there was a mount with a central grotto.

38   Burley-on-the-Hill, Rutland, c.1690. This copy plan of 'yᵉ ground-plott of yᵉ Old House', of sometime before 1692, shows the start of the 1620s double walk to the east. Note also the bowling green to the west overlooked by a mount and the 'Terrase walks' on falling ground to the south.

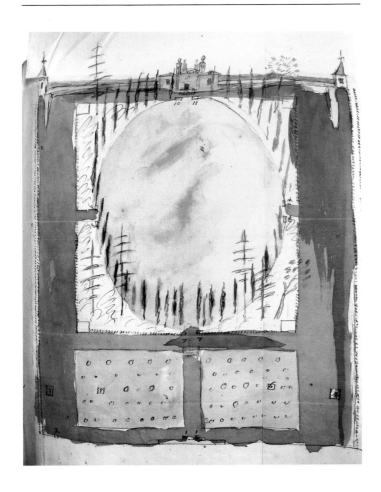

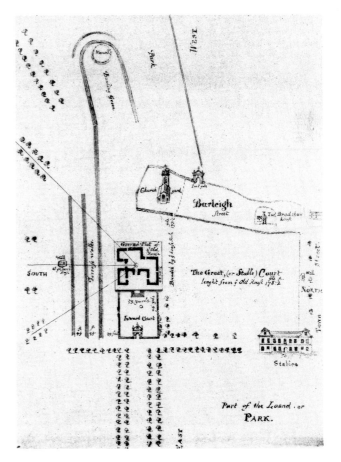

In his *Jardin de Plaisir* (1651) André Mollet showed a plate based on Honselaarsdijk, indicating an approach terminating in a demi-lune, and lateral planting to the width of the palace's moated enclosure. Avenues were installed at the Restoration by members of the English Court, including the Earl of Lindsey at Grimsthorpe and the Earl of Sunderland at Althorp. In the 1660s Pratt wrote that the approach to country houses should be

> laid out by the line, equal at least to the whole front of the house, if not somewhat more . . . and so let elms, fir-trees or rather lime-trees . . . be set at 20 foot distance from each other, on both sides of it from one end to the other and the like again cross-ways in a direct line with the front of the court . . .[22]

Versions often either without the half-rounds or without lateral walks became common at lesser places.

The traditional tree for walks had been the English elm (*Ulmus procera*), grown from hedgerow suckers. The European lime (*Tilia x vulgaris*) came into favour, and John Tradescant was paid in 1624 for going over to the Low Countries to purchase them for the New Hall avenue. Lime trees were imported from Danzig for the lines of trees either side of the canal in St James's Park in 1660 (see fig. 64) and the Long Water avenue at Hampton Court (see fig. 65) the next year. Moses Cook considered that limes grew fast, would survive in almost any sort of ground, had pleasant flowers, threw a good shade and 'no Tree keeps such a constant Pyramid-shape as this'.[23] He had propagated them at Cassiobury by layering shoots from stools of the tree, and took these skills to the Brompton Park Nursery when he became one of the nursery's partners. Sixty years after Cook, Philip Miller, author of *The Gardener's Dictionary*, was still admiring 'the regular shape it has in growing, the Agreeableness of its shade, and the beautiful colour of its Leaves'.[24]

Evelyn also advocated the sweet chestnut (*Castanea sativa*) 'for Avenues to our Country-houses, they are a magnificent and royal Ornament', though it did not have such a compact and upright shape as the lime.[25] Besides being beautiful, this tree also had the virtues of doing well on sandy soil, and being useful. Extensive sweet chestnut avenues were planted on the gravelly soils at Knole and Albury, for example (fig. 39).[26] Other species later used included the French favourite, the horse chestnut (*Aesculus hippocastanum*), and the abele (*Populus alba*).

Most avenues would be laid flat and even, requiring levelling. The avenue at Bramshill required extensive cutting and banking to achieve this.[27] The practice was continued thereafter, as attested by the causeway on axis at Castle Hill of the 1720s.[28]

A fashion developed at European palaces in the early seventeenth century for a whole layout lying along a principal axis. Slightly late, the English nobility sought where possible to develop such an axis, starting with the avenue, and continuing through gates into the forecourt, along a broad walk and up steps to the door, through the house and across the great garden to a gate in the far wall and off along a walk across the park or fields. If the doors on the ground floor of the house were opened, 'one may see from one end to the other, as far as our sight will extend'.[29]

In practice, the orientation of the axis through house, courts and gardens would often be determined not by the direction of the approach, but by pre-existing orientations, the desire to line up on a landmark, or considerations of shelter and sun. The actual approach might then be sidelong, rather than axial. Undeterred, many owners would still plant axial lines of trees across fields up to the forecourt to maintain the impression of a state approach. These might be termed 'dummy avenues', purely visual devices. An early one was seen in about 1650 at Woburn Abbey, terminated by a half-square (fig. 40). There were others at Badminton in the 1660s (see fig. 82), and scores of examples followed.[30] This formula of dummy avenue, forecourt gates and broad walk remained usual till the end of the century.

PROSPECT, ASPECT, SHELTER AND SOIL

The garden writers felt that some of the most useful advice they could give was on the best situation for a pleasant and productive garden, which might in turn influence the situation and orientation of an intended house. Parkinson, speaking to his 'courteous reader', aimed 'To shew you for everie of these situations which is the fittest place to plant your garden in, and how to defend it from

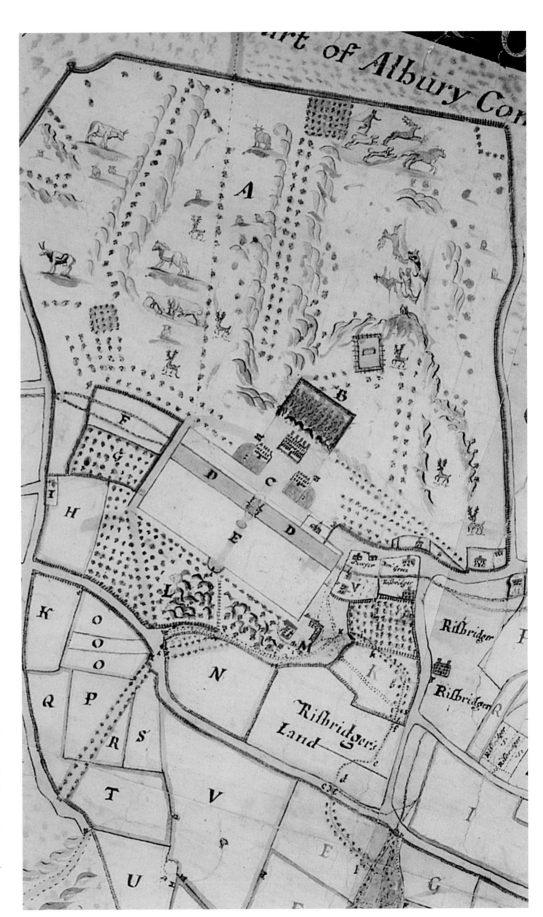

39 This estate map of Albury Place, Surrey, by Abraham Walter, 1701, shows the garden area with the planting of avenues and walks in the park, most of them sweet chestnut, which thrives on sandy soil. North is to the bottom. The legend states that 'At the Upperside of the Garden is the entrance into a Cave under a Mount of Sand which cometh out again in the Lane . . . Also . . . cometh the water out from Sherborns Springs'. A, The Park and Keepers Lodge; B, The Pyne Tree Grove; C, The Place and Courts; D, The Cannal; E, The Gardens; L, The Upper Orchard.

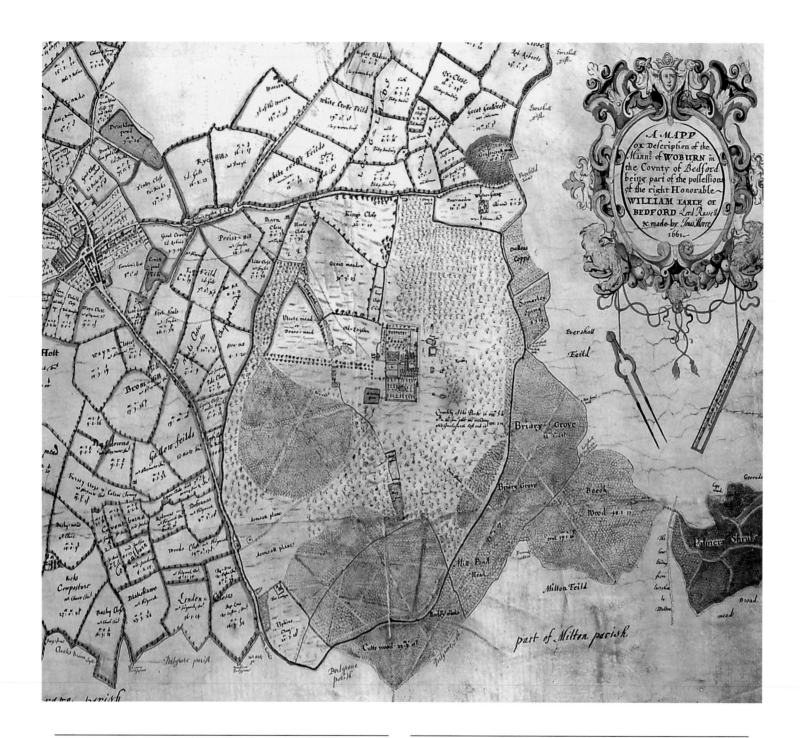

40   A section of Jonas Moore's 'Mapp or Description' of Woburn Abbey, Bedfordshire, 1661, showing the park, which displayed the latest innovations in avenues and vistos. The dummy avenue to the west has been planted with a half-square at the house end, and some woods have been cut through with stars of rides. A bowling green has been made in the park south-west of the house and a kitchen garden added to the west wall of the gardens, north of the half-square.

the iniuries of the cold windes and frosts that may annoy it, will, I hope, be well accepted.'[31] Worlidge did the same, with the best soil in mind: 'In case you have not yet laid the foundation of your intended residence, then may you consider what Ground or Soil is best for your Plantation and Partirre, without which you can never make the other complete.'[32]

In practice the best situation would always be a compromise between prospect, aspect, shelter and soil. Parkinson acknowledged that there were arguments on the one hand for the amenities of the plain, such as water and good soil, and on the other for the delights of prospect and good air:

> those places that are neare unto a river or broke to be best for the pleasantnesse of the water, the ease of transportation, of themselves, their friends and goods, as also for the fertility of the soyle, which is seldome bad neare unto a rivers side; And others extoll the side or top of an hill, bee it small or great, for the prospects sake; And againe, some the plaine or champain ground, for the even levell thereof . . .[33]

Rea, imagining some 'Gardens of Delight', preferred the level: 'The most graceful grounds for these Gardens, is an intire level . . . Hanging grounds, uncapable to be cast into a Level, seldome make handsom Gardens: such must be divided into parts, with Descents'.[34] However, most architects would seek to lift a new house out of the base of a valley. Pratt, knowing that 'The first thing to be considered is that of situation; as whether upon a plain ground, low or rising', argued for the last:

> Let it stand at the least a furlong distant from the common way out of which you turn up to it, the ground gently rising all along and the level of it both on the one hand, and on the other if not equal, yet at least not remarkably otherwise; the height of the situation will render it very pleasant when you are at it . . .[35]

Parkinson elaborated that a spot should be chosen where rising ground sloped upwards to the north, 'that it may have the comfort of the South Sunne to lye upon it'.[36] Evelyn considered that 'A place whose gentle declivitie . . . were insensibly towards the South . . . were a situation to be chosen before all others', because 'the

Sun might visite it, at three of the Cardinal points, and by this means project his raies more perpendicular'.[37]

In order to provide a garden with shelter from the cold of the north winds, and the ferocity of the west ones, plantations should protect those sides of the house, and gardens should be situated on the slope south of it. Parkinson advised this, and was supported by Rea, whose 'Gardens of Delight' would have been 'seated on the South side of the House', or else protected by 'Pear-trees, Elms, or Sicamores' on the north and east sides.[38]

An added refinement was to orientate the layout slightly to the south-east, giving exposure to the more temperate breezes from the south and catching the morning sun. Evelyn, in considering the selection of a site for a nursery ground, preferred 'some fit place of Ground, well Fenced, respecting the South-east, rather than the full South, and well protected from the North and West'.[39] Similarly, Worlidge, though seeing the 'North defended by tall Trees', considered that a new residence should exploit 'the free and open Air to the East and South'.[40]

As a consequence of all this advice many owners chose their garden fronts to be towards the south. A few owners did exploit modest slopes as suggested by Pratt, but most adhered to the level ground advocated by Rea. A general reluctance to exploit slopes seems to have been common in the middle of the century, and contrasts with both the many notable terraced gardens made in Jacobean times and those towards the end of the century. Only occasionally were houses situated in hilly terrain, and often this was because it was unavoidable, as at the Deepdene from the 1650s and Albury in 1667.

Disposition

Having decided on situation, the owner would need to consider 'disposition', the garden's layout. As noted above, he might desire a flower garden and a fruit garden, and possibly a wilderness, a bowling green and a kitchen garden. Together with the forecourt and service courts, these various walled areas would be composed into carefully planned overall layouts.

It was generally accepted that each walled garden would be square. Parkinson noted that: 'The foure square form is the most usually accepted with all',[41] as did Evelyn: 'of all the formes of Gardens, we find the Square to be most usuall; yet the oblong [& parallelogram] which is one of its species, is doubtlesse more convenient as to the circuit of the out Walls'.[42] Practitioners remained faithful to the square form into Restoration times. Worlidge considered a circular garden might have advantages for walking, as no corners would need to be turned (fig. 41), but on reflection he considered that 'The Square is the most perfect and pleasant form'.[43] The traditional *compartiment* fitted a square.

The advice to replicate *compartiments* when a larger garden was desired was followed by architects more often than by practical gardeners. At Coleshill House, where Pratt oversaw the building for a cousin from 1651, the gardens consisted of three similar square enclosures for pleasure gardens at the rear of the house. Alongside there were three further walled areas, of the same length.[44] Pratt's garden layout for himself at Ryston Hall, Norfolk, in 1669, consisted of three squares in an L-shape, being a forecourt with grass plats before the house, a rather loose-fit flower garden north of it, and a small fruit garden east of the forecourt (fig. 42).[45]

Replicating *compartiments* was not so practical when the functions and consequent space requirements of parts of the gardens were becoming differentiated. Rea, though old-fashioned in many ways, was practical enough to advise in the 1660s that a 'fruit garden' should be considerably larger than a flower garden.[46] One early fruit garden at regal scale was the ten-acre so-called 'Vineyard Garden' at Wimbledon Manor, described in 1649 as having eight triangles bordered with soft fruit on the east, and four unhedged triangles to the west, and the whole garden containing 144 lime trees, 507 standard fruit trees of various sorts, 106 fruit trees and 16 quince on lattices and 254 wall fruit (see fig. 62). Althorp House had small grass plats and no flower garden, leaving the fruit garden as the principal garden of pleasure, whilst beyond, hidden behind walls, were two kitchen garden quarters (see fig. 20).

The kitchen garden was hard to place in a layout. Being a place of base labour, it was to be concealed from the more polite areas, such as the fruit garden. At Groombridge Place, Kent, where Evelyn noted disapprovingly in 1674 on the siting of a new house within the old moat, his acquaintance Philip Packer had constructed a new walled garden to the side, across a bridge (see fig. 4). A lower level contained parterres, and an upper level was a too-obvious kitchen garden. Usually in the mid-seventeenth century the kitchen garden was simply added as a further walled area alongside older gardens, as at Woburn Abbey about 1650 (see fig. 40), and Wotton in 1651 (fig. 43), though later designs would accommodate it as a discrete space within the assemblage of walled gardens and give it a superficially ornamental appearance so that it did not detract from the principal gardens of pleasure.

The fruit and kitchen gardens are two examples of types of garden that were changing from within. The beds of flower gardens could be laid out in a variety of ways – as simple as straight beds, or as decorative as flower or heraldic forms, though the open knot, a pattern of beds in angles and straights, was

---

(Top left) 41   An idea for a round garden engraved by Frederick Hendrik van Hove for John Worlidge's *Systema Horti-culturae; Or, The Art of Gardening*, 1677. Good for walking without turns, this would have had cypresses, fir trees and fruit trees, with a fountain at the centre. The square form remained usual, however.

(Top right) 42   A bird's-eye view of Sir Roger Pratt's house at Ryston, Norfolk, c.1680. The gardens are regimented and walled into an L-shape of squares; the parterre is plain grass and gravel with four fir trees; the gate is transparent, with bars allowing some view through; and the flower garden behind the house has borders cut in squares out of the turf. The kitchen garden is to the right.

(Bottom) 43   Wotton House, Surrey, 1653. This etching of 'The house of Geo: Evelyn Esq': taken in perspective from the top of the Grotto by Jo: Evelyn 1653' shows the walled garden of grass plats, fountain, cypresses and grotto made by George Evelyn in 1651 from the mount above, itself shaped with John's help the next year. The kitchen garden was attached in simple fashion alongside the garden to the right.

F. H. Van Houe fec.

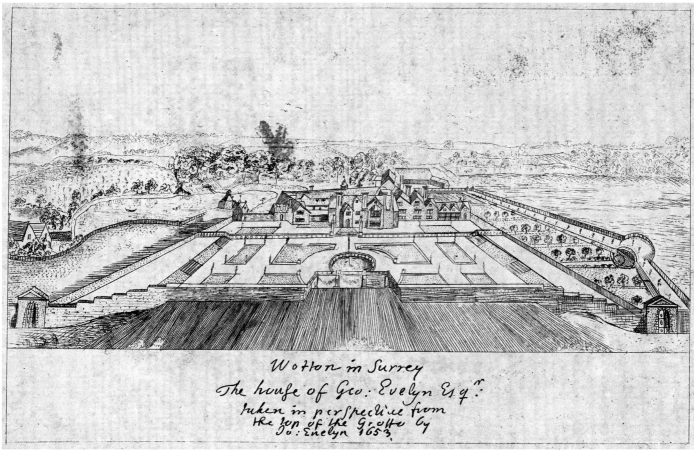

Wotton in Surrey
The house of Geo: Evelyn Esqr
taken in perspective from
the top of the Grotto by
Jo: Evelyn 1653

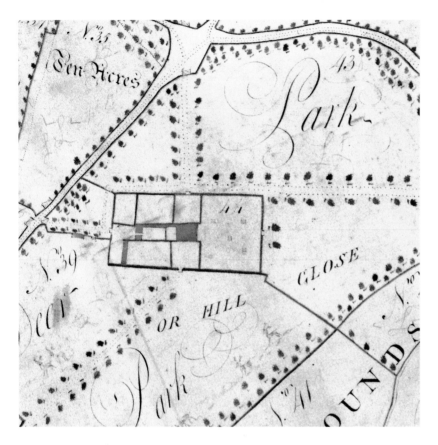

44 Thorpe Hall, Peterborough, c.1770, a planned layout in squares from Commonwealth times. All was contained within a walled rectangle with a gate central to each side. Garden and service courts fitted large squares, and sandwiched a triple square for house and courts. This layout survived through the era of the English garden.

increasingly the standard form. Owners might want grass plats, either for bowling or just as grass plats. As axes came to dominate layouts, new forms of terrace, and transparent gates and planting arrangements associated with them, were seen. The forecourt was also changing to accommodate wheeled transport. In general, though, most of the new sets of walled gardens in mid-century had adapted to allow for gardens of several types and sizes, as described below.

Experimentation with double or triple square arrangements began. Oliver St John, a Chief Justice in the Commonwealth gov-

ernment, built a new house, Thorpe Hall, near Peterborough, in 1654. The walled enclosures surrounding it were clearly devised on a drawing board, perhaps by Peter Mills, the architect of the house. The house had a square forecourt to the north, a small square garden to the south, a large square great garden to the east, with terraces, and to the west was a square enclosure for the base courts and service areas (fig. 44). Hugh May had a hand in the layout at Burlington House in the 1660s (see fig. 80). Half the garden was a square of grass plats, and half was an open grove (so called because the quarters between the hedges were open) with a cross and diagonal arrangement of walks. In 1666 the young Earl of Sunderland made his forecourt at Althorp an area the size of the house within its moat, and the walled gardens made a double square alongside (see fig. 20). This was admired by one Italian as 'the best planned and best arranged country seat in the kingdom; for though there be many which surpass it in size, none are superior to it in symmetrical elegance'.[47]

When Eaton Hall, Cheshire, was built between 1675 and 1682 for Sir Thomas Grosvenor, its architect, William Samwell, developed the layout along an axis aligned on Beeston Castle, managing to fit the whole arrangement into a double-square walled enclosure – the kitchen garden beyond was later (fig. 45). It was highly symmetrical, with service courts outside the offices flanking the forecourt, and flower gardens flanking the mansion. Behind the house was a terrace and the usual four-square grass plats.

Retaining a tight geometrical arrangement whilst allowing for gardens of different sizes led to the development of side gardens where the fruit gardens and kitchen gardens might be placed. At Horseheath Hall, built by Pratt in 1663, the Great Garden was allotted a large rectangular walled area, and narrower walled areas flanked it in the proportion 1:2:1. These widths answered the stable court, house, and office court respectively, to give a perfect square overall.[48] Sir John Bennet devised a similar if not-so-perfect geometry in the early 1670s for his walled gardens at Dawley House, Middlesex. The gardens on the south front were flanked by side gardens, probably kitchen garden areas, again in the proportions 1:2:1 (fig. 46). A similar arrangement was to be seen at Ham House, where the grass plats and open grove were

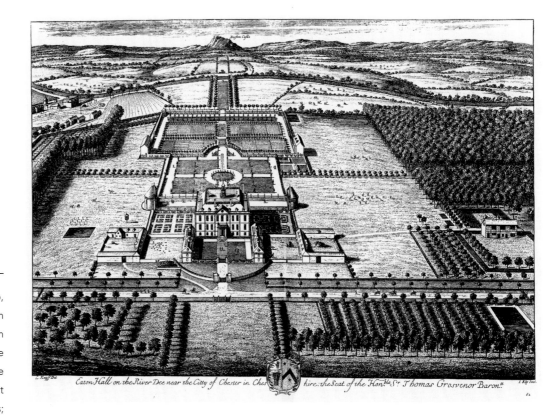

Eaton Hall on the River Dee near the Citty of Chester in Cheshire, the Seat of the Hon.ble S.r Thomas Grosvenor Baron.tt

45   Eaton Hall, Cheshire, by Knyff and Kip, c.1700. The house was built 1675–82 with an alignment eastwards to Beeston Castle, seen through the gate in the baskethandle. There were open-knot flower gardens to either side of the house and a great terrace on the garden front between facing semicircular summerhouses; the parterre of grass plats had a *jet d'eau* and four figures. The vegetable garden beyond the baskethandle and greenhouse to the left (north) were probably an afterthought.

46   Bird's-eye view from the south of Dawley House, Middlesex, by Knyff and Kip, c.1702. The four-plat forecourt was west of the house, and a service court lay to the north. The large gardens to the south had a grass-and-gravel parterre, open knots and an open grove with arbours; side gardens gave the proportions of 1:2:1 and all lay within a square with corner summerhouses. This was probably based on a pre-Civil War garden, but the fine greenhouse to the east has been attributed to William Talman, and the elaborate gate between the gardens and the south avenue was surely by Tijou. A deer-park licence of 1690, one of the last, led to the enclosure of the park, in which deer can here be seen; built in the early 1670s, the house lasted only 50 years.

Dawly in the County of Middlesex, the Seat of the Right Hon.ble Charles Lord Ofsulstone.

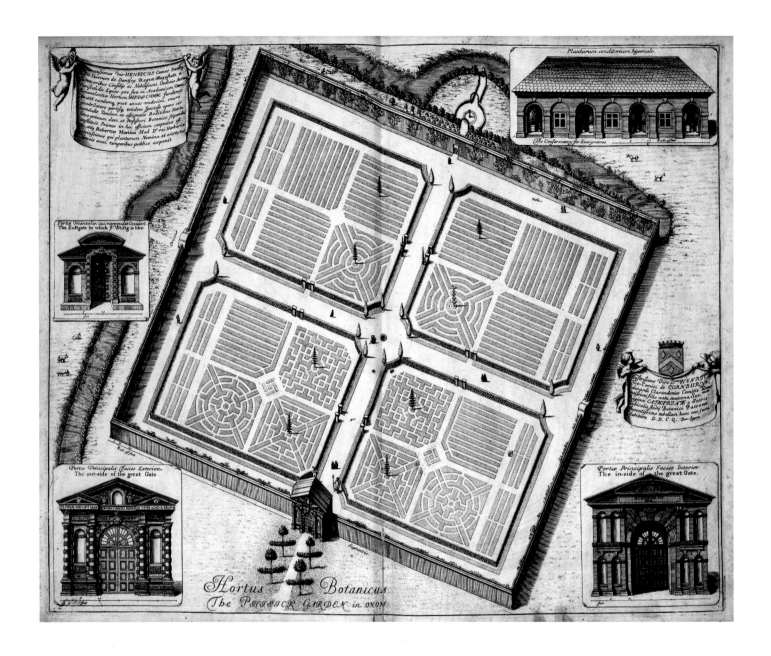

47 The Oxford Physick Garden, 1675. Jacob Bobart the Elder, as Keeper from 1642, set out the hedged quarters in open knots, a traditional but eminently practical solution; the knots became more elaborate and decorative in the more public areas. The vignette at top right shows 'The Conservatory for Evergreens'. This garden was one of the centres for plant collecting and dissemination in the second half of the seventeenth century.

flanked on the one hand by a lime trees in quincunx and on the other by a kitchen garden (see fig. 81).

OPEN KNOTS

In the seventeenth century, the word 'knot' was used loosely for any form of intricate layout in garden quarters, for example the patterns of beds shown in books by Sebastiano Serlio and Hans

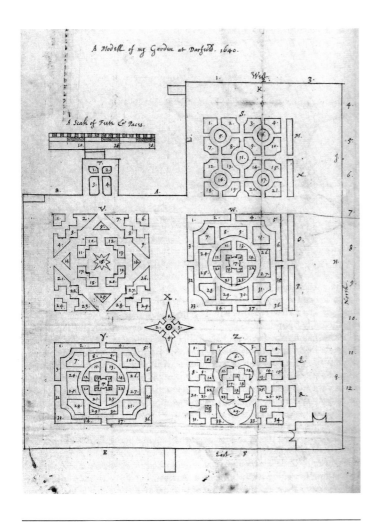

A Modell of my Garden at Darfield. 1640.

A Scale of Feete & Paces.

48 Plans of open knots for Darfield rectory, Yorkshire, 1640, by Walter Stonehouse, rector of Darfield. Making such plans was an activity common amongst his contemporaries. Such knots remained in use in flower gardens, but not in best gardens.

in his *Paradisus Terrestris*. He recommended open knots as 'more proper for these Out-landish flowers' than other forms of knot, and gave six designs, four from a published plan of the Orto Botanico in Padua, and a fifth from the Duke of Sermoneta's flower garden at Cisterna in Italy.[50] Later the Oxford Physick Garden and the Chelsea Physick Garden were both set out with extensive and elaborate arrangements of open knots (fig. 47). Rea, who considered that he was updating Parkinson,[51] illustrated a small number of open knots, calling them 'frets'.[52] Indeed, playing with designs for open knots seems to have been a common pastime, for example the Revd Walter Stonehouse working on his 'best garden' at Darfield rectory in Yorkshire in 1640 (fig. 48).[53]

The garden immediately outside the parlour was often referred to as the 'Best Garden', and at palaces sometimes 'the Great Garden'. Formerly this had been the flower garden, laid out in knots. Elaborate motifs, as seen at Theobalds, or based on hearts or flowers, were tried, especially in town gardens, but simple open knots continued to be the standard form for country house flower gardens. One was recorded at Tredegar House, Newport, about 1670,[54] and others were to be found within the Great Garden at Dawley, in the early 1670s (see fig. 46). Some rather grand flower gardens of the 1670s, such as those at Blackett's in Newcastle-upon-Tyne, Cheveley Park,[55] and Nell Gwyn's Burford House in Windsor,[56] were placed to the side of the forecourt or Great Garden. Variations on the old rectilinear geometry were seen at Ryston Hall, where in about 1671 Pratt gave himself flowerbeds sparsely cut into turf (see fig. 42).[57]

BOWLING GREENS AND GRASS PLATS

André Mollet, a Frenchman working in England but also familiar with the Low Countries and Sweden, wrote that 'England excelleth other Countreys . . . in the art of Turffing'.[58] He noted that the beautiful effect of English turf depended on frequent mowing. It was well rolled with wooden rollers for removing wormcasts, and beaten down or compacted to an even surface with stone rollers. He also advised a careful selection of turf, such as could be found on sheepwalks, to avoid coarse or tangled grass. London

Vredeman de Vries, and also the interlacing and embroidery forms. The Parliamentary survey of Theobalds of 1649 described the nine 'squares or knotts' in the Great Garden thus: 'one is sett forth with box borders in yᵉ likenesse of yᵉ Kings armes . . . one other plott is planted with choice flowers, the other 7 knotts are all grasse knotts, handsomely turfed'.[49]

Parkinson wished to distinguish interlacing designs from patterned beds, and so used the term 'open knots' for the latter

Esher Place in ye County of Surry the Seat of Tho: Cotton Esq. & Philadelphia his Wife, Daughter and Heiress of his Excellency Sr. Tho: Lynck Kt. Late Governor of Jamaica.

and Wise later added the detail that 'the Turf-cutters make choice of some part of a fine green Common or Down; such as Black-Heath, Putney-Heath, or Moulsey-Hurst.'[59]

At mid-century Evelyn, recognising that bowling greens had become an integral part of English gardens, could write that 'the incomparable divertissement which they afford us, is singular to the English Nation above all others in the World'.[60] As new gardens came to be made, bowling greens could be integrated in the layout; for example, at Sir John Danvers's at Chelsea in the 1620s.[61] As mentioned in the previous chapter, Prince Henry had a green in the Spring Garden in St James's Park, and Charles I contracted with John Tradescant to make one at Oatlands Palace in 1633.[62]

Several of the private bowling greens were placed outside the garden enclosure, often in the park, as the preserve of the menfolk (fig. 49). For example, that at Hampton Court, made in 1636,

49   Esher Place, Surrey, c.1700. One of the seventeenth-century owners built a bowling green with summerhouse on high ground in the warren to the east of the palace; other examples of parkland greens were often further away from the house and served as retreats for the men and their guests. Thomas Cotton, the owner at the time of this print, had demolished most of the remains of the Tudor palace, added wings to the gatehouse and set out the courtyard as a *parterre à l'Angloise* with *jets d'eau*.

was placed at the edge of the park, overlooking the Thames (see fig. 90). When Charles I was confined to Carisbrooke Castle in 1648–9 his gaoler, Colonel Hammond, constructed a green of 350 by 250 feet in the vacant east bailey of the castle to be the King's chief recreation.[63] The greens at Burley-on-the-Hill, Rutland (see fig. 38), and Belvoir, Leicestershire (see fig. 112), took advantage of hill-top positions, both maybe in the 1670s, but from about that time most new greens were incorporated into planned walled layouts (fig. 50). At Dawley one was placed to the side of the open grove at the far end of the Great Garden and at Badminton the green was to the side of the forecourt (see fig. 117).

In the early 1630s Best Gardens were for the first time converted to simple grass plats, and the English skills in maintaining bowling greens were transferred to them. Sometimes grass plats were actually referred to as 'bowling greens' – for example, as Evelyn did in 1651 when drawing the plats in his forecourt – and the French term 'boulingrin' appears to have derived from this usage. This fashion altered the appearance of pleasure gardens, in that fencing was dispensed with and grass introduced, but the old geometry continued, often emphasised by pencil-thin cypress trees, or another evergreen, at corners. It gave a garden restfulness and made it suitable for walking, and was retained throughout Charles II's reign (fig. 51).

One of the first of the new grass-and-gravel gardens was at Somerset House in the 1630s. Inigo Jones simplified Anne of Denmark's garden for Charles I into four plats around an impressive brass fountain of Arethusa by Hubert le Sueur, set on a pedestal and bason, and cleared away a Parnassus for a bowling green.[64] Jones is known to have been a firm Protestant, and in his mature years his preference was to eschew excessive display. It is notable that none of his architectural designs was accompanied by *parterres de broderie*, but were rather grass plats, as at the Queen's House at Greenwich.

The Privy Garden at Hampton Court was converted to grass in the late 1630s (see fig. 133), and the Privy Garden at Whitehall was laid out in sixteen grass plats about 1640 (fig. 52). Lord Capel had himself and his family painted in 1641 with his grassed Great Garden at Hadham, Hertfordshire, in the background. George

Evelyn created a four-square grassed parterre at Wotton in 1652 (see fig. 43). Sir Thomas Hanmer observed from his home in Flintshire in the 1650s:

> Our knotts or quarters are not hedg'd about with privet, rosemary or other tall hearbs which hide the prospect of the worke . . . but all is now commonly neere the house layd open, and expos'd to the view of the chambers . . . the PARTERRS are often of fine turf, kept as low as any greene to bowle on . . .[65]

The architect John Webb, Jones's kinsman and inheritor of his ideals, showed himself from the 1650s to have been wedded to the grass plat form for parterres and forecourts. About the time that he was working at Wilton House in 1652 the parterres and *bosquets* were given over to large areas of grass (see fig. 35). Grass plats within square walled gardens were seen at other places associated with Webb in the 1650s, for example at Chevening, Kent, for the Parliamentarian Lord Dacre, and at Gunnersbury, Middlesex, for the Presbyterian Sir John Maynard. Webb's addition of a loggia to Somerset House for Queen Henrietta Maria in 1662 was accompanied by a further alteration to the grass plats in the western garden, with a repositioned fountain by the riverside and low terraces around.

Amongst European counties, only Ireland has lusher grass than England, and England's recent geological history provides many gravel deposits. Englishmen who had seen gardens on the Continent realised that there was a home advantage in grass and gravel. Hugh May told Pepys that he approved

> of the present fashion of gardens to make them plain, that we have the best walks of gravell in the world, France having none, nor Italy: and our green of our bowling allies is better than any they have . . . this is the best way, only with a little mixture of statues, or pots, which may be handsome . . .[66]

Likewise, Sir William Temple, from his knowledge of France and Holland, was to state that 'Two things particular to us, that contribute much to the Beauty and Elegance of our gardens, which are the Gravel of our Walks, and the fineness and almost perpetual Greenness of our Turf.'[67]

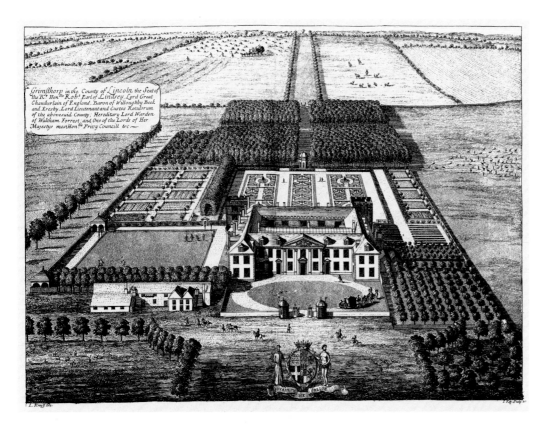

(Top) 50   Grimsthorpe Castle, Lincolnshire, seat of the Earl of Lindsey, by Knyff and Kip, *c.*1700. The gardens around the castle were pre-Civil War, with Restoration alterations. The open knots south of the house are likely to have been early, whilst alterations included the bowling green incorporated into the expanded garden. The north avenue was planted with sweet chestnuts in the 1660s. The carriage sweep had only recently been inserted into the much older forecourt. A companion view showed more of the park (to the right) which was one of the few of over 2,000 acres. The 'Four Mile Riding' was cut diagonally, across it, perhaps in the 1630s.

(Bottom) 51   Michael Burghers' 'S.E. Prospect of Madeley Manor Taken from the Garden Side', from Robert Plot, *The Natural History of Staffordshire* (1686). This view of Madeley Manor includes Mary, widow of John Offley (to whom Izaak Walton dedicated *The Compleat Angler*), walking in her garden. The plain grass and gravel is alleviated with fastigiate trees, maybe cypress or juniper; the walls are densely covered in trained trees.

(Facing page) 52   This detail of Whitehall Privy Garden from John Fisher's *Survey & Ground Plot of the Royal Palace of White Hall* (made in 1680, but published in 1747) shows the garden as grass plats with the sundial and fifteen figures. The plats had replaced Tudor railed beds with King's beasts in about 1640, and the figures had been transferred from St James's palace gardens in 1651. The bowling green was made in 1662, and the elaborate sundial in 1666. The steps down into the park are indicated top right.

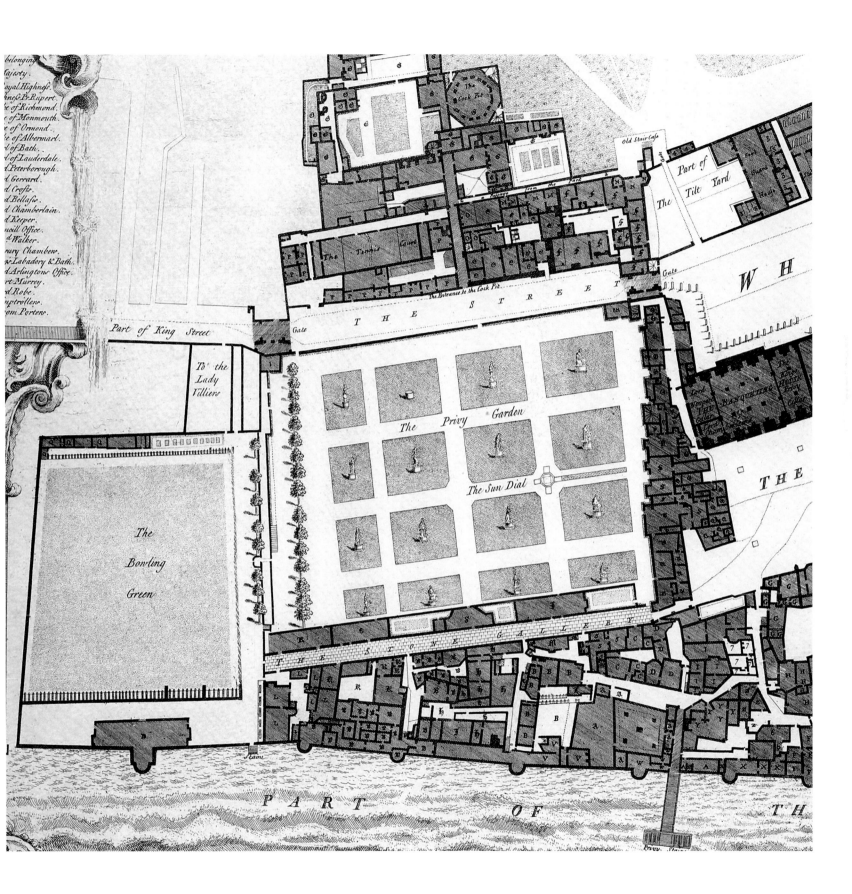

belonging
...Majesty.
...yal Highness
...nes B. Rupert.
...e of Richmond.
...e of Monmouth.
...e of Ormond.
...e of Albemarl.
...l of Bath.
...l of Lauderdale.
...l Peterborough.
...d Gerrard.
...d Crofts.
...d Bellasise.
...d Chamberlain.
...d Keeper.
...ncill Office.
...t Walker.
...ury Chambers.
...r Labadory & Bath.
...d Arlingtons Office.
...t Murrey.
...d Robe.
...mptrollers.
...om Porters.

Part of King Street

Gate

THE STREET

The Entrance to the Cock Pit.

The Cock Pit

Passage from the Park

The Tennis Court

Old Stair Case

Gate

Part of The *Tilt Yard*

Gate

W H

To the *Lady Villiers*

The *Privy Garden*

The Sun Dial

BANQUETING

THE

The
Bowling
Green

THE STONE GALLERY

S. *Stairs*

Privy Stairs

PART   OF   TH

Grass plats had become standard in Great, or Best, Gardens by mid-century, and foreigners were compelled to admit that they were unsurpassed: 'on voit pourtant un Parterre assez beau fait de gazon à la mode d'Angleterre' wrote one visitor in 1663 about the Hampton Court Privy Garden.[68] Some French parterres, though inevitably surrounded by *plates-bandes* (flower borders), had grass interiors. *La Théorie et la pratique du jardinage* was to note that this use of grass gave them the name of '*parterres à l'Angloise*, because we had the Manner of it first from England'.[69]

As the Best Garden became simple grass and gravel, the flower gardening migrated to the more private areas under the side windows of the house. May told Pepys that this was a good innovation: 'And then for flowers, they are best seen in a little plat by themselves; besides, their borders spoil the walks of another garden.'[70] Not all Englishmen were enthusiastic, in particular elderly florists who had been trained before grass plats had become prevalent. Rea noted sourly that 'I have seen many gardens of the new model, in the hands of unskilful persons, with good walls, walks, and grass plots; but in the most essential adornments so deficient, that a green meadow is a more delightful object.'[71] Similarly, Worlidge disapproved:

> The new mode of Gravel Walks and Grass-plots, is fit only for such houses or Palaces, that are scituated in Cities and great Towns, although they are now become precedents for many stately Country Residences . . . [they] have banish'd out of their Gardens Flowers, the Miracles of Nature, and the best Ornaments that ever were discovered to make a Seat pleasant. But it's hoped that this new, useless, and unpleasant mode, will like many other vanities grow out of Fashion.[72]

WILDERNESSES

The term 'wilderness' may seem puzzling since it refers to wooded areas, but the origin of these areas helps explain it. Jesus Christ spent 40 days in the wilderness, and the point of this in seventeenth-century England was that he saw no-one else for this time: the place was deserted, and he was left to his own thoughts. The idea that his 'wilderness' was a dry desert is a modern understanding. There was a Jacobean tradition of woodland for pleasure: these were outside the garden wall, often a coppice, with informal walks and seats for contemplation, and sometimes with rustic embellishments. These places of solitude and melancholy earned the name of 'wilderness' by analogy.

Such wildernesses included that next to the Spring Garden in St James's Park, mentioned above, and in time some came to be planted for the purpose. They contrasted with the French conception of woodland for pleasure, neatened up and placed within the walls. Their *bosquets* at first derived from the Italian *boschetti*, as shown by several plates published by the French gardener André Mollet.[73] They were set out as formalised groves of dense trees and shrubs, good for shade and for attracting birds. On the perimeter high palisades gave crispness to the arrangement and concealed the stems of trees, considered to be unsightly. Tunnel arbours (close walks) provided the means of communication; they were often jointed at turrets fitted out with seats and used as cabinets for retirement. Alleys were gravelled, some being *cul-de-sacs*. Italian *boschetti* were evergreen, being planted in holm oak (*Quercus ilex*). At Wimbledon Manor Mollet himself, when working for Queen Henrietta Maria in the early 1640s, had made a *bosquet* with palisades and open walks, which surveyors described as a 'wilderness' (see fig. 62).[74]

Evelyn wrote detailed instructions on how to create evergreen groves for his 'Elysium Britannicum':

> Cypresseta, myrteta, daphnes, etc. . . . which ought to be plantations apart from the taller Woods of Dry trees, and neerer in prospect to the Mansion not farr from the Parterre.[75]

He used the term 'grove' to describe his own evergreen *bosquet*, planted in 1653, at Sayes Court.[76] The Marquess of Hertford planted his old open knot at Essex House on the Strand as a *bosquet*, perhaps in the late 1650s (fig. 53).[77] In time, the name 'wilderness' transferred to such examples of tightly worked evergreen *bosquets* within the set of walled gardens, which, however, were not made in great numbers in England, probably because shade was not so highly valued as it was in more southern climes.

53 Essex House, the Strand, 1676, in a detail from the Ogilby and Morgan map of London. The gardens consisted of an upper terrace, open knots on a platform below and *bosquets* with diagonal walks and cabinets on the lowest level. These *bosquets* appear to be a deliberate conversion of an earlier diagonal arrangement of paths in a Serlio-type knot garden, and one would expect it to be planted with evergreens. The gardener when these gardens were altered around 1660 was John Rose.

TERRACES, GATES AND *DEMI-LUNES*

Italian-style viewing terraces at the end of the Great Garden may have been out of favour as they interrupted the axial development of the layout. However a new form of raised terrace, the 'great terrace', intervened between house and the slightly sunk garden. They were already known in France, for example at the Tuileries and Saint-Germain-en-Laye. An early example in England was at Horseheath Hall, Cambridgeshire, designed by Roger Pratt in the 1660s. At some places the advice to place gardens on ground falling south or south-east made 'great terraces' an obvious

choice, but the Earl of Arlington threw up one at Euston, where the ground was flat (see fig. 74). The extreme of such terraces was the second Duke of Buckingham's at Cliveden in the 1670s, which had chambers underneath (see fig. 236).[78] The Duke also created a great terrace of hitherto unseen proportions at Burley-on-the-Hill (see fig. 38).

It was the usual practice for a gate to pierce the wall at the end of the Great Garden, leading to a walk of no more than 40 feet width. However, opening up axial vistos demanded a more effective means of disclosing the view. Mollet's revised *Garden of Pleasure* (1670) advocated that there should be 'a Door of Railes or Palisado's' at the end of the garden through which 'another Walk in a direct Line to the great Walk' would take the visto out into the park.[79] Pratt installed 'transparent' gates in his own garden walls in 1671 (see fig. 42).[80] They had upper panels of iron bars instead of the usual wooden planking.

The far walls of the garden could be bowed out with a 'basket-handle', usually half-moon in shape, though sometimes half-oval. This served as an elegant transition between the square garden enclosure and the walk leading to infinity outside. Pratt, in ruminating on the decoration of niches in about 1672, remarked: 'Mem. That the Demilune at the end of a garden is most gracefully adorned with the frontispeeces, neeches etc. with about 3 steps up to them, and transparent gates between the peeres, looking down into some noble walk, grove etc.'[81]

An early and very modest example was that at Albury, designed by Evelyn in 1667 at the entry to a tunnel called 'Pausilippe', referring to that at Posillipo (see fig. 27). Others were incorporated into the perimeter of the vast enclosure at Badminton set out in the late 1660s (see fig. 104). Edward Woodroffe, an architect, made a half-moon bastion in the north wall at Gray's Inn in 1673, and another was set into the western terrace at Arlington House the following year. They become an integral part of several great layouts of the 1680s, such as those at Ragley, Longleat, Burghley and Stansted (see fig. 29).

In France, *grilles* were installed at both Fontainebleau and Versailles in the 1660s to permit vistas to continue beyond the park walls.[82] The English name for these devices was a 'grate'. Worlidge

gave an illustration of a wooden grate erected 'that the prospect of the adjacent Orchard may not be lost' from the parterre (fig. 54). Ham House had a *grille* on the main axis, and two at the ends of a cross-axis.[83] A number were inserted at Althorp about 1675 (see fig. 20).[84] Moses Cook, in discussing a garden wall at Cassiobury in 1676, observed that 'the Break in the middle against the great Walk, is a Grate' (see fig. 73).[85] As grates came into use the width of walks outside were enlarged and could lead to more interesting planting arrangements, such as *pattes d'oies* of walks.

FORECOURTS

The four grass-plat arrangement had become so well established that it became the automatic choice for forecourts and squares. At the former, visitors would dismount from horses or disgorge from carriages outside the gates. These were set within piers topped by ball finials, or, if the owner felt more exuberant, his heraldic supporters, which could be eagles, gryphons, lions or other beasts (fig. 55). Visitors would enter through them, and advance along a 'broad walk', often flagged, towards their host waiting at the front

door. It was usual for the rest of this walled forecourt to be quite plain, with two or four grass plats flanking the broad walk.

The logic of the avenue was that nothing should hinder an appreciation of the majesty of the house. Gatehouses were in the way, and many were demolished. This did not preclude pairs of single-storey lodges set into the forecourt walls either side of the

---

54   A palisade, as depicted by Frederick Hendrik van Hove in John Worlidge's *Systema Horti-culturae; Or, The Art of Gardening* (1677). The palisade enabled a view of the quincunx orchard beyond. 'Each principal walk is bordered with Flowers, each principal Corner with Flower pots, and the middle of the greater Square with Statues.'

55   Hamels, *c.*1685, engraved by John Drapentier for Chauncy's *Hertfordshire*, showing the gardens as they had been updated sometime between 1672 and 1691. Note the triple elm avenue, the gate piers with double eagles (the Brograve crest), and the wooden forecourt palisade. The gardens to the left are foreshortened by poor perspective, but the Jacobean summerhouse remained, and the terrace had acquired grates at both ends.

main gate, and these were occasionally made until the end of the century, for example at Grimsthorpe (see fig. 50). The desire to extend the axis through the house, but also to see along other vistos cut or planted within the park, led to experiments in methods of forming transparent boundaries. Owners began to replace the upper panels of their forecourt gates with bars, either wood or iron.

Then from the 1670s it became usual for the whole front walls of forecourts to be replaced by palisades in wood fixed to posts or piers at intervals. At Ingestre shortly after 1672 the division between the inner and outer courts was one such wooden palisade (see fig. 32). Soon iron palisades, or 'grates', were tried. It may have been with those at Vaux-le-Vicomte in mind that the Earl of Arlington installed them at Euston in about 1670 either side of elaborate gate piers, and supported by stone piers (fig. 56). At more provincial places, such as Longleat, the wooden palisade atop the forecourt wall, installed around 1676, was replaced by an iron version in 1678 (fig. 57).[86]

The visitor of around 1670 might be confronted by a new device, the carriage sweep, sometimes a circle, oval or ring, usually around a grass plat, itself often protected by a line of bollards. This innovation was a sign of changing travel conditions. Previously, horseback or poorly sprung coaches were the means of long-distance travel. However, by 1640 the main highways had been sufficiently well surfaced for the first stage-coach to enter service and by the 1680s London was linked by this means to 88 towns. Within London virtually all speculative development provided pitched streets. The two-wheeled gig was available from 1670.

Owners with coaches or chaises, or expecting visitors in them, would thus provide carriage sweeps outside their forecourt gates. Lord Berkeley altered his outer forecourt at The Durdans in about 1670 to accommodate a gravelled turn (see fig. 75). Another early example was seen at the Earl of Bath's seat at Stowe in

56 The King Charles Gate, Euston Hall, Suffolk. This gate, piers and *grilles* to either side were part of Lord Arlington's work in the 1670s and presaged a more widespread taste for 'transparent' boundaries of forecourts.

Devon about 1679 (see fig. 72). Owners wishing to catch up with this innovation with minimal expense could pale in part of the park for a sweep, as was the case at Bayhall Manor, Kent, about 1680 (fig. 58).[87]

The English garden in 1680

By the end of the 1670s the English had adapted the Renaissance tradition to local circumstances. One example was the way that the northern climate had led to a recasting of the advice in Italian treatises with respect to situation and prospect. Hill-

top positions were generally foregone in favour of lower ones, on ground that was level or gently falling to the south or south-east. Plantations affording protection from the west and north winds were being advised.

57   Jan Siberechts' view of the south front of Longleat House, Wiltshire, 1678, showing that the forecourt wall had been lowered. Sometime between 1676 and 1678 the wooden palisade on this wall was replaced by an iron one. The gate piers were reminiscent of the period of Inigo Jones up till the Civil War, though the fashion was briefly revived in the 1660s.

The tradition of the all-purpose four-square garden, replicated if required, gave way to layouts with the walled areas appropriate to the range of differentiated uses they accommodated – walks around grass plats for taking the air, gardens for flowers, gardens for fruit and gardens for growing kitchen stuff. Bowling greens

58   This painting by Jan Siberechts of Bayhall Manor, Kent, *c.*1680, shows a layout of the 1660s with a walled forecourt and walled garden with grass plats. Recent updating included flower borders to the plats, statuary and a fenced turnaround outside the forecourt for the carriages seen to the left.

had developed into a particular delight of the English, and the skill in keeping them led also to skill in keeping grass areas elsewhere in the garden. Greens were frequently found as side gardens after the Restoration. The flower beds in the *compartiments* of the Great Garden and the low hedges around had been cleared for grass plats.

Overwhelmingly, then, the standard garden form was a continuation of the four-square arrangement of four quarters, but the quarters of the Best Garden became grass plats, and a walk would be set out close to the perimeter, separated by beds from the walls on which fruit trees could be trained. Such a restrained layout was seen as being appropriate for hard walking when taking the air, as well as useful in being productive. The conventional English gateway became simple piers topped by caps and ball finials (fig. 59), far more restrained than the grottoes, cascades and gateways in the elaborate Italian Mannerist style seen abroad.

If English gardens had become notably different from their Renaissance-inspired predecessors, they had also taken a different path from the conspicuous elaboration and complexity of the gardens of the French court with their *parterres de broderie*, extravagant waterworks and *bosquets*. With the exception of the monarch and a few courtiers, the general mood in Protestant England till about 1680 remained one of simplicity and utility.

URBAN SQUARES

London squares adopted the building model of the *places* of Paris, with their spaciousness and good air, though the open areas took on English characteristics. The first, in 1631, had been the Covent Garden 'piazza', where the plain grass interior was protected from wheeled traffic and sedans by wooden bollards but was otherwise effectively open land.[88] The square in front of Southampton House, for which a building licence was obtained in 1661, was the first after the Restoration. Set out as if an outer forecourt, it consisted of four railed grass plats (fig. 60). Soon afterwards, the Earl of St Albans obtained the lease of land in St James's Fields in 1665, and his piazza, or square, continued in this Covent Garden mould, as did most of the squares in that century.

One important early variant to these open squares was King's Square, later known as Soho Square, in which the area within the peripheral roadway was set out as an enclosed garden for the benefit of the purchasers of the house plots. St Albans had released the land in Soho Fields, and in 1680–1 Gregory King, surveyor and statistician, provided a scheme such as a nobleman of traditional tastes might have delighted in. The four grass plats, set with sundials and trees, were centred upon a statue of Charles II, and were separated from the roadway by wooden palisades punctuated by gates with wooden posts topped with finials (fig. 61). This required a far higher degree of upkeep, the cost of which was a condition of sale of the house plots.

59   The gateway at Statfold Hall, Staffordshire, 1686. Francis Wolferstan built this gateway in 1675, at a time when others were experimenting with transparent ones. Although unremarkable, both its ball finials had been struck by lightning, prompting Wolferstan to offer a sketch for *The Natural History of Staffordshire*, engraved by Michael Burghers.

(Facing page, top) 60   Southampton House and Bloomsbury Square, St Giles's, London, c.1725, in an engraving by Sutton Nicholls. Laid out from 1661 as if an outer courtyard, it consisted of four railed grass plats, allowing pedestrians to cross from side to side and preventing carriages from passing over the turf. This general arrangement was usual in squares until the 1720s.

(Facing page, bottom) 61   King's Square (later Soho Square), Westminster, 1728, in an engraving by Sutton Nicholls. The square had been laid out in 1681 by Gregory King in four plats around a statue of Charles II – hence its name – and enclosed by wooden palisades. The idea of a square forming a private garden for residents did not prevail until later London squares.

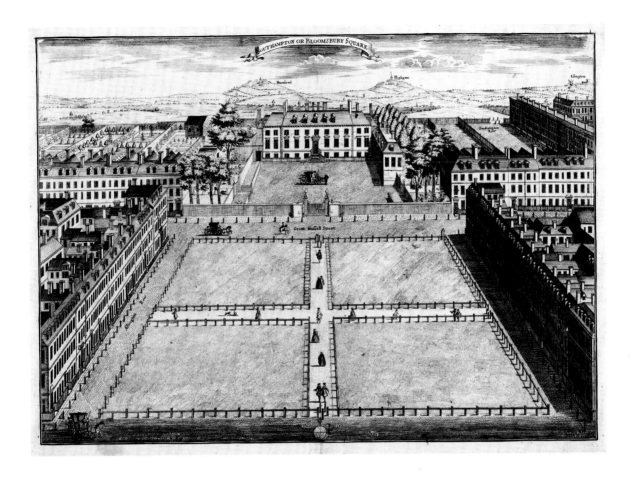

Kingly Ambitions

CHARLES II'S GARDENS AND PARKS

Although the general run of English gardens over the mid-century to some extent reflected a Protestant standpoint, with its eschewal of vanity and show, the monarch and his Court were more concerned to compete with the standards of garden-making being set in France and other Continental countries. This was against a background of Parliament being an increasingly dominant force at the centre of English life.

The French example

The French Court, in which an elaborate etiquette established any person's place in the descending ranks of status below the king, was setting the pattern for most others in Europe. The model for the administration of royal gardens in France was set by Henri

IV, who died in 1610. Other innovations were seen in the 1620s in the garden of Henri IV's widow, Marie de' Medici, at the Luxembourg Palace, where a large parterre sported an attached half-oval on axis, a visual device forming the transition from a two-dimensional parterre to a one-dimensional axial vista, and which was sometimes referred to as an *anse de panier* (baskethandle) or *demi-lune*.[1] Half a century of *broderie* patterns for parterres are represented by the publications by Jacques Boyceau in 1638, André Mollet in 1651 and a long-delayed one by his father, Claude Mollet, in 1652.

Equally impressive as the new *broderie* were the waterworks in French gardens. André Mollet's *Garden of Pleasure* (1670) stated that 'Water is said to be the Soul of Gardens'.[2] The Italians Tommaso Francini and his brother Alessandro were in part responsible for those in the Luxembourg Gardens, and were probably responsible also for a famous grotto there. In the 1630s they worked for Cardinal Richelieu, Louis XIII's chief minister, at Rueil, near Paris, where an aqueduct brought water to the head of a staircase cascade, in which small basins of water drove fountains further down, the basins of which fed further fountains, and so on.[3]

At the same time Richelieu was creating a layout on a royal scale at his ancestral home, Richelieu, in the Loire valley. The *broderie* 'Grand Parterre de la Demi-Lune' broke with Renaissance tradition in being oblong rather than square. The parterre was symmetrical only about the long axis, and at the far end, between pavilions, was a *demi-lune* semicircular evergreen hedge with niches and statues. An ironwork *grille* on axis continued the vista beyond.

CHARLES I AND HENRIETTA MARIA

Like all monarchs and princes across Europe, the English royal family looked on these French achievements in awe, but Charles I's inability to come to an accommodation with Parliament meant no new taxes and limited funds to start or complete major projects at the palaces. Perhaps Charles's most lasting achievement was the enclosure, in 1637, of New Park near Richmond Palace (today's Richmond Park). Eight miles in length, its wall enclosed both red and fallow deer.

Perhaps aware of the aqueducts to the Luxembourg Gardens and Rueil, Charles saw fountains and other waterworks at Hampton Court in his mind. He had a leat, the 'Longford River', dug for several miles from the River Crane to a reservoir in Bushy Park, providing a thirteen-foot head for waterworks in the gardens at Hampton Court. The work started in 1638 and finished the next year, but whatever waterworks were intended in the gardens were left undone, a casualty of the disputes between king and parliament.[4]

In 1639 Charles I purchased Wimbledon Manor for his queen, Henrietta Maria. The house was modified by Inigo Jones in 1640–1 (fig. 62). In the early 1640s Mollet was working in England after some years as a parterre designer in the Low Countries, Sweden and elsewhere. Many of these parterres appeared in the

first (French) edition of his *Le Jardin de Plaisir*, published in 1651 (fig. 63). He was paid in 1642 for half a year's work at Wimbledon, which included recasting the Orange Garden: 'there are four knotts, fitted for the growth of choice flowers, bordered with box in the points, angles, squares, and roundlets, and handsomely turfed in the intervals or little walks thereof', each of which had a cypress tree.[5] The 'oringe house' in the north-east corner, one of the first in England, was stocked with 60 orange trees, one lemon, one citron and six pomegranate trees in boxes.

At a higher level was the six-acre 'Great Garden'. Here the former gardens below the south front were excavated to a uniform level with the rear door of the house, and redesigned with a 25-foot-wide terrace terminated by garden houses and four 'great squares' in a line. The inward two were together enclosed by 'spired posts' and rails on three sides, and contained eight knots around marble fountains of Diana and a mermaid. The knots had cypresses, flower beds bordered with box and brick alleys. The outer two great squares were surrounded by thorn hedges set with cherry trees, and each contained four grass plats with central cypresses, arranged around central circles of grass.

At the back of the Great Garden on the main axis was a flight of ten steps and stepped walks bordered with currant bushes rising southwards to an older grassed lime walk. Above this were a maze and a wilderness either side of the axis. The former 'consists of young trees, wood[s], and sprays of a good growth and height, cut out into several meanders, circles, semicircles, windings, and intricate turnings', while the wilderness consisted of

> many young trees, woods, sprays of a good growth and height, cut and formed into several ovals, squares, and angles, very well ordered; in most of the angular points whereof, as also in the centre of every oval, stands one Lime tree or elm. All the alleys of this wilderness, being in number eighteen, are of a gravelled earth.

Meanwhile, Richelieu had died in 1642, Louis XIII in 1643, and Cardinal Mazarin became chief minister to the youthful Louis XIV. Nicholas Fouquet, appointed joint *Surintendants des finances* in 1653, commissioned a new house at Vaux-le-Vicomte, designed in

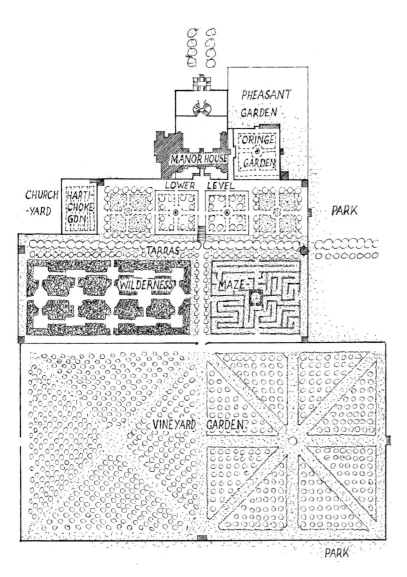

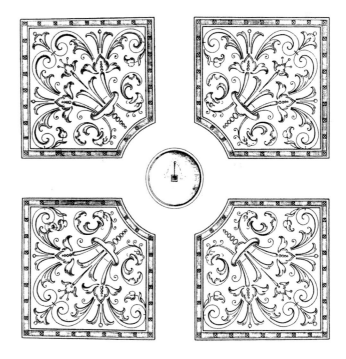

62 A reconstruction by the author of Henrietta Maria's garden at Wimbledon Manor as it appeared in 1649 after alterations by André Mollet (north is at the top). The 'Garden House fitted for the keeping of Oringe trees' was at the north-east corner of the 'Oringe Garden' and some of its orange trees were inside a lower chamber of the house. The 'Great Garden' was on two levels. The lower was level with the principal floor of the house, being a floor above the Oringe Garden, and consisted of four great squares of knots, two for flowers around marble fountains of Diana and a mermaid, and the other two with grass plots. The turfed 'Tarras' was on its upper level, reached by a flight of ten steps; the lime trees on this terrace were continued out into the park. Also on the upper level were a maze and a wilderness, here shown in designs based on Mollet's book. Through a large railed gate was the Vineyard Garden, named after the vineyard that was once here, but in the 1640s it had become a ten-acre walled fruit garden.

63 An engraved design for a parterre with eagle heads published by André Mollet in *Le Jardin de Plaisir* in 1651 and reprinted in *The Garden of Pleasure* in 1670. Symmetrical about two axes, the design, reminiscent of the 1630s, was adopted for the parterre at Bretby Hall, Derbyshire, probably in the 1680s, a rare example of French design being adopted by a non-royal nobleman.

1656, together with much extended gardens. The garden designer was André Le Nostre, from a family of gardeners who had worked under the Mollets at the Tuileries.[6] As at Richelieu, the parterres at Vaux-le-Vicomte were oblong and symmetrical about one axis only, giving great emphasis to the stupendous extent of the garden. Beyond the garden was a system of avenues cut through the forest, firmly binding even the most outlying parts of the property into an ordered whole.

Charles I's son, Charles Stuart, or Charles II as royalists declared him to be after his father's execution in 1649, eked out an impecunious though debauched exile abroad. From 1651 he resided in Paris and at Saint-Germain-en-Laye, and then from 1654 in Cologne, and finally from 1656 in Brussels. In the course of these travels he came to know gardens in the vicinities of these cities, and must have become painfully aware of the advances in French and Dutch gardens as he was constrained to stand idly by.

Charles II's gardens

Ambassadors, the King's friends and relations, the royal household, the King's ministers, petitioners and a great array of others formed a swarm of people all desiring access to the monarch. Private gardens for King and Queen were necessary to allow them to pursue private pleasures and be more intimate with their family and those close to them. In England such 'Privy Gardens' existed at Hampton Court, Whitehall, St James's and Somerset House. Space was also desirable for members of the Court to promenade in the air, and for the King to enjoy company in less formal surroundings than inside the palace. At Hampton Court, the Old Orchard and the House Park served these functions, whilst St James's Park did so at Whitehall (see fig. 24).

Lord Protector Cromwell found that he required similar arrangements and several royal palaces were placed at his disposal. While he lived, there was no question of Charles II returning, but when he died the power vacuum began to be filled by the King's allies. Charles was restored to the throne in 1660, recovering his possessions including the palaces of Whitehall, St James's, Hampton Court and Greenwich, and the royal parks and forests.

His first acts included repairs to the Great Dial in the Privy Garden at Whitehall Palace (see fig. 52), and the construction of a bowling green adjacent to the garden. A new lime avenue was added parallel to the elm one planted past St James's Palace in 1615. One of the more harmless tastes that Charles acquired abroad was for the game of pell-mell. Between the old elms and new limes a pell-mell course was set out before the end of 1660 (see fig. 71). In January 1660/1 he appointed Henry Du Puy, a servant of the Duke of York, 'Keeper of the Pall Mall' in St James's Park at the extravagant salary of £100 per annum.[7] He, and from 1672

his son Laurence, maintained the course in high state till the overthrow of the Duke, by then James II, in 1688.

ST JAMES'S AND HAMPTON COURT

Hugh May was appointed Paymaster of the King's Works, and was chiefly responsible for refurbishing the royal palaces. The works included two canal projects. By the autumn of 1660 Charles had ordered the digging of a canal through St James's Park aligned on the steps down from Whitehall Palace. A half-circle of imported lime trees was planted at the Whitehall end, and beyond were double lines of trees framing the canal (fig. 64). Three stub walks extended away from the half-circle. Samuel Pepys noticed the work in progress in September.

At Hampton Court Charles first had a bridge and the palisades to the 1630s bowling green repaired.[8] There were ideas for a canal and avenue similar to those in St James's Park, but this first required a park wall to be taken down. In December 1660 carpenters were 'imployed in . . . makeinge of a large square to sett out the worcke in the parke by for the trees; and river'.[9] During 1661 the Longford River was cleaned out, the Long Water canal was dug eastwards from the palace, lime trees were planted either side of the canal, a great half-round was planted between canal and palace, and from its ends by the palace lateral walks were planted north and south (fig. 65).

These two canal-cum-avenue projects were unlike anything seen in England before. Placing canals within lines of trees running away through parks at the rear of these palaces was very different from advice from Scamozzi and Mollet that avenues should frame the approach and be aligned on the principal front. They may have emulated Henri IV's Grand Canal at Fontainebleau, which was flanked by trees (in fact the Hampton Court canal was slightly longer). On the other hand, the half-rounds of trees and the lateral walks at the palace ends suggest familiarity with Honselaarsdijk or Mollet's book. May knew the Low Countries well through his dealings there on behalf of the second Duke of Buckingham in Commonwealth times, and these two canal projects were, then, perhaps based on his memories, adapted to suit

these palaces. The accounts identify Adrian May, Hugh's elder brother, as the person responsible for carrying out these projects, and Philip Moore for 'setting out the grounds for his Ma^ts Plantacion at Hampton Court and Directing the Planters'.

A 'Great Walke' was planted across Bushy Park to the north, aligned on the Great Hall. It had quadruple lines on each side, unheard of previously, and towards the south end there was a cross avenue, meeting the main one at an 800-foot-diameter circle and then it widened into a rectangle, presumably to embrace an intended parade in place of the Old Orchard (see fig. 90). In June 1662 Evelyn enthused over the 'sweete rows of *lime-trees*, and the Canale for water now neere perfected'.[10]

CHARLES II'S FRENCH GARDENERS

Charles had meanwhile decided upon a new garden to be taken out of the edge of St James's Park, and enlisted the by-now elderly André Mollet and his nephew Gabriel to take on the project. André was then probably living in Richmond in Surrey. Charles made the Mollets 'his Maties Gardiners and Designers of all his Gardens', responsible 'for altering & making them into the neatest formes'.[11] This description recalled Claude Mollet's position of 'desseigner en tous les jardeins de S^a Ma^té' when working for Louis XIII, and André's own title as 'intendant et desseigneur des jardins' for Frederik-Hendrik, Prince of Orange. By 'desseigneur' was meant 'draughtsman', seemingly referring to their skill at devising *broderie*. They were to be overseen by Adrian May as 'supervisor of the French gardeners employed at Whitehall, St James and Hampton Court'.[12]

In fact the Mollets were never given the opportunity by Charles II to show their skill in *parterres de broderie*, and they were chiefly required 'to keepe His Maties Royall Garden that is to be planted wth fruite trees and flowers in St James Parke betweene St James howse & ye Spring Garden wall'. The shape for this 'Royal Garden' was far from ideal, being four times as long as broad, and unconnected to the layouts at St James's or Whitehall palaces. Undeterred, Mollet devised a layout assuming that most visitors would enter at the Spring Garden end, being closer to the Whitehall steps. It consisted of twelve *compartiments*, with a fountain at the centre, and terminating at a *demi-lune* enclosed by an evergreen *bosquet* with cabinets, itself finished by a half-oval *anse du panier* (figs 66a and b).[13] The lack of a viewing position argued against *parterres de broderie* or *compartiments de gazon* with their flower bed arabesques and in favour of palisaded *compartiments*. Mollet devised

---

64　A sketch by Hendrick Danckerts of St James's Park, *c.*1670, looking towards Whitehall alongside the avenue. Note the tree guards, indicating that the avenue was newly planted.

65   Hampton Court Long Water, *c.*1667. Hendrick Danckerts' view shows the canal in the House Park aligned on the balcony, making it a compliment to the new queen. The flanking lime trees were planted in 1662. The canal was briefly the longest in Europe.

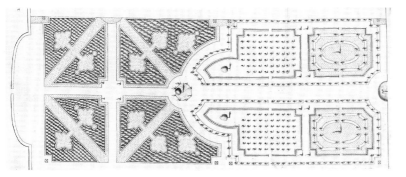
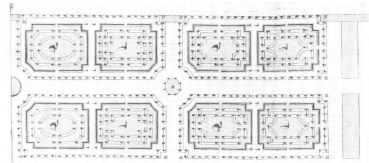

five-foot-high palisades of cypress and other evergreens around the *compartiments*, each of which had two entrances. The interiors were grassed with beds containing dwarf fruit trees, rose trees and flowers. Gabriel went to Paris in the course of 1661 for the flowers, which cost £115.

GREENWICH

The Mollets were not the only French gardeners sought out by Charles II. He had ambitions for a new palace with gardens at Greenwich, perhaps as a grand *entrée* to London for visiting royalty and ambassadors. Modifications to the Queen's House, set in the northern wall of the park, were carried out in late 1662. It was to look out over new gardens in the park. Charles had already in September 1661 had the earthwork 'Giants' Steps' cut out of the hill which rose gradually, then steeply, past the Royal Observatory, and the most likely explanation for them is that they were the initial earthworks for a spectacular staircase cascade to rival anything in France (fig. 67).[14] However his confidence faltered, and he realised that he needed a master to complete the design.

Charles's beloved sister Henrietta was in Paris to marry Philippe, Duc d'Orléans, Louis XIV's brother, in 1661, and a fête was arranged in her honour at Vaux-le-Vicomte. About the time that the Giants' Steps were being completed at Greenwich, Henrietta wrote to Charles recommending André Le Nostre as someone who might design the new gardens there. Charles II thus wrote to Louis XIV in May 1662 asking to borrow him.[15] Louis agreed, without conviction. Charles gave five geldings and a mare to Le

66a and b   The west and east ends of André Mollet's published plan for the Royal Garden, St James's, 1670. Eschewing a parterre because the garden was not overlooked, he laid it out as five quarters on each side palisaded with five-foot-high evergreens, and internal beds cut into grass and intended for flowers (for which he sent to Paris), roses and dwarf fruit trees. Beyond were two orchard quarters, backed by a wilderness of 'green trees' focussing on an ancient oak.

67   Greenwich Park, viewed east from the Observatory, from *Vivarium Grenovicanum* (1676), drawn by Robert Thacker and engraved by Francis Place. This provides a view of the earthworks of 1662 intended for a staircase cascade, but then abandoned.

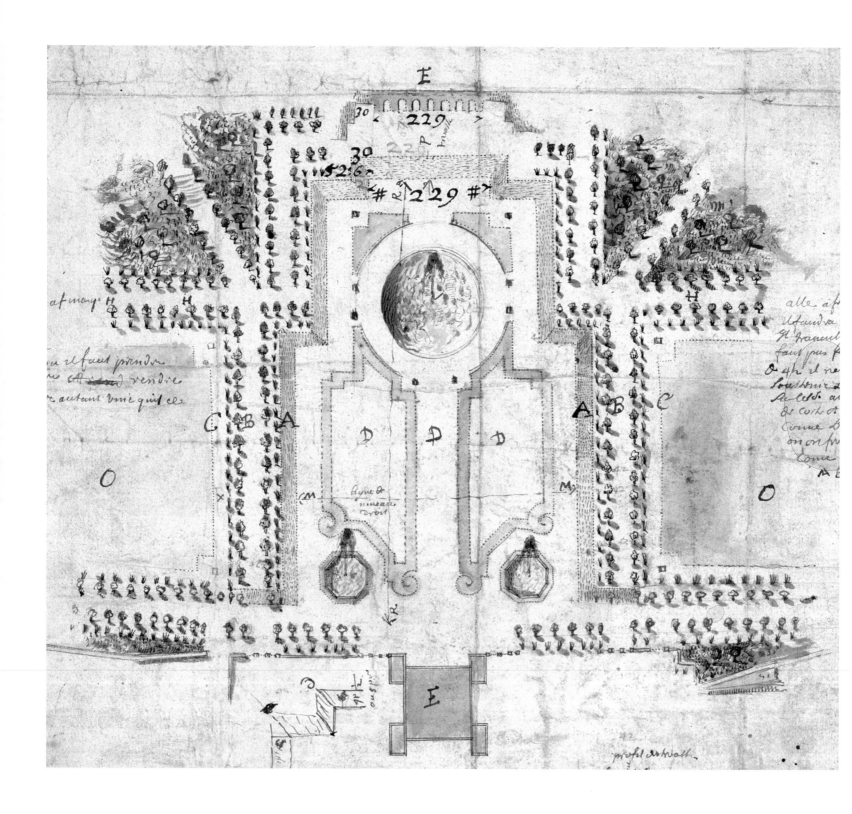

(Facing page) 68 A scheme by André Le Nostre for Greenwich Park, c.1662. Although Le Nostre never visited England, he was sent dimensions from which he devised a parterre to lie under the south front of the Queen's House similar to one he was making at Saint-German-en-Laye, with broderie within *plates-bandes* and fountains. The tree-lined walks and the terraces were made in 1663, but the parterre and fountains were left unfinished in 1665.

69 The so-called 'Pepys Plan' of Greenwich Park, c.1675–80, indicating the empty parterre platform, kite-shaped planting similar to that at Vaux-le-Vicomte and 'Boreman's Bower' at the top (south), which was new coppice planting.

Nostre and in October 1662 issued a warrant 'yᵉ Farmers of oʳ Customes' to permit 'Le Nostre our Architect' to import these horses into France without payment of customs.[16] Actually this was not a good time for him to be taken away from Fontainebleau, and it seems that he never made the journey.

However, Le Nostre did oblige with a sketch plan based on dimensions provided to him (fig. 68).[17] This showed a large area for a parterre with *plates-bandes* with corner scrolls in view from the Queen's House. Le Nostre had been told that water could be obtained, and proposed three fountains, one on axis towards the rear, and two at the corners nearest the house. The projected parterre thus had similarities with the concurrent parterre at the Château-Vieux at Saint-Germain-en-Laye. The difference was that the hillside at Greenwich had to be cut into, and Le Nostre jotted down numerous notes on forming terraces around the parterre. These terraces were to be planted with walks of trees, and further ones were to branch off to the boundaries of the park, and turn inwards again to form a kite shape, much as had been planned for Vaux and was being planned for the Grand Parc at Versailles (fig. 69).

The team at Hampton Court must have been moved straight on to Greenwich, where Le Nostre's earthworks were under way in the winter of 1662–3. John Rose, the Royal Gardener at St James's Palace, was brought over to Greenwich, and he was the most likely person to have set the design out on the ground. Adrian May's agent at Greenwich, Adrian Pratt, purchased 700 large elm trees, 500 of which were for the terraces, and 7,000 lime trees for the park walks and the nursery. Forty elms were requisitioned from Evelyn's walks at Sayes Court nearby, much to his disgust.[18] Planting started in January 1663/4. As soon as he was finished at Hampton Court in August 1664, Moore went to Greenwich, where he supervised the 'Levelling the Plaine in the Parke before the house' for the parterre. By the summer of 1665 earthmoving and planting was complete, leaving the parterre and its fountains still to be made.

However, by this time the King was being forced to accept that his plans for the new palace were out of his reach, and was ready to turn the buildings then existing into the Greenwich Hospital.

WINDSOR

Charles II was thus only partially successful in building new palaces and gardens to reflect his position as one of the leading European monarchs. However, one further and curious exploit by him in garden-making can be mentioned. He spent the summer of 1674 at Windsor. Evelyn saw earthworks thrown up on the meadows north of the castle to imitate the '*Bastions*, Bullwarks, Ramparts, Palizads, [Graft], horn-works, Conterscarps &c: in imitation of the Citty of *Maestrict*'.[19] This had been for a re-enactment of a military victory there by his natural son, the Duke of Monmouth.

This event was followed by changes to the castle by Hugh May, including the 'Star Building', extending over the old terrace walk and supported by a large bastion. As works progressed around the eastern perimeter of the castle, May remade the terrace from the bastion around to the south-east corner of the castle and had the slopes below shaped into a regular form (fig. 70). Evelyn was clearly impressed, writing in 1683, 'there was now the Terraces almost

brought round the old Castle: The Grafts made cleane, even, & curiously turf't, also the Avenues to the New-Park, & other Walkes planted with Elmes & limes' (see fig. 83). This planting included the double 'King's Avenue' (today's Long Walk), intended to continue the axis in line with the Maastricht Garden to the south of the castle to meet the Great Park. Negotiations for land purchase held up the planting, but in 1684 two and a half miles of the southern length was installed by Moses Cook and George London in elms, the central lines 138 feet apart (see fig. 145).[20]

Court and country

France, especially under Louis XIV, had an absolute (the English would say despotic) monarchy. The state was thus highly centralised. The major gardens were developed by those with power –

70   The north slopes, Windsor Castle, 1680s, in a drawing by Francis Place, showing the north scarp below the castle re-formed by Hugh May in the late 1670s into regular slopes, a process completed in William III's reign.

the royal family, the ministers and field marshals – and such places were meant to demonstrate it. In England and Wales matters were more complicated. There were two other power bases: the magnates in the House of Lords, and the elected members from the boroughs and shires in the House of Commons. Charles II was wise enough to seek an accommodation with Parliament. In truth, the potency of the monarchy to determine national life was already spent.

The boroughs had become content that the wealthier local gentry should represent them in Parliament.[21] The benefits to such gentry were great; it was the opportunity to mingle with the mighty and be close to the centre of power. It was also a chance to gain contacts with people in finance and the law, to indulge in gaming and the theatre, and to find a wife. It gave great prestige at home. The status of MP was the highest accolade for the landed gentry below that of nobility. Heirs to peerages were not ashamed to sit as MPs, so serving their apprenticeships in the Commons.

Fortunes were being made in the professions, mainly law and medicine, and in trade, for example from mines, shipping or money lending. MPs from these backgrounds increased between 1640 and 1700, as those from trade made 42% of new entrants, and those from the professions made 22%, at the expense of long-established landed gentry.[22] In terms of religion, there were members of the gentry that hankered after the old faith, but the bulk, as well as most from trade and the professions, were staunchly Church of England and anti-Catholic.

For such families seeking to rise through the social ranks, the key was Parliament. The steps forward were, having acquired a fortune, to establish a country seat with gardens, and if possible a park, to gain entry to the landed classes. This was necessary to be nominated to Parliament. Once in Parliament there were the possibilities of government office or sinecure if you showed yourself useful to the King's ministers. If your career in the service of the King was successful you would be rewarded by a baronetcy or entry to the hereditary peerage. In the seventeenth century three-quarters of those ennobled had previously been MPs.

MPs were generally selected by the county élite of whichever party, Tory or Whig, was dominant. These were the magnates, with votes in their pockets, who themselves automatically sat in the House of Lords. So how did someone come to the notice of these political superiors? Generally it was by having a reputation for a sound background, orthodox views (and would vote as told) and being a 'man of business'.

As Parliament became ever more central to the business of the nation, competition for a seat in Parliament increased, and the price of admission rose. Travel before the days of the stage coach was a slow and arduous business on horseback. Lodgings would be needed during the parliamentary session. It has been estimated that three-quarters of the MPs in the Long Parliament during Charles I's reign had incomes of at least £500 a year. After the Restoration costs escalated further, with the acquisition of a London townhouse, perhaps in one of the new squares. Then there was the maintenance of a lifestyle, involving ample expenditure on a carriage, furniture, plate, clothes and wine, commensurate with the status of MP. The phenomenon of MPs crippling their estates through election expenses was first seen in the 30 years between the Restoration and the beginning of William III's reign.

THE COURT PARTY

There was a marked divergence of outlook between the Court and the Commons. The political rhetoric of 1660–80 distinguished the Court Party, representing those holding posts at Court or in the administration, and interested in strengthening the power of the Crown in military or tax-raising matters, and the Country Party, MPs who distrusted courtiers, stressed the interests of the country as a whole, and were inclined to question the need for new taxation.

Reflecting this schism in political attitudes, there was also a divergence in ideas on how gardens should be laid out in the two decades after the Restoration. The broad swathe of the gentry pursued garden-making in a Protestant frame of mind, and had little comprehension of fashions abroad. Such people included MPs and a proportion of the King's ministers, officers and place holders, particularly those who had come to notice through Parliament.

On the other hand, there were the gardens of Charles II's courtiers, aping those of Charles himself, informed by international developments, and intended to convey messages of superiority and power. Such persons were ambitious to display their status through the houses and gardens they built. They did not have to be presently in favour – they could be aspirants to it, or those who sought to consolidate their position towards the end of a career at Court or in government. As the architect Roger North observed, 'the greatest statesmen, and favourites of fortune, after proof of all the envyed grandure upon earth, have chosen, either upon disgrace or voluntary retiredment, to imploy their time in designing fabricks and executing them'.[23] That would include their gardens.

Amongst Charles's closest circle were his family. Henrietta Maria, his mother, was given the use of Somerset House and the Queen's House at Greenwich Palace. Charles's brother, James, was effectively put in charge of St James's Palace, where he made new apartments, a riding school and a parterre surrounded by a terrace (fig. 71). Charles's cousin Prince Rupert, son of Elizabeth of Bohemia, was given lodgings in the 'wilderness' by the Spring Garden, on the edge of St James's Park. A more distant cousin, Charles Stuart, sixth Duke of Lennox, the Great Chamberlain of Scotland, possessed Cobham Hall, Kent (see fig. 130). The most notorious of Charles's mistresses, through the 1660s till the early 1670s, was Barbara Palmer, wife of the Earl of Castlemaine. In 1669 she was made Chief Steward and Ranger of Hampton Court, where Charles had a house built for her connecting to his chambers (see fig. 133).

Various royal servants and those useful in supplying money or other services naturally shared in Charles's favours. John Grenville, who had been instrumental in the Restoration, was appointed Keeper of St James's Palace and gardens in 1660, then made Earl of Bath in 1661. He was to rebuild his ancestral home, Stowe, at Kilkhampton, Devon, in 1679 (fig. 72). George, ninth Baron Berkeley, had formally invited Charles back to England. The Durdans, just by Epsom, was his fashionable villa, and he was keeper of Nonsuch Palace from 1669. He took much interest in the East African, Levant and East Indian companies, and was

made Earl of Berkeley in 1679. Richard Boyle, second Earl of Cork, a magnate with vast properties in Ireland who had lent Charles large sums of money, was Lord Treasurer of Ireland 1660–95 and was made Earl of Burlington in 1663. His best known properties were Burlington House in Piccadilly (see fig. 80), built in 1667, and Londesborough on his Yorkshire estates, where he had new wings and gardens added to the house in 1676 (see fig. 177).

There were others who, by dint of their rank or allegiance to the Crown, considered themselves close to the King. Montagu Bertie, second Earl of Lindsey, a former Cavalier soldier, was appointed to Charles's Privy Council in 1660 and made a Knight of the Garter and Lord High Chamberlain in 1661. His seat was Grimsthorpe, Lincolnshire, where he could boast a park of enviable extent. The youthful Robert Spencer, second Earl of Sunderland, could point to his father's death fighting for Charles I, and had immense wealth, which enabled him to rebuild Althorp House, Northamptonshire, in 1666–8 (see fig. 20). Lord Craven was able to give lifelong support to the interests of Charles's aunt, Elizabeth of Bohemia, thanks to wealth and possessions that included houses in London and at Combe Abbey and Hamstead Marshall. He was created Earl of Craven in 1664 and made a Privy Councillor two years later.

Some old Cavaliers became Charles's ministers at the Restoration. Edward Hyde was made Lord Chancellor and elevated to the earldom of Clarendon. He was granted the park at Cornbury, Oxfordshire, where, advised by Hugh May and Evelyn, he started to build a large mansion and plant his park. He also built a palatial town house in Piccadilly, designed by Roger Pratt. The elderly Earl of Southampton was made Treasurer, though after a few years he gave up attempting to balance Charles's finances. John Maitland, Earl of Lauderdale, who had supported Charles I's interests in Scotland, was called upon to do so for Charles II as Secretary of State. He was much engaged in improvements to Thirlestane Castle and other ancestral residences, but in 1672 he married the Countess of Dysart, owner of Ham House, where he thenceforward spent much time (see fig. 77). Henry Bennet, royalist and a suspected Catholic, spent the Commonwealth in

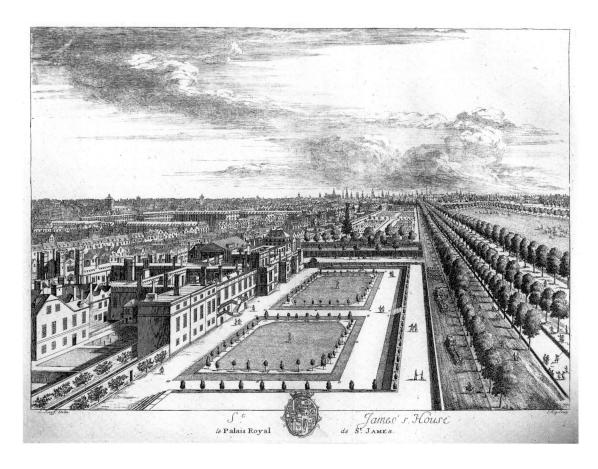

St James's House
le Palais Royal   de St. James.

71   Leonard Knyff's view of the garden of St James's Palace, *c.*1700. The two grass plats are separated from the park by a terrace providing a view over garden and out into the park. In the walks to the right pell-mell, a game consisting of hitting balls with a mallet, is being played.

72   Edmund Prideaux's sketch of Stowe, Kilkhampton, 1716, shows the house built in 1679 by the Earl of Bath on a saddle between two hills; falling ground permitted good views beyond the walls. The walled forecourt had a grand flight of steps to the door, and the two walled gardens, which had had wall fruit, were connected by *perron* stairs.

exile, and became very well travelled and multilingual. He was made a Secretary of State in 1662, and created Baron Arlington the next year.

In 1667 Arlington and the second Duke of Buckingham were amongst those that engineered the removal of Clarendon from office. For the next seven years Arlington, flushed with the rewards of being Secretary of State, spent prodigiously on Euston, Suffolk, an estate he had purchased in 1666. The house was given French-style *pavillons*, and impressive gardens and parkland were formed (see figs 74 and 233). Arlington's London house with views of St James's Park, Goring House, was burnt down in 1674, but he took the matter calmly and ordered the building of a new mansion, to be known as Arlington House (see fig. 23). His elder brother received sufficient benefits from being Farmer of the Customs to allow the rebuilding of the family home at Dawley in the early 1670s (see fig. 46).

The Duke of Buckingham did not need high office to bolster his finances. From his father he had inherited Burley-on-the-Hill (see fig. 38), though it had been burnt out by parliamentarian troops, and the great house at Chelsea that would later become Beaufort House (see fig. 122). He had also acquired considerable estates in Yorkshire by right of his wife. In 1666 he bought land at Cliveden with spectacular views over the Thames, intended for a house for his mistress, the Countess of Salisbury (see fig. 236).

After Arlington was impeached in 1674 the Duke promoted the interests of Sir Thomas Osborne, who then became Lord Treasurer and effectively chief minister till 1679. He was created Earl of Danby in 1674, and purchased Wimbledon Manor (see fig. 76). The ambassador to Paris, Ralph Montagu, heir to Boughton House, built Montagu House for himself in London, designed by Robert Hooke (see fig. 87).

There were other magnates outside the King's close circle, often with the potential to influence national events. Some were independently minded and had sided with Parliament. The Earl of Northumberland had vainly sought a moderate compromise between Charles I and Parliament. His great possessions included Syon House, Petworth and Alnwick. The Earl of Rutland, of Belvoir Castle, had formerly been a Parliamentarian. It was common to appoint magnates as Lord Lieutenants if they were supporters of the King; sometimes there were other honorific posts to bestow, as when the Marquess of Worcester (later Duke of Beaufort) was made Lord President of the Council of Wales in 1672. He had made great additions to his house and parks at Badminton from the late 1660s (see fig. 79).

The garden of pleasure

These members of the Court were well informed about innovations in French practice, but numerically they were few compared to the nobility and gentry who were as yet hesitant to embrace the French example. André Mollet was still, about 1665, evidently not convinced that his English readership would understand French vocabulary. In 1651 he had written 'du jardin de plaisir . . . nous y ordonnerons les parterres, bosquets, arbres, palissades et alleés diverses', and in front of the mansion one great advantage was 'y pouvoir planter une grande avenue'. In the English version of his book, *The Garden of Pleasure* (1670) this was rendered as 'The Garden of Pleasure consists in Groundworks, Wildernesses, choice Trees, Palissado's, and Alleys or Walks', and that in front of the house it was desirable 'to plant a great Walk'.[24] Nevertheless, when he wanted to stock the Royal Garden he was making, Mollet acquired his plants from France. In 1675 his successor, John Rose, sent his apprentice, George London, 'into France, the greatest Seat of Learning at that time in the World, especially in the Errand he went about' – in other words, gardening.[25]

Attitudes amongst the well-travelled changed when they saw the glories of Versailles for themselves. John Locke's party was shown it, 'a fine house & a much finer garden', by Louis XIV himself in 1677 and he went again several times in 1678.[26] Locke's enthusiastic description pointed out the numerous *jets d'eau*, the prospects, the great canal, the menagerie and other marvels. John Worlidge, a member of the minor gentry, writing at the same time, had evidently heard much the same: 'the Glory of the French Palaces . . . are adorn'd with their beauteous Gardens before them, which wanting, they would seem without Lustre or Grandeur'.[27] During the latter part of Charles II's reign those remembering the gardens of France began to refine their English gardens with some of the embellishments they had seen.

EMBELLISHING THE PARTERRE

Among the innovations were terraces down the sides of the parterre. Evelyn had devised some flanking his brother's grass parterre at Wotton in 1653, and Le Nostre's scheme of 1662 for the parterre at Greenwich included side terraces planted with open walks. However, it was Lord Essex's side terraces at Cassiobury of about 1675 that provided the model that was to be most followed.[28] They combined with a great terrace to form a U-shape, and with the elimination of the viewing terrace at the bottom of the garden, and a downwards sloping parterre, a view out could be obtained from these three sides (fig. 73). By the end of the 1670s there were several further examples.

Another embellishment of the parterre was the *jet d'eau*, a French term Englished to a variety of spellings. Their chief drawback was the great expense of their supply through lead pipes and stopcocks. They had been known in pre-Civil War gardens, and Mollet and Le Nostre specified them for the Royal Garden at St James's and for Greenwich. However, *jets d'eau* had in fact been omitted from most gardens between 1640 and 1670. Round about this latter date a number of noblemen decided that it was time to reintroduce them. These included Lord Arlington at Euston (fig. 74) and Arlington House. Almost all these made in Restoration times were at the crossing point of alleys dividing grass plats.

The over-size receiving pools at Eaton and Cassiobury were amongst the earliest bodies of water that could have been described as 'basons'. Most water in the garden at this time was reminiscent of, or even had been, fishponds, being generally small to medium trapezoids or rectangles, and discovered in a near piece of low ground outside the Best Garden. The garden pond was essentially the formalisation of the fishpond within a garden layout.

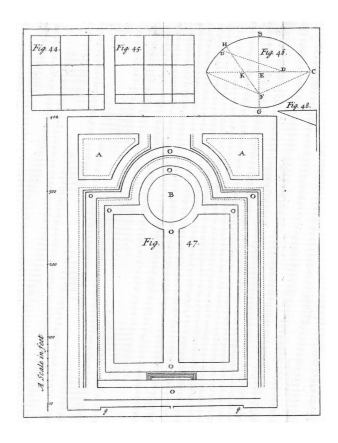

73   Moses Cook's plan of the parterre at Cassiobury House, Hertfordshire, 1676. A terrace ran under the house front and returned down the sides, forming a sunken space for a twin-plat parterre terminating at a circle intended for a fountain; a visto was continued beyond the fountain by means of a grate. This is recognisably the garden shown on the Knyff and Kip view.

Within the parterre, still mostly grass plats, some shrubs might be introduced at the corners, and this included the return of the naturally fastigiate Italian cypress. John Ray observed in 1676 how the cypress was 'now common in every garden of any note',[29] and Worlidge agreed in 1677 that: 'of all the Trees that have been propagated in our European parts, none have yet merited that esteem as the Cypress hath done'.[30] Another tree sometimes used for clipping was the fir tree, which naturally grew, and could be further trained, into a cake-stand form (see fig. 89).[31] According to

Back front of Ewston & orangerie towards y West.

Worlidge, this tree, 'by reason of the slender and aspiring trunk of the streight Firr and the facil keeping and preserving its Branches in a compleat Circular order, it doth very well become a Garden, planted at the Corners of your Squares'.[32] He himself showed the

74   A sketch by Edmund Prideaux of the 'Back front of Ewston & orangerie towards yᵉ West', *c.1725*. This view of Euston Hall shows the continuation of the great terrace to the right, the greenhouse to the left, and cypresses and figures on the grass plats around a *jet d'eau*, probably much was made around 1669. The canal was the leat to the mill, which pumped water to the fountains. A swivelling bridge was designed by Sir Samuel Morland to cross it.

tree standing at the corners of grass plats on one of his illustrations (see fig. 41).

Worlidge, keen to see flowers reintroduced to parterres, suggested that if 'you are willing to celebrate so fair a spot of Ground to the delights of Flora, then you may . . . make Grassplots, leaving only borders on their confines for your variety of plants'.[33] Some owners were indeed tired of plain grass plats, even those enlivened by cypress trees, and welcomed a more ornamented style. Whereas Worlidge was harking back to the gardens of his youth, the noblemen who threw off their Protestant reserve concerning flowers were thinking of recent examples across the Channel.

French flower gardens were the products of a passion for collecting florist flowers that had built strongly there through the

seventeenth century. Vaux-le-Vicomte had an extensive *parterre des fleurs* in beds. A formula for flower borders made standard by Le Nostre from the 1660s, consisting of a mounded bed, constrained by low box-edging and planted with shaped (ever)greens, clipped shrubs, annual flowers and bulbs, was seen for example at Saint Germain-en-Laye. Louis XIV must be counted amongst the curious, and at Versailles there were such *plates-bandes* each way from the château, including the *parterre d'eau* to the west before it was redesigned in 1683.[34] In England in the late 1670s the Lords Berkeley, Conway, Craven and Danby, at The Durdans (fig. 75), Ragley, Hamstead Marshall and Wimbledon Manor, likewise introduced *plates-bandes* around their grass plats (fig. 76).

At the centre of the grass plats might be figures. Evelyn knew their value in pleasing both eye and intellect: 'As a Garden without Water hath no life . . . so without Sculpture, it has no action'.[35] However, new statuary was unusual at the time he wrote this. Major English garden layouts of the 1660s lacking figures

75   In this painting by Jacob Knyff of The Durdans, Surrey (1679), an early example of a carriage sweep can be seen, created informally within the walled outer court and its lines of trees. To the left is the 1630s walled garden, which has a *jet d'eau* and double mount, but Lord Berkeley has fringed each grass plat with flower borders, and has demolished the far wall and cut a light through the coppice on axis.

Wimbledon *as it is seen from the great Walke of Trees in the Principle garden with a side Prospect of that part which is towards the Orange Garden And with the View of the Orange Garden and Orange house. Henry Winstanley at Littlebury in Essex fecit.*

included Badminton, Althorp and Grimsthorpe. Pieces were bought by Lord Arlington for Euston about 1670, and were placed in the traditional position at the centres of the grass plats.[36] The Duke of Lauderdale showed the range already possible in 1672. He obtained for Ham House a marble Bacchus for the 'cherry garden', stone figures for the tops of the piers into the forecourt, and lead ones painted bronze for the open grove (fig. 77).[37] Three years later he imported nine lead pieces from Holland to Edinburgh, two at least presumably going to Thirlestane Castle.[38]

---

76   Henry Winstanley's print 'Wimbledon as it is Seen from the Great Walke of Trees in the Principle garden' (1678), showing flower gardens on the garden front of Wimbledon Manor and a grass plat surrounded by a flower border with clipped evergreens. The basic form is that described in 1649, but all the cherry trees, railings and hedges, and both the fountains, had been cleared away for the then modern French forms. To the right is the orange garden with its 'orange house', reached from floor level but viewed from the roof of a gallery.

The demand for figures was only exceptionally met by imported marble; the usual source was lead castings from the Low Countries. These were not only cheaper than either marble or bronze castings, but were also much lighter than marble, which they were generally painted to resemble.

GREENHOUSES AND ORANGERIES

In mid-century the usual way of protecting tender plants was keep them in pots, which would in winter be plunged into the earth under a south wall and covered with moss or straw.[39] Orange and other citrus trees were much prized as evergreens, or 'greens', and those who wished to keep them would need a protective building with south-facing windows and a brazier or stove for the coldest nights. The greens would need to be cased up for moving indoors during winter. Henrietta Maria had had greenhouses for 60 trees made at Oatlands Palace in 1633 and at Wimbledon Manor about 1640.[40] It was not until Charles II's reign that significant numbers of greenhouses were constructed

in English gardens. Notable ones from the 1670s included the Duke of Lauderdale's at Ham House, Lord Arlington's at Euston (see fig. 74) and Arlington House, Lord Essex's at Cassiobury (see fig. 78) and, appropriately, Nell Gwyn's Burford House below Windsor Castle.[41]

It was rare for there to be a special garden for the orange trees – an orangery – at this time; they were usually found set out within well-protected enclosures adjacent to the greenhouses. Althorp had a slip alongside the walled gardens, down which the orange trees were lined out (see fig. 20), described by Evelyn as a 'Great plenty of Oranges, and other Curiosities'.[42] At Kew House about 1670 Sir Henry Capel had 'His orange trees and other choicer greens stand out in summer in two walks about fourteen feet wide, enclosed with a timber frame about seven feet high, and set with silver firs hedge-wise . . . to secure them from wind and tempest'.[43] The tiny orangery at Aspeden, Hertfordshire, and that at Hatley Park, Cambridgeshire, were in small confined areas within which the cases would be lined out either side of the

77   *Ham House, Surrey*, by Hendrik Danckerts, *c*.1672, showing the circle within the wilderness, with the Duke and Duchess of Lauderdale, statuary and open grove hedges; the trees shown (perhaps elms) probably replaced fir trees in the early 1660s. The eight plain grass plats between the wilderness and house were probably made in the 1630s, when the firs were planted.

central walk.[44] Occasionally in the 1670s tubs were set out along the breast wall or walks in the Best Garden, or around a fountain bason, as at Eaton Hall (see fig. 45).[45]

WILDERNESSES AND GROVES

In 1670 André Mollet advised that *bosquets* should consist of 'all sorts of ever-greens . . . This kind is fittest in the Gardens of Pleasure'.[46] He made another compact high-palisaded *bosquet* with diagonal walks at the end of the Royal Garden at St James's in 1661 (see figs 66a and b). English owners did not at first see the need for such expensive works and sometimes just modified existing coppices. Sir Thomas Hanmer had a vision of beautifying such woodland:

> thicketts for birds cut through with severall streight or winding gravelly walkes, or you have a variety of alleyes set with high trees as elmes, limes, abells, firrs pines or others, with fountaines Canals Grottes Cascataes statues, arbours cabinetts avearyes and seats disperst as the design and nature of the place will admitt.[47]

Such thoughts on ornamentation were shared in the wood-walks cut through coppices at The Durdans and Cassiobury in the 1670s. The Earl of Berkeley progressively cut through his wood at the former, which he embellished with a summerhouse and a grotto, and surrounded with a grass walk.[48] At Cassiobury the Earl of Essex's gardener, Moses Cook, had in the late 1670s made a splay of wood-walks, jointed at circles of trees, through a coppice to the boundary (fig. 78). A pleasurable dimension was thus added to a useful wood.

Cook recommended conifers, particularly the pine 'to set round a Bowling-Green', as such a green would be sheltered yet would not receive a heavy fall of leaves.[49] One of his walks at Cassiobury led down to a circular bowling green planted with conifers in 1672.[50] This arrangement perhaps recalled Sir John Danvers's bowling green in Chelsea, which had been surrounded by cypresses (see fig. 37).

The French liked to back up their parterres with *bosquets*, partly for wind protection, and partly because the parterre gained by the contrast with the vertical 'relief' of the trees. However, the Italian *boschetto* required excessive maintenance to keep the hedges and trees in shape, and French practice was moving towards layouts that allowed the trees more space. Most French *bosquets* dispensed with tunnel-arbours, but adopted the high hedge, usually *charmilles*, that is of hornbeam, giving 'open' walks. When at Versailles, Locke had marvelled at the 'straight hedges no wider than half-a-foot or a foot, but green from top to bottom'.[51] At the Luxembourg Gardens stars and other shapes were being formed in larger-scale designs, with wider walks.

The French *bosquet* did find a place within the walled enclosures of superior English gardens, and the term 'wilderness' was widened to include them. Evergreen trees were often at first used as the body of the planting, overcoming the bareness of trees in the English winter just when a strong green colour and shelter would have been welcome. About 1675 Dr Plot noticed the plantations of spruce firs and lesser mountain pines (probably *Pinus mugo mugo*) that had been planted in quincunx at Cornbury about 1664, probably on Evelyn's advice.[52] At Ingestre in the late 1670s, Walter Chetwynd planted a high-hedged wilderness with silver firs around each parcel to keep the evergreen look in winter.[53] At Patshull Hall, also in Staffordshire, there was by about 1680 a twelve-pointed star of walks, each walk being flanked by yard-high laurel, and each quarter being filled with Silver, Scots and Norway firs, cypress, yew and bays.[54]

A few larger wildernesses were planted with infills of deciduous forest trees. In 1698 Celia Fiennes observed of that at Badminton (fig. 79), planted in the late 1660s, that 'The Wilderness is very fine, the Trees so large as to make it very Shady, they are all of Elm, except shrubs to thicken in. In the bottom, the earth is covered with variety of plants as primroses, Periwincle, &c.' On her visit to Ingestre she saw the silver firs mentioned by Plot, which were mixed with 'some Norraway some Scots and pine trees', and observed that the interiors of each parcel were 'full of all sorts of trees scycamores willows hazel chesnutts walnuts set very thick and so shorn smooth to the top which is left as a tuff or crown'.[55]

Another form of plantation was what John James was in 1712 to call the 'grove opened in *compartiments*'.[56] This derived from the

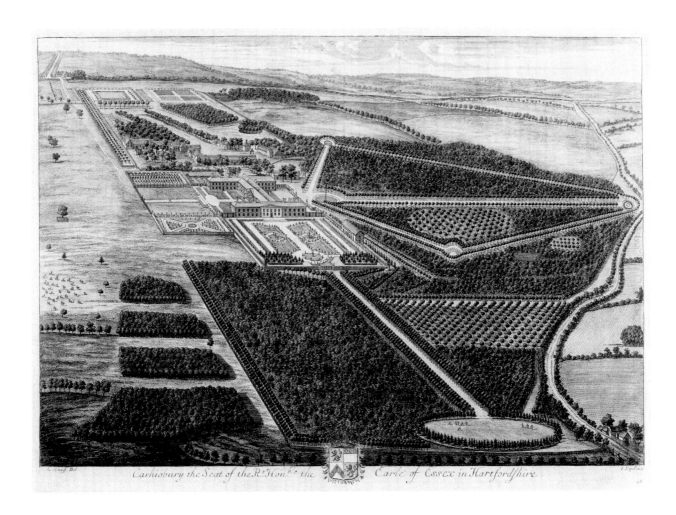

Cashiobury the Seat of the Rt. Honble. the Earle of Essex in Hartfordshire.

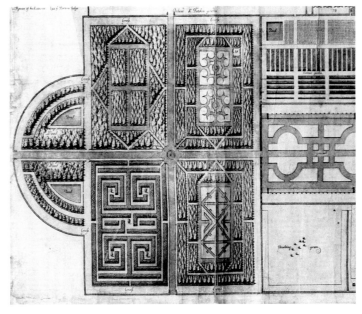

78   This Knyff and Kip view of Cassiobury House from the south-east, *c.*1700, shows the parterre below the new east wing, with side terraces and a grate continuing the axis down the double lime walk to the circular bowling green, set around by a triple ring of spruce by Moses Cook in 1672. The area of coppice and orchards north-east of the house had been cut through with a kite formation of wood-walks, an early example of ornamenting woodland.

79   Detail of a printed plan entitled *Badminton the Duke of Beaufort his House*, published between 1682 and 1699. This shows the mazes and other areas within a framework of forest trees planted in the late 1660s; these were to be recast by the second Duke in the 1700s. Closer to the house was the parterre and bowling green. Note the paucity of *jets d'eau*, a situation which had been remedied by 1698, when Celia Fiennes wrote that there were 22 of them, but thought them too small.

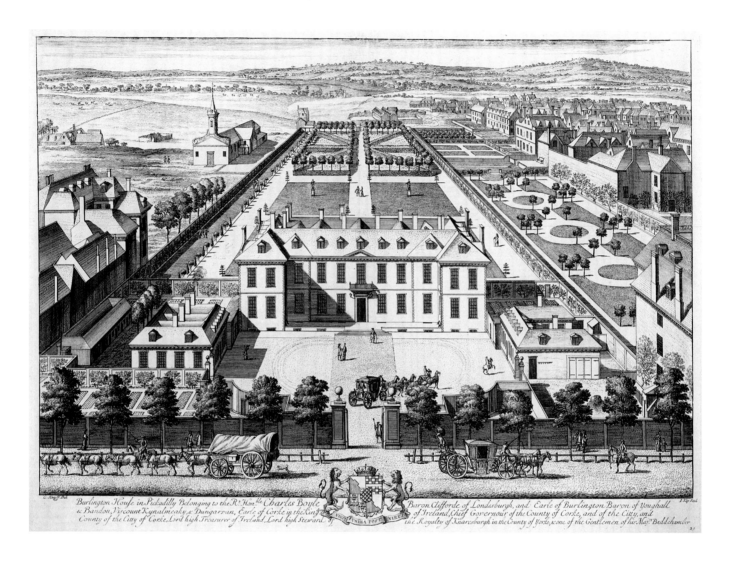

Burlington House in Picadilly Belonging to the R.t Hon.ble *Charles Boyle* Baron Clifforde of Londesburgh, and Earle of Burlington Baron of Youghall & Bandon, Viscount Kynalmeaky & Dungarran, Earle of Corke in the King. of Ireland, Chief Governour of the County of Corke, and of the City, and County of the City of Corke, Lord high Treasurer of Ireland, Lord high Steward the Royalty of Knaresburgh in the County of Yorke, & one of the Gentlemen of his Maj.ts Bedchamber

compartiment system, in that it consisted of quarters surrounded by *banquettes*, chest-high hedges, and divided by alleys. These *banquettes* were low enough to be seen over, though trees would grow through and above them, making them groves. Writing in 1714, the Revd John Laurence rehearsed the by-then traditional concept of the open grove:

> Three or four walks and double Rows of Hedges may be there contrived to open themselves at once to view, all terminating in the place where you stand; and the Triangular Spaces, by an ingenious Fancy, may be there agreeably disposed and filled up either with Borders of Flowers, or with Dwarff-Trees, or with Flowring Shrubs, or with ever-greens, or lastly, with a little Wil-

derness of Trees rising one above another, till you come to the point of a tall one in the middle . . .[57]

The quarters could thus contain any treatment considered ornamental. This might include their being 'enamelled' with the clear bright colours of bulb and wild flowers that would have been difficult to accommodate in the confines of the flower border.[58] This seems to have been the case in the 1660s at Burlington House, where a star of *banquettes* set with trees framed long grass (fig. 80). That at Ham House, set out in the 1670s, was similar, with the addition of an oval carpet walk intersecting all eight walks, and mown paths meandering their way to arbours across the long grass of the quarters (fig. 81).

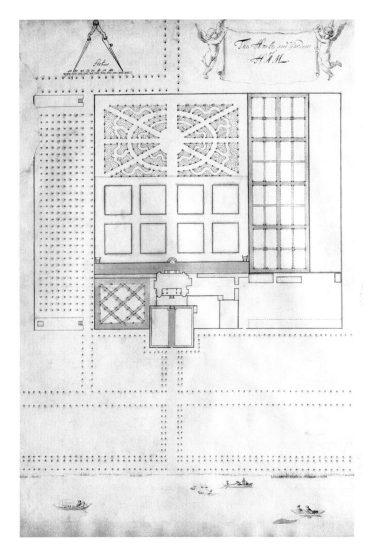

(Facing page) 80 Burlington House, Piccadilly, by Knyff and Kip, c.1700. When the house was built in the 1660s, the ball-topped finial gate on Piccadilly led straight onto a broad walk leading to the door. Half the garden was a *parterre à l'Angloise* set out in four plats and beyond that was an open grove with a Union-Jack arrangement of walks between hedges, and trees around the grove and down the central alley. The parterre was later given four figures and conifers were placed at the corners, and the forecourt was invaded by coaches.

81 'The house and garden at HAM' by John Slezer, the Duke of Lauderdale's surveyor, c.1671 (north is at the bottom). This plan of Ham House is partly a survey of the mainly 1630s layout, although the lozenge arrangement for the side garden is probably only a proposal. In the wilderness an oval carpet walk intersected the radials, and mown paths meandered their way to arbours across the grass of the quarters, probably planted with bulbs. The 'Melancholy Walk' grove to the east was answered by a kitchen garden with hedged quarters to the west.

Evelyn, an admirer of Thomas Browne's *Gardens of Cyrus*, often used the term 'quincunx' in his writings, even when referring to less geometric planting of oaks in parks, which should be 'for the great and *masculine* beauty which a wild *Quincunx*, as it were, of such *Trees* would present to your eye'.[59] In gardens, the quincunx consisted of trees with their side branches stripped up to above 10 feet, and with no undergrowth or enclosing hedges, so forming high-stemmed groves. Although Evelyn argued for the true quincunx formation, with rows at 60 degrees, in practice most were planted quadrate, at 90 degrees. The generally preferred tree was lime, though abeles (*Populus alba*) were a fast-growing alternative. The ground would have been turf, across which walks were sometimes laid. The 'Melancholy Walk' at Ham House was an impressive early example, conceivably as early as 1672.

By the late 1670s, then, the making of courtly gardens was changing. Although sharing the innovations of general English practice, such as avenues, carriage sweeps and terracing of the parterre, they included features seen in France, such as *jets d'eau*, flower borders around the grass plats, figures at their centres, new forms of grove and other garden elements including green-houses. The gardens of those in Court circles were the first to acquire these embellishments, and many outside Court circles were soon to follow.

Making and keeping courtly gardens

Charles I and Charles II both sought out French garden designers – André Mollet for parterre making, and André le Nostre for the Greenwich scheme – but the influence and financial resources required to attract these skills was seldom at hand for other garden-makers. Members of the Court wishing to lay out a fine new garden could, however, seek advice and inspiration from tours, published advice, prints, visits to other people's gardens, and personalised advice from an acquaintance, such as an architect or gentleman *savant*.

THE ADVICE OF COGNOSCENTI

Printers and authors of the Restoration were clear about their target audience. André Mollet addressed the 'chief Gentry and Nobility of this Kingdom'.[60] London and Wise were to see *The Compleat Gard'ner* (1699) being of assistance to 'The Nobility and Gentry'. Only John Worlidge was modest enough to write for 'not only . . . those who have fair estates and pleasant Seats in the Country . . . but the honest and plain Countryman in the improvement of his Ville'.[61]

Englishmen of liberal education, who had skill or knowledge of the best practice to be found in Europe, or perhaps just in England, were sought after. Those from the nobility and the wealthier gentry would provide advice to friends on houses and gardens *gratis*, and much was decided by informal means, such as social visits. Such advisors were not of course draughtsmen, but could act as critics on matters of taste, or simply provide the benefit of their own experience.

In the more specific sphere of garden design, Evelyn was an obvious person to ask for such help. He had been in most countries in Europe studying gardens, and was acquainted with theories of building and garden-making. Demonstrating his knowledge of French gardens, he 'began to set out the Ovall Garden' at Sayes Court in 1652 (see fig. 30), based on a flower garden in Paris created by Pierre Morin. He found himself transported to Albury, Euston, Wimbledon and other places to advise. For example in 1677/8 Lord Danby took him and Lord Conway (creator of Ragley Hall) to Wimbledon, which Danby had just acquired (see fig. 76). Evelyn, 'having surveyed his Gardens & alterations, returned late at night'.[62]

In the sphere of building, there were *cognoscenti* from the minor gentry or professional ranks who would seek a fee, could turn their hand to drawing and were beginning to refer to themselves as 'architects'. They would be likely to have a range of financial interests besides architecture. A few had studied buildings in Rome or Paris. Roger Pratt had been in France, Italy and the Low Countries between 1643 and 1649, meeting Evelyn in Rome in 1644. When the mathematician Christopher Wren was seeking to establish himself as an architect in the early 1660s, he thought a trip to Paris indispensable.

The traditional relationship between architect and gardener in France and Spain was one whereby the architect devised the architectural framework, and the gardener attended to the practical business of converting the spaces into gardens, mostly using familiar forms unless otherwise instructed.[63] The regularity and proportions sometimes observed in new garden layouts suggest that this could be the case in England too. The exact extent of an architect's responsibility for layout was seldom recorded, and few garden design drawings survive. Terms of service varied widely: some architects confined their help to plans of the house and courts only, whilst others offered thoughts on a 'general plan' for the gardens and plantations. In only a few cases, such as Sir Roger Pratt at Ryston (see fig. 42), or John Slezer's plans of Ham House, Lethington House and Thirlestane Castle for the Earl of Lauderdale in 1671, can the architect's contribution be observed closely.

Some gentlemen and gardeners specialised in water engineering. Sir Samuel Morland was known as an inventor, particularly of engines for raising water, primarily for domestic water supply. However, gardens provided another practical outlet. He used these skills at Euston Hall in 1670, where he advised on a combined water mill and a pump for the fountain, and devised a 'screw-bridge being turn'd with a key', presumably a swivelling bridge over the canal. He provided the Duke of Ormonde with a horse-engine to raise water at Kilkenny Castle and gardens in about 1679.[64] Having perfected a high-pressure pump to raise water from the Thames to the top of Windsor Castle, he was in 1681 declared to be the King's 'Master of Mechanics'. Soon afterwards he travelled to Versailles to give advice about the raising of water from the Seine to the gardens, though his offer of help was not welcomed.[65]

The long-established method of administering palaces, their gardens and their upkeep was for the monarch to issue a Letter of Privy Seal to the Treasury, requiring it to supply a named person with the finances to carry out specified work. In garden projects this person could be a gardener, or an aristocratic steward of a palace, but was usually a gentleman in Court circles familiar with administration. The Treasury would then appoint this person to be its 'accountant', issue him with money, and afterwards would require that person to declare a full account of the expenditure.

Because such a system would be too ponderous for performing constantly necessary repairs and minor improvements, another system evolved alongside whereby the Office of Works would order and oversee such work. Tradesman would work on stand-ard 'Crown' rates, for example for a yard of stone coping or for a tree pit dug, and submit bills detailing quantities and thus charges. Office of Works officials might 'abate' quantities or rates if they saw fit. Casual labourers would be taken on at a day rate. Bills were collected into books, one per palace, for example the 'Hampton Court Booke'. The Office of Works would then make a composite annual account for inspection and approval by the Treasury.

Most royal garden-making, as opposed to keeping, was ordered by Letters of Privy Seal. The person charged with the cutting of the Giants' Steps at Greenwich in 1661 was an official there, Sir William Boreman.[66] This command was followed by another of October 1663 to enable Adrian May to carry out several works: to bring the Longford River to Hampton Court, dig the canal there, and plant the avenues; to form the platform, terraces and walks for the uncompleted parterre at Greenwich; and various works in St James's Park.[67] May's work continued for several years, and when accounted for in 1672 by his brother Hugh, the total cost was seen to be £6,911.

At the Restoration the administration of both keeping and altering the Royal gardens was altered to be more like that in France, where *intendants des jardins du roi* were appointed. Someone from Court would generally superintend improvements to royal gardens. This person would not necessarily have any particular knowledge of gardens, though often they did. Hence Adrian May was not just responsible for the works at Hampton Court, St James's and Greenwich, but was also 'supervisor of the French gardeners' – the Mollets at the Royal Garden at St James's. This supervisory role continued and widened, and when in 1670 Hugh May took on these duties he was described as 'Supervisor of the Gardens, Walks, &c., at St James's, Whitehall, Hampton Court, &c.'. After Hugh died in 1684 he was in turn succeeded by William Legge, a close companion of James II.[68]

THE KEEPING OF GARDENS

Prior to the Restoration the gardens at the royal residences were supervised by their stewards, who would be a senior member of the Court, and keepers were counted as household servants. When they appear in documents they were referred to as 'over-seer and keeper'. The appointment of André and Gabriel Mollet in 1660 to the keeping of the Royal Garden in St James's Park changed this practice. Charles issued a warrant to the Treasury to pay the Mollets £240 yearly as the King's gardeners as from Michaelmas 1660, and for them to have the gardener's lodgings in St James's Park.[69] They thus became just like other officers of the Crown, in theory answering directly to the monarch, but in practice to the Treasury Board, like the Surveyor of the King's Works and the Keeper of the Pall-Mall. The size of the Mollets' salary suggests that they were responsible for a considerable workforce.

Concurrently, John Rose had a patent as keeper and gardener of the garden at St James's (see fig. 71), a much smaller walled area south of the palace, and this was reflected in an annual payment of only £40. Following the deaths of the Mollets, perhaps in the Great Plague of 1665, Rose was appointed 'in place of Andrew and Gabriel Mollett, deceased, for wages, for keeping the said garden' (the Royal Garden).[70] When Rose himself died in 1677 his place was taken by an eminent nurseryman, Leonard Gurle, for eight years. His replacement in 1685 was Antonio Verrio, much better known as a Court painter: James II appears to have regarded the position as a sinecure for him.

At non-royal residences head gardeners were usually servants answering directly to the owner. They were regarded as important members of households, and were paid accordingly.[71] Early in the century, Sir Francis Bacon, as Treasurer of Gray's Inn, worked closely with the gardener, paying him £16 13s 4d per annum from 1611, a wage that was unchanged till 1758.[72] At smaller country houses wages of £15 to £20 per annum were the going rate into the 1730s. When the owner was away the head gardener would be supervised day-to-day by the lady of the house, the steward or an agent.

In the second half of the seventeenth century it becomes clear that some head gardeners were working to a contract of employment, whereby they were responsible for those under them, and their tools, whilst they could expect a payment, supply of manure and the perk of selling produce that was surplus to the house's requirements. Hence John Simpson entered into a contract with Lord Hatton in 1682 to look after the gardens at Kirby Hall with these terms:

First of all y[e] saide Jo: Simpson is to keepe and maintaine all y[e] severall Gardens belonging to y[e] said hous in Good order as y[e] same is nowe in.

Item y[e] saide Jo Simp. is at his own charges to finde all tooles and seeds and railes (for lining the parterres) and workmen and weeders.

Item the saide Lord Hatton is to give and alowe unto the saide Jo: Sim. the som threescore and twelve pounds a yeare finding himself and one man dyet at such times of his lordsh: shall be there.

Item the saide John Simpson is to have all y[e] profitts of fruits and other things growing in the saide Garden over and above what is . . . in the house when his lordship is there. And also to have what dung he shall have occasion for brought to the Garden Geats [gates] and likewise Pease sticks brought to the Garden Geats.[73]

Montagu House in Bloomsbury was a major house with a garden of moderate size but a high state of keeping. In 1706 it was being maintained by Thomas Ackres on a contract worth £140 per annum, but economies were made by the second Duke of Montagu and in 1720 Samuel Peniston was being paid £100 per annum.[74] Orders for plants and other expenses would be on top of this.

The profession of gardener lacked any formal training, so the route to skill and reputation was apprenticeship to a head gardener, before becoming a journeyman until obtaining a position as a head gardener.[75] In London there was the Worshipful Company of Gardeners, which received its Royal Charter in 1605. Its main purpose was to regulate the sale of market produce in London. It could also, like all the City Companies, regulate apprenticeships to existing members of the guild. Occasionally an experienced owner concerned with standards, such as Evelyn, would himself take responsibility for training. In 1686 he took on an apprentice called Jonathan Mosse at Sayes Court, and wrote some detailed 'Directions' for him.[76]

At the end of the five- to seven-year apprenticeship the master was looking for a new apprentice whilst the gardener would be looking for a journeyman position. Meanwhile, owners elsewhere seeking a good gardener would be making enquiries. A former master often recommended a former apprentice: for example, in 1694 George London suggested Peter Aram, who had worked under him at Fulham Palace, to Sir Edward Blackett of Newby Hall.[77] Sometimes owners themselves gave a recommendation.

Because there was a general rise in the numbers of pleasure and kitchen gardens after the Restoration there was a constant shortage of skilled gardeners. A well-trained journeyman would have had little difficulty in finding employment. Because owners found themselves in competition to obtain and keep them, they could be tempted to poach talent, and a select number of highly skilled journeymen would have found themselves moving frequently. The gardens at Lisburn Castle, County Antrim, were begun in 1656 after Lord Conway brought over a Dutch gardener who previously worked for a Mr Kames of Kensington.[78]

Large garden construction projects might involve an owner in much tedious administration of itinerant labourers and numerous suppliers, and were often beyond the capability of his own men or his steward. The alternative was to turn to 'undertakers' (who we would today call contractors), to undertake a specified piece of work in exchange for a specified sum of money, and relieve the owner of much of the trouble. From the second half of the seventeenth century garden owners and the 'accountants' of royal garden projects often turned to undertakers.

The undertaker Edward Manning had walled in the New Park at Richmond for Charles I in 1634–7, and dug the Longford River at Hampton Court in 1638.[79] At the other end of the scale – and the far end of the country – Peter Hardcastle, a gardener of 'Barrow Briggs' (perhaps Barrow Bridge, near Bolton), was employed by Sir John Lowther to plant at Lowther Hall, perhaps during Commonwealth times.[80] The first major royal garden contract after the Restoration was when Adrian May used Edward Maybancke, Thomas Greene, Edward Dudley and Robert Beard, acting as joint undertakers, to carry out the bulk of the work at Hampton Court, Greenwich and St James's from 1663.[81] Lowther noted that Hardcastle 'planted with most of the Gentlemen in the north Parts'. In order to cost a piece of work, quantities needed to be estimated. For example, the calculations for the earth-moving for the parterre at Greenwich were cast up in 'floors', a floor being a square perch in area by a foot deep: 'making the Terras Walkes in the said Parke according to sundry admeasurements thereof and at the rates of iij^s ix^d and ij^s iiij^d per floore, each floore conteyneing xvj^{en} feete and a halfe square and one foote deepe'. It would take 160 floors to reduce an acre by a foot. Maybancke and his colleagues filled a pit, taking 690 floors, and excavated 10,000 more floors to create the plain for the parterre. Levelling to form the walks across the park took over 1,000 more floors. 'Levelling and new moulding the said Tarras Walkes wth new fine mould' took 1,160 floors.

Adrian Pratt, May's on-site agent at Greenwich, was responsible for purchasing the trees, but in order for them to be planted holes needed to be dug into the gravely soil and filled with good 'mould' (soil). Meanwhile, pits were dug in the Harewarren at Hampton Court 'vi foote over and ii foote and a halfe deepe'. Trees afterwards needed to be staked and watered, and sometimes protected by straw, ferns or hedge cuttings, and in due course pruned. Grassing of disturbed ground was achieved with hayseed.

As we have seen, owners and undertakers usually imported lime trees directly from the Low Countries, but by about 1670 Leonard Gurle was importing them to his twelve-acre nursery ground in Whitechapel for growing on and selling on at £6 for 40.[82] He was already the leading supplier of fruit trees in the country, sending them out to Lord Allington's Horseheath in the 1660s, Pratt's Ryston Hall in 1672, and the Earl of Bedford's Woburn in 1674. Gurle and others stocked the well-known shrubs, but more recent exotics, for example those discovered in North America, generally took at least a generation to enter the nursery trade.[83]

Parks

The royal forests, chases and parks were sequestered by Parliament in 1649, and the bulk sold off to speculators. In many cases they became hardly recognisable as parks during the 1650s. The Council of the Parliamentary government had decided that 'Whitehall House, St. James' Park, St. James' House, Somerset House, Hampton Court and the House Park, Theobalds and the Park, Windsor and the Little Park next the house, Greenwich House and Park, and Hyde Park ought to be kept for the public use of the commonwealth, and not sold'.[84] Parliament decided the same for the New Park at Richmond. These parks, at least, avoided dismemberment.

THE ROYAL PARKS:
RATIONALISATION AND REPLANTING

At his Restoration in 1660 Charles II recovered his parks and forests and sought the rationalisation of his scattered and tattered holdings. He was passionate about the navy, and was aware of the serious shortage of ship-building timber; at the same time, the poor state of the exchequer needed addressing. He thus set about allocating his medieval and Tudor forests, parks and woods to three purposes: his own pleasure, forestry or disposal.

Those parks held back from sale in 1649 were taken back by Charles II for his own amenity. They became the basis of the Royal Parks of succeeding centuries. Charles also reclaimed Woodstock Park near Oxford. In these places, repairs and improvements were desirable. The Earl of Lindsey repaired the wall at Woodstock, and Sir Lionel Tollemache did the same at Richmond New Park. In 1667 Charles extended St James's Park with the area later known as Green Park, in 1672 he began the reimparkment of Windsor Great Park, and a few years after that extended the Little or Home Park at Windsor.

Charles commanded replanting on a massive scale in his remaining forests – New, Dean and Sherwood. In the Forest of Dean alone, 11,000 acres were planted. In his *Sylva* (1664), Evelyn took up the theme of replanting in order to ingratiate himself with Charles, writing that:

> Your *Majesty* has . . . (like another *Cyrus*) by your own Royal *Example*, exceeded all your *Predecessors* in the *Plantations* which you have already made, and now design, beyond (I dare affirm it) all the *Monarchs* of this *Nation* since the *Conquest* of it . . . Nor can any thing impeach your Navigation, and the Reputation of That, whiles you continue thus careful of your Woods and Forests.[85]

Fifteen years later he could write:

> I need not acquaint Your *Majesty* how many *Millions* of *Timber-Trees* (beside infinite others) have been *Propagated*, and *Planted* throughout Your vast *Dominions*, at the *Instigation*, and by the sole *Direction* of this *Work*; because Your *Gracious Majesty*, has been pleas'd to *own* it *Publickly*, for my *Encouragement*, who, in all that I here pretend to say, deliver only those *Precepts* which Your *Majesty* has put into *practice* . . .[86]

The majority of the royal forests and parks were disposed of, however, either as rewards or for money. Their usual fate was disparkment and enclosure for agriculture. This included many medieval royal parks, Henry VIII's emparkments at New Hall, Oatlands and Nonsuch Great Park, and the more recently royal Theobalds.

PARKS AND STATUS

Deliberate and often gleeful breaking down of park pales by Parliamentary soldiers was one reason for the sorry depletion of the national stock of deer. Parkland sequestered from the bishops (in 1646) and others was sold, and most was divided into fields and let out, whilst the timber was generally felled to provide the purchasers with quick returns to offset the cost of purchase. There was also voluntary disparkment by owners, even traditionally minded nobility and gentry, either because fines and other penalties made economies necessary or because the new order undermined confidence that parks had any future in a republic. Although most of the major seats managed to retain their associated parks, many of the lesser places were effectively disparked during Civil War and Commonwealth times forever.

These blows to the deer parks of England might have been their death-knell. Gradually, though, landowners began to reassert themselves, as the extremism of the 1640s gave way to a milder climate during the Protectorate of Oliver Cromwell from 1651. The urge to enclose parkland flickered again. Sir Peter Temple made enclosures at Stowe in 1649 and two years later purchased deer. Amabel, Countess of Kent, refurbished her stand at Wrest Park in 1656, and in 1658 Ralph Verney of Claydon bought the deer from Grafton Park, which Viscount Monson, a Parliamentarian, was disparking. Several further creations and expansions took place at top seats after the Restoration, many accompanying rebuildings of mansions. A significant acreage of emparkment was under way at middling seats too, a sign of renewed determination to establish élite seats.

It must be wondered why the desire to hold parkland proved so resilient, and the answer lies in matters about which gentlemen cared the most – their ancient lineage and proof of status. The royal heralds, since 1530, and till as late as 1690, carried out visitations, county by county, in order to determine claims to gentility, and thus rights to bear coats of arms. A pedigree that stretched back centuries and was punctuated by knightly forebears would certainly clinch the matter. A more recent family would have to strive harder, including acquiring the trappings of feudal status – lordship of a manor, a manor house, and perhaps a park.

The 'magnate' families – that largely indestructible core of the élite – generally had held ancient parks for a considerable time. Their venerable pollard oaks lent an unmistakable aura of Antiquity, an understated confirmation of the legitimacy of the family's status. The truth was, however, that only a few owners could claim a long association between their families and their seats. A very considerable redistribution of land had taken place, especially in the century between 1530 and 1630, and during the vicissitudes of the Commonwealth.[87] At 1660 about 40% of the seats of the nobility and baronetcy had been acquired since the start of the reign of James I. The lack of Antiquity bit deepest with those of lesser status.

Several magnate owners wanted to increase older parks or re-empark former areas. An aspiring owner would be conscious that if he wanted his seat to reflect his new status he had better set his house in a suitably impressive park. Where a park had never existed it would be necessary to create one *ab novo*. One final option was to place a new house in an old park. By these various means most seats of the politically ambitious came over time to be set within or adjacent to their parks, a distinct change from the medieval tradition of detached parks served by hunting lodges.

Before the Civil War such houses were just a 'Lodge' or 'the house within the park'. The Countess of Bedford's new house at the More, Hertfordshire, known in 1631 as the 'great house or lodge lately erected & built within Moor Park' was known to Sir William Temple as just 'Moor-Park'.[88] Other such cases of naming one's house 'Park' were seen at Twickenham, Albury, Cornbury and Hackwood, to name a few. This practice began of course as a none-too-subtle pointer to the possession of an ancient park. It then became frequent during the eighteenth century, even where, as at Bramham, Yorkshire, in 1710, the park had just ten years before been part of Bramham Moor.

LICENSING, PENALTIES FOR POACHERS AND ROAD DIVERSIONS

The laws relating to deer parks and royal forests were traditionally widely flouted by the populace. The park licensing system had been observed by owners, not so much because the monarch would dispark unlicensed ones, but because the laws giving legal redress to owners against poachers related solely to licensed parks and warrens. The Acts, updated early in James I's reign, specified the penalties for people caught taking deer or conies (rabbits) at night.[89] Any person breaking and entering into any impaled park, and used for 'the keeping and cherishing of deer or connyes' was to be imprisoned for three months and had to pay treble damages. Furthermore, the guns and other equipment of people of an income below £40 clear could be confiscated on sight.

Unsurprisingly, emparkment and hunting was unpopular with the lower orders. Enclosure could mean loss of grazing land, rights of way or other traditional rights, and the penalties for poaching were enforced, however desperate the poacher and his family might be. When Charles I enclosed the New Park at Richmond in the 1630s he compensated those who lost grazing rights, but nevertheless it was seen as a political act, recalling the arbitrary and oppressive power wielded by medieval monarchs over their subjects. Hence this emparkment was particularly insensitive at a time when the rights and powers of the monarch were in debate.

Enforcement of James I's law completely broke down during the Civil War and rule by Parliament. Nevertheless, Oliver Cromwell ordered a licence to be made out for 200 acres at Badminton in 1656, and at the Restoration deer park licensing was fully reinstated. In 1661 there was a new 'Act to prevent the unlawful Coursing Hurting or Killing of Deere'.[90] Any person unlawfully coursing, killing, hurting or taking away red or fallow deer from 'any Forrest Chase Purliew Paddock Wood Park or other Ground where Deere are or have beene usually kept' should forfeit £20 for every offence, half to go to the informer and half to the owner of the deer. If a perpetrator did not possess £20 that person should be committed to the House of Correction for six months with

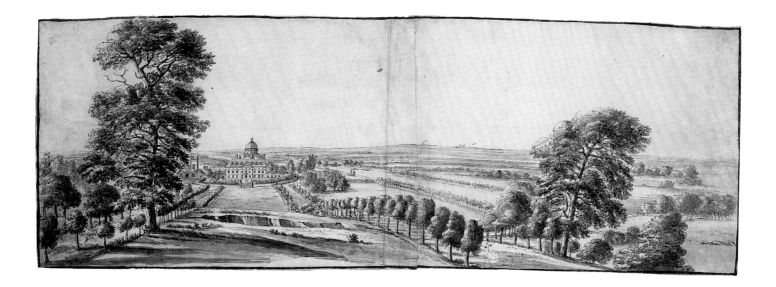

hard labour, or the common gaol for one year. This was a considerable increase over the former penalties.

Sir Horatio Townshend had expanded his park at Raynham, Norfolk, from 450 to 800 acres by about 1660. He was a supporter of the Restoration, and was rewarded with a viscountcy in 1661. Although his additional parkland was unlicensed, he was in a good position to regularise it retrospectively, and in 1662 obtained a warrant 'for the preservation of game'. Others needed the normal licences, and some of the emparkments of the 1660s were substantial: in 1661 Viscount Chaworth obtained a licence for 1,200 acres at Annesley in Nottinghamshire, in 1664 the Marquess of Worcester (later Duke of Beaufort) for 900 acres at Badminton (fig. 82), and the Earl of Bridgewater expanded the 400-acre park at Ashridge, Hertfordshire, in two bites – 240 acres in 1661 and 160 acres in 1664.[91] Lanhydrock Park, Cornwall, was one of three parks for which Lord Robartes obtained a licence in 1664.

82 The deer park at Badminton House from the east avenue by Hendrick Danckerts, c.1669, showing the parkland for which the Duke of Beaufort had acquired a licence in 1664, and then enclosed and planted with avenues. The *demi-lune* on the eastern boundary of the wilderness and the forecourt gates to the right can be discerned.

The Earl of Denbigh applied for 300 acres at Newnham Paddox, Warwickshire, in 1665. Sir William Juxon applied for 500 acres at Sezincote, Gloucestershire, in 1669.

The first Game Act was passed in 1671. Its preamble makes it clear that action was needed to protect all game, not just that in licensed parks:

diverse disorderly persons laying aside their lawfull Trades and Imployments doe betake themselves to the stealing, takeing and killing of Conies, Hares, Pheasants, Partridges and other Game, intended to be preserved by the former Lawes, with Guns, Dogs, Tramells, Lowbells, Hayes, and other Netts, Snares, Hare-pipes and other Engines, to the great damage of this Realme, and prejudice of Noblemen, Gentlemen and Lords of mannours and others Owners of Warrens.[92]

The response was to increase to £100 the income of those persons permitted to take game, and to allow lords of manors to appoint gamekeepers who would have powers to seize and dispose of all unlawfully-held animals and devices mentioned in the preamble. This power was extended from catching poachers red-handed to searches of the premises of persons suspected of poaching. The penalties were those that had once applied for enclosed parks: treble damages and costs, and imprisonment for three months.

In view of its wider application and new powers of search, the 1671 Game Act was possibly seen as more effective than the old deer park legislation, even in relation to deer-stealing. Some owners continued to have their parks licensed – for example Belton, which was five miles in circumference, an enlargement at Easton Neston in 1681, and Dawley in 1690 (see fig. 46). However, other owners appear to have become unconvinced of the need for a licence. As a consequence, the number of park licence applications dropped significantly from the mid-1670s. New game laws early in William and Mary's reign were little encouragement to obtain them.[93] Several high-status parks appear to have been enclosed without the benefit of a licence, as at Chirk Castle in 1675 and Wynnstay Park in 1678, both in Denbighshire.

Also in the Patent Rolls are the licences for road or footpath stoppages and diversions. Most were for amenity reasons, several being clearly in connection with emparkment. Hence the Earl of Southampton, Lord High Treasurer of England, obtained a licence to divert a road away from his park at Stratton, Hampshire, in 1663. The same licence that granted emparkment at Badminton also granted footpath closures; likewise with Sezincote and Easton Neston. Lord Arlington's free warren at Euston in 1671 was similarly accompanied by road closure.

Other road closures would have been for amenity and privacy in the demesnes and grounds of owners, not specifically for emparkment. A few examples will suffice. In 1667 the Attorney-General, Sir Geoffrey Palmer, obtained a closure licence for his seat at East Carlton Hall, Northamptonshire. Two years later, Elizabeth, Countess Dysart, closed a road passing by Ham House. At Cheveley, Cambridgeshire, Henry Jermyn altered the road to Newmarket in 1675. In 1681 Sir Robert Howard, the dramatist, closed footpaths and bridleways at Ashtead Park, Surrey.

PARK EMBELLISHMENT

Most ancient parks had plenty of gnarled old trees, and sometimes enclosed woodland, and more recently enclosed parks might incorporate substantial areas of coppice. Some owners, familiar with the more wooded hunting preserves of France, had already

taken the hint of what might be done with their park woods – to cut them through with rides intersecting at a *rond-point*. The Earl of Lindsey, prior to his death at the Battle of Edgehill in 1642, had initiated a system of park rides at Grimsthorpe that pierced woods.[94] The Earl of Bedford had two woods of about 50 acres apiece in his park at Woburn. Before the Restoration he had cut stars of rides in the French manner (see fig. 40).

Although the parks suitable for this form of treatment were few, it was not at all unusual to see walks, such as the mile-long one at Euston, planted through parks. Although these were in effect rides, the term 'ride' was not yet in currency, and increasingly 'walk' seemed inappropriate for planting on such a scale. So Evelyn's term, 'avenue', was over time broadened in meaning to include any ride or planted visto. Generally parkland planting was becoming more varied and complex, with walks issuing from gates and grates, and systems of walks, as at Windsor Little Park, branching off the axial visto to explore the park and its views (fig. 83). Angled walks could likewise be seen at Cornbury and Burley-on-the-Hill (see fig. 38).

The Earl of Essex's gardener at Cassiobury, Moses Cook, became an expert on planting, as his book, *The Manner of Raising, Ordering, and Improving Forrest-trees: Also, How to Plant, Make and Keep Woods, Walks, Avenues, Lawns, Hedges, etc.*, of 1676 announced. Cook dealt with these matters in great detail, such that on revising his *Sylva* Evelyn himself was content to recommend Cook's advice.[95] Cook may have seen the small circles and one large half-circle in Greenwich Park, planted in 1664. He himself planted the circles in the wood-walks at Cassiobury in the 1670s.[96] He advised that 'all Walks, of any Length, especially in Parks' should end in a circle, semicircle, triangle or other figure, either at the house end of an avenue, or where a walk intersected with another (fig. 84).[97] He made the analogy with the upright shape of a tree, in which the trunk was finished off by a circular head: 'a Walk ending bluntly without any Figure or entring into another, may be compared to a Tree with the Head off'. He gave some worked examples to show how to calculate the diameter of a semicircle to accommodate the number of *patte d'oie* walks coming into it. Another suggestion was that circles should be three times the breadth of the walks.[98]

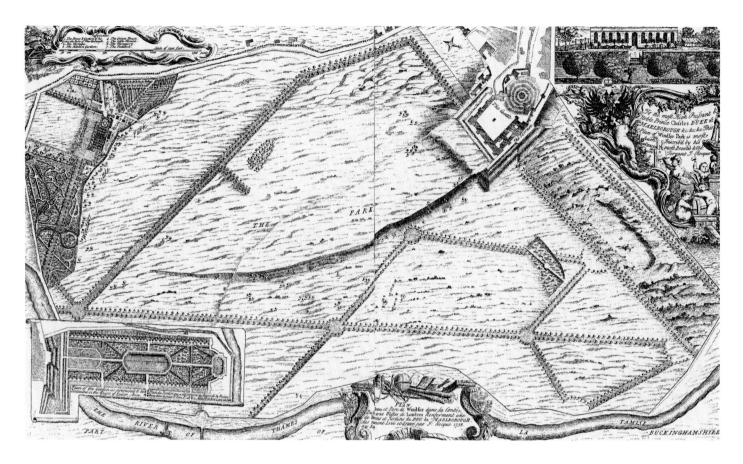

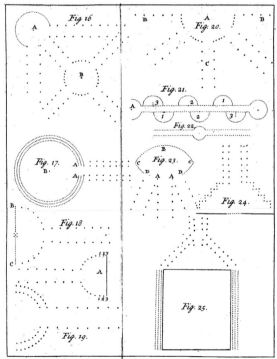

83 John Rocque's plan of Windsor Little Park, 1738. The Little Park was expanded in 1675, when the lodge was built, and then again in 1698 for the Maastricht Garden. This plan shows that although that project was abortive (the plan of 1712 from the Brompton Park Nursery is engraved at bottom left), an avenue system was planted across the park with circles at the joins, as was typical of around 1700. The plantation at the lodge was established in the 1700s, though its meandering paths were from around 1733.

84 Planting arrangements from Moses Cook, *The Manner of Raising, Ordering, and Improving Forrest-trees* (1676). Here Cook explores the various ways of starting and terminating planted vistos; there are half-circles at the house end and circles where vistos intersect in the park.

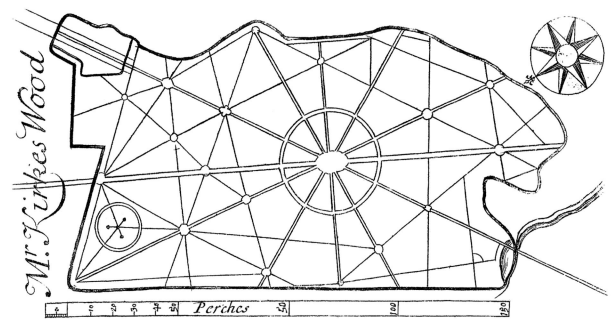

The lines in this Platforme represents the Walkes in M.ʳ Kirkes Wood (cal'd Moſeley.) neare his House at Cookeridge, (betwixt Leeds and Otley) in York= ſhire. The whole containing about Six Score Akers.
The Double line Walks are about 20. Foot wide. and ẙ Single lines about 8. Foot wide.

The half-round, at first used to terminate avenues, was the obvious choice as the springing point for radial walks, something that Cook suggested in his book.[99] Another use for circles was as the focal point for star arrangements of intersecting rides, echoes of the French practice of assembly points for a hunt amongst forest ridings. In 1679 Evelyn could cite 'the *Circle* with a *star* of *Walks* radiating from it . . . exceeding pleasant' at the Earl of Winchilsea's seat of Eastwell, Kent.[100] The most extraordinary

example of a coppice cut into walks was Moseley Wood, on the estate of the virtuoso Thomas Kirke at Cookridge, near Leeds, which was reached by a walk from the hall.[101] The 120 acres had a central star, from which radiated twelve twenty-foot-wide walks, but there were numerous subsidiary walks each eight feet wide as well. There were 65 intersections in all. Printed plans were made available to visitors from 1694 (fig. 85).

LAWNS

The parkland setting of a mansion could be enhanced by a 'lawn'. This was a medieval term for a 'place voyde of trees', or with only a thin scatter of pollards, that was permanent grassland, where deer might graze, within the matrix of coppice woods of which parks and forests had been comprised.[102] Although lawns were associated with parks, the effect of such plantings, wrote Cook,

85 Moseley Wood, Cookridge, Yorkshire, from Ralph Thoresby's *Ducatus Leodiensis* (1715). Having had this wood on his Cookridge estate cut through, Thomas Kirke printed a plan for visitors in 1694, which became famous when it was copied into John Evelyn's *Sylva* (1706) and Thoresby's *Ducatus Leodiensis*.

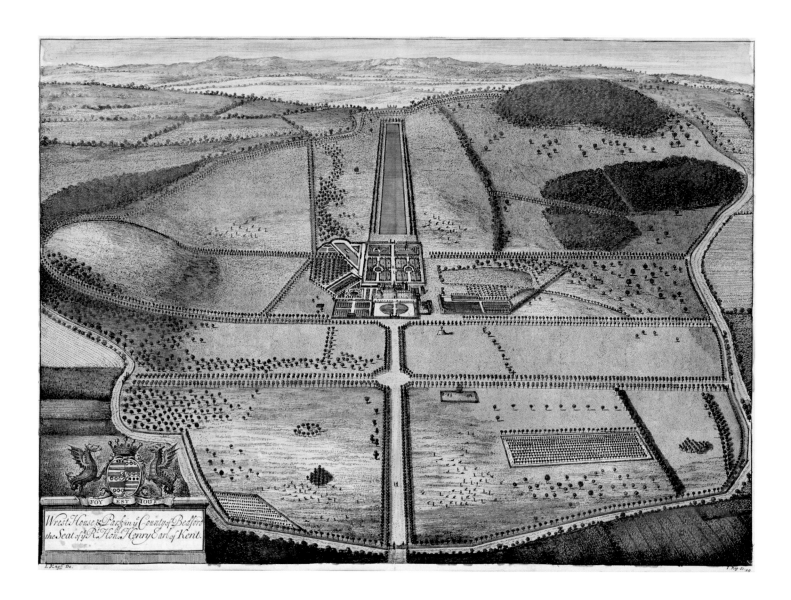

'was worth having even where owners have not the Convenience or the Quantity of Ground, if they make but 20 Acres in a Field in some good Figure leading to the House. It will be the more pleasant'.[103]

86   Knyff and Kip's view of Wrest Park, Bedfordshire, *c.*1703, dedicated to Henry, Earl of Kent, who inherited in 1702. It shows his father's parterres, wildernesses and axial canal of about 1689, but this wider view indicates the extent of the park with its woodlands and avenues, and also recent boundary planting.

For reasons of protection from wind and glare from the sun, Cook advocated the placing of houses or creation of lawns such that the latter was to the south or east. He liked the effect of a scatter of trees, provided it did not harm the vistos, and also of the ground rising to the house across the lawn. To Cook, the ideal lawn was 'a spacious Plain joining to your House', perhaps 100 acres if the place permitted.[104] The prospect should splay out from the house at an obtuse angle.

Cook advised that 'A single Rowe, to bound a Lawn round . . . would be mighty obliging to the Noblest Sense'.[105] These trees would preferably be limes, and rides could break out of the area at angles. Cook's remarks about the efficacy of a 'single row' of trees bounding a lawn could be said about a whole park. Perhaps it was he who introduced the peripheral rows around the parks at Burghley about 1683 and Wrest about 1689 (fig. 86).

Cook's idea of a lawn was suitable for an old-fashioned lodge in a park, but at modern mansions the avenue lay on the approach side, and the gardens on the other. Occasions for vast lawns were thus infrequent, but on the other hand some owners were forming parades, designed for a large concourse, such as a hunt assembling, before the fronts of houses, where Cook's thoughts on formal plantations might still apply. The grandest lawn following the Res-toration was that at Badminton, flanked by rows of trees a great distance apart (see fig. 117).[106] Boughton House had one by the 1690s.[107] The eastern lawn at Cornbury was a broad visto down to ponds,[108] while that at Althorp allowed a broad visto northwards (see fig. 20). The Office of Works had a longstanding desire for the avenue through Bushy Park to terminate at the Hampton Court end in a great parade, almost a lawn, though the idea foundered both in the 1660s and in 1689.[109] Ornamentation thus started by degrees, but already by the end of Charles II's reign avenues, star points and lawns were being made to embellish one of the owner's main sources of pride, his park.

'Rays from Versailles'

ENGLISH GARDENS · 1680–1700

Towards the end of Charles II's reign a period of intensive garden-making commenced, lasting twenty years, fuelled by an ambitious peerage rather than being led by the monarch. Whether they were supporters of James II, or the Whig lords who opposed his succession, there was a consensus that the French garden detail first introduced in the 1670s was appropriate to the seats of leading men. When the Whigs replaced James II with William of Orange, Parliament voted vast sums to promote his international standing through the royal palaces and gardens.

Power politics

Charles II may have died a Catholic, and James II was always stridently so, but the country as a whole remained solidly Protestant.

James displayed the absolutist tendencies of his father. In order to bar him from the throne an Exclusion Bill was presented to Parliament in 1678. Its promoters, led by the Earl of Shaftesbury, came to be known as the Whigs, a party for constitutional liberty, which they feared would be lost under James. Though most royalists were staunch Church of England and regretted James's religion, they abhorred these efforts to alter his rightful succession, and they came to be called the Tories.

In the event, Charles refused to yield, and in 1685 James did ascend the throne. His generals, under John Churchill, had no difficulty in crushing a rebellion by Charles's natural son, the Duke of Monmouth, and his rag-tag army of Protestant peasants. The country was prepared to endure James's rule because he was in place and his successor would be his Protestant daughter Princess Mary. Educated by a Church of England bishop, she had married

William of Orange, a stalwart defender of the Low Countries against the imperial ambitions of Louis XIV. However when in 1688 James had a son, a number of leading Whig politicians – 'the immortal seven' – decided that it was time to act once more. They invited William and Mary to enter England, whereupon James discovered that he had few supporters and felt it wise to exit to France. The Whigs then negotiated with William and Mary over the terms by which they would rule, the outcome being the first constitutional monarchy.

During William III's reign Whiggery developed from being a protest against Catholicism and absolutism into a full political philosophy. Whig ideology was underpinned by a belief in the tide of progress. The past was reinterpreted – for example the ousting of James II became a 'Glorious Revolution'. In 1694 the historian James Tyrrell, a friend of the philosopher John Locke, postulated an 'ancient', presumed Saxon, English constitution, whereby the concept of a contract between monarch and people was seemingly given a precedent.

The Whigs had always been keen to support William in his continuing struggle with Louis XIV, and this continued in the Nine Years' War, which rumbled on till 1697, and for which the Land Tax was introduced. On the other hand, the Tories supposed that William had little interest in the English throne except as a means to receive financial support for his Continental ambitions. They saw Whigs profiting from the war, paid for with taxes that fell inequitably upon the lesser gentry. Parliamentary approval for spending on these purposes did not go uncontested.

The Whigs and Tories had undergone a curious reversal of roles. Tories had been loyal to 'Church and King', but their role in opposing taxes was one formerly adopted by the Country Party. They drew most of their support from the landed gentry, and were caricatured by the Whigs as 'backwoods squires'. The Tories regarded the Whigs as warmongers, speculators and profiteers. Meanwhile, supporters of the Country Party found themselves as Whigs, who had effectively become courtiers and were enjoying their power. They drew support from those desiring the freedom to practise various brands of non-conformist Protestantism, but the power rested with those, that is the magnates

and the moneyed interest, who sought freedom from the power of the monarch.

Reductions in population levels since mid-century, causing higher wages and lower rents, coupled with past fines and confiscations, resulted in estate incomes remaining low. The more opportunistic amongst the nobility diversified their incomes through reorganisation of their estates, profits from enclosure, mines and industry, development in the suburbs of a rapidly expanding London, and government office. A single magnate, with a swelling income and at the command of numerous favours at local level, could deliver a county to the Whig interest in the Commons.

The creation of dukedoms (but also elevations in other ranks in the nobility) marked the rise of the magnates. The rank of duke had once been mostly reserved for those of royal birth. During the course of Charles II's reign he rewarded General Monck with the dukedom of Albemarle for having paved the way militarily for the Restoration, and his most prominent governors in Scotland and Ireland were likewise honoured, hence the dukedoms of Ormonde in Ireland and Lauderdale and Queensberry in Scotland. He elevated two loyal magnates: the Marquess of Newcastle upon Tyne had been a royalist commander and afterwards suffered tremendous financial losses; he was granted a dukedom in 1664. The Marquess of Worcester, seated at Badminton, was a keen adherent of the Court Party; he was created Duke of Beaufort in 1682 for 'having been eminently serviceable to the King', as well as for his thin trickle of royal blood. With the accession of William III this new practice of rewarding the great magnates for their support continued, all being Whig supporters. The Marquess of Winchester was created Duke of Bolton in 1689, and in 1694 five further dukedoms were created – Bedford, Devonshire, Leeds, Newcastle upon Tyne (second creation) and Shrewsbury. With one exception, all Queen Anne's seven ducal creations were Whigs too.

These magnates sought to dominate their counties politically. Maintaining a grip on the electoral system required not only high rank and wealth, but also that these should be made visible. A country house, garden and park of great magnificence would be a means to dispel any doubt as to status, and would act as a visible confirmation of the owner's spending power. They could crush the will of a rival to compete. Knowing that the payment of bribes and favours to electors in contested elections could be financially crippling, a competitor of inferior rank and wealth, seeing such shows of power, would be inclined to avoid a confrontation at the polls.

Even at a quite local level, it was worthwhile for a baronet or squire from an old family to establish his presence, as there could be some degree of political influence wielded, a member of the family to be nominated as Member of Parliament, and positions, such as Justice of the Peace or Sheriff, to be secured. Land and the country house were the passport to such ambition, and these intangible benefits were part of the reason for high land values.

These political and economic forces are made manifest in the statistics of garden-making.[1] The makers of fine gardens show a shift from royalty and royalist dukes and earls in the 1660s towards Whig dukes and earls, plus significant activity by newly monied men from the 1680s. By far the most prolific makers of fine gardens were the magnates, and amongst them it was the dukes and earls who contributed most. A proportion of the untitled persons carrying out projects were younger members, or members of cadet branches, of noble families, so the families of the upper ranks of the nobility accounted for half or more of the garden schemes of these times. In terms of expenditure, the proportion must have been even higher. Furthermore, the nobility was overwhelmingly influential in terms of leadership in fashion.

Viscounts, barons and baronets carried out few projects in the 1660s, but by the 1680s the gradually ameliorating conditions for landowners allowed these ranks to make a strong showing, at a third of all projects. In contrast to their social superiors, though, their ability or desire to make gardens fell away significantly in the war years of the 1690s and 1700s. Fine gardens made by those without any title were not numerous at the Restoration, but climbed to about a third overall in the four decades between 1670 and 1710. Although, as noted above, some of these owners were younger sons of aristocrats, there was an expanding category of 'new money', from the law and banking especially.

Amalgamating the contributions from all these classes, it is seen that the financial constraints felt at the Restoration had evidently eased by the 1680s, increasing disposable income. The simultaneous rise in competitive politics provided the stimulus to spend on visible show at country houses, and hence the sharply increased rate of garden-making up to about 1690. In the following two decades war conditions were bound to suppress such projects, hitting the lesser nobility and squires harder than the earls and dukes. Garden-making thus dipped slightly in the 1690s and more so in the 1700s. Hence the 1680s was the most frenetic decade for late seventeenth-century garden projects – perhaps a surprising conclusion in view of its troubled monarchical politics.

Projects and projectors

Many garden projects were associated with building projects, either on a new site or by improvement through rebuilding, refurbishment or additions, such as new wings. Whether the garden works were timed to coincide with the beginning of a house or the end was often determined by the owner's method of financing a project. Early garden works could arise if an owner took a mortgage to be serviced by future estate income, enabling the whole scheme to proceed at once. Alternatively, an owner might try to fund a scheme directly from estate income, in which case work on the garden would probably start after the completion of the house and stables. There were many combinations and variants of these options.

In the great majority of cases the house came first. The time lag between the start of building work and the start on a garden could easily be of the order of five years. The reverse – planting before building – carried risks: if the project had to be changed or abandoned, the gardens could be left fully or partially complete whilst the house was still unbuilt. There are examples of gardens being unintentionally left without accompanying houses. Roger North knew of some examples of such folly: 'It hath happened, as at lord Craven's house att Hampstead [sic] Marshall by Newbury, elegant gardens were made and kept, but the house never finished; and I have heard of some who have made gardens and never began the house.'[2] For this reason North built his house at Rougham,

Norfolk, first, and 'was not well determined of the manner of the gardens till the house and homestall were fixed'.

Garden works could drag on, resulting in very extended time-scales. The gardens at Burghley took eighteen years to complete from the early 1680s, and the new courts and gardens at Boughton House took the Earl of Montagu fourteen years from 1694. There were cases of gardens left unfinished for many years because the owner had been financially crippled by enormous building or upholstery bills.

Redesign was frequent in the highest-status gardens belonging to members of the higher nobility. It was not unusual for radical revisions to take place every generation. In some extreme cases, such as Chatsworth, the Duke of Devonshire could afford to launch new projects every decade, so that there was continuously some work afoot. However, many landowning families would have a single opportunity, say at an advantageous marriage or acquisition of a government post, to boast of fine gardens. Oliver St John, Chief Justice of the Common Pleas in Cromwellian times, temporarily had the wealth from this office to construct a house and an elaborate planned layout of gardens at Thorpe Hall, Northamptonshire, but his descendants seem to have been impecunious, despite acquiring a baronetcy. The place was largely unchanged when it was surveyed over a century later (see fig. 44). The plates in Chauncy's *Hertfordshire*, published in 1700, were prepared up to fifteen years previously, and showed several gentry gardens that had probably had only minor alterations over the previous 50 years.

Most owners in the 1680s still devised their own garden layouts, though guidance was sometimes sought. No better advice could be had than that from Sir Christopher Wren, the Surveyor-General of the King's Works, though he became too occupied by projects for William and Mary to work on many country houses. Wren's friend and colleague Robert Hooke was more active in garden layout. He favoured baskethandles at the end of *parterres à l'Angloise*, and he devised *jets d'eau* at Montagu House in London (fig. 87) and at Londesborough Hall for the Earl of Burlington in about 1678 (see fig. 177). He evidently acquired a copy of André Mollet's *Garden of Pleasure* (1670), as his general plan for Ragley

Hall, Warwickshire, designed in 1679 for a fellow member of the Royal Society, the Earl of Conway, was surrounded by a sophisticated garden layout with distinct affinities to Mollet's idealisation of Honselaarsdijk. That was not simple, as the house crowned a knoll and the ground was far from being flat. Nevertheless, with various stairs and slopes the general plan was contrived with the parterre as the centrepiece of a large rectangular enclosure, and ending at another large baskethandle. The rectangle was surrounded by a double row of trees, and was skewered lengthways, and through the house, by an axis that was continued outside the rectangle by means of avenues (fig. 88).

William Winde may likewise have had a hand in garden layout at some of his houses – for example, Combe Abbey around 1685, Castle Bromwich Hall in about 1690 and possibly Belton House in 1688 (see fig. 166). The northern architect Edward Addison must surely have contributed designs to both Hutton Hall around 1685 and Lowther Hall around 1694, as both had the unusual feature of grass parterres planted with spruce trees (fig. 89).

However, the major figure in country-house architecture from the mid-1680s was undoubtedly William Talman. By 1688 he seems to have been working as an architect at, amongst other places, Hackwood Park, Hampshire, for the Marquess of Winchester (see fig. 158); on the south front of Chatsworth, for the Earl (from 1694 Duke) of Devonshire (see fig. 95); and at Burghley House, for the Earl of Exeter.[3] The place of Comptroller of the Royal Works had been vacant since Hugh May died in 1684, and at the Revolution in 1688–9 Talman evidently found a powerful patron willing to put his name forward. Thereafter he not only had a hand in the royal projects at Hampton Court and elsewhere, but for a decade was also much in demand as a country-house architect. Few of his garden plans have survived, however, and most are for Hampton Court, in particular an idea for a retreat at Southborough in Kingston-on-Thames parish, perhaps inspired by Louis XIV's Trianon at Versailles, and in anticipation of which he bought the land (fig. 90).

Owners might not wish to supervise contracts with undertakers themselves, particularly if they were away much of the time. Sometimes the task fell to the owner's wife, but more usual solu-

87 Engraving after a drawing by James Simon, *The North Prospect of Mountague [sic] House* (1714). Montagu House, St Giles, London, was designed by Robert Hooke. The 1680s parterre was adorned by figures, flanked by terraces and terminated at an octagon fountain basin in a *demi-lune*; northwards, the view extended to Highgate. By 1706 Thomas Ackres was the undertaker to keep the garden, and in the next few years he spent copiously on plant tubs, seen here interspersed between junipers or cypresses.

88 Knyff and Kip's bird's-eye view (*c.*1700) of Ragley Hall, Warwickshire, built 1679–83 for the Earl of Conway to the designs of Robert Hooke. This view emphasises the axial arrangement and ordered planning of the gardens within a great rectangle as if this were the Netherlands; in fact, the house was at the summit of a knoll, and the ground falls away on all sides, steeply to the south (left); the rising avenue terminated in a *demi-lune*, echoed in the semicircular palisade. Inside the gates was an early carriage sweep flanked by a laundry (south) and stables (north); on the three other sides of the house there was a paved terrace. The near parterre is obscured by the house, but it dropped to a lower *parterre à l'Angloise* with scrollwork, a *jet d'eau* and baskethandle termination surrounded by a terrace with a *glacis* slope to the west. Terraced slopes lay north and south and terminated with small greenhouses with *jets d'eau*. Kitchen garden quarters occupied the lower slopes and a broad visto ran off across a field to the west and then uphill into a wood; smaller walks were planted at wide angles.

The North Prospect of MOUNTAGUE HOUSE.

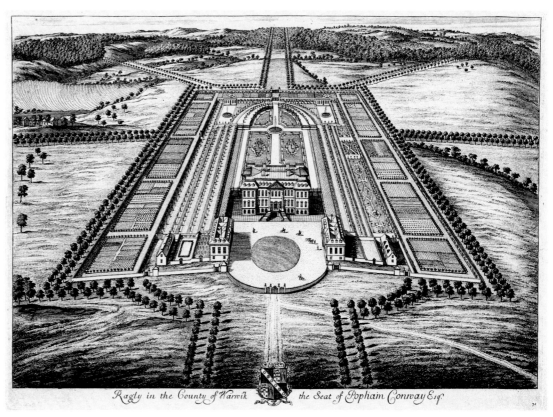

Ragly in the County of Warwik the Seat of Popham Conway Esq.

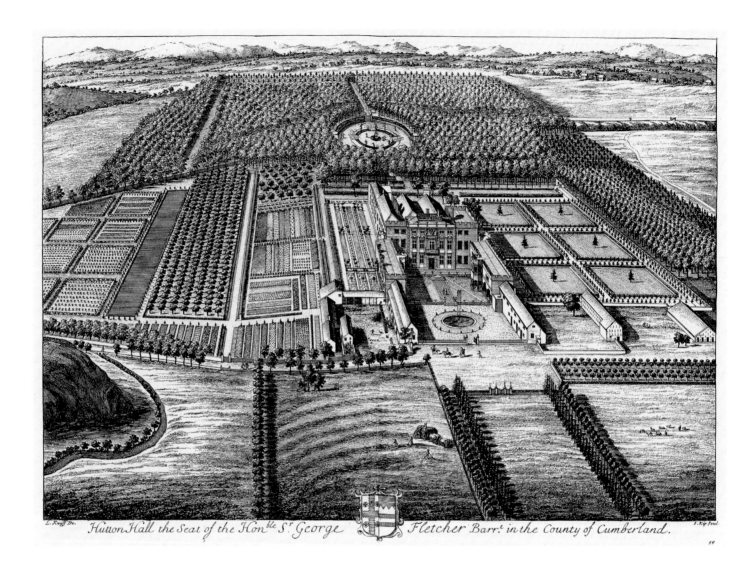

L. Knyff Del.   Hutton Hall the Seat of the Honble Sr George   Fletcher Barr^t in the County of Cumberland.   I. Kip Sculp.

tions were to ask the steward, or a neighbouring gentleman, to take it on. The Duke of Devonshire appointed a surveyor, a Mr Hewitt, or Huett, to supervise the building and garden-making works at Chatsworth from 1695 for ten years. Towards the end of this time Hewitt was also found at Calke Abbey and Melbourne.

THE BROMPTON PARK NURSERY

Although most rural seats would probably have had a resident head gardener, increasingly likely to be working to a contract, the comparatively small gardens in and around London would not justify a full-time gardener. The solution was a contract for

upkeep entered into with a gardener or nurseryman who looked after several properties. As this practice increased, some large gardens in the country were altered, and then maintained, by such

89   Hutton Hall by Knyff and Kip, *c.*1700. A garden in Cumberland was not necessarily behind in fashion: the curious water garden with surprise jets in the wood to the south-west was perhaps from an earlier era, but the double avenue from the north-east, carriage circle, open grove and huge areas of kitchen garden were up-to-date. They are associated with work on the house of around 1685 by Edward Addison. Slightly unusual was the use of conifers in the avenue and the open grove to the right.

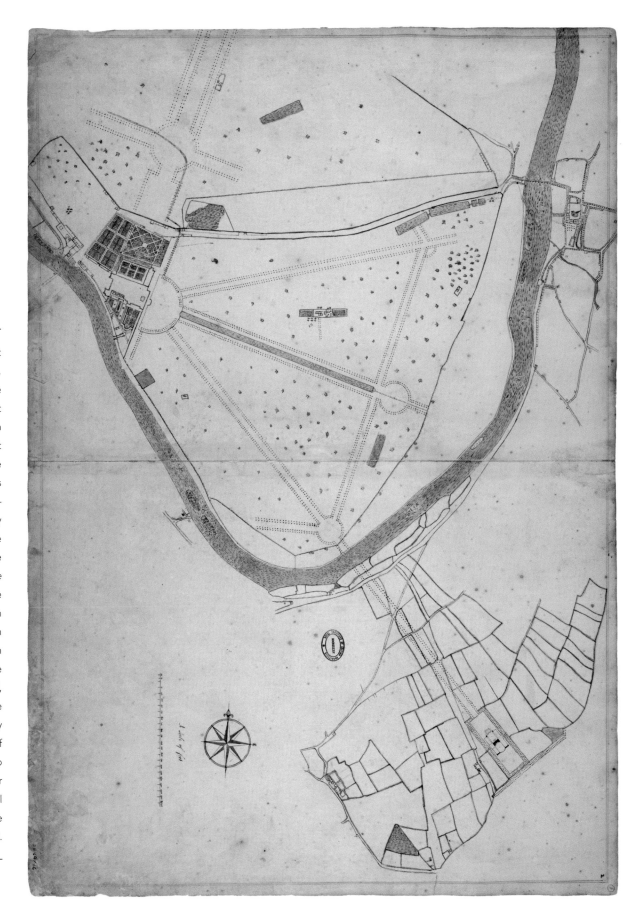

90   A plan showing Hampton Court and its parks as they were in 1694–8, made by William Talman to promote the idea of a 'Trianon' retreat across the river at Southborough in Kingston parish, an idea that was not acted upon. However, it shows the state of the gardens and avenues before the changes made in 1698–1702. The 1660s avenues in Bushy Park to the north and along the Long Water had been joined by the two diagonals from the *demi-lune* by the palace and the cross-avenue to the east. The old bowling green overlooking the river is picked out in green, as is the six-quarter kitchen garden made from the tiltyard, the wilderness made from the orchard, the melon ground made from the Privy Orchard, and the revised Privy Garden. Adjacent to the last of these is the Pond Yard, adjusted to accommodate Queen Mary's flower collection, with the three small rectangular buildings being the three 'glass-cases'.

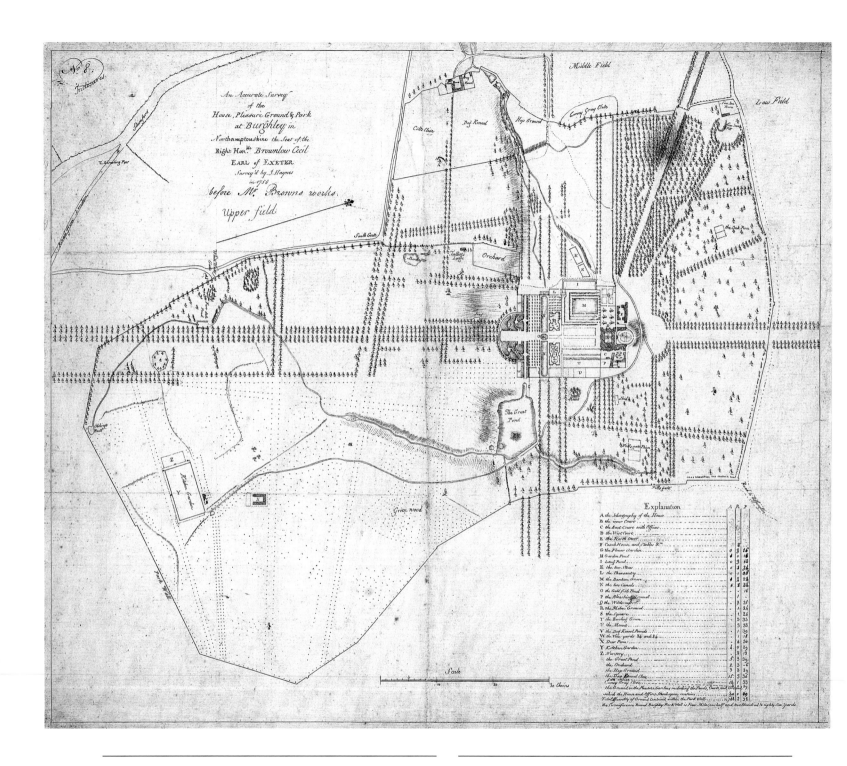

91 'An Accurate Survey of . . . Burghley . . . before Mr Brown's Alterations' by John Haynes 1755 (north is to the right). The slightly higher ground to the south-east of the house gave rise to terraces falling to a pond; following a visit in 1683 by Moses Cook and George London,

these were incorporated into a great rectangle with groves and a cross-canal and ending in a huge baskethandle. The planting in the park was even more impressive, with avenues in all directions, many being double.

garden undertakers. Being remote from the place in question, this person would normally appoint a foreman on site.

At the same time, with the increase in the number and ornamentation of 'fine-set gardens' – that is, those neatly designed and well kept – the requirement for good nurseries, florists and seedsmen was increasing. In 1681 four head gardeners joined together to establish their own nursery in the good soil of Brompton, a hamlet in Kensington, in order to ensure reliable supplies. The leading light of the nursery, Roger Looker, was gardener to Queen Catherine of Braganza at Somerset House, but he was also in charge of eight other substantial gardens besides, probably operating contracts to keep them up.[4] These included the Earl of Clarendon's gardens at Cornbury and Swallowfield, Berkshire, the Earl of Burlington's Burlington House and Londesborough, and the Duchess of Lauderdale's Ham House. Looker joined with John Field, the Earl of Bedford's gardener at Woburn Abbey, Moses Cook, the Earl of Essex's gardener at Cassiobury, and George London, the Bishop of London's gardener at Fulham Palace, to form the Brompton Park nursery.

London had been taken on in the Royal Garden at St James's as an apprentice gardener by John Rose in the early 1670s. There may have been a Wiltshire connection; Rose was from that county and London was to marry his great niece in 1679.[5] Following Rose's death in 1677 London was taken on at Fulham Palace, where he contributed to assembling a magnificent collection of exotic plants. He was meanwhile looking after the garden at Arlington House in London and two recently made gardens in Bedfordshire.

Once it became known that the quartet were willing to provide plants from their nursery, and would give time to help owners with devising their undertakings, requests for their services started coming in. The Earl of Exeter sought 'Mr Cooks and Mr Londons opinion' about his gardens at Burghley in 1683 (fig. 91).[6] Likewise, Viscount Weymouth, who had just created a walled rectangle east of Longleat, was 'desiring a little better advice than either my owne, or Mr. Tayler's' (his builder), and asked his brother to obtain Wren's opinion. This led to the four partners filling in the walled areas, taking it in turns to spend a month on supervising the

work.[7] The major earth-shaping took place from October 1683, followed by the Great Garden with a *parterre à l'Angloise* crossed by a canal. A flower garden with greenhouse was created to one side, the kitchen garden on the other, and on axis was a grate between huge piers topped by leaden stags (fig. 92). From 1694 the walled enclosure was doubled in length and further garden areas were formed, including a wilderness, a bowling green and a flower nursery. Beyond the baskethandle termination the axis led up the hill to a hexagon plantation and summerhouse, the *point de vue* of the whole (see fig. 186). The cost of this enormous enterprise was about £30,000, according to Celia Fiennes.

Cook and London were the undertakers for the Office of Works in forming and planting the King's Avenue linking Windsor Castle to the Great Park in 1684 (see fig. 145).[8] The partnership suffered two losses with the deaths of Looker in 1685 and Field in 1687, but, conscious of the growing demand for their services, Cook and London took on a new partner, Henry Wise, that year. His duties were principally in the nursery itself. In 1689 Cook retired and sold his share to the then surviving partners, whose names, London and Wise, became universally known and respected amongst the nobility and gentry for the next quarter century.

It is a matter of surmise who had devised the general plans for the two huge and costly layouts at Burghley and Longleat, and subsequent ones at Cholmondeley Castle and Chatsworth. The nursery's involvement was not certainly any more than that of making gardens to suit spaces already formed, and supplying trees. Sir Edward Blackett's new gardens and orchards at Newby in Yorkshire was one place for which London and Wise were submitting bills for trees between 1690 and 1692, and in 1694 London provided a former apprentice of his at Fulham Palace, Peter Aram, as head gardener. London probably did not provide general plans of gardens early on, yet it seems likely that he could devise sketches of the beds, planting and cutwork sufficiently well for showing to the owner and appending to contracts.

Probably because of being known to Queen Mary through her former tutor, Bishop Compton, and because of his merits anyway, London was singled out to be the English gardener to support Hans Willem Bentinck, William III's favourite, and newly ele-

vated as the Earl of Portland, in making the new royal gardens for William and Mary. London supervised the various tradesmen necessary and kept the accounts at Hampton Court and Kensington in 1689–92. Having acquitted himself well, he was turned to by many of the nobility and gentry for advice on their own projects. Evelyn could already write in 1693 of London and Wise that they had 'long experience . . . in being employed in most of the celebrated gardens and plantations which this nation abounds in'.[9]

As he was consulted and asked for advice, London found himself drawn into devising designs. He promised to take 'Draughts of ye best of those houses' he had seen to Longleat, showing Lord Weymouth how garden areas could be set out. An extremely simple sketch plan survives for a small garden for Blyth

Hall as part of a letter signed and dated by London in 1692, proof that he had started drawing by then.[10] Evelyn visited the nursery and observed that not only were Cook's skills in evidence, but that the nursery had been collecting prints and could offer designs for garden areas:

I find they have apply'd themselves to attain a sufficient Mastery in Lines and Figures for general design, and expeditious Methods for casting and levelling of Grounds; and to bring them into the most apt Form they are capable of . . . to determine the best Proportions of Walks and Avenues, Starrs, Centres etc. suitable to the lengths; and how, and with what materials whether Gravel, Carpet etc. to be layed.

They have a numerous collection of the best designs, and I perceive are able of themselves to draw and contrive others applicable to the places, when busie works and parterres of imbroidery for the coronary and flower gardens are proper or desired . . . [11]

A plan of the terraces at Dyrham may also be in London's hand.[12] In 1693 Viscount Hatton was consulting London on improvements to his Upper Garden at Kirby Hall, Northamptonshire, and his plant-collecting brother Charles was curious to know the outcome.[13] Next year Charles noted that 'I heare George London hath been at Burley on ye Hill, and drawn a designe for a very spatious garden ther.'[14] Here the Earl of Nottingham, after seeking advice from London, adapted the old terraces with low brick walls to give wider walks, and below these he set out a large semicircular sloping garden, modelled on the Hampton Court Fountain Garden.[15]

A watercolour of the cutwork that replaced the *parterre à l'Angloise* at Longleat in the late 1690s gives an impression of what London was then capable of (fig. 93).[16] His design for Herriard, Hampshire, in 1699 shows considerable ingenuity in cramming all the fashionable garden elements into a squire's walled enclosure of two-and-a-half acres (fig. 94).[17] At the different scale of parkland, London would superimpose his ideas for avenue planting on estate surveys, as at Kimberley Hall, Norfolk, and seemingly at Wotton Underwood, Buckinghamshire, in about 1712.

Documentation, including dimensioned plans, for several projects exists, notably for Longleat, two parterres at Chatsworth (fig. 95) and the kitchen gardens at Cholmondeley (see fig. 169). Owners would have been familiar with contracts with brickmakers and builders, so there were forms of contract that could be readily adapted. At Longleat the changes were made area by area, with each described on a separate plan. As soon as one was finished and had received London's approval, the plan was signed and a request for payment authorised. For example, the plan 'to level green & make slope banks', effected by a James Cook at the Bowling Green, was passed for payment of £21 with London's words: 'This is finished.'[18]

(Facing page) 92   Robert Thacker's painting of Longleat House from the rising ground east of the garden, c.1694. This shows the *parterre à l'Angloise* installed by the Brompton Park Nursery 1683–94, with a cross canal and an elaborate fountain supplied in 1691. The flagged terrace under the house ended in summerhouses. The evergreens in the *plates-bandes*, the large pots at the corners and the gravel side and end terraces can be seen; gates and grates were in wood. The flower garden to the south contained the house's first greenhouse; this garden and the parterre together formed a square with sides of 630 feet. Further major changes were under way from 1694.

93   A design attributed to George London for a cutwork parterre at Longleat House, c.1695 (north is to right; a key explains the letters). This was to replace the plats with flower borders made in 1683. This design was also implemented, with minor adjustments, at Kirby Hall, Northamptonshire, in 1995.

94 Herriard House, Hampshire, 1699. George London prepared plans for this gentleman's garden in 1699; under the house was a terrace walk with a *grille* at each end and overlooking a walled enclosure; *parterres à l'Angloise* were divided by the 'garden broad walk', surrounded by *plates-bandes* with clipped shrubs, and with some internal cutwork; the parterres were flanked by gardens for soft fruit and asparagus, with camomile paths. A cross walk led to a greenhouse at one end and gates at the other; beyond this were two kitchen gardens with grass paths behind espaliers of spruce firs, the space in between being a wide grass walk with places where the greens could be set out in lines as far as the *grille* at the wall.

It is surprising how casual the first Chatsworth contract of 1688 was. There was evidently a plan and profile (or section), and London was to make the levels accordingly. The Earl was to find 20 wheelbarrows and then turf, gravel and sand. London was then to 'finishe it fitt for Turfin, planting, and Gravilling, or sand', ready for planting, and would be paid £120 after completion of work. The Earl's gardener was presumably then to find and install the plants.[19] By the time of the Cholmondeley and the second Chatsworth contracts in 1694 the nursery had evidently consulted lawyers. The documents were structured with clauses commencing 'Whereas', 'Item' and 'Alsoe'. The description of the works was much lengthier, and there were additional clauses on staged payments – stating that work would be stopped if the owners did not pay or hindered progress – completion dates, food and lodging for foremen, and other matters.

It appears that one of London's first introductions to general plans was in collaboration with Talman in devising one of vast proportions for Castle Howard from 1698 (fig. 96). A St Andrew's cross was intended, with quadruple avenues planted in parkland, embracing to the east Wray Wood, of 66 acres, which itself was to have been cut into a star. The visto north would have been along a series of bodies of water, and to the south were to have been the gardens. There would have been great circles along the quadruple avenues, one to contain the rebuilt estate village.

As yet, though, responsibility for devising an entire major layout remained the responsibility of the owner and his architect, not London. Meanwhile, Wise's drawing skills seem to have been non-existent.[20] It would be misleading to think of London primarily as a designer. Any advice or plans supplied have to be seen as the necessary precursor to the main businesses of the nursery – undertaking construction projects and supplying plants.

In order to fulfil his obligations, London had a hectic career, dashing up the Great North Road on horseback as far as Yorkshire, or westwards to Longleat and Herefordshire, or south to Sussex and Kent. Although it is not always possible to be clear whether he visited a place merely to take orders for plants, he seems to have been the precursor of garden-making at scores of

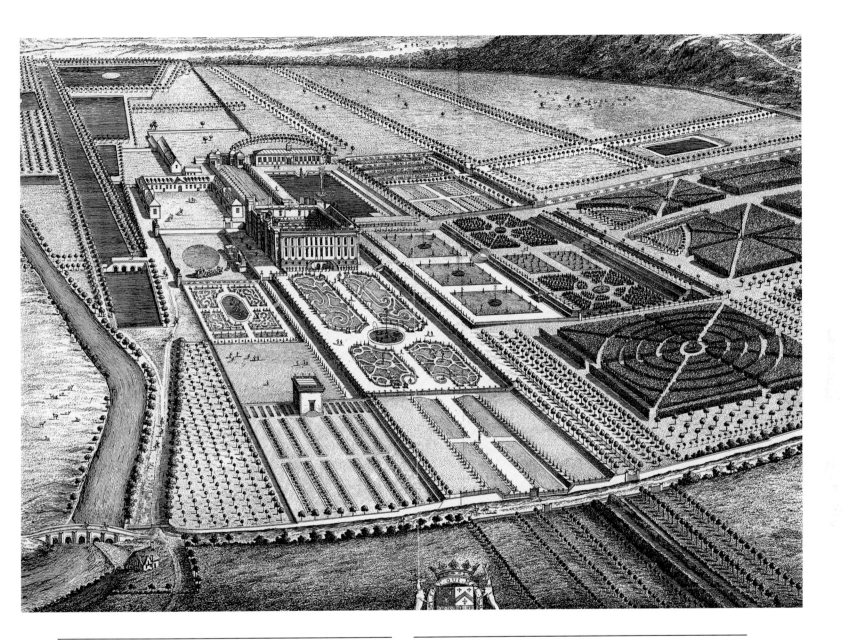

95　Knyff and Kip's view of Chatsworth House, 1699. The Duke of Devonshire's garden works, begun about 1685, included a 'great parterre' with a *jet d'eau* under the south front, three grass plats above the upper terrace, with *glacis* slopes above them; a garden of clipped greens above the middle grass plat; and quincunxes in evergreens centred around small basons. The canal to the north-west was finished in 1685, and a new forecourt was made in 1687. A flower parterre by George London in the angle between forecourt and great parterre followed in 1688–91, at about the same time as the bowling green. In anticipation of the new south front being finished, London was contracted in 1694 to make a new, lengthened, parterre with scrollwork as shown here; beyond this a 'Flora's Garden', enclosed by *grilles*, extended to the road. At the same time the outward plantations in Scots pine were planted east of the quincunxes, and a staircase cascade made to be visible from the steps down into the parterre from the south front. These gardens were already one of the most renowned of William III's reign before yet further changes after the date of this print.

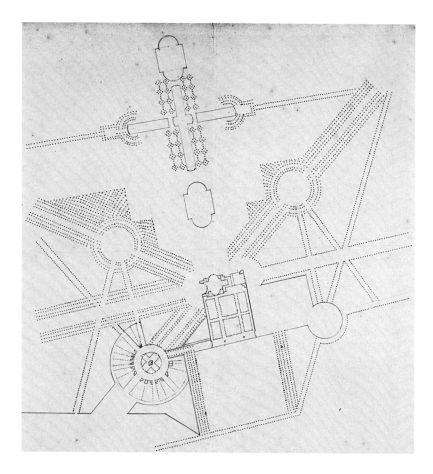

96 A general plan for Castle Howard, probably by William Talman, c.1699, showing a vast St Andrew's cross of quadruple avenues and the main front, facing west. The garden was to the south, and the village was to be rebuilt as an estate village in a circle to the south-west; the visto to the east would have been through Wray Wood, and the broad visto down the falling ground to the north was to have been embellished with basons and canals. This plan fell victim to ideas by Vanbrugh.

places. He was also invaluable as someone who could recommend good gardeners.

Under pressure, London asked Wise to visit a number of places on his behalf. Some involvement by Wise in contracts is likely, but in 1699 this aspect of his work was catapulted forward by the recommencement of royal gardens projects. London was the Office of Works official who, acting like an architect, proposed the scheme

of 'extraordinary works' at Hampton Court to the Treasury, so could hardly have awarded the work to himself.[21] From this time, Wise was engaged on a series of massive undertakings. Amongst the first was the causeway and bason in the Great Avenue through Bushy Park. The Privy Garden, the Pavilion Terrace and further avenues in House Park followed.

Undertakers were always anxious to find reliable servants as resident foremen to administer contracts. In practice, frequent redeployment on account of incompatibility with the owner, or the need for a good foreman at the next new garden undertaking, must have caused considerable movement. Indeed, that is how Stephen Switzer came to have 'a considerable Share in all parts of the greatest Works of this Kingdom'.[22] He hinted in his writings that he had worked at Blenheim, Bushy Park, Cranbourne Lodge (in Windsor Great Park), Cassiobury, Castle Howard and Grimsthorpe prior to London's death. Though on the one hand grateful for having thereby met 'the best Men and Books', he evidently hated 'the tossing of Gardeners about from one Place to another'. It is 'the greatest Blemish that is charg'd upon the Memory of one of our greatest Master-Gardeners', George London.[23]

Tilleman Bobart's career illustrates the varied life of a foreman with London and Wise. He was Jacob Bobart's younger half-brother, and trained by him at the Oxford Physic Garden (see fig. 47). In 1693 he left Oxford and explained to a correspondent: 'I am now with Mr London where my business is to manage the Royall Garden for him'.[24] In 1694 he witnessed the contract between Viscount Cholmondeley and London referred to above.[25] By 1696 he was a foreman at Hampton Court, looking after 'grass and gravel'.[26] He was afterwards taken on by Wise as assistant on the royal parks, and then in 1708 worked at Canons Ashby, Northamptonshire, before being redeployed to Blenheim, where he was granted a warrant as comptroller of the works.[27] Few of those working for the Duchess of Marlborough lasted long, and Bobart survived only till 1720, when discharged for 'abuses in the garden'. In 1724 he was living at Cannons, presumably because he was then in charge of making the Duke of Chandos's gardens on behalf of Brompton Park (see fig. 150). After Wise had been asked to form gardens for Lord Guildford, Bobart went to Wroxton Abbey, War-

wickshire, as the comptroller.[28] He died in Oxford in 1735, leaving considerable property to his son Jacob and still hoping that debts owing him from Blenheim would be paid.[29]

Brompton Park had continued to undertake maintenance, the original intention, since its inception. Having made the gardens at Chelsea Hospital, London and Wise were in 1691 awarded a ten-year contract for maintaining them (fig. 97).[30] Bobart's four years at Blenheim were in order to run the contract between the Duke and Wise; he described himself as 'on the behalf of Mr Wise the Undertaker of the Gardens and Outworke' there.[31]

OTHER GARDENERS

Experienced gardeners and nurserymen other than London were providing design advice, particularly away from the capital.

Jacob Bobart, elder brother of Tilleman, is known to have given detailed dimensions to Lord Stawell in 1690 for extensive gardens at Low Ham, Somerset.[32] Guillaume Beaumont, a French gardener, started a nursery in Bagshot, and visited numerous places in order to advise on garden-making and planting. His most devoted customer was James Grahme of Levens Hall, in Cumbria, where

97 A bird's-eye view of Chelsea Hospital from the Thames, *c.*1710, in a print sold by John Bowles. The hospital and grounds were made in 1687–92. The central walks led to steps to the river, and the canals and summerhouses were for ornament; to either side were kitchen-garden areas, no doubt worked by the pensioners themselves. This highly original layout, designed for the nature of the place, was possibly by Wren; the Brompton Park Nursery were the undertakers.

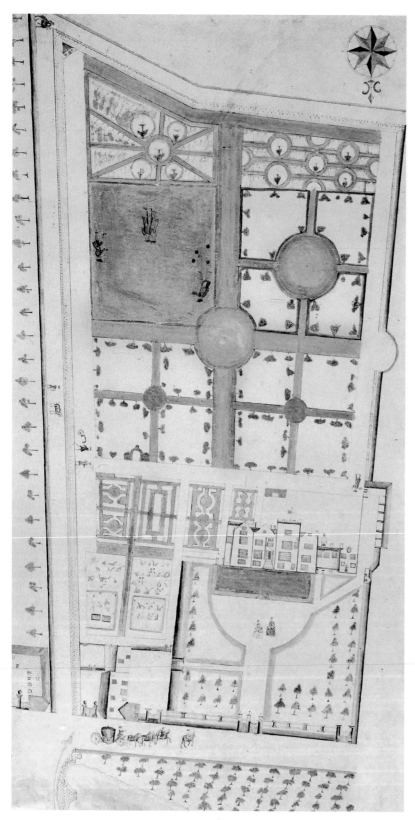

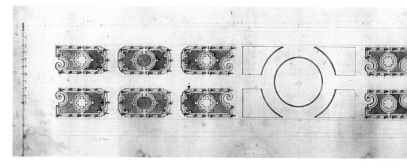

(Left) 98 'A Map of Leavens Garding' by Robert Skyring, *c*.1750 (north at bottom). This depicts the garden at Levens Hall, created from 1694 by Colonel Grahme's gardener, Guillaume Beaumont. It consisted of flower gardens by the house and four quarters with *plates-bandes* with clipped yews south of it and ending at two small wildernesses. Subsequent changes, seen here, were the clearance of one quarter for a bowling green in 1703 and the ha-ha and bastion to the west, probably of the 1730s.

(Above) 99 'Mons' Buffler, plan for a parterre', a design by Philip Buffle, or Bouffler, for Stonyhurst, Lancashire, *c*.1705. The long plot, rising slightly from the house, was to be of conventional *parterre à l'Angloise* panels; the fountain at the highest point was probably Sir Nicholas Shireburn's idea; at the far end the parterre was terminated by a viewing terrace between summerhouses.

(Below) 100 A design for Stonyhurst sent in about 1705 by Henry Wise, which can be compared to Buffle's proposal (see fig. 99). Although a departure from the conventional *parterre à l'Angloise*, it was still an unsophisticated design.

Beaumont set out the gardens and wildernesses in the course of several visits over several years, starting in 1694 (fig. 98).[33] In the same year he also visited Viscount Weymouth at Longleat and Sir Christopher Musgrave at Edenhall, Cumberland. Grahme gave him permanent lodgings at Levens in 1700, whereupon he gave up the nursery, and from this new base Beaumont advised the Tory gentry of Cumberland, Lancashire and Yorkshire on their gardens.

Philip Buffle, or Bouffler, perhaps a Frenchman, the gardener at Chelsea Hospital, clearly developed a sideline as a nurseryman. He fulfilled a significant order for Boughton House in 1711. Meanwhile he ousted Brompton Park, which had been sending pyramid yews and yew hedging since 1696, from Stonyhurst, Lancashire.[34] The first of his accounts for seeds and plants, which continued for a dozen years, was in June 1704; furthermore Buffle supplied a parterre design around that time (fig. 99) that looked more convincing than that sent by Wise (fig. 100).

The country house and garden described

By the late seventeenth century, Italian gardens were physically worn out, and had lost their power to inspire imitation. The Duchess of Marlborough was advised condescendingly in 1728 that the Duke of Parma's seat had 'a pleasant garden for an Italian one'.[35] Meanwhile, all eyes were on the rising achievements of the French Court, particularly at Versailles, where the gardens were reaching their full glory in the 1680s.

THE FRENCH MODEL

The French were fully aware of their new pre-eminence in gardens. One Huguenot, after visiting Italy in 1687, concluded that 'the Gardens and Water-works of Italy did formerly surpass those of France', but 'if we compare Frascati to Versailles . . . the celebrated Wonders not only of Frascati, but also of Tivoli, and all the most beautiful places about Rome, I mean as to Gardens and Waterworks, deserve no higher Title than that of petty Toys'.[36] Further, 'since the Face of Affairs is alter'd, we ought also to change our Language'. According to a recent translation, the Duc de Saint-Simon agreed, writing in 1700 that Le Nostre 'was celebrated for designing the fine gardens that adorn all France and have so lowered the reputation of Italian gardens (which are really nothing by comparison) that the most famous landscape architects of Italy now come to France to study and admire'.[37]

The English agreed too. A young physician, Tancred Robinson, wrote in 1683 that the gardens of Versailles were 'esteemed much the best in the world', and considered that the statuary, waterworks and other features 'all are as good as art could possibly contrive and produce'.[38] Switzer reckoned that the 'completion' of 'Gard'ning . . . seemed for *France*, and the other Northerly *European* Kingdoms of Great-Britain, which at present much out-doe Italy itself'.[39]

The prevailing object in the making of the French garden was ceremonial grandeur, an indispensable aspect of statecraft at the international level. As with the *château* itself, the purpose of the gardens was to impress and humble. With Versailles, the great age of palace gardens across Europe in the French mode had started. Among them was the garden at Drottningholm Palace, Stockholm, begun by the dowager queen of Sweden, Hedvig Eleonora, in the 1670s, employing the architect Nicodemus Tessin the Elder, and after 1682 his son, also Nicodemus. A plan of 1681 shows elements previously seen at Vaux-le-Vicomte, Versailles and Chantilly combined into a layout of great length, most of which was implemented that decade. The younger Nicodemus undertook an extended tour of France, the Low Countries and Italy in 1687 to look at houses and gardens.

In the early 1670s Philips Doublet of Clingendaal, near The Hague, had started to receive French publications on garden architecture, and details of *broderie* parterres and waterworks, from his brother-in-law, Christiaan Huygens, then in Paris, leading to a new garden laid out in 1680–7.[40] From 1685 William of Orange laid out gardens at his new hunting seat at Het Loo (fig. 101), and his cousin Count Willem Adriaan van Nassau-Odijk, who had been ambassador to France in 1678, was developing a vast scheme at Zeist, near Utrecht. Both employed a young Huguenot designer, Daniel Marot, to devise the decorative aspects of the gardens.

101 A reconstruction by Kees J. van Nieukerken of the layout of William of Orange's palace and gardens at Het Loo as at 1689 (north is at the top). The geometry was based on a great square with the centre being the door out onto the garden.

The construction of the *Grosser Garten* (Great Garden) at the palace of Herrenhausen outside Hanover had started in the 1660s. When Ernst August, Duke of Brunswick-Lüneburg, inherited in 1679 he was shocked that the garden was costing nearly 6,000 thalers a year to keep up, but soon he and his wife, Sophia, granddaughter of James I, and daughter of Frederick and Elizabeth of Bohemia, wanted something greater themselves. Sophie had been shown around Versailles by Louis XIV himself, and in 1682 hired a French designer, Martin Charbonnier, to enlarge and remodel the *Grosser Garten*. Sophie sent Charbonnier to the Low Countries

to study garden design, and there he could have seen the palace of the Statholder, William of Orange, at Honselaarsdijk, and more recent examples, such as Clingendaal.

In England the greatest palace was to be Hampton Court, which is described more fully below. A few magnates sought to have their own French-inspired palaces, the primary examples being the Earl of Chesterfield's *tour de force* at Bretby, Derbyshire, achieved over 35 years, and the Francophile Earl of Montagu's huge conception at Boughton House. Chesterfield was engaged in 'the building of his house at Bretby and the arrangement of his gardens' in 1670 (fig. 102).[41] The main parterre to the side of the house became a *broderie* design with eagles' heads, copied from the recently republished book by Mollet (see fig. 63).[42] The design was added to during his 'retirement' from Court from 1686, and Celia Fiennes noted in 1698: 'that which is most admired – and justly so to be – by all persons and excite their curiosity to come and see is the Gardens and Waterworks'. The gardens extended across a valley, which was dammed up outside the wall to drive the various waterworks. These reservoirs had apsidal ends – some of the first such devices seen in England and derived from French practice. There were at least ten fountains, and there was a water engine that played the popular tune 'Lilibolaro'. These amazing waterworks were by 'Sieur Grillet', who had worked at Chatsworth (see below), and were said to be complete by 1702, after about eight years in the making.[43] There were also greenhouses and orangery gardens. Observers were enthusiastic: even the French Marshal, Camille d'Hostun, comte de Tallard, a prisoner in England since his capture at Blenheim, who was allowed to visit on parole from his confinement in Newdigate House, Nottingham, 'seamed to be extreamly pleas[d] with the gardens and his entertyainement, and say[d] that, setting the King of France's gardens aside, there was not finer gardens in France'.[44]

French influence was also strongly evident at Boughton, where the western gardens and groves were disposed either side of a large area for parterres flanked by terraces (fig. 103).[45] As usual with the early stage of garden-making, there was a vast amount of earthmoving and waterworks. The small River Ise was canalised across the bottom of the parterres, given a large octagon bason

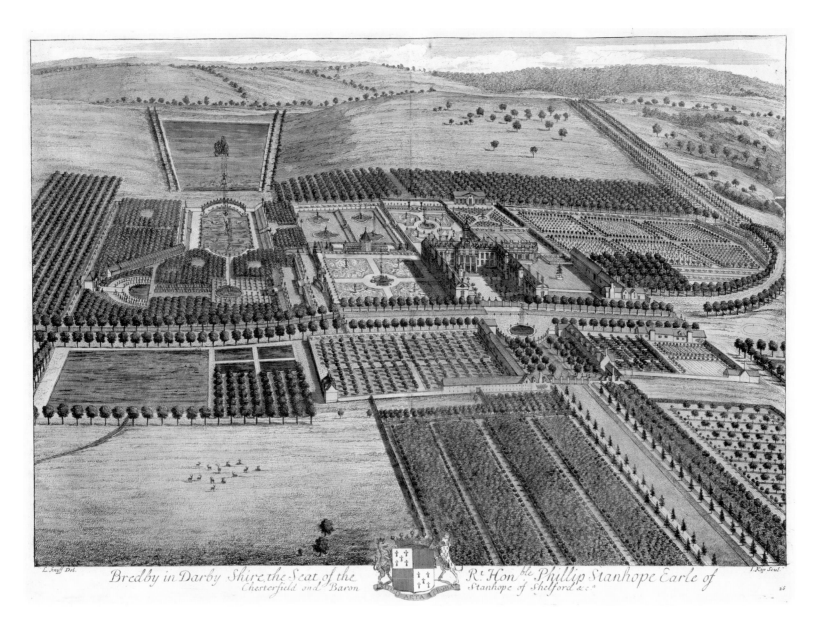

Bredby in Darby Shire, the Seat of the
Chesterfield and Baron

R.^t Honble Phillip Stanhope Earle of
Stanhope of Shelford &c.^a

on the garden's axis, and then taken through a series of turns so that an ambitious *buffet d'eau*, like that at Chantilly, faced towards the gardens (see fig. 217). It disgorged over five steps into the 'star pond', dug in a quatrefoil shape. A second source of water was brought across the park by culvert to a *grand étang* (which the Earl of Montagu's servants rendered as the 'Grandytang') just north-west of the house.

This reservoir fed a series of waterworks with numerous *jets d'eau* in the 'wilderness of apartments' north of the parterres, the

102   Bretby Hall, Derbyshire, by Knyff and Kip, c.1700. The Earl of Chesterfield's gardens at Bretby were constructed over 35 years from 1670 and added to in several stages. The parterre, taken from André Mollet (see fig. 63), was probably among the first of his additions. Sieur Grillet created elaborate waterworks, including a water organ, in the 1690s; these, with the greenhouses and aviaries, made Bretby one of the most accomplished gardens in England, admired even by the comte de Tallard.

103 'Plan de la maison et jardins de Boughton . . .' by Gabriel Delahaye, 1712 (north is to the right). These gardens were created for the first Duke of Montagu by Leonard van de Meulen. A terrace under the west front overlooked the gardens, which fell to the canalised River Ise to the west; south of the parterre with diagonal paths was a *bosquet*, and to its north a reservoir for feeding a water garden within a wilderness. West was a series of grass plats surrounded by clipped greens, leading down to a large octagon of water with nine jets and flanking basons with single jets; south of the grass plats was an extensive fruit garden. To the south-west (outside this image) the canal made a U shape so that a much-admired cascade was turned towards the house and garden.

work for which began in 1696. Steps were being finished in 1697, and the cascade was being finished in 1700.[46] Meanwhile, there was much planting south of the parterres, and a 'Broad Walk' was planted beyond the gardens, up the slope beyond to the skyline. The parterres, with their figures, fountain basons and gravel walks were being completed in 1706–7, when pleasure boats were floated on the canals. Though from the house one would espy a highly symmetrical scene, the disposition of wildernesses outside the tree-lined walks on the flanking terraces was quite different north to south, and the boundaries of the garden were mostly not walls, but iron fences outside various lengths of canals.

French influence was reinforced by the demand for French artisans at the foremost houses. Jean Tijou's unsurpassed decorative ironwork was installed at Chatsworth, and afterwards Hampton Court (see fig. 115). At the former, a French flower gardener, Pierre Audias, was employed and a Frenchman, Sieur Grillet, devised the first cascade in 1694 (see fig. 139). He may have been René Grillet from Rouen, a maker of a calculating machine (by 1673), a hygrometer and a graphometer. He established a calico printing works in Richmond Old Park in 1690 and would have had the knowledge of hydraulics to help with garden waterworks. Other immigrant Frenchmen who contributed their various skills to the English garden included Guillaume Beaumont, Philip Bouffler, Daniel Marot, Claude Desgots and Gabriel Delahaye.

French publications were amongst the most prized in the literature of gardens. Evelyn gave his name to English translations of two horticultural publications, Nicolas de Bonnefons's *The French Gardiner* (1658) and Jean-Baptiste de la Quintinie's *The Compleat Gard'ner* (1693). French garden vocabulary was steadily gaining hold. French terms such as *broderie*, *jet d'eau*, *espaliers* and *patte d'oie* slipped into English usage in William III's reign. The French style of *plate-bande* planting was quickly absorbed into English gardens even before *Le Jardinière fleuriste et historiographe* and *La Théorie et la pratique du jardinage* were translated into English.[47]

However, one could not really mistake an English garden for a contemporary French one. The disposition of French gardens was showing great variety by the 1680s, as forest rides, terraces, sheets and boundaries of water and other devices broke the outline

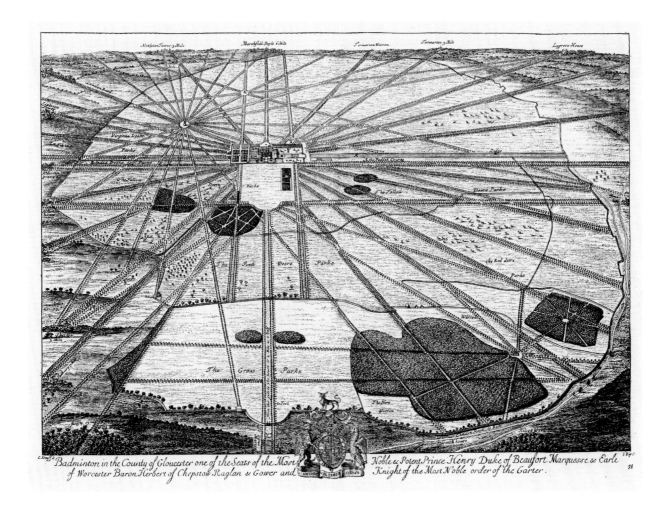

of the traditional walled rectangle, so that the French garden became intermixed with the surrounding countryside. Most English gardens remained for the time being within the enclosing wall, though the details of the late Stuart garden, as described in Chapter Four – decorative ironwork, figures, fountain groups, grates, *demi-lunes* in boundary walls, flower gardens, flowerpots, *plates-bandes*, clipped shrubs, cutwork, open walks, cabinets and halls in wildernesses, *jets d'eau*, and terraces – all had precedents in France. Celia Fiennes remarked in 1697 on the gardens at Haddon Hall, Derbyshire, by then failing to keep up with French fashion after the Earls of Rutland had moved to Belvoir Castle: 'good Gardens but nothing curious as ye mode now is'.[48]

Meanwhile, out in the park, avenue networks having the semblance of the rides in French forests, made an appearance. The greatest of all networks, that at Badminton from the 1680s, was shown in its full glory in a view by Knyff and Kip (fig. 104). It had about twenty vistos radiating from the house lanthorn, twenty-two from a hillock to the south-east and six from the semicircle enclos-

---

104   Badminton House from the north by Knyff and Kip, 1699. This bird's-eye view overlooks the parks at Badminton from north to south. In reality, the avenue network was never as complete as this, but the ambitious plan was evidently for 20 vistos radiating from the house lanthorn, 22 from a hillock to the south-east and six from the semicircle enclosing its parade; they were planted to be vistos resembling rides through a forest on the French model, and would have been cut through woodlands where necessary.

Wansted House in Essex the Seat of · · · · · the R Hon

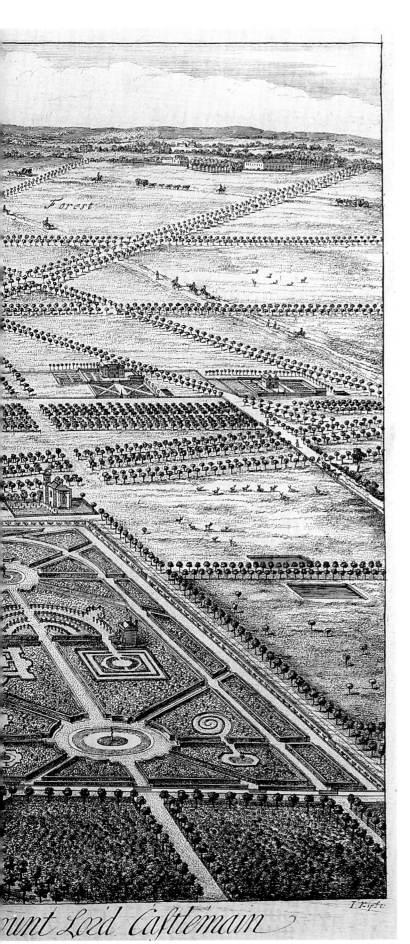

ing its parade. Several of these were planted across the Duke's neighbours' land.

That park avenues made little sense outside hunting preserves was not the point: the English conception of them was as vistos, in the same vein as dummy avenues to the front of the house. Several owners thought of aligning them on far-distant landmarks. Sometimes they were extended outside parks. Wanstead provides an even clearer example. By 1691 Josiah Child had a 'vast number of elms, ashes, limes, &c. planted in rows on Epping forest' (fig. 105).[49] It would not have been possible to hunt this land; it was very close to London, and regarded as common grazing land. The bewildering criss-crossing of walks was thus purely for visual effect, intended merely to give the visitor the flavour of an ancient hunting preserve.

ENGLISH DISPOSITION

In 1686 Sir William Temple considered that:

> The best Figure of a Garden is either a Square or an Oblong, and either upon a Flat or a Descent; they have all their Beauties, but the best I esteem an Oblong upon a Descent. The Beauty, the Air, the View make amends for the expence, which is very great in finishing and supporting the Terras-walks, in levelling the Parterres, and in the stone-Stairs that are necessary from one to the other.[50]

In most gardens in England and Wales the walled rectangle had become the norm, replacing the walled square of Restoration

---

105   Wanstead House from the east by Knyff and Kip, c.1713, after the gardens by George London had been finished, but before work had started on the new Palladian house. Josiah Child's criss-crossing avenues of the 1670s on the denuded Epping Forest to the west evoked the forest as a hunting ground. The twin semicircular pools were reshaped as an octagonal reflecting bason in 1714; the wilderness to the north may have been designed in this curious fashion to open up views of the Roding valley to the east.

times. Temple liked the way that a falling garden gave prospects. 'Vallies' and water were enjoyed from the walled areas at Stowe, Trentham (fig. 106), Easton Neston, Melbourne Hall and many other gardens. Side terraces, like those at Cassiobury, became the norm. Ragley was given them about 1679, and thereafter they were made at Longleat, Beaufort House and Belton. Although some side terraces were only three feet high, they could be massive, like those in the unfinished layout at the Earl of Macclesfield's Gawsworth,

---

106 'W. & by S. Prospect of Trentham Hall taken from yᵉ Hill near yᵉ Cistern' by Michael Burghers, 1686, showing a set of rectangular walled gardens south of the house. The side axis of the house was marked by the fountain and a large gateway, through which canals could be seen in the middle distance.

Cheshire. In William III's reign, his Privy Garden at Hampton Court and many further places acquired them (see fig. 16).

At some places, for example Erddig (see fig. 223), Denbighshire, and Harrowden, Northamptonshire, asymmetrically arranged garden areas were set to either side of the principal parterre, from which they would have been obvious. However, it was more usual to arrange garden areas, at least those in view from the Great Terrace, symmetrically either side of the axis. That did not mean that the interiors of wilderness quarters had to be identical; indeed at places like Ledston, Yorkshire, and Wrest, Bedfordshire, they were deliberately differenced. But it did mean that parterres, terrace walks and low planting had to mirror each other.

The axial progression of avenue, forecourt, house, walled gardens and visto was generally adhered to, but not so slavishly as formerly. The fashion for baskethandles persisted. Where the lie

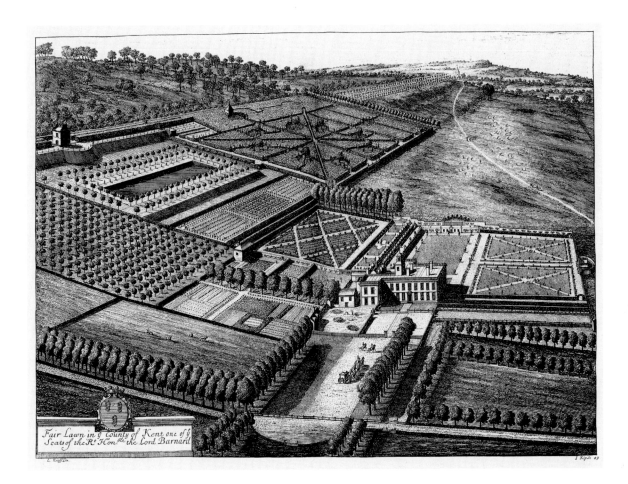

Fair Lawn in y̆ County of Kent one of y̆
Seats of the Rt Honble the Lord Barnard

of the land, constraints such as a river or road, or other consider-ations suggested it, the great rectangle might be developed along an axis to the side of the house (fig. 107). There was precedent for this at Wilton, where the outline of the 1630s garden was main-tained, although the details were reworked in the new mode in William III's time (see fig. 205).[51]

The usual means of holding up a terrace was the 'breast wall' (today we would say 'retaining wall').[52] The increase in terraces of all kinds from the late 1670s provided new opportunities for such wall-building. They varied in scale from the walling sup-porting the terraced walk at Arlington House, to the low wall supporting the Grand Terrace at Brympton d'Evercy, Somerset, both from the late 1670s. The peak of their construction was in the 1680s, after which grassed *glacis* slopes were preferred, not just as a necessity, but as an ornament to a garden. Hence the walls

supporting the terraces around the Great Garden at Kirby were replaced by *glacis* in the early 1690s.[53] Sir Thomas Willoughby surrounded his new bowling green at Wollaton, Nottingham-

107 Fairlawne, Kent, by Knyff and Kip, c.1700. The forecourt, house, grass plat and terrace with grotto under had been set out axially perhaps around 1640. Terracing to the north looked down across the garden, and late in the century Christopher Vane developed that axis, rising up the hill, for soft fruit, vegetables, fruit trees and a reservoir. It led to an upper terrace with a two-storey outlook pavilion. A recent addition in this view was a very elaborate wilderness with a curving path pinched along each axis and linking eight cabinets surrounded by cypresses, and each with a central tree; this was superimposed on a Union Jack arrangement of straight paths.

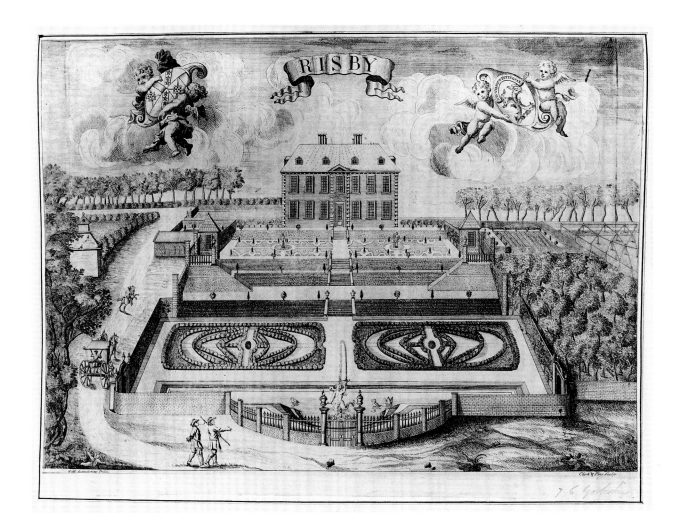

(Facing page) 108 *Wollaton Hall and Park* by Jan Sieberechts, 1697. The southern gardens (to the left) remained simple at this date, with just a few clipped greens and figures. The back of the greenhouse can be seen, and to the east there is a bowling green on a knoll shaped into *glacis* slopes. There was a plan to replace the kitchen garden to the south with a wilderness.

109 A view by William Lansdowne, engraved by John Clark and John Pine, of the south-east aspect of Risby Hall, Yorkshire, *c.*1720. The gardens, created in the 1680s by Sir James Bradshaw, lay within a rectangle terraced down to groves and a canal. The visto continued through iron gates, thus giving the visitor a full view of the gardens along the approach before being taken up and round to the entrance front.

shire, with three *glacis* slopes, one below another (fig. 108). At Petworth terraces were reformed as multiple *glacis* slopes.[54] At Kiveton, Yorkshire, in about 1704 (see fig. 162) and Chirk Castle about 1705 (see fig. 234) the necessity of coping with falling land was turned into a virtue by well-formed slopes.[55] Such was the change of fashion that when Switzer came to write *Ichnographia Rustica* (1718) he discussed the support for terraces purely in terms of making *glacis* slopes.

After about 1680 more terracings descended slopes below the house, reflecting the elevated positions for new houses. Sir James Bradshaw's carefully planned gardens of the 1680s at Risby, Yorkshire, faced south, and fell from a great terrace with summerhouses at each end down to a cross-canal within the walls (fig. 109). The

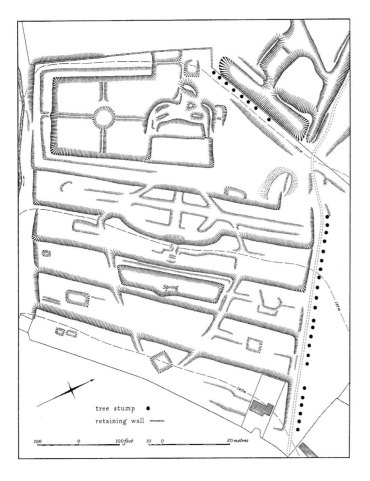

tree stump ●
retaining wall ▬▬▬▬

100   0   100 feet   10   0   50 metres

---

110   A drawing made in 1974–5 of earthworks for the 'Falls' at Harrington Hall, Northamptonshire. Sir Lyonel Tollemache, fourth Baronet, created an extensive set of terraces overlooking the Jacobean house at Harrington (robbed foundations of the house can be seen to the west, where there is a jumble of earthworks, and a four-quartered garden appears to its south) after inheriting from the second Lord Stanhope in 1677. Some of the terraces had pools, and it is likely that they also had fruit gardens and groves. A county historian wrote in 1712 that 'for a descent of Garden Walks there is nothing so remarkable'; however, these gardens appear to have been abandoned at Tollemache's death in 1726.

---

visitor, approaching from the south along the avenue, encountered this scene head-on through a grate in the garden wall.

There were situations where owners were forced by the fall of the land into multiple terraces. At Powis Castle the fall was so

---

(Facing page, top) 111   New Park, Richmond, by Knyff and Kip, c.1700. The Earl of Rochester, uncle of Queen Mary and a courtier, rebuilt the keeper's lodge in 1692 and under the garden front formed the parterre with terraces round and wildernesses beyond. In 1698 he was granted the woodland at the corner of the New Park as far as the mount, and within two years created the hanging garden and *glacis* slopes shown in this print. The outer woodland was not re-formed: instead, he merely cut through and planted vistos between the ancient trees.

(Facing page, bottom) 112   Belvoir Castle in 1731, one of a set of views by Thomas Badeslade that shows the spectacular series of *glacis* slopes to the north-east, made around 1700 for the first Duke of Rutland, who had probably inherited the bowling green and a wilderness with contoured paths to the south, which the shape of the ground prevented from being entirely regular. The outer plantation to the east, which has straight and curving rides, was probably the work of the third Duke around 1725.

---

steep that terraces had to be expensively blasted out of rock.[56] Some owners even welcomed hillsides that would give the opportunity of forming slopes. Sir Lyonel Tollemache dug and banked to achieve an extensive set of terraces and slopes overlooking his house at Harrington, Northamptonshire, in the 1680s (fig. 110).[57] About 1698 the Earl of Rochester cut a massive platform supported by a *glacis* slope into the hillside above his house at New Park, Richmond (fig. 111). Terracing above the house at Dyrham, Gloucestershire, consisting of part-wall, part-*glacis*, ornamented with yews and hollies, was being laid in 1704 (see fig. 173).[58]

As at Windsor, the craggy slopes at Belvoir were tidied up into spectacular *glacis* slopes (fig. 112).[59] Such places drew Switzer's admiration

> Terrace-Walks that are cut out of a natural Hill very much exceed all others, plac'd upon which we view the adjacent Country with the utmost Delight . . . For who is there that ever saw those noble Elevations of *Belvoir, Nottingham, Burleigh on the Hill, Winchester*, and many other places, would not think them appointed by Nature for the Residence of great and sublime Spirits . . .[60]

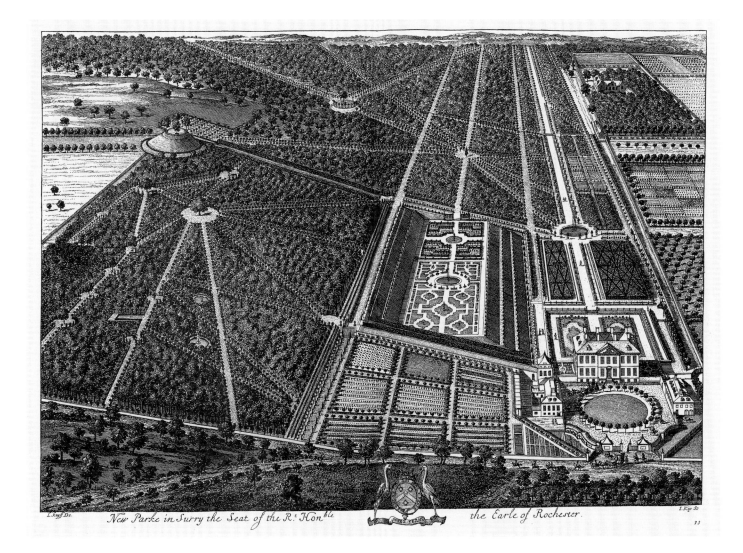

L.Knyff De.   New Parke in Surry the Seat of the Rt Honble   the Earle of Rochester.   I.Kip Sc.

33

To his GRACE JOHN DUKE of RUTLAND; MARQUIS of Granby; EARL of Rutland;   BARON Roos of Hamlake, Trusbut and Belvoir, and BARON Mannors of Haddon; LORD
LIEUT.t and CUSTOS ROTULORUM of the County of Leicester; CHANCELLOR of   ij Dutchy of Lancaster; One of the LORDS of his MAJESTY.s most Hon.ble Privy Council,
and KNIGHT of the most Noble Order of the Garter. This North West Prospect of   BELVOIR CASTLE in the County of Leicester the Seat of his Grace; is most humbly Inscribd.

Whether wall or *glacis* slope, steps would be needed. Gardens from early in the century often had steps at the ends of the terraces, sometimes within turrets. However, in the late seventeenth century flights of steps were generally placed at the midpoint on axis and built in more expansive fashion, broad in width and shallow in tread. Sometimes, on narrow terraces, a *perron* arrangement was employed. Just after the turn of the century Alexandre Le Blond gave detailed advice on the formation of stairs, with several designs for magnificent examples erected at Saint-Cloud, the Tuileries and the Luxembourg gardens, besides others less grandiose.[61]

Only a few turrets and summerhouses were built into garden walls mid-century, but there was a minor revival late in the century. A pair of facing summerhouses could be useful in providing seating and shelter in gardens or on terraces used for taking the air. This function was already obvious at, for example, the early pairs at Grimsthorpe about 1670 (see fig. 50), Gray's Inn in 1672,[62] and Eaton about 1676 (see fig. 45). As late as the 1730s a music room was erected to face a greenhouse across the walled area at Castle Bromwich, Warwickshire.[63] Grates might be flanked by summerhouses, which emphasised the dimension of a visto from the garden. An early example was the pair of flat-roofed banqueting houses at Drayton House, Northamptonshire, about 1680.[64] At Stansted Park, Sussex, by about 1686 summerhouses terminated walks at the outer corners of the parterre (see fig. 29).

At the front of the house, the carriage sweep was becoming general. At many places, for example Patshull in 1680, gates and an inner court with a broad walk remained between the sweep and the door.[65] Alternatively, the broad walk and grass plats might be converted to a sweep, allowing passengers to alight at the door itself. At Burlington House the grass plats either side of the broad walk were gravelled and became *de facto* a sweep (see fig. 80). Some of the other larger inner courts were converted to sweeps, as at Grimsthorpe by 1702 (see fig. 50). Where the gate was directly onto a highway, a half-moon might be scooped out of the property on the far side in order to enable the carriage to turn round in the highway, as at Bretby (see fig. 102).

Ragley, built in the 1680s, was an early example of a layout being conceived *ab novo* with a sweep around a circle of grass (see fig. 88). House, offices and stables all fronted directly onto it and the rest of the sweep was enclosed by an iron palisade. This solution was also adopted at Buckingham House (formerly Arlington House) in 1702, which was influential in connecting house and wings by colonnades (fig. 113). Generally the form of a sweep was gravel around a circular or oval grass plat, protected from the wheels of carriages by stone bollards. A few variations were found. The sweep at New Park, Richmond, Surrey, of the 1690s was planted round with a circle of trees (see fig. 111), whilst at Acklam, Yorkshire, the gravel sweep was a rectangle with rounded corners, enclosing a bowling green. Talman may have been the person who about 1690 thought out the complex arrangement of a ramped rectangular sweep enclosing a four-plat *parterre à l'Angloise* at Lowther Hall, Westmorland (see fig. 243).

THE QUEST FOR PROSPECT

Although the great walled rectangle was adhered to, further ways were found of opening up vistos. As discussed in Chapter Four, iron grates became popular during the 1680s, in the front wall of forecourts, in *demi-lunes* beyond the parterre and let into walls on cross-axes. The supports were often brick or stone piers with ball finials. In one unique case, Aqualate Hall, Staffordshire, Edwin Skrymsher, who had studied at Trinity College, Oxford, topped his piers with thirteen busts in imitation of the Sheldonian Theatre (fig. 114). About 1695 Celia Fiennes encountered the grates at Broadlands: 'the Gardens are walled in . . . severall places with

---

113   View from Buckingham House, depicted in *A Prospect of St James's Park* (1752), a print based on a drawing of 1736 by Jacques Rigaud. This shows the paved forecourt made by the Duke of Buckingham with a central octagon bason with seahorse fountain; beyond is the lime walk planted across the park at the Restoration, and to the right is the canal that led to Whitehall Palace.

114   'N.N. West Prospect of Aqualate House' by Michael Burghers, 1686. The heads atop the pillars in the iron palisade mimic those at the Sheldonian Theatre in Oxford.

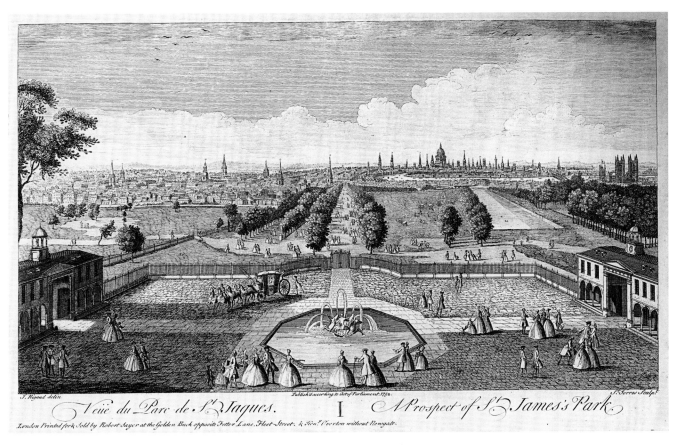

J. Rigaud delin.   Publish'd according to Act of Parliament. 1752.   J. Torres Sculp.

Veüe du Parc de St. Jaques.   I   A Prospect of St. James's Park.

London Printed for & Sold by Robert Sayer at the Golden Buck opposite Fetter Lane, Fleet-Street, & Hen.r Overton without Newgate.

To the Worpl.l the
Learned and ingenious Gent.
EDWIN SKRYMSHER of
AQUALATE Esq.r
This 20 Table being ye N.N. West
Prospect of AQUALATE House,
as a thankfull aknowledgment
of his singular favours
is gratefully dedicated
by R.P. & D.

M. Burghers delin. et sculp.

open grates to look through'.[66] In the case of two 1710s examples, Westbury and Cannons, the grates were made as much for the view inwards as outwards, inviting travellers to have a glimpse of the impressive scene inside.[67]

The next innovation in ironwork was the decorative wrought-iron gate, generally replacing the wooden gate between the piers. In the 1670s French artisans mastered the art of what Celia Fiennes referred to as 'carved' ironwork.[68] One of the first examples in England was that of the early 1680s at Patshull, described as 'the many stately gates of iron-work curiously painted and guilt'.[69] Patshull was close to areas famous for its early iron industry, but these gates probably did not compare to the beautiful *repoussée* work, which was the technique of hammering cold sheet iron on a bed of pitch to achieve a mild relief suitable for decorative elements such as masks and leaves. This was developed by the Gautier family and by Jean Tijou. The iron bars for such works, incidentally, were generally imported from Sweden.

Tijou came to England about 1686 and was for twenty years foremost in decorative ironwork. Evelyn noted 'the Yron Gate . . . wrought in flowers' at Castle Ashby in 1688,[70] and Fiennes described the 'door of iron, carv'd the finest I ever saw, all sorts of leaves flowers figures birds beast wheate in the Carving' that she saw at Burghley.[71] At Hampton Court, Tijou's greatest commission, he was asked to make a fabulously expensive 'iron fence' with twelve decorative panels and three gates to enclose the Fountain Garden from the House Park (fig. 115).[72] Other Tijou

gates include those at Cholmondeley, paid for in 1695 (fig. 116), at Wimpole, which were identical to one of his published designs, and at Wanstead.

A number of *demi-lune* grates, as at Cassiobury, were wider than the walk they revealed, and required supports, as forecourt palisades usually did. Iron grates did not comprise the complete side of a garden area till 1688, however, when Wren set one up between summerhouses atop the river wall to the Thames at the new Chelsea Hospital (see fig. 97). Similar but longer lengths of ironwork were installed to allow views over parkland in the 1690s at Badminton (fig. 117). Chatsworth acquired two sets of railings in about 1694, one beyond the other, enabling the vista from London's great parterre to be continued southwards (see fig. 95). However, these examples were in 1701 eclipsed by the extended 'iron fence' at Hampton Court, which by 1702 enclosed the Pavilion Terrace.[73]

Antoine-Joseph Dezallier d'Argenville's *La Théorie et la pratique du jardinage* described how *grilles* had been dispensed with in France where there was lower ground or a ditch outside a dropped section of a wall. In the words of John James's 1712 translation, 'At present we frequently make Thorough-Views, call'd *Ah, Ah*, which are Openings in the Walls, without Grills, to the very Level of the Walks, with a large and deep Ditch at the Foot of them, lined on both Sides to sustain the Earth, and preventing the getting over'.[74] The device made the boundary invisible 'et fait crier ah ah, dont ils ont pris le nom'. One of the book's plates showed how 'the End of this Terrass is terminated by an Opening, which the French call a Claire-voïe, or an Ah, Ah' (see fig. 154).[75]

The English had timidly been using *claire-voies* already for some years, without going so far as to drop the wall right down to the ground. At Newby in the early 1690s there were short sections of parapet between piers at the ends of the garden terrace. At Levens in 1693 a bastion topped by a waist-high iron rail projected outside the line of the wall with a ditch outside (see fig. 98),[76] and at Fairford a few years later the same arrangement could be seen at the parterre's baskethandle (fig. 118).[77] The idea was repeated more spectacularly in 1700 at the grand half-circle overlooking the Thames at the south end of the Broad Walk at Hampton Court.[78] At Wanstead in 1701 the east perimeter of the circular bowling

---

115 One of twelve panels (this one with a thistle centrepiece) from the Tijou screen at the river end of the Privy Garden, Hampton Court, erected in 1689. Originally commissioned for the screen towards the House Park in 1689, the panels were set up in the Privy Garden in 1701/2, allowing a view of the Thames from the state apartments. Removed in 1731, they were returned in 1901, and restored and gilded in the 2000s.

116 The White Gates at Cholmondeley Hall, Cheshire, by Jean Tijou. Formerly in the forecourt of the old house, they were repositioned close to the modern castle in the nineteenth century and were restored in the 2000s.

117   A bird's-eye painting of Badminton House from the north by Thomas Smith, *c.*1710. It illustrates how in the late 1660s the first Duke of Beaufort had regularised the house, gardens, orchards and village into a huge rectangle, with *demi-lunes* on three of the sides; on the fourth side was the forecourt giving onto the park lawn. To the west (left) he planted a four-acre wilderness of elms with mazes. Before he died in 1699 the Duke had planted numerous further avenues and erected an iron fence on the north side of the wilderness (far left). The second Duke's work included refashioning the parterre into a conventional *parterre à l'Angloise*, reworking the interiors of the wilderness quarters, and bringing the tally of fountains up to nine.

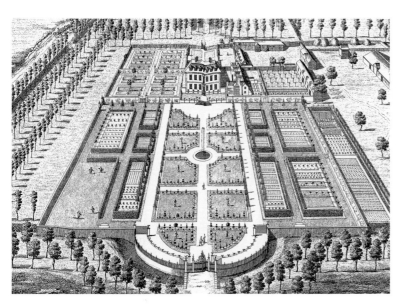

Peripheral canals were dug between the 1690s and the 1710s, but they tended to be totally enclosed within the garden area, and to have had iron fences beyond the water. This appears to have been the case with those at Boughton, and with the canalisation of the Roding at Wanstead soon after 1706, the canal by the temple at Wrest soon after 1709,[81] and the canal around the Fountain Garden at Hampton Court in 1710.[82]

Although the English sought a prospect of the countryside beyond the garden, adherence to the walled rectangle meant that this was achieved largely through terracing within the walls combined with gates and grates on the axes. They tried, but seemed cautious about, such French devices as the *grille*, *claire-voie*, and wet ditch.

PARTERRES AND WILDERNESSES

Sir William Temple advocated *plates-bandes* (flower borders), *jets d'eau* (fountains) and figures (statues) to enliven the parterre:

> The part of your Garden next your House (besides the Walks that go round it) should be a Parterre for Flowers, or Grass-plots bordered with Flowers; or if, according to the newest mode, it be cast all into Grass-plots and Gravel Walks, the driness of these should be relieved with Fountains, and the plainness of those with Statues; otherwise, if large, they have an ill effect upon the Eye.[83]

The English parterre remained the traditional four grass plats, but enlivened with flower borders they became simple versions of what the French were calling the *parterre à l'Angloise*. *Broderie* designs were found at Bretby and then Hampton Court, but overall *broderie* was scarce. Probably there were never more than twenty examples of it in the whole of England.[84]

The term *compartiment* had new applications in French theory and practice. They were still the parts of a parterre that needed to be seen all together for full effect, but now they could be irregular and fit together like jigsaw pieces. Le Blond showed borders in the form of scrolls canting in opposite directions off short straights, described as 'Scroll-work', and running across the in-work between

118   This detail of Fairford House, Gloucestershire, drawn and engraved by Johannes Kip, c.1708, shows Samuel Barker's new gardens, made probably after 1706, when he acquired his wife's fortune, but before his death in 1708. The layout was highly organised, as was the tradition, divided into thirds, with the *parterre à l'Angloise* in ten plats, with borders with shaped yews and smaller evergreens, and with central figures; the outer thirds had hedged kitchen garden quarters and a bowling green. The baskethandle was given an elaborate ironwork gate on axis and low palisades to either side with a ditch outside; this was the English compromise version of the French *claire-voie*.

green was a combination of iron rail and gates on axis, probably by Tijou, and *claire-voies* with the wall at waist height along the arcs to the sides (see figs 149a and b).

John James described the French use of 'wet ditches', which were canals around the perimeter of a garden, essentially a flooded version of the *claire-voie*.[79] Occasionally, as at Hampton Court, Herefordshire, water formed the boundary of a garden in England (fig. 119). Such garden canals seem to have carried French connotations. Having seen the gardens at Hinchingbrook, flanked by a canal, John Percival observed in 1701: 'They are order'd much after the French fashion being Sorounded on one Side by a Canal w^ch: hinders no prospect as generally a wall does.'[80]

opposite *plates bandes*, forming a 'Parterre of Compartiments'.[85] The first of the few examples of scrollwork in England appears to have been at Ragley about 1683 (see fig. 88) and Melton Constable, Norfolk, shortly after. They were comparatively restrained, with more compass-strokes and straights and looser scrolls than those in French pattern-books.

The introduction of flower borders necessitated edging on both sides, generally of 'Dutch box', to prevent intermixing of soil or gravel.[86] The border would be slightly raised in the centre into an 'ass's back'. Evergreen clipped shrubs would be lined out down the middle of the border, leaving the sloping sides for planting with annuals and bulbs.[87] A thin strip, or *allée*, of inert material, usually white sand or shells, would separate the cut edge of the grass from the inner box edge of the border.

The usual larger evergreens were the yew (*Taxus baccata*) and the golden holly (*Ilex aquifolium* 'Aureamarginata') that Worlidge had so admired. As for yew, 'our modern Planters have brought into our Gardens to adorn our Walks, the Eugh Tree'.[88] In 1706 Evelyn looked back on his experiments with yew 50 years before, and claimed that he could '(without vanity) be said to have been the first which brought it into fashion' for hedges and pyramids as a 'succedaneum to Cypress'.[89] Especially after the death of so many cypresses in the fierce winter of 1683–4, alternating yew pyramids and golden holly globes were the general pattern for the taller clipped shrubs in élite gardens. Interspersed between them would be savin (*Juniperus sabinus tamariscifolia*) and other lower, clipped evergreens.

There were some variations from this norm, whereby rare and expensive trees or unusual shapes could give special effect. Hence,

119 *The South East Prospect of Hampton Court in Herefordshire* by Leonard Knyff, 1699. Lord Coningsby, financially buoyed by being Paymaster-General in Ireland, created these gardens with the help of George London from 1692. Being on the valley floor, the boundaries to the south and east, even a baskethandle, could be canals; another point of interest was the oval bowling green between evergreen spandrels, a device first seen at Danvers's house in Chelsea.

120 A bird's-eye view of Denham Place, Middlesex, from the west, c.1705. The house and pavilion over the canalised stream dated from Restoration times, but the gardens shown here were predominantly Sir Roger Hill's creation of the 1690s. The gate piers with lead figures aloft, the extravagant ironwork at the entrance, and the quantity of statuary in evidence are noteworthy; the garden with lozenge paths and shaped yews is extraordinary. Across the canal were kitchen quarters and fruit trees within hedges.

for example, at the Privy Garden at Hampton Court in 1701 there were, at strategic positions, eight pyramid hollies, four pyramid phillyreas, four round-headed alaternus and four shaped yews.[90] 'Shaped yews' were those cut into tiered and other complex forms. An extraordinary collection was assembled at Denham Park, Middlesex, in about 1692 (fig. 120).

A variation on the *parterre à l'Angloise* was to cut a pattern out of the turf, often dispensing with the flower borders, clipped shrubs and all, thus composing a pattern in grass and sand alone. This treatment, explained London and Wise, 'of Angles of several Forms, Squares, Circles, Semi-circles, Ovals, and Branch-works; all which compos'd together the *French* call *Gazon coupé*, and we Cut-works in Grass'.[91] *Gazons coupés* had been infrequent in France, although in the late 1660s the Parterre de Latone at Versailles was turf cut into scallop shells and scrolls, and the Parterre de l'Orangerie of about 1680 was more of a strapwork design in sand alleys.[92] Within a few years there was an example at Bretby between the garden front and a terrace (see fig. 102), and there was a strapwork example as the principal parterre at Belton (see fig. 166). The turf of the new south parterre being made at this time at Chatsworth was also in cutwork, though, unusually, it also had a flower border. The most splendid cutwork of all was the design that replaced a *parterre à l'Angloise* at Longleat in the late 1690s (see fig. 93).

SCULPTURE AND WATER

Figures were bought for Ragley about 1679, by when a great influx was under way. Of the 69 gardens depicted by Knyff and Kip, 39 had figures. It can be surmised that about 100 gardens had them at William III's death. Some high-status places can be cited without figures by 1700, but often such gardens had been made soon after the Restoration, when statuary was scarce. Whereas in Italy, and to a lesser extent France, figures might well collectively give a political message, there are no known cases in the seventeenth century of English collectors imbuing figures with a meaning beyond, for example, considering it appropriate to place a figure of Flora in the flower garden or Neptune in the fountain. Even at Hampton Court, William III's selection does not appear to have been politically inspired.

Lead castings had been imported from the Low Countries, but by the 1680s some were being made in London. John van Nost, originally from the Low Countries, and apprenticed to another Dutch sculptor in England, Arnold Quellin, became adept at metal casting, producing bronze and lead pieces in competition with imported ones. When Quellin died in 1686 Nost took over the business, and developed a famous yard in the Haymarket specialising in figures and urns in lead.

Only exceptionally were marble figures imported, such as those for the Hampton Court Privy Garden in 1701. A few stone carvers who had been employed on tomb monuments and architectural embellishment turned their hand to figures. The usual material was native stone, especially Portland stone, for the figures as well as the pedestals. The most prominent carver supplying stone garden figures was Caius Cibber, born in Denmark, but who had worked in Italy and the Low Countries before arriving in London in about 1660. He supplied seven stone figures to Belvoir in about 1680.[93] The next year he made a figure of Charles II for King's Square in Soho (see fig. 61), and in 1685 went on to Thoresby, Nottinghamshire. Two years later he made two sphinxes, a triton for the fountain, a figure of Flora and other pieces for Chatsworth.

Perhaps the earliest urns in English gardens were the 'large stone vases' that Lord Coleraine is said to have brought back to Longford Castle from Italy in 1680.[94] The rounded faces of urns provided an opportunity for relief carving and by the 1680s there were fine examples in Dutch gardens, such as Hans Willem Bentinck's Zorgvliet.[95] Probably at the suggestion of Bentinck, two exquisite pairs of urns and vases were carved in marble by Cibber and Edward Pearce for Hampton Court in 1690. Pearce, one of the best of the native-born carvers, had been responsible for the very fine floral panels on the piers at Hamstead Marshall in 1673. In 1694 he made a new base for Arethusa, originally from Somerset House (see Chapter Three), and then at the Hampton Court Privy Garden (see fig. 128).[96]

Figurative sculpture adorned the fountains of Versailles, much being installed between 1675 and 1685.[97] William of Orange had a triton fountain at Het Loo in the 1680s.[98] The English were quick to imitate. About 1680 a dolphin fountain was set up at Longford Castle (see fig. 14), and a seahorse sculpture was working at Patshull.[99] A triton fountain arrived in Chatsworth's flower garden in 1687, and a seahorse in the great parterre in the 1690s.[100] At Hampton Court, Herefordshire, a Neptune sculpture was added to a large bason in about 1699.[101] However, the number of such extravagant pieces was always small. Simple *jets d'eau* were much more common, generally being placed at the crossing point at the centre of parterres, though they were sometimes found in fore-courts. From about 1680 and into the 1690s the number of new *jets d'eau* increased greatly.

Octangular or rectangular ponds were being admitted to gardens in small numbers – there was a square one in a walled area at Drayton by about 1680.[102] Roger North considered that a moat 'is a Delicacy the greatest Epicures in Gardening court, and we hear of it by the Name of a Canal'.[103] Many agreed with him, and an explosion of interest in garden basons and canals was under way from about 1680, and at the same time the situations and uses for water became more various. Though usually for purely decorative purposes, some ponds had a function as reservoirs for *jets d'eau*, notably at Hackwood about 1683 (see fig. 219),[104] and the 'Grandytang' at Boughton about 1696 (see fig. 103). The Earl of Portland had a canal serving as a reservoir at Bulstrode shortly after the turn of the century (see fig. 189).

The axial parkland canals in St James's and Hampton Court parks were copied in Wrest Park in the early 1680s (see fig. 86), but rarely elsewhere. It was more common to find smaller versions adorning gardens, often on axis between wildernesses. An early example of this was at the Ranger's Lodge in Windsor Little Park about 1675, and a substantial canal was dug between groves at Melton Constable in about 1685. At Wanstead by about 1701 a canal ran down the middle of the parterre (see fig. 105). The same year at Chatsworth 'a great rock wch Stood within the compass of the garden has been levell'd, & in its place is a canal making 322 yards long 25 broad'. Flanked by lime walks, it led to 'an iron gate thrô which one may see a rude prospect'.[105]

If a valley crossed a garden from side to side, then a cross-canal or 'broad water' would be the more economical possibility. Cross-canals would not necessarily be prominent from the house, but might be discovered upon a perambulation of the garden. At Longleat in 1683 a canal was dug right across the principal parterre (see fig. 92). Former monastic ponds at Newstead, Nottinghamshire, were regularised about 1695 as a central element between the parterre and a grove known as 'Devil's Wood'.[106]

☙

WILDERNESSES

The verticality, or 'relief', of the wilderness came to be seen more frequently at the far end of the parterre but within the great rectangle. Sir William Temple discussed suitable arrangements, his groves being fruit gardens or evergreen trees:

> However, the part next to the House should be open, and no other Fruit but upon the Walls. If this take up one half of the Garden, the other should be Fruit-Trees, unless some Grove for Shade lie in the middle. If it take up a third part only, then the next third may be Dwarf-Trees, and the last Standard Fruit; or else, the Second Part Fruit-trees, and the third all sorts of Winter greens, which provide for all Seasons of the year.[107]

Hence the planting of evergreens remained an option, as when the Duke of Devonshire made two groves of fir trees at the top of his garden in the late 1680s (see fig. 95).

La Théorie et la pratique du jardinage referred to standard high-hedged wildernesses as 'groves of a middle height with tall palisades'.[108] The walks were kept neat by the strong structure of the palisades:

> Palisades, by the Agreeableness of their Verdure, are of the greatest Service in Gardens . . . They serve to inclose and border the Squares of Wood, to divide them from the other Parts of the Garden, and to prevent their being enter'd but by the Walks made for that Purpose.

The English wilderness of the late seventeenth century followed this form. The palisades were generally of hornbeam (*Carpinus betulus*), and over ten feet high, but low enough so that 'the Heads of the trees may be fully seen over them'.[109] The body of the planting could just be elms or other trees.[110] The Hampton Court wilderness had high hornbeam hedges and the quarters were filled with elms, the survivors of which were felled on safety grounds around 1900. Walks were of gravel, though a strip of grass might be kept at the base of the palisades.

Sometimes wildernesses would, for pragmatic reasons, be placed to the side of the house, but having them rising at the far end of the parterre, and for the axis to run through them, was the ideal. The wildernesses at Burghley of 1683 and Belton and Wrest about two years later were examples of these high-hedged geometrical layouts within garden walls, intersected by open walks interspersed by cabinets. French practice was that the trees should 'never arrive to the great Height of the Forest-Trees, scarcely exceeding thirty or forty Foot high'.[111] If necessary, the trees were lopped to ensure that they remained of medium height. This was done at some places in England, but at others the tufts of the forest trees overtopping the palisades were preferred. Not the least of the pleasures of such wildernesses was the contrast between the sheer-sided clipping, denoting control, and the tufts of the ornamental trees disobediently bushing out above them.

Star arrangements of walks were frequent in square wildernesses, and diagonals, or St Andrew's crosses, in rectangles. These simple forms continued in the 1690s, when they were joined by a small number of walks of more interesting geometry, and circular or more complex cabinets. Circular, oval or other curving walks could provide endless loops cutting the straights. When the gardener at Stainborough, Yorkshire, was corresponding with his employer, the Earl of Strafford, in 1713 about trees for a new wilderness, a circular walk of this nature was referred to as a 'verso' walk, presumably with the meaning 'to turn about often' or 'to turn round and round'.[112] The oval carpet walk at Ham House (see fig. 81) of about 1671 was an early sign of this desire for more intricate arrangements. By 1700 Fairlawn, Plaxtol, Kent, was given walks that were pinched in along the axes, and swelled out to cabinets along the diagonals (see fig. 107), and a few years after that the lower part of the gardens at Shardeloes, 'formed out of a morass by Sr William Drake', was given a complex layout with minor walks in circles and cusped curves (fig. 121).[113]

One type of planting that seemed peculiarly English was evergreen spandrels around oval or circular bowling greens, allowing them to fit within a rectilinear walled space and yet to receive the shelter from the planting. Moses Cook's evergreen planting around the oval bowling green at Cassiobury (see fig. 78) was copied at Hampton Court in Herefordshire, where in the 1690s

an oval green was made within spandrels (see fig. 119). Wise unsuccessfully proposed an oval green for Cliveden (see fig. 144), but London's nephew Thomas Ackres made a circular bowling green surrounded by an evergreen grove set with arbours at Knole, for which he had signed a contract in 1710 (see fig. 206).

By these various means the austerity of Commonwealth and Restoration times came to be reversed from the 1680s. The *parterre à l'Angloise* routinely came to incorporate *jets d'eau*, figures and flower borders with low shrubs and alternating yew pyramids and golden holly globes. Great terraces became standard, and side terraces, which also helped the new glories of the parterre to be seen, were introduced. Indeed this was the age of terracing, as *glacis* slopes came to be used in order to extend garden spaces up or down hill. Garden reservoirs, basons and canals were dug in a variety of positions. A wilderness of gravel alleys and high hedges in a tightly geometric layout was often found beyond the parterre but still within the walled enclosure.

The keeping of plants

The last quarter of the seventeenth century was remarkable for the increase in known plants and the attention given to their cultivation. It seems that by then the Puritan reserve respecting ornamental, rather than useful, plants had everywhere been overcome. As John Aubrey wrote:

> I doe believe I may modestly affirme that there is now, 1691, ten times as much gardening about London as there was Anno 1660; and wee have been, since that time, much improved in forreign plants, especially since about 1683, there have been exotick plants brought into England no lesse than seven thousand.[114]

Exotic shrubs, mainly from the Mediterranean, including evergreens such as orange trees, kept in tubs, were imported in this period in large numbers, and required their accompanying greenhouses. In addition, the rapidly expanding world of trade brought hitherto unknown plants of all forms from all climatic

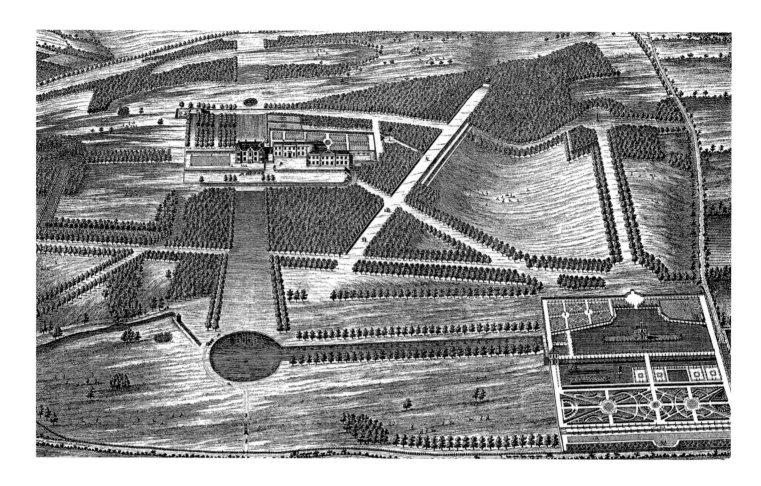

zones. Hence a wealth of plants was acquired from the Ottoman empire, succulents came from the Cape of Good Hope, orchids from forests, and conifers from North America. Meanwhile, florists, arborists and nurserymen had greatly increased the number of cultivated varieties of flowers, fruit and vegetables.

121   This bird's-eye view of Shardeloes House, Buckinghamshire, from the north-east by Badeslade and Toms of *c.*1730 shows several periods of garden development. A lodge was built in the park in Jacobean times; the formal gardens with canals at bottom right (perhaps the site of an earlier house) were 'reclaimed from a morass' *c.*1695; and the wilderness with curved paths was planted a few years later. The vistos from the house and the circular bason were maybe of the 1710s, whilst the park planting, the angled hedged walk up to a small pavilion, and the obelisk were probably by James Gibbs and Charles Bridgeman, *c.*1725.

France remained an important source of flowers and vegetables for England through the seventeenth century, but the Dutch yielded to none in horticulture, and provided many of the essential ingredients of the English garden. Their skills and technology in growing florist flowers and fruit was unsurpassed. The Dutch had trading outposts in many far-flung parts of the world, symbolised by the globe fountains in William III's parterre at Het Loo. By the 1690s the Amsterdam Hortus Botanicus had become the most lavishly stocked in the Low Countries, or indeed the world, surpassing the famous one at Leiden.

Various specialised buildings and areas were required to house this wide range of plants. The influx of tropical plants required special hothouses, or 'stoves'. Hardy flowering plants, including florist flowers, had always best been kept in beds of six to eight feet wide, but the specialist flower gardens of the late seventeenth century were often laid out in ornate arrangements of such beds.

Hardy trees and shrubs were accommodated in the wilderness, and bulbs in the open grove. Meanwhile, increasing skills and techniques in the productive gardening of fruit and vegetables led to improved designs for the kitchen garden.

GREENHOUSES AND ORANGERIES

By orangery, or 'orangerie', was meant the garden area where the trees would be set out in the warmer months. Their winter home was the 'greenhouse'. These structures usually had a central door through which the plants could be carried in their tubs, and closely spaced south-facing windows. The three other walls had no windows, in order to reduce variations in temperature. Some form of heating would keep frost off the plants. During the 1680s and through to the 1700s many English garden projects incorporated greenhouses. Occasionally an upper storey was added as a bothy for the garden boys, and sometimes a pediment or cupola provided ornament. Talman took the trouble to produce interesting façades for his greenhouses at Chatsworth, Dawley, Dyrham and Wanstead.[115]

The Parterre de l'Orangerie at Versailles of about 1680 was cutwork in grass with the cases ranged along the borders, whilst other French orangeries had *broderie* parterres or St Andrew's cross patterns. *La Théorie et la pratique du jardinage* referred to a form of border 'quite plain, and only sanded, as in the Parterres of Orangery', where the cases stood in the summer.[116] At Squerryes, Kent, by about 1705 there was a small greenhouse and 'greenhouse court' with a large fountain, continuing the practice of such well-enclosed areas (see fig. 156),[117] but many English owners by this time were setting out their tubs atop breast walls or along the parterre's great walk, where visitors could enjoy them most freely. An apron of hardstanding for movement and setting out in front of the greenhouse was convenient, as at Southwick Priory, Hampshire, in the 1690s. At two gardens of the early 1700s, Dyrham and Tring, a canal provided practical centrepieces of garden areas used as orangeries in summer.

The Dutch had meanwhile devised an amphitheatrical form of orangery. Hans Willem Bentinck marshalled his cases into con-

centric semicircles at Zorgvliet about 1676, and then at Heemsteede and Zeist about 1685 circular orangeries with tiers were made around basons.[118] Before the 1680s were out, close copies had been made in England at Bretby (semicircular; see fig. 102) and Stansted (nearly circular; see fig. 29), and an old rectangular garden in the Pond Yard at Hampton Court had been converted to a tiered orangery around a small canal (see fig. 16).

STOVES

Henry Compton, appointed Bishop of London in 1675, was 'one of the first that encouraged the Importation, Raising and Increase of Exotics, in which he was the most curious Man of that time . . . and by the recommendation of Chaplains into foreign Parts had likewise greater Advantages of improving it as any other Gentleman could'.[119] Compton had jurisdiction over the Anglican Church in North America, and had plants, seeds, drawings and specimens sent from the West Indies and Virginia by the Reverend John Banister in the years 1678 to 1692.

At the London end, Compton rejoiced in 'above 1,000 species of Exotic Plants in his Stoves and Gardens' at Fulham Palace. These new plants were distributed to the Physic Garden at Oxford and the Society of Apothecaries' newly established one in Chelsea, and from these places outwards to eager nurserymen and collectors. Compton's gardener, George London, was also, from 1681, in a position to disseminate the bishop's introductions through the Brompton Park nursery.

Other British plant-collecting expeditions included one mounted by John Watts, Curator of the Chelsea Physick Garden, who sent the gardener James Harlow to Virginia in the mid-1680s, and Hans Sloane's journey to Jamaica as physician to the Governor, the Duke of Albemarle, in 1687.[120] Although the Duke died within a year, Sloane remained in Jamaica studying the natural history of the island. He returned to England in 1689 with 800 specimens of Jamaican plants and seeds.

William Darby, nurseryman of Hoxton, north London, was remembered as 'one of the first in England who chose the Culture of Exotic Plants' from about 1677. George Rickets had another

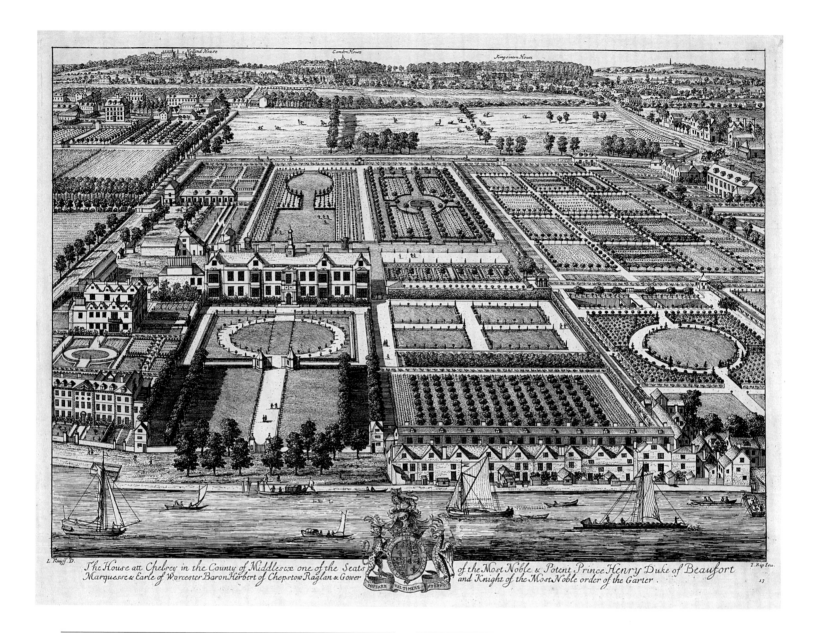

The House att Chelsey in the County of Middlesex one of the Seats of the Most Noble & Potent Prince Henry Duke of Beaufort Marquesse & Earle of Worcester Baron Herbert of Chepstow Raglan & Gower and Knight of the Most Noble order of the Garter.

122   Beaufort House, Chelsea, by Knyff and Kip, c.1700. This is a garden of many phases: once the property of Sir Thomas More, it was extensively remodelled by the Marquess of Winchester in the 1550s and great changes were made by the Duke and Duchess of Beaufort following their acquisition in 1681. The Inner Court was given a carriage sweep and decorated with clipped yews; the Great Garden was remade for the Duchess's collections of trees, shrubs and florist flowers; the sunken area behind the house was lined out with Scots pine, spruce, silver fir, laburnums, laurels, guilder roses, lilacs and other shrubs, leaving a bowling green and a circle referred to as 'the great grass walk'. The sunken area to the east was laid out as a flower garden with an outer hedge of sweet briar, inside which was a rectangular grass walk enclosing four quarters for flowers around a *jet d'eau*; the parlour garden east of the house was laid out in four squares, and the terrace was breached at the house end. Next to it, the fruit area appears to have become also an orangery garden, with innumerable plants in pots down the sides; along the south side a building with 20 windows onto the roadside may have been the Duchess's hothouse.

famous nursery at Hoxton, and his catalogue, printed by Worlidge in the third edition of *Systema Horti-culturae* (1688), showed that Rickets had a selection of 'Housed-Greens, Winter-Greens, Flowering-Shrubs, Flowering-Trees, Flowers, and other curious Plants, as well Exotick as English'.

Amongst the most avid of collectors was the Duchess of Beaufort, evidently a major customer of the Oxford Physic Garden: 'The great Favour she held towards Virtuosos in her own way, I have in several great Instances heard from Monsieurs the Bobarts, both very eminent in Botanick Amusements'.[121] She assembled 750 species from many parts of the globe at Badminton by 1699.[122] She had a second greenhouse at Beaufort House, Chelsea, built against a wall 18 feet high and 110 feet in length (fig. 122).

Heating was essential for keeping exotics from the tropics. Moses Cook related what happened when his employer, the Earl of Essex, received some unknown exotics:

My Lord had thirteen sorts of strange Seeds sent him, as I remember, from Goa; I never saw the like . . . I rais'd ten of the thirteen Sorts, tho some of them lay almost a year in the Ground; but I also must tell you, I lost all my ten sorts the first Winter, but one Sort, and that the second, for want of a Green-house.[123]

Charles Hatton, fired with enthusiasm, wrote to his brother, Viscount Hatton of Kirby Hall: 'I have settled a correspondence with Mr Bobart, and he hath . . . promis'd me some curious plants wch I designe for y^r Lordshippe', warning him, 'w^thout a stove you cannot keepe them'.[124]

Heating greenhouses with braziers or pans of charcoal could generate fumes, which would damage the plants, so stove pipes to carry away the fumes were essential. The Dutch were the technical masters of the greenhouse and its heating in the second half of the century, and greenhouse construction in England owed much to their example. The Roman hypocaust system, of hot air passing through flues in walls and floors, was experimented with. One advantage was that the stove could be tended from outside the greenhouse. The hothouses of Amsterdam and Leiden seem to have been of this form, and at Chelsea in 1685 Evelyn admired

'what was very ingenious the subterranean heate, conveyed by a stove under the Conservatory, which was all Vaulted with brick; so as he leaves the doores & windowes open in the hardest frosts, secluding onely the snow &c'.[125]

The Dutch developed this idea further in the 1680s, combining underfloor heating with 'glass cases' above, which were very efficient in trapping the sun's rays. This was the idea behind the three 'glass cases' at Hampton Court built by a specialist Dutch carpenter, Hendrick Floris, in 1689.[126] Charles Hatton described these glass cases as 'much better contrived and built than any other in England'. They also attracted the attention of the Duchess of Beaufort, who had been making enquiries through John Bale (or Ball), a servant of the Duke's at Beaufort House. In September 1692 he was able to report that the Queen had three hothouses in a line, and each was 55 feet in length. They were backed by a wall, behind which was a shed 'to shelter those y^t make ye fires under ye stove'. Each had '4 fire plases to each of wch is a grate in ye forme of a little wagon'. The 'wagon' had four wheels, and 'when ye fire is made in it & Burns Clear it is Runn into ye Valt' by means of rails and pushed or pulled by 'an Iron Crooke'. Meanwhile 'all ye front is glass windows, of wch there are 14 doors to each'.[127]

Precious and exotic plants were often grown in decorated flowerpots so that they could be brought inside the house to be displayed. Although frequently earthenware, the pots could be of Delftware, lead or stone, and they came in a rich variety of shapes and sizes.[128] Flowerpots were not common in Commonwealth or early Restoration times, but became the height of fashion from about 1680. Large fluted pots formed the corners of the *parterre à l'Angloise* at Longleat in about 1683 (see fig. 92). William Pierrepont, a supporter of William III, had over 50 decorative pots, as well as a number of the more common sort, set out along the breast wall around his parterre at Pierrepont House, Nottingham, soon after 1689 (fig. 123). At Burley-on-the-Hill breast walls a few feet high were built of brick in 1697 with buttresses every ten feet for flowerpots.[129]

William and Mary themselves had a huge collection of exotics in ornamental pots at Honselaarsdijk that was transported to

Hampton Court in 1692 and kept in the glass cases there.[130] The number of both flowerpots and tubs bought for Hampton Court between 1689 and 1702 was exceptionally large.[131] In addition, a number of lead flowerpots, painted to resemble stone, or perhaps gilt, were supplied for the stop pedestals – those at the tops and bottoms – of the steps in the Privy Garden in about 1700.

FLOWER GARDENS

An aspect of the increasing French influence upon English gardens in the 1680s was a passion for flowers, and this gave rise to numerous flower borders surrounding English grass plats. Enthusiasts might also create specialised flower gardens close to the house. The traditional florists' flowers were bred to produce a bewildering number of varieties: tulips in broken colours, gillyflowers (carnations), hyacinths, anemonies, auriculas, ranunculuses and narcissi. The older species bulbs and annuals, including crown imperials and species of *Crocus*, *Cyclamen*, *Iris*, lilies, Marvel of Peru (*Mirabilis jalapa*), pansies, forget-me-nots and various kinds of *Amaranthus*, were being supplemented by the new plants coming in from various parts of the world. Queen Mary and the Duchess of Beaufort were known for their collections of both exotic plants and florist flowers. The Queen had an 'auricula quarter' at Hampton Court, whilst the Duchess had her collections of auriculas and polyanthus, as well as an extensive collection of striped plants built up in the 1690s.[132]

English plant lovers still often bought tulips from Paris until the end of the century. Meanwhile, nurserymen strove to meet the

123 Pierrepont House, Nottingham, *c.*1705. This bird's-eye painting shows a town-house garden belonging to a branch of the Pierrepont family. It had revetted terraces on all sides, and wooden steps at the centres of each; the highest terrace, by the house, had balustrading, and elsewhere there was a low parapet wall. The base of the garden was an open knot for flowers, similar to designs published by Leonard Meager from 1670, centred around a large figure; 78 flower pots were set out on the balustrade and parapet walls.

demand for the large quantities of flowers required for borders. William Lucas's catalogue of 1677 advertised the seeds of over 70 different flowers.[133] Another of the Hoxton nurseries was specialising in anemonies in 1691; this was Mr Pearson's, 'accounted very honest'.

However, the most prized flowers were often the rarest, and these might be displayed in specialised flower gardens. The usual position was to the side of the forecourt, house or Best Garden. At Het Loo, William and Mary had their private gardens, where flowers figured prominently, under each side of the palace. Switzer implied that the tradition persisted twenty years later when suggesting that side courts 'if they are adjoining to the private Apartments of Ladies and Gentlemen' should be set out with 'Flowers, and Edgings, of Thyme, &c. according to the common Method'.[134]

The exact form of the beds is often unclear, but traditional open knots from Jacobean times clearly still had a place at small country houses such as Westbury Court, Gloucestershire. However, more interesting designs suggestive of flowers or foliage were tried, an early example being at Wimbledon Manor (see fig. 76), and a later one the Privy Garden at Hampton Court (see fig. 128). In the 1680s the French 'parterres de pieces coupées pour les fleurs' inspired the flower garden at Chatsworth made by London in 1687; it consisted of scrolls and other devices around an apsidal-ended bason (see fig. 95). About 1707 Secretary Johnston had a French-style flower garden under his side windows at Twickenham.[135] Bulbs could be planted in open groves and wildernesses, but, with the increasing use of *glacis* slopes, a common practice became to set out bulbs in lines and patterns on banks where the mowing could be left till later.

SHRUBS

Open groves, in which the *banquettes* were purposefully kept chest-high so that the interiors could be displayed, continued in popularity. Viscount Hatton, guided by his brother Charles, had an extensive grove at Kirby, started in 1689, in which, it was said in 1712, he had collected every known species of tree and shrub.[136]

This plantation may have been exceptional, but it was not unique in accommodating a wide range of trees and shrubs. The early 1700s open grove beyond the parterre at Wanstead appears to have been an example of the traditional way of shrub planting (see figs 149a and b).

When the flowering shrubs were allowed to grow, such a grove would develop into a high-hedged wilderness, with the body of the planting being mixed, using ornamental or exotic trees instead of the more standard elms or other forest trees. A contract drawn up in 1699 by the second Viscount Townshend for making a wilderness at Raynham specified the garden-maker agreed to plant the quarters 'with yᵉ sevˡˡ. Varietys of Flowering Trees Undermentioned yᵉ walkes to be laid all with Sand and yᵉ Center places to be planted with Spruce and Silver Firs'.[137]

The trees included lime, horse chestnut, wild service, laburnum, Guelder rose, lilac, bladder senna, wild olive and conifers. Bare stems of trees and shrubs were considered unsightly, and when the shrubs overtopped the hedge the logic would be to allow the hedge to grow higher to continue to hide the stems. Enjoyment of the shrubs could then be from a mown 'close walk' within the quarter, reached through narrow gaps in the high hedge.

THE KITCHEN GARDEN AND HOTBEDS

Evelyn was a great promoter of kitchen gardening as translator of Jean-Baptiste de la Quintinie's *Instruction pour les jardins fruitiers et potagers* (1690) and author of *Acetaria: A Discourse of Sallets* (1699). In the latter he recommended to those who aspired to a long life to eat 'salladings' and raw fruit. Sir William Temple's readers, who may have thought of raw fruit more as a purgative, might have been alarmed at his boast that he could eat 30 to 40 cherries a day or 'a like proportion of Strawberries, white Figs, soft Peaches or Grapes' without ill-effect.[138]

Moses Cook had observed that 'An Oval is no ill Figure for a Garden', and reported that he had made an oval kitchen garden at Cassiobury.[139] Elsewhere, however, kitchen quarters were preferred square or rectangular, with a cross of alleys and a peripheral one, though they could be any shape necessary to fit spaces

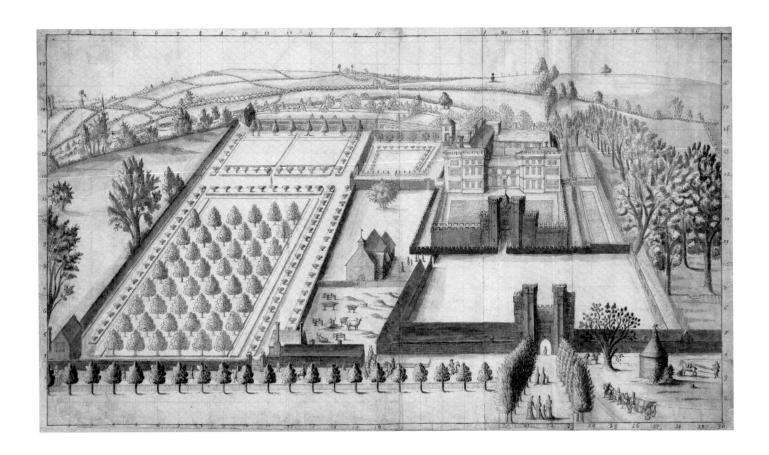

available. At this time most kitchen gardens were integral with the walled gardens around the house.

It appears that places remote from cities often had large kitchen gardens, whereas those close to markets, especially around London, did not need them. A glance through *Britannia Illustrata* (1707) identifies many of the new kitchen gardens of the quarter century beforehand. They were getting larger: particularly impressive examples were planned or made at Combe Abbey, Lowther, Cholmondeley (see fig. 169) and Castle Howard (see fig. 197), some of which were associated with George London.[140] Kitchen gardens had wall fruit, but they were not intended for fruit trees in the open ground.

Until William and Mary's reign there had been a distinction between the kitchen garden, a mostly utilitarian area, and the fruit garden, a part-ornamental one. The fruit garden was often close to the parlour, best garden or bowling green, whilst the kitchen garden was preferably more hidden from view. However,

the introduction of dwarf fruit trees gave more scope for a kitchen garden to include fruit as well as vegetables (fig. 124). The perimeter alleys were given a border about six feet wide towards the cultivated ground, in which were 'dwarf' trees. Thomas Langford, steward at Gorhambury, Hertfordshire, wrote in 1681 of dwarfs that

These *Trees* have been of late much affected and coveted, because they are of special advantage for Table-fruit, (whether

124 Lullingstone Castle, Kent, *c.*1700, a sketch done for Sir Percyval Hart, aspiring politician, for a print that was never engraved. The Harts expanded the garden by new northern gardens behind the church; to the east (top) was a kitchen garden, to the west (bottom) a fruit garden; the borders around both were stocked with dwarf fruit trees trained into goblets.

Pears, Apples, Plums (or Cherries) being but of low Stature, and may be *planted* in the *borders* of *Garden-walks*, without doing any thing else there about them any prejudice, by overshadowing them.[141]

Being grafted onto dwarfing rootstock, they did not impede growing conditions in the quarters, and were low enough for most picking to be done from the ground.

The alternatives for laying out a kitchen garden were now many. The old hedged quarters could still be enclosed by hedges or railings supporting soft fruit, the hedges could be replaced by espaliers of fruit trees trained onto lattices of ash in the latest Dutch manner, or there could be no physical barrier at all, just a border set with dwarfs at intervals. Sometimes, as at Hatherop Castle, Gloucestershire, the dwarfs were interplanted with gooseberries or blackcurrants, giving a kitchen-garden version of the *plate bande* in the parterre. A kitchen garden no longer needed to be hidden away; it seems to have been a London and Wise trademark to make them partly ornamental. Some were set out with diagonals, some combined elements of the parterre with the cultivated areas, and other experiments gave rise to a great variety in layout, as seen in Knyff and Kip's prints.

Hotbeds were for the cultivation of plants from tropical countries that needed warmth to force germination, growth or flowering, and were situated adjacent to the kitchen garden. The plants in question included melons, cucumbers, green amaranths, Spanish pepper and the roots of passion flower. The required moist heat from below was generated by rotting manure. Moveable frames or 'mellon-Glasses', without bottoms and with a glass top sloping south to protect plants against the wind and catch the sun's rays, were placed on top.

Although popular in the Low Countries, the English were at first apprehensive about the unwholesome heat, and also the unnaturalness of forcing 'Praecoces' such as early salads, asparagus, and other 'forward Plants and Roots for the wanton Palate' on a heap of fermenting dung, 'which being corrupt in the original, cannot but produce malignant and ill effects to those who feed upon them'. London appears to have had no qualms, though, and

installed hotbeds at Burghley House about 1683 (see fig. 91) and Hampton Court in 1689. Thereafter hotbeds were not unusual adjuncts to the more ambitious kitchen gardens.

William III at war

The Whigs arranged for William of Orange to accede to the thrones of England, Scotland and Ireland in 1689 because he had proved to be a dogged adversary of Louis XIV. William was a military hero, but more importantly he was engaged in a war of wills, defending Protestant values against Catholicism and the tyranny of absolutism. A Protestant king needed to show that he was a bulwark against Europe's leading Catholic one. Parliament voted large sums in order to support William's majesty, including an immensely expensive project to create a major European palace for him at Hampton Court. The Nine Years' War against Louis XIV cost the English nation the stupefying figure of £40 million. The £83,000 spent on the royal gardens in his reign might thus not seem excessive when their role in statecraft is appreciated.[142]

HAMPTON COURT

William III was much involved in the decisions regarding Hampton Court, as he had been in his palaces and gardens in the Low Countries (see fig. 101). He had already built up a gardens organisation for his residences there, and he imported many of the individuals to England in order to give him the standard of care that he was used to. The central figure was Hans Willem Bentinck, William's closest friend and superintendent of his Dutch gardens. William 'doe Erect an Office, to be called the Superintendency of all their Gardens, and doe Give the same to Wm. Earl of Portland wth a Salary of 200£ a Year'.[143] His deputy was George London.

Wren's initial plans for Hampton Court, drawn up in early 1689, were ambitious: a complete rebuilding except for the Great Hall. The Great Avenue, aligned on the Great Hall, and the Long Water avenue east of the palace were to become the principal axes. Reviving the original idea for the Great Avenue as the main approach, he planned a 'Great Courtyard' suitable for a vast concourse of coaches. Entrance to the palace would have been under the Great Hall to an Entrance Court, on the eastern side of which there was to be a domed Council Chamber and the King's and Queen's apartments to either side. Wren employed Nicholas Hawksmoor as his assistant from about 1680, and often gave him the tasks of sketching out the courts and gardens.

Between them, Wren and Hawksmoor produced numerous schemes for Hampton Court's gardens, parterres and avenues. Hawksmoor was paid £10 for 'taking the plans of the gardens and out parts of Hampton Court for Mr. London'.[144] One plan shows how the gardens would have been altered (fig. 125). The Old Orchard was to disappear in favour of the Great Courtyard, and the tiltyard was to go as well. The old Privy Garden, the Mount Garden and gardens alongside the Water Gallery, dating from Henry VIII's time, were to be combined into a single parterre, attached to the King's apartments, with two fountains and extending to the Thames. Because of the association between kingship and territorial possessions, this was an important point for William in an iconographical sense. The Pond Yard area was to be reworked into further parterres. On the east front the whole area within the semicircle of limes was to become the 'Great Parterre', one of Europe's largest, and to have a central fountain. Narrow canals were to run around the parterre inside the limes and then north and south along the lateral walks.

Radial avenues were to focus on Queen Mary's study at the centre of the east front. Standing at the exact centre of this room, the Long Water and these radials corresponded to each of her three windows. Most likely the radials were conceived by Wren, and planted early.[145] The Kingston Avenue was aligned on the spire of Kingston church, and the Ditton Avenue was planted at the same angle to the south. A cross avenue ran past the end of the Long Water and intersected the other avenues.

In the event, the proposals for rebuilding were scaled down to a rebuilding of the state apartments, but then work went ahead rapidly. Parts of the general plan for the gardens had to be rethought too. With the abandonment of the Great Courtyard,

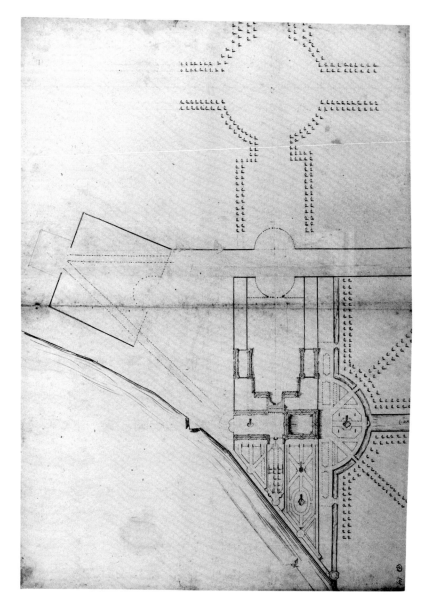

125   Sketch of a general plan by the Office of Works for the rebuilding of Hampton Court palace, in Nicholas Hawksmoor's hand, 1689. The axes north and east, established by Charles II, would have been the basis of the layout; the approach would have been from the north, reaching a vast parade in front of the Great Hall. The Privy Garden and Pond Yard would have been redesigned to achieve a connection to the Thames, and a fountain garden was planned within the half-moon of walks to the east. These ideas were not forgotten, but drastic compromises had to be made by George London in revising the gardens from 1690.

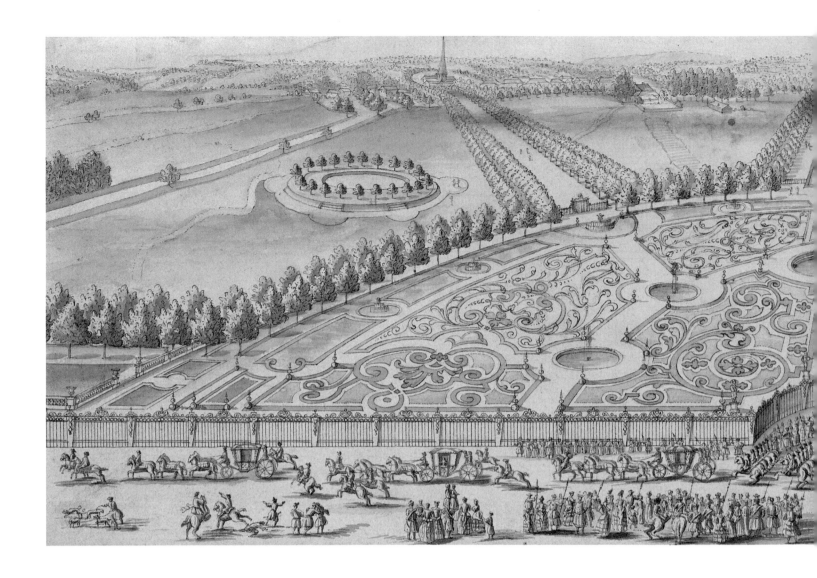

126   A design drawn by Daniel Marot for the Great Garden, Hampton Court, 1689, showing how he would have filled the half-moon to the east with a parterre. He thought that a concourse was needed on the east front, so that the Great Parterre would have been detached from the palace's other gardens behind an elaborate *grille*. The design was based on two concentric rings of *jets d'eau*, consisting of one large bason, ten others, and two *buffets d'eau*; inside the inner ring he would have had cutwork with scrolls running through, and in the outer ring *parterre de broderie*. When made, the cutwork and the *broderie* were switched, to bring the *broderie* forward to be under the windows of the palace, and the concourse was not wanted, as visitors continued to arrive by the traditional way via the west front.

the Old Orchard had a reprieve. The Tiltyard walls remained, the space divided up by new walls to become a kitchen garden of six quarters. The old Pond Yard survived, though it was adapted to be suitable for Queen Mary's plant collections.

A greenhouse was intended on the ground floor of the south front of the state apartments, and this and the Privy Garden thus became intimately linked; the state apartment's axis was that of the garden's, whilst the garden was to be the orangery to the greenhouse. The garden would need widening to match the new width of the front and also to enable higher side terraces to be thrown up. For the time being however, it was the works yard, so had to await its remodelling. Hence the Mount Garden and Water

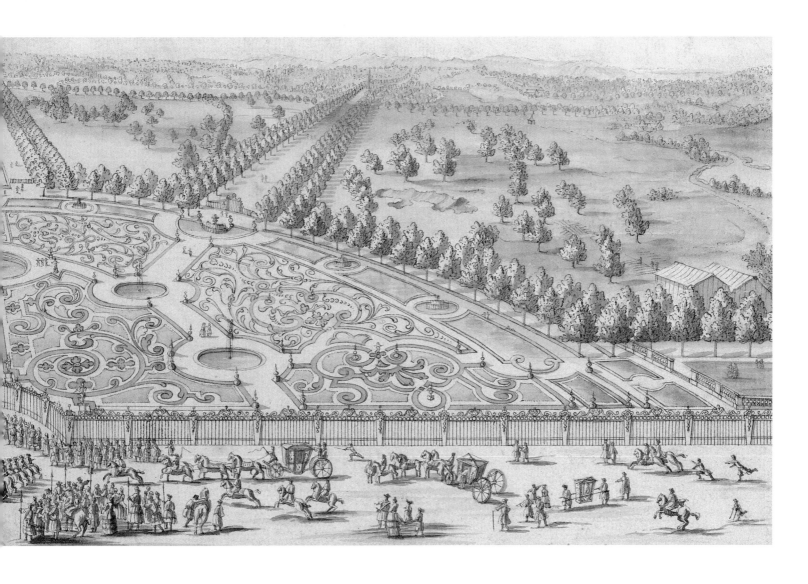

Gallery survived for the while, the latter being fitted up as a temporary apartment for Queen Mary. The only area where plans could fully go ahead was in the Great Parterre.

A Letter of Privy Seal in May 1689 required the Treasury to supply Portland with money. Work on levelling must soon have been under way. Wren preferred a fairly simple grass and gravel layout for the Great Parterre but before this could be fixed William brought over a favourite architect of his, Daniel Marot, 'Architecte du Prince d' Orange', from the Low Countries.[146] A view by Marot, dated August 1689, illustrated his conception (fig. 126). It was to have an inner semicircle containing *gazon coupé*, and an outer arc with *broderie*, divided by walks extending the radials into the parterre. Every intersection of walks was to have a *jet d'eau*, and within the semicircle he designed eight more instead of a canal, making thirteen in all, after which the garden was known as the 'Great Fountain Garden'. The Longford River was repaired, and 3,123 yards of elm pipe were laid from the Conduit House in Bushy Park to the parterre, where a network of lead pipes supplied the fountains. This scheme, with the *gazon coupé* and *broderie* reversed, added superior French flair to the already grandiose ideas of William's official architects at the Office of Works. This huge garden became the general concourse for courtiers, petitioners and sightseers, allowing the Privy Garden to be reserved for the monarchs' personal use.

The Old Orchard still needed recasting. A new arrangement appeared, with diagonals, alleys between mid-points of the sides, a pinched oval walk intersecting all these straight ones, and a number of cabinets (see frontispiece). The overall design was very similar to one of Marot's published designs for a *bosquet*, so his hand is likely here too (fig. 127). In addition, two semicircular turf mazes, called 'Troy Towns' (a term explained below), either side of an alley, were incorporated into the arrangement, and a unicursal maze was set out within the awkward trapezoidal shape of one of the quarters.[147]

In the seventeenth century most mazes were hedged. One at Tothill, in Westminster, had been made about the start of the century, and John Aubrey remarked in 1687 that it was still 'much frequented in summer-time in fair afternoons'.[148] A pair of mazes was made at Wrest in this decade, one being in yew, the other in blackthorn (see fig. 86), but in general they appear to have been regarded disdainfully. As Switzer was to observe, mazes 'seem to be calculated for an inferior Class of People'.[149] On the other hand, some foreign designers remained faithful to them. André Mollet illustrated a couple of designs for mazes,[150] and Louis Liger assisted potential makers with his published designs.[151] Mazes were also still being made in the Low Countries.[152]

More perplexing were the Troy Towns. Their origins are obscure, but were probably connected with religious observance, and not gardening. The general pattern is of a path passing back and forth around the central point. Virgil described the origin of a Roman game called 'Troy', in which horsemen of that city circled back and forth, making an obvious analogy with the characteristic miz-maze pattern of a Troy Town. Although several rustic Troy Towns were made about this time, they were unusual in high-status gardens.

By November 1691, when London relinquished keeping the accounts, the considerable additional avenue planting in the House Park had been completed, and the Great Fountain Garden had been made. The new wilderness had been formed, and the Pond Yard adapted for plant collections. The plans to extend the Privy Garden to the river were then suspended without lowering the Mount Garden or demolishing the Water Gallery. Some

interim arrangement was needed, and a flower garden was set out for Queen Mary (fig. 128). There appears to have been no statuary, borders or other further embellishment beyond the beds and Arethusa with its new base, carved by Edward Pearce.[153]

KENSINGTON PALACE

William and Mary's other gardening project in these early years of their reign was at Kensington. Being an asthmatic, William found that the coal-smoke of Westminster did not agree with him. Nottingham House, on a higher piece of ground adjacent to Hyde Park, was thought to have better air, and so was purchased in June 1689 as a private retreat. The house was approached by an elm avenue from the south. Around the house were clustered outbuildings and a few small gardens incorporating a mount, a banqueting house and a bowling green. To the north was an old orchard taken out of Hyde Park in 1664 and due to revert to the Crown in 1705.

Both house and gardens clearly needed some adaptation for royal usage. The Office of Works set about building new wings on each corner of the house. William wanted a safe passage from Whitehall, his place of business, to Kensington. The preferable route would have been through Hyde Park if it had not been a notorious haunt of footpads. So in 1690 the illuminated 'King's Road' or '*Rue de Roi*' – quickly translated by Londoners as 'Rotten Row' – was built to the orders of Captain Michael Studholme, the Surveyor of his Majesty's Highways. Celia Fiennes saw this phenomenon a dozen years later:

> The whole length of this Parke there is a high causey of a good breadth, 3 coaches may pass, and on each side are rowes of posts on which are Glasses-cases for Lamps which are lighted in the evening and appears very fine as well as safe for the passenger. This is only a private roade the King had which reaches to Kensington, where for aire our great King William bought a house and fitted it for retirement with pretty gardens.[154]

London set to work in 1689 and by April 1690 he had carried out gravelling and gardening works, mainly paving, worth £1,540

in the five acres of gardens.[155] He also provided a collection of greens from the Brompton Park nursery, which was not far away. A visitor from Yorkshire to several London gardens in December 1691 wrote about these:

> Kensington Gardens are not very great nor abounding with fine plants. The orange, lemon, myrtles, and what other trees they had here in summer, were all removed to Mr. London's and Mr Wise's greenhouse at Brompton park, a little mile from them. But the walks and grass are laid very fine, and they were digging up a flat of four or five acres to enlarge their garden.[156]

This last remark perhaps indicated the start of a new garden, the 'Slope Garden', on the ground that dipped gently down from the house to Kensington High Road (fig. 129). Protection was needed from the public gaze, and hence the garden ended in dense planting. The design had dissimilar arrangements of parterre and wilderness either side of the avenue. On the west side was a *parterre a l'Angloise* with a cross-walk, backed up by a palisaded wilderness with spirals, a *halle* and cabinets. On the east, wilderness followed parterre, but the theme of each was a circle, perhaps to disguise the angled eastern boundary. Another difference was the increased complexity, with more extravagant display of clipped

127 'Jardin en Bosquet d'Espalliers de diferentes figures' by Daniel Marot, 1703. The core of this design within the perimeter path is a St Andrew's cross overlaid by a lozenge and figure of eight; it is very similar to that implemented in the wilderness at Hampton Court (with a hornbeam maze and a Troy Town) c.1690, giving credence to the supposition that Marot, as William III's personal architect, was the author of several garden designs at Hampton Court and Kensington Palace.

128 Sutton Nicholls's etching of about 1696 of the Hampton Court Privy Garden after it had been widened c.1690, and before it was extended in 1699. Although possibly a cutwork design, it was more probably a flower garden, like Queen Mary's at Het Loo; the figure of Arethusa had come from Somerset House and was to go to Bushy Park; its base was newly carved by Edward Pearce.

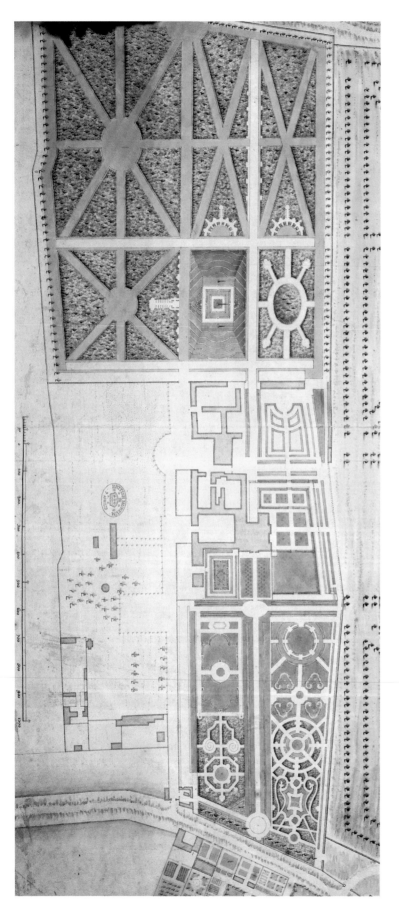

shrubs. Nothing quite like this had been seen in England before, and it was 'counted a Master piece of Art in the new regular manner of greens and gravel gardening'.[157] Several of the decorative touches once again suggest that the design was by Marot.[158] This new garden was probably completed in early 1693, for the head gardener, Hendrick Timmermans, was paid for looking after the 'new gardens' from that date.

MAINTAINING THE ROYAL GARDENS

With the completion of the Slope Garden, construction of these royal gardens was largely over for the time being. Bills dropped from the very high levels between 1689 and 1692 of about £20,000 per annum to about £4,000. The total expenditure on the royal gardens from 1689 to 25 March 1696, it was calculated, had amounted to about £83,000, over three quarters attributable to Hampton Court. Actually only £66,000 had been disbursed, leaving the rest as debts to the workmen. When Mary died of smallpox in December 1694 new gardening projects ceased altogether, and without Mary's devotion her plant collection went into decline. William was mostly in the Low Countries in the middle years of the 1690s, pursuing his struggle against Louis XIV and enlarging Het Loo.

---

129 'Design for Kensington Gardens' (the so-called 'Sandby Plan'), which was probably drawn up as ideas for expanding the gardens were initiated about 1720. It shows the Slope Garden between the palace and the high road. The central path terminates at a large 'alcove' building designed by Wren; parterres for flower display give way to wildernesses with cabinets and spirals showing the influence of Marot. The tapering of the eastern side was cleverly disguised by the use of circles; the circular compartment enclosed by high greens had a statue in the middle with eight walks centring on it. The plan also shows the 30 acres of plantations north of the palace, planted in the first few years of Anne's reign; behind the greenhouse of 1704 was the evergreen tree and shrub area, rising by ascending ranks to give the appearance of a mount. Immediately to its west was the orangery, a former gravel pit cut into five levels for the display of the greens.

Maintenance contracts with working gardeners at Hampton Court had begun from midsummer 1693. Hendrik Quellenburgh contracted for work in the Privy Garden and Upper Orangery, whilst Samuel van Staden looked after the grove by the Wilderness; from midsummer 1695 each took on additional areas from London. Caspar Gemperle began in midsummer 1693 to contract for providing materials and keeping the fires going at the stoves, and also added further areas two years later. Grass and gravel, much of it in the Great Fountain Garden, was maintained by London, with Tilleman Bobart as foreman. Together with Henry Peacock, the bowling-green keeper, Henry Badger, the mole catcher and the rolling-horse keeper, the full complement at Hampton Court was 80 men and women.

At Kensington the intricate parterre and wilderness work was one reason for there being another huge complement of gardeners, 72 altogether. Timmermans required a staff of forty men and ten women to keep the pleasure gardens, whilst the head gardener in the kitchen garden, William Kirke, had another sixteen men and four women there.

The royal gardens were 74 acres in size, the largest being Hampton Court with 46 acres and Kensington with 17 acres. The remainder was the Royal Garden and the house garden at St James's, and small areas at Richmond Palace and Windsor. The total annual cost, including officers' salaries, was £3,055 12s 8d. Portland negotiated a contract with the Treasury worth £5,000 a year from 1696, but this was to include his own sinecure of £200 a year and the cost of existing contracts, as well as repairs by tradesmen such as plumbers, carpenters and glaziers, estimated at £831 1s 0d a year.

William III and Portland had inevitably brought their Dutch preferences to bear on the royal palaces. In part this was a result of their awareness of modern French taste, seen in Marot's *broderie* at Hampton Court, the Great Fountain Garden's iron fence, and in sophisticated wilderness designs. In part their taste was more personal. Portland had tunnel arbours and urns at Zorgvliet, his home in the Low Countries, and these were seen at Hampton Court and later at his English home, Bulstrode.

The gargantuan effort expended on the royal gardens had been primarily for international consumption, and had only a small influence on the mainstream of English garden-making. There was no sudden change between English gardens of the 1680s and the gardens of William's reign. *Broderie* remained rare, as were tunnel arbours and urns. Curiously, the semicircular shape of the Great Fountain Garden, actually an inherited feature, was copied occasionally, presumably as a compliment to the monarch. Henry, Viscount Sidney, the Lord Lieutenant of Ireland, made a semicircular parterre at Dublin Castle gardens in about 1690,[159] and there were others, at Burley-on-the-Hill about 1696 and Dawley, about 1707.[160] Likewise *pattes d'oie* of avenues, probably of the early 1690s, were seen at Osterley and Cobham (fig. 130).

William III at peace

After the Nine Years' War came to an end Portland was sent as envoy to the French court the following year. As Superintendent of the Royal Gardens, he took the opportunity of taking his deputy, George London, with him. Between January and June 1698 they saw many of the great gardens around Paris, including the Tuileries, Sceaux, Chantilly and Clagny. London met Jean-Baptiste de la Quintinie at the *potager* at Versailles, and Portland approached André Le Nostre for designs for a refurbishment of the Maastricht Garden at Windsor. In a letter to Portland dated 1698, Le Nostre wrote: 'Remember the beautiful gardens of France: Versailles, Fontainebleau, Vaux, and especially Chantilly'.[161] However, he was much too old and feeble to travel to England himself, and sent instead his nephew, Claude Desgots, who accompanied London on his return to England. They visited Windsor together in July, and Desgots produced an elaborate design for the Maastricht Garden area.[162] Not to be outdone, Wren and Hawksmoor devised their own scheme (fig. 131).

William was meanwhile mostly in the Low Countries, and made no immediate move to improve his English palaces. Even the catastrophic fire at Whitehall in 1697/8 elicited little response, despite various schemes from Wren and the Office of Works (fig. 132). At last, however, in mid-1699 William decided to pursue improve-

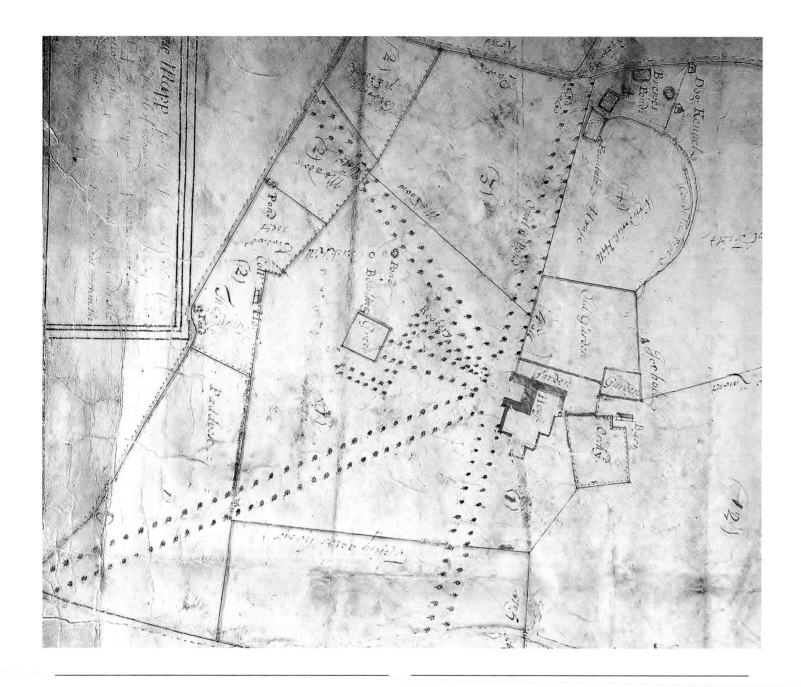

130 'A Map of Cobham Deer Parke and the Paddock' by George Russell, 1718. The parkland bowling green at Cobham Hall was probably created by one of the dukes of Lennox prior to the Civil War, but the *patte d'oie* of avenues was seemingly planted during William III's reign by Sir Joseph Williamson, who had been Principal Secretary of State 1674–8, in homage to Hampton Court.

(Facing page) 131 A design by Wren for a new Maastricht Garden at Windsor Castle, 1698. This was to be centred on the Star Building bastion, making it narrow as compared to a rival scheme by Claude Desgots. Wren envisaged floral cutwork, a grand fountain, a long canal, stepping-in groves, and further fountains and a pavilion at the river's edge; on a cross-axis he proposed a wilderness terminating at an eight-columned temple.

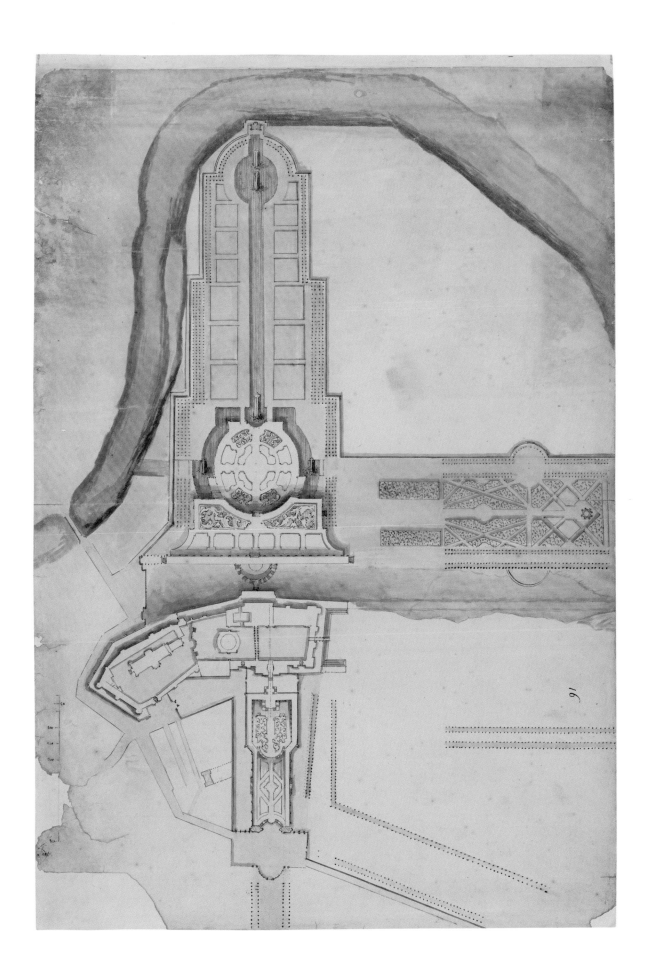

ments to Hampton Court. Some of the new works had been planned ten years before, but had remained unfulfilled. Amongst these were the lengthening of the Privy Garden. However, the largest works were newly devised schemes for providing extensive and highly polished walks, along which members of the Court could stroll.

London drew up an estimate of £5,558 for the works decided upon in 1699, consisting of walls between the wilderness and Great Fountain Garden and down to the Thames, and steps and drains in the Privy Garden.[163] A Letter of Privy Seal was sent to the Treasury, and the work was carried out.[164] Henry Wise was amongst the undertakers – his first involvement at Hampton Court.

Meanwhile, Portland had resigned all his posts in pique because of the rising influence of a rival royal favourite, and although London remained in post, and was responsible for the maintenance contract, Portland's departure undercut his authority. Talman took control in his capacity as Comptroller of Works. For some reason the time-honoured Letters Patent system was not used, and Talman ran a series of 'extraordinary' accounts. Whereas 'ordinary' works were those ordered at the discretion of the officials, mainly repairs and small improvements, 'extraordinary' works were those approved by the Treasury Lords themselves, on behalf of the King, after estimates and abatements. All bills were copied into the 'Accounts Ordinary and Extraordinary' at year end. Both London and Wise had already encountered the extraordinary works system, for it was used for their construction of the gardens at Chelsea Hospital between 1688 and 1692, work that had been worth £5,145.[165] Most of Wise's changes at Hampton Court from 1700 were 'extraordinary'.

132 'Plan of the Palace, Gardens, Canals, and Decorations', a drawing of 1697 showing Wren's proposals for replacing Whitehall Palace after it had burned down. The moated parterre at bottom (east), overlooked by the surviving Banqueting House, would have had nine fountains and sections of *broderie*; Charles II's canal in St James's Park was retained and partly mirrored, framing a space for extensive formal walks; William III disliked Whitehall and showed no interest in the scheme.

Planting of additional limes and horse chestnuts inside the Great Avenue in Bushy Park began on 2 August 1699. In October five-feet-high triangular tree guards were being erected. Wise was also employed to make a 60-foot-wide roadway down the centre of the avenue and to surface it with gravel. Further, he made a bason of water at the crossing. These works cost £4,934 after abatements of the undertakers' rates. In order to keep the King informed, Talman had to write abroad to William Blathwayt, who, as Secretary of War, accompanied the King. On 12 September 1699, he wrote that: 'Wee are making a Road of 60 ft. broad through the Middle Park and a Bason of 400 ft. diameter in the middle of the circle of trees, which will be very noble.'[166]

At the same time, bricklayers' and masons' work began on a wall past the tennis court to Hampton Court Road, which would match the terrace wall of the Privy Garden. There were also some works in the Privy Garden, such as stone steps up onto the terraces, and gravelling and turfing in the Wilderness. These works were all that the royal gardens administration took direct charge of.

A programme of works for 1700 was required, and Talman submitted an estimate. Shortly thereafter Wise submitted his own, cheaper, estimate for similar works.[167] The two major items were the Broad Walk across the east front of the palace, to be 39 feet wide from the river to the Kingston Road, and two levelled and enclosed 'divisions' extending the Fountain Garden to the same length. A low wall in which iron railings were to be set was built to enclose the two divisions from the park, and railings were placed on the wall and joined to those around the Great Parterre. Also the Longford River needed to be diverted out of the northern division into the park. Wise obtained approval for his scheme in February 1699/1700, and had carried out his works by about June.

Talman was employing other tradesmen in the gardens. One of these was Jan van Nost, who in 1701 carved gate piers topped by lead flower pots supported by boys of incredible detail and quality at the 'Flower Pot Gate' at the north end of the Broad Walk. However, Talman's works cost over £10,000 instead of the £6,480 that had been estimated. Much of the reason for this was

that William was demanding further improvements, in particular the Pavilion Terrace alongside the Thames, extending half a mile between the huge 'Circle Wall next yᵉ Thames' at the south end of the Broad Walk and the terraced oval enclosure around a new bowling green.[168] It had waist-high railings overlooking the Thames on one side and yews and hollies and a railing looking out onto the park on the other.

The Earl of Ranelagh, who had proved himself architecturally at Ranelagh House by Chelsea Hospital, was appointed 'Sur-intendent generall of oure Buildings & of our works in our parks' on 22 June 1700, filling the vacuum created by Portland's resignation.[169] In July he was urging the Works' officers to prepare an estimate for the terrace, and a few days later he was pressing them to demolish the old Water Gallery. This took place, and on 25 September the officers were able to report to the Treasury that the banqueting house, expanded from an old Tudor tower, was nearly finished, and that the wall around the bowling green was being built. In the latter part of 1700 Wise made up the level of the new bowling green and turfed it. A new avenue was planted east of the bowling green, and 10,000 cubic yards of soil were removed from the Mount Garden preparatory to remodelling it yet again as part of the Privy Garden (figs 133, 134 and 135).

One unexpected drain on finances was the continuing failure of the fountains in the Great Parterre (or Fountain Garden as it became known). New lead pipes and brass cocks for them were installed and the fountains themselves were paved. In 1700 Robert Aldersey, an 'enginemaker', was called in to give advice.[170] In 1701 he charged £400 for 'bringing the water more plentifully to Hampton Court', and he devised a system for raising water for the fountains. He agreed with Ranelagh and London to maintain the system for £200 a year, from Christmas 1701.

Works progressed more slowly in 1701, and at one stage in September, William Blathwayt wrote from Het Loo on behalf of the King to the Treasury urging it to give Talman the money for works to proceed.[171] The foundations were laid for four pavilions at the new bowling green in April. The other major building work in the gardens this year was the 'new Glass Case',

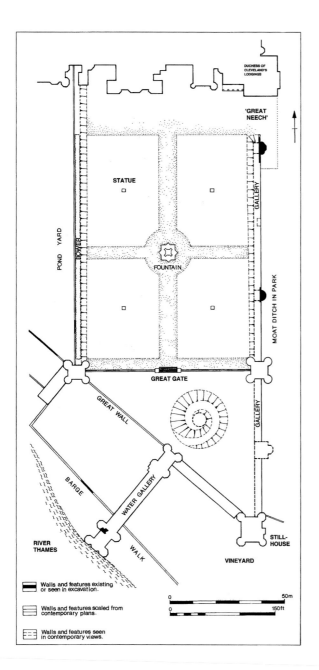

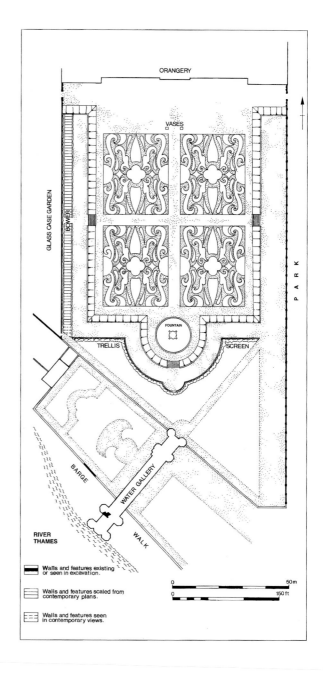

the large greenhouse that replaced the three hothouses in the Glass Case Garden. There was also great activity concerning statuary, ironwork and a domed arbour in the wall between the gardens and Hampton Court Road. This was oiled and painted an iron colour by Thomas Highmore, the Serjeant Painter. Louis Laguerre, Tijou's son-in-law, then decorated it. A small garden south-east of the new banqueting house was transformed into the King's aviary, sometimes referred to as the 'vollery ground', with a semicircle of cages containing a collection of exotic birds (see fig. 16).

Wise removed the final 16,751 cubic yards of soil from the Mount Garden, lengthened the western side terrace in the Privy Garden and laid the gravel and grass of an entirely new design for the whole of the extended Privy Garden as a *parterre à l'An-*

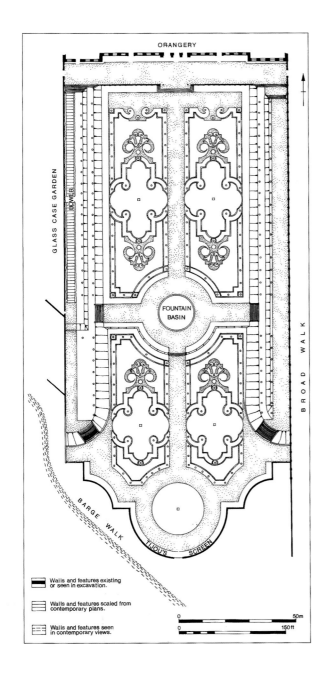

133   A reconstruction by Daphne Ford of the Privy Garden and Mount Garden at Hampton Court as they appeared in 1680. Either Charles I or Cromwell had set out the Privy Garden as four grass plats around a fountain; the statuary in the plats was installed in 1651, and a figure of Arethusa was moved here from Somerset House in 1655 and set up on a black marble fountain in the centre of the garden. The Mount Garden and Water Gallery remained to the south.

134   A reconstruction by Daphne Ford of the Privy Garden and Mount Garden at Hampton Court as they appeared in 1695. The side terraces have been widened and heightened, with a tunnel arbour to the west and a view of the Great Parterre to the east. Since it was planned to extend the garden to the river's edge, the figure of Arethusa had been moved south and given a new white marble base by Edward Pearce, making it into a fountain. By the time a halt was called to the works, the 1530s mount had been spread around what remained of the Mount Garden, but the Water Gallery survived. The flower garden reflected Queen Mary's interests, but may have been viewed as a temporary expedient.

135   A reconstruction by Daphne Ford of the Privy Garden, Hampton Court, as it appeared in 1702. Huge quantities of soil had been removed to the Pavilion Terrace to the east, and at last there was a view to the Thames. The new parterre, a *parterre à l'Angloise* with *plates-bandes*, internal scrollwork, and cutwork flourishes, may well have derived from designs by Daniel Marot. The Tijou screens were set up on the boundary with the bargewalk.

gloise to replace the *gazon coupé*.[172] Tijou's twelve screens at last had a resting place in the iron fence at the bottom of the garden. However, on inspecting the finished garden in June 1701, William was dismayed to find that the Thames could still not be seen properly, and ordered the entire body of the garden to be lowered again, which meant that all plants needed to be taken up, more earthmoving undertaken, and the plants moved back again. At

last, the ambition of a dozen years was achieved, with a design that may well also have dated back to Marot's time at Hampton Court, in which scrollwork divided the parterre into grassed compartments (see fig. 16). Works were almost complete in early 1702 when William's horse stumbled on a molehill in the House Park and threw him. The resulting injuries developed complications that killed the Protestant hero.

6

Queen Anne's Years

Queen Anne's reign (1702–14) nearly coincided with the War of the Spanish Succession, or the 'Marlborough Wars', terminating at the Treaty of Utrecht in 1713. Although the financial penalties of war meant that the ability of landowners to make new gardens was diminished to some extent, conceptions of what made a fine garden were reconsidered. On the one hand, the aesthetic of Versailles was developed by increasing attention to detail, neatness and elegance close to the house. On the other, there were experiments with ideas for a more masculine, simple, grand and rural approach to country-house settings, as being both more suited to England's natural assets in grass, gravel and tree growth, and an expression of the country's bid to catch the torch of Classical culture supposedly let fall by nations of the south.

CR

War and peace in Queen Anne's reign

The creation of a Whig ideology owed much to two men, Charles Montagu and John Somers. Montagu, of Horton Hall, Northamptonshire, who had managed the economy with skill and boldness during the Nine Years' War, was Chancellor of the Exchequer in the late 1690s. John Somers, a constitutional lawyer, developed the argument that James II had not been usurped but had vacated his throne; he became Lord Chancellor from 1697, when he was ennobled.

Montagu and Somers had enlightened attitudes towards literature and science. The former was a lifelong friend of Isaac Newton, providing him with the post of Warden of the Royal Mint in 1696, and the mastership in 1699. Montagu, Somers, Newton and John Locke together tackled the problem of the debasement of the currency brought about by clipping the edges of coins. They were also interested in the new science. Montagu was President of the Royal Society 1695–8, and Somers its chairman 1699–1704.

With power being eagerly contested by Whigs and Tories, the value of persuasive writing was well appreciated. Montagu had some poetical pretensions, but was more effective in enlisting the support of others through patronage. Somers and Jacob Tonson, a publisher and supporter, arranged to supply impecunious poets with mutton pies from Christopher Cat's tavern near Temple Bar, and hence was founded the Kit-Cat Club. It drew in Joseph Addison, an excellent Latin poet and translator, the playwright William Congreve, John Vanbrugh, at that time also a playwright, and Richard Steele, the dramatist and essayist. It also drew in Whig politicians and, by the end of Anne's reign, a large number of Whig dukes and earls.

Montagu had met the young Addison soon after the latter had gained his MA from Oxford in 1693. Addison's poem 'To the King' and his celebration of the Peace of Rijswijk were dedicated to Somers and Montagu respectively. As a recruit of great promise to the Whig interest, Addison was provided with a pension in 1699 to enable him to travel. He would thereby gain knowledge of European affairs and the French language, with a possible diplomatic career ahead. For Addison, it gave him the opportunity to travel onwards to Italy and drink from the same wellspring of inspiration as Horace and Virgil, the countryside between Rome and Naples.

The Whigs had a more doctrinaire geopolitical understanding of Europe than the Tories. They believed that Louis XIV sought a universal monarchy, with all the states of Europe subjugated to his crown, ambitions that they believed had to be held in check for the safety of the Protestant nations. Louis's actions had driven the English to a nationalist position, seen for example when Edmund Gibson wrote in the dedication to his new edition of William Camden's *Britannia* in 1695 that England 'has been a great Sufferer by foreign Modes and Fopperies'.[1] However, she 'now resolves to quit them all, and convince the World that she has every thing within herself and can live without borrowing'. His dedicatee was Sir John Somers.

William III granted the barony of Halifax to Montagu, but Whig dominance of government was faltering in 1700. It was the Tories that became the chief ministers, reinforced when Anne, who had decidedly Tory sympathies, came to the throne. The War of the Spanish Succession was actually begun by a Tory administration. The Tories, more concerned about local issues and the taxes paid by the landed interest, were inclined to see war as a burden best alleviated soon. Hence Anne and her ministers soon came to depend for the prosecution of the war on the support of the Whigs, who insinuated themselves into power from 1705 till 1710. Addison, for example, became Under-Secretary of State for the South from 1706 to 1709.

THE VICTOR OF BLENHEIM

On the death of the last Hapsburg King of Spain in 1700, Louis XIV declared one of his grandsons, Philippe, duc d'Anjou, to be the successor, and started garrisoning fortresses and ports in the Spanish Netherlands. Alarmed by the power that France and Spain could wield acting as one, an alliance of England, the Low Countries and Austria was formed in 1701. John Churchill, Earl of Marlborough, was William III's commander of British forces in the Low Countries, and his wife, Sarah, was Princess Anne's closest friend. Towards the end of 1702 he was elevated to a dukedom by Anne, by then Queen.

In August 1704 Marlborough's troops crushed a Franco-Bavarian force under the Marshal of France, the comte de Tallard, at Blenheim, in Bavaria. The rejoicing at this famous victory back in England was enthusiastic. In January 1704/5 Parliament agreed that the Queen should present the Duke with Woodstock Park, and at the same time she ordered the construction of a palace there at Parliament's cost. This was to be a monument to military prowess – its Great Hall came to be decorated with trophies, and a 30-ton marble bust of Louis XIV captured by Marlborough at the siege of Tournai in 1709 was to be hoisted aloft to the roof of the garden front, much to the disgust of later French tourists.[2] The creation of a palace for the country's greatest military hero echoed the episode fifteen years before when monies were allo-

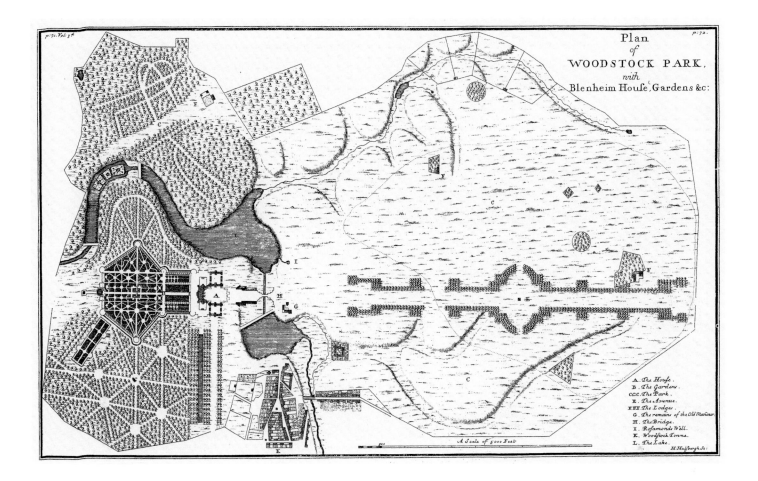

136   An engraved plan of about 1717 showing Blenheim Park as envisaged by Vanbrugh and Hawksmoor on completion. Begun early in 1705, the 'military' garden of 77 acres was enclosed by a ditch and ramparts faced with stone-built walls. By the house was a 250-yard parterre with clipped greens and shells in cutwork (simplified by the date of this plan); this led to the 'Woodwork', a hexagonal wilderness. There were eight circular bastions at corners of the rampart, and outside them were avenues within the wooded park. The walled kitchen garden was made at the same time, enclosed by fourteen-foot high brick walls; the bridge over the Glyme, erected in the late 1700s, is seen on axis towards the north. Work slowed to a crawl in 1710 as the Duke of Marlborough's political star waned, but it seems that Vanbrugh had ideas for flooding the valley that were not achieved until the time of Lancelot Brown. The avenue through the park was simply a visto, as the approach was from the east (bottom).

cated for a new palace at Hampton Court for William III. This was not a specifically English way of honouring a great general: one parallel is the Austrian empire's general, Prince Eugene of Savoy, who was sufficiently enriched by his lengthy campaigns to build the Belvedere palace in the suburbs of Vienna, and the Schloss Hof outside it.

The Duke of Marlborough wanted Vanbrugh to be his architect, and designs were settled between January and March 1704/5. Hawksmoor became Vanbrugh's very necessary assistant, and together they planned the vast gardens, kitchen gardens, outworks and avenues at Blenheim (fig. 136). The park consisted of a largely level gravel bed, though dissected by steep-sided dingles, the chief of which had the River Glyme winding through it. In organising the approaches and outworks Vanbrugh keenly sought the most advantageous situation and prospect for the new palace, which

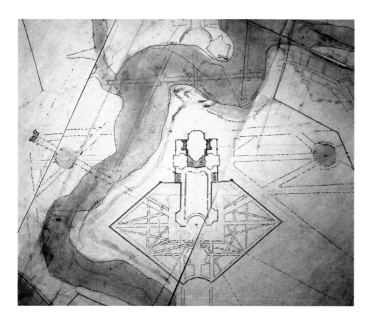

137 Nicholas Hawksmoor's 1705 sketch of the initial idea for a wilderness at Blenheim Palace to fit the natural topography; the low ground of the Glyme valley is identified.

was placed close to the rim of the Glyme's abrupt little valley so that its effect, as seen from most of the park, could be emphasised. This position was towards the southern end of the park, which enabled a broad level planted 'Mall' from the highway to the east. However, as at Castle Howard, the principal fronts were not determined by the approach, for the palace was orientated north-south, giving an opportunity for a dummy Great Avenue almost a mile and a half long through the central and northern parkland.

The idea for the gardens was also a deliberate manipulation of the setting. Hawksmoor seems to have drawn up the first plan for the gardens and avenues. This showed how they might respond to the natural topography south of the palace (fig. 137). Although passing by the north front of the palace in an east-west direction, the valley then turned south. Hawksmoor's plan showed how the perimeter wall of the gardens would crown the precipitous fall to the west, and would be of hexagonal form, so that the western-most point would fit the topography closely. This was adjusted

and the final design consisted of a parterre under the house with scrollwork defining grass *compartiments* and flanking counter-walks, leading to an hexagonal wood-work (or wilderness), bringing the enclosed southern garden to 77 acres. Envisaged not so much as a garden wall but as the curtain walls to a Roman or medieval city with bastions at changes in direction, it was even sometimes called the 'military garden'.

Vanbrugh knew Henry Wise well enough through the Office of Works. The system of commissioning work was for Wise to give estimates based on the same rates as for Office of Works projects, and for these to be approved, the rates perhaps being 'abated' by Vanbrugh, and then to put in bills at the end of every month. In April 1705 Wise's men were digging the foundations for 'Blenheim' palace and preparing the ground for the gardens and eight-acre kitchen garden. In June the foundation stone was laid, and Vanbrugh reported that the 'Garden wall was set agoing the Same day with the House'. In October some of the bastions were finished, and planting of the wood-work was proceeding. The innumerable alleys were many miles in length, and a strange ser-pentine walk was threaded through the perimeter planting of the vast wood-work, presumably to confuse its bounds (see fig. 136). In 1706 the Great Avenue to the north and the approach avenue eastwards were planted. Remarkably, for such a huge undertaking, the gardens were all but finished in three years. After five years Wise had been paid £13,686 for his undertakings.

GARDEN-MAKING DURING WARTIME:
VANBRUGH, HAWKSMOOR, ARCHER AND WISE

Other owners discovered that the War of the Spanish Succes-sion was not a good time to incur the expense of making new gardens. Taxes bore heavily, whilst the high interest from Gov-ernment loans to fund the war meant that all borrowing, includ-ing mortgages, was expensive. While Blenheim and royal projects took centre stage, other garden-making was more depressed than it had been for two decades.

Vanbrugh's star was rising. He had already displaced Talman as the Earl of Carlisle's architect for the rebuilding of Castle

Howard in 1699, and three years later was granted the comp-trollership of the Works at the accession of Queen Anne, again displacing Talman. Hawksmoor, who had been assistant to Wren for twenty years, was in most matters Vanbrugh's assistant too, providing invaluable practical knowledge. Few architects gave such consideration to the overall scene as did Vanbrugh. It has often been observed that he must have been acquainted with the principles of landscape painting. As a vistor to town and country houses, he would frequently have encountered landscapes by Jan Griffier or the Italian masters who depicted Classical landscapes with temples, bridges and obelisks. In his imagination, and often in reality, he invested the approaches, forecourts and vistos at his English country houses with Antique and monumental tones. This was seen in his obsession to span the Glyme at Blenheim by means of a Classical bridge supported by a single arch of Hercu-lean proportions. Its foundations were begun in 1708, and the arch made in 1710. At Hampton Court, he built oversize masonry piers for the proposed Lion Gate in 1713, intending that the wilderness and melon ground would be cleared for a parade to terminate the Great Avenue.[3] At Castle Howard he built gateways, a Roman wall and an obelisk on the approach (see fig. 272).

Vanbrugh was content to let Hawksmoor labour on the ideas for fortification boundaries and winding walks; he himself was in general less interested in the gardens themselves. It was Hawksmoor, for example, who pressed for early planting at Castle Howard. At Kimbolton Castle, Huntingdonshire, Vanbrugh reported in 1708 to the Earl of Manchester: 'Up the Middle of the Garden and Canall, wch is now brim full of Water, and looks mighty well: The Espalier Hedges will be in great perfection this Year, and the Fruit Trees are now Strong enough to produce abundance'.[4] Nevertheless, all he had done was to redesign the garden within the old walls, a much less adventurous scheme than his joint efforts with Hawksmoor at other places (fig. 138).

The architect Thomas Archer had had the benefit of some years in Rome, so may have had a reputation for understanding matters Italian. Back in England he made himself useful to the Duke of Devonshire on architectural works. The domed cascade house at Chatsworth, built from 1702 (fig. 139), is attributed to Archer, and

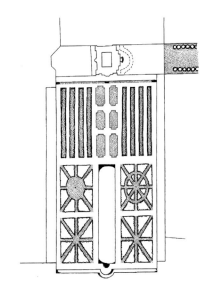

138 A reconstruction of the gardens at Kimbolton Castle in 1728, based on an account by a French tourist, Pierre-Jacques Fougeroux, and a later map (north is at the top). The arrangement, which was probably much as Vanbrugh had left it in 1708, was an adaptation of a large Great Garden of an earlier generation. Six plats of grass gave way to a canal, and the view to the park was over a boundary canal; the parterre was flanked by *allées* between pleached limes and the *bosquets* had grass paths throughout.

139 'The Cascade at Chatsworth' by William Stukeley, 1725. This shows the cascade as lengthened in the 1700s, when Thomas Archer's temple was built at its head, and flanked by groves of firs that were fully removed in the early 1730s.

his contribution to gardens seems to have included several water-works. He may have been responsible for a less ambitious cascade on the axis of the parterre at Bramham around 1710, and he was probably responsible for a three-arched structure with cascades that appeared about 1715 at Hurstbourne Priors, Hampshire, also known as 'Down-Husband', at the end of an axial canal (fig. 140). Switzer illustrated it in his *Hydrostatics* and observed that Lord Lymington 'seems to take the Model of one he has at *Down-Hus-*

140 *The Grange, Hurstbourne Priors* by Jan Griffier the Younger, 1748. The cascade, an early example of the fashion for such features, was probably designed by Thomas Archer in the 1710s. In 1728 Stephen Switzer wrote that Lord Lymington had taken as his model a cascade at Villa Aldobrandini in Frascati. The parterre may have been more elaborate when the cascade was built.

band, near Whitchurch' from a cascade at Villa Aldobrandini at Frascati.[5] It is possible that Archer also designed general plans for the gardens and plantations at Hurstbourne Priors, as he may also have done at Heythrop and Stainborough around 1710 and after-wards at his own house, Hale Park, Hampshire.

QUEEN ANNE AND HENRY WISE

Wise became the nation's leading gardener in Queen Anne's reign, emerging from the shadow formerly cast by George London (fig. 141). At the reign's outset, London had taken the opportu-nity of an interview with the Queen about his position as Royal Gardener to present a petition by the tradesmen who remained unpaid for their work on the garden of Hampton Court. Irri-tated, she declared that she intended to 'restrain the expense' of the royal gardens, and called for Wise.[6] He proposed a new con-

141 *Henry Wise* by Sir Godfrey Kneller, probably painted while Wise was still the Royal Gardener, between 1702 and 1728. The painting descended within the senior branch of the family, living at Woodcote, in Warwickshire, before passing to the Waller family; it was purchased by George VI at Christie, Manson & Woods in 1947 from the collection of the late Sir Arthur Waller, fifth Baronet.

tract, by which he would maintain the royal gardens at Hampton Court, the Maastricht Garden at Windsor, Cranbourne Lodge in Windsor Great Park, and Kensington Gardens for £1,600 per annum (or £20 per acre instead of £57 per acre), with a salary for himself of £200 per annum. He was responsible for all wages, implements, wheelbarrows, rollers, horses and dung. He was also obliged to make good any losses of trees, shrubs or evergreens. He was immediately appointed the new Royal Gardener. He gained

the Queen's confidence and before long was Deputy Ranger of St James's Park.

Despite her professed wish to restrain expense, Anne became as keen on garden projects as her hated brother-in-law, William. Her first significant project was a 30-acre wilderness on the north side of Kensington Palace (see fig. 129). This had actually been begun in William's reign, but Anne, who liked this palace, decided to continue. A local schoolmaster observed that

> Her Majesty has been pleas'd lately to Plant near Thirty Acres more towards the North, separated from the rest only by a stately Green House not yet Finish'd; upon this spot is near 100 Men dayly at Work, and so great is the Progress they have made, that in less than Nine Months the whole is Level'd, laid out and Planted, and when Finish'd will be very Fine. Mr. *Wise* her Majesties Gardener has the Management of this Work.[7]

Vanbrugh and Hawksmoor were responsible for the new greenhouse, which was soon to house a 'noble collection of foreign plants and fine neat greens' over winter. One compartment of the new plantation was reshaped from a former gravel pit into a sunken orangery garden, formalised into five levels with yews between perfect geometrical slopes. Another was filled with graduated planting of evergreens. The effect was described by Addison as 'a seeming mount, made up of trees rising one higher than another, in proportion as they approach the centre'.[8] A larger area was parcelled off from Hyde Park in 1705 to provide a paddock for deer and antelope.

At Hampton Court Wise was in 1707 ordered to replace the *broderie* in the Great Fountain Garden with a *parterre à l'Angloise* arrangement (fig. 142).[9] Three years later he dug transverse canals parallel to the lateral arms of limes, so that the park was seen over water along the length of the boundary with the garden. The Office of Works' plan for a new approach through Bushy Park was revived by Vanbrugh, who intended that it should terminate at a huge parade in front of Henry VIII's Great Hall, replacing the Wilderness. The Arethusa Fountain, which had been in store since its removal from the Privy Garden in 1700, was erected atop a large pier in the centre of the bason in Bushy Park in 1712. Van-

brugh designed and built some monumental piers topped with lions. In the event, the project foundered and some iron gates by Tijou, quite inadequate for this position, were thrown up between the Lion Gate piers, and the Wilderness survived.

Anne may not have been able to hunt, as formerly, but she much enjoyed speeding along in a chaise with two huge wheels. At Windsor the three-mile Queen's Walk (later Queen Anne's Ride) was laid smooth and gravelled through the Great Park in 1707–9, and soon another chaise riding was laid down the Long Walk (see fig. 145). Further ridings were cut 'through the heath in Windsor Forest for the convenience and ease of her Majesty's hunting there'. Nothing quite like these chaise rides had been seen before in England, but with these improvements Anne could drive

40 or 50 miles in a summer's afternoon through park and forest. Wise also smoothed out 20 miles of chaise ridings at Hampton Court in 1710.[10]

A new Maastricht Garden was decided upon in 1708. Gravel would be dug and used on local roads whilst negotiations for land acquisition proceeded. Afterwards the pit would form the central bason of a design of formal plantations. The final plan of 1712 showed the pit as an apsidal-ended bason of gigantic proportions (fig. 143). As the walls, iron railings and the trenching and planting of the palisades proceeded, estimates for the project escalated, to the disquiet of the Treasury. At Anne's death the project paused, and severe flooding provided a convenient excuse for setting it aside for good.

142 The Great Parterre or Fountain Garden at Hampton Court. Made in about 1707, this must be a presentation drawing by someone working for Henry Wise to show how the parterre would look after elimination of all the box, as Queen Anne is said to have wished. Wren had always wanted a very simple parterre, and it seems that he got his way, as Wise's 'new Turfing & Gravelling the great Fountain garden' in 1707 also eliminated the four small inward fountains and the path connecting them.

WISE ELSEWHERE

Wise was better as an undertaker rather than designer. Parterre designs for Stonyhurst in 1705 (see fig. 100) and Cliveden (fig. 144) about the same time were not implemented; Sir Nicholas Shireburn and Lord Orkney must have thought that they were not very suitable for their situations. Wise stated in 1713 that he had taken on 'one Man constantly in pay and sometimes more' for 'the making several surveys and Draughts of Her Majesty's

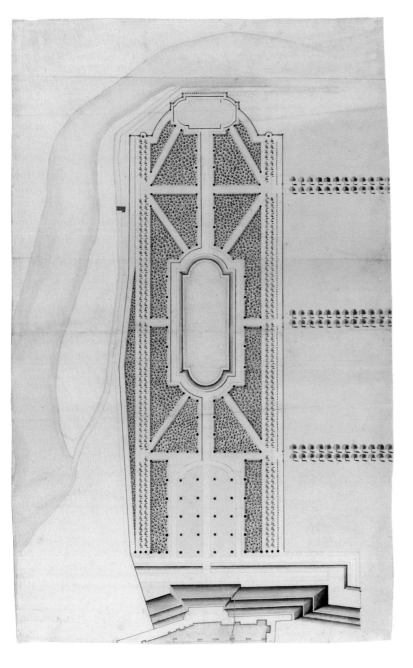

143   A version of Wise's scheme for the Maastricht Garden, Windsor Castle, 1712. This adopted the axis through the Star Building bastion; a plain parterre was to lie below the slopes but most of it was a 'great plantation' around a huge bason. The end was to be an iron grille giving a glimpse of the Thames.

144   A garden design, probably by the Brompton Park Nursery, for Cliveden House, c.1706 (north is at the bottom). A *parterre à l'Angloise* backed by a plantation centres on an oval bowling green; the parterre's side terraces were to be placed in line with the staircases at either end of the great terrace. This conventional design did not take advantage of the unusual and spectacular site.

Palaces, Gardens Parks and Plantations'.[11] It is possible that this was at first Tilleman Bobart, who was paid for three survey plans of Windsor Great Park in about 1705.[12] However, Wise was also employing a young surveyor, Charles Bridgeman, perhaps from 1705. Bridgeman's early survey drawings of Blenheim, Hampton Court and Kensington were unpolished, but he soon acquired an assured hand.[13] In time Bridgeman's surveys for Wise covered all the royal parks and Blenheim (fig. 145).

Meanwhile, Wise continued to supply plants to country houses. His chief assistant in running the nursery side of Brompton Park was Joseph Carpenter, whose passion was fruit. Thomas Coke had asked for London to attend him at Melbourne, Derbyshire,

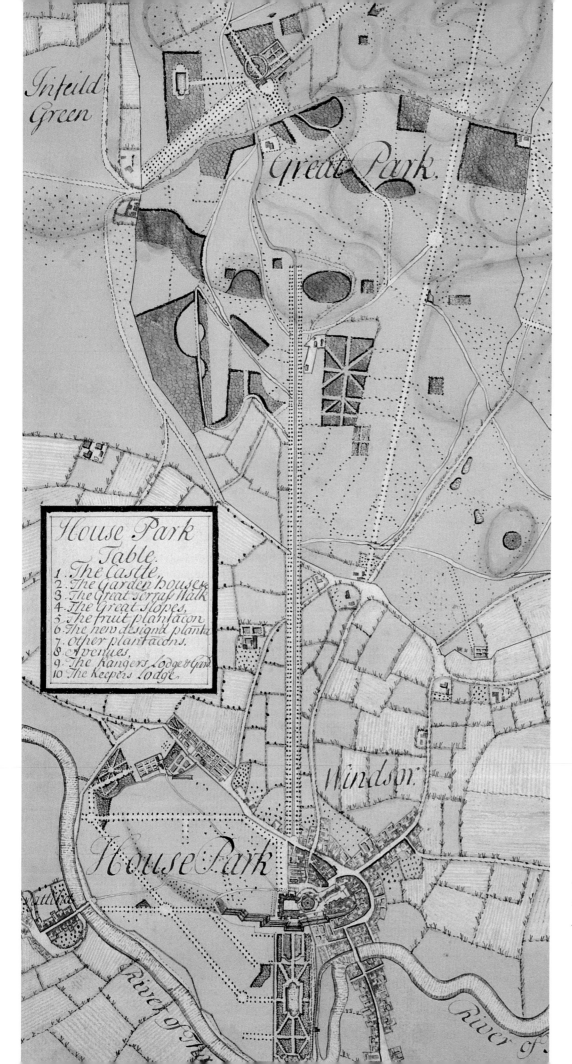

House Park Table.
1. The Castle.
2. The Garden house.
3. The Great Terfass Walk.
4. The Great Slopes.
5. The fruit plantacon.
6. The new designd planta.
7. Other plantacons.
8. Avenues.
9. The Rangers Lodge & Gard.
10. The Keepers Lodge.

145   Windsor Castle and Great Park in about 1712, a further example of Bridgeman's maps of the royal parks (north is at the bottom). This detail of his very large Windsor map indicates the House Park avenues of the 1700s, the Maastricht Garden design by Henry Wise of 1712, the slopes under the castle of the late 1670s, the avenue of 1684 southwards to the Great Park, and the Ranger's Lodge in the Great Park.

(Facing page) 146   Melbourne Hall, Derbyshire, in about 1710. This undated plan shows the recent transformation of the old gardens on three levels (north is to the left). The upper level had been laid down to a conventional *parterre à l'Angloise* in 1704 following the advice of Henry Wise. The middle level became a garden to show off statuary and the water garden was excavated for a large pool with three fountains, driven by the millpond, which occupies the bottom right part of the plan. The irregular wilderness to the side was devised by a Mr Huett, a Huguenot surveyor then working at Chatsworth; the owner, Thomas Coke, has evidently had a try himself at improving the wilderness layout, but the design on this plan survived.

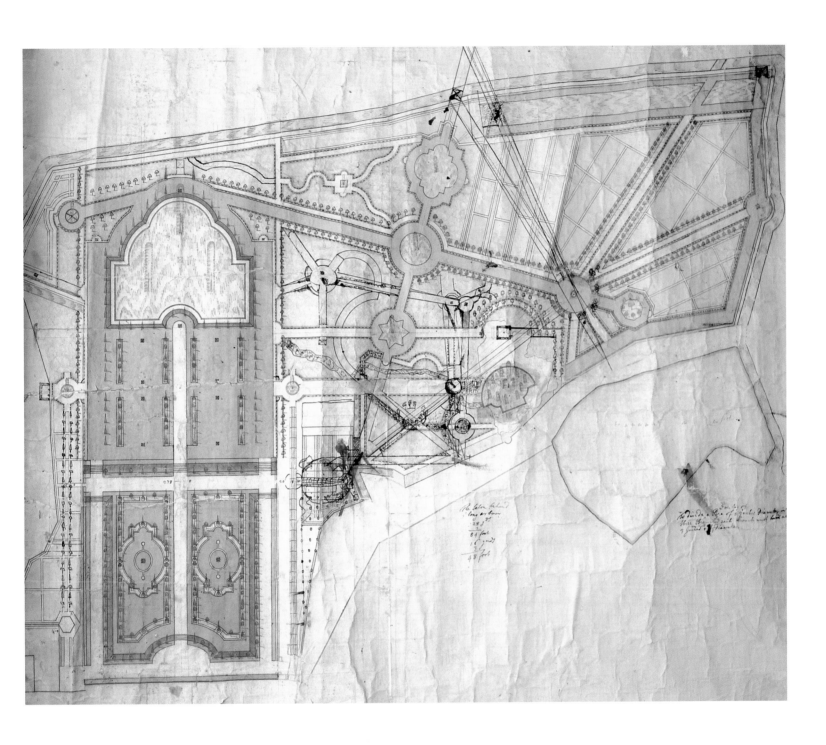

and from 1699 Wise supplied the plants.[14] In 1704 Brompton Park sent plans for a *parterre à l'Angloise* for Melbourne, incorporating all the old gardens on three levels, one 'to suit with Versailles', as the nursery jokingly remarked (fig. 146). Wise then supplied £158 worth of pyramid and round-headed evergreens, and hedge yews

for the wilderness; on another occasion 3,000 feet of Dutch box, 720 hedge yews, 1,500 iris, 100 tulips, 1,000 Dutch elm, 3,000 hornbeam, and other items. Meanwhile, the plot between the millpond and the garden was filled with a wilderness to a design by Mr Huett, or Hewitt, a Huguenot surveyor then working at Chatsworth.

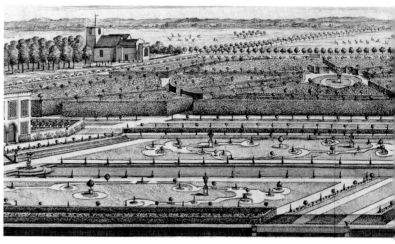

(Left, top) 147 Newdigate House, Nottingham, as shown in a plan at the back of London and Wise's *The Retir'd Gardner* (1706). This was a revision of the garden of the house where the Marshal of France, the comte de Tallard, was paroled after his capture by the Duke of Marlborough at the Battle of Blenheim in 1704. The 'explanation' makes it clear that access to Tallard's garden was via a terrace under the house (D) overlooking a cutwork parterre with coloured infills made from sand, brickdust, pit-coal, spar, cockleshells, etc.; beyond was a banqueting house with stairs (O) and an upper grass-walk terrace with borders (N, K); at this level was a parterre with borders for flowers and clipped greens with grass verges, which was separated from the grass quarters by lines of white spar (M); a third parterre was of cutwork with a central fountain and places for pots (L).

(Left, bottom) 148 *The South West Prospect of his Grace ye Duke of Marlboroughs House in St James Park*, an etching by John Harris after a sketch by James Lightbody, *c*.1715. Henry Wise made these gardens for the Duchess in 1710, very plain as suited her taste, and a portent of the plain parterres of George I's reign. The house looked over the Mall in St James's Park, seen in the foreground; 50 years earlier this had been the wilderness end of the Royal Garden.

(Above) 149a and b Bird's-eye view by Knyff and Kip of the parterres at Wanstead House from the south of the inner gardens, *c*.1713. The top and the bottom form a panorama and the oval bowling green takes centre stage, with the canal set within open groves planted with shrubs to the west and the Tijou ironwork at the start of the visto to the east; to the north was a terrace ending in a bowling-green house, and behind that the high-hedged wilderness.

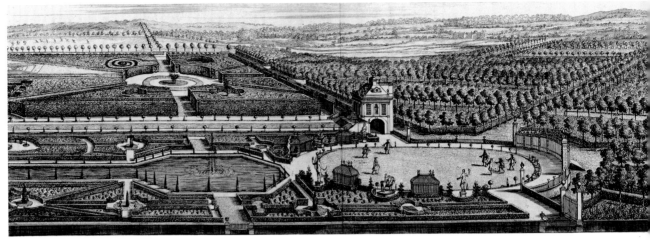

After being captured by the Duke of Marlborough, the comte de Tallard spun out his captivity in some style at Newdigate House, Nottingham, and Brompton Park appears to have made his elaborate parterres there (fig. 147). Wise was also asked by the Duchess of Marlborough to set out plain grass plats and gravel walks in the gardens of Marlborough House, St James's, from 1710.[15] This was a very different garden from Melbourne, largely because the Duchess, even more so than the Queen at Hampton Court, wanted a very simple and restrained garden (fig. 148).

GEORGE LONDON'S LAST WORKS

Wise may have been shown royal favour, but London was still much sought after. As well as old acquaintances, such as William Blathwayt at Dyrham and the Earl of Portland at Bulstrode, there were new customers, the most outstanding being the Childs of Wanstead, immensely wealthy from banking. His first undertaking there was very much in his customary manner, and an opportunity to reassemble the team he had had at Hampton Court (fig. 149a and b). The architect of the garden buildings was probably Talman, and Tijou was brought in too. London's debt to Marot was evident in his use of cutwork in grass, scrollwork, open walks, and curves, loops and spirals in wildernesses.

London had his own band of apprentices. For example, he had taken on Switzer in 1699, and he had several foremen running his many contracts at country seats. At his death in January 1713/4 he was working on Stainborough for the Earl of Strafford (see fig. 260), who had been partly responsible for negotiating the Treaty of Utrecht, and 'that noble Design of the Right Honourable the present Earl of Carnarvon, at Edger [Edgware] in Hertfordshire, before the finishing of which he died'.[16] These last gardens, at Cannons, were phenomenally costly but Carnarvon could afford them, thanks to being Paymaster of the Forces. Although the architect for Cannons changed several times, it seems that London's general plan for the gardens and plantations was doggedly adhered to from 1713 until about 1721 (fig. 150).[17]

Both London and Wise, like John Rose before them, amassed significant landed property. London bought a farm called Southborough, in Kingston-on-Thames parish, from his friend Talman,[18] and in 1709 Wise purchased the manor of Lillington, Warwickshire, which included Warwick Priory, to which he later retired (fig. 151). It was these landowning credentials, rather than eminence in their trade, that allowed London and Wise to describe themselves as 'gentlemen' (fig. 152).

In the new century there were others who offered themselves as undertakers. At Melbourne, the construction of Coke's parterre and wilderness in 1704 was undertaken by a Derbyshire man, William Cooke, not Brompton Park. Five years later, Cooke was offering his services at Calke Abbey, Derbyshire. However, there were no English undertakers with the capability and expe-

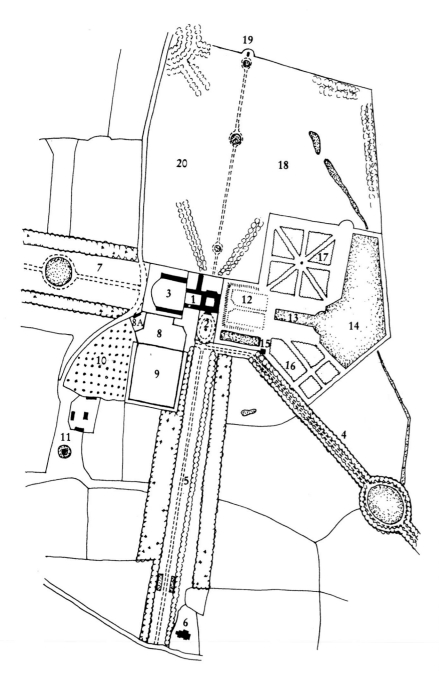

150 Reconstruction by the author of the layout of Cannons as completed in about 1722. The general plan had been made by George London shortly before he died in 1713. 1, Cannons House; 2, Great Court; 3, Stable Court; 4, Edgware Avenue; 5, Whitchurch Avenue; 6, St Laurence's, Whitchurch; 7, Stanmore Avenue; 8, Garden and melon ground; 9, Kitchen garden and slip; 10, Orchard; 11, Marsh house and dove house; 12, Parterre and terraces; 13, Canal and grass panels; 14, Great Bason; 15, Gardener's lodge and canal; 16, Alcove Wilderness; 17, Star Wilderness; 18, North Garden; 19, Equestrian statue of George I; 20, Physic garden. The layout was conventional in most respects, though the grandeur of such elements as the avenues with reflecting basons, the seven-acre 'Great Bason' within the garden and the outer plantations of 61 acres to the north was extraordinary for the time.

At Boughton House, the Earl (now Duke) of Montagu brought in Leonard Vandermule, who in 1706 was making the parterre (see fig. 152).

England among other nations

Towards the end of the first decade of the eighteenth century the war was becoming increasingly unpopular in the country. Anne formed a new Tory-dominated ministry in 1710 and fresh elections provided a Tory majority in the House of Commons. The new leaders were Robert Harley, created Earl of Oxford and Lord High Treasurer in 1711, as Chancellor of the Exchequer; and Henry St John, Viscount Bolingbroke from 1712, as Secretary of State. They keenly sought peace with the French. Anne dismissed the Duke of Marlborough from his command, and the way was clear to negotiate.

Antagonism between the parties was running high. Their leaders were ever more anxious to secure the allegiance of propagandist writers. The Whigs lost Jonathan Swift, who had been Sir William Temple's secretary, to the Tories, but the youthful Alexander Pope was for a while attracted to Addison's coterie centred in Button's coffee house. After losing his office as Under

rience to match Brompton Park, and foreign undertakers were sometimes called upon. Following William III's death, Viscount Montgomery returned from exile to Powis Castle with Adrian Duval, a gardener from Rouen.[19] William Winde designed the lower terraces to the gardens, and Duval supervised the work on cut and fill from 1703, and perhaps the staircase cascade (fig. 153).

Secretary of State for the South in 1709, Addison had joined with his old friend Richard Steele in writing for the daily journal *The Tatler* (1709–10), *The Spectator* (1711–12, 1714) and later *The Guardian* (1713).

Addison was an admirer of the new science, and of Locke and the other Whig ideologues, and at the same time sought a revival of the Classical republican ideal of virtue, adapted to the times in which he lived. He regarded the journals as an

151   Drawing of the view from Warwick Priory by Canaletto, *c*.1750. This is the garden of the Royal Gardener, Henry Wise, at his estate in Warwickshire. In the foreground is the simple garden of the 1720s, with a bason, figure and vases, and a viewing terrace along the south side. To the right is St Mary's church. Guy's and Caesar's towers of Warwick Castle are in the distance to left of centre, and the spire of St Nicholas's is off to far left.

152   Henry Wise's heraldic achievement. Henry Wise of Brompton, afterwards Warwick Priory, was granted arms in 1720: 'Sable, three chevronels ermine between as many adders argent. Crest – a demi lion rampant argent holding in the paw a rose branch proper in the mouth a snake vulnerating him in the shoulder and entwined about the body vert'. This was a variation on the arms of Wise of Sydenham, Devon, to whom Henry was doubtfully connected, but the rose branch was his own invention.

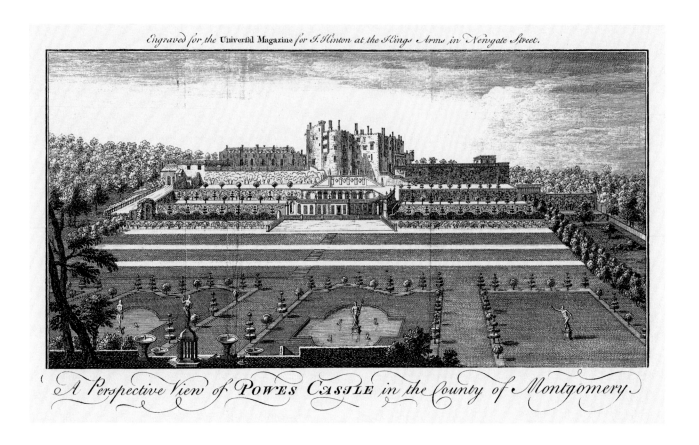

A Perspective View of POWES CASTLE in the County of Montgomery.

opportunity to re-present his learning as arguments in favour of a moderate, balanced and harmonious life. He did so in an easy and polished style, attracting the admiration of a range of readers far wider than he would have gained through another

---

153   *A Perspective View of Powes Castle in the County of Montgomery* by Samuel and Nathaniel Buck, re-engraved for the *Universal Magazine*, 1742. The Jacobite Marquess of Powis returned from exile in 1703 with Adrian Duval, a gardener from Rouen. William Winde designed the lower terraces, of which the central third was treated architecturally, with arcades, balustrades, blank windows and a greenhouse, combined with a series of steps. Clipped yews, lead figures by Andries Carpentière and urns adorned each level. Duval supervised the work of cut and fill and probably the staircase cascade driving *jets d'eau* at each level. The top of this cascade can be seen bottom left; it fed apsidal-ended pools surrounded by borders with cut and divided yews.

---

volume of poetry. *The Spectator* became the nation's *arbiter elegantiarum*. Addison was 'ambitious to have it said of me, that I have brought Philosophy out of Closets and Libraries, Schools and Colleges, to dwell in Clubs and Assemblies, at Tea-Tables and in Coffee Houses.'[20]

The rise in Classical learning, and interest in Classical times amongst those without the learning, gave Addison, Pope and others profitable opportunities in translation from the Classics. Tourists to Rome found paintings by Claude, informed by the buildings and countryside around Rome, and rendered with a quality of light and subject matter that infused the poetic imagination with idealised landscapes of Classical Antiquity. To a nation familiar with painting merely as portraiture, such works suggested a world of new possibilities. The reign of Queen Anne, marred as it was by war and ferocious party contest, was a time of adjustment, as learning, taste and refinement were valued as never before.

The Whig world view saw a special place in it for Britain ('Britain' because the crowns of England and Scotland were united in 1707). Lord Somers was the recipient of the third Earl of Shaftesbury's 'Letter Concerning the Art and Science of Design', written in 1711/12.[21] Shaftesbury, grandson of the founder of the Whig party, was a strong Parliamentarian, and thus keen to show that ''tis not the Nature of a Court to improve, but rather corrupt a *Taste*'. English taste, he wrote, had been blighted by 'one single Court-Architect', in other words Wren, over several reigns. He felt that an improved 'National Taste' was forming because 'Almost every-one now becomes concern'd, and interests himself' in both public and major private projects. He argued that despite the great achievements of the French under a dominant monarchy, the British genius promised even greater.

Shaftesbury thought that Britain's destiny was to take a leading role in the arts. The inheritors of the Classical tradition, the Italians, and then the French, had squandered their inheritance through degenerate (what was to be called 'Baroque') art. It was now down to Britain, free of the dead hand of autocracy, to rediscover the true Classical tradition. Shaftesbury wrote in 1709 of the 'rising Genius of our Nation', and prophesied that when the Marlborough wars ended, 'united Britain' would be 'the principal Seat of Arts', amongst which he counted architecture.

Whig prognostications for the future argued that the new constitution would enable Britain to take a leading role amongst the powers in Europe, acting as arbiter between the others, a prediction that turned into fact. In the event, the Treaty of Utrecht, ending the War of the Spanish Succession, was the first international treaty to mention a 'balance of power' explicitly. It was signed in 1713, though without the agreement of Britain's allies, and the Whigs accused the Tories of betraying the national interest.

EMULATING AND SURPASSING THE FRENCH

France may have been at war with Britain, yet it remained the country to emulate in artistic matters. A problem arose that travel to France had been prevented for 23 years from 1690, first by William III's war, and then the War of the Spanish Succession, with just a five-year interlude following the Peace of Rijswijk. A curiosity for information on French gardens built up, no doubt fuelled by hints such as Addison's on 'the Magnificence which is easily discoverable from the French Designs'.[22] He had gone to Italy via France, visiting Fontainebleau and other royal palaces and forests (see fig. 251).[23] He later observed that 'our English Gardens are not so entertaining to the Fancy as those in France and Italy, where we see a large Extent of Ground cover'd over with an Agreeable Mixture of Garden and Forest'.[24]

Not until 1709 did an authoritative work on the French garden design tradition appear. Published anonymously, *La Théorie et la Pratique du Jardinage* was a collaboration between the architect Alexandre le Blond, who had worked under Le Nostre, and who devised the plan of the book and provided the drawings for the plates, and Antoine-Joseph Dezallier d'Argenville, a gentleman connoisseur who provided the polished prose text.[25] Together they sought through the book to 'Form a right Taste of what concerns . . . the Designs of Parterres, Grass-Plots, Groves, Arbour-work, Cascades, and other suitable Ornaments'.[26] James Johnston, formerly Secretary of State for Scotland, obtained a copy, and, having a 'good Opinion of the Original', he encouraged his architect, John James, to translate it.[27] Johnston used his influence in Parliament to assemble a lengthy list of subscribers, including the majority of the powerful who were active in garden-making.

In his first book, published three years later, Switzer complained of 'The Misfortune that most of my Profession are under, in not having been abroad'.[28] He commented enviously that the originator of 'Mr. *James*'s Translation . . . has had the most magnificent Gardens in all France to view, and he has certainly chose the very Marrow and Beauty of all those excellent Designs'.[29] He confessed 'that, in this Point, I must expect to fall very far short of him; which will be excus'd, when 'tis consider'd, that I have writ this Treatise in a Country that does not yet abound with such truly noble Gardens as *France* does'. As to suitable designs, Switzer observed that 'many may be collected out of Mr. *James*'s Book' (fig. 154).[30]

154 'The General Disposition of a Magnificent Garden all Upon a Level', Le Blond's general plan for a garden on falling levels of 1709 as re-engraved by Michael van der Gucht for John James's translation of Dezallier d'Argenville (1712). Within a rectangle of 46 acres were courts and kitchen gardens either side of the forecourt and house, behind the house was a *parterre de broderie* surrounded by *bosquets* in a high state of upkeep, then a cross-canal and larger and more rustic plantations. The boundaries were walls punctuated by *claire-voies*, and at the far end was a ditch with water, allowing unimpeded views out.

155 Leyton House in a detail of John Rocque's *Map of London*, 1746. In about 1712 a Huguenot, David Gansel, made gardens west of his house, starting with parterres, then plantations, leading down to a canal on the flood plain of the Lea; few English gardens followed Le Blond and Dezallier d'Argenville as closely as this.

In one case, Leyton House, Essex, a garden was made by a Huguenot refugee, David Gansel, to a general plan inspired by Le Blond's plates (fig. 155). However, it was not his general plans that drew most attention, but plates of parterres and *bosquets* that could be plundered for enriching English designs (see fig. 170). For example, some of the halls in the plantations at Southill and Belton were simplified versions of those shown in his plates (see fig. 166).[31]

It is little wonder that fashion-conscious owners asked for-eigners to draw up their schemes. The Earl of Jersey had been ambassador both at The Hague and in Paris, and no doubt found the draughtsman of his very polished plans for Squerryes Court, Kent, of about 1705 in the latter city (fig. 156).[32] In 1713, the very year the War of the Spanish Succession concluded, one of the Duke of Marlborough's commanders, Lord Orkney, requested

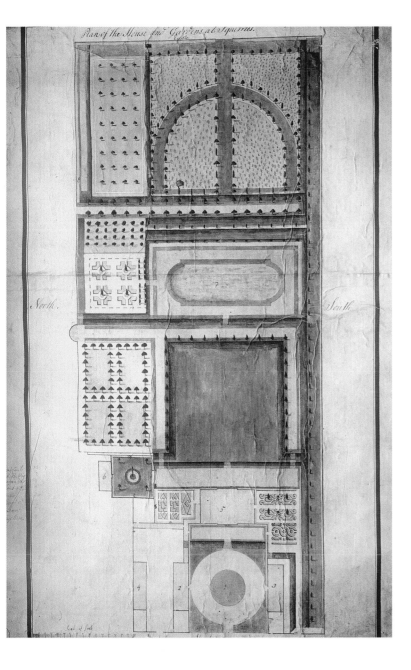

parterre designs from Claude Desgots for Cliveden (fig. 157a and b). The second Duke of Montagu employed a Dutchman, Gabriel Delahaye, who produced a similarly refined garden plan for Boughton in 1712 (see fig. 103).

Despite this continuing admiration for French gardens, authors hoped that England had the potential to surpass them in some respects. For example, James remarked in his dedication that 'we may hope to see, ere long, our English Pleasure-Gardens in greater Perfection, than any the most renowned, in France, or Italy, since our Woods and Groves, our Grass and Gravel . . . are allowed to surpass in Verdure and natural Beauty, whatever is to be found in those Countries.'[33] The claim for the superiority of English grass was not new, or even English.[34] James's claim for the superiority of its gravel was based on the reputation of hoggin, a mix of gravel and clay to make a bound surface, used over much of England in contrast to the loose gravel preferred by the French for their alleys, or the sand used by the Dutch. James's overall point was repeated by Switzer, who was sufficiently emboldened by his vision of 'Forest, or Rural, Gardening' (see below) to hope that with its general adoption 'we may hope to excel the so-much-boasted Gardens of France, and to make that great Nation give way to superior Beauties'.[35]

Switzer also emphasised the quality of patronage in Britain. The Earl of Carlisle's labyrinth wood at Castle Howard showed 'the highest pitch that Natural and Polite Gard'ning can possibly ever arrive at'.[36] He named several dukes and earls as 'amongst some of the greatest Ornaments of Arts and Sciences, especially Gardening, that History has Produc'd'. Their seats 'and such-like august Designs as these, which are to be seen in many Places now, denote that Greatness of Mind that reigns in the English Nobil-

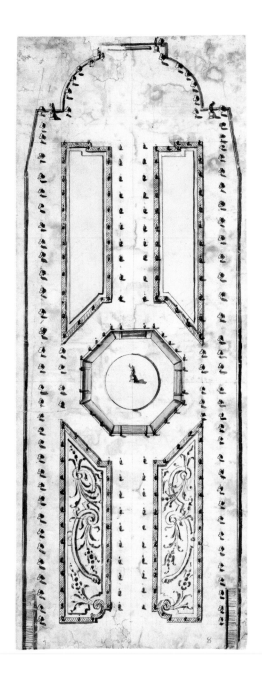

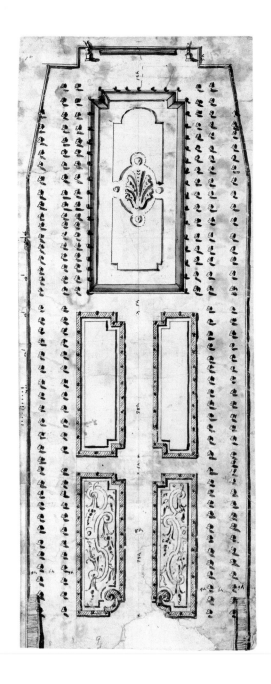

157a and b   Claude Desgots' alternative designs for an extended
parterre at Cliveden House, 1713. Probably not implemented, the
parterre would have commenced with *broderie* designs on a scale
appropriate to the site; one had a central sunken area with a figure,
and the other was smaller, to make space for a sunken area with cutwork.
The tree-lined walks presaged those planted in 1723.

ity and Gentry. And it cann't but argue a true Gust and Relish
of . . . what may reasonably be expected from futurity.'[37]

This hope ripened to fruition over time, if Batty Langley was reliable in claiming that 'our British Nation does at this Time consist
of the most noble grand Planters and Encouragers of Gardening
of any in Europe'.[38] The Revd William Harper could, in 1732,
look back at a remarkable period: 'Our Palaces, both Royal and

others, seem to *Rival* the best Models of Foreign Antiquity in their *Avenues, Vistas, Walks, Wildernesses,* variety of *Fruits* and *Flowers,* and every Thing, that is *Grand* and *Magnificent* in that kind.'[39]

'The nice touches and embellishments of art'

New levels of sophistication in the adornment of avenues, gardens and parks were reached as Queen Anne's reign progressed. Wren, the country's leading architect, advocated balance and proportion:

> There are natural Causes of Beauty. Beauty is a Harmony of Objects, begetting Pleasure by the Eye. There are two causes of Beauty, natural and customary. Natural is from Geometry, consisting in Uniformity (that is Equality) and Proportion . . . Geometrical Figures are naturally more beautiful than other irregular . . . Strait Lines are more beautiful than curve.[40]

It is to be expected, then, that in gardens more unified schemes of parterre and wilderness within the traditional walled enclosure were sought, and embellishments to these pleasure gardens refined.

AVENUE AND FORECOURT

Moses Cook's advice had been 'Do not mask a fine Front, nor veil a pleasant Prospect (as too many do) by making the Walks too narrow'.[41] A half-mile avenue would need to be 40 feet broad, a longer one proportionately wider. The Great Walk through Bushy Park, intended as the new approach to Hampton Court, was initially planted at 260 feet wide (see fig. 90), and it was still 170 feet wide after Wise had lined it with horse chestnuts in 1699.[42] The term 'great avenue' seems to have been reserved for a special class of such outsize vistos. Cook and London were responsible for two in the early 1680s, the two-and-a-half mile one linking Windsor Castle to the Great Park (see fig. 145), and the 200-foot-wide one at Longleat. The next was in Queen Anne's reign, the 300-foot-wide lime avenue through the park north of Blenheim

Palace (see fig. 136). This was surpassed by the far shorter, but 400-foot-wide, approach at Bramham, which sprang from a 450-square-foot parade (see fig. 188). Cannons was provided with an approach 1,000 yards long with a one-acre reflecting bason, and a western visto over 300 feet wide, embracing the service court and its wings, 1,303 yards long (see fig. 150).[43] Before he died in 1718, the last Viscount Dunbar planted a double elm avenue nearly 300 feet wide at Burton Constable, Yorkshire. Most of the larger avenues remained smaller than these, at around 80 to 100 feet wide, so the 100-foot-wide dummy double avenue with canal at Cholmondeley, dug around 1713, was of a quite typical width, whilst the 150-foot-wide double avenue stretching an immense distance away from the front at Castle Ashby, Northamptonshire, which was being finished in 1715, was approaching the 'grand avenue' class.

A new form of avenue planting, consisting of blocks of trees, was seen. There was one precedent, the plantations, about six trees each way in a block, planted by 1683 alongside the way to Hackwood from Basing Castle, Hampshire (fig. 158). In 1706–7 similar blocks were planted as part of the Great Avenue at Blenheim, being embedded into the outer edges and half-square terminations (see fig. 136). They came to be known as 'platoons', perhaps to be in keeping with the military overtones of the 'fortification way' of gardening. Wise planted further platoons in Hyde Park as a ride at this time,[44] and in 1713 planted some around Lord Halifax's Upper Lodge in Bushy Park.[45]

Switzer's commendation of Halifax's 'Forest works' may suggest that he had been involved at Bushy Park as Wise's assistant.[46] About 1712 he visited Heythrop, where alternating clumps and platoons were planted, confining a broad and long vista to the north (see fig. 253).[47] Platoons also lined the middle walk at Grimsthorpe, where he worked. When in *Ichnographia Rustica* Switzer described his idealised 'Manor of Paston', 'Plattoons or Poletoons' lined his middle walk (see fig. 254),[48] and an illustration indicated platoons surrounding an example of a grand lawn in a forest (see fig. 179).[49] Hence, platoons could be planted either with lines of trees or without to form vistos, or alternatively used to surround half-squares or lawns.

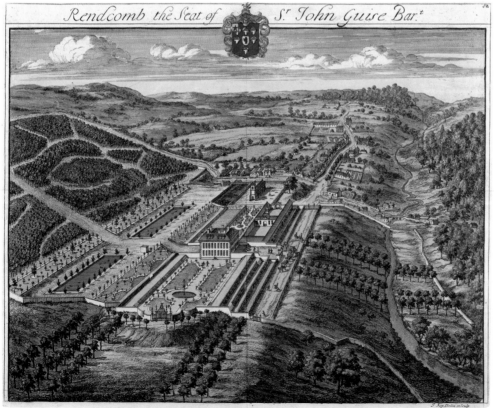

158 'A Topographicall Discription of the Lands . . . known by the name of Hackwood Parke', an estate survey by Thomas Smith, 1683 (north is at the bottom). The sixth Marquess of Winchester rebuilt the Tudor hunting lodge in Hackwood Park, Hampshire, in 1683–8, possibly using Talman as architect. Walks extended in each direction and the avenue from the north ran between platoons. The east walk ran through Spring Wood, which had a circular ride, and out into the eastern parkland; another walk intersected it and was flanked by twelve platoons, possibly the earliest example of such planting.

159 Bird's-eye view of Rendcomb House, Gloucestershire, drawn and engraved by Johannes Kip, 1712. Sir John Guise, third Baronet, had recently added elaborate gates by William and Simon Edney to the far end of his father's garden of about 1690. The borders in the slope above may well have been for bulbs, and the reservoirs above drove the fountain; the ancient wood had a number of glades, though a visto was cut through it on the side axis of the house.

During the late seventeenth century bridges were simply necessit-ies that were incidental to the layout, and not objects worthy of attention. Vanbrugh, however, saw their ornamental possibilities. A little bridge, paid for in 1705–6, with miniature obelisks on the parapets, was built on the north avenue at Castle Howard.[50] This was in contrast to his Great Bridge at Blenheim, decided on in 1706, but brought to reality over several years.[51] It was only ever used by estate traffic, and the Great Avenue never flanked any sig-nificant roadway. Archer too saw the possibilities, and faced a dam at Heythrop with an ornamental bridge in about 1710.[52]

Reflecting basons were introduced at about the two-thirds point of avenues, and on a windless day reflections provided an inverted view of the destination. The first may have been that at Hampton Court, dug to London's specification in 1699–1700 within the circle of the Great Avenue through Bushy Park (see fig. 16). Others were dug at Woburn Abbey (see fig. 288), Tring, Wanstead (see fig. 287) and Cannons (see fig. 150), all places where London is known, or suspected, to have worked. The octagon at Wanstead was formed about 1715 by Adam Holt, who had perhaps been Lon-don's foreman there. Bridgeman designed an octagon bason on the approach to Sacombe, Hertfordshire (see fig. 224), like those at Tring and Wanstead, and a round-headed canal aligned on the entrance front of Stowe, dug in 1716–18 (see fig. 269).

ENTRANCE COURTS AND GATES

The fashion for iron gates set within the forecourt palisade resulted in a generation of native English ironworkers mimicking Tijou's techniques. They supplied scores of sets of gates, gener-ally quite locally. Robert Bakewell provided gates in and around Derbyshire, as well as the arbour at Melbourne. William and Simon Edney of Bristol appear to have had a copy of Tijou's *New Booke of Drawings* of 1693, as their designs were adapted from it. They made gates for Rendcomb, near Cirencester, erected in time to be illustrated in Atkyns's *Glostershire* (1712), which were placed in the half-moon at the end of the parterre garden as a

160   Gates at Chirk Castle made by the Davies brothers of nearby Bersham in 1719 for the outer court and moved to the edge of the park, to form the lodge gates, in 1770. They have been restored to their original white by the National Trust.

transparent termination (fig. 159). The fine forecourt gates at Tre-degar House were delivered by the Edneys in 1715.[53] At the other end of Wales, the Davies brothers of Bersham, near Wrexham, were particularly known for Chirk Castle and its gates, commis-sioned in 1711 but not delivered for several years; they were paid for in 1721 (fig. 160). There are many other gates by them in north Wales, Cheshire and Shropshire, including those at Hawkstone, paid for in 1725, or attributed to them, as at Eaton Hall. Other fine examples of this period include the gates at Hamels, Hert-fordshire, supplied by a Mr Warren in the mid-1710s (see fig. 240). and the iron forecourt gates at Grimsthorpe, made by a smith called Edward Nutt in 1730.

At larger houses, where a large number of carriages might wish to enter the court, the carriage sweep proved inadequate, and so 'great' or 'grand courts' were made sufficiently large for a con-course and pitch-paved right across.[54] Het Loo had such a court around a fountain, for the horses to drink (see fig. 101), as did Buck-ingham House, facing St James's Park (see fig. 113). Vanbrugh and Hawksmoor designed those at Castle Howard and Blenheim in

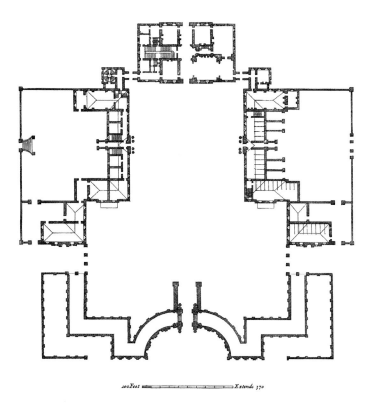

100 Feet ————————————— *Extends 370*

161 A general plan for the house, offices and Great Court at Easton Neston as illustrated in *Vitruvius Britannicus* in 1715, probably on the basis of designs made by Hawksmoor in about 1701. The parapeted moat and gatehouse enclosing the Great Court were never built; such militaristic overtones were typical of the Vanbrugh circle's treatment of outworks in the 1700s.

1702 and 1705 respectively without fountains (see fig. 172). Switzer knew these examples, and observed that: 'It has formerly been the Method, to place a Fountain in the Middle of Court-Yards, or to make, in its Room, a large circular or oval Plott; but this is altogether disus'd at present . . . now the Manner, to pave the grand Court all over'.[55] He suggested that the surface chosen should be stone, 'pitch'd Chequer and Star-wise'. That may have been so in London and major seats, but at quieter country houses gravel remained the norm.

Vanbrugh and Hawksmoor carried on devising some imaginative schemes for enclosure of such courts with quasi-medieval or military-style outworks. Hawksmoor designed some for Easton Neston, Northamptonshire, before 1715 (fig. 161). About that year Vanbrugh enclosed the court at Claremont with ramparts, as did Colen Campbell at Wanstead. Vanbrugh's schemes for Sacombe (see fig. 224), Eastbury in 1718 (see fig. 194), and Lumley about 1720 (see fig. 244) had gravel rectangles without any central island of grass from the start. In 1717 Vanbrugh's forecourt at Kings Weston was even going to have a gateway topped by a pyramid.[56]

CUTWORK AND SCROLLWORK

The literature on how to form pleasure gardens was very inadequate early in Anne's reign. A book explaining how the labyrinth at Versailles was based on the fables of Aesop was published by the Dutch cartographer Nicolaes Visscher in four languages, including English.[57] It evidently found its way to England, because a plate of the former labyrinth at Versailles came to be re-engraved for Switzer's *Ichnographia Rustica* (see fig. 238).[58] More directly apposite was Louis Liger's *Le Jardinier fleuriste et historiographe* (1704). It incorporated some parterre designs collected over many years, and some plates of *bosquet* designs, though these were of poor quality. Jacob Tonson determined that the book should be translated into English, along with François Gentil's *Le Jardinier solitaire* (1704).[59] In order to make these works more applicable to England, he persuaded London and Wise to annotate the result as *The Retir'd Gard'ner* (1706).

The design of a curlicue cutwork grass border in Liger appears to be a variation on one set out by Le Nostre at the Maison Royale de Saint-Louis at Saint-Cyr about 1685.[60] His Plate VI, of a cutwork parterre, was similar in general form to the parterre at the Château de Petit-Bourg overlooking the Seine, perhaps laid out about 1650,[61] and to panels in the Tuileries, installed by Le Nostre soon after 1664.[62] Liger's designs were widely ignored, except for the cutwork in grass. The Duke of Leeds created some fine examples at his new Yorkshire mansion at Kiveton (fig. 162). It was based on Liger's Plate VIII, but without *broderie* (fig. 163). Cutwork was continued by others in this reign, for example at Eaton about 1710 and Stowe about 1713.

The East Prospect & Garden Front of KIVETON HOUSE The Seat of the most Noble THOMAS OSBORNE Duke of LEEDS Marquis of Carmarthen, Earl of Danby, Viscount Latimer and Dumblane, Baron Osborne of Kiveton, and Baronet.

162 'The East Prospect and Garden Front of Kiveton House', drawn by Thomas Badeslade and engraved by Michael van der Gucht, *c.*1712. It shows the first Duke of Leeds' mansion, erected in 1698–1704. *Glacis* slopes have been used to open up views of the lower garden and wildernesses from the higher one, and of the higher one from the great terrace; the quantity of figures and urns was prodigious. The cutwork pattern was based on one in Louis Liger's book.

163 'The Form of a Parterre with Cut-work and Imbroidery in the Middle, and the Borders of Grass', plate VIII in Louis Liger's *Le Jardinier fleuriste et historiographe* (1704), probably derived from French examples of 50 years before. The book was published in English in 1706 by Jacob Tonson with annotations by London and Wise. The cutwork was adapted by the Duke of Leeds for Kiveton with the *broderie* interior replaced by grass (see fig. 162).

Vol. 1.   p. 235.

VIII

DIRECTIONS *to* Gardeners, *who have not had the Opportunity of Travelling, with Regard to some Particulars in laying out of* Gardens, *and some Technical Words frequently mentioned in this* Treatise.

A Pyramid Plant is reprefented thus in a Draught; and when we have Occafion to place feveral of them upon a Ground Platt, they muft be all fet upright with that which we firft defign; fo likewife the Shades muft be all placed the fame way.

A *Headed Plant* is reprefented thus.

A *Pyramid Plant*, cut and divided, may be reprefented thus.

A *Collonade*, or *Arcade*, in a Garden is generally planted with *Yew-Trees*, and may be exprefs'd thus; the Bafes and Capitalls may be carv'd and gilt, or elfe made of *Wood*, painted with *Verdegreafe Green*, to be taken off, and put on when the *Trees* want

M 2   Clip-

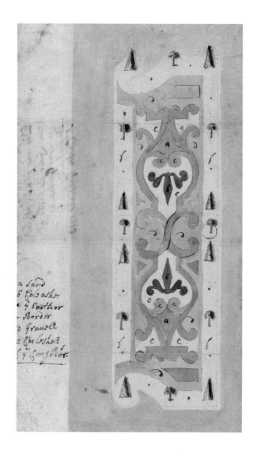

164   Terms for clipped plants from Richard Bradley's *New Improvements of Planting and Gardening, both Philosophical and Practical* (1731). Bradley distinguishes between the pyramid plant (most yews), the headed plant (the golden holly) and the pyramid plant, cut and divided (more elaborate clipping into layers). He also included the arcade of yews grown against timber formwork, in fashion since Dezallier d'Argenville's book was published in English.

165   'Draught of a Knot for the Lower Quarter of the Long Garden at Bush-hill Drawn by Mr Clarkes Gardiner 1713'. This naïve sketch for a parterre design for Bush Hill, Edmonton, indicates the coloured materials to be used in a form of embellishment that was briefly popular in Queen Anne's reign; they included yellow sand, black coal ashes and white crushed cockleshell. The recipient was probably Sir Samuel Vanacher Sambrooke, Baronet, elder brother of Jeremy Sambrooke of Gubbins.

Otherwise, English parterres continued to sport *plates-bandes* and side terraces, many inspired by the scrollwork in the Privy Garden at Hampton Court and at Blenheim. Imitations were seen at Wanstead (see fig. 184), Kings Weston, Gloucestershire, and Melbourne (see fig. 146).[63] Most *parterres à l'Angloise* in the early 1710s continued to incorporate scrollwork, for example at Waldershare Park, Kent, Stainborough Park, and Caversham Court, Berkshire. Despite his own advocacy for plainer parterres, Switzer admitted that turf 'cut into Shell and Scroll-work with Sand-Alleys between them' provided 'the finest Kinds of Parterre Works of Esteem with us' and gave three designs.[64] He likened a couple of them to the Privy Garden at Hampton Court and to the parterre at Blenheim 'and some others, that are accounted amongst the best of their Kind' on account of their proportions and design.[65]

Parterres continued to be embellished with yews and shrubs, *jets d'eau* and figures. The bulk of new clipping was of the traditional

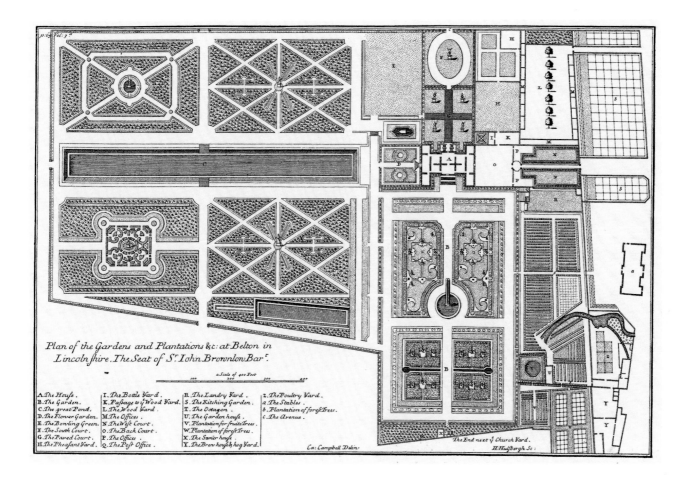

Plan of the Gardens and Plantations &c: at Belton in
Lincolnſhire. The Seat of Sr. John Brownlow Bart.

a Scale of 400 Feet

A. The Houſe.
B. The Garden.
C. The great Pond.
D. The Flower Garden.
E. The Bowling Green.
F. The South Court.
G. The Paved Court.
H. The Pheaſant Yard.

I. The Bottle Yard.
K. Paſſage to ye Wood Yard.
L. The Wood Yard.
M. The Offices.
N. The Weſt Court.
O. The Back Court.
P. The Office.
Q. The Poſt Office.

R. The Landry Yard.
S. The Kitching Garden.
T. The Octagon.
U. The Garden houſe.
V. Plantation for fruite Trees.
W. Plantation of foreſt Trees.
X. The Somer houſe.
Y. The Brew houſe & hog Yard.

z. The Poultry Yard.
a. The Stables.
b. Plantation of foreſt Trees.
c. The Avenue.

The End next ye Church Yard.

Ca: Campbell Delin: H. Hulſbergh Sc:

pyramid yews and globe hollies, but 'shaped greens' were more in evidence in the 1700s. Such pieces were those cut into tiered and other complex forms instead of simple shapes. The botanist and agricultural writer Richard Bradley, in explaining 'Technical Words', gave three shapes for clipped shrubs; 'pyramid', 'headed' and 'pyramid, cut and divided', that is conical, globe-headed and tiered (fig. 164).[66] Another occasional refinement was to use coloured infills in parterre borders (fig. 165), as the comte de Tallard had done in Nottingham.

James's translation of *La Théorie et la pratique du jardinage* became available when English parterre design was on the cusp. In some places the plain parterre was making its appearance, whereas elsewhere an attachment to French forms was maintained. A drawing in the Castle Bromwich archive for a parterre with scrollwork ending in dolphin heads probably relates to a payment

of five guineas by Sir John Bridgeman to 'Cross the gardener' for 'the Draughts of Castle Bromwich Gardens Wildernesses etc.' in 1716/17. It is clearly derived from a plate in James's book. Slightly earlier, Sir John Brownlow copied a 'parterre of Cutwork for Flowers' from James in a hall in his new wilderness at Belton (fig. 166).[67]

166   'Plan of the Gardens and Plantations &c: at Belton', engraved by Henry Hulsbergh, *c*.1717. The plantations may have been added soon after Sir John Brownlow's marriage in 1712 and certainly before his ennoblement in 1718. Dezallier d'Argenville's general influence is evident, and the flower garden within one of the halls is a direct use of one of Le Blond's designs; the cutwork resembling strapwork was a notable feature, but perhaps this and the *bosquet* beyond dated from the late 1680s.

167 Easton Neston House in 1719 as depicted in Peter Tillemans' 'Prospect of the Lord Lempsters House Taken in the Garden'. This view from the lower end of the garden walled in about 1686 by Sir William Fermour, using advice from Wren and Hawksmoor, is dominated by the yew pyramids in the *plates-bandes*. By the house are several of the Arundel marbles that Fermour (by then Lord Lempster) brought here in 1692; to the right can be seen a fluted Corinthian column with Apollo aloft, one of the first examples of a column in an English garden.

SCULPTURE

Richard Osgood, John van Nost and his principal assistant, Andries Carpentière, produced a range of bronze and lead pieces. Nost's blackamore and Indian kneeling slave sundial bases were installed at Hampton Court, Wanstead, Dunham Massey, Okeover and Melbourne in the first decade of the century. He supplied a wide variety of other pieces to Melbourne, including *amoroni*, a boy and swan, a triton, and in 1705 the spectacular 'Vase of the Seasons', set in a circle in the wilderness. He supplied about another dozen properties with pieces. The two pairs of urns and vases carved by Cibber and Pearce for Hampton Court seem to have inspired other owners to acquire similar works.[68] The Duke of Leeds acquired sixteen urns for Kiveton. Also in Yorkshire, Robert Benson had the square 'Four Faces' urn carved from stone for Bramham. The Earl of Carnarvon commissioned gilded vases to flank the great walk of the parterre at Cannons in about 1714,[69]

at the same date that Lord Cobham had gilded garden vases placed in the openings of the arcade around the parterre at Stowe (see fig. 215).[70]

In 1652 an Antique column, purchased earlier in Rome by Evelyn, had been erected in the inner *bas court* at Wilton, but Antique ornament of any kind remained unusual in English gardens.[71] The other exception was the famous and revered Arundel marbles, originally assembled before the Civil War by the Earl of Arundel, a great quantity of which Lord Lempster had bought in 1691 and moved to Easton Neston. Before Lempster died in 1711 his architect Hawksmoor had set up a broken Antique column from the Temple of Apollo at Delphos in the parterre and topped it with a statue of Apollo (fig. 167). This and other Antique statuary were placed on pedestals with an 'L' cut into their faces.

FLOWERS, ARBOURS AND ARCADES

The craze for exotics was easing off, and the number of new greenhouses declined. Bradley attributed this to 'all those pompous Edifices which I have seen in *England*, for the keeping of Exotick Plants, the true Design of such Buildings has been so little understood, or regarded, that scarce three of them have answer'd the End they were built for'.[72] Likewise, fewer flower gardens were seen by the house, and fewer flowerpots and tubs for greens are visible on engravings. Switzer pointed out that flower gardening might be desirable in town gardens, as the owner would probably still be in residence when most flowers bloomed, but when at his country seat in the late summer and autumn he should not be spending time 'in the more trifling and fading Beauties of Flowers'.[73]

London and Wise commented that 'we cover our Portico-Galleries with Limes, which do very well', whereas that in the Hampton Court Privy Garden had actually been in wych elm. Such tunnel arbours were seldom seen again, the exception being for the Earl of Portland himself, at his home at Bulstrode (see fig. 189).

Arcades, consisting of trees trained into open arches with a trellis framework, were well known in France and the Low Countries. Liger gave an illustration of one, commenting, 'I have nam'd a great many sorts of Compartments, in which Horn-beam is

made use of; yet methinks none of them look so beautiful and magnificent as a Gallery with Arches.'[74] A few examples, generally surrounding parterres, were seen, at Squerryes, Wrest and Forde Abbey, and, as with palisades generally, yew increasingly came to be used in England for such features.

James's translation of *La Théorie et la pratique du jardinage* was to have a profound effect on English wildernesses and outward plantations, but in the short term it sparked a much greater interest in arcades than Liger's book had done. Dezallier d'Argenville had observed that palisades pierced through with arches composed 'a kind of Order of Rural Architecture'.[75] Le Blond's illustrations of palisades, mostly shown surrounding the parterre, which were supplemented in the second French edition, were clear and attractive, and were put into practice in England over the next fifteen years. The first examples were seen at the Marquess

of Wharton's garden at Winchendon, Buckinghamshire (see fig. 192), Lord Cobham's at Stowe (see fig. 215), and the Marquess of Lindsey's at Grimsthorpe, all around 1713, but the fashion for them dwindled through the 1720s, and the last was made in the 1730s (fig. 168).

168 Valence, near Westerham, in about 1750, in a drawing by John Donowell labelled 'A View of Es^q. Turner Garden with a Beautiful rural Caskaid that flows out of a thick Wood into a Large Basson in the Garden & then wastes it self underground'. From 1732 William Horsmondon-Turner, soon to be Member of Parliament for Maidstone, formalised the cascade with a reclining water nymph at its head and surrounded the viewing area below with arcades; although arcades were decreasing in popularity at this date, cascades on axis were on the rise.

Beyond the parterre, but within the walls of the garden enclosure, all 'inward' wildernesses continued to be composed as geometrical exercises on a drawing board. Talman's 'scrach of a Garden' for the Duke of Newcastle, perhaps at Welbeck Abbey, Nottinghamshire, of about 1703 showed a variety of garden areas, but all symmetrical and confined to a simple rectangle ending at a *demi-lune*. Dezallier d'Argenville in 1709, Switzer in 1718, and Langley in 1728 all included lengthy sections on geometry and how to set out from a plan.[76] The characteristic signs of textbook patterns for wildernesses are the symmetry, angles of 90, 60 or 45 degrees, and their complexity. The advice was to set them out with great precision with high palisades, and ideally the trees within the wilderness quarters would be lopped to a uniform height. For example, in 1707 the Pensioners at Gray's Inn ordered the gardener to cut the lime trees 'next the Tarrass Walke flat and even at the topps'.[77]

Alternative ways of filling palisaded wilderness quarters continued in practice, with forest trees, orchards, kitchen-garden plots, and especially exotic trees and shrubs all being possible. Switzer rather exaggerated the incidence of exotics in arguing against them and in favour of his more rural manner: 'The Method of Sowing and Raising Wood is certainly much cheaper than planting Exotics, &c. the Way that has been followed in all our Modern Wildernesses'.[78] At Badminton there had been proposals in about 1710 to recast the interiors of wilderness quarters as gardens of clipped shrubs.

Designs for wildernesses were often simplified or the patterns adapted for economy or specific circumstances; for example, the extent of the plot, or shape of the land, could force an irregular layout. The Earl of Rutland found this on the slopes at Belvoir about 1695, where he had to lay out his walks along the contours. At the other end of the scale, as at Inkpen Old Rectory, Berkshire, a small, steeply sloping, polygonal enclosure was exploited to the full by extending the walks to each corner, irrespective of the odd angles created. The same was true of some larger wildernesses, as at Melbourne, set out from about 1704, where the only space

available to Thomas Coke was a declivity of awkward shape to the right-hand side of the axis (see fig. 146).

Some English designers of wildernesses elaborated them in sometimes unsophisticated or idiosyncratic ways. Prior to 1715 the second Duke of Montagu set out some eccentric wildernesses at Boughton in the form of labyrinths of irregular polygons and square within square (see fig. 217). A labyrinth of about 1714 for one of the Duke's other residences at Beaulieu was similar in plan.[79]

Liger illustrated stars, *pattes d'oie*, labyrinths and arcades.[80] A star in a garden would have hornbeam palisades with narrow gravel alleys under them, and a grass swathe down the middle of the walks. His garden *patte d'oie* consisted of rolled gravel walks converging on a round grass plot. These instructions met with little response.

Dezallier d'Argenville had offered much encouragement for the ornamentation of woods, for 'they make the greatest Ornament thereof', and ''tis certain, that a Country-Seat without them is defective in one of its principal Particulars'.[81] He described woods of middle height with tall palisades, groves opened in *compartiments*, quincunxes and evergreen woods, 'which are made use of in fine Gardens'. He mentioned the star and St Andrew's cross arrangements and also the *patte d'oie*, but English readers took much more interest in Le Blond's more complex arrangements of *allées* and his ideas on *halles*.

A few owners immediately copied or adapted Le Blond. Sir John Brownlow's new wilderness at Belton, mentioned above, had four quarters with a canal down the axis, all derivative in some respect from *La Théorie et la pratique du jardinage*. Vanbrugh provided Earl Cholmondeley with a 'generall scheme for what is left to do' at Cholmondeley in 1713. Part of the alterations, or perhaps just a proposal, around that time was a spiral labyrinth to the side of the axial avenue, which had been taken into the garden as a yew-lined walk (fig. 169). It was a literal copy of a plate by Le Blond, derived from a design for Chantilly.[82] This labyrinth was also copied in part at Wentworth Woodhouse, at Rosendaal in the Low Countries and at La Granja in Spain.

Dezallier d'Argenville advised that 'You should always observe to make something Noble in the Middle of a Wood, as a Hall of

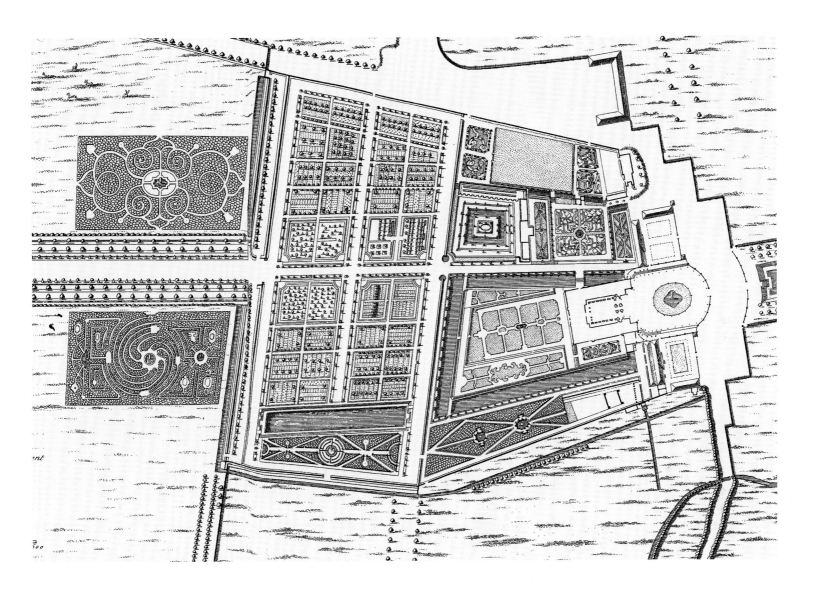

Horse-Chesnuts, a Water-work, Cascade, or the like'.[83] Le Blond's plates gave designs for three halls and four cloisters, and there were many other halls indicated on his plates of whole gardens (fig. 170).[84] Switzer's plan of a plain and a water parterre surrounded by terraces appears to have been an elaboration of Le Blond's 'great Hall of Horsechesnuts' (fig. 171).[85]

Salles and cabinets, small palisaded spaces designed to afford privacy, had been shown in André Mollet's designs published in 1670,[86] and were also found in designs associated with Daniel Marot. The wilderness at Belton had a bewildering number of tiny cabinets entered by just one walk, where the visitor might

169 'The Geometrical Plan of the House, Gardens and Adjacent Parts of Cholmondeley', engraved by Henry Hulsbergh, *c.*1715. In 1694 the third Viscount Cholmondeley had contracted with George London to make the new ground to the west (left) into a 'plantation of fruit trees' and other divisions, as well as the avenue beyond the gates and the concentric orangery in the older gardens. However, in 1704–13 Lord Cholmondeley (elevated to an earldom in 1706) made great changes to the house and as this work finished he turned to garden improvements; these included bringing the avenue within the gardens and planting the wildernesses to either side; the western one was a spiral labyrinth taken from James's *Theory and Practice of Gardening* (1712).

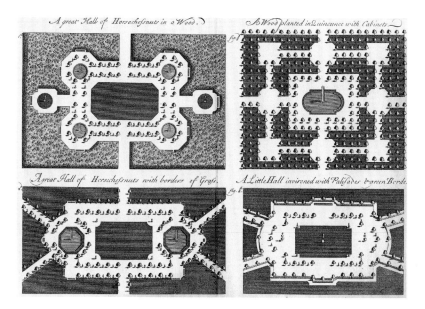

A great Hall of Horsechesnuts in a Wood.

A Wood planted in Quincunce with Cabinets

A great Hall of Horsechesnuts with borders of Grass.

A Little Hall invirond with Palisades & green Borders.

170 *Bosquet* designs by Le Blond, 1709, re-engraved by Michael van der Gucht for John James's 1712 translation of Dezallier d'Argenville. Such *bosquet* and quincunx designs were an inspiration to those thinking of creating halls in the outward plantations of England in the 1710s and 1720s.

171 'A Plann of Plain Grass with Terress and Parterres of Water', engraved by J. Harris for Switzer's *Ichnographia Rustica* (1718). Switzer envisioned a plain parterre with figures descending to a bason with five *jets d'eau*, then a cascade and quatrefoil receiving bason, and finally a canal on axis; the soil thus thrown up would have gone into a pair of substantial side terraces with treed walks. This whole arrangement was conventional in size and proportions, though the various elements were new or used in a new way.

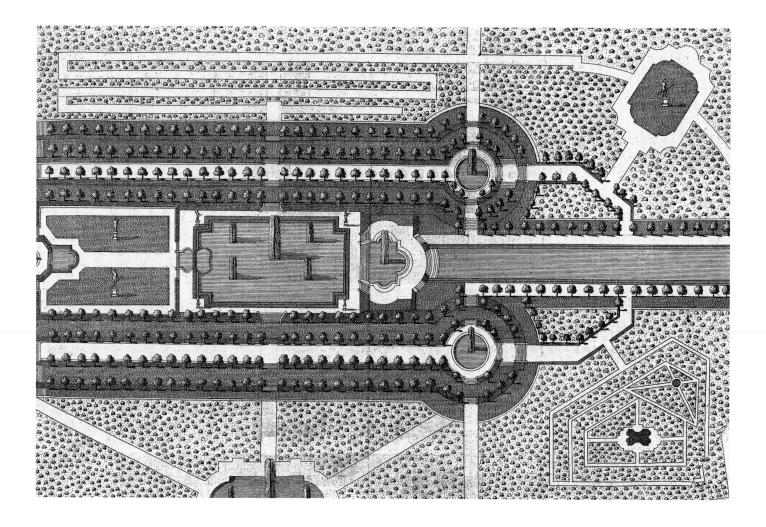

find a seat. Elsewhere it was common for cabinets to form nodes at the junction of two or more straight alleys, as was seen in the wood-work at Blenheim (see fig. 136). Occasionally cabinets were enlivened by *jets d'eau*.

French *bosquet* designs tended to have gravel alleys throughout, as a consequence of the planting being evergreen, and some English ones followed this model. However, Bretby and Chatsworth had wildernesses with 'carpet' (grass) walks, and this treatment was not unusual. The southern wilderness at Castle Howard was planned to be grassed throughout (fig. 172), as was William Blathwayt's on the hill above Dyrham (see fig. 173), and the large extensions to the gardens at Boughton in the early 1710s. Often it was only the main walks that were gravelled, and the minor ones would be grass. The publication of Dezallier d'Argenville's and Le Blond's book seems

to have encouraged a few owners to try gravelling throughout once more, a good example being the wilderness at Belton of the early 1710s, but by and large an increasing number of walks were of grass.

---

172 Detail from the aerial view of Castle Howard engraved by Henry Hulsbergh, *c*.1715, showing the mansion and the wood-work south of it. An estate plan of 1728 reveals that this scheme was accomplished. Huge walls, bastions and Roman corner towers enclosed this wood-work in the 1700s; further suggestions of Antiquity were provided by the axial temple and the obelisks set at intersection points within the planting. The large plain parterre was unprecedented; eight 40-foot obelisks, vases by Daniel Hervé and a 50-foot pillar were installed on it in 1720–4. To the west is the start of the huge kitchen garden.

213

In the quest to open up views, baskethandle terminations remained popular, generally accommodating iron palisades. More palisades or 'iron fences' along whole sides of gardens were seen in the 1700s. The entire end of the garden at Kimbolton, for example, became an iron fence, giving a view of the park (see fig. 138). The palisade around the Fountain Garden at Hampton Court has been mentioned. Probably the most extensive set of iron fences ever was those by a Jean de Montigny enclosing the 27 acres of the Marquess of Carnarvon's gardens at Cannons from 1715.[87] One visitor noted that 'the greatest pleasure of all is, that the divisions of the whole being only made by ballustrades of iron, and not by walls; you see the whole at once, be you in what Part of the Garden or Parterre you will'.[88]

However, these devices were expensive in the extreme, and their demise came about with greater use of the fortification-style ditches and terraces (see below). Some of the later examples of iron palisades were in town, as at Gray's Inn, where an Elizabethan wall was replaced by them in 1720,[89] and those around the enclosed area at St James's Square when it was redesigned in 1727.[90] The once so-admired iron fences at Cannons were to have a sad end. By 1735 they were being dismantled. In 1740 the Marquess, by then Duke, of Chandos, let it be known that if anybody wanted the remainder, quantities could be 'taken down from the gardens at Cannons, which may be had at a moderate price: it would be too much to let them go as old iron'.[91]

Cascades tended to be situated on axis, built into the garden's walled enclosure and visible from the house. As the example of Thomas Archer reveals, in Queen Anne's reign skills in making them were not confined to French and Dutch experts, and they multiplied. Once again it was Chatsworth that set new standards, when its stepped cascade was much enlarged between 1703 and 1708 (see fig. 139). A 30-acre reservoir on the hill above was completed in 1712, the same date that the cascade house was completed. Jets arched over the steps, said Daniel Defoe, and 'Out of the mouths of beasts, pipes, urns etc, a whole river descends the slope of a hill a quarter of a mile in length, over steps, with a terrible noise and broken appearance.'[92]

A near rival was the water-works at Dyrham, fed from a bason with a Neptune fountain at the head of the cascade (fig. 173). This was so long, and the bason was so high on the hill, that it could not be contained within the garden enclosure, and was made in the park. Work seems to have got under way about 1704, and in 1715 one visitor, seeing it completed, marvelled at the 'cascade from a very steep hill of 224 steps, the finest in England except the Duke of Devonshire's'.[93] A third remarkable cascade was at Powis Castle, on the slope opposite the garden terraces. It was a true staircase cascade, with jets on its various levels, and it disgorged into three apsidal-ended basons surrounded by borders with clipped shrubs (see fig. 153). One dinner guest reported in 1705 that 'the water-works and fountains that are finished there are much beyond anything I ever saw whose streams play near twenty yards in height the Cascade has too falls of water which concludes in a noble Bason.'[94]

Some other cascades were of the *buffet d'eau* type, following on from that at Boughton House. Lord Halifax, who purchased the rangership of Bushy Park in 1708, had an ambition for one. He rebuilt the Upper Lodge, and saw the opportunity for a cascade arising from the Longford River, which takes high ground at this point. Upstream, the river was widened to form a reservoir, and at the fall of ground a cascade visible from the garden front was constructed. However, Halifax needed advice from an expert, and in 1710 wrote from Bushy Park to some servant of the Duke's at Montagu House:

> I desire you would write to Boughton to Mons.[r] Vandermulen to send me an exact account of the cascade, viz., how many feet the water falls, the dimensions of the steps, the breadth of each step, the distance from step to step, and, if he can, to make such a draft of the whole, by a scale, as we may follow the example as far our ground admits of it.[95]

The result had deeply rusticated stonework in which there were recesses for painted 'perspectives' simulating the interiors of grottoes (these were brought indoors in winter). The receiving bason

the garden wall at the end of an inward wilderness, as devices to conceal its limit. An early, unbuilt, example of a garden temple was that included by Wren on his plan for the Maastricht Garden of 1698; it shows a circular building with eight attached columns (see fig. 131). Wren set a 'niche', a large arch within a pedimented structure, at the bottom end of the Slope Garden at Kensington Palace in 1703. Archer's domed cascade house at Chatsworth was constructed in 1703–12 at the uppermost limit of the garden (see fig. 139).

These were all at or near the edge of the garden enclosure, intended to conceal its limits, and they turned the visitor's gaze back on the garden. Archer's pavilion at the end of the canal at Wrest, designed in 1709, took a rather different approach. This was not just because it was huge and impressive, an adaptation of Michaelangelo's domed design for San Giovanni dei Fiorentini in Rome, but because it looked as much outwards as inwards (fig. 175). It was to have stood at the centre of a six-pointed star of vistas pointing all ways, although some planting was frustrated by adjoining landowners.

FRUIT AND KITCHEN GARDENS

In 1706 *The Retir'd Gard'ner* included a chapter by Gentil on 'How to lay out a Piece of Ground of Four Acres' for a 'fruit and kitchen garden', with a plan not unlike the *potager* at Versailles, centred upon a bason of water.[98] The six-foot borders around the 'squares', or quarters, were to be planted with dwarf fruit trees,

was a square with apses on the sides (fig. 174). Switzer, who may have contributed to its design or construction, and would at least have observed it being built while he was planting in the park, illustrated this structure in his *Hydrostaticks*.[96] Obviously admired, it was also illustrated by Jacob Bogdani and Bernard Lens and was the progenitor of that at Brackenstown in Ireland in 1719.[97]

The number of freestanding buildings greater than mere summerhouses was on the rise. Bowling-green houses of great grandeur were constructed at Hampton Court in 1700 and Wanstead (see fig. 149a and b) in about 1702, whilst others, such as Hanbury Hall, had more modest wooden buildings. Increasingly, summerhouses of Classical form were to be found set into

whilst three-foot borders under the walls nourished wall-fruit. This publication thus encouraged the combined fruit and kitchen garden seen in William III's reign, which was to remain unaltered in general form till the mid-century, although *espaliers* usually replaced the dwarfs. *Espalier* training of fruit trees had become popular on the Continent, and was soon being recommended by English authors.[99] In the 1730s Philip Miller could look back to observe of dwarfs that 'These were formerly in much greater Request than they are at present . . . and since the introducing of Espaliers into the English Gardens, Dwarf-Trees have been destroy'd in most good Gardens.'[100]

As a place of base labour, the kitchen garden needed to be unobtrusive. One tactic was disguise. The palisades of the wilderness could just as well screen off kitchen quarters or orchards as forest-tree planting. William III had orchard quarters at Het Loo, and so did the Earl of Portland at Bulstrode in the late 1700s. So, about the same time, did the Duke of Leeds at Kiveton, and Sir Robert Walpole at Houghton. Switzer afterwards urged his readers in this direction.[101]

---

174   *A View of the Cascade, Bushy Park Water Gardens* by the studio of Marco Ricci, c.1715. The Earl of Halifax made inquiries about the Boughton cascade in 1710 and afterwards constructed a similar and much admired one at Upper Lodge, Bushy Park. Switzer, who may have been involved in planting platoons in the park at this date, described it in *Hydrostatics* (1728). It had deeply rusticated stonework in which there were recesses for paintings of the interiors of grottoes; these were brought indoors in winter.

175   An anonymous bird's-eye view of the Duke of Kent's gardens at Wrest Park, c.1721. The domed pavilion designed by Thomas Archer in 1709, perhaps after a church by Michelangelo in Rome, is prominent. Completed in 1712, it was initially conceived as being set in parkland at the centre of a star of six walks, so was probably the first major garden building beyond the garden wall in England, but by 1715 it was described as 'at yᵉ end of his Grace's garden'. Alongside the canal are plantations of 1717, possibly by Thomas Ackres, and a canal with an apsidal swelling behind the pavilion was dug by the Duke's gardener in 1718; the Cain Hill pavilion can be seen far right.

One drawback of wildernesses as a setting for kitchen quarters was that they did not provide fruit-walls. Another tactic, then, was to remove the walled fruit and kitchen garden from the vicinity of the pleasure garden altogether. Some kitchen gardens had always been set away from the house, of course, but that was for lack of alternatives. At Belvoir Castle the nearest flattish land was at the bottom of the hill on which the castle stands (see fig. 112). At Newby Hall, the gardens of the old house were retained as the kitchen gardens when the new house and fruit gardens were established on a different site in about 1690. At Squerryes, the new kitchen garden of about 1705 was placed on the only nearby south-facing land.

However, architects in Queen Anne's reign sought ways to distance the kitchen garden from the pleasure garden when opportunities arose. Hence at Blenheim, Vanbrugh's kitchen garden, with tall walls for fruit, and looking like a fortress, was outside the perimeter of the pleasure garden (see fig. 136). At Bramham, the kitchen gardens were placed either side of the vista to Black Fen, concealed by buildings and the wood (see fig. 188). In the early 1710s, at Heythrop and Cannons, the kitchen gardens were also placed very discreetly. Vanbrugh repeated his free-standing militaristic idea at Claremont (see fig. 227) and Sacombe (see fig. 224). From this time it became general for kitchen gardens to be entirely disconnected from pleasure gardens.

The topic of kitchen gardens cannot be left till the fate of the humble box plant is related. Miller thought that 'best and most durable Plant for Edgings in a Garden, is . . . the Dwarf Dutch-Box'. It had once been an expensive import, but in the 1700s English gardeners discovered how to propagate this plant 'by parting the Roots'. Miller reported that by the 1730s 'it is now so common, that it may be purchased from the Nurseries at a cheap Rate'. Box was being expelled from the parterre, but with the removal of hedges to surround kitchen quarters, an acceptable edge between soil and gravel was still required. Box was thus given a new place in kitchen garden borders: 'These Edgings are only planted upon the Sides of Borders next Walks, and not (as the Fashion was some Years ago) to plant the Edgings of Flower-beds, or the Edges of Fruit-borders in the Middle of Gardens'.[102]

Parks and the mansions to which they were attached had drawn close to each other over the previous century, and an increasing number of new mansions were surrounded by parkland as their owners assumed the trappings of Antiquity and status. Emparkment via a royal patent was no longer a consideration, as licensing was abolished altogether at the start of Queen Anne's reign as part of her financial settlement.[103]

By the end of the seventeenth century, hunting was no longer synonymous with deer hunting. Lesser landowners had been indulging in fox hunting since Elizabethan times. It gained in popularity because it was without formality, did not require the apparatus of a deerpark, and the opportunity for fast gallops over open fields was more thrilling. Fox hunting spread up the social ladder. The Duke of York (soon to be James II) had donned a red coat and hunted fox with Lord Grey at Uppark in the early 1680s.[104] The Duke of Richmond leased, and then in 1697 purchased, Goodwood for its proximity to the Charlton Hunt. In 1711 Joseph Addison's fictitious squire, Sir Roger de Coverley, in defending his class, declared that its members 'take it ill of you, that you mention Fox-hunters with so little Respect'.[105] On another occasion he referred to himself as an 'old Fox-hunter'.[106]

Deer hunting was on the decline in parks: where it continued, as at Windsor, the deer were carted to the forest to be hunted with dogs, and hunting was banned in Windsor Great Park itself.[107] During the early eighteenth century the last of the great estates were succumbing. Even the Duke of Beaufort ceased to hunt his deer in 1762.[108] The principal purpose of parks and their deer was, instead, display and aesthetic effect as seen from the mansion and general amenity, including different forms of sport, such as shooting and fishing, as well as warrens, domestic stock, and woods for fuel and timber.[109]

Planting within the park was becoming ever more adventurous. An increasing number of networks of rides were being established every decade till the 1720s. By the 1700s it had become common for full circles to be cut out of woodland, and new ones were planted to form the end of walks, or where two walks intersected.

In addition, the 1700s saw plumps or clumps being employed for park decoration. The term was sometimes adopted for tree nurseries planted in the open parkland, such as the two large roundels in the park at Blenheim in the 1700s marked as 'Nurseries for trees' on one map.[110] Clumps then began to be placed ornamentally to emphasise the swell of the ground: the Earl of Portland's 'Star Clump' on a knoll in Moat Park at Windsor of about 1700 is an example. At the end of the same decade, clumps were planted on the hill above Waldershare, a landscape in which London is suspected of having had a hand (fig. 176). There were modest clumps at Claremont soon after 1716 (see fig. 173), and a plan by Colen Campbell suggested a number of large clumps and an 'asterisk', or eight-pointed star, of trees for the park at Thoresby soon after that.

'An agreeable mixture of garden and forest'

The demands of fashion since the 1680s may have led inexorably to further embellishments, but at heart the English had a more reserved view of ostentation than the French, and, for example, the old fondness for plain grass plats had never quite been forgotten. At the same time, a taste for having 'outward' plantations adapted to pleasure was on the rise, and, being away from the house, their walks could sometimes take pragmatic, non-geometric, courses. A new form of circumvallation arose, the mock fortification, seen chiefly as a boundary to these outward wooded gardens. Hence Queen Anne's reign saw not only increasing sophistication in the fine-set garden, but the initial stages in country-house gardens becoming one with the countryside around.

'PLAIN BUT NOBLE GRASS AND GRAVEL'

In 1707 Wise was ordered to simplify the Great Fountain Garden at Hampton Court, the largest *broderie* design in England, and equal to the largest in France, to a *parterre à l'Angloise* arrangement (see fig. 142).[111] Supposedly this was because Queen Anne disliked the smell of box, but more likely it was because of the expense,

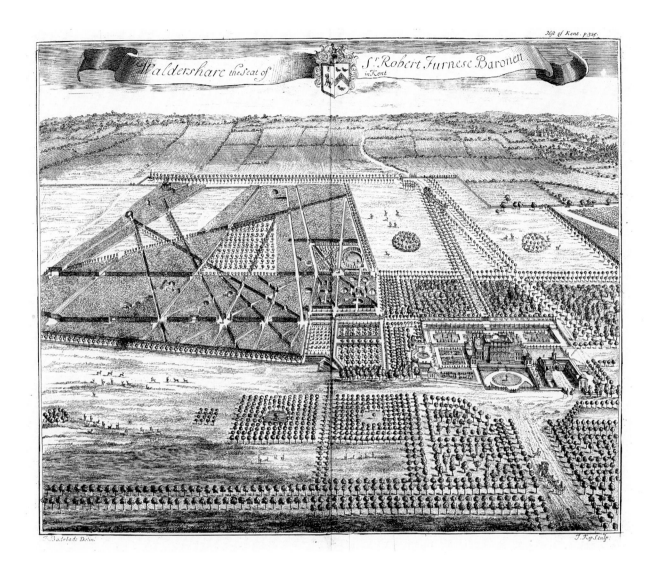

Waldershare the Seat of Sr Robert Furnese Baronett in Kent

T. Badeslade Delin.

J. Kip Sculp.

and a preference for a more English way of designing parterres. Switzer related that 'The Box-work at Hampton-Court was pull'd up . . . and the Gardens laid into that plain but noble maner they now appear in.'[112]

A few owners, even at the height of the admiration for Versailles, had contrarily preferred unadorned grass plats or bowling greens to any form of design with borders or cutwork. The Duke and Duchess of Beaufort did so at Beaufort House, their house in Chelsea, about 1685 (see fig. 122), and so did Christopher Vane at Fairlawne (see fig. 107), and Sir Robert Atkyns at Sapperton, Gloucestershire, a few years later, and the Earl of Jersey at Squer-

176   Bird's-eye view by Thomas Badeslade of Sir Robert Furnese's gardens and plantations at Waldershare House, Kent, 1719. The house and the garden with terracing had been established in the 1710s by Furnese's father, who by the time of his death in 1712 had also added the wildernesses and circular bowling green. Sir Robert carried on the work with large outward plantations to the west, based on an avenue system with a star planted by his father. Waldershare thus followed Wanstead in starting with highly polished gardens, and then moving on to plantations, and George London's hand may be suspected here as well. The clumps on the hill above the house were an early example of this form of park embellishment.

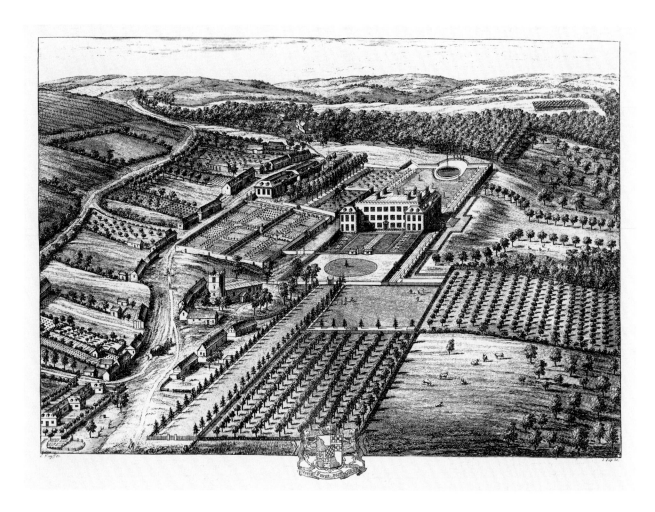

ryes in about 1705 (see fig. 156). At Londesborough the Earl of Burlington had earlier simplifed his parterre against the trend (fig. 177). The Knyff and Kip view shows a parterre with side terraces

177 Bird's-eye view by Knyff and Kip of Londesborough Hall, Yorkshire, from the south-west, c.1700. The Earl of Burlington employed Robert Hooke to add the wings to the house in 1676, and the gardens shown here were associated with those changes. The bowling green and orchards on two sides were laid out in 1678; the avenue into the park and the parterre behind the house probably date from not long after. Burlington died in 1697 and Knyff shows that he or his heir had stripped the parterre back to its permanent elements: the figures, the *jet d'eau*, the side terraces and their clipped yews – preference or parsimony?

enlivened with pyramid yews, and terminated with a grate with a baskethandle filled with a bason with a *jet d'eau*, in many ways similar to the parterre at Ragley, where Robert Hooke had also been the architect. The difference was that at Londesborough the walks, beds and clipped shrubs had already been removed from the body of the parterre by the time Knyff visited; it was an undivided grass plat ornamented only by five figures on pedestals. A visitor remarked in 1701 that Londesborough was not beautiful, 'having no gardins nor furniture', but then it would have been inconceivable to most at that time that such a plain design could be regarded as a garden.[113]

Castle Howard seems never to have had walks, borders or yews in the space between the garden front and the 'wood within the walls' (see fig. 172). Perhaps one should not expect any before 1712,

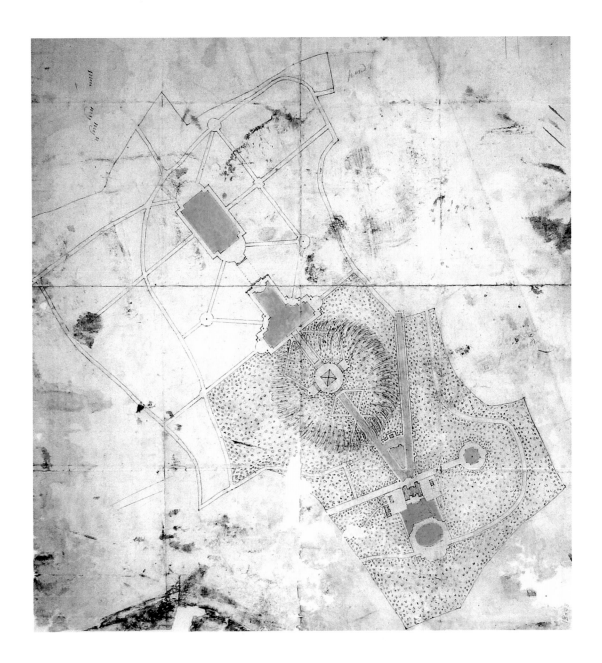

as this area served as the works yard, but no attempt was made to establish a decorative scheme for another decade. This plainness seems to have been Vanbrugh's preference, for his own retreat at Chargate, Surrey, appears to have displayed simply grass, gravel and wood (fig. 178). A French tourist made a sketch of the gardens of Kimbolton, showing that the parterre consisted of six unadorned grass plats, an arrangement established when Vanbrugh was reforming the gardens in 1707 (see fig. 138).[114]

178   Drawing of a scheme by Sir John Vanbrugh for his own garden at Chargate, near Esher, c.1712. This garden was made in a wooded heath with a belvedere erected at the highest point; the absence of any parterre is notable for this date. A pronounced ridge south-west from the belvedere is indicated by the positions of the two grassed openings, one a bowling green; the path layout also had to respect property boundaries. After being sold to the Earl of Clare the property became 'Claremont'.

The sheer extent of turf in the English garden was a distinct difference from French practice. Partly for climatic reasons the French had difficulty in creating such good grass, and they did not play bowls, like the English. The French *boulingrin* was one of the few cases of an extensive grass area, though it needed the dank conditions promoted by sinking the area and surrounding it with *bosquet*. Liger provided a plate to illustrate an elaborate scheme in grass and sand with clipped shrubs and within a palisade.[115] The difference between the parterre and the *boulingrin*, he explained, was that the first was surrounded by shrubs, the second generally by tall trees.

The French seem to have been genuinely envious of the quality of grass that could be achieved in England. Dezallier d'Argenville wrote: 'their Grass-plots are of so exquisite a Beauty, that in France we can scarce ever hope to come up to it'.[116] Claude Desgots explained to the Earl of Orkney in 1713 that he would not presume to issue instructions on forming turf because nowhere was it more beautiful or so well looked after as in England.[117] The French tourist Pierre-Jacques Fougeroux noted in 1728 that the weather encouraged good growth, texture was provided by mowing twice a week, and all irregularities were flattened by

> rollers made either of stone or of iron, half an inch thick. These rollers are hollow in the middle, and measure about eighteen inches in diameter. Four iron bars run through the centre of the roller, and to the end of them are attached two shafts. I saw a horse put between the shafts, with very wide leather boots on its feet; they were fastened by buckles half way up the leg. The soles of the boots contain large nails to prevent the horse from slipping on the grass.[118]

Switzer followed Vanbrugh in his love of grass. He wrote a chapter on grass and gravel: 'those natural Ornaments of our Country-Seats, by which we much excel all other Nations, and are indeed the Glory of all our Gardens'.[119] His ideas on the 'Extensive Way of Gardening', 'which the *French* call *La Grand Manier*' would redefine the pleasure grounds to include the outward plantations at country seats.[120] Grass was an essential element of both inward and outward gardens.

Switzer was initially content with the old form; parterres should be longer than broad, and have a 'Terrass Walk on each Side'. He included prints showing cutwork and borders, and his designs for plain parterres sometimes had central walks, sometimes yews (see fig. 171). Embellishments that remained acceptable were *jets d'eau* and figures. Maybe the prints were several years older than the text in which he was endeavouring to help readers visualise 'that simple, plain, and unaffected Method I have propos'd'.[121]

The impulse to go the whole distance and banish clipped yews was stirred by Addison's article 414 in *The Spectator*, which observed that 'Our Trees rise in Cones, Globes and Pyramids', and asserted that 'I would rather look upon a Tree in all its Luxuriancy and Diffusion of Boughs and Branches, than when it is thus cut and trimmed into a Mathematical Figure'.[122] Pope elaborated the point in *The Guardian*, mocking clipping into figurative forms, a tradition from Elizabethan times that remained in townsmen's and tradesmen's gardens.[123] The botanist Peter Collinson recalled how in about 1712, when he lived with relatives in Peckham, he often accompanied them to nursery gardens, especially one run by a Mr Parkinson in Lambeth, to buy clipped yews 'in the shapes of birds, dogs, men, ships, &c.'[124] A representation of a boar hunt or hare chase cut out in box could be seen in Daniel Bullen's nursery in Dublin, perhaps also in the 1710s. The tradition of having 'trees in the most aukward figures of men and animals' was thus sufficiently alive to be worth ridicule from Pope.[125]

Switzer evidently agreed with this sentiment as regards country-house gardens. Whilst parterres and flower borders might be appropriate in town gardens, in the country he would be 'opposed to those crimping, diminutive, and wretched Performances we every-where meet with . . . in Clipt Plants, Flowers, and other trifling Decorations'.[126] As his ideas developed, he became more firmly opposed to borders and yews.

In *Ichnographia Rustica* Switzer distinguished 'Bowling-green or plain Parterres' from 'Parterres of Embroidery'.[127] By the former he was referring to the old *parterre à l'Angloise*, though stripped down to 'plain grass and gravel', without the refinements of 'Borders, Greens and Flowers'.[128] This form of parterre was 'of the most

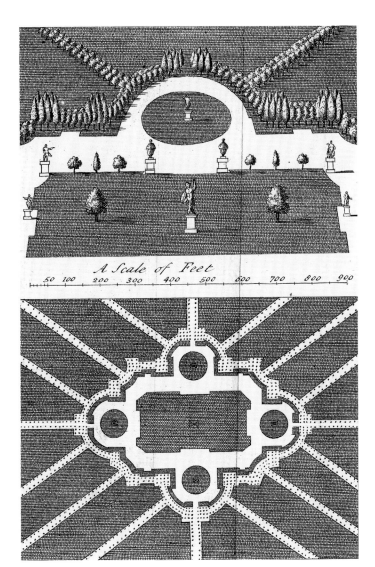

the inward parts of gardens his system 'cashiers those Interlacings of Box-work, and such like trifling Ornaments, and substitutes the plain but nobler Embellishments of Grass, Gravel, and the like'.[129]

Switzer thought there was a place for plain parterres in outward plantations. Just one plate seems to have represented his vision (fig. 179).[130] This was an aerial view and plan of 'a large open Lawn in the Middle of a Park or Wood', consisting of a grass rectangle within a gravel walk with figures, yews and shrubs along the edge and centre. Platoons joined by rows of trees provided the wooded setting.

It was bold of Switzer to have proposed the dissolution of the highly elaborated parterre of Queen Anne's reign. It is certain that he was impressed by Addison's article in *The Spectator* for he printed it *verbatim* in his *Nobleman, Gentleman, and Gardener's Recreation* (1715) with the omission only, perhaps out of deference to Wise, of the sentence that criticised 'our great Modellers of Gardens', who 'have their Magazines of Plants to dispose of', for stuffing their designs with clipped shrubs. Whilst Addison suggested what he disliked, it was Switzer who had the conviction to follow through the logic to practical prescription.

FORTIFICATIONS

Owners had attempted for half a century to reconcile the walls around their gardens with their desire to see the country beyond. Devices already seen included rails set within gates, grates, *claires voies* and iron fences. The next development was 'reducing Fortification into Gardening', as Switzer put it.[131] At this time, tall, upright city walls were vulnerable to modern artillery, a consideration given extra urgency by the frequent wars of the seventeenth century. The science of fortification had devised new methods, such as low-profile defences in the form of outer earthworks and inner low walls, designed with ever-more elaborate angled bastions to permit enfilade fire onto any advancing enemy. Publications on fortifications were numerous, amongst the best of which were those by a Dutch expert, Menno van Coehoorn, though seldom in English. However, the campaigns in Flanders during

---

179 Plan and view of a 'large open Lawn in the Middle of a Park or Wood', from Switzer's *Ichnographia Rustica*, 1718. Grass embellished by no more than *jets d'eau* and figures, this was the first time a gardening manual had proposed a plain parterre. The surrounding planting was in platoons, made to seem like 'turrets' between the lower linking planting.

Use, and is, above all, the beautifullest with us in England, on Account of the Goodness of our Turf'. Another reason he added, paraphrasing Pope, was 'that Decency and unaffected Simplicity which it affords to the Eye of the Beholder'. He asserted that in

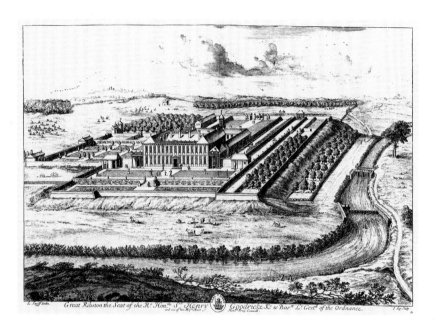

180 Bird's-eye view of Ribston Hall, Yorkshire, from the south, by Knyff and Kip, c.1700. In the closing years of James II's reign, Sir Henry Goodricke, perhaps fearing another civil war, fortified his garden with bastions permitting enfilade fire, perhaps to control the bridge crossing the River Nidd; this was perhaps a uniquely late example of country house fortification. Goodricke was afterwards William III's Lieutenant General of the Ordnance. Note also the nine-plat *broderie* garden with cypress trees and corner pavilions, possibly surviving from earlier in the century.

the Nine Years' War and the War of the Spanish Succession made Englishmen all too well aware of the principles and terms associated with fortifications.

Fortifications around English houses were not necessarily mere toys.[132] In 1688 it was noted that Sir Henry Goodricke of Ribston Hall, Yorkshire, was 'environing his garden with a kind of fortification' that incorporated military-style bastions (fig. 180). He may have been preparing for another civil war in James II's reign, and was shortly to secure York for William of Orange, who rewarded him with the post of Lieutenant-General of the Ordnance. The fortifications at Blenheim were indisputably a garden device, although defending not a city but a wood-work against nothing more threatening than cows and deer.

Switzer, who had directed the planting of yew hedging in the wood-work in 1706, was enthused by this idea of a fortified garden, which 'was first deliver'd to us by a Gentleman, that is deservedly honour'd with some considerable Posts belonging to the Architectural Province, &c. in his Majesty's Works.' This was Vanbrugh, who had experienced military service himself, and at Blenheim employed fortifications as a nice conceit for a martial genius that would enable the visitor to 'look either forward or backward, and view with Pleasure the rude and distant Scenes of Nature'.[133]

Although the Blenheim fortifications were around the entire 'inward' garden, the wood-work contained was on a scale beyond anyone's experience, and was more comparable to 'outward' woods as far as size was concerned. When Vanbrugh came to devise other fortifications the distinction between inward and outward plantations could be blurred, as when Wray Wood at Castle Howard received ramparts and bastions from about 1705 (fig. 181). Twenty years on, a visitor there noted the 'Wall built in the Fortification way with several Bastions, a Gravel Walk runs Parallel with it'.[134]

Switzer considered this method 'without Doubt, the noblest Way of fencing in a Garden', and with the benefit of hindsight, thought that: 'It is somewhat of Wonder, that it has not been made Use of before now. The first was the *Ambit* of the Gardens at *Blenheim*.'[135] He had presumably made, if not designed, the fortifications around the wood at Grimsthorpe, which differed from Vanbrugh's versions (fig. 182). Each of the eight alleys terminated in arrowhead bastions 'in the latest manner', and was composed of hedge and ditch, a cheaper alternative to a masonry wall and ditch. Switzer was fascinated by the idea of fortified gardens, and went on in *Ichnographia Rustica* (1718) to suggest a fortified parterre, or 'A Hexagone in Fortification Work'. In his *Practical Kitchen Gardener* (1727) he also conceived a fortified octagonal kitchen garden (fig. 183).

OUTWARD PLANTATIONS

The wilderness of the first half of the seventeenth century, an area outside the garden, wild but embellished, had been neatened and geometrised in the second half of the century as it was brought

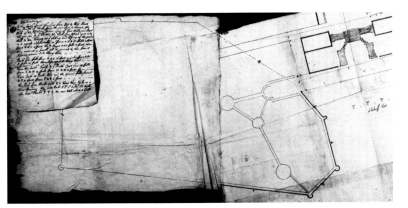

181　Sketch plan of the boundaries of Wray Wood, Castle Howard, *c.*1705. The inscription states that 'the Prick Line Markt with R is Wray Wood Wall as is – Now Standing the lines Markt S S S is more of the Old Wall – The lines Markt with T T is the new Wall which is built'. The bastioned outline is comparable to Vanbrugh's fortified wood-work at Blenheim, and the irregularly disposed paths are similar to those at New Park, Richmond.

182　William Stukeley's sketch of 'The Duchesses Bastion' at Grimsthorpe Castle, 1736. The militaristic forms of fortification have been continued, but with traditional hedge and ditch; a bastion was set at the end of most arms of a twelve-point star cut through the wood. In the early 1710s Switzer appears to have been George London's foreman at Grimsthorpe, where he wrote *The Nobleman, Gentleman, and Gardener's Recreation* (1715).

inside the walled enclosure. Timothy Nourse, an Oxford-educated member of a gentry family, was aware of this, but he was amongst those who, at the end of the century, still smiled on the conceit perpetrated by the old wildernesses: 'let this . . . Wilderness be Natural-Artificial; that is, let all things be dispos'd with that cunning, as to deceive us into a belief of a real Wilderness or Thicket, and yet to be furnished with all the Varieties of Nature.'[136]

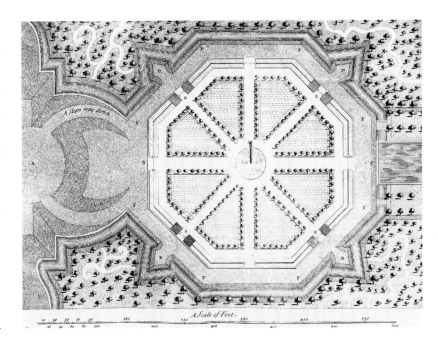

183　A fortified kitchen garden: Stephen Switzer's 1727 'Plan of an Octangular Kitchen Garden' engraved by J. Clark for *The Practical Kitchen Gardener*. The octagon of walls is defended by a moat with bastions 'after the latest manner'; the soil from the fosse would go towards the making of the surrounding terraces.

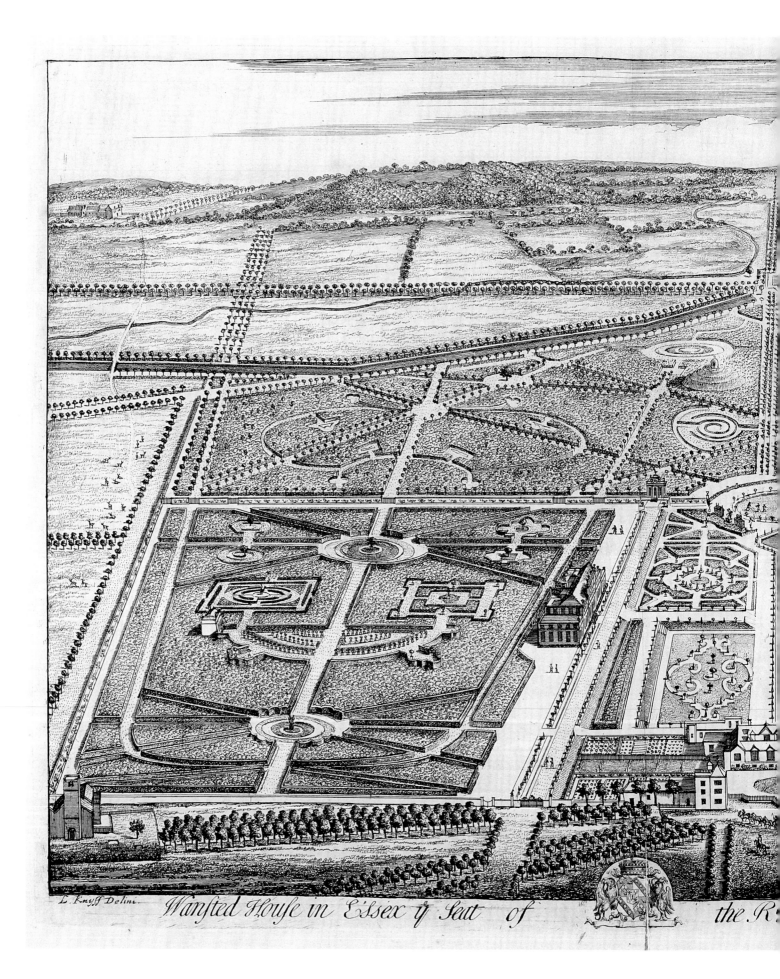

L. Knyff Delin. Wansted House in Essex ÿ Seat of ——— the R:

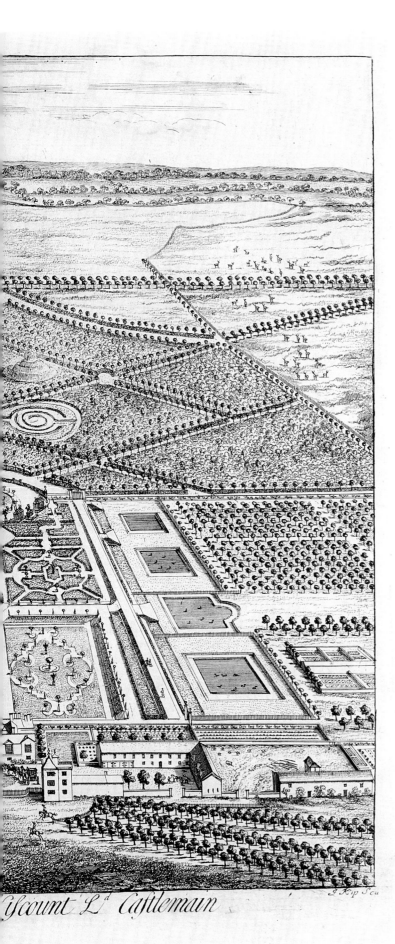

Nourse promoted the economic advantages of coppice woods, and also the ornamental: 'A Plantation of *Coppice-Wood*, as it is most profitable to a private Undertaker, so is it most pleasant and ornamental, if near a Gentleman's House'.[137] He thought it graceful to 'cut Glades or Avenues which may give a View and Prospect of the Seat'. Switzer thought so too, seeing that the neater 'inward' wilderness could be complemented by the rural 'outward' wood. The latter could be more 'simple' in character, with carpet walks and rough and ready maintenance – for example, the palisades could be trimmed with scythes fixed to poles, rather than shears.[138]

The 'wildernesses' at the far end of Greenwich Park (see fig. 69), planted by William Boreman for fuel for the palace, were followed in 1700 by Wise making the 'Lower Wilderness' at Hampton Court. Probably designed by London, this consisted of twin geometric plantations beyond the eastern end of the Long Water and either side of the vista, half a mile from the gardens enclosure. It too was probably envisaged as a source of fuel as well as an amenity. Unfortunately, it was prone to flooding from the Thames, and was almost destroyed in 1722. Notwithstanding, these cases were royal precursors of the 'outward' wilderness.

New plantations had become common by the turn of the century, but most were dwarfed by London's new plantings. He appears to have been much influenced, on his visit to Paris in 1698, by the French manner of treating woodland, and was to be prominent in creating outward plantations later in the 1700s. His plantations at Wanstead covered the slope down from the bowling green to the River Roding, picking up the vistos through the earlier gardens and wilderness (fig. 184). Switzer wrote of 'Sir Richard Child's at Wanstead in Essex . . . begun in 1706, a design worthy of an English Baronet, and equal to the greatest

184 Bird's-eye view of Wanstead House from the west by Knyff and Kip, *c.*1713. The Elizabethan house remained, and behind it were the gardens leading down to a circular bowling green created in the early years of the century. The vast outer plantations were established from 1706; the spirals and curving paths are reminiscent of the much smaller ones at Kensington Palace.

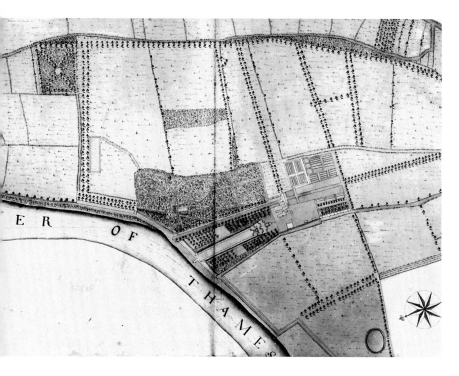

French Peer . . . one of Mr London's last undertakings'.[139] It was a scheme of such extent, originality and complexity that most visitors were overwhelmed. That of course was gratifying to Sir Richard, and in order that the visit might not be forgotten he had views drawn in about 1714 by the then aged Knyff. At Cannons London contrived 63 acres of outward plantations beyond the walls and iron fence.

THE ORNAMENTATION OF WOODS

The arrangement of walks, the insertion of halls and cabinets, and other devices could ornament outward plantations and give them additional interest. Most of the types of woods described by Dezallier d'Argenville were within garden walls, but he also expanded upon 'forests, or great woods of high trees' and coppices, outside. The former had no palisades, nor gravel walks, only ridings for hunting; coppices were the same but were cut on rotation, except for the 'standers', or standards. A plate by Le Blond, labelled as 'A Great Wood of Forrest trees', actually showed designs for *bosquets* of seven acres and under, some devised by Le Nostre for Clagny

in 1675, so English readers may have gained the impression that outward woods should be more ornamented than Dezallier d'Argenville had meant.

An example of a pre-existing coppice wood being treated ornamentally in Queen Anne's reign was the Duke of Ormonde's at the lodge to Richmond Old Park (fig. 185). Although the walks were not in a geometric arrangement John Macky observed 'the Wood cut out into Walks, with the plenty of Birds singing in it'.[140] There were also the Marquess of Wharton's copse at Winchendon, and the extensive woods at Waldershare (see fig. 176). The readiness of owners to forego purely economic uses may be a sign that coal was becoming more readily available even in the countryside, diminishing the value of wood as fuel. The Duke of Bolton had little compunction in felling some of the quarters of Spring Wood, a 60-acre coppice at Hackwood, just before 1722.

Certainly, many English outward plantations came to be ornamented, although, as at Richmond Lodge, adapted according to boundaries, topography and other considerations. The principal ornamentation at first was networks of alleys. These typically were given carpet walks, and were lined either with trimmed standard trees or palisades. The star device was much employed: Dezallier d'Argenville wrote that 'great Woods of tall Trees . . . are usually planted in a Star, with a large Circle in the Middle, where all Ridings meet'.[141] The Dutch referred to such a wood as a 'sterrenboss'.

England had seen several stars. Moses Cook, quite probably, invented them when he cut the star of tree-lined walks through

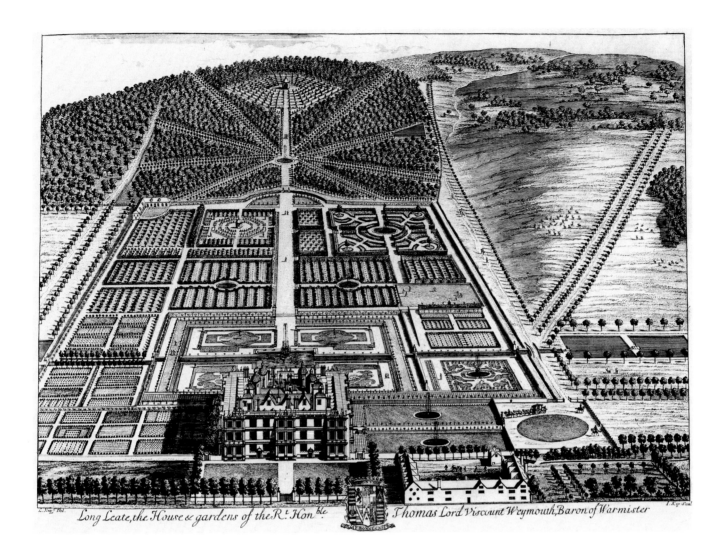

Long Leate, the House & gardens of the Rt. Honble ... Thomas Lord Viscount Weymouth, Baron of Warmister

the coppice above the gardens at Longleat (fig. 186). London may have advised Evelyn's grandson about his star in Dampier's Wood at Wotton (fig. 187). Robert Benson of Bramham cut numerous walks through his Black Fen wood with three large circles and three small ones at the main intersections (fig. 188). Grimsthorpe's star of palisaded alleys was an early 1710s adaptation of the planted grove with the simple cross of walks seen on the Knyff and Kip view.

A star on the summit of a hill gave prospects all round and was understandably popular. At Broadlane Hall, Flintshire, about 1685, a star wood was planted on the slopes of the mound of Hawarden Castle, leaving the mound as the centrepiece. Cain

186   Longleat House by Knyff and Kip, *c.*1700. Viscount Weymouth undertook a further series of improvements after the end of the Brompton Park contract in 1694; by 1700 the garden had doubled in length with fruit gardens, a bowling green, a wilderness, and a flower nursery with a replacement greenhouse. Meanwhile, the *parterre à l'Angloise* was replaced by cutwork. The flagged terrace under the garden front was extended through the flower garden and given grilles, and the garden became a *parterre à l'Angloise* with great lengths of *plates-bandes* for flowers replacing the earlier and simpler design. It was also given a large fountain with tritons supporting a bowl catching water from numerous jets. A carriage circle was formed outside the forecourt. Improvements were to continue until Weymouth's death in 1714.

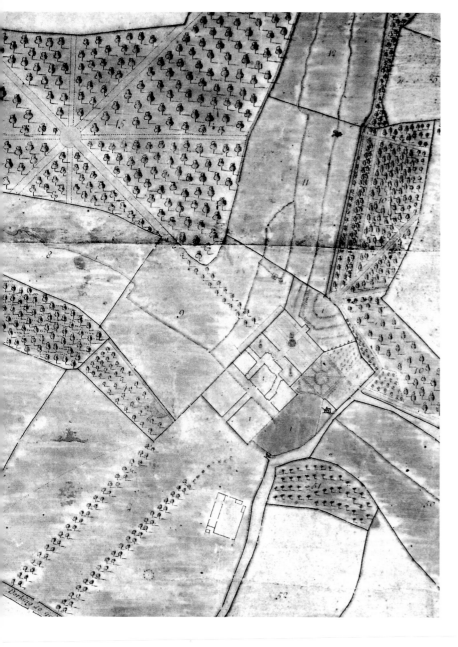

Hill, at Wrest, was planted as a seven-point star from 1703, gaining a stand at its summit some years later.[142] Hills near Chirk Castle (see fig. 234) were given a similar treatment, each star centring around a large tree.[143]

Stars were not the only arrangement of alleys employed. At several places the *patte d'oie* was seen, and at Brympton d'Evercy and Kiveton plantations outside garden walls were given the complex arrangements familiar from inward wildernesses. When London came to devise the outward plantations at Wanstead from about 1706 he borrowed forms from earlier wildernesses. The pinched oval in the Hampton Court wilderness, and spirals like those in the Slope Garden at Kensington Palace, were deployed once more (see fig. 184).

A liking for bowling greens outside the garden enclosure, favouring hilltop positions if feasible, reawakened pre-Civil War tastes. Although most bowling greens had been drawn into the garden enclosure after the Restoration, some were now allowed to escape into outward woods, at Cassiobury, Esher, Windsor Castle and Wimpole. The last three were in elevated positions. Vanbrugh's own outward wood at Chargate – later named Claremont after he sold it to the Earl of Clare (soon to be the Duke of Newcastle) – was adapted with a large hall, filled with a bowling green, on the ridge of the hill (see fig. 178). The Duke of Chandos made himself a bowling green as a retreat two miles northwards, uphill from Cannons, in about 1720.

All this cutting of vistos and openings must have created much devastation, however temporary, causing an affront to those with affection and respect for their trees and woods. The Countess of Warwick was saddened in 1673 when her husband had a coppice

187 Detail of an estate survey of Wotton House, Surrey, 1739 (north is to bottom left). The old forecourts and dummy avenue of the Evelyn family seat remain, as do the parterre, grotto and mount rising up the hill behind the house that were created in the 1650s. Jack Evelyn (the diarist's grandson) was being advised by George London from 1706, and the star cut out of Dampier's Wood may be the walks that are recorded as being reset with lime in 1710.

(Facing page) 188 *The Plan of Bramham Park in the County of York* by John Wood and Henry Hulsbergh, c.1725. The house and garden were created in the 1700s; the Black Fen to the left (east) had been cut through with these walks prior to an estate survey of before 1713; some of the meandering walks also existed by then. The feeble cascade on the axis of the house was replaced by extensive new water-works on the line of the stream (D, E, F, G, H).

The Plan of Bramham Park, In the County of York
the Seat of the R.t Hon.ble the Lord Bingley.

A The House.
B Parterre with the Cascade, Water falls
  21 feet on thirty Steps.
C Terrasses that Surround the Garden.
D The great Reservoir.
E Piece of Water.
F Obelisk, the Water falls from y.e Base 12 feet.
G The Great Cascade, the Water falls 25 feet

H Water falls 17 feet.
I Coach Road through the Gardens.
K Park.
L Kitchen Gardens.
M Bridges that make the
  communication of the Park.

N Great Stair Case.

A Scale of 2540 Feet or half a Mile.
140   540   1540   2540

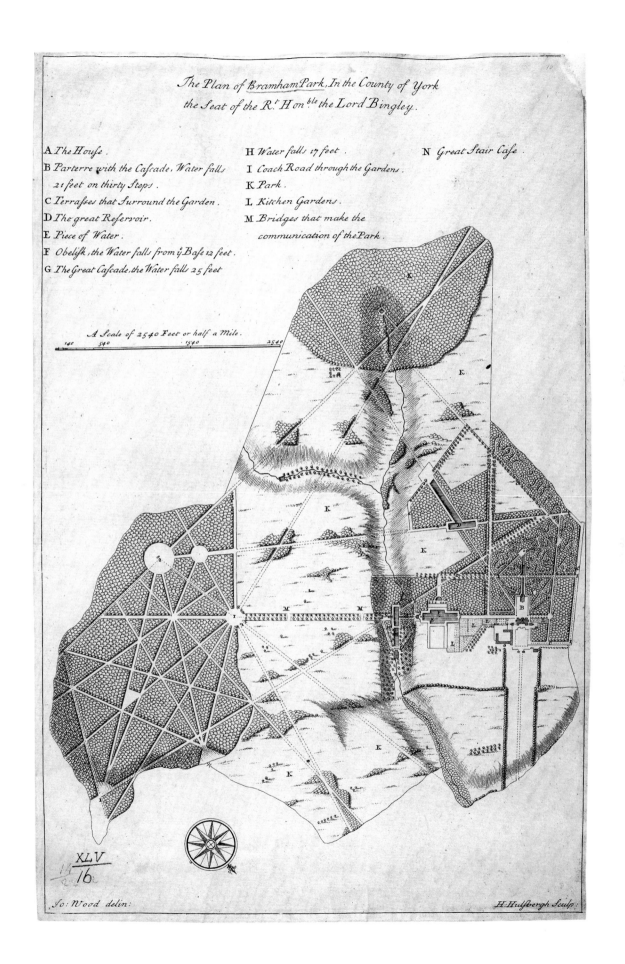

XLV
16

Jo: Wood delin:

H. Hulsbergh Sculp:

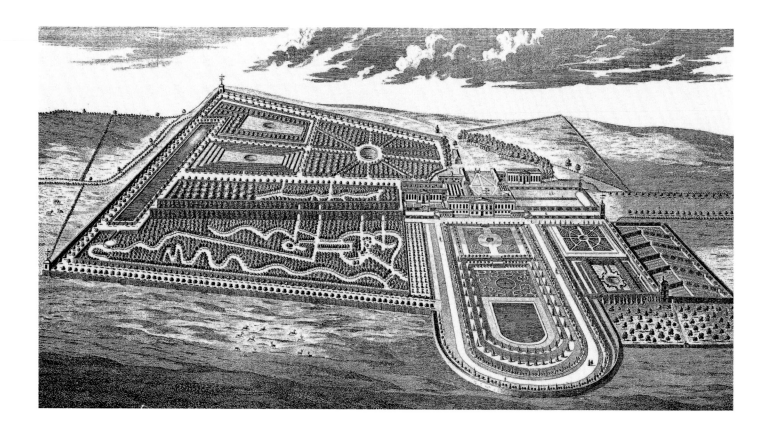

189 Bird's-eye view of Bulstrode House from the south by T. Willson and T. Bowles, c.1725. The house had been built in 1686 by Judge Jeffreys, but later passed to the Earl of Portland, who built the garden front in 1706. George London was responsible for the gardens shown here. The parterres and pool under the garden front stepped down and were surrounded by terraces with pyramid yews; to the east the older gardens were filled with a grove and a tunnel arbour. Outside the turreted wall there was a new kitchen garden. To the west a huge area was walled in (including an old coppice), the northern part of which was a grove with fruit trees in the quarters; other areas led up to a canal, which served as the reservoir for the gardens' water-works. The coppice was cut through with a combination of straight and meandering walks, an early example of such treatment.

wood felled at Leez Priory, Essex, and recorded her emotions poetically.[144] Switzer related how in 1699 'Mr London design'd a Star' for Wray Wood at Castle Howard, but how the Earl of Carlisle shied away from the devastation that the 8-pointed star would cause to the huge beech standards within the coppice.[145] In the 1720s the Duchess of Chandos would not permit her husband to cut down trees to improve his south visto at Cannons.[146]

The Wray Wood example caused Switzer to criticise designs that were too rigidly geometric and did not suit actual places.[147] He objected

> to *Gardeners*, who having wrought a little while at some or other of the great Works of this Kingdom, immediately put on an Apron, get a Rule and pair of Compasses, with other things belonging to this Work; thus equipt, what Wonders are we not to expect from so profound a Set of *Mathematicians* and *Designers*?

This practice led to 'many a noble Oak, or sometimes whole Lines of these and other umbragious Trees, fell'd, to humour the regular and delusive Schemes of some Paper Engineer'. Ways had to be found to make woods ornamental without felling their chief glories. The Earl of Rochester, Ranger of Richmond New Park, had taken up this challenge when in 1698 the King, by patent,

'Giveth & Granteth unto Lawrence Earle of Rochester All that parcell of Woodland & all Timber & other Trees scituate within the Northwest part of New-Parke.' He had lost no time in converting this area for his pleasure. The largest of the old pollard oaks were planted round with circles of young trees and became some of the nodes of a network of tree-lined walks leading up to 'Henry VIII's mount', from where the faraway St Paul's Cathedral could be espied (see fig. 111). The irregular arrangement of straight walks had no obvious precedent, unless seen as a rustic interpretation of the palisaded labyrinth at Versailles.

In describing a plate intended for (but not included in) *Ichnographia Rustica*, Switzer noted how, in an ideal arrangement, the walk across the garden front at Castle Howard would have continued to the east up the slope to the summit of Wray Wood.[148] The open circle there would have been the obvious centre for London's star, but in fact the wood's 'Distribution and Figure . . . is by no means Regular' because the Earl's response was 'by no means cut it out into a Star, or any Mathematical Figure; but follow Nature, and where-ever we find natural Openings and Glades, there, to make our Lawns and Walks, be they either strait, or Serpentine, still humouring, and not straining, the Place by Art.' The Earl thus gave the wood 'that Labyrinth diverting Model we now see'. In part, this was by straight walks between openings, much like those at New Park, and indeed a plan of about 1705 shows

that this was the case in parts of the wood nearest the house (see fig. 181). Switzer mentions 'serpentine' walks, and a visitor in 1712 wrote that on the other side of the open circle at the summit he went along 'winding mazes' to reach a 'level square' with flower borders.[149] Further on, there were other openings with, variously, a swan fountain and fruit trees, a lead statue painted white of a satyr ravishing a nymph, a figure of Diana holding a buck, a shepherd and his dog, a waterfall, and a square wooden summerhouse.

The Earl of Portland incorporated an old coppice wood into his gardens at Bulstrode and cut it through with a combination of straight and meandering walks, possibly when London was working there around 1705 (fig. 189). A third example was Bramham, where winding walks in the wood backing the parterre were recorded on a map of 1713.[150] It is conceivable that at Bulstrode Portland was remembering the winding walks strung with cabinets that he might have seen in 1698 in the Bosquet de Louveciennes at Marly.[151] It is equally possible that a number of owners were settling on similar solutions for a common problem: how to cut walks through coppice with standards in order to bring them into the dressed grounds while minimising the devastation. Whichever solution was chosen, owners' acceptance of the need to depart from the rule of geometry was a portent of things to come.

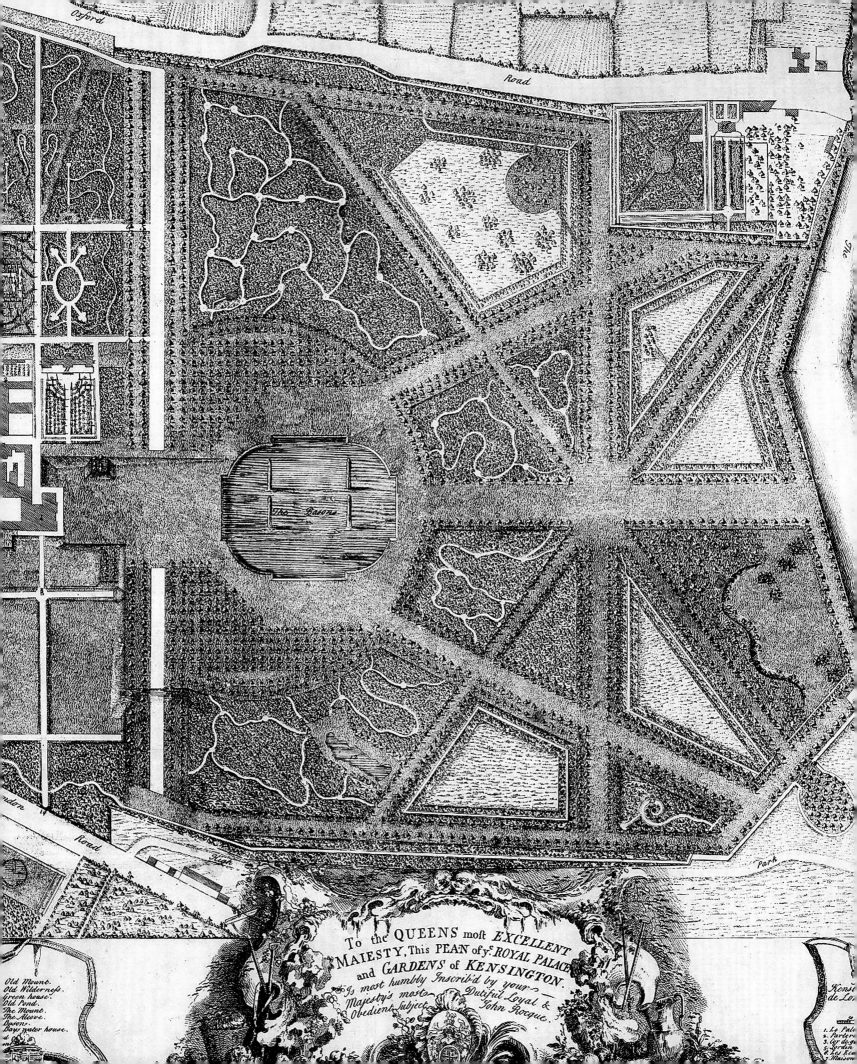

Oxford

Road

The

The Basins

London

Road

Rich

Park

To the QUEENS most EXCELLENT
MAIESTY, This PLAN of yᵉ ROYAL PALACE
and GARDENS of KENSINGTON.
Is most humbly Inscrib'd by your
Majesty's most   Dutiful Loyal &
Obedient Subject   John Rocque.

Old Mount.
Old Wilderneſs.
Green house.
Old Pond.
The Mount.
The Aleove.
Basons.
Bayswater house.

Kens
de Lo

1. Le Pala
2. Parter
3. ler deg
4. Jardin
5. Les Ecu
Maison

Gardens in the Augustan Age

England in early Georgian times saw great changes to the social and economic order. This was also a time of radical new thinking on garden-making. Initially there was a breakdown in the distinction at country estates between inward gardens, within the wall, and outward plantations, outside it. A more extensive and open style developed, in which elaboration was reserved for the plantations rather than the parterre. In the process, many of the long-established elements of gardens were abandoned, and many others were introduced or reintroduced.

Stephen Switzer was party, with Charles Bridgeman, to the rapidly moving changes in garden design in the late 1710s, having produced plans for merging gardens with woods, planting new outward plantations, ornamenting woods with meandering walks, basons and halls, and surrounding them with fossees. Alongside the new garden style, which reached its full flowering in the 1720s, yet other conceptions of gardening were developing from specu-

lating what Antique gardens might have looked like, and applying the principles of history painting to garden design.

The early Georgian background

The 1701 Act of Settlement had been intended to secure a Protestant succession to the throne. After William III, it would go to his sister-in-law, Anne, and her children, or failing them James I's granddaughter Princess Sophia of the Palatinate. Since Sophia died in 1714, two months before Queen Anne, who had no surviving children, the throne should automatically have been offered to Sophia's son, George Louis, Elector of Hanover. However, Viscount Bolingbroke had undermined the position of Robert Harley, Earl of Oxford, who lost office as Lord High Treasurer just before Anne's death, and was in secret but incomplete negotiations for the return of James II's son, the 'Old Pretender', known as James III by the Jacobites.

The Duke of Shrewsbury, as Lord High Treasurer, and the Lords Justices of the Realm, who included the Earl of Carlisle, the Marquess of Lindsey, the Duke of Bolton and the Earl of Abingdon, forestalled Bolingbroke's plans. From now on, these and other Whig magnates controlled the affairs of the country. Bolingbroke fled, becoming the Old Pretender's Secretary of State, and was attainted in his absence. Oxford was imprisoned in 1715 and impeached the next year for his conduct of the Treaty of Utrecht, which ended the War of Spanish Succession, in 1713 and for dealings with the Jacobites, but was acquitted. The Earl of Strafford, his colleague in the peace negotiations, escaped censure, and retired to Stainborough and his projects there.

Used to Herrenhausen, with its flat terrain, formality and surrounding canals, George I felt quite at home at Hampton Court. Whereas Charles I and Charles II had envisioned ambitious changes to their palaces, and William III had partially succeeded in making improvements, George I does not seem to have had any such dreams. He was cut off from everyday life and politics in England by long absences in Hanover, and his inability to speak English. The Whig grandees regarded this as quite satisfactory; they were enabled to act as though they were European princelings, commandeering the highest levels in matters of politics, taste, manners, patronage and building. As if to emphasise their quasi-princely status, nine more were raised to dukedoms in the early years of George I's reign. The only threat to the new status quo was when the Earl of Mar, who had been Secretary of State for Scotland from 1705 to 1714, led a failed Jacobite uprising in Scotland in 1715.

POLITICS AND MONEY

The peace inaugurated by the Treaty of Utrecht signalled a marked revival in garden-making. Some of the Duke of Marlborough's military commanders started to build and lay out gardens, such as the Earl of Orkney at Cliveden and General Sir Richard Temple at Stowe. So also did those noblemen who had made for-

tunes as a result of the war, such as the forces' paymaster-general, the Earl of Carnarvon, at Cannons, the Earl of Cadogan, Marlborough's quartermaster, at Caversham, and Stephen Bisse, victualler of the navy, at Wimbledon House. However, the principal factor in this revival was the tremendous surge in trade that followed the war, as London became the leading commercial city in Europe, surpassing Amsterdam.

At the pinnacle of the financial world was the First Lord of the Treasury, to which post the Earl of Halifax was recalled at George's accession. On Halifax's demise the next year, the Earl of Carlisle briefly succeeded him. Meanwhile, Sir Richard Onslow of Clandon, who had been Speaker of the Commons some years previously, became Chancellor of the Exchequer. In late 1715 Sir Robert Walpole was appointed to both positions. The principal challenge for chancellors in the 1710s was the national debt, consisting of many millions of pounds of Government bonds sold to pay for the recent war. When Walpole resigned over an unrelated issue in 1717, the new Chancellor was John Aislabie, whose interest in gardens was expressed at his home at Studley Royal in Yorkshire, as well as at his stepson's Hall Barn, Buckinghamshire, within easy reach of London (fig. 190). Aislabie devised a scheme whereby holders of bonds could exchange them for stock with a good rate of interest in a company that Harley had founded back in 1711, the South Sea Company. The South Sea Bill was passed early in 1720. This granted the South Sea Company a monopoly of British trade with the islands of the South Seas and South America. An investment in the company seemed like a sure winner. The price of shares rose throughout 1720, prompting a speculative frenzy that saw them rise tenfold.

Those running the South Sea Company saw their stocks rise. Sir Theodore Janssen, a director, purchased a baronetcy in 1714 and Wimbledon Manor in 1717. Peter Delaporte, another director, bought Esher Place, and began a new garden with fortification boundaries (fig. 191). John Fellowes, Sub-Governor to the company, purchased Carshalton House in 1715, and then a baronetcy in 1718. In 1720 he was paying Bridgeman and Joseph Carpenter of Brompton Park for improvements to the garden. Francis Hawes, cashier to the Customs and another South Sea

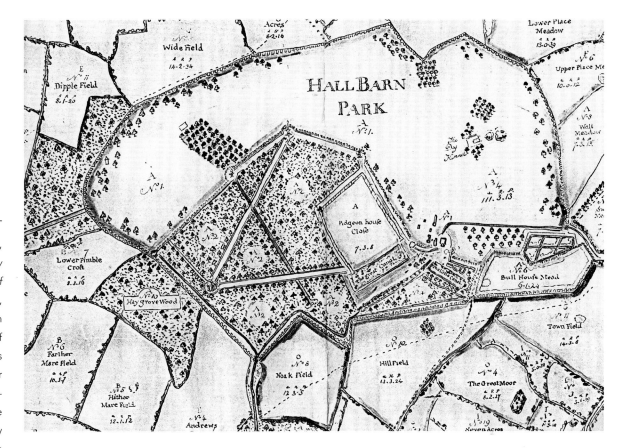

190 Hall Barn, Buckinghamshire, as shown in a detail of *A Survey of the Estates in the Parishes of Beaconsfield . . .* by John Richardson, Jr, 1763. A coppice with beech standards was given a boundary of terraces, jointed at bastions with urns and an obelisk, giving views out over the park. Under way on the north-west side of the wood in 1717, the work was completed by 1724. Many meandering paths (not shown on this map) were inserted through the old coppice, which was converted into a yew-hedged wilderness of rooms and corridors.

191 This plan by John Rocque of the gardens at Esher Place, 1737, encapsulates the downfall of Peter Delaporte, a director of the South Sea Company from 1715, whose estates were seized after the South Sea Bubble burst in 1720. He had been clearing away buildings and parterres to make vistas east and west, and was making fortification boundaries with bastions, but these had to be left unfinished. The sinuous ha-ha to the south-east was installed by William Kent for a later owner, Henry Pelham, in the mid-1730s.

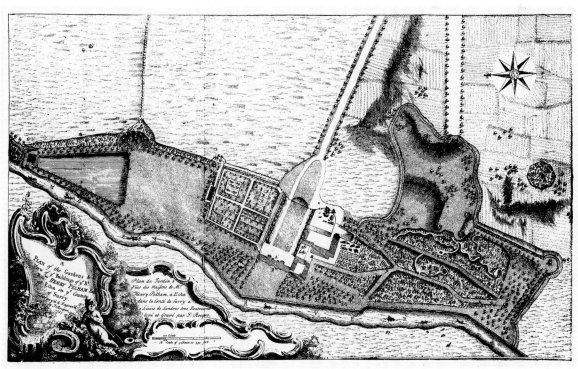

director, was also employing them 'for laying out the Gardens at Purley'.

The bubble burst towards the end of 1720. Respectable clergy and gentry lost their savings. The rich were not immune. The Duke of Wharton, who had engaged in ostentatious displays of wit and magnificence at his houses in London and at Winchendon (fig. 192), was ruined. Some, like Walpole, were lucky and sold early. Among them was the Duchess of Marlborough, enabling her to carry out further work at Blenheim. Benjamin Styles, a stock jobber, purchased Moor Park from the Duchess of Buccleuch from his profits. Likewise, Sir Gregory Page's trustees speculated on his behalf, making £200,000, which enabled them to purchase Wricklemarsh Manor in Charlton, Kent. Styles, and then Page (when he came of age) subsequently spent large sums on both houses and gardens.

---

192 Framed by arcades, this view, probably by Peter Tillemans, depicts the Duke of Wharton's gardens at Winchendon from the east, c.1720. Bridgeman may have had a hand in the garden in 1716, and in 1718 Switzer admired the 'Columns, Pilasters, Niches, &c.'; the parterre to the right under the wilderness terrace contained some expensive statuary. Ruined by the South Sea Bubble, the Duke had to sell up in 1724.

However, most members of the Houses of Commons and Lords had lost money and were enraged. As a result of a parliamentary inquiry, Aislabie was found to have encouraged and promoted the South Sea scheme with a view to his own profit, and had combined with the directors in their pernicious practices to the ruin of public trade and the credit of the kingdom. He was kept as a close prisoner in the Tower of London. The South Sea Company directors were arrested and their estates forfeited. Four who were Members of Parliament were expelled, including Janssen, who was forced to relinquish Wimbledon Manor. Delaporte's estates were sold, with his garden fortifications only half complete. Robert Surman, a cashier of the company, escaped ruin because of his youth, and moved to Valentines in Ilford, north-east of London, where he was to spend large sums on a canal, being dug in 1724. Aislabie no doubt had profited, as the House of Commons had declared. Despite this, and having spent great sums on Studley Royal, he seems to have been only temporarily embarrassed by the collapse, as he retained the property, and was able to carry out further major works on its gardens from 1727.

Walpole, who had been against the South Sea Company scheme from the outset, was perceived as competent, and was reappointed First Lord of the Treasury and Chancellor in 1721. He found other ways to dissipate the national debt, and eventually

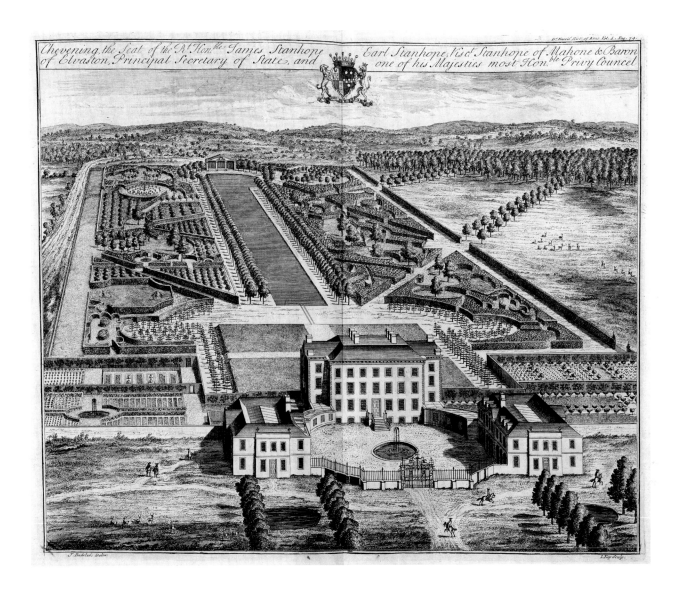

Chevening, the Seat of the R.t Hon.ble James Stanhope of Elvaston, Principal Secretary of State, and Earl Stanhope, Visc.t Stanhope of Mahone & Baron one of his Majesties most Hon.ble Privy Councel

193   Chevening House, Kent, from the north, drawn by Thomas Badeslade and engraved by Johannes Kip, 1719. In about 1718 Lord Stanhope had the far wall of the old Best Garden demolished in order to extend his pleasure garden. A *patte d'oie* of avenues was incorporated and the canal may also have been part of the earlier layout. The canal was terminated by a circular bason and a Classical pavilion. On both sides a high-hedged wilderness with a highly varied layout was set out: to the east the quarters contained a bowling green, fruit orchards and a circular orangery; to the west the plantations were solid, with cabinets around older parkland trees, some contained in a hall, and straight and winding walks.

stability returned. From this time on, Walpole played a pivotal role in government to such an extent that he presided over the meetings of the ministers. His jealous enemies mocked him as the 'Prime Minister'.

The benefits of office could still be very great. Walpole had plans to rebuild his house at Houghton before he resigned in 1717, and revived them when he was made Chancellor for the second time. The huge pile was then under construction from 1721 for a decade. Other Lords of the Treasury who went on to make important formal gardens included James Stanhope, who bought Chevening in 1717 (fig. 193) and was elevated to the earldom of

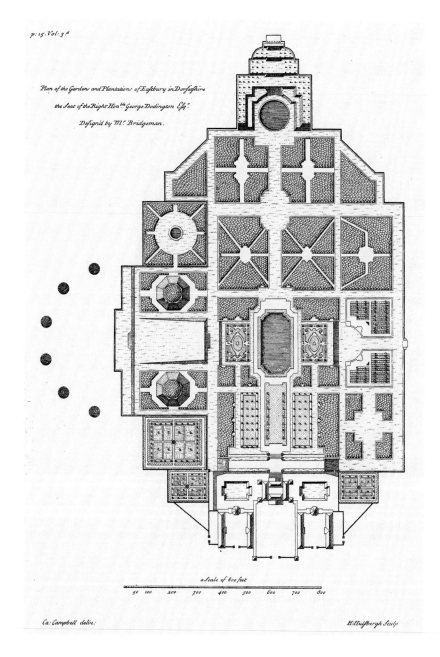

Plan of the Gardens and Plantations of Eastbury in Dorsetshire
the Seat of the Right Hon.ble George Dodington Esq.ʳ.

Design'd by M.ʳ Bridgeman.

a Scale of 800 feet

50   100   200   300   400   500   600   700   800

Ca: Campbell delin: H: Hulsbergh Sculp

194   This plan of the gardens and plantations of Eastbury House, engraved by Henry Hulsbergh for Colen Campbell's *Vitruvius Britannicus*, was based on a plan by Charles Bridgeman of c.1718 (north is to the left). Vanbrugh designed the enormous house and Bridgeman the equally expansive plantations stretching eastwards over gently undulating downland. Most of the planting was carried out, with some modifications, as revealed by surviving earthworks. The axis was terminated by a pool in a dip, and earth steps rose to a Corinthian temple over 60 feet high to the top of its finial. Early publication of this scheme 'Design'd by Mr. Bridgeman' was perhaps hoped for, but it had to wait until 1725, by which time the estate had been inherited by George Bubb Dodington and several small modifications were afoot.

Dorset (fig. 194), where he restarted work in 1724, when he became a Lord of the Treasury.

Below such people were the newly wealthy lawyers, bankers, and physicians (and even a poet, Pope) who required their own new country seats or villa residences. The boom in country houses and their accompanying gardens and garden buildings surpassed that in William III's reign, peaking in the early 1720s, but began to decline in the early 1730s.[1] Around London, the banks of the Thames in the region of Richmond and Twickenham were particularly popular, and to the east the near parts of Essex, at Leyton and Wanstead, saw many new and improved residences.

In towns, squares were ever-more popular, with lords and lawyers rubbing shoulders. The old four-plat arrangements were no longer favoured; oval or octangular gardens were left after generous paving was provided for carriages. To the west of London, Grosvenor Square was developed in 1725, being filled by a *bosquet* arrangement with an equestrian statue of George I by John van Nost placed at the centre in 1726 (fig. 195). St James's Square was redesigned by Bridgeman in 1727 with a large central bason. In Bath, Queen Square was set out in 1727 by the architect John Wood as a wilderness with tall palisades, and cabinets radiating from a central bason into areas of flowering shrubs. The Grove in Bath was remade in 1732 as 'The Orange Grove' (named after the Prince of Orange, not the tree).

Stanhope the next year; John Wallop, made Viscount Lymington in 1720, who had inherited Hurstbourne Priors (see fig. 140); Richard Edgcumbe of Mount Edgcumbe, Cornwall; Henry Pelham, brother of the Duke of Newcastle, who bought Esher Place in 1729; Sir William Yonge of Escot, a house designed by Robert Hooke; and George Bubb Dodington (Pope's 'Bubo'), who inherited a barely started house and garden at Eastbury House,

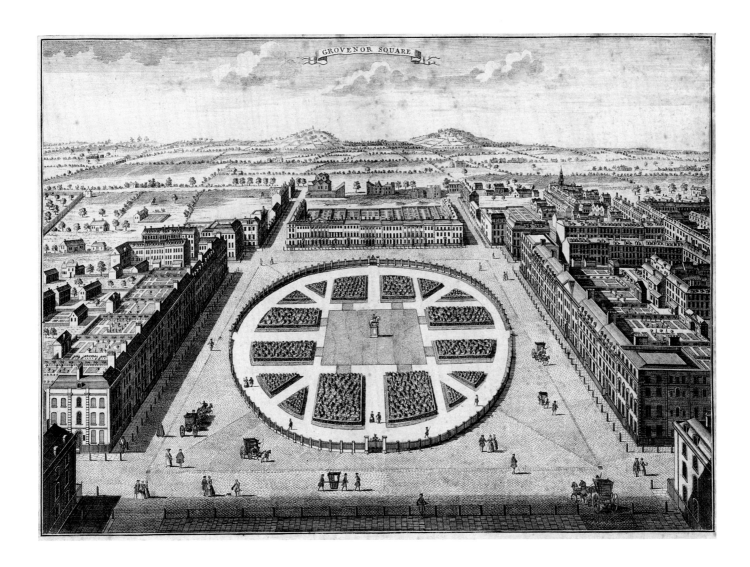

Nature and the imagination

In his text for *La Théorie et pratique du jardinage* Dezallier d'Argenville used the word 'rural' as a term of approval; for example, he described the 'great woods of tall trees' at St Germain-en-Laye, Fontainebleau and the Bois de Boulogne as 'wild and rural'.[2] Further, he mentioned the 'Rustick Order of a Grot or Cascade'. No longer did 'rural' or 'rustic' necessarily denote the artless and crude; instead these terms could imply affinity with the natural countryside and its unaffected simplicity.

In 1712, the same year that John James's translation of Dezallier d'Argenville appeared, Addison placed a series of essays in the *Spectator* intended to promote the pleasures of the poetic imagination; they were eagerly consumed by the public. He argued that 'if we consider the Works of Nature and Art, as they are qualified to entertain the Imagination, we shall find the last very defective,

195 Grosvenor Square, Westminster, a print attributed to Sutton Nicholls, *c.*1735. The original idea for the square, which was being finished in 1725, was to lay the centre out as a parterre; however, the design adopted was a *bosquet*, perhaps influenced by Thomas Fairchild's recommendation of wilderness-work in *The City Gardener* (1722); at the centre was a gilded lead equestrian statue of George I.

in Comparison of the former'.[3] He continued: 'there is in Nature something more Grand and August . . . it gives us a nobler and more exalted kind of Pleasure than what we receive from the nicer and more accurate Productions of Art'. He had several young followers, one being Alexander Pope, who parroted: 'there is certainly something in the amiable simplicity of unadorned nature, that spreads over the mind a more noble sort of tranquility, and a loftier sensation of pleasure, than can be raised from the nicer scenes of art'.[4]

In order to illustrate his argument, Addison contrasted the open countryside, as representing Nature, and fine-set gardens, as representing Art. Horace and Virgil had written about the country life, as also had the English pastoral poets, whereas gardens did not excite the poetic imagination to anything like the same degree. Addison's and Pope's objections to clipping, a form of Art, cited in the previous chapter, struck a chord with those who had no liking for the foreign fashion for tonsuring shrubs and trees, but the essay's more far-reaching importance was to be in promoting the wider countryside, and Nature in general, as worthy of a more profound sort of admiration than could be had for great gardens:

> The Beauties of the most stately Garden or Palace lie in a narrow Compass, the Imagination immediately runs them over, and requires something else to gratify her; but, in the wide Fields of Nature, the Sight wanders up and down without Confinement, and is fed with an infinite variety of Images, without any certain Stint or Number.[5]

Confessedly inept as an improving landowner himself, Addison felt that English gardens, neat and elegant as they were, did not feed the imagination as did the artificial rudeness of the French way of mixing garden and forest. He was evidently intrigued by Sir William Temple's essay 'Upon the Gardens of Epicurus . . .', in which a short passage gave a second-hand account of gardens described as being in China.[6] Temple had applied the term 'sharawadgi' to the irregular art of laying them out.[7]

Temple had warned that, although imported screens and porcelain gave an idea of this form of art, he would 'hardly advise any of these attempts in the figure of gardens among us' as they would be likely not to succeed. Nor was Addison suggesting the 'Chinese' way of gardens to his readers. Having argued that Nature was superior to Art in stimulating the Imagination, he was merely pointing to this concealed art that created a careful disorder to simulate Nature. He asserted that the 'Chinese . . . laugh at the Plantations of our Europeans, which are laid out by the Rule and Line'. Instead, his pleasure in unconfined prospects and the beauty of nature (the country), the main thrust of the essay, suggested ways to appreciate and describe 'landskips', including prospects from gardens.

One of his young admirers and acquaintances, Samuel Molyneux, followed Addison's preference for the wild scenes of Nature over gardens, to which he made some visits in 1712–13. He professed to be unimpressed by Hampton Court ('I did by no means think it adequate in the whole to the notion I had of the Palace of a great Prince'), and commented that though the Slope Garden at Kensington and the new form of the gravel pit were 'in its way very agreeable yet in my opinion all this falls so low and short of the sublime unconfinedness of nature'. He added that 'there is something infinitely more exalting in the beautiful Scaravagie of noble grown Trees in a wild wood', so that the wood above New Park at Richmond (see fig. 111), with its extensive views, took his fancy:

> Here art has nothing Sawsy and seems to endeavour rather to follow than alter nature, and to aim at no beautys but such as she before had seem's to dictate . . . a fine wood so interspers'd with Vistos & little innumerable private dark walks thro every part of it lin'd on both sides with low hedges with the unconfin'd Prospects you meet every now and then of the Garden below[,] the Country and the River beyond . . .[8]

Addison's views gave authority to new trends in gardening towards plain grass and gravel and making extensive and informal walks through the outward plantations to viewpoints. One reader was Switzer, who took the *Spectator* article as a manifesto for his own system, introduced in *The Nobleman, Gentleman, and Gardener's Recreation*.[9] He also quoted extensively from Pope's poems on *Windsor Forest* and *Essay on Criticism*.

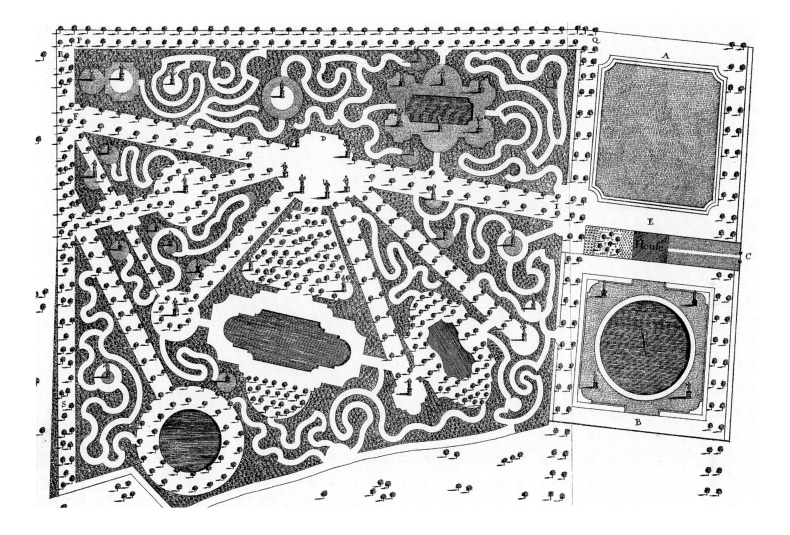

Switzer expanded his book and renamed it *Ichnographia Rustica* ('design of the country') in 1718. He wrote of outward plantations that 'these kind of Woods, as they are more Natural and Rural than the Set Wildernesses and Groves, so much us'd of late amongst us, yet they are a great deal less expensive, an Acre of this being made full five times cheaper than the other'. In extolling 'Rural Gardens', he thought 'such seem to be Gardens for the Politer and Greater Genius's of Britain, especially if to it be added Water the Spirit and most enchanting Beauty of Nature'.[10] The 'Rustic Order' was the general theme.

Batty Langley also thought his own 'method . . . most grand and rural'. He lived not far from Chiswick House, where the winding walks were conceivably 'Imitatio Ruris', and he referred to his own meandering walks as 'Rural'. Planting too could be 'rural' if trees were randomly disposed; for example, Langley showed a plate with a 'rural Grove' and a walk 'planted rural after Nature's own Manner' (fig. 196).[11] His book included fourteen plates of 'a

---

196   'A Garden that Lies Irregularly to the Grand House', from Batty Langley's *New Principles of Gardening* (1728). This plate, designed and drawn by Langley and engraved by Thomas Bowles, shows a plantation to the side of the house, 'wherein at D is a *pleasant Cabinet*, from whence we have five different Views, of which the Middle one [is] through a *rural Grove*' with randomly placed trees; at far left the 'Walk R S is planted rural after *Nature's own Manner*'.

---

rural garden after the new manner' and others laid out in similar style.[12] 'Rural' had here become the eschewal of artifice, planting randomly after Nature's own order.

This rhetoric of the 'rural' spread to the readers of garden books. In the early 1730s John Loveday saw the new plain parterre at Wanstead and the woods and water beyond (see fig. 287) and exclaimed:

> the Garden just in view from the house is truly wild and Rural, a very spacious Lawn just before the house – Woods about it – Water at the bottom of the View; the River runs through the Water. Here are fine Walks under Arbours of Trees, Statues placed in other parts.[13]

TASTE OF THE ANCIENTS

The literature of George I's reign is sometimes referred to as the 'Augustan Age', after the period's self-conscious imitation by English authors of the writings of Virgil and Horace in the time of the Emperor Augustus. Addison, Pope and Swift admired the stylish satirical writings of the golden age of their Roman counterparts, which they aspired to emulate. A parallel emphasis was placed on recapturing Antiquity's qualities in architecture, sculpture and gardens.

The Earl of Shaftesbury's prophecy in his 'Letter Concerning the Art and Science of Design' (see Chapter Six) that the British would pick up the mantle of Classical taste was the theme of Colen Campbell's preface to *Vitruvius Britannicus* (1715), in which he stated that Italian architects had lost 'the great Manner and exquisite Taste of Building . . . for the Italians can no more now relish the Antique Simplicity, but are entirely employed in capricious Ornaments'. Hence they had lost any special insight into Classical architecture: 'As to the Antiques . . . the Italians themselves have now no better Claim to them than they have to the purity of the Latin.'[14] Campbell sought to establish that the architecture practised by Palladio, translated to England by Inigo Jones, and recently reawakened amongst modern British architects, was the new national taste, and made the British the true

inheritors of the Antique. Indeed, 'in some Things we surpass our Neighbours', and Campbell hoped that his book would show that native designs 'would admit of a fair Comparison with the best of the Moderns'.

Lord Somers, an ally of Shaftesbury, had been appointed to oversee the education of the young Richard Boyle, 3rd Earl of Burlington. It was no surprise, then, that Burlington, as he grew into manhood, felt the weight of Shaftesbury's writings. Robert Castell acknowledged that Burlington was giving the arts of the Ancients 'new life when they languish, and even rescue them from Decay and Oblivion' and hoped that his own book *The Villas of the Ancients* (1728) was 'worthy the Patronage of my Lord BURLINGTON', its dedicatee. In his quest for a true Classicism Burlington was not alone, for Sir Andrew Fountaine of Narford Hall, Norfolk, a great connoisseur and collector since his Grand Tour, had corresponded with Burlington on the latter's second tour to Italy in 1719. There was also Lord Herbert, who designed Marble Hill. Both were described by the architect Robert Morris alongside Burlington as the 'preservers' of 'Ancient Architecture' and 'Protectors of Antiquity'.[15] The Earl of Mar, himself an architectural visionary, wrote in 1728 that he too sought 'the true ancient simple taste', which, he regretted 'is no more to be found' in Italy.[16]

The general eagerness of the British to adopt symbols of Antiquity is shown by the forests of columns and obelisks planted in their gardens in the reign of George I. Columns were suitable for commemoration because of their ability to support figures. They were becoming larger, and were often placed at the termination of major vistos. However, it was obelisks that became particularly characteristic of the 1720s. Although Egyptian in origin, they were seen by every tourist in Rome, marking intersections of roads or garden walks. The Villa Mattei had an obelisk in its *prato*, or theatre, and the Villa Medici contained an Antique one in a central position in its garden.[17] The Piazza del Popolo, the entrance to Rome for every visitor from the north, centered on one.

Full-sized obelisks had made an appearance in England in 1702, when Aislabie, no doubt with such Roman precedents in mind, paid for one, designed by Nicholas Hawksmoor, for the market square at Ripon, which he represented in Parliament.[18] The next

English obelisks may have been by Vanbrugh, or Hawksmoor acting as his assistant, at Castle Howard, in two of the circles of the immense southern wilderness (see fig. 172). In 1714 they erected one, dedicated to the Duke of Marlborough, where the approach to Castle Howard made a right-angle turn, and another was proposed in 1716 by Hawksmoor for the Avenue at Blenheim. Vanbrugh introduced further obelisks on the south parterre at Castle Howard once it had ceased to be the works area. Gilded vases on pedestals by Daniel Hervé, eight 40-foot obelisks and a 50-foot pillar were all installed in 1720–4 on the otherwise plain parterre (fig. 197). A visitor in 1724 remarked of the obelisks that: 'The parterre garden is almost filled with them'.[19]

At Dunham Massey a small obelisk at an intersection of walks in Langham Grove is dated 1714.[20] At Narford about 1719 Fountaine set up one at the intersection of his avenue with the public highway (fig. 198). Four obelisks were seen in the four plats of the parterre at Wentworth Woodhouse, and Vanbrugh proposed two large ones at Eastbury in 1724. These symbols of Rome became employed in scores of English gardens to indicate the primary construction lines and intersections of a garden's layout, being placed at the end of water, at the intersection of walks, on bastions, or at small distances beyond the fossee.

Burlington's quest to recover architectural Antiquity was sparked when he returned from a Grand Tour in 1715, and found his copies of *Vitruvius Britannicus* (1715) awaiting him. He made a resolve that he would promote the purer architecture practised by Palladio and publicised by Campbell. A domed temple started by James Gibbs at the end of the lime walk at Chiswick was too close, Burlington soon reflected, to the modern Italian style (later known as 'Baroque'). He employed Campbell in 1717 to help him design a *bagnio* on Palladian lines, which he then built at the end of a toe of the *patte d'oie* in the outward plantation that he was establishing (see fig. 291). As Burlington's ideas matured further, he saw that Palladio was just a door to the understanding of his real interest, Roman Antiquity itself. His architecture has been described as 'Neo-Classic'.[21]

Construction of Burlington's new villa at Chiswick started in 1725. He came to wish for gardens to suit, and started thinking about the principles. Pope had previously claimed that unadorned Nature 'was the taste of the ancients in their gardens, as we may discover from the description extant of them'.[22] No doubt alluding to Virgil, Horace and other Roman poets who wrote about the rural life, Switzer even ventured that 'Agriculture and Gard'ning, abstracted from the Profits of it, was so very solid, durable, and delightful an Employ' that it was 'plac'd above the most Refined Pleasures of Antiquity (not inferior to the Seraphick Entertainments of Musick and Poetry) [as] ancient History undeniably proves.'[23] After citing the outward woodland at Castle Howard, New Park and Cassiobury, Switzer speculated that 'the Romans had doubtless the same extensive kind of Gardens'.[24] He thought that 'The Ancient Villa's and Possessions of the Greeks and Romans were undoubtedly of this kind, in which they spent the happiest of their Moments, and Reap'd not a little Advantage thereby; in those early Days of Innocence and Antique Virtue.'[25]

Encouraging as such thoughts may have been, they were of little help in designing actual gardens. Some Englishmen who might have been curious about the real gardens of the ancients had visited Rome – for example, Thomas Archer in 1691–5, William Kent in 1709–19, Fountaine in 1718 and Burlington once more in 1718. There may have been confusion between authentic Antiquity in ruin and decayed Renaissance gardens, no doubt deliberately fostered by the guides, but the gardens of Rome were the best visual evidence available for those of Antiquity. Fountaine set out a semicircular gravel piazza on the garden front of his house when he returned from Rome, and when Burlington built his villa at Chiswick it was given a rectangular forecourt with a semicircular ending, a piazza before his villa. It was adorned with *termini*, or terms, which Burlington could have seen in a number of Roman gardens, and which he had Giovanni-Battista Guelfi sculpt in 1729. Framing the visto to the side was a miniaturised version of the *laberinto* at the Villa Ludovisi, complete with statuary.[26]

Burlington's desire to recreate the appearance of Antique gardens is revealed in a seemingly minor matter. In the gardens of Rome some high palisades that had become unfurnished at their foot were underplanted.[27] Dezallier d'Argenville knew of French examples of this, at Versailles and Saint-Cloud, and described

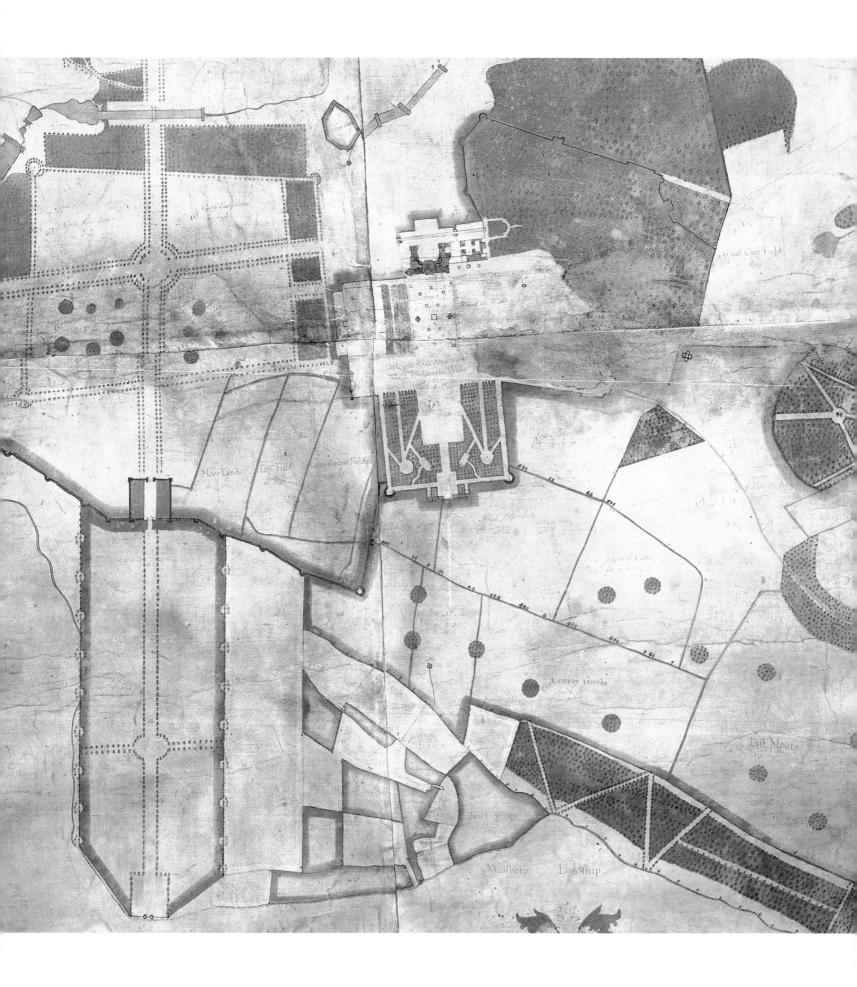

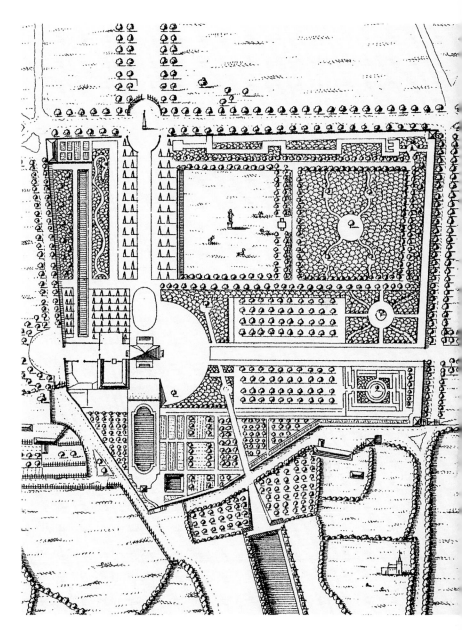

(Facing page) 197 Central portion of an estate map of Castle Howard by Ralph Fowler, 1727. The house is situated on a ridge running east-west; the wood-work south of the house and the obelisks on the plain parterre are evident. Half of Wray Wood, to the north-east, was enclosed by a terrace; the approaches consisted of avenues punctuated by gatehouses, and at the main crossing point there was a high obelisk; the parkland was studded with 'plumps', or clumps.

198 A detail of the 'Plan of the Garden and Plantations of Narford . . . ' engraved by Henry Hulsbergh, 1725. This layout, by Sir Andrew Fountaine, a Classical enthusiast and amateur architect, dated from about 1718. It was set within a garden wall, but the inward plantations were of unusual form: its obelisk at the entrance, piazza by the house, groves, labyrinth walks and Classical architecture made it reminiscent of a Roman villa. A deer paddock, visible over a *fossee*, had a deer house; an Ionic temple overlooking a pool was set within high hedges in order to conceal the fact that it was on the garden's boundary; these buildings and the deer enclosure were amongst the sources for Lord Burlington's alterations at Chiswick soon after.

how the defect was remedied by filling up the lower part with box or yew trained on a trellis.[28] Burlington seems to have made a note of this, and the right-hand hornbeam walk of the *patte d'oie* at Chiswick was underplanted with yew in the early 1730s.

Burlington's changes to his garden to make them conformable with ancient Roman gardens followed closely on the building of his villa, and were shown on paintings by Pieter Andreas Rysbrack from 1728 and drawings by Jacques Rigaud in 1733. His principal walks and vistos were flanked by palisades in yew. The unusual appearance of this hedgework was a result of its decoration by stone figures and scores of *termini*, contrasting with the dark of the palisades. Around 1734 Burlington set about forming a visto behind the villa terminated by a hemicycle, much as could be seen at the Villa Mattei, and here he placed some Antique figures and lines of urns of his own design to form in effect a sculpture garden.

The interiors to Burlington's plantations formed a complete contrast. He had acquired adjacent property in 1727, which enabled him to plant further wilderness areas, the creation of

which was captured by a Rysbrack painting of about 1729 from the new terrace. This shows the planting of palisades defining some violently meandering carpet walks in the new western wilderness (fig. 199). John Rocque's plan of 1736 (see fig. 291) shows that the northern wilderness had gone through the same process. Cabinets, a bowling green and an opening of simple grassland unfolded to the unexpecting visitor. Pope's design for Marble Hill had already shown tightly twisting paths in 1724 (fig. 200). A quite different

approach from Bridgeman's was evident, with much in common with the extremes of 'rural' gardening proposed by Batty Langley.

As Burlington was altering his gardens, Robert Castell was meanwhile on his own mission of unlocking the rules of designing Roman villas and their gardens. The fullest extant descriptions of Roman villas and their surroundings are Pliny the Younger's epistles concerning his villas at Laurentum and in Tuscum. Pope had jokingly referred to his garden at Twickenham as 'My Tusculum' in 1720. Robert Castell pored over the same text as the best source in his quest to discover the Antique rules on the situation and disposition of villas. His interpretation of the epistle on Tuscum was that alleys beyond the end of the hippodrome, 'by many and various Windings' passed though one place where 'the box describes a thousand different forms', then 'a little Meadow' and 'after a most elegant Taste, a sudden Imitation of the Country seems accidentally introduced'.[29]

Castell's rather free translation of Pliny suggests that he was making the text conform to thoughts already being suggested to Burlington. In a lengthy disquisition on the 'first Rise of Gardens', he suggested that the first villas had no gardens as such, just places where various plants and trees were found to grow best. He continued:

> But this rough Manner, not appearing sufficiently beautiful to those of a more regular and exact Taste, set them upon inventing a Manner of laying out the Ground and Plantations of Gardens by the Rule and Line, and to trim them up by an Art that was visible in every Part of the Design.

The 'Imitation of the Country' hinted at a hypothetical third manner of laying out gardens, consisting of 'Hills, Rocks, cas-

199 Detail of a painting by Pieter Andreas Rysbrack of Chiswick House, c.1729, showing the western wilderness being set out. This field, Judd's Close, had been acquired in 1727, and a 'river' dug through it; the spoil was mounded up along the roadside creating the terrace from which this view is taken. The work shown here is maintenance of the recently planted western wilderness with hedged meandering paths and cabinet.

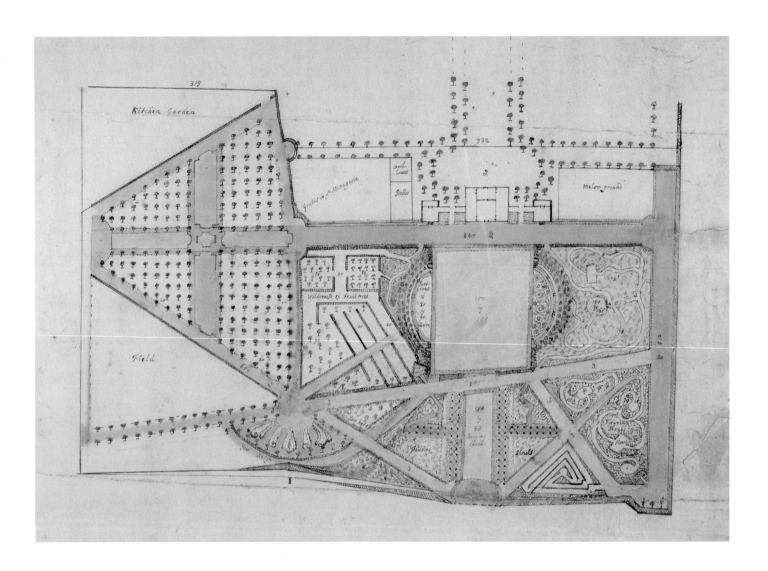

cades, Rivulets, Woods, Buildings, &c . . . thrown into such an agreeable Disorder, as to have pleased the Eye from several Views, like so many beautiful Landskips'. He saw that this could have

been the same as Temple's and Addison's understanding of 'Chinese' gardens, whose Beauty consisted in 'a close Imitation of Nature; where, tho' the Parts are disposed with the greatest Art, the Irregularity is still preserved'.

Castell showed what he meant in his plan of the villa in Tuscum (fig. 201). The 'Vivarium or Park' was rough Nature, the inward gardens were set out 'by rule and line', and two circular halls in dense planting represented the third. One was the 'Pratulum or little meadow in the garden', the other 'Imitatio Ruris', 'The imitation of the natural face of some country, in the garden'. Twisting water courses ran through meadows and irregularly-disposed trees. This imagery was perhaps derived from specimens

200 Pope's design for Marble Hill, Twickenham, 1724. This is the only known design drawing in Pope's hand; it can be dated by reference to the property that Pope assumed was available. As well as space for a bowling green and flower parterres, it includes a very early example of madly meandering paths through plantations. It was superseded by a more practical scheme by Bridgeman, who kept the idea of a bowling green within a grove on the principal visto.

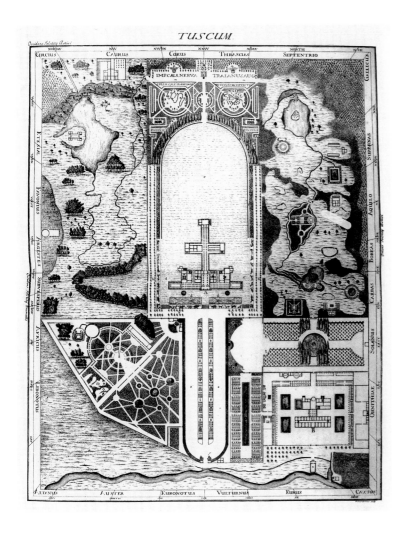

to the Duchess of Marlborough to save the ruins of Woodstock Manor on the grounds that 'it wou'd make One of the Most Agreable Objects that the best of Landskip Painters can invent'.[32] Dezallier d'Argenville too extolled 'The Pleasure of seeing . . . for four or five Leagues round, a vast Number of Villages, Woods, Rivers, Hills, and Meadows, with a thousand other Varieties that make a beautiful Landskip, [which] exceeds all that I can possibly say of it.'[33] Later, in June 1712, Addison remarked in his article 414 in the *Spectator*: 'there is something more bold and masterly in the rough careless Strokes of Nature, than in the nice Touches and Embellishments of Art'. The painting metaphor was not lost on Pope.

The standard French work on the theory of painting was Charles Alphonse du Fresnoy's *De Arte Graphica* (1667). This poem in Latin took a highly intellectual approach, and was seen as representing the theory of art approved by the French Academy. It had been translated into prose by John Dryden, the Poet Laureate in William III's reign, whose subtitle read 'Translated into English, with an original preface, containing a parallel between painting and poetry by Mr. Dryden'. Dryden's thoughts along this line had been inspired by an assertion by Philostratus, a Greek sophist of the third century AD, translated as: 'The *Art* of *Painting* has a wonderful affinity with that of *Poetry*; and that there is betwixt them a certain common imagination.'[34]

Pope saw parallels between 'history painting', scenes displaying moments of great heroism or virtue from Antiquity, and the purpose of poetry in moral instruction. His interest in the unity of the arts was ignited, and in 1713–14 he spent much time under

of ancient groves being captured and framed, as if on display, within some of the new outward plantations at the time (see 'Wildernesses after the rural manner', p. 287 below).[30]

'OUR KIND ARTS UNITE'

Fashions in gardens need not be allied to fashions in other arts, like painting or poetry. On the other hand, there sometimes is a correspondence between them, such that each can be seen as a different expression of the prevailing mood, although through different media. A generation familiar with the landscapes of Nicolas Poussin and Claude made the small step to employ the language of painting to describe actual views.[31] Vanbrugh made his appeal the instruction of Charles Jervas, a pupil of Godfrey Kneller. He had painted the famous portraits of Kit-Kat club members and later became a neighbour of Pope's at Twickenham. To Pope, Jervas was a painter from whom he could learn some of the art of painting, and a talker with whom he could explore the relationship between the arts. Pope made some progress in painting, undertaking a number of passable portraits, and becoming vain enough to insert some strokes into a landscape being painted by Peter Tillemans.

At this time a second edition of Dryden's Du Fresnoy was proposed, which Jervas was to 'correct'. Pope composed an 'Epistle to Mr Jervas' (1715) to be a preface to the work, which included a testament to their friendship:[35]

> Smit with the love of Sister-arts we came,
> And met congenial, mingling flame with flame;
> Like friendly colours found them both unite,
> And each from each contract new strength and light.

Pope made commitment to their joint project clear in writing that 'Images reflect from Art to Art'. He then invoked a journey to Rome in the imagination:

> What flatt'ring Scenes our wand'ring Fancy wrought,
> Rome's pompous Glories rising to our Thought!
> Together o'er the Alps methinks we fly,
> Fir'd with Ideas of fair Italy.
> With thee, on Raphael's Monument I mourn,
> Or wait inspiring Dreams at Maro's Urn:
> With thee repose, where Tully once was laid,
> Or seek some Ruin's formidable Shade;
> While Fancy brings the vanish'd Piles to view,
> And builds imaginary Rome a-new.

Pope told Jervas that 'I long to see you a History Painter'.[36] Alas, Jervas never was. Pope, however, maintained his interest in pictorialism, and would observe how views could be 'picturesque', that is suitable as the subject of a history painting.

Pope's major literary project from 1714 to 1720 was the translation of Homer's *Iliad*. His commentary on it gave him the opportunity to show how poetry and painting could unite. At a time when image and dialogue could not be combined, except ephemerally on stage, Pope was anxious to stimulate his readers' imaginations to supply images. Hence he would mention incident, movement and colour, thus offering hints for a pictorial interpretation of the scenes in the text.[37] In an essay introducing the second volume of his *Iliad*, Pope claimed that Homer had done so too, and pointed to 'what Use Homer every where makes of each little Accident or Circumstance that can naturally happen in a Battel, thereby to cast a Variety over his Action . . . [this] makes his Work resemble a large History-Piece'.[38]

With his labours on the *Iliad* drawing to a close Pope could begin to relax. From 1717 he started his 'summer rambles' to the country houses of owners who had befriended him. He had known Lord Bathurst for several years, and was delighted to find him in 1718 working on vast schemes of planting at Oakley Wood, which Bathurst had bought in 1716 to join to his Cirencester property (see fig. 11). Pope discussed improvement with Bathurst, but his schemes remained 'all very fine in our own imagination'.[39] Some echoes of their enthusiastic joint planning can be heard years later in Pope's 'Epistle to Burlington', in which Pope saw estate improvement as a process of landscape painting:

> Consult the Genius of the Place in all;
> That tells the Waters or to rise, or fall;
> Or helps th' ambitious Hill the Heavens to scale,
> Or scoops in circling theatres the vale;
> Calls in the Country, catches op'ning glades,
> Joins willing woods, and varies shades from shades;
> Now breaks, or now directs, th' intending lines;
> Paints as you plant, and, as you work, designs.[40]

As the *Iliad* had proved commercially successful Pope could afford to seek a new, larger, home, and in 1718 he took the lease of a house on the Thames from Thomas Vernon of Twickenham Park. Lines that Jonathan Swift wrote in 1714 represented Pope's own mood:

> I've often wished that I had clear
> For life six hundred pounds a year

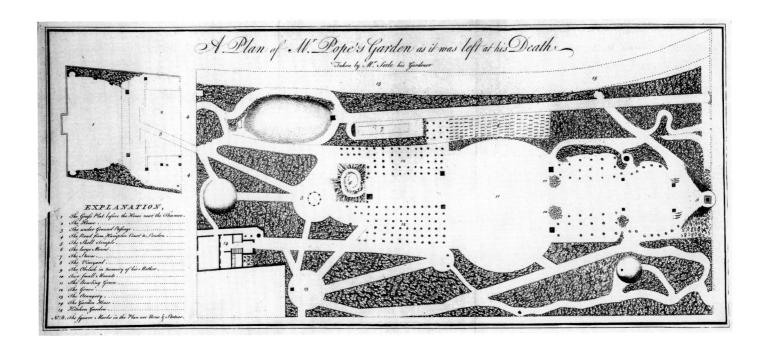

A handsome House to lodge a friend,
A River at my garden's end,
A terrace Walk, and half a Rood
Of Land, set out to plant a wood.
Well, now I have all this and more,
I ask not to increase my store . . . [41]

Burlington advised on alterations to Pope's villa from 1719. One was a passage under the highway at the back of the villa in order to reach the garden on the far side. It was managed so that, from

202 A plan of Pope's garden at Twickenham, made after his death by his gardener, John Serle, in 1745. Although not particularly accurate – for example, the walk under the road was not at such an angle – it does show the sequence of groves and grass at the centre overlooked from the mount. The circular bowling green could be viewed as a 'light' in a history painting, with the groves providing the encircling shades, and the further grove and grass being a trick of perspective. Although laid out using familiar elements, the arrangement was a novel application of the rules of painting to a garden.

an open temple decorated with shells in a cabinet in the garden, boats on the Thames were visible from the slightly sloping passage.

Pope's other, absorbing, activity was garden-making. In the winter of 1719–20 he had 'a vast deal to do with Gardeners', making bowers, avenues, and a rising mount.[42] The last of these was positioned just by the entrance to the passage, so was presumably constructed with soil from its excavation. In 1721 the gardens were sufficiently advanced for Pope to encourage visitors to view his Mount, 'Great Walk' and a 'Green', and John Gay, the poet, congratulated him on the finished gardens. From 1722 there was increasingly frequent mention of the grotto made in the basement of his house; this was finished in 1725. Its embellishments were a spring discovered during construction, porches at either end, doors that could be closed to create a camera obscura inside, and a pebble floor. Pope considered his grotto at Twickenham to be natural, seemingly on the basis that he lined it with samples of raw minerals.

An idea of the garden's design after 25 years was provided by a pamphlet on the grotto, sold to visitors, by John Serle, Pope's factotum and gardener, which came with *A Plan of Mr. Pope's Garden as it was Left at his Death* (fig. 202).[43] A 'Great Walk' led away from the Mount down the centre of the layout between quincunxes to a bowling green, and this arrangement was repeated a second time at a smaller scale. Pope boasted in a letter of this view: 'I will carry you up a Mount, in a point of view to show you the glory of my little Kingdom.'[44] Quincunxes and greens were enveloped by dense planting, through which ran irregularly arranged *allées* leading to other cabinets, not very different from wildernesses by Bridgeman at the time. The arrangement as a whole was quite different, though, with no parallels elsewhere.

Philip Southcote, creator of Woburn Farm from 1735, considered 'Mr Pope and Kent were the first that practiced painting in gardening'. Pope told Joseph Spence that the plantations either side of his Great Walk were narrowed for distancing 'as they do in painting', and gave the advice that 'The Lights and shades in gardening are managed by disposing the thick grovework, the thin, and the openings.'[45] Serle's plan suggests that the garden layout was on precisely these principles. The view to the spacious bowling green would have been directed by the quincunxes. When bowls was in progress, the players would have been in a very prominent position in the view from the Mount. The distancing by means of the narrowing quincunxes beyond, and the smaller scale of the second green, would have given the impression of a much greater depth to the garden than actually existed.

The obvious source of ideas for this layout was the new edition of Dryden's Du Fresnoy. The advice to painters was made in a large number of 'precepts', many of which could be reinterpreted for the sister art of gardening. These included:

IV, regarding 'The Disposition or Oeconomy of the Whole Work'; here it is advised 'Let your Compositions be conformable to the Text of Ancient Authours'.[46]

XI: 'Let the principal Figure of the Subject appear in the middle of the Piece under the strongest Light', suggesting a central open area.

XXXI, regarding 'The Conduct of the Tones of Light and Shadows', which includes clauses such as 'The passage of one into the other must be common and imperceptible, that is by degrees of Lights into Shadows and of Shadows into Lights',

and 'Let the Lights and Shadows be so discreetly managed, that light Bodies may have sufficient Mass or Breadth of Shadow to sustain them', which suggested merging the open area into surrounding groves.

XXXIII: 'The greater Light must strike forcibly on the middle', reinforcing the suggestion of an open central area.

XLV: 'Let the Field, or Ground of the Picture, be pleasant, free, transient, light, and well united with Colours which are of a friendly nature to each other'. Elsewhere it is advised that '*Terre Verte* (or green Earth) is 'light'.

Pope may thus have envisaged the bowlers on his green as the central group in the 'Light' of a history painting, the quincunxes to be the shadows, and the repetition of quincunxes and green a device to create an illusion of greater depth to the garden.

Pope met Bridgeman in the early 1720s, if not before, and evidently had respect for him, expressed when he apologised in 1724 for postponing a visit to the new Earl of Oxford at Wimpole: 'I am heartily disappointed, and so is another man, of the Virtuoso-Class as well as I; (and in My notions, of the higher kind of class, since Gardening is more Antique & nearer God's own Work, than Poetry) I mean Bridgman, whom I had tempted to accompany me to you.'[47] Pope and Bridgeman were that year collaborating on Mrs Henrietta Howard's gardens at Marble Hill. She had become mistress to the Prince of Wales in 1720, and in 1722/3 he made a settlement in her favour to be administered by the Earl of Ilay and others. Amongst the swarm of gallants seeking to assist Mrs Howard were the Earl of Peterborough and Pope, who was spending time in June 'studying & in drawing new plans'.[48] His general plan was a cramped arrangement of bowling green, flower parterres, alleys, arcades, a wilderness of flowering shrubs with tightly winding walks, a wilderness of fruit trees, a melon ground, a kitchen garden and other areas (see fig. 200).

In September 1724 Ilay arranged for further land to extend the design to the river's edge.[49] Pope wrote to his publisher that he had been 'very busy in laying out of a garden, shall be busier next month'.[50] This appears to have been in conjunction with Bridgeman, who was promising his plan a few days later. The result was an oval bowling green surrounded by an arcade, behind which were dense plantations with meandering walks. The view narrowed beyond the bowling green, then opened up for a broad visto between quincunxes to the Thames (fig. 203). Pope superintended the making of the gardens – the accounts include a garden roller 'by the order of Mr. Pope'. He begged trees off Lord Bathurst in October, and the quincunxes down to the Thames were planted that winter. The descent from the bowling green to the riverside meadow was managed by a series of slopes. In 1725–6 Bridgeman was working on Richmond Gardens for the Prince and Princess of Wales and Pope wrote to Lord Oxford that 'I have just turf'd a little Bridgmannick Theatre myself. It was done by a detachment of His workmen from the Prince's, all at a stroke'.[51] The overall design at Marble Hill, with an oval lawn and arcades, was a careful compromise on Bridgeman's part, as it incorporated elements of Pope's earlier plan and was spacious enough to permit a layout according to his painting principles. It achieved Pope's aims: the view from the villa would have been of players in a 'Light', with a wide prospect of river, fields and hills beyond.

Pope seemed to regard painting principles simply as an aid to his own designs, and did little to promote them; we know of his painterly rules only because he proffered them in conversation in 1739 to contemporaries who understood that way of thinking. Kent, Southcote and Spence were amongst the vanguard of another generation who saw these principles as an expressive simile to explain a new aesthetic of setting out gardens 'without line and level'.

Garden undertakers

After London's demise in 1713/14, Henry Wise, as the sole surviving partner in the Brompton Park nursery, sold the business to two of his servants, Joseph Carpenter and William Smith, for £6,100 with 38 years remaining on the lease of the premises, his own house excluded.[52] The nursery had Tilleman Bobart as foreman at Blenheim, and probably Switzer at Grimsthorpe, so they continued to be employed. Bridgeman made plans of gardens for Wise

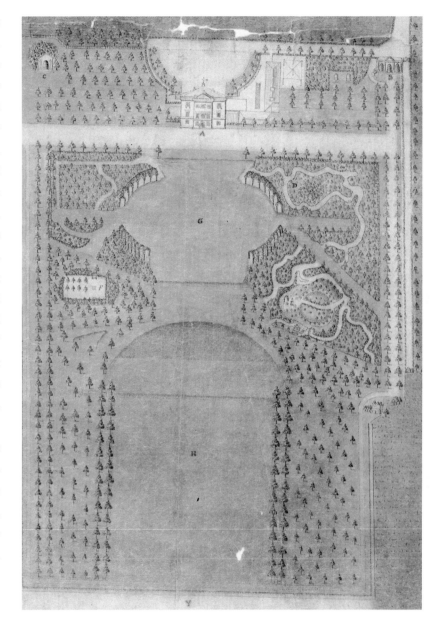

203   A survey of Marble Hill, Twickenham, prepared c.1752, when for legal reasons the Countess of Suffolk transferred the land to her brother, the Earl of Buckinghamshire. This records Bridgeman's design of 28 years earlier: the bowling green was encircled by arcades, and Pope's ideas for tightly twisting paths within plantations had also been adopted. Extra land towards the river (at bottom) was acquired in late 1724 so that it could be planted as a visto flanked by groves; the slope down was shaped into low earthworks in 1726.

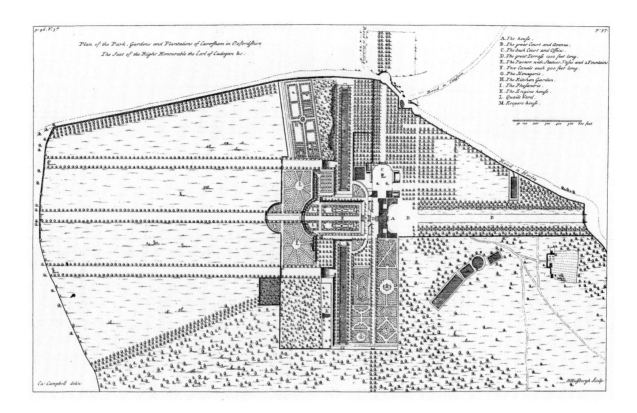

204 Colen Campbell, 'Plan of the Park, Gardens and Plantations of Caversham', engraved by Henry Hulsbergh, c.1719. William Cadogan, Marlborough's quartermaster, was made Earl Cadogan in 1718, the year that he signed an agreement with Switzer to make the garden (later credited to Thomas Ackres). Traditional elements, such as the large walled rectangle, the baskethandle and the parterre were combined with up-to-date *bosquet* designs and a separate service courtyard, as at Cannons. The menagerie, quail yard and pheasantry suggest an obsession with birds.

as Royal Gardener, but was not a trained gardener, and may never have had a formal association with Brompton Park. His skills were employed instead in devising layouts, though he often called upon the nursery to supply plants.

With the monarch being indifferent to garden-making, the position of Royal Gardener was both less interesting and less remunerative. Furthermore, in 1715 a new post of Surveyor of Gardens and Waters was created for Vanbrugh, giving him over-sight of relevant contracts, principally Wise's, and responsibility for repairs and new works in the palace gardens. This effectively demoted Wise, who was in his early sixties, suffering from rheumatism and colic, and acknowledging that it was time to retire. In 1716 he requested that Carpenter share the position of Royal Gardener with him, which was accepted. Wren was still Surveyor General of the King's Works, but he too was old. In 1718, as taste turned towards a more purely Classical style in architecture, William Benson, who was in favour with George I for having designed some water-works at Herrenhausen, successfully insinuated himself into Wren's post with false reports on the state of the Parliament buildings. Within a year he had proved his incapacity, and was replaced by Sir Thomas Hewett, a country gentleman who was not only a leading proponent of Classical architecture but who had also proved himself capable as Surveyor-General of the King's Woods for twenty years.

Colen Campbell, who was in league with Benson, did not lose the opportunity when producing an engraving of Caversham for

256

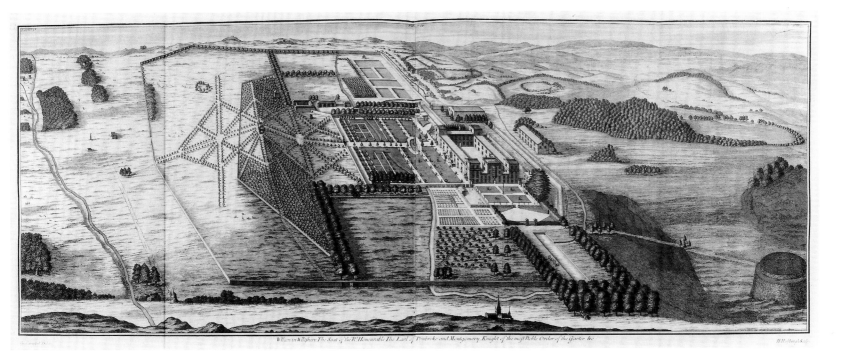

Wilton in Wiltshire The Seat of the Rt Honourable The Earl of Pembroke and Montgomery, Knight of the most Noble Order of the Garter &c.

Vitruvius Britannicus of stating that 'These gardens were form'd by Mr. Acres, where he has left lasting Monuments of his Capacity. Anno 1723' (fig. 204). Benson sent a letter to the Treasury Board acquainting it with what he claimed were the the King's orders that Wise and Carpenter should be replaced by Ackres, whose contract would be for 'half what they have hitherto cost, occasioning the saving of £1600 per annum'.[53] However, the First Lord of the Treasury, the Earl of Sunderland, was offended by Benson's presumption in by-passing the Board, and ordered the letter to be burned in his presence.

Bridgeman struck out on his own as a designer and undertaker (of which more later), being engaged by many owners, and in some respects taking over from where London left off. In time, he was to develop a business keeping town-house gardens in London: for example, he was appointed to Montagu House in 1725. There is some evidence that Bridgeman also maintained out-of-town gardens, since in 1728 he entered into a contract with Lord Wilmington to keep the gardens at Compton Place, near Eastbourne.

Switzer had left the employ of the Brompton Park nursery soon after 1715, his interests having broadened into practical improve-

ments in gardening and agriculture, and he was not confined to garden projects. He dedicated the second and third volumes of his *Ichnographia Rustica* (1718) to Lord Coningsby and the Earl of Pembroke, so it seems likely that he was involved at Hampton Court in Herefordshire and at Wilton House. Canals and cascades may have been his business at the former, and at the latter *plates-bandes* were removed to reconcile parterres to the prevailing taste (fig. 205). The agreement with Earl Cadogan 'for making parterres, terrace walks with two canals, kitchen gardens, orchards, etc.' at Caversham was made in 1718 for the agreed sum of £1,392 4s 9d.[54]

---

205   Colen Campbell, 'Wilton in Wiltshire', engraved by Henry Hulsbergh, 1725. In the late 1680s the eighth Earl of Pembroke, among other changes, had the canal dug, and the parterre embellished with *plates-bandes* and clipped greens with a Neptune fountain at its centre. Towards the end of his long life he acceded to changes in taste by removing both the *plates-bandes* and the forecourt's clipped greens. John Loveday saw 'the plain Garden here' in 1731. One of the first acts of the ninth Earl in 1734 was to level the walls of the 1630s garden and make ha-has.

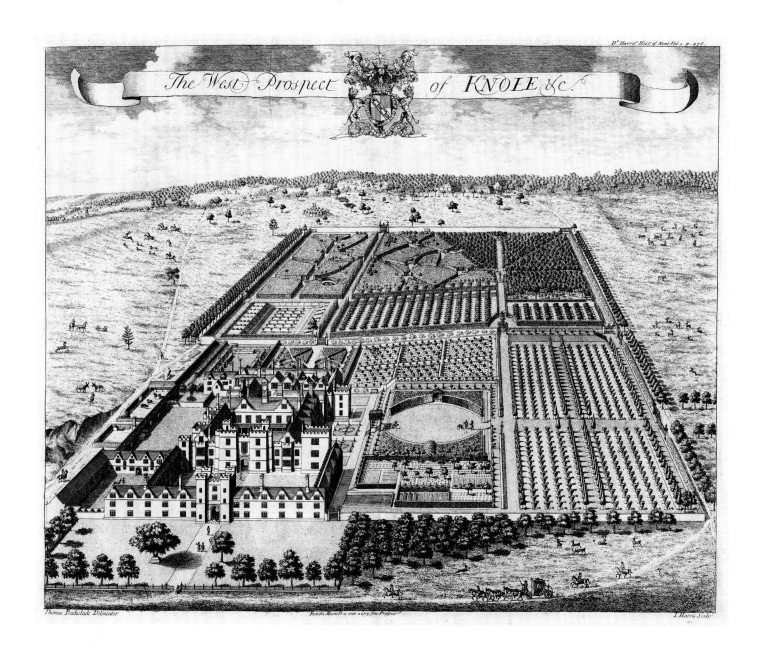

The West Prospect of KNOLE &c.

From the early 1720s, Switzer's writings had much less to do with pleasure grounds and more with fruit gardens, kitchen gardens, seed strains, techniques of agriculture and horticulture and improvement generally. He travelled much in giving advice on such matters, ran a seed stall in Westminster Hall and set up his own nursery on Millbank in 1727. Owners for whom he worked included Henry Hoare, the banker, and the Earl of Orrery. Whilst residing at the latter's seat at Marston, Somerset, Switzer had a free run of the library, which assisted in his writing of *Hydrostaticks and Hydraulicks* (1729). He could well have supplied seeds of lucerne grass and advised the Tories on techniques in the kitchen garden, as he later also did to the Society of Improvers in the Knowledge of Agriculture in Scotland from about 1731. It was only in the 1730s that he returned to garden design, notably producing general plans for Gibside, near Newcastle upon Tyne, and Nostell Priory, Yorkshire (see fig. 270).

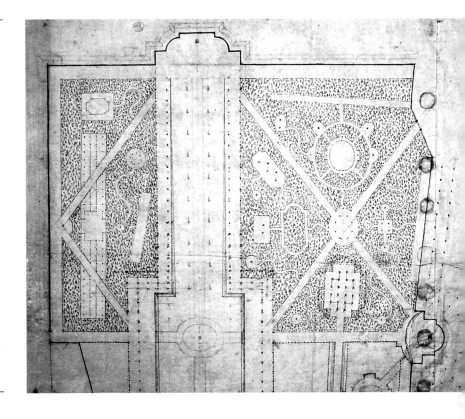

(Facing page) 206 'The West Prospect of Knole' by Thomas Badeslade and John Harris, c.1715. The extensive area for 'goblets' of dwarf apples and pears was a legacy of London and Wise, who were supplying the sixth Earl of Dorset in 1698. In 1710 the seventh Earl signed a contract with Thomas Ackres for alterations, including a little parterre under the south front, a bowling green, a 'canall', which could not hold water, so became a sunken area east of the house. There were also improvements to the kitchen garden and dwarf fruit areas. Roughly coeval was the low grove and walk set with cypresses extending to the iron gate in the further wall, new planting with cabinets either side of this walk, the *patte d'oie* in the wooded area and several *grilles* and gates.

207 A plan for the wilderness at Houghton Hall, c.1717, probably by Bridgeman. Lines beyond the boundary indicate that this was to be a ha-ha, not an upstanding wall. The design is an exercise in inventing as many different forms of hall or cabinet as possible, all linked by meandering paths; the clipped yews along the central vista were soon to be outmoded. This design was implemented in altered form by Kingsmill Eyre in 1720.

Much is known about several other undertakers. Thomas Ackres, briefly mentioned above, a nephew and executor of George London, lived in St James's parish, Westminster. Like many of the independent gardeners, his bread and butter was undertaking maintenance at London houses. He appears as such at Montagu House in 1706, charging £140 per annum, though his services were dispensed with in 1709.[55] He was at Wrest from 1706 at the latest until 1728, undertaking alterations for the Duke of Kent in his rapidly changing garden. At one point, in 1715, he was asked for a plan. He signed a contract with the Earl of Dorset in 1710 for several alterations at Knole (fig. 206).[56] After his attempt to become Royal Gardener in 1718 he was seen at Ampthill and Caversham. He was evidently well known, for Pope remarked in 1725 that 'I have long been convinced that neither Acres, nor Wise; nor any public Professors of Gardening, are equal to the Private Practisers of it.'[57]

Kingsmill Eyre was a gentleman who had assisted the Earl of Shaftesbury with improvements at Wimborne St Giles, Dorset, in the late 1700s. A few years later he was making himself useful within the Walpole circle.[58] When the garden at Houghton was adapted in the late 1710s, Bridgeman produced a plan (fig. 207), but Horace Walpole remembered that: 'It was laid out by Mr. Eyre, an imitator of Bridgeman'. Eyre seems to have implemented the plan in his own way and organised the supply of trees. He may also have worked at Chevening.

At Londesborough Burlington had a head gardener, Thomas Knowlton, who from 1726 was his representative at several places in Yorkshire, including Dalton Hall (fig. 208) and Aldby Park. Lord Herbert likewise had his own circle, which included the architect Roger Morris, and Lord Petre had a mysterious surveyor, 'the Sieur Bourginion', or 'Bourguignon', to draw his amazing and intricate designs in the 1730s.[59]

In the late 1720s a cocksure newcomer, Batty Langley, began writing on gardening and building, seeking to attract the notice of 'The Nobility and Gentry of Great Britain'.[60] He appears to have been knowledgeable about plants and surveying, and had

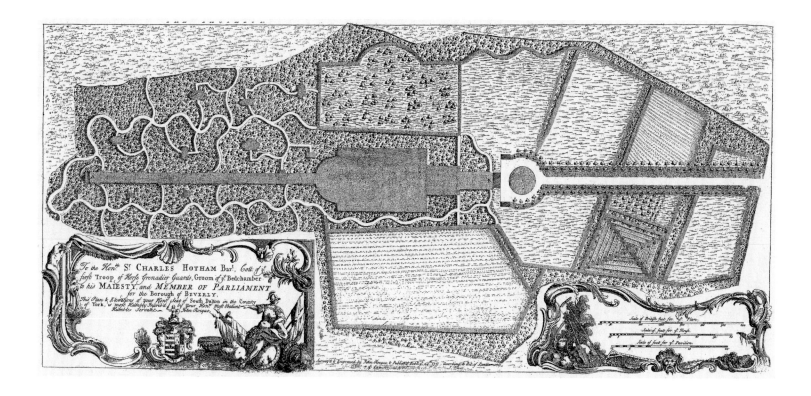

some involvement in gardens local to Twickenham, his home, such as Twickenham Park and Secretary Johnston's (fig. 209), but appears to have had limited success in gaining a wider circle of employers.

GEORGE II AND QUEEN CAROLINE

Bridgeman was to become the Royal Gardener, for when Carpenter died in 1726 Wise asked for Bridgeman to take Carpenter's place. Two years later, Wise gave up being Royal Gardener altogether. That left Bridgeman the sole holder of the position and his career then became entwined with some major royal projects.

George I's only foray into garden-making was the enclosure of a paddock from Hyde Park with a brick wall, starting in 1726, for a menagerie of wild animals. A great star of walks was planted to subdivide the area into 'Lawns, Quarters, & Walks', and excavation for the Great Bason (today's Round Pond) and dam-building to flood the six fishponds in Hyde Park for a single body of water (today's Serpentine) was begun. The following year George

II succeeded his father. His queen, Caroline, had her own ideas for the Hyde Park paddocks. The tigers were sent off to the Tower of London, and Bridgeman was required to turn the whole area, together with the Upper Garden, into an enormous outward plantation, with miles of serpentine walks threaded with cabinets

208   Plan and elevations of Dalton Hall, Yorkshire, by John Rocque, 1737. In 1729 Lord Burlington sent his gardener at Londesborough, Thomas Knowlton, to Dalton to devise a new layout for Sir Charles Hotham, as seen on this plan. On the garden front the view opened out by stages onto a lawn with an apsidal end; the great walk beyond led to a Classical pavilion, with planting to each side threaded with complex meandering paths with frequent cabinets. In the rest of the layout a planted framework enclosed various areas, and carpet walks were set out along the edges. These areas included one with older trees that seems to have been left as *imitatio ruris*; £294 was spent on 'the garden seat at the end of the wood'. This was the pavilion of 1733–4, probably designed by Colen Campbell.

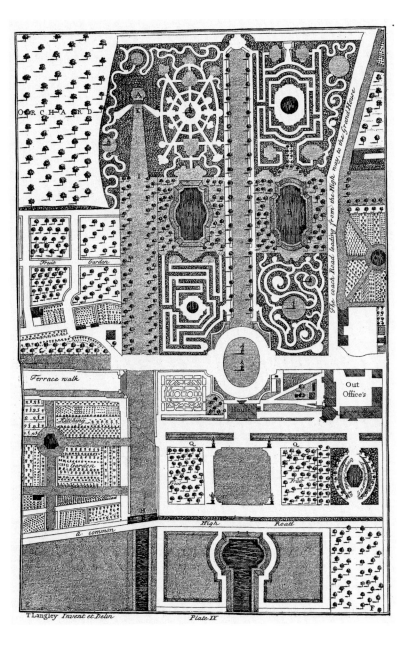

209 'A beautiful Garden at Twickenham', from Batty Langley's *New Principles of Gardening* (1728). Despite being reversed and 'improved' by Langley this is easily recognisable as James Johnston's garden by the Thames. Langley would have modified the groves into labyrinths, shaped the pools and set them within a quincunx, and would have replanted vines as further wildernesses; he suggested that the parterre could have been a small, plain one with corner statues flanked by parcels of dwarf fruit trees, over which views could be had, and the grove below the greenhouse could be re-formed as an 'Amphitheatre of Oranges, Mirtles &c.'. Langley had no known involvement here, so this seems to be simply an imaginary reworking of a famous garden.

masonry steps by slopes, the grassing-over of the cutwork in the parterre, and the removal of the yews on the terraces.[62]

However, Caroline's chief love was Richmond Gardens. Prince George and Caroline fell for the place in 1719, took on the lease in 1722, and gave the maintenance contract to a local nurseryman, Thomas Greening. In 1725 a field by the Thames was turned into a garden by Bridgeman. A Swiss traveller, César-François de Saussure, noted in June 1726 that Caroline was taking 'great interest in the gardens' and had 'greatly embellished them'.[63] Soldiers had been at work there, digging a canal and forming associated earthworks (fig. 211). In 1729–34 Bridgeman laid out the 'new Terrass', extending all the way along the river to the Queen's House at Kew. His position as Royal Gardener had been more demanding than he could have dared think.

(fig. 210). The Great Bason was completed in 1728 and the Serpentine by 1731. Already by May 1731 'two Yachts are to be placed in the Serpentine River . . . for the Diversion of the Royal Family'.[61] At that point, George I's new wall was rebuilt as a ha-ha. Meanwhile, the Queen had the old Slope Gardens down to the Kensington High Road grassed over. At Hampton Court she oversaw a mild re-formation of the Privy Garden, with the replacement of

The rules of garden layout

John James's translation of Dezallier d'Argenville, *The Theory and Practice of Gardening* (1712), and Switzer's *Nobleman, Gentleman, and Gardener's Recreation* (1715), are very different books, though in some ways complementary. The former relates to gardens of the town and the suburb, with stylised layouts giving the impression of firm geometric control, whereas the latter deals with the management of country estates. In practice, most designers took what they

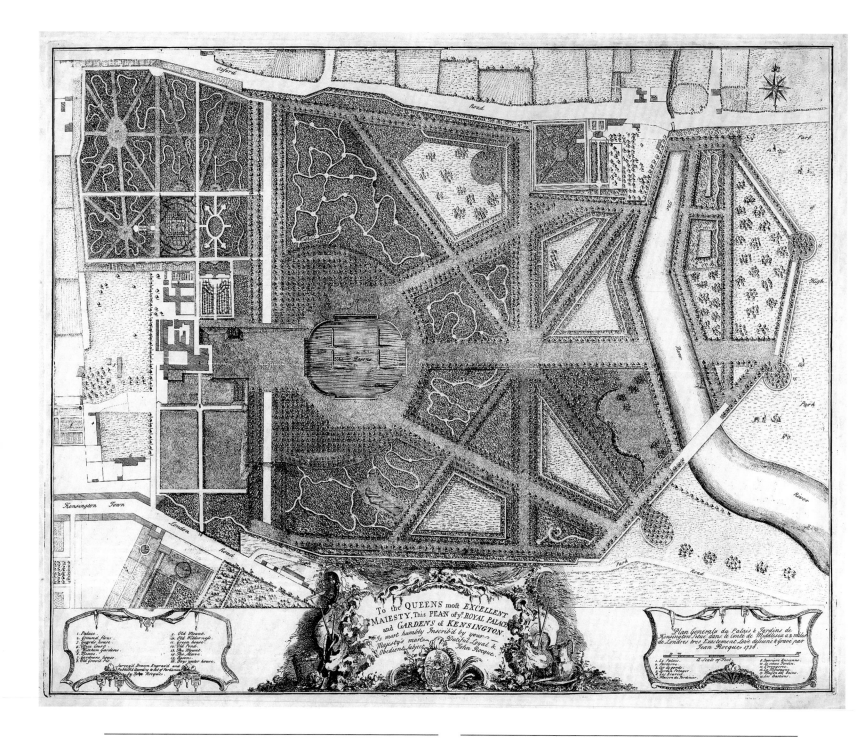

210   John Rocque's 'Plan of yᵉ Royal Palace and Gardens of Kensington', 1736. In 1726 George I had ordered Joseph Carpenter, his Chief Gardener, to plant a great star with paddocks for his collections of animals between the radials, and a brick wall over a mile in length to enclose the area. He started enlarging a pond into the Great Bason (today's Round Pond) and amalgamating ponds into a lake (the Serpentine). After he died, Queen Caroline made this her project, with a new Chief Gardener, Charles Bridgeman. She banished the animals, established plantations between the radials and rebuilt the wall as a fortified fossee with bastions. Meandering paths with small cabinets were threaded through both these plantations and the wilderness planted by Queen Anne. The bason and lake were completed in 1731, and two yachts were floated on the latter. The Slope Garden was grassed over during these years.

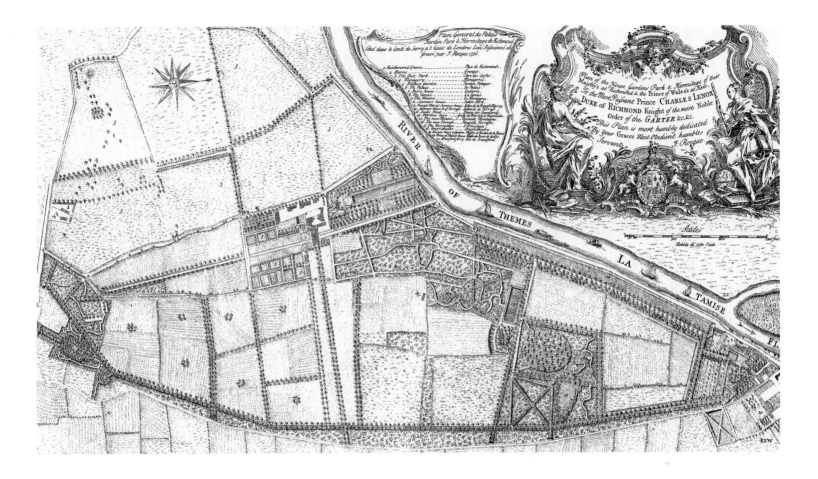

needed from both. At least Switzer would have agreed with Dezallier d'Argenville that 'the greatest Skill in the right ordering of a Garden is, thoroughly to understand, and consider the natural Advantages and Defects of the Place; to make use of the one, and to redress the other'.[64]

Alexandre Le Blond provided several worked examples of layouts to accompany Dezallier d'Argenville's text. All presumed that there would be a parterre immediately below the house, and that beyond it would be *bosquets*. Although the parterre and its Great Walk should show exactness and symmetry, the *bosquets* should have diversity:

If two Groves are upon the Side of a Parterre, tho' their outward Form and Dimensions are equal, you should not, for that reason, repeat the same Design in both, but make them different within. For it would be very disagreeable to find the same Thing on both Sides; and, when a Man has seen one, to have Nothing to invite his Curiosity to see the other . . . the greatest Beauty of Gardens is Variety.[65]

211 John Rocque's 'Plan of the House Gardens Park and Hermitage of their Majesty's at Richmond', 1736 (north is to the right). This shows all Queen Caroline's improvements since her husband's accession in 1727, including the Hermitage (1731) and Merlin's Cave (1733) by William Kent. Works by Bridgeman included the planting of clumps in the south-eastern cornfields, a thick belt on the eastern boundary, the plantations between this belt and the old wood, incorporating an oval hall with transplanted old trees, an amphitheatre with stepping-in sides and meandering paths, and in 1734–6 the extension of the Duke of Ormonde's terrace along the river to the Queen's House at Kew. Although charming, the arrangement of the whole was somewhat haphazard.

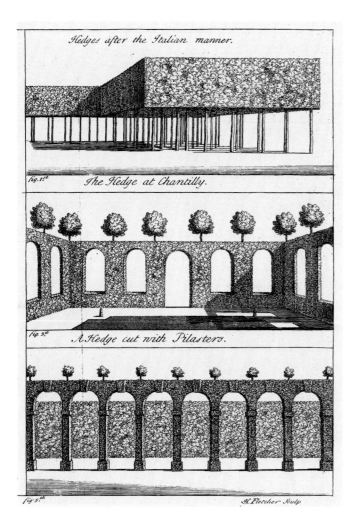

212 A plate from the second edition of *The Theory and Practice of Gardening* (1728) re-engraved by Henry Fletcher from the plate included by Dezallier d'Argenville in the 1713 and 1722 editions of *La Théorie et Pratique du Jardinage*. These inventive ways of training trees were previously unknown in England, but over 20 arcades were made after 1713, a late example being the 'hedge cut with Pilasters' copied at Chiswick in about 1727.

He then went on to catalogue and describe the various forms of parterres, walks, *bosquets*, cabinets, arbours, figures and other components of the French garden, with many plates to illustrate the designs.

In 1713 Dezallier d'Argenville updated his book as 'L. S. A. J. D. A.' (an acronym of 'Le Sieur Antoine-Joseph Dezallier d'Argenville'). It contained six new plates, devised by him, which 'contain the newest Designs of their kind, and indeed those that are of most Use and best Taste in Pleasure-Gardens'.[66] These included designs for 'extraordinary hedges' (fig. 212) and 'ascents and steps of grass-work', and layouts at irregular sites. There was also much new text, including large additions to the chapter 'Of the Disposition and General Distribution of Gardens' discussing the need

to pay close attention to 'natural advantages and defects' because of limited areas. One of the plates showed a circle on the highway with a gate into a small rectangular forecourt one way, and an avenue the other, just as at Chiswick (fig. 213).[67] Several obvious borrowings of design details show that this edition was circulating in England by the late 1710s. A third French edition, with barely perceptible changes, appeared in 1722. For reasons that are unclear it now gave the author as Le Blond. In 1728 John James Englished that edition, and the plates added since 1712 were modified for his translation.

Dezallier d'Argenville's new text for 1713 enunciated 'four fundamental Maxims to be observ'd' in the disposition of a garden. The first, 'to make Art give Place to Nature', was so that '[Art] should be made use of . . . only to set off the Beauties of [Nature]'. He advocated working with 'the Nature of the Place', so that 'the Parts of a Garden . . . ought to be so placed, that one might think them to be set there at first by the Author of Nature'. This approach would tend to counter the too-evident 'manual art' of so many places, by which 'every thing is done by Dint of Money'. Instead of costly 'trifles', he preferred 'that noble Simplicity we see in Steps, Slopes, and Banks of Turf, natural Arbours, and plain Hedges without Lattice-work'.[68]

The second maxim, 'never to cloud and darken a Garden too much', was to encourage 'the free Prospect of every thing about us'. For this reason, parterres should accommodate nothing more solid than small yews and flowering shrubs lest the sight be constrained, and 'Openings should be preserved . . . where the Prospect of the Country can be seen to advantage'. He illustrated the

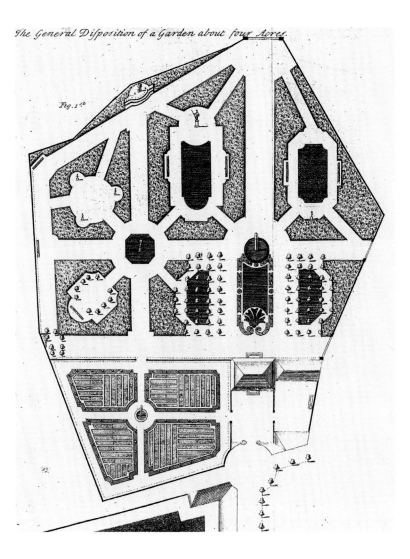

The General Disposition of a Garden about four Acres.

Fig. 1.te

213 A garden of about four acres, from the second edition of *The Theory and Practice of Gardening* (1728), re-engraved by Henry Fletcher from the plate included by Dezallier d'Argenville in the 1713 and 1722 editions of *La Théorie et Pratique du Jardinage*. This is a demonstration of how to form a small regular garden from an irregular plot, countering the argument that the first edition provided ideas for rectangular areas only. It shows a carriage sweep made on a public road, a kitchen garden with fruit trees in borders, a visto beyond the *parterre à l'Angloise* continued through a *grille*, and a *bosquet* with four dissimilar quarters around a central figure.

made a garden look small. In his plans he had 'endeavoured, as much as possible, to stop the Eye in the halls'. 'Hedges, Walks of Trees, or Woods judiciously placed . . . or making Blinds of Wood against the Walls' would divert attention from the garden's boundaries: 'The pleasure of a garden is to have the View stopt in certain places, that you may be led on with Delight to see the more agreeable Parts of it, as fine Groves or Woodwork, Green-Halls adorned with Fountains and Figures, &c.'[70]

Pope's 'Epistle to Burlington' (1731) versified the same principles, in the same order, by making Nature the arbiter of design, arguing for variety and surprise ('Contrariety and Change'), and layouts that appeared large because the boundaries were disguised:[71]

> To build, to plant, whatever you intend,
> To rear the column, or the Arch to bend,
> To swell the terrace, or to sink the Grot;
> In all, let Nature never be forgot.
> But treat the goddess like a modest fair,
> Nor over-dress, nor leave her wholly bare;
> Let not each beauty ev'rywhere be spy'd,
> Where half the skill is decently to hide.
> He gains all points, who pleasingly confounds,
> Surprises, varies, and conceals the Bounds.[72]

The parallels are striking. Pope explained in the dedication of the *Epistle*: 'It has been above ten years on my conscience to leave some testimony of my Esteem for your Lordship among my writing',

point with 'General Plans' for hypothetical irregularly shaped properties.[69] In one plan for a four-acre garden he described how the sight lines would have run through to a grille or an 'Ah, Ah' in the boundary one way, to some small grass steps adorned with flower pots another way, and to statues in other ways, 'so that the View is agreeably terminated every way'.

The third maxim was to avoid going to the opposite extreme: 'not to lay it too open'. The designer should avoid the unimaginative design whereby 'you discover the whole at one View from the Vestibule of the House'. 'Contrariety and Change' should be sought. The last maxim, 'to always make it look bigger than it really is', was a further reminder that views over the country could and since by 1731 the poem had a primarily political theme, the passage above probably dates from the time when Pope was laying out his own garden at Twickenham about 1720.

Joseph Spence, who made Pope's acquaintance in 1726, had also absorbed Dezallier d'Argenville's maxims. In Part II of his *Essay on Pope's Odyssey* (1727) he placed a dialogue in the 'Gardens of Horatio', apparently Richmond Gardens, and

> When I had the Pleasure of Conversing with the Gentleman, who design'd these Gardens, (as indeed the Finest in the Nation owe their Beauty to his Directions) I was very much pleas'd with a Maxim which he then mention'd; 'That as the greatest fault in a Prospect was Confinement; So the meanest thing too in a Design, was to have the Bounds and Restraint of it immediately visible.'[73]

This gentleman would, of course, have been Bridgeman.

Langley was aware of the first edition of James, but may not have known Dezallier's additions, and James's new translation came out in 1728. Langley drew up a list of 37 'general Directions' for the disposition of gardens. Few of these were very original, being derived from Addison, James and Switzer. However, they reflect the amalgam of ideas to be seen in the gardens of the time, including the promotion of plain parterres, quincunxes to either side, shady walks, mounts, meanders and cabinets, and the rejection of flower borders with their clipped shrubs. Variety and surprise were central to his ideas: 'new unexpected Objects at every Step we take . . . we can never know when we have seen the whole. Which (if I mistake not) is the true End and Design of laying out Gardens of Pleasure.'[74]

BRIDGEMAN'S 'SIMPLE THOUGH STILL FORMAL STYLE'

Horace Walpole looked back to 'Bridgeman's simple though still formal style' as representing garden-making in the reign of George I (fig. 214). He remembered that 'though he still adhered much to strait walks with high clipped hedges, they were his only great lines; the rest he diversified by wildernesses and with loose

214 A pencil sketch by Sir James Thornhill of 'old Master Charles Bridgeman', made c.1721, perhaps while they were working on Wimpole.

groves of oak, though still within surrounding hedges'. He added: 'But the capital stroke, the leading step to all that has followed, was (I believe the first thought was Bridgeman's) the destruction of walls for boundaries, and the invention of fosses'.[75]

Walpole was condensing a long and varied career for the sake of his narrative. Between Bridgeman's first undertakings on his own, in about 1715, until his death in 1738 he assisted private owners in about 45 projects, some small but many vast, from London squares to rural megalomania. He far surpassed Switzer in the quantity of such work, and his designs characterised the time.

Generally, architects were instrumental in recommending Bridgeman to owners. At first he seems to have been strongly dependent on Vanbrugh, for work at Stowe from 1714 (fig. 215), Sacombe, Hertfordshire, from 1715, and then Eastbury and Clare-

mont, no doubt based on trust earned from their acquaintance at Blenheim. However, Gibbs, as demonstrated early at Chiswick, Lowther and Hartwell House, Buckinghamshire, was clearly as interested as Sir John in garden buildings and design, and his orbit soon intersected with Bridgeman's, so that they were found together at Wimpole, Down Hall, Cliveden, Tring, Shardeloes, Dawley, Hackwood, Gobions in Hertfordshire, and Badminton. Bridgeman had much less to do with Colen Campbell or the architect earls.

The emergence of Bridgeman's style can be observed through his surviving drawings.[76] He was by origin a surveyor, and several surveys by him survive, but he also developed a style of presentation drawing for both proposed and completed schemes to which he adhered throughout his career, from Blenheim in 1709

to Amesbury in 1738. These are in pen and watercolour, and are variants on his survey style, for example showing similar hatching for landform and shadows for slopes. A few are signed, and the majority of finished drawings are given cartouches. Most were from either the early part of his career, when working for Wise, or

from the last ten years, that is 1728 onwards. The exception is a plan for Eastbury of about 1719 preparatory to publication (see fig. 194). This was a magnificent advertisement for his work, though the intended publication in *Vitruvius Britannicus* was deferred until 1725. His splendid bird's-eye view of Stowe in about 1723 (fig. 216) and that of Boughton in about 1730 (fig. 217), if it is his, may also have been studies for prints.

216　Detail of a bird's-eye view of Stowe House from the south-west, c.1723, probably by Charles Bridgeman, perhaps as a study for a print. His early work north of the diagonal way to the church was supplemented after about 1720 by the plantations south of it, to complement Vanbrugh's buildings. The plantations contained canals, amphitheatres, grovework and meandering walks; a large octagon of water was formed at the bottom of the older abele walk on axis. The extensive ha-ha boundary is notable.

In the busiest part of his career, from Houghton in the late 1710s till Lodge Park, Gloucestershire, in about 1729, Bridgeman was in the habit of producing simplified pen and ink drawings. These have solid or dotted lines indicating boundaries and breaks of slope, simple scales, dots either to define the geometry or give tree positions, and often some notes, generally about levels. There are a small number of preliminary drawings, done in pencil when devising the geometry or levels. Another way of indicating proposals was to amend survey plans, and this he did for Boughton about 1730 and Brocket about 1734. It is these pencil, pen and amended drawings that show Bridgeman at work.

Bridgeman's reputation had already spread to the newly monied at a time when many were seeking to create gardens. He was particularly busy working for several of the South Sea directors and wartime entrepreneurs up to late 1720, when the Bubble burst. This proved not to be much of a setback to Bridgeman, as his reputation was spreading by word of mouth amongst

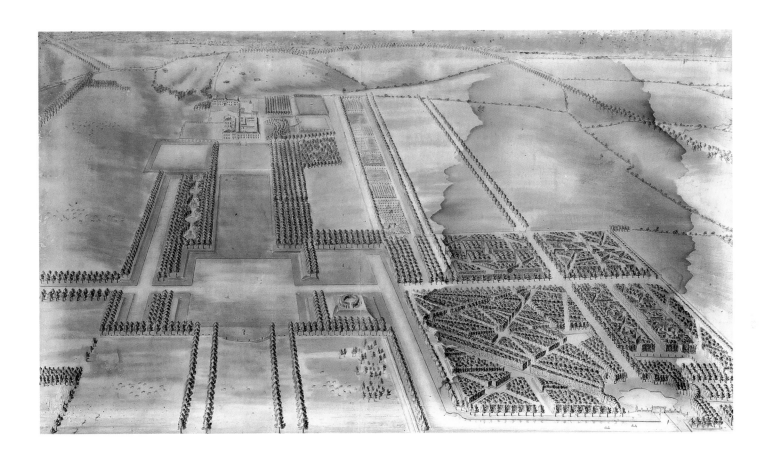

greater landowners. Lord Perceval, after visiting Stowe in 1724, remarked: 'Within these two years, [Stowe] has gained the reputation of being the finest seat in England . . . It is entirely new and tho' begun eleven years ago is now almost finished . . . Bridgeman laid out the ground and plann'd the whole, which cannot fail of recommending him to business.'[77]

The house at Stowe was situated on a hilltop with the axis aligned on a spire in Buckingham (subsequently lost). The gardens fell southwards to a minor lane, beyond which a walk of abeles, or white poplars, continued the axis down the slope towards a small stream. After Bridgeman had modernised the parterre of about 1680 with cutwork, arcading and a cross-canal, he turned his attention to the approach and new plantations. To the north, an axial canal was dug in 1716–18, with the spoil making a mount at its far end. Either side were quincunx plantations. The forecourt appears to have been dispensed with altogether. Lord Cobham then evidently decided that the minor

lane should not present an obstacle to the southwards prolation of the gardens, and Bridgeman became busy on plantations of over twenty acres on both sides of the abele walk, which were substantially complete by 1719. Vanbrugh noted in that year that Cobham was spending all he had to spare on his gardens, and from this time the architect devised temples, a column and a pyramid to complement the plantations. Those to the west were dense, but threaded through with meandering walks, and

217   Boughton House from the west, c.1729, by either Charles Bridgeman or Thomas Badeslade, whose plan of about the same date was published in the fourth volume of *Vitruvius Britannicus* (1739). This view, drawn after the broad water and mount had been completed in the mid-1720s, but before the avenue planting of the 1730s, illustrates the conversion of the elaborate French-inspired gardens of the 1690s to the simpler taste of the late 1720s.

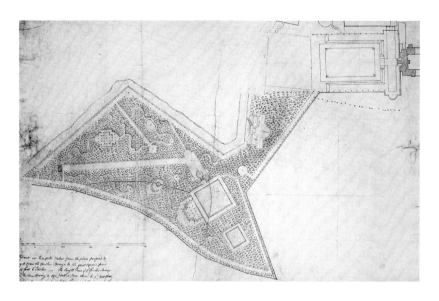

218 Scheme for outward plantations at Rousham House, Oxfordshire, for Colonel Robert Dormer, c.1718, in Bridgeman's hand. The earlier great terrace under the house and parterre flanked by low terraces have been simplified, and the slopes above the River Cherwell have been planted; halls, an amphitheatre, groves, meandering paths and cabinets make a garden full of surprises.

embraced a quincunx with southward views, at the head of which was the 'brick temple'. To the south-west was another canal, earthworks, a column, temples and meandering walks, and at the stream an octagon bason was dug with a spouting obelisk, or 'guilo', at its centre, all seen by Perceval.

Bridgeman was also planning changes for Colonel Robert Dormer's parterre at Rousham, and his outward plantations were to have meandering walks, basons and earthworks (fig. 218). The Earl of Oxford, who had acquired Wimpole through marriage to the Duke of Newcastle's daughter, summoned Bridgeman thence in 1720 to participate in discussions on plantations south of the house. Bridgeman suggested wilderness planting like others he was planning. Other wildernesses were planned for Matthew Prior at Down Hall, Essex (see fig. 237), at Scampston and Ledston, both in Yorkshire, and several other places. The grandest of his wilderness layouts was one of 60 acres made out of Spring Wood at

Hackwood from 1722 (fig. 219), which in turn came to be dwarfed by the 114-acre extension of Kensington Gardens for George I from 1726 and finalised by Queen Caroline, as described above (see fig. 210).

Bridgeman is particularly associated with the 'theatre', sometimes 'amphitheatre', of rising concentric terraces providing a purely decorative handling of slopes and hillsides. Orangery gardens, especially Wise's at Kensington, had shown that earthworks could be attractive, but these new amphitheatres were on a different scale and were not for use as orangeries. Dezallier d'Argenville's first edition had described how a hillside could be contrived into 'Landing-Places, or Rests, at several Heights, and easy Ascents and Flights of Steps for Communication . . . called Amphitheatres'.[78] In the second edition, he said much more about them and included an extra plate (fig. 220).[79] Figure 1 on the plate shows turf steps suitable for the end of a piece of water; Figure 3 shows steps raised at the end of a walk. These were surely the inspiration for Bridgeman's grass steps in the late 1710s at Sacombe, Eastbury and Stowe. A small theatre at Rousham was followed about 1722 by the many-stepped 'Queen's Theatre' at Stowe facing the canal (fig. 222), a theatre at Hackwood in a hall, and slopes around the entrance court at Ledston. Dezallier d'Argenville's Figure 5 illustrated 'Stairs mixt with Slopes and Landing Places', the inspiration for Bridgeman's most grandiose amphitheatre, at Claremont, the high point of his theatre-mongering, for the Duke of Newcastle in about 1725 (fig. 221).

Bridgeman often employed older garden elements, such as canals, and octagon basons in or at the end of them, but he mixed these with many other design ideas from *La Théorie et la pratique du jardinage*. One of his particular delights was halls in canted, niched and compound squares, rectangles, circles and other shapes within plantations, with no two being identical. Usually, Bridgeman used his own invention to produce his variations, generally of the same geometry as in *La Théorie*, but simpler in detail.

When it came to the boundaries (treated more fully below, under 'The Sight without Confinement'), Bridgeman appears to have shared Addison's and Dezallier d'Argenville's liking for

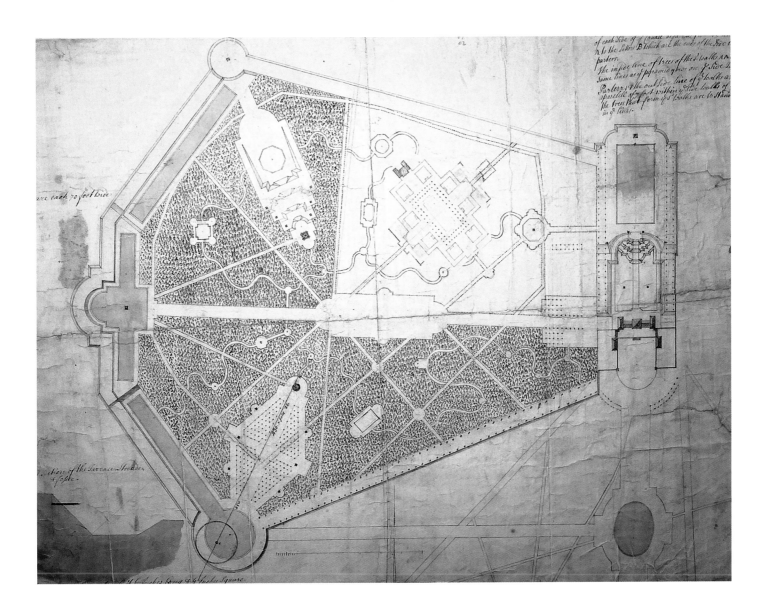

extent, judging from his remark (quoted above) in the description of the 'Gardens of Horatio' in Spence's *Essay on Pope's Odyssey* (1727). Bridgeman was an early promoter of low fossees, at Houghton in about 1717, and Wimpole and Down Hall, instead of the more costly fortifications. At Houghton the fossee was to have been carried around the whole inward plantation (see fig. 207). For those owners who balked at the costs involved in enclosing a large plantation with fossees he reverted in the early 1720s to stockades – in French, *chevaux de frize* – notably at Stowe and Hackwood, as Vanbrugh and Switzer had done at Grimsthorpe

(see fig. 182). Nevertheless, he made several more fossees, and even some impressive fortifications with bastions, at Stowe and Kensington Gardens in the late 1720s.

---

219 Plan for Spring Wood at Hackwood House, c.1725, in Bridgeman's hand (north is below). A coppice wood with westwards visto (see fig. 158) was given surrounding fortifications, with halls, meandering paths and cabinets cut out of the wood in one of the grandest of such schemes; the unfinished quarter contained aviaries.

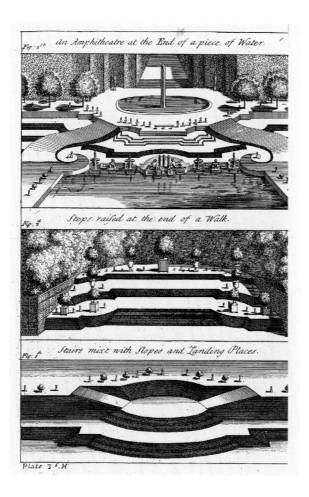

220 Grass ascents and steps, a plate re-engraved by Henry Fletcher for the 1728 edition of *The Theory and Practice of Gardening* from the plate included by Dezallier d'Argenville in the 1713 and 1722 editions of *La Théorie et pratique du jardinage*. In the lowest design, gravel slopes lead down to 'an oval Half-pace', from which three steps descend to a 'Counter-Terrass'. By 1728 the craze for these 'ascents and steps of grass-work' was already well under way.

221 Plan of the amphitheatre and circular pool at Claremont, *c*.1724, in Bridgeman's hand. The inspiration for the amphitheatre may well have been a plate in Dezallier d'Argenville (see fig. 220). These earthworks, aligned on a circular pool that had been dug by 1717, were perhaps the grandest anywhere. The pool was modified by Kent in the 1730s, but he retained the amphitheatre, which has been restored by the National Trust.

Bridgeman was a skilled exponent of Dezallier d'Argenville's advice to consider the 'natural Advantages and Defects of the Place'. He exploited the slopes and dell at Rousham to their full potential, and at Stowe he selected positions for bastions that gave them and the buildings on them maximum prominence. At Ledston he was presented with an area above the entrance court that was hemmed in by roads, but he was able to see possibilities: the court was extended into a parterre surrounded by double terraces, the old dummy avenue was kept as a garden visto, and the surrounding area was a plantation in which meandering paths took the visitor to halls and cabinets, diverting attention from the constraints of the area. The gardens at Hackwood were an adapt-

ation of a coppice wood, made by inserting halls and meandering walks as if the whole was planned at once. Such examples show Bridgeman working adeptly within existing boundaries and with the prospects, which were both assets and difficulties of places, the more so as they became larger and took in substantial areas of countryside.

The prolated garden

The levelling of walls, so that the parterre and the outward plantation were united in the 'rural and extensive' garden, had far-reaching consequences. Switzer declared that the 'extensive Way of Gardening' that he promoted as consisting

rightly in large prolated Gardens and Plantations, adorn'd with magnificent Statues and Water-works, full of long, extended, shady Walks and Groves; neither does it altogether exclude the use of private Recesses, and some little retired Cabinets; this seems to be the general Idea of the Plan or Ichonography of a well-contriv'd Seat.[80]

222   'View of the Queen's Theatre from the Rotunda' at Stowe House by Jacques Rigaud, engraved by Bernard Baron, 1734. The rotunda, a temple with a statue of Venus (1720–1), stood on a low mount overlooking a canal dug in 1721, which led to amphitheatric earthworks and Queen Caroline's Monument (a pillar). As can be glimpsed on the right, a *chevaux de frize* ran alongside the terrace overlooking the fields.

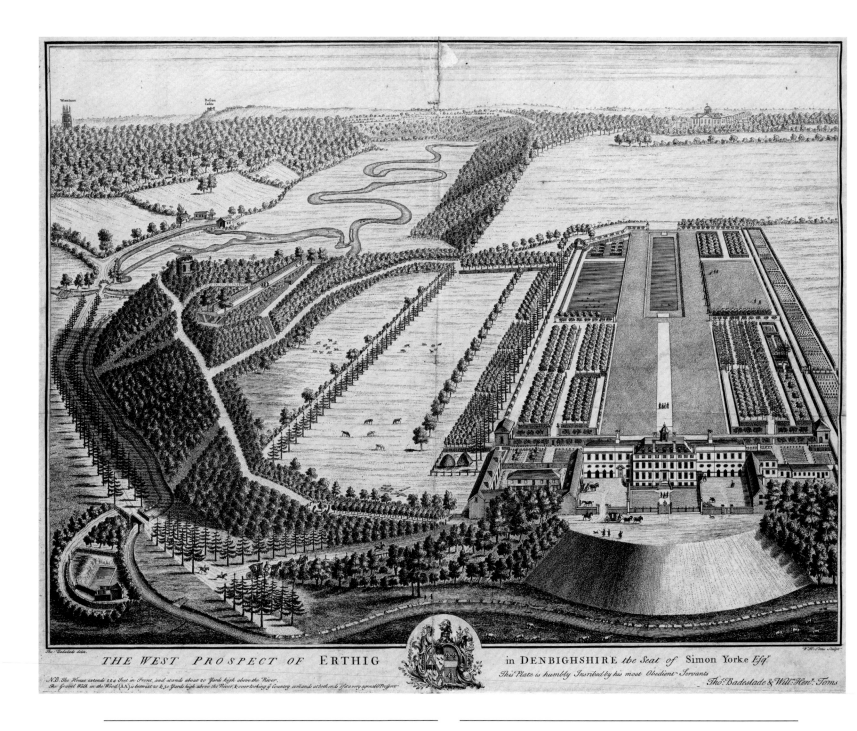

223 *The West Prospect of Erthig in Denbighshire* by Thomas Badeslade and William Henry Toms, 1740. The large rectangle, set out in 1718–25 with a pool, canal and bowling green east of the house, tripled the size of earlier gardens at Erddig; the walls were complete in 1725. A kitchen garden was set out along the outside of the south wall, and a shelter belt was planted by the north wall. An amphitheatre designed for the end of the visto was abandoned in favour of a *claire-voie* and in 1720–1 gates for the forecourt were commissioned from Robert Davies of Bersham. On inheriting the house in 1733 Simon Yorke grassed over the parterre and set out the walks to a gravel walk and a tower on the hill to the north, but did not dispense with the walls, which still survive.

The familiar elements of a 'fine set' garden – the *parterre à l'Angloise*, terraces, *jets d'eau*, walls and grilles – quite suddenly evaporated from newly made gardens. The plain parterres, that is of grass and gravel, and outward plantations with fence or fortification boundaries, tried out at a few places in Queen Anne's reign, rapidly became the new look.

The distinction between inward and outward wildernesses was becoming redundant. Outward plantations, being part-garden and part-forest, linked the polite and ordered geometry of the pleasure garden to the pastoral scenes of the wider countryside. To Switzer, their early advocate, 'prolated' gardens opened more than prospects. As they grew they were seized upon as places where imaginary scenes could be brought to view, and perhaps even realised through mood-setting garden buildings.

'THE SIGHT WITHOUT CONFINEMENT'

Some owners continued on the assumption that gardens were to be fine set and within walls. The garden at Kings Weston was extended on axis in the mid-1710s by wildernesses within new walls. Likewise, John Meller, the new owner of Erddig from 1715, extended his garden by building a new wall (fig. 223),[81] Perhaps the last place to acquire walled pleasure gardens was Castle Bromwich Hall, which appears to have been idiosyncratically old-fashioned in this respect in the late 1730s.[82] Elsewhere, Addison's word 'confinement' became something to be avoided. Within months, William Stukeley, the antiquary, wrote of Blenheim: 'The garden is . . . taken out of the park, and may still be said to be part of it, well contriv'd by sinking the outer-wall into a foss, to give one a view quite round and take off the odious appearance of confinement and limitation to the eye.'[83]

There was no shortage of other writers to extoll the joys of open prospect. However it was Switzer, the practical man, who first announced clearly that walls had to go:

Neither would I advise the immuring, or, as it were, the imprisoning by Walls (however expensive they are in the making) too much us'd of late; but where-ever Liberty will allow, would throw my Garden open to all View to the unbounded Felicities of distant Prospect, and the expansive Volumes of Nature herself.[84]

In expanding on 'Ingentia Rura . . . that extensive Way of Gard'ning', he explained that it 'directs that all the adjacent Country be laid open to View, and that the Eye should not be bounded with high Walls, Woods misplac'd, and several Obstructions, that one sees in too many Places, by which the Eye is as it were imprisoned'.[85] When in *Ichnographia Rustica* Switzer added more thoughts to his general theme, he attacked those advising owners to build walls:

The first Thing Gentlemen commonly do after their Houses are built, is to set out their Garden Walls; In this there is some Surveyor or Bricklayer that is very ready, it being some of the best picking they can have; and the Gardener himself is doubtless as fond of them as any thing, and thinks his Garden can't be fine, except it has a Brick Wall round it . . .[86]

Instead of walling a garden, the same money 'would have embellish'd a hundred Acres of Ground in this rural Way'.

Most owners decided that they could do without walls as there were other reasons why they could be dispensed with. The security formerly provided by a brick wall was increasingly the duty of gamekeepers, policing the Game Laws, which meant that the woods and parkland were efficiently patrolled, and privacy ensured. That left defence merely against cattle and deer, and sunk fences had demonstrated how this might be achieved without upstanding walls.

Quite suddenly, in the mid-1710s, it was the fashion for new pleasure gardens to be constructed without any walls and for the Best Garden to give way onto tree-lined walks and outward plantations. As a consequence, gateways, baskethandles, iron fences, grates and all the trappings of enclosure were thenceforward rarely seen. The pleasure ground was thereby much enlarged, and its boundary became the fence of the plantations. The rapidity of this change in fashion was disorientating, as shown by John Bromley's will of 1718, which specified that his gardens at Horseheath, Cambridgeshire, 'be finished according to plan, unless they

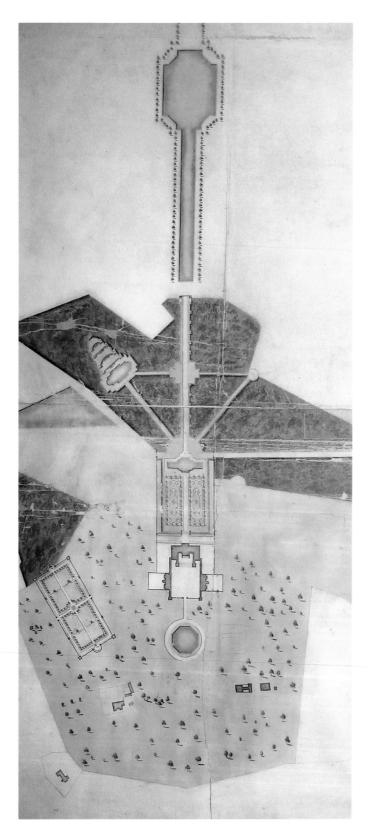

224　General plan for improvements at Sacombe House, Hertfordshire, c.1715 (north is to bottom left). The house and kitchen garden, with massive walls, were by Vanbrugh. Bridgeman, who came in under Vanbrugh's wing, here suggests an octagon reflecting pool on the approach and a parterre with scrollwork in the manner expected from Brompton Park. However, beyond the cross-canal at the end of the parterre a coppice wood has been ornamented with walks and an amphitheatre, and beyond the wood the axis is continued by a long canal terminating in a large octagon; the shape of the canal can be seen today on aerial photographs. This must have been one of Bridgeman's earliest commissions.

225　The south front of Raynham Hall, Norfolk, 1725. Edmund Prideaux's sketch shows grass and gravel where there had until recently been Jacobean walled gardens. However, the second Viscount Townshend was evidently reluctant to expunge the clipped greens that he had installed in his parterre in the time of William III.

would be better contrived with garden walls, iron gates and all other things necessary'.[87]

An early example of this new approach was shown on a plan, attributed to Bridgeman and made seemingly sometime in 1715–17, for Sacombe (fig. 224).[88] The plan might be mistaken for one of London's schemes, with its octagonal bason in the avenue and the scrollwork parterre with side terraces. However, Vanbrugh had placed the kitchen garden out in the park, and the parterre garden had no end wall. Instead, there was a narrow cross-canal, and the garden merged into a coppice wood. A *patte d'oie* was planned, with one alley terminated by ornamental earthworks, and a lengthy canal on the central vista beyond the coppice.

Wall removal at older gardens was sporadically under way from the late 1710s. In about 1718 Earl Stanhope had the far wall of the old Best Garden at Chevening demolished in order to extend his pleasure garden along the park canal to a round pond and a pavilion. It became flanked by wildernesses with kitchen and planted quarters (see fig. 193). Lord Burlington removed the north wall of his gardens at Chiswick perhaps the next year in order to bring the very recent outward plantation into the gardens proper. At Esher in about 1720 Peter Delaporte swept away the parterre and walls down to the river (see fig. 191).

Some older walled gardens survived as kitchen gardens when the new pleasure grounds were made elsewhere. The more usual case was exemplified at Raynham, where in 1727–32 the century-old garden walls were taken down and replaced by sunk fences. A visitor noted that the hall 'stood quite free of walls', and that Lord Townshend had rebuilt 'his kitchen garden and fruit garden quite out of sight of the house' (fig. 225).[89] The Earl of Pembroke lowered his walls at Wilton in 1734. In fact, during the mid- and late 1720s walls were removed wherever gardens were being redesigned.

Most new kitchen gardens were now built away from the garden enclosure, often behind the stables, from which they would receive the manure. By the time that the kitchen gardens were made at Rokeby about 1724 (see fig. 283) and Londesborough in 1725 they were at considerable distances from the houses, so that their sight and smells did not intrude on the politer areas by the house, and located to take advantage of south-facing slopes and water supply.[90] In his 1731 book *New Improvements of Planting and Gardening, both Philosophical and Practical*, Richard Bradley could write a chapter on 'the Situation of the Kitchen-Garden' without once mentioning the house.[91]

Fruit gardens had been a great proof of the gardener's art, and John Laurence in his *Gentleman's Recreation* (1716), Switzer, in his *Practical Fruit Gardener* (1724), and Langley in his *New Principles of Gardening*

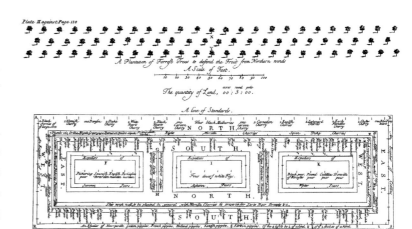

226 An ideal fruit garden with apples, pears, cherries, mulberries, figs, plums, nectarines, etc., from Batty Langley's *New Principles of Gardening* (1728). Langley supported the extensive use of *espalier* training. Although expert gardeners hankered for the fruit garden of the past, owners generally preferred combined kitchen and fruit gardens.

(1728) (fig. 226) were still giving directions on how to form and plant them as if they had a future. However, it was not to be. Owners who were improving their seats in the 1720s were seeking to eliminate walls altogether, and chose to situate their productive gardens away from the house in the new 'fruit and kitchen garden' form. Hedging his bets, Langley offered a plan for this type of garden too.

Vanbrugh's fortifications at Blenheim and Castle Howard were the precursors to low terraces and sunk fences of various forms. Whilst others were experimenting with *fossees*, he and Hawksmoor remained loyal to fortifications. At Claremont in about 1716 Vanbrugh appended angular bastions to a garden fortification that was highly irregular in plan (fig. 227). Round-bastioned mock fortifications around woods or new planting accompanied building work designed by Vanbrugh at Duncombe Park about 1718 (fig. 228) and Seaton Delaval in 1719.[92]

Developing the theme of fortification, Switzer gave general directions in *Ichnographia Rustica* for the 'Terrace-Walk and Graff' or 'Terrace-Walk and Water' around gardens (fig. 229).[93] The 'graff', on the outside, was 'what supplies the Inside, and raises up

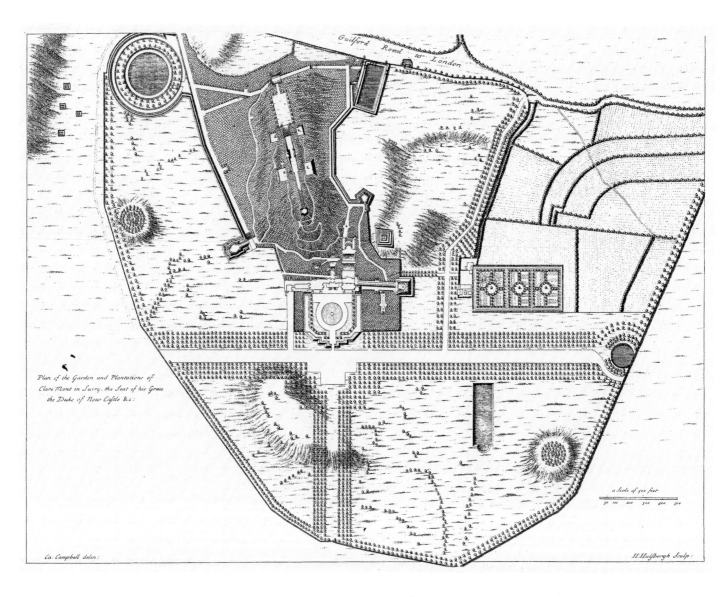

Guilford Road to London

Plan of the Garden and Plantations of
Clare Mont in Surry, the Seat of his Grace
the Duke of New Castle &c:

a Scale of 500 feet
50 100 200 300 400 500

Ca: Campbell delin:

H. Hulsbergh Sculp:

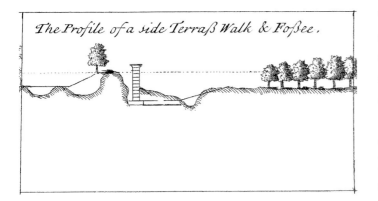

The Profile of a side Terraß Walk & Foßee.

(Facing page, top) 227 Colen Campbell, 'Plan of the Garden and Plantations of Clare Mont', engraved by Henry Hulsbergh, c.1717. Prior to his sale of the estate to Lord Pelham in 1711, Vanbrugh started ornamenting this wood at Claremont by creating a bowling green on the crest of the hill (see fig. 178). Work was taking place on the Belvedere in 1715, and seats were supplied for the bowling green in 1716. Another 50 acres were acquired in 1716, allowing the construction of the fortified boundaries with bastions, the bason surrounded by two rows of trees, quadruple avenues crossing in front of the house with the corners stepped back rather than forming a half-round, and a kitchen garden. The park acquired two clumps on knolls and double peripheral rows of trees.

(Facing page, bottom) 228 The terrace at Duncombe Park, Yorkshire, that surrounds the plantations, similar to that surrounding Wray Wood at Castle Howard. It was probably made in 1718. An Ionic temple was later built on one of the bastions, a Tuscan temple on another; here a bastion encloses an oak tree.

(Above) 229 'The Profile of a side Terrass Walk & Fossee' by Switzer, engraved by J. Clark, 1718. Switzer provides a cross-section through the side terrace of a parterre, with a wall and fossee (or 'graff') providing the boundary with fields outside. The terrace would be three and a half feet above the level of the parterre, so that 'one may look either forward or backward, and view with Pleasure the rude and distant Scenes of Nature, as well as the more elaborate works of Art'.

the Terrace'. (Switzer explained that 'graff' was the Dutch term for dry ditch, though most used the French term *fossé*, generally Englished to fossee, to describe these terraced sunk fences.) It should be five feet deep and fifteen feet wide at the bottom. Mean-while, the terrace wall would be seven and a half feet high, giving a two-and-a-half-foot-high parapet, suitable for sitting on. The terrace walk on the inside would be twelve to fifteen feet wide, or twenty feet in the greatest designs. Bastions would be located as convenient, where a change in direction was wanted.[94]

Several fortifications were simplified into short straight lengths without bastions. The Earl of Strafford, at his second house at Boughton Park, was in 1719 'puling downe the wals and other Work at the house', for which he was congratulated by his cousin Lord Bathurst. His complex wood-work with palisades had a lengthy raised terrace around the south and west sides, which was being finished in 1721 (fig. 230).[95] At Hall Barn, John Aislabie initiated a polygonal ha-ha, with bastions, with the intention to enclose the whole of the 80 acres of garden and grove (see fig. 190). Lord Perceval remarked on the effect of emerging from the grove onto this terrace in 1724: 'The walks are terminated by Ha-has, over which you see a fine country, and variety of prospects, every time you come to the extremity of the close winding walks that shut out the sun.'[96] The western terrace at Wentworth Woodhouse of 1734 was both one of the finest and one of the last of these great fortification works.[97]

Soon the raised terrace came to be flattened, so that the terrace walk was at ground level. Fossees could be ditches with fences in the base. A variant was the brick wall in a ditch at Euston of pre-1725.[98] An alternative term was a 'ha-ha', a variation on Dezallier d'Argenville's 'ah-ah' for a *claire-voie*, but in the English context generally applied to lengthier sunk fences or fossees.[99] Switzer provided a plate illustrating how the view down a canal could be carried onwards over a fossee, labelled 'Ah Ah', to ground at the same level beyond.[100] Bradley copied Switzer in describing the 'Haha! Or Fossee . . . they mean a Ditch, or Moat to Enclose a Garden, whether the Ditch has Water in it, or not'.[101]

Boundaries to the outer plantations were still mostly walls, palings or agricultural hedges, though throughout the 1720s the fossee or ha-ha was extended around increasing lengths of boundary. The initial intention at Eastbury was for most of the plantations to be within a wall, though a length of fossee was intended on the main east cross-axis. Construction stopped in 1720 at

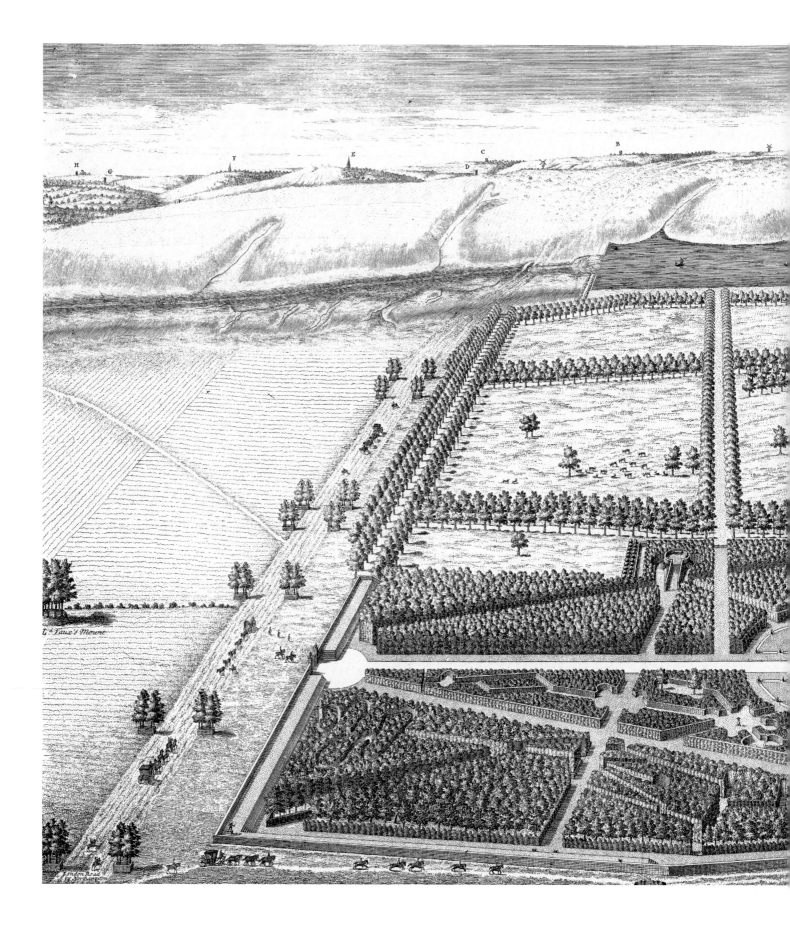

H G F E D C B

t. Vaux 't Morent

London Road
to Serbarton

George Dodington's death; when his nephew restarted work four years later he constructed a fossee round the whole. At Bramham the contract for 'Terraces that surround the Garden' was dated 1727.[102] The engraver George Vertue, visiting Easton Neston in 1734, observed that the far wall of the Great Garden had been replaced by 'a fossee which lays the country open to your view'.[103] In 1731 Loveday admired the way that Kensington Gardens and Hyde Park were 'separated only by a Haw-Haw so that the Coaches seem to go into the Gardens', and five years later he saw at Hinton St George, Somerset, how 'by the help of an Haw-Haw you take in a good View for a low Situation'.[104]

PLAIN PARTERRES

Switzer's vision of parterres stripped of their borders and greens, in order to achieve the 'plain but noble' effect of grass and gravel, was a well-judged prediction. Cutwork was last made in the late 1710s, and by 1720 *jets d'eau* and side terraces were omitted from new designs as well. Few flower borders were made, and few pyramid yews were planted after the mid-1710s; Cannons, Cholmondeley, Sacombe, Eastbury and Caversham were amongst the last. Perhaps the very final occasion that pyramid yews were designed for a country-house garden was Bridgeman's plan for Ledston Hall of about 1722.

The propaganda against clipped greens had been gaining force. Princess Caroline held a 'gardening conference' at Richmond Gardens in 1719 at which Pope was present. He provided a comic account on the current debate on shaping trees:

---

230 *Boughton Within Two-Miles of Northampton* by Thomas Badeslade and John Harris, 1732 (this Boughton is not to be confused with the Duke of Montagu's Boughton House). The Earl of Strafford was in 1719 'puling downe the wals and other Work at the house' to make way for a plantation with walks, cabinets and figures; straight lengths of raised terrace without bastions enclosed them on the south and west sides, completed in 1721. This was an early simplification of the 'fortification way'.

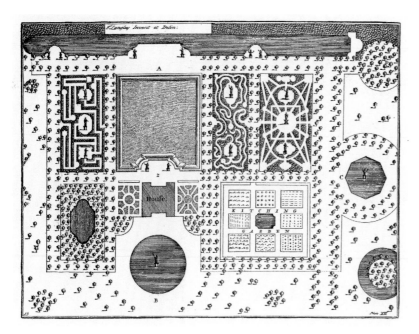

231 'Grand Parterre of Grass', from Batty Langley's *New Principles of Gardening* (1728). Langley's 'Design of a small Garden situated in a *Park*' shows the parterre as simple unadorned grass without a grand walk, suitable for this rural location, and flanked by *bosquets* in various forms. There would have been flower gardens under the side windows and a carriage circle around a pool.

There were some who cou'd not bear Ever-greens, and call'd them Never-greens; some, who were angry at them only when cut into shapes, and gave the modern Gard'ners the name of Ever-green Taylors; some who had no dislike to Cones and Cubes, but wou'd have 'em cut in Forest-trees; and some who were in a passion against any thing in shape, even against clipt hedges, which they call'd green walls.[105]

Langley's *New Principles of Gardening* (1728) stated that 'the plainer Parterres are, the more Grandeur', and 'since Parterres are most beautiful when entirely plain, I therefore recommend the removal of all Kinds of Ever-Greens from thence, and to have no more Gravel Walks about them than are necessary for Use.'[106] One of his engravings illustrated how 'the front of the House opens upon

a fine large plain Parterre' (fig. 231).[107] He pointed to the parterre at Ham House, which, thanks to absentee owners and neglect, had been spared borders and yews, as 'grand and beautiful', and wished that the borders could be removed from the Fountain Garden at Hampton Court.[108]

New parterres, such as those at Shotover, Oxfordshire (fig. 232), and Narford (see fig. 198) from just before 1720, were thus usually made with grass and gravel only. Owners of old parterres began simplifying them by eliminating gravel and ornament, as at Euston (fig. 233), Melbourne, Houghton and Chirk (fig. 234). To the theorists it was particularly important to grass over the old great, or middle, walk, a relic of symmetrical layouts, although the parterre's perimeter gravel walks might be kept for walking in inclement weather. Hence Philip Miller's *Gardener's Dictionary* stated that: 'These Pieces of Grass should not be divided in the Middle with a Gravel Walk, (as is too frequently seen;) for it is much more agreeable to view an entire Carpet of Grass from the House.'[109]

The removal of clipped greens already planted was a more protracted affair. Whatever was written, owners commonly retained their yews and hollies, recently procured at great expense, along walks and terraces. At Stowe, the yews remained to be recorded by Bridgeman undertaking his bird's-eye view about 1724 (see fig. 216), and at Houghton the yews along the vista were sketched in place in 1727. Over the next few years owners of established parterres were understandably reluctant to rip out their greens, but had to bow to the inevitable. A description of Easton Neston in

(Facing page) 232 Bird's-eye view of Shotover House, Oxfordshire, from the east, drawn and engraved by George Bickham, 1750. The house, gravel terrace, plain parterre and ornamental water were all completed around 1720 by General James Tyrrell. This was an early example of a parterre conceived from the outset as grass and gravel only. The plantation to the west with meandering paths and surrounded by terraces and bastions was probably made soon after. The temple of 1725 (hardly visible) was Kent's first garden building. The Gothic Temple, inspired by recent work at All Souls College, Oxford, was built by William Townesend, perhaps in the 1730s.

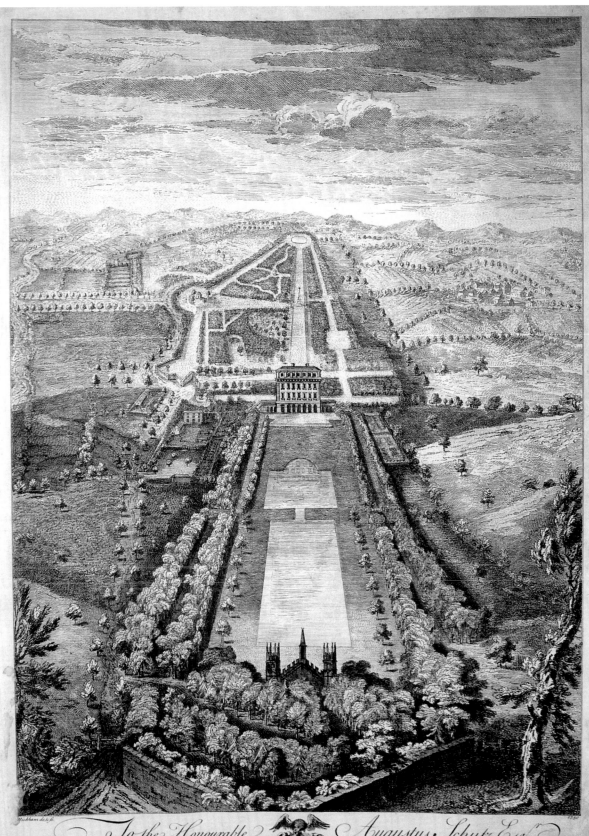

To the Honourable Augustus Schutz Esq.r
This Plate of Shotover House & Garden Is humbly inscribed by Geo. Bickham.

1734 mentioned 'the evergreens of which are taking up to bring it to the modern taste'.[110] At Broadlands Lord Palmerston wrote to his son in 1736 that he was 'giving away all the fine pyramid greens

to those that will fetch them'.[111] In 1737 Philip Miller could look back and write about the 'Aquifolium' (holly): 'there was scarcely a small Garden of any Worth, but was fill'd with these Trees, which were clipp'd either into Pyramids, Balls, or some other Figures; but . . . the Fashion of clipp'd Greens going off, so now they are almost wholly neglected.' He regretted that cedars of Lebanon 'are by many People kept in Pyramids, and shear'd as Yews, &c.', as by training 'they lose their greatest Beauty . . . the Extension of the Branches'. As to the 'Taxus': 'it may be too often seen, especially in old Gardens, what a wretched Taste of Gardening did generally prevail, from the monstrous Figures of Beasts &c. we find these Trees reduced into; but of late this taste has been justly exploded by many persons of superior Judgement.'[112]

Switzer considered sculpted figures to be 'one of the noblest Ornaments of our best Gardens and Plantations, which not only

233 Edmund Prideaux's sketch 'Ewston Front next the Garden on the South', c.1725, showing Lord Arlington's great terrace of c.1669 under the south front of Euston Hall, Suffolk, which continued to the left to become the terrace opposite the greenhouse and ended at a canal. This view was achieved by demolition of the walls and gates of the garden that the terrace overlooked. Any parterre it possessed was grassed over and extended for 500 yards to reach the reservoir, here shown recast as a shaped bason, feeding the canal that was to the west. This work was probably ordered by the second Duke of Grafton soon after he inherited in 1723.

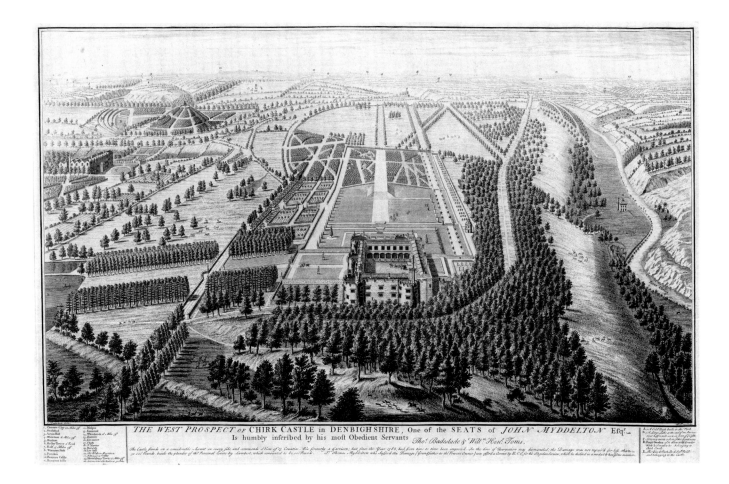

THE WEST PROSPECT of CHIRK CASTLE in DENBIGHSHIRE, One of the SEATS of JOHN MYDDELTON Esqr.
Is humbly inscribed by his most Obedient Servants Thos. Badeslade & Willm. Henry Toms.

make a magnificent Appearance, but 'tis there also we Hieroglyphically find the great Ideas of Valour and Renown'.[113] Langley likewise approved of figures,[114] and illustrated a plain parterre with a circumambient gravel walk, eight figures and a central octangular bason.[115] This was the form he suggested to Secretary Johnston for revising his garden in Twickenham.[116] As far as older gardens were concerned, their pieces might remain in place, though new plain parterres were seldom adorned with them. Instead, they found a new place in the plantations amongst the halls and in niches, and overlooking the basons and canals, in the 1730s.

An urn was a carving representing Antique receptacles with lids for the ashes of the dead. The *boschetto* at the Villa Ludovisi in Rome had urns set into the surrounding hedgework together with terms,[117] whilst the Villa Borghese had alternating urns and figures around the rear court. Urns were always uncommon in

English gardens, but found their champion in Gibbs who made designs for some at Wimpole and Cliveden, and who included many designs in his *Book of Architecture* (1728).[118] Elegant shapes with or without fluting were preferred to the flamboyant relief carving of 30 years beforehand. The mason who supplied urns

---

234 *The West Prospect of Chirk Castle* by Thomas Badeslade and William Henry Toms, *c.*1735. Sir Richard Myddelton made the eastern gardens in 1708 with slopes, clipped yews, a bowling green and a wilderness, all within the rectangle of walls, but in about 1720 his cousin Robert Myddelton simplified the parterres, an example of the way that *parterres à l'Angloise* with their *plates-bandes* and (sometimes) scrollwork were being treated by this date. One visitor in 1733 observed that 'There are no Gardens laid out.'

to Cliveden in 1725 was Thomas Greenway of Bath. In 1730 he advertised his Bath Stone garden ornament in Dublin: 'Having lately imported a large number of Flower Potts, urns and Vases, of the newest and most fashionable pattern, and also several other ornamental pieces . . . [he] proposes to sell the above Pieces at very reasonable Prices.'[119] Burlington designed his own urns in a Classical style for his garden changes at Chiswick in the 1730s.

The gravelled great terrace of former times subsided with the rise of the plain parterre. Without an intricate pattern to look

upon, their purpose was defunct, and it became usual for grass without glacis slopes to meet the steps down from the house. Axial canals within gardens also fell victim to plainness. The canal between the parterres at Wanstead and that down the axis of the wilderness at Belton (fig. 235) were both filled in by about 1730.

Loveday saw a number of 'plain gardens' on his tours from 1731.[120] One was at Wilton, where the Earl of Pembroke had been removing his 1690s parterre (see fig. 205). Miller, copying both Switzer and Langley, extolled 'plain parterres', which were 'more beautiful in England than in any other Countries, by reason of the Excellency of our Turf, and . . . Decency and unaffected Simplicity'.[121] He advised that

In a fine Garden, the first thing that should present itself to the Sight, should be an open level Piece of Grass, full as broad as the Length of the Front of the Building, which may be sur-

rounded by a Gravel Walk, for the Conveniency of walking in wet Weather.

With the abolition of walls, treed walks became a convenient way to frame the parterre, render shade and connect to other walks in the plantations. At Claremont about 1715 the new circular bason was surrounded by two rings of trees (see fig. 227). At Shotover a treed walk flanked the plain parterre, bason and canal.[122] When the parterre was made at Cliveden in 1723 it was beautified by treed walks down its sides (fig. 236). At other places such walks were lined out along the fortifications surrounding the gardens.

Where a plain parterre, especially a large one, was surrounded by walks or plantations comparisons might be made with lawns in parks by those who favoured the rural rhetoric. The key to Bridgeman's plan of Down Hall of 1720 (fig. 237) indicated 'The Lawne' for the parterre. Switzer had used this term in *Ichnographia Rustica* as an alternative to parterre, and continued rather grandiosely to refer to plain parterres as 'lawns'.[123] Langley similarly used 'plain parterre', 'open plain' and 'lawn' interchangeably. Hence the 'lawn' became domesticated and passed from park into garden terminology: for example, Loveday wrote of the 'very spacious Lawn just before the house' at Wanstead in 1736.[124]

236 Study for a print of Cliveden House, made by John Donowell perhaps in the 1750s, when Cliveden was on the tourist circuit. The parterre, which had been laid to grass, was flanked by treed walks. In the 1720s the *perron* steps had replaced a pair at the ends. The Earl of Orkney must have decided against any form of wilderness that would obscure the view of the River Thames.

'WILDERNESSES AFTER THE RURAL MANNER'

The new 'rural garden' consisted not only in a simplified parterre, but also in a much expanded and ornamented wilderness. It was as if the object of a walk was no longer those features within view of the house, but the unfolding discovery of many and various points

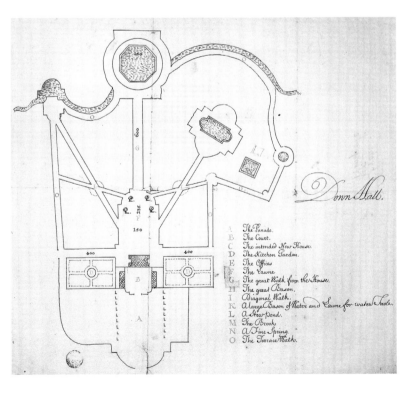

237 Plan of Down Hall, Essex, in Bridgeman's hand, 1720. Down Hall was close to Wimpole, where Bridgeman was employed at this time, but work was cut short by the death of its owner, the poet Matthew Prior, in 1721. Bridgeman has devised a miniature country-house layout, with a hall, an octagon bason and a canalised stream with a terrace alongside. The forecourt is labelled 'The Parade' and the plain parterre 'The Lawne'.

of interest further off. Some gardens at country seats already had adjacent plantations, but if not, Switzer encouraged owners to plant 'a Wood or Coppice of twenty or thirty Acres, more or less . . . And if the House is to be built, by the time that 'tis finish'd you may see a great progress in the advancing Coppice'.[125]

Wildernesses did not suddenly become 'rural', for the influence of James's translation of Dezallier d'Argenville was strong. Plantations in geometrical blocks reminiscent of formal *bosquets* with tall palisades and with gravel alleys were still being created in the 1720s, as were the halls and arcades shown therein. Pope lampooned this type of wilderness as at Timon's villa:

> No pleasing Intricacies intervene,
> No artful wildness to perplex the scene;
> Grove nods at Grove, each Alley has a brother,
> And half the platform just reflects the other . . .[126]

Through that decade, though, symmetrical wildernesses were becoming less common as freer arrangements were preferred, often responding to the lie of the land and mixed with fields. Gravel was practical on the most trodden parts close to the house and on axes, but increasingly carpet walks were the norm elsewhere.

Not only could the plantations each side of the great walk be differenced, but the general plan could also be varied. At Chiswick, in or about 1716, an unequal *patte d'oie* in hornbeam radiating from the northern garden gate was planted (see fig. 291). Encouraged by Switzer, and by the second edition of James's translation of Dezallier d'Argenville, published in 1728, many owners were happy for their outward plantations to be irregular in plan, and to have quite different arrangements of walks and halls either side of the axis.

Quincunxes made a pleasant transition between the parterre and the wilderness planting around, allowing free movement within, and their dappled shade contrasting with the dense shade of forest planting. The French frequently planted them. Liger mentioned 'sorts of Groves, that are neither enclos'd by Borders of Horn-beam in Palisades, nor tufted within, but consisting only of Trees with high Stems, such as Elms in right Angles.'[127] Most of Le Blond's garden plans incorporated one or more quincunxes. Both Liger and Le Blond presumed that the lines

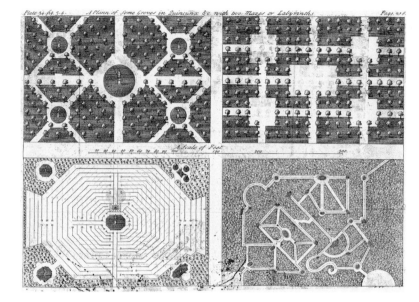

238 'A Plann of some Groves in Quincunx &c. with two Mazes or Labyrinths', from Switzer's *Ichnographia Rustica* (1718). The example top right was copied from James (see fig. 170); the grove top left is planted in true quincunx formation, according to Switzer; that at top right is not, but was the generally accepted form of a quincunx or high-stemmed grove; bottom right is the Versailles labyrinth designed by Charles Perrault in 1666.

and rows of such plantations should be quadrate rather than at 60 degrees. Dezallier d'Argenville explained: 'The Quincunces we make now-a-days, are very different from those of the Ancients . . . They now plant their Quincunces in Lines returned at right Angles . . . which renders the Walks more regular, and of equal Breadth throughout.'[128] This revisionism was rejected by Switzer, who considered Dezallier d'Argenville to have been 'mistaken', and attempted to demonstrate how a noble regular grove could be made in quincunx by means of his own plan (fig. 238).[129] Although strictly speaking he was correct that a true quincunx should be planted at 60-degree angles, most English high-stemmed groves were quadrate.

In about 1716 Burlington planted a high-stemmed grove in his rear garden at Chiswick through which one passed before reach-

ing the gate into the outward plantation (fig. 239). Bridgeman's plan for Eastbury indicated groves between the house and the bason that was central to the plantations (see fig. 194). Before the South Sea Bubble burst in late 1720 sufficient garden areas at Esher had been cleared of walls that the plain parterre down to the river could be flanked with high-stemmed groves (see fig. 191). Bridgeman showed how they could also flank an approach when in about 1719 he planted some either side of the canal approaching the house at Stowe. During the 1720s it became common for groves to flank plain parterres by the house. Bridgeman and his contemporaries also filled halls with high-stemmed groves. This may have been first proposed at Houghton (see fig. 207) and Rousham (see fig. 218). Another device of the 1720s, maybe in imitation of Narford, was paired groves on both sides of a principal walk, breaking the uniformity of the palisades, as if they were platoons engulfed by encircling forest planting.

The visitor could explore the interiors of the main quarters of the wilderness by means of serpentine, or meandering, subsidiary walks. The early examples of such paths at Castle Howard and Bramham were followed by many others, so that by about 1720 they had become common. Bridgeman's plan for the inner plantation at Houghton of about 1717 showed them, and his designs for Eastbury showed increasing lengths of them. The wood-works

239   The grove at Chiswick House, c.1733, one of eight drawings of Chiswick by Jacques Rigaud commissioned by Lord Burlington. The high-stemmed grove was planted about 1716 within a walled garden area; although a response to fashionable taste, it was not well-considered and proved victim to better ideas. When the villa was constructed around 1725 the grove shut it in too much, and it was opened up for a visto a year after Rigaud's drawing.

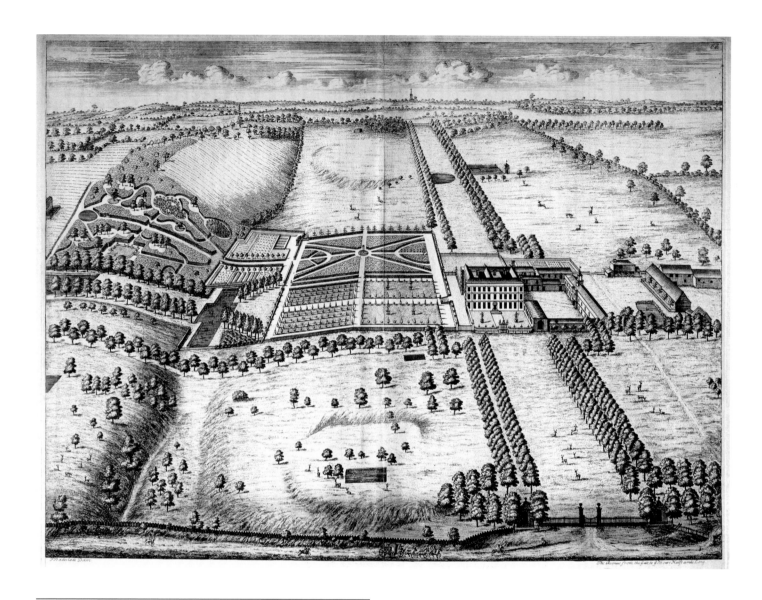

240 *Hammels in the County of Hertford...* by Thomas Badeslade and John Harris, 1722 (north is to the right). Ralph Freman purchased Hamels in 1713, and at first concentrated on repairing and improving the walled gardens to the south and the wilderness alongside (compare fig. 55). However, in 1717 'a walk was cut thro the south wood', probably to extend the axis of the wilderness across the valley; this seems to have commenced 'the wood-work', where in the years up to 1722 the wood was reinforced by a great variety of new trees and shrubs. The resulting layout was elaborate, with meandering paths and various openings, no doubt in response to the older trees present; the gardens and wood-work together were 28 acres.

at Hamels (fig. 240) and Chevening displayed even more confident serpentine walks.

The halls in the interior of Bridgeman's plantations were generally reached along meandering walks. These often threaded through small circular cabinets, so that the wilderness walks of the late 1720s could resemble beads on a necklace. The most extravagant example was at Kensington Gardens, with 42 cabinets along the meanders through the quarters round the Round Pond (see fig. 210).[130] Cabinets continued to be included in most plantations into the late 1730s. Walks, cabinets and halls were still mostly contained by tall palisades, often Dutch elm (*Ulmus x hollandica* 'Major') or

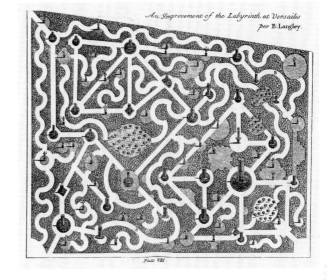

241 'An Improvement of the Labyrinth at Versailles', as proposed by Langley in his *New Principles of Gardening* (1728); he would have added many meandering 'rural' paths and cabinets with *jets d'eau* to the straight lines of the original.

242 Detail from a survey plan of Jeremy Sambrook's estate at Gobions, by Thomas Holmes, *c.*1725 (north is to bottom right). This shows designs for walks that were added *c.*1730. Walks across fields connected the house to coppice woods, within which walks and halls had been cut out. One hall had a canal, another an amphitheatre, and another specimens of ancient trees. 'Gubbins', which was much admired, was visited by Queen Caroline in 1732.

hornbeam, with yew being employed for shaping into arches or in areas of low light levels.

At first, the meanders serpentined gently through the planting, which would be the usual woodland trees, but at Hackwood, then Kensington Gardens and Wolterton, Bridgeman's increasing tendency to convolute the walks can be seen. This was picked up by Langley, who showed in his *Practical Geometry* (1726) how to produce 'arti-natural lines', 'not a small help to invention in designing gardening after that rural manner'.[131] His schematic designs in his *New Principles of Gardening* (1728) showed some extreme geometric meanderings of his 'rural Walks'.[132]

Increasingly, plantations were treated as solid blocks through which *pattes d'oie* and meandering walks were burrowed, and out of which halls and cabinets were carved. The labyrinth at Versailles designed in 1672 by Hardouin-Mansart, with a 'considerable Thickness of Wood between Hedge and Hedge', was a famous example of this approach – hence perhaps the attention paid to it by Switzer, who contrasted it to the tight 'single hedged' maze at Hampton Court.[133] Langley soon after attempted 'An improvement of the Labyrinth at Versailles' by adding numerous serpentine walks (fig. 241). The same approach, of excavating halls and connecting alleys from pre-existing coppice woodlands, was the method also in the wider landscape at Gobions (fig. 242).

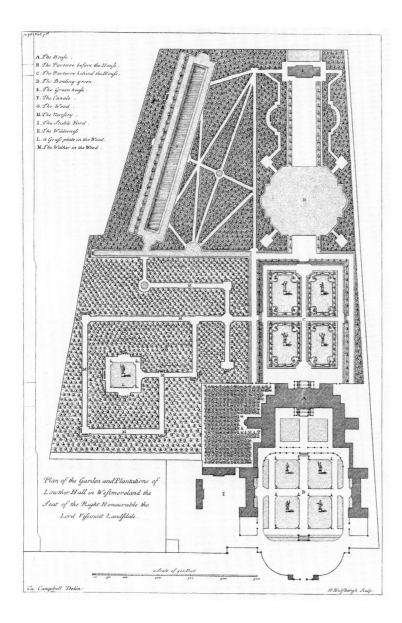

A. The House.
B. The Parterre before the House.
C. The Parterre behind the House.
D. The Bowling-green.
E. The Green house.
F. The Canale.
G. The Wood.
H. The Nursery.
I. The Stable Yard.
K. The Wilderness.
L. a Grass plate in the Wood.
M. The Walks in the Wood.

Plan of the Garden and Plantations of
Lowther Hall in Westmoreland the
Seat of the Right Honourable the
Lord Viscount Landsdale.

a Scale of 500 Feet

Co. Campbell Delin.   H. Hulsbergh Sculp.

243 'Plan of the Garden and Plantations of Lowther Hall . . . ', drawn
by Colen Campbell and engraved by Henry Hulsbergh, 1717. This
unexecuted design, intended to replace the 1690s layout, was most
probably supplied by Gibbs, who is known to have worked on plans for
the new house in 1717. The scrollwork parterre within the side terraces
with clipped greens harks back to the 1700s, whereas the new planting
with cabinets up the hillside to the left and labyrinth arrangement were
newly fashionable in the late 1710s. The principal visto would have run
gently uphill through a bowling green to a greenhouse.

Halls could contain any feature thought to be of interest. Some
early ideas for 'prolated' gardens consisted of *parterres à l'Angloise* set
within dense plantations. Gibbs's unexecuted plan for the gardens
at Lowther, of about 1717 (fig. 243), was for a scrollwork parterre
enveloped by new planting. Likewise, at Caversham, Switzer's
layout had a scrollwork parterre with figures, vases and fountains.
Large areas of plantation surrounding the house and parterre
screened the boundaries and kitchen garden. Bridgeman's first
plan for Eastbury House in 1718 had massive plantations centring
on a bason and two cutwork parterres. Before long, halls contained plain parterres, bowling greens, circular or octagular water
bodies and even flower gardens. Bridgeman's designs show high-
stemmed groves, small amphitheatres, terraced slopes, canals of
various forms, and combinations of these. Gobions had a bowling
green in a hall. Halls were also a favourite place for seats and
garden temples. Langley, in his enthusiasm, envisaged meandering walks leading to

> Flower Gardens, Fruit Gardens, Orangerys, Groves, of Forest
> Trees, and Ever-Greens, Open-plains, Kitchen Gardens,
> Physick Gardens, Paddocks of Sheep, Deer, Cows, &c. Hop
> Grounds, Nurseries of Fruit and Forest Trees, Ever-Greens,
> &c. Vineyards, Inclosures of Corn, Clover, &c. Cones of Fruit
> Trees, Forest Trees, Ever-Greens, Flowering Shrubs, Basins,
> Fountains, Canals, Cascades, Grottos, Warrens of Hares and
> Rabbits, Aviaries, Menazeries, Bowling-Greens; and those
> rural Objects, Hay-Stacks and Wood Piles . . . [134]

In larger wildernesses there might be natural features of interest, or views from the top of a slope. In keeping with the desire
to be 'rural' mature trees such as the oak standards in a coppice,
or veteran oaks in former parkland, could be retained, and put
on display, as it were, framed by the encircling planting of a large
hall. One of Langley's plates showed a '*rural Grove* of Forest Trees'
(see fig. 196).[135] Actual examples could be seen at Gobions and
Richmond Gardens, and a square one was formed at Dalton, the
home of a relative of the Earl of Burlington (see fig. 208). The
groves of old parkland trees at Lumley Castle were enclosed about
1730 within halls of more varied geometry (fig. 244).

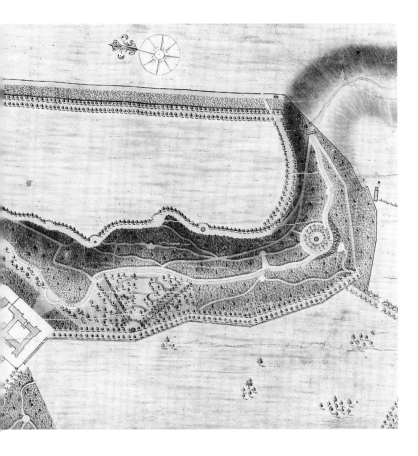

244 Detail from a general plan of Lumley Castle, County Durham, in the style of Charles Bridgeman, c.1729 (north is to the left). This shows the ambitious plans by the second Earl of Scarborough for reworking the irregular beck north and east of the castle. A chaise ride along the western boundary was to connect to another running along the beck's eastern rim, making a circuit starting at the castle; the latter ride, which was to take the natural line of the break of the slope, was to be studded with circles *en route*, some with a temple or an obelisk. A walk was to pass alongside the water (here and there formed into small cascades) and areas of 'rural' groves, a triangular regular grove, an amphitheatre and a double circle. Elsewhere, the slopes were thickly planted and threaded by meandering wood-walks; the eastern paddock was encircled by gallops.

DISPOSING AND PLANTING OF FLOWERING SHRUBS

Dedicated collectors of plants in William III's time laid out their money on flower borders, special flower gardens and greenhouses within the walls of the garden. However, the types of plant being collected were changing as fresh waves of new trees and shrubs flooded in from the known world. At the same time, flower borders were being expunged from the 'plain parterre', flower gardens next to the house were being grassed over and the number of new orangeries was decreasing. New parts of the garden had to be employed for distributing the plant collections. The answer was that the care and attention of plant-collecting virtuosi were now lavished on the plantations.

The collectors' ranks were being swelled by commercial men. Charles Dubois, who had shown an early interest in plants by being instrumental in the introduction of rice to Carolina in the 1690s, was cashier general to the East India Company from 1704. He used his contacts and wealth over many years to gather a vast number of new introductions in his garden at Mitcham, Surrey, in due course much admired by Philip Miller of the Chelsea Physick Garden and other botanists. The slightly younger James Sherard was an apothecary who served his apprenticeship with John Watts, the curator of the Chelsea Physick Garden. He was successful in business and became a fervent botanist in the 1710s, to which occupation he turned exclusively in the 1720s, amassing an extensive collection in his garden in Eltham, south London. Such amateur virtuosi thus joined a community of enthusiasts already populated by some members of the nobility and some professional gardeners.

Meanwhile, the taste of the 1720s began to turn against palisades because they confined the sight. The changing reactions to the wilderness at Hampton Court in different editions of Defoe's *Tours* serve as an illustration. In 1724 'nothing of that kind can be more beautiful', whereas the comment in the 1742 edition was 'nothing can be more disagreeable than to be immured between Hedges, so as to have the Eye confined to a straight Walk, and the Beauty of the Trees growing in the Quarters, intirely secluded from the eye'.

Tall palisades were dispensed with at many more rustic outward plantations in the 1720s. As with their greens, however, owners were reluctant to destroy what they had recently striven to acquire, and fine examples of high palisades continued to excite admiration into the 1730s. Loveday observed the 'fine high hedges and long Walks' in Kensington Gardens in 1731.[136] When he saw Hinton St George, he noticed that the 'Wilderness and Maze are in the Park, the hedges of it are in great perfection'. Although plenty of illustrations up to the 1740s and beyond show that high hedges remained in top gardens, such as Claremont and Studley Royal, they were ultimately doomed, first along the meanders and cabinets, and later along the principal walks. Kent's work at Chiswick from 1733, for example, included removing sections of hedge in order to open out views.[137]

These two factors – plant introductions and the fashion against palisades – came together in new ways of planting flowering trees and shrubs in wildernesses. Low hedges, as in open groves, were already familiar. James described the *banquettes* of open groves as not exceeding three or four feet, which were 'no Hindrance to the enjoying of a pleasant Prospect through the Trees'.[138] If shrubs and trees were planted in ascending height away from the walk, all could be seen, whilst the foliage would conceal the unsightly stems of the next tallest trees behind. Hence Thomas Fairchild's advice was: 'I recommend to plant the tallest Sort of Trees in the Middle of each Quarter, and so let them decrease in their Stature till we come to the Hedge Sides that enclose them.'[139] In 1727 Richard Bradley recommended the 'Dwarf Yew Hedge, which hides the Litter of the falling Leaves'.[140] Such a hedge, maybe three feet high, would allow an unimpeded view of the exotics from the walk. Langley similarly described a system whereby the flowering trees and shrubs would be graded by size, and then planted in 'a perfect Slope of beautiful Flowers'.[141]

In fact, the graduated slope had already been seen at Sherborne Castle, Dorset, in 1724 by Pope, who noticed 'a semi-circular Berceau, and a Thicket of mixed trees that compleats the Crown of the Amfitheatre'.[142] He indicated 'flowering shrubs' on his plan for Marble Hill (see fig. 200). Miller too described the new form of planting in the 1730s. He had become scornful of older groves, 'very few of their Designers ever studying the natural Growth of Plants'. Their palisades had 'the stiff Appearance of Art'. Another design principle, articulated by Langley, was that the flower colours would be 'so intermix'd, as for every Flower to be an Opposite or ground to throw forward the Beauty of the other'.[143]

The *banquettes* of the open grove, now this new way of wilderness planting, remained the means to display bulbs and low shrubs. Langley preferred to see bulbs 'in the inward parts of an open Wilderness, &c. planted promiscuously in the Quarters thereof; but not in regular Lines, as has been the common Way'.[144] The 1730s wilderness had changed its appearance and was enjoyed in a very different way to that of the 1700s.

OF TERRACES AND CASCADES

Earthworks were a very common form of ornamentation in the 'prolated' garden, and alongside Bridgeman's amphitheatres older forms were refreshed too. New mounts, like those at Wanstead, were seen at Eastbury and Stowe. These may have been in part to gain a view, but were also perhaps a reference to the tumuli in the surrounding landscape. Pope, himself a mount-builder, observed in 1727 that Lord Bathurst should have had mounts at Richings, Buckinghamshire, for the sake of variety.[145] The mount at Boughton, by far the largest anywhere, was begun in 1723, and must have been an idea of the eccentric second Duke of Montagu (see fig. 217).[146]

Although orangeries were on the decline generally, the tiered Dutch form continued to be favoured. In the early 1720s Langley attempted to persuade Secretary Johnston that he needed an 'amphitheatre' for his orange trees with a bason and within a grove at his garden in Twickenham (see fig. 209),[147] and when Burlington sought to set out his newly acquired orange trees and other 'greens' at Chiswick in 1729 he chose a Dutch orangery, distinguished only by his placing of an obelisk in the central bason and an Ionic temple to oversee the greens (fig. 245).

Meanwhile, terraced slopes were elaborated. Some ramparts were made at the base of the hill below the statue of Marcus Aurelius at Wilton shortly after 1723. The whole hillside at Oatlands was shaped into bastions and slopes by the Earl of Lincoln, the Paymaster-General of the Forces in the mid-1720s, somewhat

like those at Windsor (fig. 246). Switzer proposed terracings for Erddig, and made some at Leeswood. Spectacular examples of ramps and slopes were made shortly after 1730 in the hillside below the house at Castle Hill (fig. 247), and on flatter ground at Exton Hall, Rutland. On the other hand, Langley derided Bridgeman's modest slopes at Marble Hill, and objected to designs that 'break their Slopes into so many Angles, that their native beauty is thereby destroy'd', recommending 'one grand Slope only with an easy Ascent'.[148]

The outstanding element of the new 'prolated' garden, however, was waterworks. Many canals and basons were dug, often in the traditional way in being along principal axes. The English fascination with water became obsessive, with the size of water features increasing and the ways in which water could be used becoming more varied. The canal at Cannons might have

been seen as traditional, as it lay on the house's axis, but it gave onto the 'Great Bason', a polygonal lake, beyond (see fig. 150). In 1718 a plan was devised for Caversham with two canals, extending both ways from the parterre (see fig. 204). At Sacombe and the Duke of Norfolk's Worksop Manor, canals terminated in octagon basons (fig. 248). Bridgeman remembered Wise's Maastricht Garden when he came to devise the extensive plantations

245   The Chiswick House orangery, a painting of c.1729 by Pieter Andreas Rysbrack. Lord Burlington had acquired an orange-tree collection through his purchase of Sutton Court in 1727. This tiered arrangement had been much used in the Netherlands, but the obelisk in the pool was Burlington's own invention. The domed drum with Ionic portico was built without delay.

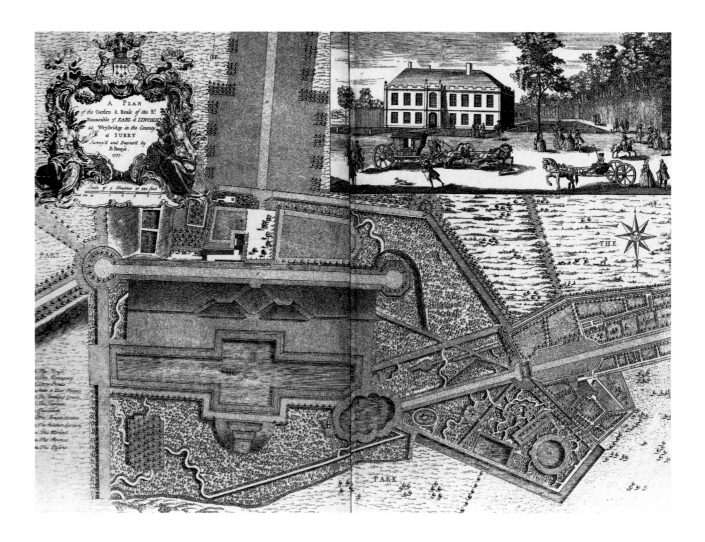

246 Oatlands House as shown in 'A Plan of the Garden, & House . . . at Weybridge' by Bartholomew Rocque, 1737. Lord Burlington produced designs for rebuilding this former ranger's lodge in 1725 and although that did not proceed, an extensive earthworks garden was laid out for the seventh Earl of Lincoln. The approach was down a platooned avenue to a gravelled area in front of the old house. Behind the house was a massive crossways terrace with bastions at each end; below the terrace were ramps down to a canal. On axis, facing the ramps, was an amphitheatre, backed by a plantation with serpentine paths and various cabinets, one with a quincunx, another with a mount, another with a statue, and so forth; west of the canal was a multifoil basin overlooked by an obelisk. This interesting layout has been overlooked in favour of the changes by the ninth Earl in the 1740s.

with a central bason at Eastbury in 1718. Many smaller canals and basons were found in new gardens, some in halls, some on cross-axes, and some just where there was low ground. Apsidal ends to basons were given a boost by Dezallier d'Argenville's *La Théorie et la pratique du jardinage*, and Burlington was one of those to incorporate them in his basons at Chiswick of about 1718, with the earth thrown up formed into small mounts (see fig. 291).

Cascades retained their fascination. At Ebberston, Yorkshire, and at Sir Thomas Hewett's Shireoaks, Nottinghamshire, series of shallow steps were arranged to be seen from the principal living room. Bridgeman made cascades at Kedleston and Moor Park in the early 1720s. At Gnoll, outside Neath, Thomas Greening, as garden undertaker, created a cascade in 1727–30 below a reservoir,

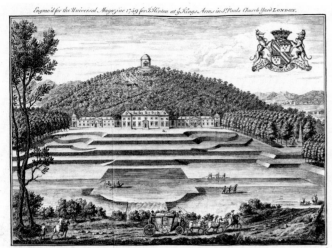

247 Castle Hill, Devon, in an engraving made in 1748 from a drawing by John Wootton of about 1733 for a painting. A new house had been built by Roger Morris from 1728, 'as my Lord Burlington or Lord Herbert shall direct'. Extensive earthworks in four risings were formed below the house between curved quadruple lines of trees punctuated by obelisks on platforms. At the base of the hill the river ran crossways, with an intersecting canal and cascade on the house axis; the hilltop temple was built as a fort.

248 This 1720s plan of Worksop Manor, Nottinghamshire, shows proposed adaptations of the eighth Duke of Norfolk's extensive layout of around 1710 to bring it abreast of fashion (north is at the bottom). The alterations included the arcaded plain parterre west of the house and the quincunx hall and meandering paths in the plantations nearby. No changes were proposed to the cutwork south of the house, but the large bason at the head of the canal, which could almost be by Bridgeman, was executed.

with steps and glides over a vertical height of 87 feet.[149] The steep cascade at Stanway, Gloucestershire, with a fountain in the receiving pond was unusually spectacular.

The more successful of these cascades relied upon plentiful supplies of water from higher ground. Lord Bingley must have acknowledged that his cascade at Bramham was no real orna-ment. Anxious to achieve something more impressive, he tried again. John Wood's duties there in 1724–5 probably included this work. His map shows 'the Great Reservoir', a T-shaped canal fin-ished in 1728, a 'peice of water' (the obelisk pond immediately above the cascade), and 'the Great Cascade' itself, with a fall of 25 feet (see fig. 188). Some owners, however, accepted that such stepped cascades were impractical for their situation and chose the simple *buffet d'eau* (single-fall) form instead. In 1733 John Hore of Newbury, who was engineer of the Kennet Navigation, was paid for renovating the water-works at Shaw House, near Newbury. He dug a new leat from higher up the river to supply a *buffet d'eau*, visible from the house front and discharging into a new semicircular bay of the River Lambourn. Burlington's cascade at Chiswick, which relied on a donkey engine to raise its water to a tank, was less successful.

'THE ANTIENT MANNER OF TEMPLES IN GROVES'

The mood and character of a garden can be suggested or emphasised by its buildings. Classical architecture lent an air of Antiquity, and, away from the presence of the house and its inward gardens, rural gardens became fertile places for the imagination to summon up ideas and scenes of Antique virtue, the complement to the poetry and 'history painting' of the time.

Having imaginative flights of fancy was not the same as carrying them out, of course, and the influence of the Arcadian scenes of Claude, and the 'horrid' scenes of Salvator Rosa, complete with twisted trees and *banditti*, on real gardens was limited. Similarly, the frissons of danger experienced by travellers, such as Evelyn passing over the Alps, or Celia Fiennes descending Blackstone Edge, were emotions that were taken no further, even though they were strangely pleasurable.[150] When the third Earl of Shaftesbury declared that: 'Even the rude Rocks, the mossy Caverns, the irregular unwrought Grotto's, and broken Falls of Waters, with all the horrid Graces of the Wilderness it-self, as representing NATURE more, will be the more engaging, and appear with a Magnificence beyond the formal Mockery of princely Gardens', he was enjoying the 'rude Rocks' with their 'horrid Graces' as a contrast to fine gardens, not advocating that these scenes should be brought into them (fig. 251).[151]

Readers of Classical literature developed images in their minds of the groves of ancient Greece or Rome. William Stukeley's drawing of 'The antient manner of Temples in Groves'

249 'The antient manner of Temples in Groves', a sketch attributed to William Stukeley. Readers of Classical literature or its translations developed images in their minds of the groves of ancient Greece or Rome: here the trees are in quincunx and the temple is Doric. Architects could create such scenes in reality to give a garden associations with a Classical past.

illustrates how, in his mind, such temples had been embedded in high-stemmed groves (fig. 249). Feeling such pleasures of the imagination could tempt architects, in outward plantations and in parks at least, to deliberate manipulation of mood through association. That required a common understanding between the architect and the observer of his buildings through shared experience and reading.

Most garden temples had hitherto been on axis, facing the garden front of the house, on or near the boundary – even the extraordinary temple at Wrest was at the property boundary. By 1715 Vanbrugh was planning a four-pillared Doric portico to be set on axis in the wilderness wall at Castle Howard (see fig. 172). His Corinthian temple at Eastbury, which was being planned about 1718 with an internal dimension of 50 feet, was amongst the greatest and last of this genre.[152]

Classical garden buildings from 1720 were in fact chiefly notable for avoiding such obvious placement. Distributing them

to accord more with topography and views than with the axes of the house was the new way. Both Vanbrugh and Gibbs can be seen as leaders in this respect, especially where encouraged by the possibilities afforded by extended plantations. Gibbs, who left a record of many designs for temples, square, circular and octagon pavilions, Classical seats, obelisks and urns in his *Book of Architecture* (1728), started modestly enough. One well-known and early octagon summer-house of his was that added to the end of the greenhouse in Secretary Johnston's garden at Twickenham in 1716. One design for a 'summer-house in the form of a Temple' looks much like one installed by the bowling green at Tring Manor House around 1720.[153] By this time he had probably also advised on the architectural gardens at Chiswick and Hartwell with their clipped yew palisades. At Hartwell House Gibbs gave Sir Thomas Lee many garden buildings to terminate vistas within a wilderness of *allées* and a *patte d'oie* (fig. 250). Here, at Tring and possibly at Chiswick, Gibbs devised columns on which walks in plantations

250   One of a set of eight paintings of the gardens at Hartwell House, Buckinghamshire, by Balthasar Nebot, 1738. This shows a *patte d'oie* arrangement of yew alleys associated with Gibbs, who may have visited Hartwell as early as 1715. The view is much compressed, as the angles between the walks were actually about 45 degrees; clearly the owner, Sir Thomas Lee, agreed that each alley should be terminated by some architectural object.

Veuë du Chasteau de Fontaine bleau du costé du Jardin

1 le Roy allant a la chasse. 3 l'Hostel de Condé. 5 Court des Cuisines. 7 la Chapelle. 9 Court des fontaines. 11 la Capitainerie. 13 la petite Escurie. 15 La fontaine autrefois appellée
2 la Heronniere. 4 le Bourg de Fontainebleau. 6 Court de l'Oualle. 8 Salle des Suisses. 10 Court du Cheval blanc. 12 l'Hostel de Turenne. 14 Le Mail. du Tibre.

251 Adam François Van Der Meulen's view of the park at Fontainebleau, engraved by Adriaan Frans Boudewyns, c.1680. In the background is the château and the Grand Parterre, work on which had kept Le Nostre away from Greenwich in 1662. The park was notable for being studded with large rocks; when Lord Shaftesbury wrote that 'rude Rocks . . . appear with a Magnificence beyond the formal Mockery of princely Gardens' he may have had similar scenes in mind. The evocative rock formations inspired the Barbizon painters in the nineteenth century.

could focus. It is likely that he designed the domed pavilion at Chiswick, which was placed conventionally, at the end of an axis on the boundary. Gibbs worked at Cannons in 1715–19, and a larger version of the Chiswick pavilion was placed within the vast plantation there. It was described in 1728 as 'a pavilion containing a pretty saloon, most elegantly designed, with three projections, flanked by columns and crowned with pediments. The central saloon, which is decorated within by Corinthian pilasters, is surmounted by a cupola.'[154]

Gibbs populated Bridgeman's designs for converting the Spring Wood at Hackwood into a rural garden in about 1722–5 (see fig. 219). One addition was a temple 'upon the upper ground of an

Amphitheatre, back'd with high Trees that render the Prospect of the Building very agreeable'.[155] Others were a domed cruciform pavilion and a menagerie housing pheasants. He also worked with Bridgeman shortly afterwards at Gobions, where Gibbs provided a temple, a dovecot and another bowling-green house. At both these places the designs were on a new scale, away from the house, but the buildings were set in dense old coppice woodland converted into rural gardens, and had few or no views beyond their confines.

After a visit by Vanbrugh to Stowe in 1719 Lord Cobham had embarked in the 1720s on an ambitious programme of garden buildings. By 1724 Vanbrugh had designed many, situated in walks, quincunxes and halls, including temples, pavilions, seats, a 'Witch's House' and a pyramid, in conjunction with Bridgeman's laying out of about twenty acres of new plantations. Rising through the plantings either side of the Queen's Theatre (a canal with an amphitheatre at one end) were Prince George's column and Caroline's monument.

Gibbs took over at Stowe after Vanbrugh died in 1726. The 50-acre Home Park had been enclosed within a garden arm in 1724 and Gibbs responded to this enlargement. His *Book of Architecture* (1728) included designs for an open pavilion built on the far side of the Home Park, looking back over it and to the recent buildings and gardens.[156] This was known as 'Gibbs's Building' (though it was also variously known as the Temple of Fame, the Belvidere, and the Fane of Diana). He also designed the Boycott Pavilions, which were lodges at the entrance into the park.

Burlington, almost unwittingly, was amongst the innovators. Around 1718 his mentor, Sir Andrew Fountaine, at his home at Narford, formed a deer paddock with a deer house seen over a fossee, set within complex plantations within a wall (see fig. 198). At Chiswick Burlington too created a deer enclosure. He replaced the eastern wall of his garden with a fossee, and built deer houses at each end of it for storage of hay. What had formerly been a kitchen garden area thus became a small deer paddock (see fig. 291). Fountaine's deer house was rusticated with a round-arch opening. This was soon afterwards imitated at Chiswick as the Rustic Arch on the right-hand arm of the *patte d'oie*. Fountaine also

252 *View of the Hermitage in the Royal Garden at Richmond* by J. Gravelot and C. Dubosc, c.1735. This 'rustick' structure, designed by Kent, authorised in November 1730 and started in 1731, was located off the oval with the ancient trees (see fig. 211). Although Classical in plan, its ruinated state suggested that the hermit lived amongst the remains of a great civilisation, guarding its philosophical treasures; there were busts within of great thinkers – Robert Boyle, John Locke, Isaac Newton, William Wollaston and Samuel Clarke.

built an Ionic 'portico' on axis with the house and overlooking a bason between high hedges. Around 1723–5, during Burlington's period of intense interest in Palladio and Jones, he too made a secluded bason with a waterside temple. This had a portico modelled on Jones's design for the church in Covent Garden. These buildings at Chiswick were to be joined by 1727 by a column, and an Ionic temple standing over Burlington's orangery, similar to that at Narford (see fig. 245). Although Burlington followed Fountaine architecturally, the *patte d'oie* buildings and the two temples were amongst the first to be set off the principal axes.

Kent's name has been left to last because he introduced another form of garden building. Not that his early achievements in temple-mongering were unexpected, bearing in mind the task given him by Burlington in editing *Designs of Inigo Jones* (1727, 1731). His early designs at Shotover and Holkham (see Chapter 8) were Classical, and placed in layouts almost certainly the responsibility of others. However he had seen, and no doubt enjoyed, the mossy overgrown water-works of century-old Roman gardens, and if he knew Switzer's *Hydrostaticks* (1729) he would have observed that several illustrations were to that taste. Switzer boasted on his page that the plates included some 'of rural Grotesque'. The cascade at Villa Aldobrandini at Frascati, 'being situate in Cover, and of Rustick Appointment can't be an inelegant Figure'.[157] He praised Thomas Archer's cascade at Hurstbourne Priors and that at the Upper Lodge in Bushy Park (see Chapter Six).[158] There was a grotto at Carshalton, Surrey, designed and built in a similar manner by the owner, Thomas

Scawen, in 1724: 'planted on the Top with Flowering *Shrubs*, disposed in the wildest Manner they possibly can be, for the out-side Appearance ought to look Rural.'[159]

Lady Burlington was one of the ladies of the bedchamber to Queen Caroline, and this was probably the route by which Kent was commissioned to make designs for buildings for the new plantations in Richmond Gardens. He devised a hermitage near the forest oval, authorised in 1730 and started in 1731 (fig. 252), and the grotto called 'Merlin's Cave', by the side of Duck's Pond, designed in 1733.[160] Apart from being 'rustic' rather than Classical, these buildings were notable for being backed up by 'rural' planting of evergreen trees and flowering shrubs. Evidently pleased with the experiment, the Queen ordered a temple in Kensington Gardens overlooking the Serpentine, and backed by similar natural, rustic, planting. In 1733 Kent persuaded Burlington to experiment with the 'rural' look in a section of the garden at Chiswick, as will be discussed in Chapter Nine.

8

Ichnographia Rustica

Ichnographia Rustica, by which is meant the general Designing and Distributing of Country Seats into Gardens,
Woods, Parks, Padducks, &c. which I therefore call *Forest*, or in a more easy Stile, *Rural Gard'ning*.

(Stephen Switzer, 1715)

The levelling of garden walls and a new emphasis on wider prospect and outward plantations encouraged owners to consider the appearance of the parts of the estate thus made open to view. This was especially so in parks, being the private domains of the owner devoted to pleasure. The wider the view, and the more irregular the land, however, the more impossible it was to impose a controlling geometry. It had been found impractical for some of the great park schemes of the recent past, such as Bramham and Cirencester, to be designed around axes aligned on the house. Switzer deflected that point by proposing that the demesne or park be a design of plantations and paddocks, complete in its own right, and largely independent of the house and

garden. In other cases, owners embellished with regular plantations and canals where feasible, but were relaxed about geometry where it was not.

Towards the end of the 1720s owners began to display their ornamental grounds at the entrance to their parks, rather at the forecourt gate, leading to a new scale of improvement. Park designs responded more to the shape of the land, with skyline plantations, towers and vistos, and valley-bottom bodies of water with bridges, thereby taking in whole parks. This generation, being the first to extend their gaze into the wider landscape, there encountered the antiquaries. The interpretation of earthworks and masonry structures was in its very early days, and distinctions between Druidical, Roman, Saxon and medieval were not yet clearly drawn. Nevertheless many landowners took an interest when their monuments were attributed to one period or another, especially when that would reinforce aesthetic or political preferences – for Roman traditions, or Saxon 'liberty'.

A 'farm-like way of gardening': Beauty and utility

The Ancients were a topic to which Switzer returned about 1730. Fortified by Robert Castell's conclusions on the 'first Rise of Gardens' (see above, p. 249), he asserted of rural gardening: 'that this was the Method used by the Romans of old, the curious Drafts and Accounts of the Ancient Villa's . . . fully evince'.[1] Furthermore, 'the Roman genius, which was once the Admiration of the World, is now making great advances in Britain also'. In 1733 he published the first volume of *The Practical Husbandman and Planter*, which included 'A Dissertation on the Ancient and Modern Villa's'.[2] He dedicated the book to the new Earl of Halifax, averring that 'like the Romans of old, you esteem no Part of Life equal to that which you pass away in the Field', probably referring to his improvements at Apps Court, Surrey.

Conventionally, the Virgilian lifestyle was seen as a source not only of pleasure, but also of profit. The juxtaposition of use and beauty had been a powerful theme in seventeenth-century English pastorals, both because it resonated with those in retirement from politics, and because it was an ideological theme of Protestantism. So when Switzer many years later described his system of rural gardening as 'a judicious Mixture and Incorporation of the Pleasures of the Country, with the Profits', his readers would have understood.[3]

Similarly Sir John Clerk was rehearsing an old idea in pointing to productivity, not evergreen plants, as the distinguishing mark of Paradise: 'Now of all Grounds the orchard claims the Praise / As most ressembling Antient Paradise.'[4] Addison used the old rhetoric in the *Spectator*: 'But then why may not a whole estate be thrown into a kind of garden by frequent plantations, that may

turn as much to the profit as the pleasure of the owner?' and suggested that walks might be set out along field margins and planted with trees and flowers. Switzer thought the same: 'Since all agree, that the Pleasures of a Country Life cann't possibly be contained within the narrow Limits of the greatest Garden; Woods, Fields, and distant Inclosures should have the Care of the industrious and laborious Planter.'[5]

THE MANOR OF PASTON

Switzer's three volumes of *Ichnographia Rustica* (1718) 'collated some Materials' on agriculture and the pleasures of a country life in an orderly and methodical manner. His ideas went far beyond ornamenting the landscape with plantations, and placing a few walks along field margins. The key to his practical ideas was the 'Arm of the Garden' running through an estate, allowing the owner to inspect his whole property without leaving his walks. While at Blenheim in 1710 he went across to the first Duke of Shrewsbury's estate at Heythrop (fig. 253). He there saw one such 'arm of the garden', which was 'the first attempt of the kind I ever saw, and which in a great measure has prompted these thoughts'.[6] It seems likely that a small sliver of land, hedged and ditched on both sides, that ran between the main garden enclosure and outward woodlands, was his inspiration.

In order to illustrate his ideas he showed how an estate (his imaginary 'Manor of Paston') composed of fields and a few scattered water bodies and woods could be transformed. His 'survey' plan showed the field boundaries, and his 'proposals' plan showed how the ditches and banks of the field boundaries could be regarded as stockades, and, with new stockades backing onto the old ones, could form a 'terrace', along which a six- or eight-foot-wide walk could be laid (fig. 254).[7] That arrangement would keep the cattle out, and if the 'Hedge-Rows being mix'd with Primroses, Violets, and such natural sweet, and pleasant Flowers; the Walks that lead through [would] afford as much Pleasure as . . . the most elaborate, fine Garden.' Switzer would have taken walks past fishponds: 'it's ten to one but they are in some cunning Hole or other where 'tis impossible to see them'.[8] If it was not possible to incorporate

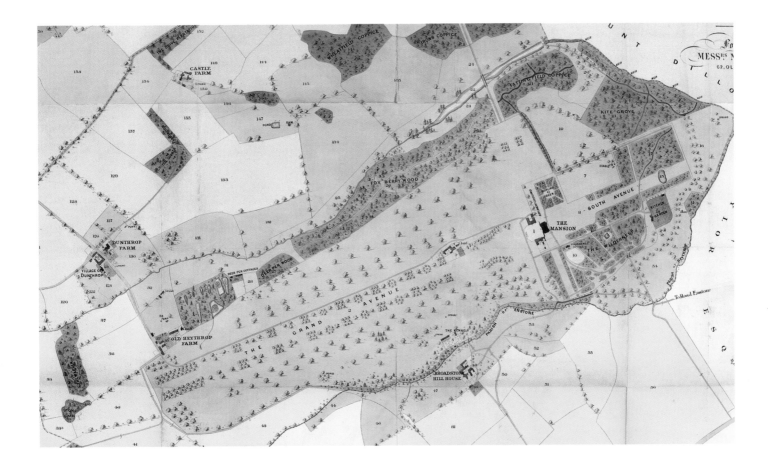

them into the garden, then 'One wou'd carry some Arm of the Garden to view them'.

Switzer queried why designers should esteem only large regular walks, and why

> for diversity, should not rather mix therewith Serpentine Meanders; and instead of levelling Hills, or filling up Dales, should think it more entertaining to be sometimes on the Precipice of a Hill viewing all round and under us, and at other times in a Bottom, viewing those goodly Hills and Theatres of Wood and Corn that are above us . . . ?[9]

He in fact preferred the serpentine: 'Of all the Lines that a Designer ought to use in natural Gard'ning, the loose Serpentine Line seem to be the most entertaining; because thereby the Owner does not see all his business at once, but is insensibly led from one Place to another'.[10]

These ideas on 'arms of the garden', laid out irregularly to gain access to fishponds and views, were developed by Switzer into an idealised plan (fig. 255), perhaps loosely based on Blenheim, which demonstrated

> At or near the House, a little more exactitude is required; so after that view is over one would sometimes be passing thro'

253   'Plan of the Heythrop Park Estate', a detail of a sale map of 1870 (north is to the left). The landscape had hardly changed since the Duke of Shrewsbury laid it out in the early eighteenth century, with an avenue in round and square platoons and flanked by parallel lines of trees. The arm of the garden that inspired Stephen Switzer was the narrow connection running east from the bowling green plantation in Union Jack form to the woods and coppices on the slopes above the artificial water.

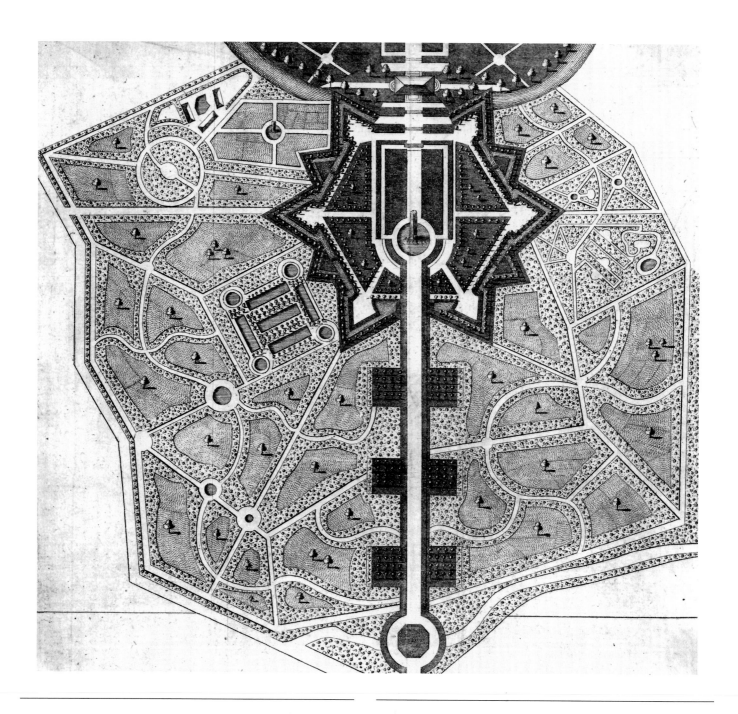

254   'The Manor of Paston Divided and Planted into Rural Gardens',
engraved by Michael van der Gucht, 1718. This plan from Switzer's
Ichnographia Rustica for an imaginary estate with a moated and fortified
garden and platooned axial walk was designed to illustrate how hedges
could be doubled to provide wooded walks between fields.

(Facing page) 255   This 'Plan of a Forest or Rural Garden', engraved
by Michael van der Gucht for Switzer's *Ichnographia Rustica* (1718) and
perhaps derived remotely from Blenheim, illustrated Switzer's ideas of
redesigning a park to accommodate all the pleasures of a country life –
a wilderness, twisting paths in more remote plantations, lakes for boating
and rides running between fields to outlying gardens.

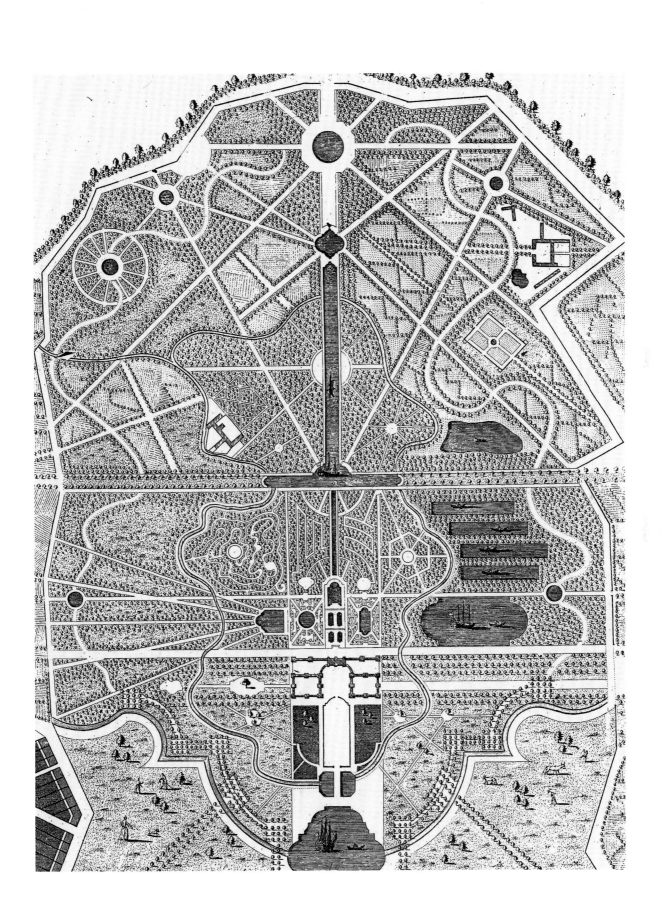

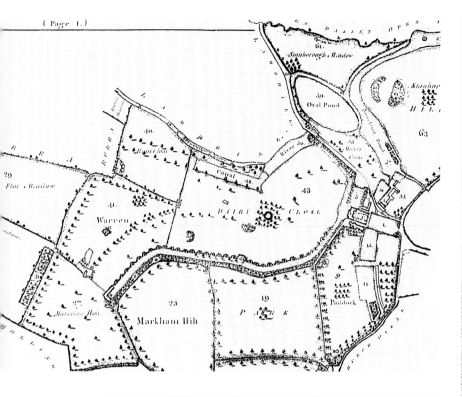

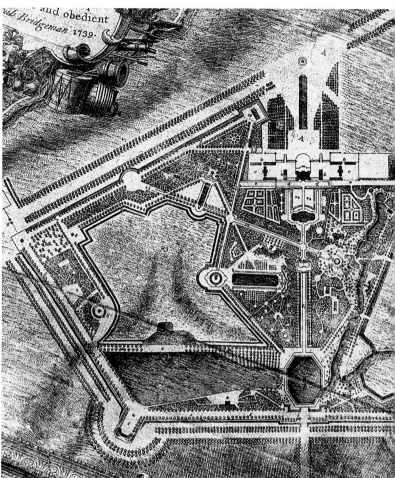

(Above) 256 Detail of an estate plan of Farnborough Hall, Warwickshire, surveyed by Edward Linnell, 1772 (north is to the right). 'The Terrace', three quarters of a mile long and broad enough for two horsemen, rises steadily from by the hall to the obelisk; the west side (the side with the view) is crinkled for trees to be planted on their own mounds a chain apart. The largest swelling, a third of the way along the terrace, supported an Ionic temple. Although begun perhaps as late as 1738, the design has more the flavour of the 1720s.

(Right, top) 257 Detail of *A General Plan of the Woods, Park and Gardens of Stowe . . .* published by Sarah Bridgeman, 1739. This shows Stowe at the close of Bridgeman's career (he died in 1738), with the eleven-acre lake completed and the fields east and west of the gardens with ramparts enclosed. The naturalistic water and planting along the eastern edge of the gardens were started in 1733, with Kent supplying designs for the buildings.

(Right, bottom) 258 A watercolour by Bernard Lens III of a scene in Bushy Park, *c.*1720, showing fashionable gentlefolk enjoying the open air of the gardens of the Upper Lodge, where the chief attraction was the cascade (see fig. 174). In the 1770s the ranger, Lord North, who had no use for the lodge, demolished it and built a 'tea room' for his pleasure in its place.

little Padducks and Corn Fields, sometimes thro' wild Coppices, and Gardens, and sometimes by purling Brooks and Streams, Places that are set off not by nice Art, but by luxury of Nature, a little guided in her Extravagancies by the Artists Hand . . .[11]

Rural walks proliferated in the 1720s, though taking several forms. At Corby Castle, Cumberland, a riverside walk led to a temple, and later riverside rural walks included one at Rokeby (see fig. 283), and the Long Walk, a private walk to the Dropping Well at the spa town of Knaresborough, opened to the public from the 1730s for a small fee. At Farnborough Hall, Warwickshire, a lengthy bastioned terrace climbed a hill to a viewpoint (fig. 256), and there were circuit walks. At Dalton Hall they were modest, just margins to fields (see fig. 208), whereas at Stowe the new walk around the Home Park was constructed at much expense, with fortifications and garden buildings (fig. 257). Nearer to London, a day visit to Hampton Court might include perambulating Bushy Park, with the Longford River and cascade (fig. 258).

RICHINGS, DAWLEY AND STOWE

Switzer's system of estate improvement was ingenious, although the trouble and expense of construction were maybe not as practical as he declared. Perhaps that was why few owners adopted his system. On the other hand, improvement for the national good, as contrasted to personal aggrandisement by the Whig grandees, became a political theme. As the Whigs had gained power it was the Tories who sought to defend ancient freedoms supposedly established in Anglo-Saxon times. Hence some Tories wanted to invoke Saxon architecture, for example Lord Bathurst of Cirencester Park in 1721 at the Wood House, a timber cottage lost in the woods. After that fell down, he built 'Alfred's Hall', mentioned above, near the same spot in 1727–32, using salvaged medieval stonework (fig. 259). It was not unusual for ancient families to live in new houses in view of their abandoned castles. In 1727 a mason began to build 'Wentworth Castle' (fig. 260), on the summit of the hill above the Earl of Strafford's new seat, Stainborough Hall, of which the keystone reads: 'Re-built by Thomas Earl of Strafford

in the Year 1730', a curious statement for a new construction. One interpretation recalls that the hill had earthworks considered to be Anglo-Saxon by the antiquary Roger Dodsworth.[12] A visitor in 1732 wrote of it: 'I delight in the . . . building of the Castle tho' [it] is neither Egyptian nor Grecian but of a more proper order, the Saxon'.[13] Some years later, at Stowe in 1741, the association of Saxon styles with ancient liberties was further reinforced when Gibbs designed a Temple of Liberty in a Gothic style, which he called 'Saxon', reflecting the politics of Lord Cobham, who had gone into opposition.

Switzer, who had earlier worked for Whig magnates, found himself in the employ of some of the opposition politicians in the 1720s. Led by Lord Bolingbroke, they included Bathurst at Cirencester and Richings. Bathurst had acquired the latter, near Slough, by marriage in 1704, and during his political rise in the early 1710s planted an outward wilderness with axial canal and radiating walks. After the accession of George I and the eclipse of his political hopes in 1714 he concentrated on Cirencester, but in the early 1720s he was once more spending time at Richings. Bathurst supplied trees from his nursery there to Pope for Marble Hill in 1724. Switzer was probably involved at that time; he dedicated his *Practical Kitchen Gardener* (1727) to Bathurst ('Best of Masters, best of Friends'), and wrote that he admired Bathurst's 'hearty and sincere love for your country and a generous concern for the good of all mankind', as well as his retirement into fields and gardens, and his contemplation of the stupendous works of nature.[14] In addition to showing two plans for kitchen gardens incorporating ideas for multiple levels, and octangular and fortified forms (fig. 261), Switzer approved Bathurst's 'method of rural kitchen gardening'.[15] This had 'kitchen garden quarters', instead of blocks of forest trees, within wildernesses: 'the insides of the Quarters (are) for sowing of Corn, Turnips, etc. or for the feeding of Cattle'. They were reached by meandering walks, which concealed them from casual gaze from the principal alleys. Switzer gave a description of a 'regulated epitome' of the place, indicating the kitchen garden quarters, the canal and an *enfilade* surrounding the whole.[16]

In 1740 Lady Hertford wrote of verses pinned inside a covered seat at Richings by Addison, Pope, Prior, Congreve and Gay, and

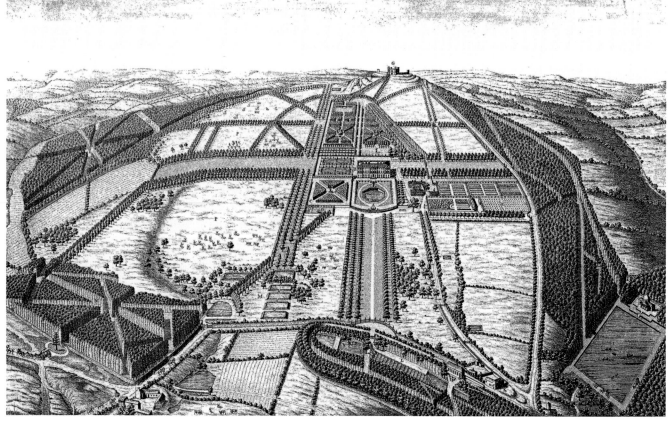

The Plan of a Kitchen Garden on three Levels with a Canal at bottom.

A Scale of Feet.

(Facing page, top) 259 *The North East View of* KING ALFRED'S HALL, Cirencester Park, based on a 1763 drawing by Thomas Robins. Lord Bathurst began this 'Wood House', or 'Alfred's Hall' in 1721 deep in the wooded Oakley Park, in part using materials from Sapperton Manor, which he demolished (see fig. 11). He was not averse to myths being created around the building, as the subscript starts: 'Tradition says that a Treaty was sign'd here with Gormandus the Dane . . .'. This was perhaps the earliest Gothic revival building in a landscape.

(Facing page, bottom) 260 *A Prospect of Stainborough and Wentworth Castle* from the east by Thomas Badeslade and John Harris, 1730. The new house, facing downhill, was built from 1710. In 1711 the Earl of Strafford asked George London to produce a plan for the gardens, surely the origin of the scrollwork parterre south of the house and the flanking wildernesses planted in 1713. After London's death in 1713/14 Thomas Archer provided general ideas and is likely to have assisted with the various cascades and water features on the estate. The park was enlarged with land to the south and east, and park plantations were enlarged and cut into stars. In the 1720s the public road to the north was moved away from the hall, allowing kitchen and other gardens to be built near the stables; the land thus taken in included the hill on which Wentworth Castle (G) was built 1727–30. One of the earliest mock castles in the century, it was built to emphasise Stafford's ancient lineage.

(Right) 261 'The Plan of a Kitchen Garden on Three Levels with a Canal at the Bottom' engraved by J. Clark for Switzer's *The Practical Kitchen Gardener* (1727). The square buildings let into the walls lent an air of fortification, but were used to house the gardener and his men, tools and fruit, and those by the canal were for the owner's pleasure, like some at Sacombe House, Hertfordshire.

of a greenhouse supposedly on the site of 'St Leonard's Chapel'. She described the place as Bathurst left it,

> laid out in the manner of a French park, interspersed with woods and lawns. There is a canal in it about twelve hundred yards long [corrected to 555 yards], and proportionably broad, which has a stream continually running through it, and is deep enough to carry a pleasure-boat. It is well stocked with carp and tench; and at its upper end there is a green-house, containing a good collection of orange, myrtle, geranium and oleander trees. In one of the woods (through all which there are winding paths) there is a cave . . . There are several covered benches . . . there is one gravel walk that encompasses the whole . . . a flock of sheep graze the lawns fine . . . [17]

Bolingbroke had been rejected by the Old Pretender in 1715, and afterwards affected the lifestyle of a rural philosopher at La Source, near Orléans. He developed a comprehensive philosophic system. Pure deism – disbelief in supernaturally revealed religion and a belief in the understanding of the nature of God through a study of his works – and a system of vigorous principles upheld by a mind supposedly unhampered by self interest, were the mainstays. His patriotism was widely shared by those opposed to Walpole's government, which was seen to be sacrificing England's interests to those of Hanover. Bolingbroke returned briefly to England from France in 1723 after a pardon, and then in 1725, with help from his friend Bathurst, bought Dawley in Middlesex. The Earl of Tankerville had built a replacement mansion there, orientating it eastward, and revising the gardens around, but it was on the market after the second Earl decided to settle at Uppark. From Dawley the remarkably energetic and resilient Bolingbroke gathered the remnants of the old-guard Tory party for an assault on Walpole.

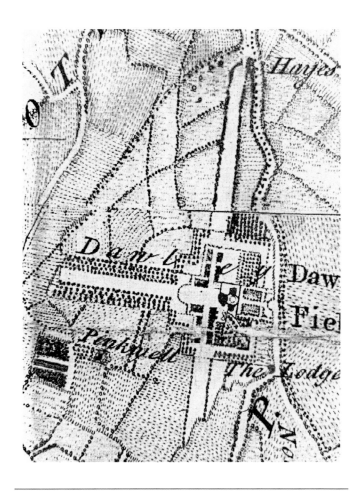

262 Dawley House, in a detail from John Rocque's map of Middlesex, 1754. The Earl of Tankerville moved the road eastwards, built a new house on a slightly different site, and extensively reorganised the gardens and avenues around the house. When the estate was sold to Lord Bolingbroke in 1724 Tankerville's work was incomplete, so Bolingbroke brought in Gibbs to finish it off. The work was completed 1727 and the old house demolished soon after. Bolingbroke, leader of the Tories, renamed the estate 'Dawley Farm' to make a point about responsible land ownership, and disparked the demesne (compare fig. 46).

The chief method at Bolingbroke's disposal was a propaganda campaign by himself and his old literary friends through journals and published poetry. He joined forces with William Pulteney, who had been Secretary of War in 1714–17, but who had become disaffected at the rise of Walpole, in the production of the journal, *The Craftsman*, for ten years from December 1725. Swift visited England in 1726 and 1727, talking politics and seeing much of Pope, and so old friendships were rekindled. These men had a real and visible target – the 'vanity of expense' by the Whig lords.

On taking possession of Dawley, Bolingbroke at once became ostentatiously engaged in the conversion of his 'agreeable sepulchre' to a suitably rustic retreat. He put the inscription 'Satis beatus ruris honoribus' – 'Happy enough with the rewards of the country?' – above his door to symbolise an awakened sensibility to estate improvement. Gibbs 'new modelled' the recently rebuilt house during 1726. Bolingbroke wrote to Pope and Swift in February 1727 that 'I am in my farm, and here I shoot strong tenacious roots: I have caught hold of the earth, (to use a gardener's phrase) and neither my enemies nor my friends will find it an easy matter to transplant me again'. So that his renaming of Dawley as 'Dawley Farm' might be fulfilled, 'he has fitted up his farm, and this scheme of retreat is not founded upon weak appearances'.[18] Bolingbroke had paid a large sum of money to have the mansion house painted with 'Rakes, Spears, Prongs, etc., and other ornaments merely to countenance calling this place a farm', according to Bolingbroke's half-sister, Lady Luxborough, who added that 'he had his hall painted in stone colours, all the implements of husbandry placed in the manner one sees or might see arms and trophies in some General's hall; and it had an effect that pleased every body'.[19] To complete the moral tone, Pope noted, 'his great Temperance and Economy are Signal'.

Bridgeman was called round on the recommendation of his friend Pope. Whether he was employed or not, further major changes to the gardens were required to reorientate them in a new position around the new house, instead of the 1670s mansion (fig. 262). The older avenues were mostly preserved, but the old *parterre à l'Angloise* was swept away in favour of lawns. Bolingbroke kept the westward avenues and northward Long Walk as features and field boundaries. Using the main avenues and the hedgerow lines existing at emparkment in 1690, he turned Dawley back into farmland, and put tenants onto some of it.

Switzer complimented the Lords Bathurst, Bolingbroke and Cobham, for their endeavours in 'rural kitchen gardening'.[20]

They were 'great encouragers' of the farm-like way of gardening as well. Cobham was a friend of Pope, and was becoming disenchanted with the Walpole ministry. So Switzer may perhaps have felt that, on the strength of the enclosing of the Home Park within the great ha-ha at Stowe (see fig. 257), Cobham could also be said to be practising the farm-like way of gardening. A few years later, in his essay 'A Further Account of Rural and Extensive Gardening' (added to the 1742 edition of *Ichnographia Rustica*) Switzer referred to Bathurst and Bolingbroke as 'improvers'. He also used the term 'la ferme ornée' in relation to Richings and Dawley.[21] It is not clear whether Switzer coined the term himself or whether Bolingbroke invented it for his own activities at La Source. The bases of the *ferme ornée* were the political and moral aspects of estate improvement, rather than artistic impulse. The point had to be made by Lady Luxborough to a bemused correspondent in 1749: 'My brother's calling it (Dawley) a Farm was only meant that it really was one; for he then kept £700 per annum in hand: but that the house was much too fine and large to be called a Farm. But on the other side, its environs were not ornamented, nor its prospects good.'[22]

SENSE

Alexander Pope's 'Epistle to Burlington' of 1731 promoted the aesthetic taste and judgement of Burlington, who represented the supposed Roman values of simplicity, restraint, elegance and clarity of expression. At the same time Pope contrasted such values to the wanton display and tastelessness of the Whig palaces, an example of which he described:

> At Timon's Villa let us pass a day,
> Where all cry out, 'What sums are thrown away!' . . .
> To compass this, his building is a Town
> His pond an Ocean, his parterre a Down:
> Who but must laugh, the Master when he sees,
> A puny insect, shiv'ring at a breeze! . . .
> I curse such lavish cost, and little skill,
> And swear no Day was ever pass'd so ill.[23]

Most of his readers could think of a few recent mansions that would in part fit this description. Many assumed that Pope was attacking the Duke of Chandos's seat of Cannons, and counter-critical material included William Hogarth's engraving *Man of Taste* (1731), depicting Pope, hunchbacked, whitewashing Burlington's gate and bespattering the Duke's coach passing by. Pope disingenuously claimed that he had merely invented the caricature of the 'Patron with no Sense'.

Pope had to reconcile his acquaintance with Bridgeman and Kent, who, as the artists concerned, had been party to huge extravagances by Whig lords, and the original scheme of the poem – recognition of the taste of Burlington – with Bolingbroke's new scheme of the moral responsibility of wealth. His method was to distinguish the respective responsibilities of patron and artist into 'Sense' and 'Taste'. The unfortunate combination of artist's taste and lack of patron's sense yields a vulnerable product: 'Without it, proud Versailles! thy Glory falls'. He is not here attacking Le Nostre, as artists were not charged with the responsibility of Sense: 'Jones and Le Nôtre have it not to give'. Jones, the supreme British architect, was an appropriate choice. Charles I had incensed Parliament with the 'Senseless' expense of the Whitehall Banqueting House and lost his head in front of Jones's masterpiece.

Pope then expounded on the nature of worthwhile improvement, providing compliments to his friends in passing:

> Who then shall grace, or who improve the Soil?
> Who plants like Bathurst, or who builds like Boyle.
> 'Tis use alone that sanctifies Expense,
> And Splendour borrows all her rays from Sense.
> His Father's Acres who enjoys in peace,
> Or makes his Neighbours glad, if he increase:
> Whose cheerful Tenants bless their yearly toil,
> Yet to their Lord owe more than to the soil;
> Whose ample Lawns are not asham'd to feed
> The milky heifer and deserving steed;
> Whose rising Forests, not for pride or show,
> But future buildings, future Navies, grow:

Let his plantations stretch from down to down,
First shade a Country, and then raise a Town . . .[24]

The allusion to plantations 'from down to down' invoked Bathurst's massive scheme at Cirencester thirteen years before (see fig. 11). As Pope wrote in the 'Epistle to Lord Bathurst', he considered all this to be prudent investment:

To balance Fortune by a just expense,
Join with Economy, Magnificence;
With Splendour, Charity; with Plenty, Health;
O teach us, Bathurst! yet unspoil'd by wealth![25]

'Incomprehensible vastness'

In 1742 Switzer remarked that 'in all cases the Lawn or Parterre should not be too large, since 'tis a very wrong way of thinking, to imagine that true Greatness consists in Size and Dimension'.[26] He laid some of the blame for lawns of 50, or even 100 acres, that made their houses look small at Bridgeman's door: 'This aiming at an incomprehensible Vastness, and attempting at Things beyond the reach of Nature, is in a great measure owing to a late eminent Designer in Gardening, whose Fancy could not be bounded.' Paraphrasing Pope's description of Timon's villa, Switzer then went on to say that Bridgeman's lakes were 'generally designed so large, as to make a whole Country look like an Ocean' (fig. 263).

Castle Howard, Blenheim and Heythrop were early examples of gigantism in park layout, and large-scale emparkment seemed to be under way more frequently in the 1720s. These were not for deer hunting but for improving the setting of a house, and often led to elaborate schemes of park ornamentation. The Duke of Dorset bought out the remaining freeholders on adjacent commons in 1720 in order to expand the park at Knole to 660 acres. In 1723 the Duke of Kingston, with an eye on Sherwood Forest, obtained an 'especial Lycence to take in and Enclose within his Park at Thoresby in Com. Nottingham 1217 Acres 3 Rood & 30 Perch being his own Inheritance and for the enjoyment of free Chace &

263 This detail from a 1735 engraving of William Hogarth's *A Rake's Progress No. 2* shows Bridgeman among the tradesmen vying for Tom's custom; he is holding a drawing inscribed 'Garden plan'. This is an older Bridgeman than the Thornhill sketch (see fig. 214) but recognisably the same man. Hogarth is satirising Bridgeman's expensive schemes of 'incomprehensible Vastness', deplored also by Switzer.

free Warren in the same when inclosed'. The Duke of Richmond expanded his holding at Goodwood from 200 acres to over 11,000 in the 1720s, which included extensive parkland.

THE APPROACH

Some owners, feeling that their display of ornamentation should begin at the entrances to their parks, repositioned their lodges from forecourt gates to park gates. At first, this would be where the axial avenue met the highway. At Hamels, a pair of lodges, the width of the avenue, were erected in 1716–19 at the roadside (see fig. 240). Cannons famously had lodges at the start of the

Edgware Avenue, defended by army pensioners. In 1726 Stowe gained the Boycott Pavilions, designed by Gibbs. Claremont and Esher Place were both given lodges at their park entrances in 1733, and about that time Kent had ideas for lodges at the start of the southern avenue at Holkham, two miles south of the house, which turned into a triumphal arch with pyramidal-roofed pavilions (fig. 264).

Ironwork gates too began to be set at park entrances instead of forecourts. About 1730 George Wynne had two sets of screens, the Black Gates and the White Gates, set up at the roadside to permit views into his park at Leeswood. They reputedly cost £1,500 and may have been by the Davies brothers (see fig. 1). They were remarkable for being overtly Palladian in design instead of the usual Baroque form. Likewise, some fine iron gates were supplied by James Foulgham of Nottingham for the north end of the ride at Rufford Abbey in 1734.

Conventional planting in lines for approach avenues was still practised, as, for example, at the 1730s lime avenue to Buxted Park, Sussex. The old standard width had been around 100 feet, and this was envisaged for Goodwood, as shown in *Vitruvius Britannicus* in 1725. The avenue at Caversham, as designed in 1718, was rather wider, at 160 feet. Bridgeman gave that at Wimpole a width of 270 feet, reminiscent of the old 'grand avenues', and a bason part-way along its length, much as London would have designed.

Alternatives to trees in lines were the visually more exciting platooned or clumped arrangements. Miller pointed to the advantages of them for the rider: 'In large Parks this Method of planting in Clumps has a very good Effect; for as a Person rides through the Avenue, the Opening between the Trees, to the Turf where the Deer are feeding, is much more agreeable, than in passing between strait Rows of Trees.'[27] At one extreme of width were the platoons on the approach to the Earl of Lincoln's Oatlands, set 500 feet apart, and ending at an even wider parade (see fig. 246). In 1731 the Duke of Chandos was planning the dummy Whitchurch Avenue at Cannons to be extended by planting large platoons of elms to three miles distant, achieved in 1736.[28] Lord Petre designed the approach to Gisburn, Yorkshire, to be between platoons and mounts (figs 265 and 266). At Londesborough, Lord

264 An engraving by Matthew Brettingham of 1748 showing Kent's design, made in about 1733, for the Triumphal Arch, the southern entrance and lodge to Holkham Park. The pyramids were never built. A couple of miles from the house, at the far end of the park, this may have been intended as the London lodge. It is an early example of a lodge being placed at the entrance to the park rather than the forecourt.

Burlington started a double avenue in the late 1720s. Not completed until land was purchased in the late 1730s, it was extended to the York Road in 1742 as platoons. Platoons also formed the Column Ride at Tottenham by about 1740.

The most celebrated approaches of this time, however, were the sidelong ones given by Vanbrugh to Blenheim, Castle Howard and Stowe, devised largely for scenographic purposes. Vanbrugh wrote to the Earl of Carlisle in 1724 that Lord Cobham favoured the indirect approach when 'the approach right forward' would be 'difficult and unreasonable', and had been impressed by an example he had seen in Germany.[29] At Castle Howard a similar argument had been made, allowing the house's full width to be seen high on the ridge from either north or south on the five-mile long double avenue. This was aligned to pass some way to

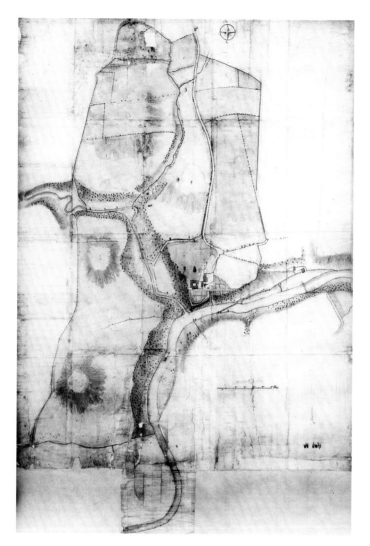

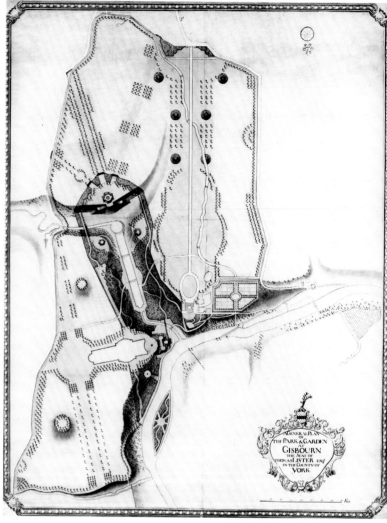

265   A survey of Gisburn Park, Yorkshire, 1735 (north is at the bottom). The well-described topography formed the basis of the general plan for the park and garden (see fig. 266).

266   *A General Plan of the Park & Garden at Gisbourn* by Sieur Bourguignon, 1735 (north is at the bottom). The entire park at Gisburn is ornamented with mounts, platoons, clumps, belts, canals, and cascades to form lawns, inward plantations and park plantings, but there is no parterre at the house.

the west, intersecting at a circle with the sidelong approach to the forecourt (see fig. 197).

Approaches could incorporate lawns, a point considered as far back as 1705, when Hawksmoor sketched an oval lawn set within plantations in the northern park at Blenheim (fig. 267). Switzer

observed in *Ichnographia Rustica* that 'a great Fault in many of our Designs, in bringing our Avenues close to the Court-Gate, by which Means we very often lose the Beauty of a very noble Lawn'.[30] He advised that a depth of at least a quarter of a mile deep would give 'the most Champion view', and advised against

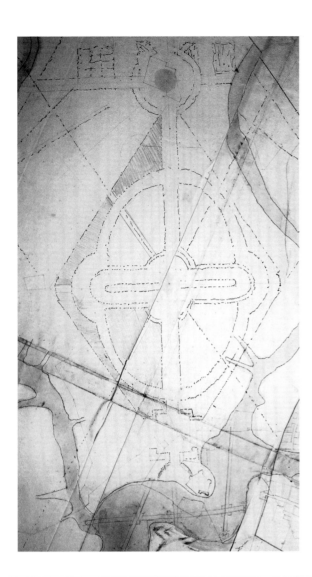

267   Part of a plan of a proposal for the park at Blenheim, probably by Nicholas Hawksmoor, 1705 (see fig. 137). This vast cross with an oval leading to a circle was displaced by an avenue incorporating platoons (see fig. 136), but geometrical arrangements for park lawns were to gain popularity from the 1720s.

268   Detail of a survey of the Ditchley House estate, Oxfordshire, by Edward Grantham, 1726 (north is at the top). The old Ditchley was amongst the buildings and kitchen garden to the north-east of the new house, designed by Gibbs in about 1720 to stand in the park. An axial drive approached a carriage sweep via an octagonal lawn in front of the house; diagonal avenues radiated from the house and the sides of the lawn. From 1729 the terrace overlooking the park north of the house was expanded into a revetted great terrace; there never was a parterre.

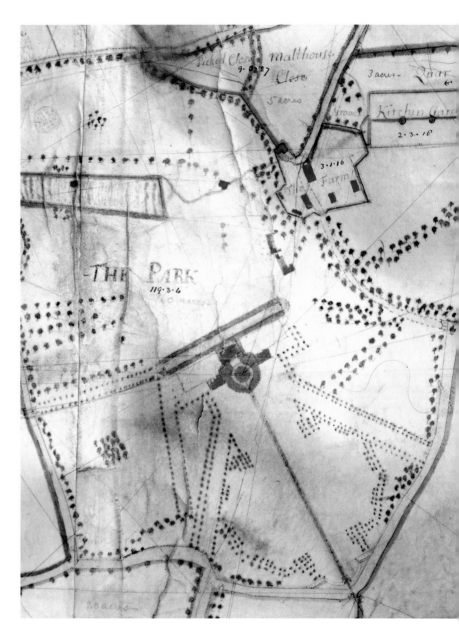

placing woods too close to the mansion.[31] He recommended that lawns be enclosed by ranks of trees where the approaches met in front of the house. About 1722 a modest octagonal lawn at Ditchley was indeed planted where avenues converged on the house front (fig. 268). Half-rounds, or half-squares, at the house end

of avenues were rarely made by the 1720s; amongst the last was that at Houghton, associated with the rebuilding of the house from 1721.

The need to enclose a forecourt came under question. At first, walls and iron palisades were replaced by simpler post and rail fences. The gravel sweep at Ebberston Lodge, Yorkshire, was enclosed about 1718 against the deer park by this method.[32] Simi-

larly, at Marble Hill the gravel circle was separated from the field beyond only by a post and rail fence, the minimum necessary to keep out stock (see fig. 203). The removal of any enclosure against the parkland may have first been effected at Stowe. There, about 1720, a sweep was set out under the entrance front with no barrier between it and the grass that extended out into groves flanking the canal (fig. 269). At Antony, Cornwall, set out by Gibbs in the early 1720s, stone arcades flanked the sweep round a grass circle but the end was entirely open to the park.[33]

During the 1720s, then, the very idea of a forecourt had faded to the point of vanishing, particularly where the approach was through open parkland. Hence Bridgeman's plan for Lumley of about 1730 suggested gravelling the whole of the old forecourt and taking the walls down so that it would be open to the lawn down to the river (see fig. 244). Bourguignon's plan for Gisburn

269 *View from the Portico of the House to the Park* at Stowe by Jacques Rigaud, engraved by Bernard Baron, 1734. This is one of a set of views by Rigaud commissioned by Bridgeman. The canal, flanked by groves, was dug in 1716–18, and the soil used to form a mount where an equestrian statue of George I by John Nost was set up by 1720. This was one of the first examples of a forecourt being dispensed with altogether.

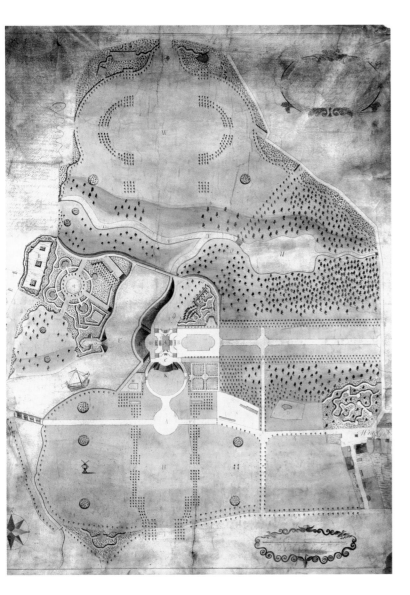

270 Stephen Switzer's 'View of the New House, Offices and Park at Nostel, Yorkshire, with yᵉ Improvements made and to be made in yᵉ [severall] Plantations in yᵉ Park', c.1735. The platoons, clumps, amphitheatres and formal plantings were not exceptional for this date and the sense of scale, the glad use of ancient trees and the naturalistic water and belts typify the grander manner of the 1730s.

house were sought out. Hence several domed temples and obelisks were placed on the bastions of fortification boundaries in order to advertise their placement for views. Vanbrugh designed a cupola on columns, the Rotunda, for the western bastion at Stowe in 1721 (see fig. 222), and installed a similar cupola at Duncombe Park. Kent's first garden building was a domed temple on a bastion at Shotover House for which William Towneshend the mason was paid in 1725 (see fig. 232).

The desire to create interesting views within the park and outer plantations led to a keener interest in avenue orientations that picked up neighbouring landmarks. This was an old pastime, for the Kingston Avenue at Hampton Court, planted in 1689, was on alignment with the spire of Kingston church, but it was one still much indulged in. Lord Bathurst's numerous vistas in Cirencester Park established in the 1720s were designed to align on neighbouring churches,[34] and Bridgeman spent his time at Wimpole in 1721 'in contriving how the diagonal may take Whaddon steeple exactly in the middle'.[35]

Where such landmarks were lacking, there was no shortage of ideas on how to supply them. Towers with a hint of Antiquity made interesting objects of view and invoked the historical depth of the English countryside. They could have practical purposes as park lodges for keepers or other servants, or as standings where a hunting party might breakfast and admire the view, though it was always important that they could be seen. One of the first examples was a two-storey square tower with ogee roof on Park Hill, a mile away from Wimborne St Giles House. It was nearly aligned with an avenue and referred to by the third Earl of Shaftesbury in 1707 as 'yᵉ designed Summerhouse'. Another two-storey

of 1735 showed a large oval sweep with no barrier whatsoever between grazing animals and the door. Likewise, Switzer's plan of the same date for Nostel Priory showed two sweeps open to parkland (fig. 270).

VISTOS, TEMPLES AND BELVEDERES

Whereas in the late seventeenth century cupolas were erected on houses in order to obtain the best views, in the days of prolated gardens and circumambient walks viewpoints away from the

square tower, on How Hill on the far skyline from Studley Royal, is thought to have been designed by Vanbrugh in 1719 and to have marked the axis along the Long Canal.

Vanbrugh's romantic streak came to the fore as he designed more distinctive towers in his 'castle' style, with castellations. His belvedere atop the wooded hill behind Claremont was being finished off in 1715 (fig. 271). The three-storey 'summer-house' at Swinstead of about 1720, with architectural similarities to this

---

271 The Belvedere at Claremont from the bowling green; the building, atop a hill, is in Vanbrugh's 'castle' style, with castellations.

272 The Carrmire Gate and Pyramid Gate on the southern approach to Castle Howard. The obelisk seen through the Pyramid Arch was designed by Vanbrugh and set up in 1714 (in honour of Marlborough) where the approach makes a right-hand turn. The Pyramid Arch itself was designed in 1716, and is dated 1719, the year of its completion, when curtain walls were begun either side of it. Based on English town walls known to Vanbrugh, these were completed in 1722; the Carrmire Gate in the foreground was erected in 1725. This sequence is an example of Vanbrugh's liking for the theatrical.

---

belvedere, was outside the park pale but visible from Grimsthorpe, and is attributed to Vanbrugh. At Castle Howard he went further back in time. The straight approach road passed through an archway of 1719 topped by a pyramid, a variation on the forecourt gates for Kings Weston, proposed in 1717 but not built, though now transferred to the approaches. Being placed where the road passed over a ridge, this position gave an opportunity for several hundred yards of 'fortification' being constructed in 1725 from the gate in both directions along the ridge (fig. 272).[36] Ancient city walls were Vanbrugh's inspiration, suggestive of past military prowess and provoking the imagination.

Owners who liked to think that they were recovering the Roman tradition felt validated when Roman antiquities were found on their land. Inigo Jones had assured the Earl of Pembroke that Stonehenge was a Roman structure. Lord Burlington was delighted that he had a Roman road running through Londesborough, and furious with William Stukeley for arguing that Stonehenge was built by the Druids. Another option for park pavilions, then, was large temples and triumphal arches in the Classical tradition. Batty Langley showed 'Ruins after the Old Roman Manner for the termination of Walks avenues &c', looking much like the ruins of Rome.[37] Literal ruins were, though, a bit impractical, and most park buildings invoking the Roman past were for the view, used by riding parties or lived in.

Nicholas Dubois, who had been a siege engineer, devised a plan for Charles Howard for Audley End, Essex, in 1725, which included a temple on a hill within elaborate military fortifications, though it remained on plan. At Ditchley Park, Oxfordshire, Gibbs 'gave several drawings for temples, for the woods in the park, as also Triumphal Arches for the Termination of the three long Vistas, cut through the woods, seen from the House' in 1728.[38] At Tring, where Gibbs was involved, a pyramid was placed in the park in the mid-1720s. A triumphal arch, 'Heaven's Gate', was set up in 1739 on Sidown Hill at the end of the broad vista running south from Highclere Castle.[39]

Large obelisks silhouetted against the sky, and memorial columns, could be placed at a considerable distance from the house. Gibbs described a design for two pavilions at Kedleston 'opposite to one another, on each side of a Vista proposed to be cut through a Wood, and to be terminated with an Obelisque upon a Hill fronting the House'.[40] On the axis south of Holkham Hall the land rises to a hill, one of the few in the area. Kent designed an obelisk, built in 1729–32, for its crest (fig. 273). A great obelisk dedicated to Queen Anne was built by the Earl of Strafford on the far side of the park at Stainborough in 1734.

The column to the Duke of Marlborough at Blenheim has been mentioned. Lord Bathurst, another Tory whose honours were bestowed by Queen Anne, was planning a Doric column in her honour in his park at Cirencester in 1736, though it was not erected till 1741. It was within a circle and linked to his other vistos by platooned avenues, each platoon being on a hummock. A fifteen-foot-wide cutting had to be made to allow an uninterrupted view.

As rides and *enfilades* took the mounted visitor further afield, the views back across the ornamented park and towards the house were given thought. Buildings in outward plantations and even faraway woods gave opportunities for such landmarks not only to be seen but to have a view themselves. Dezallier d'Argenville explained that 'the Ends and Extremities of a Park are beautified with Pavil-

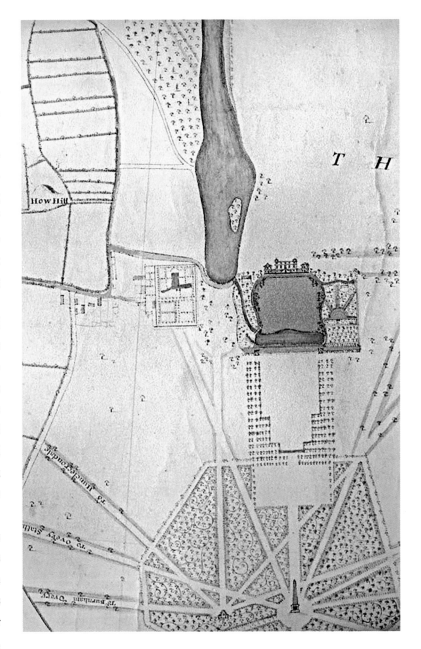

273 Detail from *Holkham in the County of Norfolk, the seat of the R^t Honble Thos Earl of Leicester*, 1754–9, an example of an estate survey of the mid-eighteenth century illustrating earlier formal parkland planting. Vistos were cut through the woods from the obelisk and temple (some of the objects in view can be seen named to the west). South of the house a lawn drops to a pool; at either end are pavilions by Kent. Beyond, a grove steps in to frame the principal visto.

ions of Masonry, which the French call Belvederes, or Pavilions of Aurora . . . always built upon some Eminence, they open and command the country round about'.[41] An English example would be the Belvedere, later known as the Bellmount Tower, consisting of a room raised aloft above a high arch, two miles across the park at Belton, at the termination of the eastern avenue. It was shown on a bird's-eye view by Thomas Badeslade published in 1739, and it was to have a view itself, as well as serving riding parties.

At Castle Howard in 1723 Vanbrugh, Hawksmoor and Lord Carlisle were debating an appropriate form of building at the end of the eastern green walk. Hawksmoor proposed a rusticated and domed belvedere 'After yᵉ Antique. Vide Herodotus Pliny, and M: Varo', but Vanbrugh objected to the idea of a belvedere, arguing that the location in question was not a hilltop: 'the Name of Belvedere is generally given to some high Tower . . . But this Building I fancy wou'd more naturally take the Name of Temple which the Situation is likewise very proper for.'[42] This resulted in the Temple of Diana, later named after the Four Winds, on which construction started in 1726. In 1729 Kent designed what was to become the Temple of Ancient Virtue at Stowe, situated overlooking the small valley east of the church. The same year he was working on a temple for the highest point of the hill at Holkham, erected in 1730. This and the obelisk, mentioned above, provided the focal points for numerous vistos cut through woods that were aligned on local landmarks.

Colen Campbell was Aislabie's architect for a 'garden room' for Hall Barn in 1724, and, in the late 1720s, for a series of buildings placed on high places or halls in the gardens at Studley Royal. A Temple of Venus was situated in line with the Upper Canal, and high up on the western slopes a greenhouse, used mainly as a banqueting house (fig. 274), was built in 1727–32. Nearby was a rotunda called the Temple of Fame on a bluff overlooking the Long Canal. The Doric Temple, dedicated to Hercules and overlooking the Moon Ponds, was erected in 1728–33.

One of the most ambitious schemes of populating parks with Classical buildings was by Ambrose Phillips, of Garendon, Leicestershire, between 1734 and 1737. He had made studies of antiquities and architecture in Rome in 1730, and afterwards ornamented

274 *A View of the Banqueting House and Round Temple at Studley*, one of a set of four engraved views of Studley Royal by Anthony Walker, 1758. Colen Campbell designed several of the buildings of between 1727 and 1733 that adorn the woodland setting of the canals. High up on the western slopes was the Greenhouse, finished off as a Banqueting House with a coffin-shaped lawn in front (as seen here). The nearby rotunda, called the Temple of Fame, stood on a bluff overlooking the lower canal. These structures are contemporary with the balustrade and fishing houses on the dam, the Rustic Bridge above the upper canal and the Doric Temple, offset from the lower canal and dedicated to Hercules. The amphitheatric works at the Doric Temple and by the upper canal may be of the early 1730s, as may be the Moon and Crescent Ponds, completing a remarkable scene of formal elements fitted comfortably into the wild and irregular valley of the River Skell.

(Facing page) 275 Plan of Garendon Hall, Leicestershire, by an estate surveyor, 1777 (north is to top right). Having made studies of Roman architecture in Italy in 1730, Ambrose Phillips designed a new house and garden with a cross-canal serving as its southern boundary; the eastern elm avenue terminated at an 80-foot-high obelisk. Phillips also ornamented the park with vistos and a number of Classical buildings of his own design (not shown). The eight-point star had a circular 'Temple of Venus' at its centre, and a triumphal arch formed a lodge between the park and Charnwood Forest at the point where the western ray met the park boundary; the south-eastern boundary of the park was planted with a winding *enfilade*. This was an early example of a park, rather than a garden, being embellished by buildings.

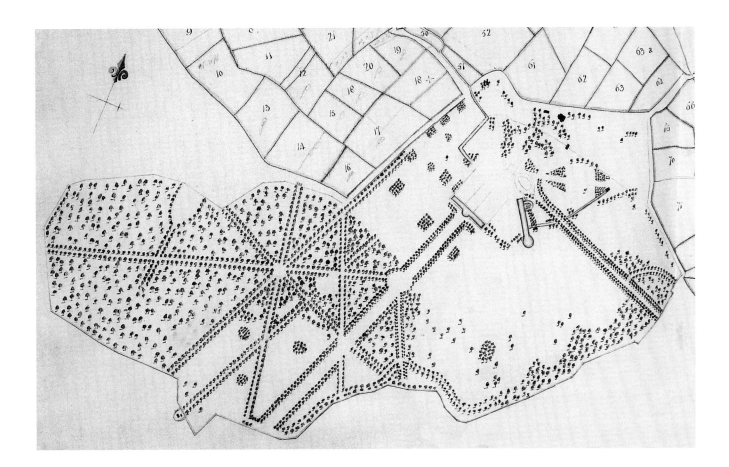

his park with large plantations with Classical buildings at focal points (fig. 275).[43] A double avenue ran south from the house to an 80-foot-high obelisk on a hill. It was set in a *rond point* within dense woods, from which one visto ran to the Temple of Venus, the centre of an eight-point star, and another ran to a triumphal arch based on the Arch of Titus at Rome.

More or less contemporary with Garendon was the collection of buildings in the landscape at Castle Hill, eventually even more diverse. In the early 1730s a domed temple was planned for the summit of the hill behind the house (see fig. 247), though when built this was altered to a 'Gothic Castle'. This was followed by a pyramid, a rotunda, a Classical seat, a Spa Bath House, a Chinese Temple, a Sybil's Cave, a Satyr's Temple, a Hermitage and cascades.

As can be seen from the names they were given, temples and other ornamental buildings in outward plantations and parks, at first intended to invoke a general Antique air, were afterwards associated with Augustan virtues, such as ancient virtue or filial piety, and then given proper nouns, such as the Fane of Diana or Temple of Bacchus, from Classical or other myth to suggest imaginary histories. Those who were slow to join this game of fancy could be wrong-footed. Mrs Delany reported to Jonathan Swift in 1733 that 'Alfred's Hall' in the woods at Cirencester, actually built in 1727, 'is now a venerable castle and has been taken by an antiquarian for one of King Arthur's'![44]

PARK PLANTATIONS

Even when there were no belvederes or towers, great vistas could be formed by imaginative planting arrangements. The conventional star arrangement was still employed in the new parkland at Stainborough in the late 1720s (see fig. 260). One of the largest

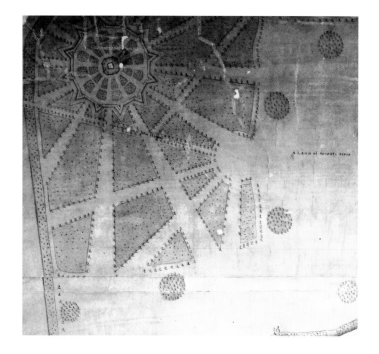

276　Detail from a large plan for the park at Foremark Hall, Derbyshire, *c.*1738 (north is at the bottom). The owner, Sir Robert Burdett, had come of age in 1737 and was sheriff in 1738, providing a likely date for this plan. The Temple of View was one of the ideas that suggest the influence of Batty Langley (see fig. 277).

277　'An Elegant, Large, Open Large Cabinet, or Lawn, in a Thicket on yᵉ Top of a Hill, with a Temple of View in its Center'. This design from Langley's *New Principles of Gardening* (1728) attests to the continuing popularity of stars of vistos.

star systems was in Viscount Lymington's plantations in Hurstbourne Park, Hampshire, centred upon a pavilion perhaps by Thomas Archer. The star formation was particularly popular where the centre could be placed on the summit of a hill (fig. 276). Langley illustrated the idea, including a 'Temple of View' on a summit (fig. 277). At Rokeby in the 1730s Sir Thomas Robinson planned a temple on a hill beyond the park wall, to be the focus of broad radial vistas through a plantation (see fig. 283), similar to Bridgeman's ideas for radial vistas within the park at Brocket Hall.

However, there were alternative forms of planting. There was the gargantuan ride, following the example of Lord Bathurst's rides in Cirencester Park. He widened the Broad Avenue, aligned on Cirencester church steeple, about 1728, much to the disgust of Pope, who objected to the necessary felling. This avenue was surpassed by the Grand Avenue cut through Savernake Forest for nearly four miles from Tottenham Park (fig. 278). The system of rides at Silverstone, Northamptonshire, was cut through heathland as an extension of Stowe from the 1730s.

Great lawns began to be formed once more behind the house, or even far off in the park, by plantations. For Wolterton in about 1724 Bridgeman devised a double ring of trees to convert the ground falling from the garden's fossee down to the lake as an oval lawn. Langley gave illustrations of circular, square and triangular 'Lawns, or Openings . . . into a Park, Forest, Common, &c.'[45] One was an 'oblong lawn', obviously inspired by the flat behind the Queen's House at Greenwich; perhaps Langley was unaware that this area had been intended as a parterre by Le Nostre.

278　An aerial view of Tottenham Park from the north-west by Pieter Andreas Rysbrack, 1753. The house was built to Lord Burlington's designs in 1721, and great changes were then made to the gardens and park. The older grassed visto to the south-west was answered by another to the north-east that passed over a ha-ha garden boundary. An avenue with embedded platoons was planted on axis, whilst the quadruple Marlborough Walk, on the line of a Roman road, seen to the east, was opened up through Savernake Forest. Tottenham Coppice, either side of the Great Walk, was cut through with walks, one serpentine, and a banqueting house was built about 1730 in a circular room at the top of the slope. Wings were added to the lodge in 1737, and this seems to have been accompanied by the lawn, flanked by urns on pedestals, behind it. The octagon, seen at the edge of the painting, was erected in another circle in 1743.

A View of the West Front of the Hall at Kelmarsh. The Seat of [coat of arms] in the County of NORTHAMPTON. WILLIAM HANBURY Esqr.

J. Mynde sculp.

A plan of an unknown place by Bridgeman shows a lawn encircled by platoons,[46] and a plan for the park at Brocket in about 1734 shows a less regular lawn with new planting defining a vast hippodrome shape.[47] Switzer devised a 'grand lawn' 1,340 feet wide and 2,100 feet long for Nostel Priory in 1735, but away from the house (see fig. 270). Lord Petre's scheme of 1737 for Worksop included

279 *A View of the West Front of the Hall at Kelmarsh . . .* engraved by James Mynde. Although published in 1791, this must be based on a much earlier image, perhaps of *c.*1740. This front, built in 1728–37 for William Hanbury, was designed by Gibbs. The lawn, flanked by groves stepping down to the widened River Ise (an arrangement reminiscent of Marble Hill), shows that owners of middling country houses had quickly absorbed the taste for garden lawns without a parterre.

a lawn within a platooned starburst at the end of the canal. So during the 1720s and 1730s the number of platoons planted to define vistas and great lawns increased greatly. Miller observed of the new fashion that 'they have lately introduced a more magnificent Method of planting Avenues; which is to plant the Trees in Clumps, or Platoons, making the Opening much wider than before, and so place the Clumps of Trees at about three hundred Feet Distance from each other'.[48]

Several owners formed 'parades' in front of their houses, designed for the assembly of hunting parties. If sufficiently large, they could reach the dimensions of a great lawn. At Wimpole in 1721 Bridgeman and possibly Gibbs formed a 'Grand Parade' stepped in at both ends. At the same time, Bridgeman devised a toy-scale 'Parade' in front of Down Hall (see fig. 237). The intended approach to the Duke of Richmond's hunting seat at

Goodwood was to have been along a double avenue to a rectangular parade. At Atherton Hall, Lancashire, there was another large rectangular parade enclosed by groves and paired kitchen gardens, out of which led a broad and long dummy avenue. However, the largest parades were those devised by Lord Petre in the 1730s. For his own home at Thorndon Hall the plan was for a lawn approaching 100 acres enclosed by lines of trees before the house.

Stepped planting, like side-screens in a theatre, could provide a stage set to show off the house (fig. 279). Rocque's map of Richmond Gardens even referred to a level, stepped arrangement of planting there as the 'amphitheatre' (see fig. 211). The first occasion for this device's use appears to have been at Eastbury, where four steps framed the mansion as seen from the axial approach . A late example was Bridgeman's design for the plantations converging on the park front at Badminton, coordinated with a pair of obelisks and domed temples by Gibbs (fig. 280).

In fact, these theatrical devices were equally commonly arranged to be seen from the house, drawing attention to some garden structure. At Kedleston, three sets of ramps and platforms of diminishing size, flanked by stepped groves, rose up a hill in front of the house to an obelisk crowning the slope. Ston Easton was given a similar arrangement in the late 1720s (fig. 281), and so was Holkham at a larger scale, with its groves stepping in to Kent's obelisk as seen from the house. Bridgeman's plan for Lodge Park of about 1729 showed platoons on the rising ground beyond

the stream stepping in to a terminal point (fig. 282). He devised some stepped-in groves for Boughton about 1730 for the rising slope beyond the garden, whilst at Rokeby Park the plantations were to frame the temple on the hill outside the park (fig. 283). Bridgeman's last idea for theatrical planting was on a hillside up to a proposed octagon temple at Amesbury.

Some park planting designs displayed great complexity. Langley gave two hypothetical plans for parks showing networks of single, double and triple avenues so that the observer 'in every of its Parts [is] entertain'd with different Views, open Plains, Groves, Thickets, open and private Fish Ponds, and in brief every Thing that's pleasant' (fig. 284).[49] There were few actual designs like that, but Lord Petre's layouts of the 1730s for Thorndon Hall and Gisburn showed the parks criss-crossed by immensely varied forms of avenue, using combinations of lines, platoons, clumps and mounts.

---

280   An ink and wash drawing inscribed 'Bridgman's Design for Badminton', attributed to John Wootton, c.1733. In 1733 Gibbs proposed replacing the house's lanthorn with a pediment, and building low transverse wings terminated by pavilions on the north front. This was co-ordinated with ideas from Bridgeman, resulting in a pair of obelisks and domed temples by Gibbs that controlled the expanding stepped groves. The Duchess of Beaufort wrote that 'The draught Bridgeman sent down for Badminton is one of the Grandest things I have seen, and will I believe answer in the execution as well as it does upon paper.'

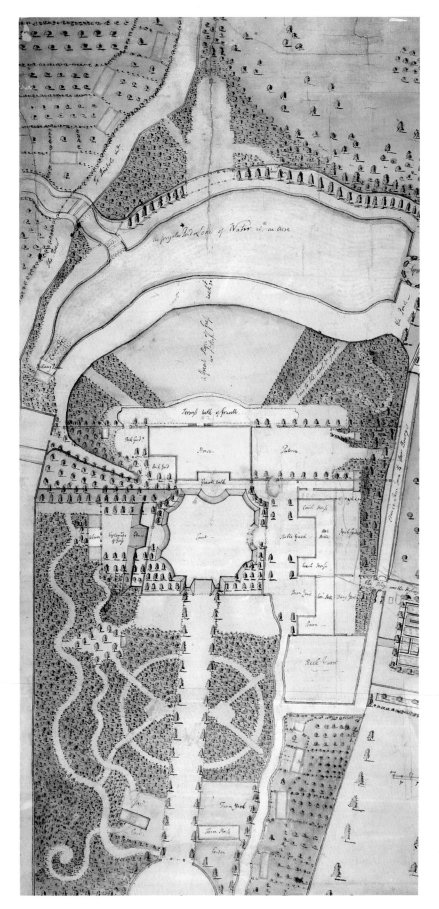

Clumps mostly followed early examples in being placed to emphasise knolls. By the time that Castle Howard was mapped in 1727 it had a scatter of 'plumps' over the south-east parkland (see fig. 197). Tring had a few clumps in its newly made parkland, clearly shown on knolls on a map of 1719. Other examples situated on knolls include Bridgeman's ideas for Lodge Park in 1729; Newburgh Priory, Yorkshire, very soon after; Danbury, Essex, in about 1735; Lord Petre's ideas for two clumps at Gisburn of the same year; and Leeds Castle, Kent.

The other reason for clumps was to encourage game. This was seen on Campbell's plan for Goodwood of about 1724, which shows some at the centres of fields. Clumps were similarly placed in the embellishment of Richmond Gardens in the late 1720s (see fig. 211). Switzer's plan for Nostell Priory dated 1735 shows some symmetrically placed clumps, but also 'a cornfield planted for the benefit of game', with three square clumps set within it (see fig. 270).

The old form of belt was a single row of trees planted just within the park pale, deemed sufficient to soften the line of the paling or park wall. Such rows, but partly multiple, appeared soon after 1716 at Claremont (see fig. 227). The new park at Tring was given a single row, and so was that at Shardeloes (see fig. 121). Goodwood was designed about 1724 to have a single row, widening in places to two, and Petre's plan for Gisburn showed a single row varied by additional planting in places (see fig. 266). Caversham was to have triple rows alongside a highway (see fig. 204).

Bridgeman's plan for the parkland at Eastbury started a new variation on the belt. There would be dense planting at the park pale, though the single row would be retained on the inside of this planting. Further examples, almost all by Bridgeman, were at Wolterton about 1724, Richmond Gardens a few years later,

281 Detail of an estate survey of Ston Easton House, Somerset, c.1740. The owner, John Hippisley-Coxe, planned formal gardens, probably when he married in 1739, but made no attempt to regularise the old millpool; beyond was an amphitheatric arrangement of trees closing the visto.

282 General plan for plantations in a park, identified by the author as Lodge Park, Gloucestershire, c.1729 (north is to the right). Almost certainly by Bridgeman, this shows a great avenue westwards from the lodge, a serpentine lake taking the shape of the valley, an arrangement of platoons on axis stepping in to some terminal structure, and paddocks enclosed by belts; a network of rides seems also to have been contemplated. Bridgeman's ideas were largely implemented.

283 *The Geometrical Plan of the Park and Plantations of Rookby, in the County of York,* engraved by Peter Fourdrinier, 1741 (north is to the right). At Rokeby, plantations defined a lawn stepping in to an obelisk, with a star plantation with a temple beyond. Great care was taken to plan the network of vistos, which are faintly indicated; the park is given privacy by dense belts. The kitchen garden was located on productive soil, out of sight.

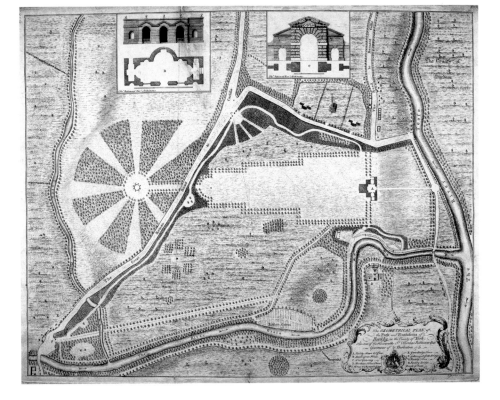

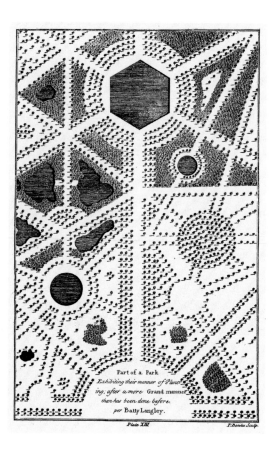

284 'Part of a Park Exhibiting their Manner of Planting after a more Grand Manner than has been done Before', engraved by T. Bowles for Langley's *New Principles of Gardening* (1728). Park design could display great complexity in the late 1720s and the 1730s. Here Langley gives a hypothetical plan showing networks of single, double and triple avenues so that the observer 'in every of its Parts [is] entertain'd with *different Views, open Plains, Groves, Thickets, open* and *private Fish Ponds*'.

Lodge Park in 1729, and Lumley Castle about 1730. At Brocket, Bridgeman intended a thick belt along the highway, and Switzer's plan for Nostell Priory of 1735 showed a belt, with an inner row of trees, of varying thickness in order to reduce the lawn inside to a regular shape.

Extensive woodland plantations, much deeper than mere belts, sometimes followed emparkment. The main work on forestry was still Evelyn's *Sylva*, which had a fifth edition in 1729. The planta-

tions at Cirencester have been mentioned above. Colen Campbell wrote that the 'Plan of the Park' at Goodwood

for the Variety of Extension of Prospect, spacious Lawns, Sweetness of Herbage, delicate Venison, excellent Fruit, thriving Plantations, lofty and awful Trees, is inferior to none. The great Improvements Mr Carné has made in this delightful Place, will be lasting Monuments of his Art and Industry, and Carné's Oaks shall never be forgot. This Park has an easy Descent to the East, South and South-West, with the Prospect of a rich and beautiful Landskip, bounded by the Sea for 30 Miles in Sight.[50]

A much more extensive scheme was afoot from 1728 at Chatsworth, where the second Duke of Devonshire began a process of providing a setting for the house at the scale of the whole valley (fig. 285).[51] Field boundaries in the meadowland and on the rising slopes facing the house were being removed in the late 1720s in order to create a park-like feel, though a painting by Peter Tillemans showed that the area was chiefly for horses, not deer. The 'new scotch fir wilderness' areas from the 1690s were considered to be too close to the house and some were grubbed out. Then the skylines both above the house and across the valley were planted up with tens of thousands of trees, predominantly firs. Small circular clumps detached from the main body of planting were installed in about 1730.

LAKES AND BRIDGES

Canals had generally been dug straight and often along axes. At Cholmondeley a canal was dug outside the garden enclosure, down a dummy avenue. At Easton Neston there was one down the visto, continuing the axis across the fields. Aislabie formed his canals and cascades at Studley Royal, where for several years from 1718, with at times 100 men at work, the Long Canal was formed. It was held by a masonry dam discharging by a *buffet d'eau* cascade into the roughly circular lake below.

Lord Bathurst had a mostly straight-sided canal dug at Richings in the 1710s, but this terminated in a curved section.[52] From the

late 1720s a number of serpentine canals and lakes were created, seemingly for their 'rural' associations, in the same way that walks were being serpentined. Nicholas Dubois' elaborate scheme for serpentine canals at Audley End was of the late 1720s. At Longleat House the canal through the parterre was serpentined gently, and a dam was raised so that the canal in the field above could be enlarged and supply a cascade, finished in 1736 (fig. 286). The finished edges were, again, gentle serpentines formed by Thomas Greening, amongst other undertakers.[53] West Wycombe, Buckinghamshire, likewise had a serpentine through its garden, and another was dug between the pond and lake at Holkham.

285   *A South West View of Chatsworth* by Thomas Smith, 1743, engraved by François Vivares and published in 1744. This records the second Duke of Devonshire's achievements from 1728. In that year he put the parterre down to grass and carried out planting on a huge scale high up the hill above the house and on the skyline, guided by the scale of the landscape itself. In 1732 he was ready to open up the gardens by removing plantations and over the next few years felled thousands of trees, including 'stubbing up all the Fir trees in the Gardens', thereby removing the Scots pine wildernesses planted in 1695. A huge jet 90 feet high was installed in the canal in the 1730s, a predecessor to the Emperor Fountain of 1844.

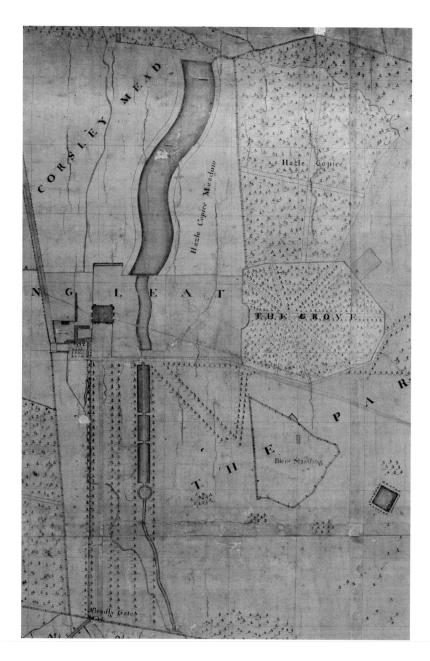

286 Detail of an estate map of Longleat House, surveyed by John Ladd, 1747. When the second Viscount Weymouth came of age in 1731 he inherited magnificent gardens in sad decay. They were cleared away for grass, and in 1736 walls were being demolished; the canal through the garden enclosure was made into a gentle serpentine in the rural manner, and a dam was thrown up to form a broader upper canal, with a cascade down the dam. A yacht was ready by 1737.

At Blenheim in the late 1710s Vanbrugh had plans for turning an old causeway to Woodstock Manor into the dam of a lake, which certainly would have been ornamental, and for a lower lake, both to be left with natural edges (see fig. 136). Perhaps the first bason actually made that might be aggrandised with the title of a lake was the seven-acre 'Great Bason' at Cannons, completed about 1721. As it filled a shallow valley with side-streams, even the great expense in regularising the sides could only result in an irregular polygon (see fig. 150).[54] More garden lakes were made, such as the eleven-acre lake at Stowe (see fig. 257). New lakes were floated partly or wholly into larger gardens and, as ornamentation extended into them, into parks, with less attention to regularisation than before. For example, the 30-acre monastic lake at Nostell Priory (see fig. 270) was tidied up only in places, and not given a regular perimeter. Some architects and owners did not care that their lakes lacked geometrical shape and were content that their outlines should be determined by the contours of the valley. William Freman of Hamels noted on his visit to Thoresby in 1724 that 'a grand cascade is now making opposite to the garden front, & a lake of 60 acres made by damming the river to raise the water for the cascade', although this natural-sided lake was seen primarily as a means to drive an engine for the cascade, rather than as an ornament in itself.[55] One of the largest lakes was the Serpentine in Kensington Gardens, made in 1726–32 by Charles Wither, the Surveyor-General of His Majesty's Woods and Forests, from a chain of six ponds (see fig. 210). About this time other substantial lakes were floated at Ditchley, Blickling, Holkham and Londesborough.

Some wanted to shape their water into naturalistically rather than geometrically serpentine outlines. Bridgeman planned a lake taking the serpentine shape of the valley through Lodge Park in 1729. At Euston there was 'a pretty rivulet cut in a winding and irregular manner with now and then a little lake etc.' of about 1729.[56] At Castle Howard in 1732 a visitor reported that 'they have already begun to make a Serpentine River that will wind along a beautiful Bottom, and lose it self in a Wood'. This was of naturally meandering form, not the rigid geometry of a true serpentine.[57]

Larger bodies of water introduced new scope for decoration. At Wanstead in the early 1720s a 'fortification', not unlike a coastal fort from the time of Henry VIII, was erected on an island surrounded by channels of the River Roding, though whether mock battles were conducted, as they were later at other places, is not recorded (fig. 287). Certainly, Lord Castlemaine enjoyed pleasure craft – for example, the gondola seen by Macky floating on his octagon pond.[58] Lord Cobham had several craft on the eleven-acre lake at Stowe by about 1730.[59] Lord Torrington, the former Admiral Byng, appropriately had a three-masted man-o'-war on his large octagon at Southill.[60] Serpentine rivers and the ends of lakes gave scope for primarily decorative bridges. The Rustic Bridge at Studley Royal was made in 1728.[61] Burlington, whose own bridge at Chiswick of about 1727 was 'Palladian', in other words of mathematical timber frame construction, designed another with a 60-foot span for Euston in 1729.[62] At Stowe in 1733 another wooden 'Palladian' bridge spanned the new 'Upper River'.[63]

RIDINGS AND *ENFILADES*

In order to appreciate the new buildings, plantings and lakes in one's park, it would be necessary to show them off by means of ridings or *enfilades*. Ridings were for enjoyment on horseback, and so could be turf, whilst *enfilades* were more specifically designed to take visitors to the best points of view, and if this was to be by chaise, would require a metalled surface. Switzer, who would have been aware of Queen Anne's chaise ridings, promoted the idea of the 'Ambit, Circuit or Tour of a Design, such as in large Designs can be done only on Horseback, or in a Chaise or Coach'. He remarked that the French called such a circuit an 'Anfilade'.[64] He thought this *enfilade* should be six or seven yards wide, and be 'carried over the tops of the highest Hills that lie within the Compass of any Nobleman's or Gentleman's Design', so that from some building or clump the whole design could be viewed.

An early *enfilade* was created at Tring by a series of short avenues jointed at small circles. By this means the track was taken up through the steep Park Wood on the far side of the park. This wood was cut through with sloping alleys which centred upon an obelisk by Gibbs. The track continued along the rim of the valley,

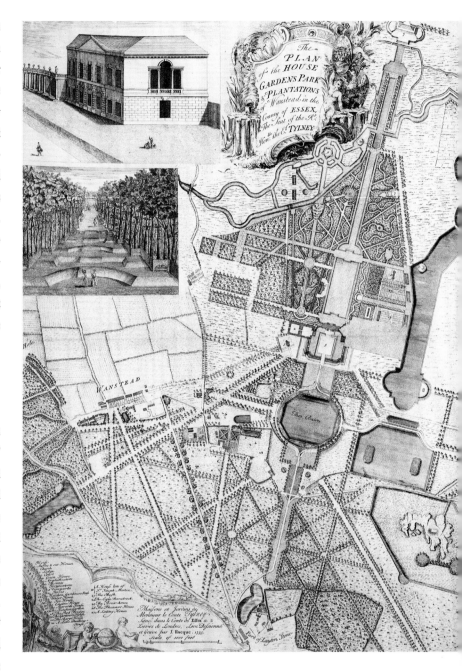

287   The eastern section of *The Plan of the House Gardens Park & Plantations of* WANSTEAD . . . by John Rocque, 1735 (north is to the left). Meandering paths were made through London's plantations in the early 1720s, and a fort built on an island; the elaborate parterre was laid to grass in the late 1720s. The Great Lake to the south continued westwards; another part of the plan shows an island shaped into a map of Britain.

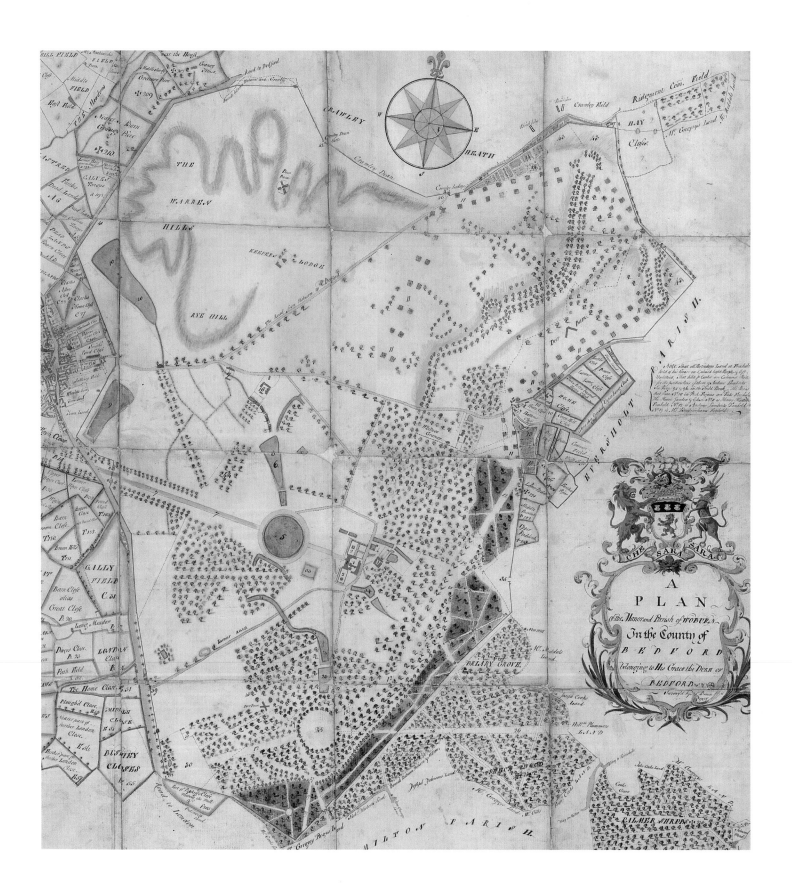

A
PLAN
of the Manor and Parish of WOBURN
In the County of
BEDFORD
Belonging to His Grace the Duke of
BEDFORD

and on the descent the expedient was taken of a winding section to link back to the parkland avenues below. In 1729 Bridgeman devised an *enfilade* for Lodge Park. He selected the break of slope between valley sides and fields above as the line for the *enfilade*, which thereby simultaneously enjoyed the prospect over the serpentine river and shelter from the plantations. About 1730, choosing a ridgeline again, he designed a bastioned *enfilade* overlooking the new garden at Lumley Castle that was to occupy the valley of a beck behind the castle (see fig. 244). It also ran along the belt surrounding the parkland beyond, and down to the castle, making a circuit suitable for ladies in chaises.

Switzer mentioned an *enfilade* around the perimeter of Richings, and showed it on his 'regulated epitome', suggesting that it was in place by the late 1720s. At Newburgh Priory about 1730 rides were incorporated into extensive woodland belts, one running down the edge of three hayfields, with a fossee inwards. At Rokeby a serpentine drive was set out around the park perimeter, planted with a great variety of trees. Bridgeman set out another *enfilade* at Woburn when he was brought in to dispose the 'Grand Park' in 1733; a serpentine line took the ridge north of the house, and the return was via a platooned avenue on lower ground (fig. 288). Lord Petre obviously thought the *enfilade* obligatory, and indicated tracks between the single-line belt and the park pale on the perimeters of his designs for Thorndon Hall in 1733 and Gisburn in 1735 (see fig. 266).

Considerable planting took place in the park at Houghton in 1717–18, and when Badeslade surveyed it in 1720 he showed that where avenues intersected the peripheral belt, rides had been left

---

288 Woburn Abbey as depicted in *A Plan of the Manor and Parish of Woburn* by Thomas Brown, 1738. The park has grown since 1661 with the incorporation of large areas to the north; the western approach was ornamented with a circular bason and a wider visto, probably by the third Duke of Bedford after he inherited in 1711 (compare fig. 40). The fourth Duke, who inherited in 1732, showed off the recent emparkments to the north by means of an *enfilade* ride along the curving crest of the hill, with a return gallop along a platooned ride.

within the belt so that riders could connect to other avenues.[65] An even greater scheme for rides was hatched towards the end of the 1720s. There was an intention to extend the park further to an enormous scale, for which Bridgeman prepared a new plan in 1728. Sir Thomas Robinson wrote in 1731:

> The enclosure of the Park contains seven hundred acres, very finely planted, and the ground laid out to the greatest advantage . . . Sir Robert and Bridgeman showed me the large design for the plantations in the country, which is the present undertaking; they are to be plumps and avenues to go round the Park pale, and to make straight and oblique lines of a mile or two in length, as the situation of the country admits of. This design will be about 12 miles in circumference, and nature has disposed of the country so as these plantations will have a very noble and fine effect; and at every angle there are to be obelisks, or some other building.[66]

Isaac Ware produced a 'Geometrical Plan' in 1735 showing these improvements, and from this it is clear that almost all the earlier planting was to be replaced, in favour of a much simpler, but vaster, scheme of dead straight peripheral rides, each over a mile long and flanked by very large platoons, giving views one way and then the other (fig. 289).

At Boughton House the rides came to break almost entirely free of parkland. It started about 1727, when the Duke of Montagu planted a ride to Geddington Chase, and cut that wood into a star. Soon afterwards he consulted Bridgeman, who seems to have stimulated ideas for a network of avenues around the estate, linking up with Weekly Hall, Geddington Chase and Grafton Wood. Virtually the whole system was complete by 1737 (fig. 290). The total length of the avenues was 23 miles, and the rides within woodlands were almost as long.

In twenty years the English conception of the pleasure ground had expanded from the area within the garden walls to ornamented outward plantations, and then to entire demesnes or estates, in which garden, park and even the wider landscape formed one ornamental whole. It was an astonishing shift in form and scale, a revolution in the setting of the country house.

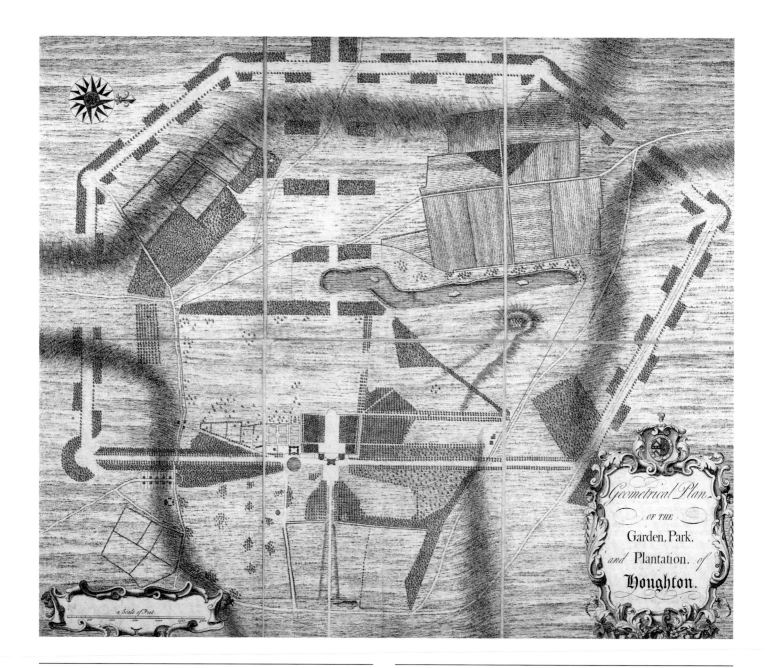

289 'Geometrical Plan of the Garden, Park, and Plantation of Houghton, from Plans, Elevations, and Sections . . . of Houghton in Norfolk' by Isaac Ware (1735). This shows Bridgeman's megalomaniac scheme, which was being implemented in 1731. An outer circuit of gallops along higher ground had alternating blocks of planting either side; to the east (bottom) can be seen Sir Robert Walpole's intended cutting, which would have opened a visto that way, but was left unfinished in 1742.

(Facing page) 290 The rides at Boughton House as depicted in *A Map of the Hundreds of Huxlow, Polbrook & Navisford* by William and J. Ballard (1737). Bridgeman's proposals to the second Duke of Montagu of about 1730 stimulated ideas for a network of rides around the whole estate, linking up with Weekly Hall, Geddington Chase and Grafton Wood. The rides within Geddington Chase were surveyed in 1735, and virtually the whole system was complete for this map; the total length of avenue was 23 miles, and the rides within woodlands covered almost the same distance.

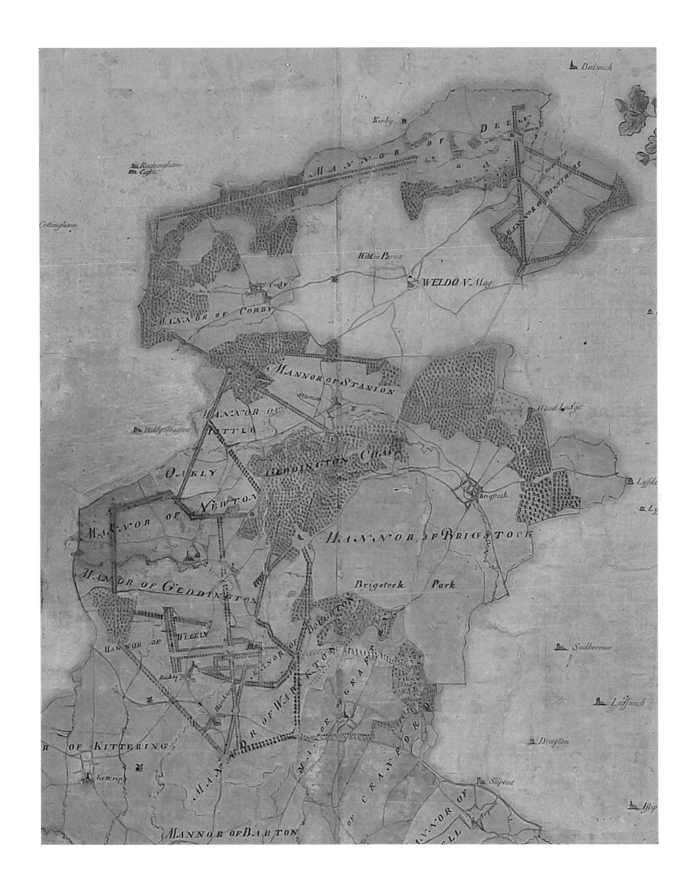

Postscript

Lost but Rediscovered

In 1757 Joseph Spence identified the moment when the 'natural' taste of mid- to late Georgian times was created: 'Mr. Kent was the sole beginner of the national taste. At Kensington Garden (below Bayswater) and Chiswick – the latter, October 1733'.[1] Whether or not that precision was warranted, William Kent's way of gardening has often been seen as the opening act in the 'Natural Style'.

Kent adopted a 'rural' style of shrub planting topped by Scots pines as the setting for his rustic buildings – including the Hermitage in Richmond Gardens, the Queen's Temple in Kensington Gardens and the cascade at Chiswick House (see Chapter Seven). He created open lawns in front of each. Their edges were modified to become rural planting, including the formation of groves by removing hedges and thinning the dense planting behind. Irregular water was seen at Chiswick, Stowe and elsewhere. More buildings were added. The sharp corners and bastions were rubbed off ha-has. A naturalistic 'look' took shape. Larger areas of

Bridgeman-designed gardens, such as Claremont and Rousham, were given the treatment in the late 1730s. In the 1740s Kent was amongst those who gloried in the sensual swells and declivities of the park, enhancing them by planting and showing them off from chaise ridings.

All the elements of the more 'natural' garden had been initiated within generally regular gardens and parks, so Kent's success was not so much the single-handed invention of a new style as a response to the collective reimagining of the English landscape by Classically educated owners as Greek or Roman. The creation of hundreds of neo-classical parks was in full swing in the 1760s. Nevertheless, formal or regular gardens survived in several ways. Whether or not they had been erased on the ground, they very often left a substantial record in artistic, literary, archival, cartographic and archaeological terms. These are the materials of researchers and conservationists today, allowing them to imagine the topography and qualities of the places dressed in their former garb.

The aim of this chapter is to expand on this rediscovery of the gardens of the period, so that historians and archaeologists may find the oddities of late survivals less surprising, and will be able to see the survival of their research material in better context. It should no longer be necessary to question whether gardens such as these really existed.

Naturalism with formality: The case of Chiswick House

Lord Burlington claimed to be the introducer of what Philip Southcote thought was 'the fine natural taste in gardening'.[2] Yet the plan of Chiswick by John Rocque, published in 1736 (fig. 291), and later paintings and prints yield only glimpses of what was meant by this. A closer look shows that the changes to Chiswick (and also to Kensington, Stowe and Claremont) were confined to small areas, almost vignettes of rusticity, within much greater formal layouts.

Although Rocque's plan represents a snapshot in time, just as Kent's changes were beginning, it is also a record of the quick succession of alterations at Chiswick up till that point. The villa and forecourt occupied the space that had been the parlour garden west of the old house, whilst to the north there had been an ornamental fruit garden within walls, and through a gate could be seen a paddock, across which a treed walk had been planted. Burlington's first works in 1716 included the Pantheon ('D' on Rocques' plan), perhaps by James Gibbs, terminating the 'grande allée' that ran through the fruit garden, the gate in the wall and along the walk. Colen Campbell advised on the *bagnio* (F), designed by Burlington himself and built at the north-west corner of the paddock. The *allée* to it from the gate, and another to the other corner, formed an unequal-angled *patte d'oie*. That was followed by the replacement of the fruit garden by a quincunx, and the planting of the paddock as a wilderness for the *allées* to pass through.

Back from his second Grand Tour in 1719, Burlington made further changes inspired by Sir Andrew Fountaine. A 'rustic arch'

(E), modelled on the deer house at Narford, was built about 1720 at the extremity of the eastern arm of the *patte d'oie*. The eastern wall of the fruit garden was taken away and a ha-ha built a few feet away, and the area thus revealed became a deer paddock, reached via a 'deer house'. The north and west walls of the fruit garden were likewise taken down, exposing a western slope down to the brook, alongside which a pool was dug, and mounts thrown up from the spoil and planted. Hedges replaced the wall to the north. A similar sized pool was then made in the outward plantation between the brook and a temple (H).

The villa was built in 1726–7 and Burlington was anxious that the gardens should also be Roman in spirit. The forecourt to the south (A) was filled with cedars brought over from Sutton Court. The visto to the west (B) was flanked on one side by a miniaturised version of the *laberinto* at the Villa Ludovisi in Rome, and on the other by one of the planted mounts. Also in 1727 Burlington leased a field, Judd's Close, to the west. Beyond that he acquired the small estate of Sutton Court, including its park, deer and collection of orange trees, cedar trees and statuary. A canal (or 'river') was dug in 1728 along the irregular edge of Judd's Close, and a terrace formed against the public road from the spoil, with a small earthwork theatre looking up the river. The rest of the close was planted up as a high-hedged wilderness with tightly winding minor paths (see fig. 199). The older wilderness too was threaded through with paths winding through openings of various kinds, probably the inspiration of – or inspired by – Robert Castell's thoughts on Roman villa gardens.

In the wilderness a bason was dug with concentric terraces for setting out in the summer, and an obelisk placed at the centre. An Ionic temple with a portico (K) like that at Narford was erected to oversee the scene. After a few more years Burlington decided to bring the orange trees over. Architectural hedges with pilasters and a green curtain, as shown in the second edition of John James's *Theory and Practice of Gardening* (1728), were placed in the deer paddock, preparatory to a greenhouse for the winter. Statues of Hercules and a gladiator acquired from Sutton Court were moved here. In 1732 an obelisk was placed in a circle adjacent to a gate on the public road at the end of the terrace.

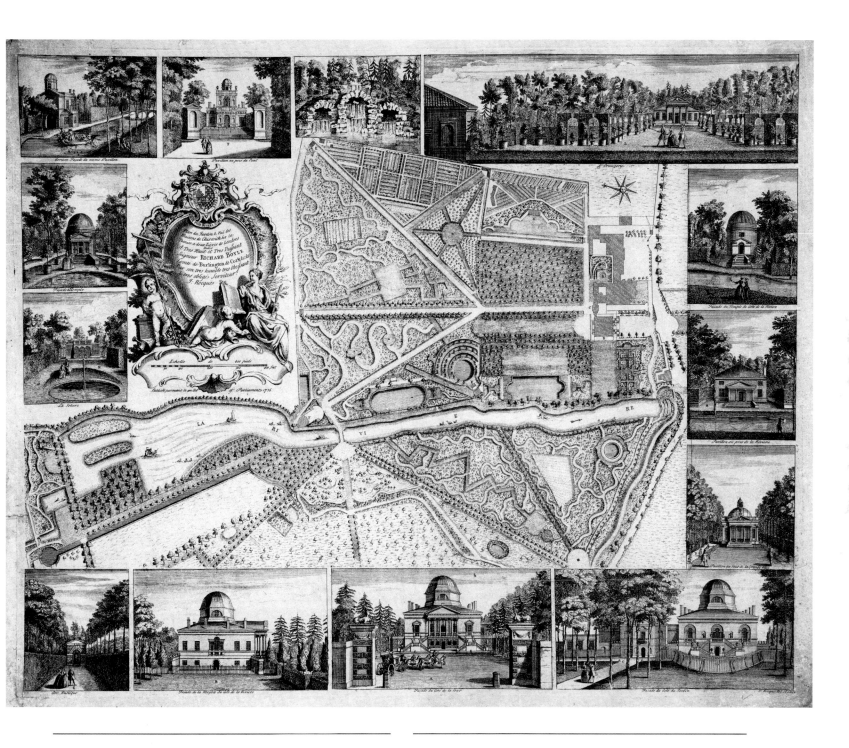

291 'Plan du Jardin & Vue des Maisons de Chiswick . . . ' by John Rocque, 1736 (north is to the left). The garden had undergone several phases of change by this date, not always well integrated with those before. Lord Burlington's earliest changes, the grove and the *patte d'oie* of about 1716, were still evident. The pools and many of the buildings followed his Grand Tour in 1719; the villa, the river, the orangery and the tightly twisting paths were from the late 1720s. The underplanting of hornbeam hedges with yew can be seen in the bottom left vignette.

292 *A View of the Garden of the Earl of Burlington, at Chiswick; Taken from the Top of the Flight of Steps Leading to yᵉ Grand Gallery in yᵉ back Front* by John Donowell, 1752. This visto had been cut through the grove north of the house in about 1734; the urns, cypresses and sphinxes, leading to some Roman worthies, gave it the conceit of a processional route to the abode of the dead.

This was the point at which the gardens were drawn by Rigaud and surveyed for the plan published a few years later by Rocque. By this time Kent was suggesting his changes. He envisioned a rustic cascade backed by rural planting to replace the small amphitheatre, and a rural treatment from it to the far end of the river. This would entail the removal of the *labirinto* and other hedgework to give open views down to the river. This work probably began over the winter of 1733–4.

Meanwhile, Burlington had developed a passion for garden statuary. He ordered terms for the forecourt in 1729, and started designing urns. He replaced the western part of the quincunx with a third visto from the villa, along which he lined out urns interspersed by sphinxes and trees. This led to a hemicycle in the wilderness hedge, where he displayed three earlier acquired Antique draped figures, other urns and stone seats (fig. 292). The lion and lioness by the hemicycle, and a boar and a wolf at the villa end, were carved in imitation of Antique originals in Rome.

The formality retained is of as much interest as the formality lost. The sloping lawn down to the river, free of hedges, and the cascade backed by rural planting, were together a prototype for the garden in the 'natural' taste, but at the same time, or perhaps a year or two later, the formal visto to the hemicycle was embellished. Furthermore, Burlington, though he lived till 1752, showed no desire to reconcile the forecourt, eastern part of the quincunx, pools, orangery or *patte d'oie* to Nature. One must conclude that he saw a mix of regular and rural areas as being the ideal, in line with his personal conception of ancient gardens. It was a few more years before Kent was to transform a whole scene, as at Claremont and Rousham, typically with naturalistic water bordered by lawns rising up swelling ground and shading into the edges of 'rural' groves.

In the period of uncertainty around 1740 a number of owners created gardens in the new taste, but set them in a predominantly geometric frame. Lord Petre's design for Worksop, dated 1737, was a mix of the park ornamentation of the late 1720s, taken to the ultimate possibilities of elaboration, with small garden areas after Kent's notion within the wilderness.[3] Other attempts were less convincing. A plan for Boringdon Hall, Devon, of about 1740 shows the park encircling the house, and a new wilderness enclosed within a rectangular fossee. Within this formal frame the design is highly laboured, with twisting meandering walks, 'rural groves' and other elements from a decade before, intermixed with buildings evidently inspired by those of the mid-1730s at Stowe.[4]

The last formal gardens

The tide of fashion was flowing towards the 'natural' way in the mid-eighteenth century, although it would be a mistake to imagine that there had been an overnight conversion of the gardens of England and Wales to the new style. The formal tradition continued, especially in parks, into the 1740s. It also continued in Ireland and far to the west in Virginia and Carolina. Geometric design faded, but only by degrees.

Spending on English gardens in the century covered here, between the 1630s and the 1730s, had been ruinously high. It is not to be expected that an owner, having invested so heavily in demonstrating his status, should wish to alter his gardens at the first whiff of a new fashion. The hesitant, piecemeal, advance in taste becomes clear at Blenheim, Longleat, Lowther and scores of other élite places. Much of the firm information on 'regular' gardens comes from estate surveys of the mid-eighteenth century, made in time to capture formal elements before they were expunged or irregularised. Usually, it was those who succeeded to estates, and who had no particular loyalty to another generation's taste, that were in the vanguard of change.

Meanwhile, Bridgeman carried on designing until his death in 1738, and Switzer provided designs for Rhual Hall, Flintshire, in 1735, Nostell Priory in 1735, and Beaumanor, Leicestershire, in 1737. A formal design of extraordinary boldness that would not have disgraced Bridgeman was provided for Weald Hall, Essex, in 1738 (fig. 294). Suburban gardens, such as Stamp Brooksbank's at Hackney House, north from London, funded from his banking career, continued in a contracted Bridgeman manner through the 1730s (fig. 293). Certain grander owners, such as the Duke of Montagu at Boughton and George Bowes at Gibside, continued to form regular layouts into the 1740s, and Thomas Knowlton was still setting out platoons at Aldby Park in 1746.

Hence, formal designs were being made into the 1740s, and some surprisingly archaic if isolated ideas cropped up thereafter. In the 1760s avenues were being eradicated or 'broken' in large

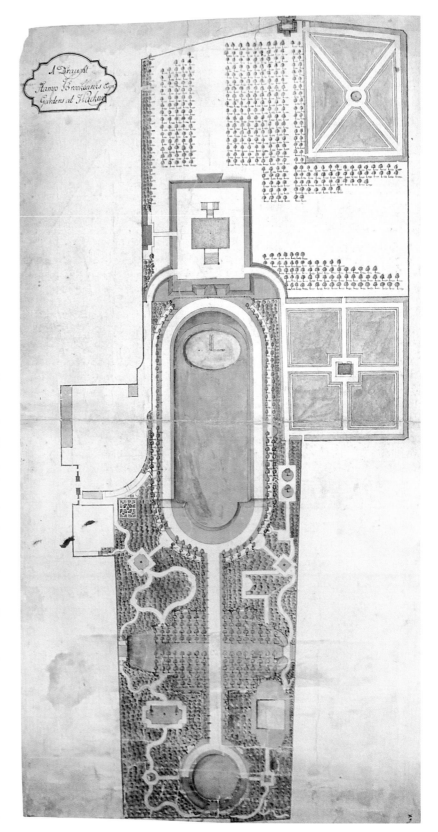

293 Brooksbank's gardens at Hackney, c.1735. Stamp Brooksbank rose to be a Whig MP in 1727, a Director of the Bank of England in 1730, and a Governor in 1742–3. His villa, designed by Colen Campbell, was built in 1727–32; it stood in an estate of eighteen acres, surrounded by a wall. The small but fashionable layout provided a lawn, groves, meandering walks and kitchen gardens within a constrained plot; the view east over the Lea valley was framed by stepping-out groves.

345

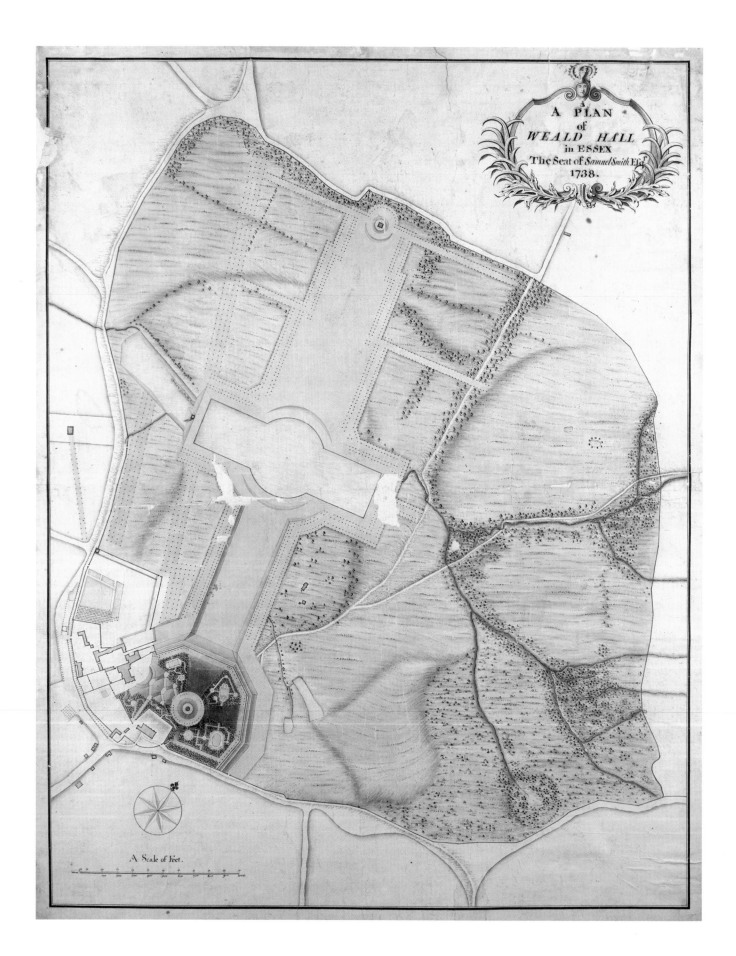

A PLAN
of
WEALD HALL
in ESSEX
The Seat of Samuel Smith Esq.
1738.

A Scale of Feet.

numbers according to the dictates of the natural taste. At this time Earl Temple, whose endeavours at Stowe were bringing the gardens to a new acme of naturalism, had refaced the house's garden front and in 1767 built the Corinthian Arch on the crest of the hill opposite, through which house and landscape would first be seen by the visitor. In order to bring visitors to the arch he planted a double avenue from Buckingham a mile and a half distant, terminating it with a *demi-lune*, slightly larger than that which the first Duke of Buckingham had once planted at New Hall. This Grand Avenue at Stowe may appear to have been an astonishing anachronism, but one is reminded that the 'Natural Style' was a conceit at a time when formal design remained the familiar. Tourists of the 1750s and 1760s would happily visit layouts of the 1720s or earlier alongside the new genre exemplified by Painshill, Piercefield, Monmouthshire, and Hackfall, Yorkshire.

SCOTLAND AND IRELAND

Although connections between garden-making in England and Scotland were strong, the latter had its own tradition with its own designers, and is best treated as a separate subject.[5] Certainly, the Scots were in no way behind in the craft of gardening, and many Scots gardeners were tempted south to gain relatively lucrative positions, much to the irritation of Switzer, who growled about 'Northern lads'.

In the seventeenth century the political climate of Ireland was unsettled, and great houses on the scale of those in England were infrequent, and uncomfortably often sacked or burned. Although the Earl of Ormonde, for example, was from a family long-established in Ireland, many Irish peers were English by recent descent, having been rewarded with lands and titles for services rendered. When improving the gardens at Lisburn from the 1650s for Viscount Conway, George Rawdon turned terraced slopes into walled terraces with *perron* stairs, as one might expect of an Englishman familiar with the gardens of the previous half century.[6]

The Restoration in 1660, and the relatively settled condition of Ireland thereafter, allowed several Irish landowners to think of garden-making to emulate their English counterparts. The Earl of Ormonde, newly elevated to a dukedom after exile with Charles II, set about improvements to Kilkenny Castle, perhaps more inspired by Continental gardens than English ones. On the other hand, James II's most ardent supporter in Ireland, the Earl of Tyrconnel, laid out the gardens at Carton House, County Kildare, around 1685 in the manner then current in England, with a set of walled gardens within a great rectangle, filled by a *parterre à l'Angloise* under the house, wilderness beyond and fruit gardens to the sides. The motte at Antrim Castle, County Antrim, was cut with a spiral walk like that at Warwick Castle.

Kilruddery House, County Wicklow, was laid out within a great rectangle too. Around 1690 the Earl of Meath, of English descent and a supporter of William III, filled the central vista with a lengthy water parterre and then continued it over a small baskethandle and up a hill in the park by a double lime avenue. The side gardens included an open grove, an oval bowling green within planted spandrels, a quincunx, a cherry garden and a kitchen garden. Though usually thought to be 'French', Kilruddery was no more French than several English gardens of the time, though the water parterre was certainly unusual. The strongly Protestant Viscount Massereene set out a wilderness at Antrim Castle about 1715 similar to contemporary ones in England. Its several curiously contrived vistos were cut through the planting on alignment with interesting objects outside, such as the castle's round tower, a church spire and a chapel. Mrs Delaney noticed the hedges in 1758, remarking that: 'The garden

---

294 *A Plan of Weald Hall in Essex, the seat of Samuel Smith Esq'*, 1738. Despite the title, Smith had died in 1732. Although sometimes attributed to Sieur Bourguignon, this plan has more in common with Bridgeman's designs. A hillock by the house was shaped into a huge octagonal mount with some facets being grassed vistos, others planted with labyrinth walks and cabinets; the facet above the house was shaped into an amphitheatre. North from the mount was a broad avenue down to a large cross-canal with central bason and stepped groves up to an eyecatcher building. In the 1740s a Gothic belvedere was built on the mount.

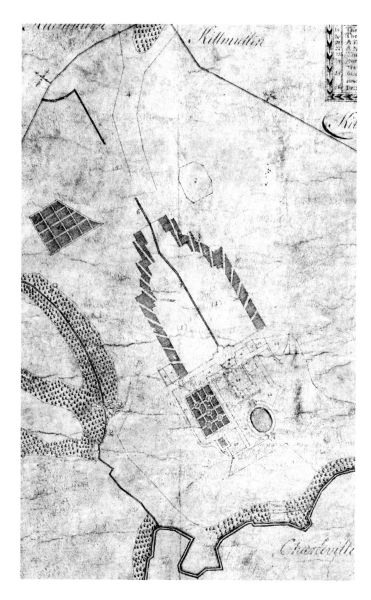

was reckoned a fine one forty years ago – high hedges and long narrow walks.[17] An oval bason fed a canal on two levels running down one of the alleys.

In the mid-1720s a large flat lawn was created on the garden front of Castletown House, County Kildare, and surrounded by plantations with rooms linked by meandering walks. The vistas cutting through this plantation were reminiscent (though on a grander scale) of those published by Batty Langley at this time. A magnificent parade was formed at Powerscourt, County Wicklow, in the mid-1730s by plantations cut through by diagonal vistos, and these plantations stepped theatrically inwards towards an intended staircase cascade on axis. Also at Powerscourt the hillside south of the house lent itself to being shaped as a vast amphitheatre of slopes down to an oval pond, such as would have made Bridgeman envious (fig. 295). In 1741 a newspaper reported that Richard Wingfield, first Viscount Powerscourt, was 'remarkable for employing great Numbers of Labourers, from his unbounded Charity, feeds 150 poor People every day'. Also in the 1730s Sir Edward O'Brien was setting out a huge and complex layout at Dromoland Castle, County Clare, somewhat similar to the designs of Lord Petre.

AMERICA

The awe and wonder of the gardens of the English political and economic élite reverberated in the faraway American colonies, though political and economic conditions were markedly different from those of the home countries and also varied from north to south. The low concentration of high-status gardens in the northern colonies such as Massachusetts and Pennsylvania prior to 1740 is probably because of the different social status, ambitions and activities of the settlers. There may have been significant gardens that have disappeared with inadequate record, as seems quite likely in Jamaica, Antigua and other colonies in the West Indies, but the evidence is awaited.

Seldom did a titled person condescend to make the tiresome journey across the ocean to visit what had the reputation of being a wilderness, but if they did it was usually to represent the

295 The central section of *A Map of the Demesne Land . . . of Powerscourt*, County Wicklow, by Thomas Reading, 1740, showing the gardens started in about 1738. North from the house a rising lawn was enclosed by a belt that was stepped in to confine the grand central visto; diagonal vistos were inserted through this belt. A staircase cascade was planned on axis above the lawn, but never implemented. To the south was a terrace with a view of the Sugarloaf Mountain overlooking parterres with a walled kitchen garden on the west; the valley below the parterre was shaped into an amphitheatre on several levels, focusing on an oval pool on axis formed by damming the valley to its south.

Crown as a governor. Such men naturally sought something like the gardens they had left behind at home. So too did plantation owners in Virginia and Carolina. They were in America chiefly to seek profit from rice and other crops supplied to the trade between Bristol and the West Indies, and they were often English minor gentry or younger sons who knew from home about the importance of visible signs of status.

Sir William Berkeley, Governor of Virginia 1641–52 and 1660–77, erected a considerable house at Green Spring, about five miles west of the future Williamsburg in the late 1640s, and afterwards set out gardens, including a bowling green. Like many early colonists he was perforce an eager and knowledgeable plantsman, and was reported to have '15 hundred fruit-trees, besides his Apricocks, Peaches, Mellicotons, Quinces, Wardens, and such like fruits'.[8] This quantity of trees would have occupied over ten acres alone, and it seems that the whole enclosed area at Green Spring was about 27 acres within a large square, with the central walk aligned with the house. It was an extensive if simple version of the planned enclosed rectangle, with a mix of differentiated areas, as seen in England in the Restoration period.

This form was particularly well suited to Virginia, a colony where gardens were vital for the basic necessities, and might need to be defended. Arthur Allen was a successful early settler, and was sufficiently well thought of to be made Speaker of the House of Burgesses of Virginia. His one-and-a-half-acre garden at Bacon's Castle of the 1680s was a rectangular enclosure, though with only the north side in brick, the others being palisaded with bay.[9] Here the enclosed area was essentially a kitchen garden. This general form continued at many places until the 1750s, in defiance of changing taste. At the Kingsmill plantation, perhaps in the 1730s, Colonel Lewis Burwell set out a two-and-a-half-acre palisaded garden on axis below the house, beginning with three terraces, down which were flights of Welsh granite steps, landing in the main garden, which was divided into four equal quarters by walks.[10] A cousin had a similar garden at Carter's Grove nearby, started in 1751.

Other Virginian plantation owners sought to keep abreast of taste back in England, and in about 1690 William Byrd I planted avenues three ways from his house at Westover. The College of William and Mary in Williamsburg was founded in 1693 with Bishop Compton being named on the charter as the first chancellor. The next year John Evelyn mentioned to a correspondent that arrangements had been made by George London, 'his Majs Gardner here', to have 'an ingenious Servant of his' sent to Virginia 'on purpose to make and plant the Garden, designed for the new Colledge, newly built'. A central walk led to the grand steps of the college building. Either side were borders with evergreens, then counter-walks and *parterres à l'Angloise* with *plates bandes* with more evergreens, probably alternating globes and obelisks.[11] The layout was reminiscent of Gray's Inn Walks, but planted in the 1690s way with evergreens rather than elm trees.

An even more determined attempt to create a fine-set garden was made by Alexander Spotswood, Lieutenant-Governor of Virginia 1710–22, as an expression of his status and power. He enclosed a park behind the Governor's Palace at Williamsburg and stocked it with deer. While still on good terms with the Council of Virginia, he persuaded it to pass an Act in 1710 to pay for a courtyard and garden.[12] Both were to be within four-foot-high brick walls topped with wooden palisades. The forecourt arrangement appears to have been a cross of flagged walks, with the cross-walk reaching to flanking offices, and grass plats in the quarters. The garden was under an acre but had summerhouses at the far corners. The body of the garden was divided into squares by alleys, and each square had lozenge shapes within. It appears to have been an open knot, a reduced version of, for example, that at Grimsthorpe, which may have dated from the 1630s (see fig. 50). In fact, the whole ensemble had a curiously old-fashioned look for the 1710s, but then Spotswood was a soldier and the son of a physician, perhaps not imbued with the latest fashions.

Spotswood laid out further garden areas in about 1717. Outside the west gate of the garden he set out kitchen garden areas and then a set of three terraces ('falling gardens') overlooking a canal. There was a 'bannio', or bathhouse, by 1719. In 1717 he was forming vistos flanked by trees south from the palace, which brought him into dispute with local notables, no doubt as concerned about his political ambition as his profligate spending.

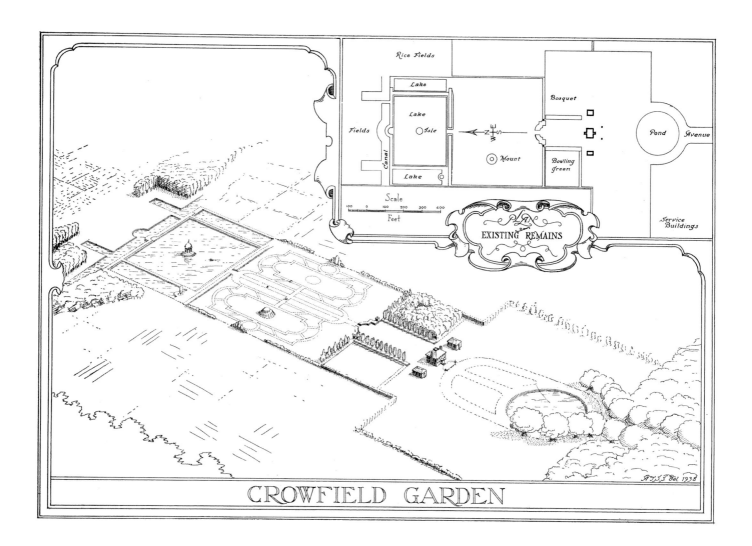

Within the illustration:
Rice Fields · Lake · Lake · Lake · Isle · Fields · Canal · Mount · Bosquet · Bowling Green · Pond · Avenue · Service Buildings · Scale · Feet · 100 · 0 · 100 · 200 · 300 · 400 · PLAN EXISTING REMAINS

CROWFIELD GARDEN

William Middleton, from the family at Crowfield Hall in Suffolk, was given land in South Carolina by his father in 1729, and there built a Carolinan Crowfield. It was approached by an avenue of live oaks (*Quercus virginiana*) which ended at a half-round

with a reflecting bason in front of the house. Behind the house was a flower parterre with low side terraces and a baskethandle end.[13] On one side was a bowling green and on the other a *bosquet*. Beyond were wildernesses, one having a mount at its centre. The main axis continued to a large square pond with a 'Roman' temple on an island. Outside this pond were canals (fig. 296).

A visitor, aware of the value of 'rural' delights, described the place in 1743:

as you draw nearer new beauties discover themselves, first the fruitful Vine mantleing up the wall loading with delicious Clusters; next a spacious bason in the midst of a large green presents itself as you enter the gate that leads to the house . . . From the

296   'Crowfield Hall, South Carolina' by Augustine Stoney, 1938. This drawing records the bones of a 1730s garden with a reflecting bason on the avenue, parterre, side terraces and baskethandle termination, with a sunken bowling green to one side, an arrangement of paths with a mount, formerly within an outward plantation, and, beyond, a large pool with a temple on an island. Its creator, William Middleton, had relied on his own or others' memories of gardens seen in England.

back door is a spacious walk a thousand feet long; each side of which nearest the house is a grass plat ennamiled in a Serpertine manner with flowers. Next to that on the right hand is what immediately struck my rural taste, a thicket of young tall live oaks . . . Opposite on the left hand is a large square boleing green sunk a little below the level of the rest of the garden with a walk quite round composed of a double row of fine large flowering Laurel and Catulpas which form both shade and beauty.

My letter will be of unreasonable length if I dont pass over the mounts, Wilderness, etc., and come to the bottom of this charming spott where is a large fish pond with a rising out of the middle – the top of which is level with the dwelling house and upon it is a roman temple. On each side of this are other large fish ponds properly disposed which form a fine prospect of water from the house.[14]

Apart from the temple, this sounds like a late George London design, but of course was twenty years too late to be so.

William Byrd II, of Westover, was in England from 1714 till 1726 with only a short break, and rebuilt his house in brick and altered his gardens not long after his return. John Bartram, the Philadelphian botanist and horticulturist, wrote in 1738 that Byrd had been 'very prodigalle . . . with new Gates, gravel Walks, hedges, and cedars finely twined and a little green house with two or three orange trees with fruit on them; in short he hath the finest seat in Virginia'.[15] Byrd had erected an iron palisade with fine iron gates at the entrance from the park outside. The piers were topped by eagles, no doubt taken from his presumed heraldic achievement. He also cleared out the old gardens between the house and river and laid them down to lawn interspersed by figures. A grove was planted to the side of the house, while a new garden was set out within planting. These gardens appear to reflect those that Byrd would have seen during his stay in England, including the innovation of the plain parterre.

Henry Middleton, younger brother of William, was educated in England in the 1730s, and in 1741 he acquired through marriage a plantation outside Charleston.[16] He renamed the house, situated on a bluff over the Ashley River, 'Middleton Place', and contrived a formal landscape around it (fig. 297). A wide carriage turn was made under the landward side of the house. Under the garden front was a great terrace that led to two side terraces enclosing a broad parterre divided into four by alleys and with a baskethandle end open to the river. Below it were five grass terraces taking the shape of the baskethandle and overlooking a half-moon of ponds divided by a central causeway. These earthworks, said to have been accomplished over ten years by slaves in the off-season from the rice crop, were described in 1791: 'much labour has been employ'd to distort nature, & to transform a very pleasing variety of Grounds into regular terraces adorn'd with straight Rows of Trees.'[17] Beyond the end of one garden terrace was a sunken octagonal garden, perhaps a bowling green, and to one side of the carriage sweep was a large enclosure, perhaps surrounded by a ditch and hedge, that probably contained a kitchen garden. At the western end a long bason was excavated, perhaps for water supply.

Henry Middleton appears to have had Bridgeman's great earthworks in mind when forming his own terracing. Like his brother William, and also William Byrd, he was not an experienced contriver of gardens himself, and did not have access to one, so had to fall back on memories and perhaps memorabilia gathered when in England. Such men would have admired the English gardens with an established reputation, and would not necessarily have been impressed by the newly fashionable. This produced two characteristics of their elaborate creations: first, their designs contained the elements one would have expected in England a decade or two previously, and second, they showed idiosyncrasies that doubtless derived from their own experiences and preferences.

Survival of geometric elements

In Britain, the élite families usually altered their gardens and parks in due course, so the grander formal gardens were recast by or during the 1760s. Humphry Repton was to write that of the hundreds of properties he had seen, only six retained flower gardens below the principal front. The antiquarian and then Arts and

Charleston Road

Legend

A. The Mount
B. The Great Oak
C. The Main Dwelling
D. The Tomb
E. The Kitchen
F. The Spring House
G. The Rice Mill

Scale of Feet

0   100   200

Plan Showing
Site of Garden
on River

Ashley River

Stable

Servants'
Quarters

Rice Fields

River

MIDDLETON
PLACE
IN SOUTH CAROLINA

A. T. S. Stoney
surv. & del.
1938.

Crafts fascination with older formal gardens identified a number of survivals at minor or secondary seats – Canons Ashby, Levens Hall, Melbourne Hall, Owlpen Manor and Snowshill Manor being amongst them. Modern surveys and archaeological field-work have revealed a surprising degree of further survivals of garden areas and elements, only occasionally of complete gardens, and more usually of formerly unidentified remains (such as walls and slopes), elements incorporated in later layouts, earthworks of abandoned gardens, and parterres that were grassed over.

Any survey of gardens in the mid-eighteenth century would have shown the predominance of regular gardens and extensive survival of geometric elements in parkland even after there had been a nod to the new 'natural' taste (fig. 298). Some owners were reluctant to fell their walled gardens, and were content to retain

(Facing page) 297 'Middleton Place, South Carolina' by Augustine Stoney, 1938 (north is to the right). The house, on a bluff above the Ashley River, was completed in 1741 by William Middleton's younger brother, Henry; below it was a great terrace and side terraces flanking a parterre with a baskethandle termination; below that, grandiose elaborate earthworks led down to pools, echoing English practice in the 1720s. The reservoir-cum-canal and gardens to the north could well have been a kitchen garden in the 1740s.

298 St Giles's House, Wimbourne, c.1760, by Thomas Vivares. Earthwork remains of Williamite side terraces remain under the south front despite the fourth Earl having made the river and the ha-ha. This engraving is a reminder that many incongruities would have been temporarily evident in mid-eighteenth-century gardens. Another version of the print shows the terraces erased.

299 Owlpen Manor, Gloucestershire, by the American architect Francis Adams Comstock, c.1924. The transparent gates between piers with ball finials are typical of the Restoration period, as are the wooden palisades to either side, although here they were surprisingly late, being paid for in 1723. Survival of such elements at small manor houses was a matter of chance and lack of money.

history. At the upper end of the social scale, Boughton House descended twice through heiresses to the dukes of Buccleuch, whose main residence was Drumlanrig in Scotland, and so escaped the hand of the improver. Governmental tight-fistedness could induce great inertia, as at Hampton Court, which substantially survived thanks to the maintenance contract system and despite all the scorn heaped upon it in the heyday of the English garden.

However, most of the survivals were of lesser houses that ceased in the eighteenth century to be the principal residences of a family. This was not uncommon when a male line died out and the property passed to daughters or cousins. As they would live elsewhere, the old houses might become dower houses or tenanted farmhouses. One must not forget younger sons and the once wealthy families that simply fell on hard times, and for survival became gentleman farmers who rubbed shoulders with the many wealthy yeoman farmers around them. Their houses might then remain in relative obscurity until they were rediscovered by antiquaries in the nineteenth century. Certain parts of England have many such places, for example the Cotswolds (fig. 299), and Wales has a particularly rich heritage of seventeenth-century gardens in various states of preservation.

old ones for fruit and vegetables, despite their interruption of views. Then there were many families whose circumstances did not permit them to convert their old-fashioned gardens to the new taste as speedily as they might have wished. Many had to live with what they inherited until an advantageous marriage, a government position, receipt of mining royalties or simply because they could bear being out of fashion no longer and were willing to sacrifice in other directions. The lower down the social scale, the more the avenue and fruit-walls lingered.[18] In many cases it took till the 1780s or later for gentry gardens to catch up with the taste of social superiors.

Then there were families who never had or never took the opportunity to make changes, so that their old-fashioned gardens avoided conversion to the new taste. Generally, the reasons for any such places retaining their formal layouts can be found in family

Revivals

An antiquarian interest in gardens began to make itself evident from the 1780s. It was accompanied by an aesthetic rediscovery of formality through the Picturesque, since an architectural foreground could provide a frame for the roughness and texture of the landscape in the middle ground. Hence Richard Payne Knight persuaded the Earl of Powis not to blow up the terraces at Powis Castle, as proposed by the improver William Emes, as a smooth green slope would have been a poor substitute for the terraces, with their massive balustrades, overgrown yews, and rampant ivy, as a foreground to the distant views of mountains. His fellow theorist of the Picturesque, Uvedale Price, did remove his old-fashioned terraces around his house at Foxley, probably during the 1770s, and came to regret it.

These thoughts led to historicism in gardens, both old and new. One of the first parterres actually to be made in the nineteenth century was that at Chiswick House by Lewis Kennedy, who used Alexandre Le Blond's flower-garden design as the centrepiece of a semicircular parterre outside the conservatory of 1814. The same plate had been used at Belton in the 1710s, and became, rather more loosely, the model for William Sawrey Gilpin's design for a parterre at Audley End in the 1830s. The Earl of Harrington and his gardener William Barron, in laying out new gardens at Elvaston Castle, Derbyshire, in the 1830s borrowed a plate from Daniel Marot's *Oeuvres* showing a tunnel arbour, a record of that at Het Loo. William Andrews Nesfield, who devised the most splendid High Victorian parterres of all, likewise borrowed heavily from historical sources.

This reliance on pattern books may have been acceptable when the effect was to be Italianate, but in fact the most intense interest in formal design in Victorian times came to be reserved for the gardens of the Elizabethan and Jacobean periods, as representing Englishness in a way that Continental Baroque could not. Nevertheless, because garden history was still a rather imprecise subject, garden architects embellishing gardens with what they thought represented the ancient style actually relied heavily on the architectural detail and clipped shrubs (increasingly referred to as 'topiary') of William III's reign. So topiary was added to Levens, and new mazes were created, usually modelled on the surviving one at Hampton Court, as at Castle Bromwich and Hatfield. Ancient clipped yews, as overgrown and grotesque as possible, seemed to be a proof of Antiquity – a quality that could not be bought. As an aside, the appearance of Antiquity can be misleading. Although the majority of older garden yews do date from 1690–1720, it has often become difficult today to distinguish them from those planted in the historicist and Arts and Crafts times, say 1830–1930.

The 1980s saw the start of a new fashion for topiary and formality. Since that decade, many familiar elements have been reintroduced into cutting-edge gardens. Knots and parterres have been seen again to the designs of Rosemary Verey, the dowager Marchioness of Salisbury, Sir Roy Strong and many others. The landscape architect Kim Wilkie has subtly introduced Bridgeman-inspired earthworks and ponds to several country-house gardens. A roaring cascade has been created at Alnwick Castle. Charles Jencks has become known for his modern take on amphitheatric earthworks at an increasing scale. Indeed, bold formal elements are often an innovatory aspect of contemporary gardens. And so the wheel comes round. The forms of regular gardens endure as a wellspring of inspiration for designers of the present and future generations.

Abbreviations

BL	British Library, London
BM P&D	Department of Prints and Drawings, British Museum, London
CCA	Canadian Center for Architecture, Montreal
CSP	Calendar of State Papers, Domestic Series, published by His Majesty's Stationery Office
GAC	Government Art Collection (UK)
MoL	Museum of London
MSGD	Bodleian Library, Oxford, Gough Drawings and Maps
NLW	National Library of Wales
NRS	National Records of Scotland
PL	Pepys Library, Magdalene College, Cambridge
RCHME	Royal Commission for the Historical Monuments of England
RCIN	Royal Collection (UK), Inventory Number
RIBA	Royal Institute of British Architects, London
RO	Record Office
TNA	The National Archives (UK), Kew
V&A	Victoria and Albert Museum, London
YCBA	Yale Center for British Art, New Haven, CT

Notes

PROLOGUE

1   Mark Laird, *The Formal Garden, Traditions of Art and Nature* (London: Thames and Hudson, 1992), 45.

2   *The World*, 12 April 1753.

3   *The World*, 3 April 1755.

4   David Jacques, 'Who Knows What a Dutch Garden Is?', *Garden History*, 30/2 (Autumn 2003), 114–30, at 125.

5   Walpole, 'On Modern Gardening', in Walpole, vol. 4, 247–316.

6   Barrington, 124.

7   Switzer 1715, 1–97.

8   Felton 1785.

9   Felton 1829, viii.

10   Repton 1803, 123.

11   Repton 1806, Part 1.

12   William Bray (ed.), *Memoirs, Illustrative of the Life and Writings of John Evelyn, Esq. F.R.S.... Comprising his Diary, a Selection of his Familiar Letters...* (two vols, London: Henry Colburn, 1818–19).

13   Loudon, 65–8.

14   Repton 1803, 123.

15   W. Carew Hazlitt, *Gleanings in Garden Literature* (London: Elliot Stock, 1887), 174.

16   Amherst, 205.

17   Blomfield, vi.

18   Ibid., 59.

19   Ibid., 167.

20   Triggs illustrated, *inter alia*, Brickwall, Canons Ashby, Hampton Court, Kingston House, Levens Hall, Melbourne Hall, Montacute House and Risley Hall.

21   Charles Holme (ed.), *The Gardens of England*, three vols (London: The Studio, 1907–11), vol. 1, includes Holme's own lengthy but derivative 'History of Garden-making'.

22   These are the first examples usually accepted by both the succeeding generation of commentators, such as Joseph Spence, and modern authors looking for unequivocal style change.

23   H. F. Clark, 'Eighteenth Century Elysiums: The Rôle of "Association" in the Landscape Movement', *Journal of the Warburg and Courtauld Institutes*, 6 (1943), 165–89, at 167.

24   Temple, 132.

25   Pevsner, 140–6.

26   H. Frank Clark, 'Lord Burlington's Bijou, or Sharawaggi at Chiswick', *Architectural Review*, 95 (May 1944), 125–9, at 125.

27   Pevsner, 144.

28   Hadfield, 179–94.

29   Hussey 1967, chapter three; also Robinson, 92.

30   Green, xi.

31   Hussey 1967, 13.

32   Vanbrugh's letters were published in 1928.

33   Willis 1977, 1.

34 William Alvis Brogden, 'Stephen Switzer: "La Grand Manier"', in Willis 1974, 21–30, at 21.

35 William Alvis Brogden, 'Stephen Switzer and Garden Design in Britain in the Early 18th Century', PhD thesis, University of Edinburgh, 1973.

36 John Phibbs, 'Projective Geometry', *Garden History*, 34/1 (Summer 2006), 1–21, at 3.

37 Caroline Dalton, *Sir John Vanbrugh and the Vitruvian Landscape* (Abingdon: Routledge, 2012), 52–7.

38 Myers, 21–2.

39 Samuel de Sorbière, *Relation d'un voyage en Angleterre: où sont touchées plusieurs choses, qui regardent l'estat des sciences, & de la religion, & autres matieres curieuses* (Paris: Thomas Jolly, 1664) and Béat Louis de Muralt, *Letters Describing the Character and Customs of the English and French Nations...* (London: Thomas Edlin, 1726).

40 *Diary of a Tour in 1732 Through Parts of England, Wales, Ireland and Scotland, Made by John Loveday and Now for the First Time Printed from a Manuscript in the Possession of his Great-Grandson John Edward Taylor Loveday* (Edinburgh: William Blackwood and Sons, 1890).

41 John Harris, '"Gardenesque": The Case of Charles Grevile's Garden at Gloucester', *Journal of Garden History*, 1/2 (April–June 1981), 167–78, at 167.

42 Travers Morgan Planning, *Royal Parks Historical Survey: Hampton Court and Bushy Park* (three vols and two boxes of plans), August 1982, produced for the Department of the Environment, by whom published in limited circulation, and carried out by the author in 1981 whilst at Travers Morgan; most of the other Royal Parks were surveyed by Land Use Consultants.

43 Thurley, 23–42 and 79–118.

44 Tom Williamson, 'Garden History and Systematic Survey', in John Dixon Hunt (ed.), *Garden History: Issues, Approaches, Methods*, Dumbarton Oaks Colloquium on the History of Landscape Architecture, 13 (1989), 59–78, at 60.

45 Ibid., 78.

46 John Adey Repton, letter concerning Oxnead Hall, in Britton, 98.

47 Christopher Taylor, 'The Place of Analytical Fieldwork in Garden Archaeology', *Journal of Garden History*, 17/1 (January–March 1997), 18–25, note 5.

48 RCHME 1975 was the first of a 5-volume series completed in 1985.

49 Pattison, for example.

50 David Jacques, 'Garden Archaeology and Restoration', *Transactions of the Association for Studies in the Conservation of Historic Buildings*, 16 (1993), 13–23.

51 Thurley, 79–118.

52 Walpole, vol. 4, 53; Blomfield, 1.

53 Woodbridge, 9.

54 Walpole, vol. 4, 53.

55 Harris 1986, 8–9: Harris wryly pointed out that the garden style for the two decades prior to 1735 has been termed Rococo, Elysiums, natural, irregular, informal, early landscape, formal landscape, transitional, poetic, proto-romantic, proto-picturesque, emblematic, Addisonian, Popeian and enlightenment.

56 Williamson, 33 et seq.

57 Conan 1999; Conan 2005.

58 Conan 1999, 77–90.

59 Harwood et al., 91–4.

60 Charles Quest-Ritson, *The English Garden: A Social History* (London: Viking, 2003, 1).

61 Timothy Mowl, *Historic Gardens of Dorset* (Stroud: Tempus, 2003), 13–14.

I THE PHENOMENON OF FORMAL GARDENS

1 Jacques 1999, 36.

2 Wales, though a separate country, was politically within the territory of the English Crown, sending members of Parliament to Westminster, and 'England' is sometimes used in the text in the sense of 'England and Wales'.

3 Jacques and Rock, 217.

4 Wasson, 13 and 45.

5 London Metropolitan Archive, MS 28953: 'Copies of the Charter and Bylaws of the Worshipful Company of Gardeners'.

6 The 'CABAL' government was named after Charles's chief ministers in the late 1660s – Clifford, Arlington, Buckingham, Ashley-Cooper and Lauderdale.

7 Worsley, 75.

8 Temple, 117.

9 Switzer 1715, xxxvii.

10 Laurence, preface.

11 Campbell 1725, 10.

12 Jacques 1998, 5.

13 Macky, vol. 1, 24.

14 Aubrey 1898, under 'Philip Herbert, Earl of Pembroke'.

15 Speed, *Map of Staffordshire* (1610); Sir Simon Degge, 'enumeration of Parks about the time of the Civil War', printed in Sampson Erdeswicke, *A Survey of Staffordshire* (ed. Revd Thomas Harwood, London: J. B. Nichols and Son, 1844), xix–xxi; 'Map of Staffordshire' ('sculpt 1682'), in Plot 1686; Richard Wilkes, 'A View of Staffordshire' (1735) in Revd Stebbing Shaw, *The History and Antiquities of Staffordshire* (London: J. Nichols, 1801), following p. xxiv; William Yates, *A Map of the County of Stafford* (1775).

16 Roberts, plate 256 and p. 258; anon., 'A Review of the Great Park', 1662.

17 Willis 1977, plate 24; Charles Bridgeman's plan of 1709.

18 The measurement of Grade I and II* parks and gardens was carried out for internal purposes by English Heritage in 1992.

19 Cantor and Squires, 15.

20 Switzer 1718, vol. 3, xiv.

21 De Jong, 24.

22 Taigel and Williamson, 8.

23 Jacques 2001, 365.

24 O'Halloran, chapter four.

25 Evelyn 1955, 16 October 1671 and 10 September 1677.

26 Cook, xix.

27 Jacques 1995, 31.

28 Jacques 1999, 16–25.

29 Jill Francis, '"My little Gardine at Dassett Paled": Sir Thomas Temple and his Garden at Burton Dassett in Warwickshire, c.1630', *Garden History*, 41/1 (summer 2013), 21–30, at 21–3.

30 Camden, 247.

31 Ibid., 442.

32 Ibid., preface.

33 Harper, 13.

34 Defoe, vol. 1 (1724), Letter 1, 110.

35 Sally Jeffery, 'J. Gibson's "Short Account of Several Gardens near London" of 1691: A Note on the Author', *The London Gardener*, 12 (2007), 67–77, 68.

36 Peter Willis (ed.), *Furor hortensis: Essays on the History of the English Landscape Garden in Memory of H. F. Clark* (Edinburgh: Elysium Press, 1974), 31–40.

37 NRS, GD/112/21/77: personal account books kept by John, Lord Glenorchy.

38 Fougeroux, 105–42.

39 Evelyn 1955, for 22 January 1677/8.

40 John Harris and Gervase Jackson-Stops (eds), *Britannia Illustrata: Knyff and Kip* (Bungay: The Paradigm Press, 1984), 6–7.

41 Information from Simon Scott, of Boughton, who found the letter in the Wentworth Papers, BL Additional Manuscripts. See Scott 32 and 39–42.

42 Bailey, vii.

43 As Rigaud and Baron.

44 As Badeslade and Rocque.

2   PROFIT AND PLEASURE

1 Gervase Jackson-Stops, 'Cliveden, Buckinghamshire – II', *Country Life*, 3 March 1977, 498–501, at 500.

2 Patrick Little, 'Fashion at the Cromwellian Court', *The Court Historian*, 16/1 (June 2011), 25–42, at 26–7.

3 Goody, 190 and 204.

4 Ernest Law, *The History of Hampton Court Palace* (three vols, London: George Bell, 1885, 1888 and 1891), vol. 2, 30.

5 John Nickolls (ed.), *Original Letters and Papers of State Addressed to Oliver Cromwell* (London: Whiston, 1743), 115.

6 CSP Dom, Interregnum, vol. 15, 16 April 1651.

7 W. L. Sachse (ed.), *The Diurnal of Thomas Rugg 1659–1711*, Camden Third Series, vol. 91 (London: Royal Historical Society, 1961), 10–11.

8 Temple, 77–8.

9 Worlidge, 9, 43 and 50.

10 Evelyn 1955, for 27 August 1678.

11 Ibid., for 14 July 1675.

12 Mollet 1670, preface.

13 Evelyn 1664, 29.

14 Bacon, 271.

15 Parkinson, 458.

16 Gunther, 55.

17 Parkinson, 608.

18 Evelyn 1664, 21, 29 and 30.

19 Worlidge, 85–6.

20 Evelyn 1664, 66.

21 Worlidge, 1.

22 Percival, 168.

23 Evelyn 1955, for 14 August 1654.

24 Percival, 50, 86, 89 and 96.

25 Ibid., 136 and 151.

26 Gunther, 56 and 167.

27 Harris 1995, plate 10.

28 Karin Seeber, '"Ye making of ye Mount": Oxford New College's Mount Garden Revised', *Garden History* 40/1 (Summer 2012), 3–16, at 5–6.

29 D. Field, 'Field Survey of the Marlborough Mount', Field Survey Report AI/15/1999 (London: English Heritage, 1999), 5–6; the mound is in fact prehistoric in origin, like a smaller Silbury Hill.

30 Aubrey 1982, 682–4.

31 Fiennes, 24–5.

32 Ibid., 84–5.

33 Temple, 112–13.

34 Worlidge, 9 and 31.

35 Preface by 'Philocepos', i.e. John Evelyn, in John Rose, *The English Vineyard Vindicated* (London: John Crook, 1666).

36 Pepys, for 22 July 1666.

37 Jacques 1989, 50, 52.

38 Worlidge, 41.

39 Joseph Addison, *The Spectator*, no. 269, 8 January 1711/2.

40 TNA, WORK 5/1, fols 282r, 290r.

41 TNA, AO 1/2481/292.

42 Evelyn 1955, for 9 February 1665.

43 TNA, WORK 5/1, fol. 21r etc.

44 Ex inf. Jan Woudstra.

45 Dunbar, 226–7.

46 TNA, WORK 5/52, fols 275, 376 and 428v.

47 Staffordshire RO, Eccleshall Court Rolls, 1598–9.

48 John Stow, *A Survey of London* (two vols, London: John Windet, 1598), vol. 2, under 'Suburbs without the walls'.

49 Ibid., vol. 1, under 'Ealdgate Ward'.

50 Lawson, 58.

51 Jacques 1989, 49.

52 John Steane, 'The Grounds of Magdalen College 1480–1880', *Oxoniensia*, 63 (1998), 91–104, at 99.

53 'Spring Gardens', in *Survey of London*, vol. 20, *St Martin-in-the-Fields, pt III: Trafalgar Square and Neighbourhood* (London: London County Council, 1940), 58–65.

54 Evelyn 1955, for 10 May 1654.

55 David Coke and Alan Borg, *Vauxhall Gardens: A History* (New Haven, CT, and London: Yale University Press, 2011), Chapter One.

56 Revd Sir John Cullum, *The History and Antiquities of Hawsted, and Hardwick, in the County of Suffolk* (1784; 2nd edn, London: J. Nicholls, 1813), 140.

57 John Evelyn to Thomas Browne, 28 January 1657/8, in Geoffrey Keynes (ed.), *The Works of Sir Thomas Browne*, second edn (four vols, London: Faber and Faber, 1964), vol. 4, letter 178, p. 301.

58 Browne, *Garden of Cyrus*, note 4 to Chapter 5.

59 De Jong, 21.

60 Francis Bacon, Viscount St Albans, *New Atlantis*, appended to *Sylva Sylvarum* (London: William Rawley, 1627), 31–2.

61 Aubrey 1898, under 'William Harvey'.

62 Evelyn 1955, for 1 August 1655.

63 Aubrey 1718–19, 4, 163.

64 Pierre Gassendi, *The Mirrour of True Nobility and Gentility: Being the Life of the Renowned Nicolaus Claudius Fabricius Lord of Peiresk*, translated by William Rand (London: Humphrey Moseley, 1657), 'The Epistle Dedicatory'.

65 See John Evelyn to Thomas Browne, 28 January 1657/8 (op. cit., in note 57 above), where Evelyn lists 'Beaugensor' (Boisgency); for the connection with Jacques Boyceau, see Hazlehurst 1966, fig. 3.

66 Douglas Chambers, 'The Tomb in the Landscape: John Evelyn's Garden at Albury', *Journal of Garden History*, 1/1 (January–March 1981), 37–54, at 40 and 43.

67 Bacon, 269.

68 Browne, *Garden of Cyrus*, 'The Epistle Dedicatory'.

69 Hanmer, xviii.

70 Evelyn 1664, 64–6.

71 Ibid., 66.

72 Evelyn 1658, 'Epistle Dedicatory'.

73 Evelyn 1664, 58.

74 Hanmer, 130 and 135.

75 Worlidge, 80.

76 Peter Goodchild, 'John Smith's Paradise

and Theatre of Nature', *Garden History*, 24/1 (Summer 1996), 19–23, at 20; citing Smith, 20.

77 Ibid., 21; citing Smith, 191.

78 Ibid., 19–23.

79 Reid, 3.

80 Percival, 54, 116 and 151.

81 For example, Jan van der Groen, *Den Nederlandsen hovenier* (Amsterdam: de Wed: van Gysbert de Groot, 1669), and Jan Commelin, *Nederlantze Hesperides* (Amsterdam: Marcus Doornik, 1676).

82 Blith, third impression (1653), 153.

83 Ibid., 155–6.

84 Ibid., 153.

85 Evelyn 1664, 18 and 23.

86 Evelyn 1955, entries for 14 May 1656, 20 May 1656, 13 May 1657, 23 August 1660, etc.

87 Evelyn 1664, 3rd edn (1679), 239.

88 Rea, 3.

89 Sandra Nicholson, 'The Role and Use of Fruit in the 17th Century Garden', MA dissertation, Architectural Association, London, 2003.

90 Temple, 110.

91 Cook, 72 and 93.

92 Evelyn 1955, entries for 27 August 1678, 17 April 1680 and 28 March 1688.

93 Mollet 1670, 4.

3   ENGLISH GARDEN DESIGN

1 Parkinson, 3–4.

2 Rea, 1.

3 Worlidge, 20.

4 Jacques 2001, 367.

5 Rea, 2.

6 Evelyn 2001, 32.

7 David Jacques, 'The *compartiment* System in Tudor England', *Garden History*, 27/1 (Summer 1999), 32–53, at 33.

8 John Raymond, *An Itinerary Contayning a Voyage, Made through Italy, in the Yeare 1646, and 1647* (London: Humphrey Moseley, 1648), introduction.

9 Ray, as cited in Hunt, 30–2.

10 Evelyn 2001, 460.

11 Ibid., 194–5.

12 Evelyn 1955, for 21 July 1679.

13 Worlidge, 36–7 and 63.

14 Wren Society, vol. 7, plate XXV: Anon., Plan of Buckingham House and Grounds, c.1721.

15 Hunt, 145 and 155.

16 Aubrey 1898, under 'Sir John Danvers'.

17 Hunt, 126–30.

18 Vincenzo Scamozzi, *L'Idea dell'architettura universale* (Venice: published for the author, 1615), vol. 2, 356–60.

19 Evelyn 1955, for 25 August 1654.

20 Evelyn 1664, 3rd edn (1679), 'Advertisement'.

21 Bezemer Sellers, illustrations 9–15.

22 Gunther, 55.

23 Cook, 96–7.

24 Miller, article on 'Avenues'.

25 Evelyn 1664, 25.

26 The remains of these avenues can be seen today.

27 Krystyna Bilikowski, 'Historic Parks and Gardens', *Hampshire's Countryside Heritage*, No. 5 (Winchester: Hampshire County Council, 1983), 4: redrawing of a map of the estate by Isaac Justis, 1699; the earthworks remain today.

28 This is evident on the ground today.

29 Mollet 1670, 2.

30 Harris 1979, plate 47: Hendrik Danckerts, drawing of Badminton down the north avenue, c.1669.

31 Parkinson, 1.

32 Worlidge, 7.

33 Parkinson, 1.

34 Rea, 3.

35 Gunther, 45 and 55.

36 Parkinson, 1.

37 Evelyn 2001, 93.

38 Rea, 3.

39 Evelyn 1664, 6.

40 Worlidge, 8.

41 Parkinson, 3–4.

42 Evelyn 2001, 99–100.

43 Worlidge, 18.

44 Berkshire RO, D/Epb P 1: William Brudenell, *A Platt of the Mannor of Coulsill and Parish of Coulsill…*(1666).

45 Gunther, 167–83 and 305–8.

46 Rea, 3.

47 Magalotti, 250.

48 Royal Commission on the Historical Monuments of England, *Horseheath Hall, Cambridgeshire: An Earthwork Survey*.

49 Amherst, 329.

50 Parkinson, 4 and 5.

51 Rea, 'To the Reader'.

52 Peter Goodchild, 'John Rea's Gardens of Delight: Introduction and the Construction of the Flower Garden', *Garden History*, 9/2 (Autumn 1981), 99–109, at 105 and 109.

53 Hadfield, 103.

54 National Library of Wales, Tredegar MS 1077: Anon., *Plan of the Ancient Mansion and Gardens of Tredegar As They Were in the Early Half of the XVII century* (nineteenth-century tracing of c.1670 plan).

55 Harris 1979, plate 67a.

56 Knyff and Kip, plate 14.

57 Gunther, 178.

58 Mollet 1670, 9.

59 London and Wise 1706, vol. 2, 779.

60 Evelyn 2001, fol. 86.

61 Hunt, 126–9.

62 Leith-Ross, 95.

63 Jack D. Jones, *The Royal Prisoner* (London: Lutterworth Press, 1965), 74–5, 88, 91, 104 and 107.

64 Colvin, vol. 4, part 2 (1982), 269–70.

65 Hanmer, xviii.

66 Pepys, for 22 July 1666.

67 Temple, 114.

68 Balthasar de Monconys, *Journal de voyages de Monsieur de Monconys* (two vols, Lyons: Horace Boissat and George Remeus, 1665–6), vol. 2, 78.

69 James, 33.

70 Pepys, for 22 July 1666.

71 Rea, 1.

72 Worlidge, 19.

73 Mollet 1651, plates 25–8.

74 Parliamentary survey, 1649, printed in Amherst, 315–30.

75 Evelyn 2001, 147–8 and 313.

76 Prudence Leith-Ross, 'The Garden of John Evelyn at Deptford', *Garden History*, 25/2 (Winter 1997), 138–52, at 141.

77 Ogilby and Morgan.

78 Campbell 1717, plates 70–4: 'General Plan of Cliefden house'.

79 Mollet 1670, 1; this advice was new since the edition of 1651.

80 Gunther, 303.

81 Ibid., 45.

82　These remain and are identified by signs such as 'Grille des matelots' (at Versailles).

83　Dunbar, 226.

84　Harris 1995, plate 10: Johannes Vostermans (attrib.), *View from the South, c.*1675.

85　Cook, 196.

86　Harris 1979, plates 66a and 66b, 67 and 85.

87　Ibid., plate 68b.

88　Longstaffe-Gowan, 30–3.

4　KINGLY AMBITIONS

1　Hazlehurst 1966, 50–74.

2　Mollet 1670, 1.

3　Kenneth Woodbridge, 'The Picturesque Image of Richelieu's Gardens at Rueil', *Garden History*, 9/1 (Spring 1981), 1–22, at 9.

4　TNA, AO 1/2481/291.

5　Amherst, 315–27.

6　Hazlehurst 1980, 1, 19. Although Le Nostre's name is frequently modernised to 'Le Nôtre', I have adopted the form invariably used in his lifetime.

7　TNA, C 274/33, 30/25; TNA, C 274/34, 11; TNA, T 51/3, 318.

8　TNA, AO 1/2481/292.

9　TNA, WORK 5/1, fol. 400r.

10　Evelyn 1955, for 9 June 1662.

11　TNA, T 51/14, 225.

12　Laurence Pattacini, 'André Mollet, Royal Gardener in St James's Park', *Garden History*, 26/1 (Summer 1998), 3–18, Appendix, 17–18.

13　Mollet 1670, 11–12.

14　David Jacques, 'Garden Works in Greenwich Park, 1662–1728', *The Court Historian*, 11/2 (December 2006), 149–54, at 151.

15　Mrs Evelyn Cecil, Lady Rockley, *A History of Gardening in England* (London: John Murray, 1910; third edition of Alicia Amherst, *A History of Gardening in England*, London: Quaritch, 1895), 186.

16　TNA, T 51/10, fol. 137.

17　Hazlehurst 1980, plate 289.

18　Harris and Hunter, 117.

19　Evelyn 1955, for 21 August 1674.

20　TNA, AO 1/2/2479/274.

21　Wasson, 22–6.

22　Ibid., 89.

23　North 1981, 5–6.

24　Compare Mollet 1651, chapter 11, and Mollet 1670, 1.

25　Switzer 1715, 80.

26　Friedman, 177.

27　Worlidge, 3.

28　Cook, 190 and 242 and figs 17 and 47.

29　Ray, 228.

30　Worlidge, 71.

31　The 'fir tree' was the spruce from Norway, *Picea abies*, from which deal boards were made.

32　Worlidge, 17 and 76.

33　Ibid., 19.

34　Hyde, 148.

35　Evelyn 2001, 204.

36　Harris 1964, plate 31: 'Back front of Ewston & orangerie towards ye west'.

37　Dunbar, 226.

38　Harris 1979, plate 100.

39　Jan Woudstra, '"Much Better Contrived and Built Then Any Other in England": Stoves; and Other Structures for the Cultivation of Exotic Plants at Hampton Court Palace 1689–1702', in Michael Lee and Kenneth Helphand (eds), *Technology and the Garden*, Washington, D.C.: Dumbarton Oaks Colloquium, 35 (2011).

40　For Oatlands, see Leith-Ross, 96.

41　Cook, 241, and plate 47.

42　Evelyn 1955, for 14 July 1675.

43　Gibson, 185.

44　Chauncy 1700: John Drapentier, 'Aspeden Hall . . .'.

45　Harris 1979, plate 133: Jan Griffier the Elder (attrib.), *View of Sudbury Hall, c.*1682.

46　Mollet 1670, 13.

47　Hanmer, xix; with additions as seen in the original manuscript.

48　Fiennes, 342–3.

49　Cook, 117.

50　Ibid., 190.

51　Friedman, 177.

52　Plot 1677, 172.

53　Plot 1686, 41 and 381.

54　Fiennes, 228–30.

55　Ibid., 175.

56　James, 57, and plate 7.

57　Laurence, 'The Clergyman's Recreation', 23.

58　Jan Woudstra and James Hitchmough, '"The Enamelled Mead": History and Practice of Exotic Perennials Grown in Grassy Swards', *Landscape Research*, 25/1 (2000), 29–47, at 35.

59　Evelyn 1664, 114.

60　Mollet 1670, Preface.

61　Worlidge, A6.

62　Evelyn 1955, for 18 February 1677/8.

63　Information from Carmen Anon Feliu, who was involved in the restoration of the gardens at La Granja and Aranjuez.

64　Lamb and Bowe, 21.

65　Dickinson, 74.

66　TNA, E 351/3428.

67　TNA, AO 1/2481/292.

68　Jacques and Van der Horst, 64.

69　CSP Dom, Charles II, vol. 38, June 1661.

70　Ibid., vol. 147, 8 February 1666. Ent. Book 23, p. 16.

71　O'Halloran, chapter five.

72　Jacques 1989, 41–65.

73　Northamptonshire RO, Finch Hatton 2447.

74　Bedfordshire RO, X800: extracts from accounts prepared by Mark Antonie, 1706–20.

75　O'Halloran, chapter two.

76　Mark Laird, 'Sayes Court Revisited', in Harris and Hunter, 129.

77　Harvey 1974, 68.

78　Lamb and Bowe, 25.

79　TNA, AO 1/2481/291, 307 and 308.

80　Cumbria RO, Lonsdale MSS, Sir John Lowther, 'Memorable Observations', 1655.

81　TNA, AO 1/2481/292.

82　Harvey 1974, 46.

83　Ibid., 51.

84　CSP Dom, Interregnum, vol. 1, 24 May 1649.

85　Evelyn 1664, 'Epistle Dedicatory'.

86　Evelyn 1664, 3rd edn (1679), 'Epistle Dedicatory'.

87　Robinson, 42.

88　Temple, 130.

89　*The Statutes of the Realm*, 1225–1713, 12 vols, London: G. Eyre and A. Strahan, 1810–28: 3° James I, chap. 13, 'An Acte against unlawfull hunting and stealing of Dere and Connies'.

90　Ibid., 13° Carolus II, chap. 10.

91　These deer park licences can be found in the Patent Rolls, indexed in TNA, C 274/33 to 37.

92　*The Statutes of the Realm*, 1225–1713, 12 vols, London: G. Eyre and A. Strahan, 1810–28: 22° and 23° Carolus II, chap. 25 – 'An Act for the Better Preservation of the Game, and for Securing Warrens not Inclosed, and the Severall Fishings of this Realme'.

93 Ibid., 3° Gul. and Mar., chap. 10; 4° Gul. and Mar., chap. 23.

94 Todd Longstaffe-Gowan, 'Grimsthorpe Castle, Lincolnshire', *Country Life*, 21 May 1998, 50–5.

95 Evelyn 1664, 3rd edn (1679), 239.

96 Cook, 30 and 187.

97 Ibid., 186 and 189.

98 Ibid., 190.

99 Ibid., 196.

100 Evelyn 1664, 3rd edn (1679), 239.

101 George Sheeran, *Landscape Gardens in West Yorkshire 1680–1880* (Wakefield: Wakefield Historical Publications, 1990), 25.

102 Sir Thomas Elyot, *Dictionary of Syr T. Elyot Knyght* (London: Thomas Berthelet, 1538; reprinted 1545), extract from entry for 'Sal us' (*sic*).

103 Cook, 200.

104 Ibid., 197–8.

105 Ibid., 70–1.

106 Harris 1979, plate 47: Hendrik Danckerts, drawing of Badminton down the north avenue, *c.*1669.

107 Boughton House, Northamptonshire, Map #3; George Nunns, *surv*, and John Booth, *fecit*, 'A Map of the Mannors of Boughton, Warkton, Weekly, And part of Geddington... surveyed Anno 1714', 1715.

108 Oxford Museum: Thomas Pride, Map of the Cornbury estate, 1787.

109 TNA, WORK 34/32.

5 'RAYS FROM VERSAILLES'

1 Jacques 1999, 40.

2 North 1981, 81.

3 Harris 1982.

4 Harvey 1974, 54.

5 George Royle, 'Family Links between George London and John Rose: New Light on the "Pineapple Paintings"', *Garden History*, 23/2 (Winter 1995), 246–9, at 246.

6 E. C. Till, 'The Development of the Park and Gardens at Burghley', *Garden History*, 19/2 (Autumn 1991), 128–45, at 136.

7 Green, 10–11.

8 TNA, AO 1/2479/274.

9 Evelyn 1693, 'Advertisement'.

10 Hunt and De Jong 1988, cat. 103: George

London to Edward Mellish, 24 January 1692/3, including a plan for a parterre at Blyth Hall, Nottinghamshire.

11 Evelyn 1693, 'Advertisement'.

12 Gloucestershire RO, Blathwayt E236.

13 Sladen, 154.

14 Thompson, 206, for 29 September 1694.

15 Finch, vol. 1, after 112: William Cullingworth, 'Map of the House, Court and Gardens', 1783.

16 In the possession of John Harris.

17 Jeffery, 53 and plate 14.

18 Jacques and Van der Horst, 32.

19 Jan Woudstra, Colin Merrony and Michael Klemperer, 'The Great Parterre at Chatsworth: Refining Non-Invasive Archaeological Methods as Investigation Techniques', *Garden History*, 32/1 (Spring 2004), 49–67, at 63–5.

20 The maps dubbed the 'Wise collection' by Green are likely on stylistic grounds to be by Bridgeman.

21 TNA, T 1/67.14.

22 Switzer 1715, x and xxix–xxx.

23 Ibid., xxii.

24 Bodleian Library, Oxford, Bodl. MS. Eng. hist, c. 11, fols 19–20 (transcription by Helen Watt and Brynley Roberts).

25 Cheshire RO, Cholmondeley papers, DCH/A/242.

26 TNA, AO 1/2482/298.

27 Whistler, 90.

28 Batey and Lambert, 204–8.

29 TNA, Prob 11/674/104.

30 Wren Society, vol. 19 (1942), 61–82.

31 Green, 144–6.

32 Pattison, 56–64.

33 Annette Bagot, 'Monsieur Beaumont and Colonel Grahme. The Making of a Garden, 1689–1710', *Garden History*, 3/4 (Autumn 1975), 66–78, at 67.

34 Stonyhurst College, Lancashire, Archives.

35 Hunt, 98, quoting BL, Add. MS 61,479, fol. 173v.

36 Maximilien Misson, *A New Voyage to Italy: With a Description of the Chief Towns, Churches, Tombs, Libraries, Palaces, Statues and Antiquities of That Country* (two vols, London: R. Bently et al., 1695), vol. 2, 60–1; Letter XXVI.

37 Lucy Norton (ed.), *Saint-Simon at Versailles* (London: Hamish Hamilton, 1980), 59.

38 Ray: Tancred Robinson to John Ray, Paris 1683.

39 Switzer 1715, 39.

40 Hunt and De Jong, 29–30 and fig. 15.

41 Chesterfield, 35.

42 Mollet 1670, plate 11.

43 Fiennes, 172.

44 Chesterfield, 63.

45 'The History of the Park and Gardens', in Colson Stone Partnership, 'Boughton House: Survey and Restoration Management Plan', 1995.

46 Northamptonshire RO, Boughton MSS: Anon., 'An Acco^t of the Debts of the severall Cred^{rs} of the most Noble Ralph late Duke of Montagu (upon simple contract) proved by Comi^con [Commission] in the Country', 1712, fol. 190.

47 Laird and Harvey, 169–70. The original works consulted were Liger and Dezallier d'Argenville, third edn (1722).

48 Fiennes, 102.

49 Gibson, 186.

50 Temple, 126–7.

51 Jacques 1997, 28–9.

52 This term was frequently employed by Celia Fiennes.

53 Jacques 1997, 12–13.

54 Gervase Jackson-Stops, 'Wilderness to Pleasure Ground', *Country Life*, 26 June 1975, 1686–7, fig. 2: Anon, Survey of Petworth, 1706.

55 *Chirk Castle* (London: The National Trust, 1989), 40 and 42; Thomas Badeslade, 'The West Prospect of Chirk Castle' and 'The North-East Prospect of Chirk Castle', 1735.

56 *Powis Castle* (London: The National Trust, 1994), 42.

57 RCHME 1979, 75–7 and plate 26.

58 Gloucestershire RO, Blathwayt E236: Anon., Sketch for the terraces, *c.*1704.

59 Knyff and Kip, plate 7, 'Windsor Castle'.

60 Switzer 1718, vol. 2, 168.

61 James 1712, 119–21 and 126, and plates G and H.

62 Jacques 1989, 41–65.

63 Staffordshire RO, Bridgeman MSS, D1287/3/8c: John Bridgeman, Account book, 1716–19 and 1732–47.

64 Samuel Buck; *The south view of Drayton-House...*, 1729.

65 Fiennes, 228–30, 'My Great Journey to Newcastle and to Cornwall', 1698.

66 Fiennes, 57.

67 For Westbury, see Atkyns, plate opp. 798, and Johannes Kip, *Westbury Court*, engraving, c.1707. For Cannons, see Jacques 1998, 6.

68 Pierre Gauthier was the King's master locksmith in the naval dockyards of Marsailles.

69 Plot 1686, 359.

70 Evelyn 1955, for 20 August 1688.

71 Fiennes, 68–70.

72 TNA, AO 1/2482, fol. 298, under Jean Tijou.

73 TNA, WORK 6/5, fol. 94.

74 James, 77.

75 Ibid., 28 and plate 3.

76 This bastion remains.

77 Atkyns, plate opp. 430.

78 TNA, WORK 5/51, fol. 490, for 'Iron Work done for yᵉ Circle Wall next yᵉ Thames' by Tijou.

79 James, 25 and plate 1.

80 Percival, 85–6.

81 Bedfordshire RO, Lucas MSS: Peter Tillemans, set of nine watercolours of Wrest, c.1721–9.

82 TNA, T 1/126.21.

83 Temple, 118.

84 Atkyns, plate opp. 470.

85 James, 37 and plate 2B.

86 Laird and Harvey, and Thurley, 43–77.

87 Thurley, 56.

88 Worlidge, 71.

89 Evelyn 1664, fourth edn (1706), Book 2, 158.

90 TNA, WORK 5/52, fols 572 and 582.

91 London and Wise, vol. 2, endplate, 'Explanation of the Plan of M. *Tallard*'s Garden'.

92 Lablaude, 63–7.

93 The bulk of the information here and below comes from Gunnis.

94 Triggs, 13.

95 Jacques and Van der Horst, plate 7.9.

96 Jacques 1995, 28–9, 31 and 34.

97 Lablaude, 80, 91 and 93.

98 Hunt and De Jong 1988, plate 34a: C. Allard, 't Konings Huis van de Tuin–zijde, met de Fontein van Venus', c.1700.

99 Fiennes, 228–30.

100 Ibid., 97.

101 YCBA, B1978.43.13: Jan: Stevens, 'The South Prospect of Hampton Court in Herifordsheir Don by Mʳ Stevens', c.1705.

102 Samuel Buck, 'The South View of Drayton–House…', engraving, 1729.

103 North 1713, 33.

104 Bodleian Library, Oxford, MSGD, a3, fol. 4; William Gibson (attrib.), Survey of Spring Wood, c.1727.

105 Percival, 155–7.

106 Harris 1979, plate 254: Peter Tillemans, 'South Front of Newstead Abbey from the Park', c.1725.

107 Temple, 118.

108 James, 46.

109 Miller, article on 'Bosquet'.

110 Jacques and Van der Horst, 158–61.

111 James, 50.

112 Jan Woudstra, 'The Early Eighteenth Century Wilderness at Stainborough', in Patrick Eyres (ed.), 'The Georgian Landscape of Wentworth Castle', *New Arcadian Journal*, 57/8 (2005), 65–84, at 75.

113 Lysons, 497.

114 Aubrey 1847, 93.

115 Harris 1982, 44.

116 James, 35 and 38–9, and plate 6.

117 Woudstra 2003, 37–8.

118 Jacques and Van der Horst, plates 3.8 and 3.10.

119 Switzer 1718, vol. 1, 70.

120 Sloane, vol. 1, preface.

121 Switzer 1715, 54

122 Jacques and Van der Horst, 175.

123 Ibid., 177.

124 Thompson, vol. 1, 87, for 4 July 1688.

125 Evelyn 1955, for 6 August 1685.

126 Thompson, vol. 1, 148, for 26 April 1690.

127 Jacques and Van der Horst, 179–80.

128 Ibid., Chapter 10.

129 Finch, vol. 1, 113.

130 These are illustrated in the manuscript 'Hortus Regius Honselaersdicensis', Vatican Library, Rome.

131 TNA, WORK 5/53, fol. 292, Josiah Kemp, 'Potter', for March 1702/3.

132 Jan Woudstra, '"Striped Plants": The First Collections of Variegated Plants in Late Seventeenth-Century Gardens', *Garden History*, 34/1 (Summer 2006), 64–79, at 70.

133 Harvey 1972, 14–23

134 Switzer 1718, vol. 2, 149.

135 Langley 1728, plate IX.

136 Sladen, 152 and 154; Morton, 493.

137 Taigell and Williamson, 11 and 89.

138 Temple, 143.

139 Cook, 238–9.

140 Knyff and Kip 1707, plates 41 (Lowther) and 47 (Combe).

141 Thomas Langford, *Plain and Full Instructions to Raise all Sorts of Fruit-Trees that Prosper in England* (London: Richard Chiswel, 1681), 68.

142 Jacques and Van der Horst, 72.

143 TNA, C 274/37, 14.

144 TNA, AO 1/2482/298.

145 Tree positions as surveyed by Travers Morgan Planning in 1982 indicated that the semicircle, when planted in 1661, did not have the radials, and that they were inserted later, requiring adjustment to make good corners.

146 Woudstra 1997, 555.

147 Badeslade and Rocque, plate 4–5: John Rocque, 'Plan of yᵉ Royal Palace and Gardens of Hampton Court', 1736.

148 Matthews, 135.

149 Switzer 1718, vol. 2, 189.

150 Mollet 1651, plates 28 and 29.

151 London and Wise, vol. 2, 743, and plate XIV.

152 Jacques and Van der Horst, 165.

153 Ibid., plate 7.7.

154 Fiennes, 293.

155 TNA, AO 1/2482/298.

156 Gibson, 181–2.

157 Molyneux, 70.

158 Woudstra 1997, 553–63.

159 Charles Brooking, *A Map of the City and Suburbs of Dublin* (London: published for the author, 1728).

160 TNA, MPH 246: Anon, 'A Plan of Dawley', c.1714–22.

161 Bernard Jeannel, *Le Nôtre* (Paris: Fernand Hazan, 1985), 104.

162 National Museum, Stockholm, THC 7631: Carl Hårlemann, after Claude Desgots, unexected plan for the Maastricht Garden, c.1698.

163 TNA, TI/67.14.

164 TNA, AO1/2482/299.

165 Wren Society, vol. 19 (1942), 87.

166 BL, Add. MS 20,101, fol. 69.

167 TNA, T1/67.39.
168 TNA, WORK 5/51, fol. 548, and 5/52, fol. 574, under 'Henry Wise'.
169 TNA, WORK 6/2, fol. 125.
170 TNA, WORK 5/52, fols 449r and 586.
171 BL, Add. MS 20,101, fol. 69.
172 Thurley, 30–2.

6   QUEEN ANNE'S YEARS

1   Camden, dedication to Sir John Sommers.
2   Jacques and Rock, 224.
3   TNA, WORK 34/32: John Vanbrugh (attrib.), proposals for a parade and an approach across the wilderness, c.1712.
4   Vanbrugh, 19.
5   Switzer 1729, vol. 2, 411, and plate LV. 'Down Husband' was the colloquial name, to distinguish it from 'Up Husband', i.e. Hurstbourne Tarrant.
6   Green, 55–6.
7   John Bowack, The Antiquities of Middlesex; Being a Collection of the Several Church Monuments in that County: Also an Historical Account of Each Church and Parish . . . (two vols, London: S. Keble et al., 1705), vol. 1, 20.
8   Addison.
9   TNA, T1/107.3.
10 TNA, T1/126.21.
11 Green, 103.
12 Roberts, 538, note 70.
13 Bridgeman's earliest autographed plan for Blenheim is dated 1709.
14 Melbourne House archive.
15 Lucy Porten, '"All [I] Ever Wanted . . . [was] a Clean Sweet House and Garden, Though ever so Small." Sarah Churchill and the Gardens of Marlborough House', The London Gardener, 10 (2005), 65–78, at 71.
16 Switzer 1715, 84.
17 Jacques 1998.
18 TNA, PROB 11/538/234.
19 Powis Castle (London: The National Trust, 1994), 44.
20 Joseph Addison, The Spectator, no. 10, 12 March 1710/11.
21 Anthony Ashley Cooper, third Earl of Shaftesbury, 'A Letter Concerning the Art, or Science, of Design', 6 March 1711/12, in Characteristicks of Men, Manners, Opinions and Times, 5th edn (three vols, London: John Danby), vol. 3, 395–410, at 398, 400, 401 and 404.
22 Addison.
23 Joseph Addison, Remarks on Several Parts of Italy, Etc., In the Years 1701, 1702, 1703 (London: Jacob Tonson, 1705).
24 Addison.
25 Runar Strandberg, 'The French Formal Garden after Le Nostre', in Elisabeth MacDougall and F. Hamilton Hazlehurst (eds), The French Formal Garden, Dumbarton Oaks Colloquium 3 (1974), 41–67, at 65. Le Blond was 'Architect-General' in Russia from 1716.
26 James, 4.
27 Ibid., 'Dedication'.
28 Switzer 1715, viii, xii and xiii.
29 Switzer 1718, vol. 2, 136.
30 Ibid., vol. 3, 106.
31 James, plate 8C.
32 Woudstra 2003, fig. 3.
33 James, 'Dedication'.
34 Pepys, for 22 July 1666; Jacques and Van der Horst, 126.
35 Switzer 1718, vol. 1, 273–4.
36 Switzer 1715, 87.
37 Ibid., 85.
38 Langley 1728, 155.
39 Harper, 13.
40 James Elmes (ed.), Memoirs of the Life and Works of Sir Christopher Wren (London: Priestley & Weale, 1823), 'Appendix, Tract I', 119–20.
41 Cook, 186.
42 This dimension has been perpetuated by replanting and can be observed today.
43 Jacques 1998, 6–7.
44 TNA, WORK 32/312: Charles Bridgeman (attrib.), 'Kensington Gardens and Plantations with Hyde Park', c.1708.
45 TNA, T 1/179, fol. 35: Henry Wise, 'An Estimate of new Planting Severall Lines & Platons of Elms & Abeals, in . . . Bushy Park', c.1713; the arrangement was shown on subsequent maps.
46 Switzer 1715, 87.
47 Macky, vol. 2, 110–11.
48 Switzer 1718, vol. 2, before 115.
49 Ibid., vol. 2, 207.
50 Whistler, 78.
51 Ibid., 114–15.
52 The attribution of this bridge to Archer was by Mavis Batey, who had studied Heythrop in depth.
53 Edwards, 20–1; these palisades remain.
54 Switzer 1718, vol. 2, 141–4.
55 Ibid., vol. 2, 142.
56 Kerry Downes, 'The Kings Weston Book of Drawings', Architectural History, 10 (1967), 9–88.
57 Nicolaes Visscher (ed.), Labyrinte de Versailles / The Labyrinth of Versailles / Der Inn-gart zu Versailles / 't Dool-hof tot Versailles (Amsterdam: Nicholaus Visscher, 1682), following 81.
58 Switzer 1718, vol. 2, plate 34, fig. 4.
59 Liger's text on parterres, with the illustrations, was not printed in volume 2, but in volume 1, with Gentil's dialogue between gentleman and gardener.
60 Hazlehurst 1980, plate 261.
61 Woodbridge, fig. 186.
62 Hazlehurst 1980, plate 137.
63 Atkyns, plate opp. 476: Johannes Kip, 'Kingsweston', c.1707.
64 Switzer 1718, vol. 2, plate XXIX, fig. 1.
65 Ibid., vol. 2, 190.
66 Bradley 1731, 163.
67 James, plate 6B, figure 2.
68 Jacques and Van der Horst, plate 7.7.
69 Macky, vol. 2, 8.
70 BL, Add. MS 15,776, Jeremiah Milles, 'Travels in England and Wales 1735–1743', fol. 2: 'An account of the journey yt Mr Hardness & I took', 1735.
71 Christopher Hussey, 'Gardens of Wilton House, Wiltshire – II', Country Life, 1 August 1963, 264–7, at 267.
72 Bradley 1725, preface.
73 Switzer 1715, xxix.
74 London and Wise, vol. 2, 745, and plate XVI; London and Wise added that limes were used in England.
75 James, 46 and 63; see also the second edition, 1728, 61.
76 James, part 2, chapter 1; Switzer 1718, vol. 2, Geometrical instructions; and Langley 1728, part 1, section 1.
77 Jacques 1989, 55.
78 Switzer 1715, 335.

79 John Cornforth, 'Castles for a Georgian Duke', *Country Life*, 8 October 1992, 58–61, at 59.

80 London and Wise, vol. 2, 740–7, and plates XII and XIII.

81 James 1712, 48.

82 Ibid., plate C10.

83 Ibid., 49.

84 Ibid., plates 8C and 9C.

85 Compare James 1712, plate 8C, fig.1, with Switzer 1718, vol. 2, opp. 195, plate 30.

86 Mollet 1670, 14, and plates 31–4.

87 Baker and Baker, 159.

88 Macky, vol. 2, 10.

89 Jacques 1989, 41–65.

90 Willis 1977, plate 16b: Sutton Nicholls, *St James's Square*, revised version, 1727–8.

91 Baker and Baker, 152–62.

92 Defoe, 1742 edn, vol. 3, 89.

93 William Matthews (ed.), *The Diary of Dudley Ryder, 1715–1716* (London: Methuen & Co, 1939), 249.

94 *Powis Castle* (London: The National Trust, 1994), p. 44.

95 *Royal Commission on Historical Manuscripts*, I, 'Report on the MSS of the Duke of Buccleuch at Montagu House' (London: HMSO, 1899), 357: Charles Montagu, Earl of Halifax, letter to unknown correspondent, 9 August 1710.

96 Switzer 1729, plate XXXIV.

97 Malins and Glin, 16, quoting Lord Molesworth to Lord Coningsby, 26 May 1719.

98 London and Wise, vol. 1, 14.

99 Bradley 1731, 566.

100 Miller, article on 'Dwarf-Trees'.

101 Switzer 1715, 335.

102 Miller, articles on 'Edgings' and 'Buxus'.

103 1° Anne, chap. 1, 'An Act for the Better Support of Her Majesties Houshold and of the Honour and Dignity of the Crown'.

104 Roger Longrigg, *The English Squire and his Sport* (London: Michael Joseph, 1977), 77–8.

105 Joseph Addison, *The Spectator*, no. 34, 9 April 1711.

106 Joseph Addison, *The Spectator*, no. 335, 25 March 1711/2.

107 Roberts, 24.

108 Robinson, 114.

109 Cantor and Squires, 30, notes this changing role of parks.

110 James Bond and Kate Tiller (eds), *Blenheim: Landscape for a Palace* (Gloucester: Alan Sutton, 1987), plate 50.

111 TNA, T 1/107.3.

112 Switzer 1715, 83.

113 Percival, 106.

114 Jacques and Rock, fig. 34.

115 London and Wise, vol. 2, 784.

116 James 1712, 68.

117 *Cliveden* (London: The National Trust, 1994), 48.

118 Jacques and Rock, 218.

119 Switzer 1715, 241.

120 The term appears to derive from French court painting of Classical scenes depicting noble subject matter, and is close in meaning to 'history painting'.

121 Switzer 1718, vol. 2, 190.

122 Addison.

123 Pope 1713.

124 A. B. Lambert, 'Notes relating to botany, collected from the manuscripts of the late Peter Collinson', in *Transactions of the Linnean Society of London*, 10, 1811, pp. 271–3.

125 Francis Elrington Ball, *A History of the County Dublin*, Dublin: University Press, 1917, p. 122.

126 Switzer 1715, xiii–xv.

127 Switzer 1718, vol. 2, 184.

128 Ibid., 73.

129 Switzer 1718, vol. 1, xix.

130 Switzer 1718, vol. 2, 206, and plate 32, figs 2 and 3, opp. 187.

131 Ibid., 164 and 174, and plate III, opp. 3.

132 Ridgway and Williams, 53.

133 Switzer 1718, vol. 2, 164.

134 YCBA: Robert Tracey, 'Iter Boreale', 1732, fol. 25.

135 Switzer 1718, vol. 2, 174.

136 Timothy Nourse, *Campania Foelix, Or, a Discourse of the Benefits and Improvements of Husbandry* (London: Thomas Bennet, 1700), 322.

137 Ibid., 111.

138 Switzer 1715, xxvi.

139 Switzer 1718, 84.

140 Macky, vol. 1, 69.

141 James, 49.

142 Bedfordshire RO, L33/286, fol. 3: E. Laurence, 'Rest-Park in Bedfordshire', 1719.

143 Atkyns, plate opposite 366.

144 Mary Rich, Countess of Warwick, 'The Occasional Meditations of Mary Rich, Countess of Warwick', ed. Raymond Anselment, *Medieval and Renaissance Texts and Studies*, vol. 363 (Tempe, AZ: Arizona Center for Medieval and Renaissance Studies, 2009), 'Upon the Cutting Down of the Wilderness'.

145 Switzer 1718, vol. 2, 198.

146 Baker and Baker, 155.

147 Switzer 1715, xiii, xvii and xx.

148 Switzer 1718, vol. 3, 101–3, and plate 37, opp. 44; he remarked of his ideas that 'any Body that has seen my Lord *Carlisle*'s Wood at *Castle-howard*, will easily discern is taken from thence'.

149 Gloucestershire RO, D421, fol. 32: Thomas Player, 'Description of a journey into Yorkshire', *c.*1712.

150 Bramham Estate: Anon, 'A Map of Bramham Parke the Seat of the Rt Hon[ble] Robert Benson', *c.*1710–13.

151 Harris 1986, 19–20.

7   GARDENS IN THE AUGUSTAN AGE

1 Worsley, 85.

2 James, 50.

3 Addison.

4 Pope 1713.

5 Addison.

6 Temple, 131–2.

7 The origin of the term has long been debated; for recent scholarship compare Murray, 34–8, and Jan Woustra and Lei Gao, 'Re-solving Sharawadgi: Some Thoughts on its Chinese Roots', *Shakkei*, 17/1 (Summer 2010), 2–9, at 7–8.

8 Molyneux, 69 and 70.

9 Switzer 1715, 256–9.

10 Switzer 1718, vol. 1, 272–3.

11 Langley 1728, xii and plate VI.

12 Ibid., xiii and plate XI.

13 Markham, 250.

14 Campbell 1715, introduction.

15 Morris, xii.

16 Terry Friedman, 'A Palace Worthy of the Grandeur of the King', *Architectural History*, 29 (1986), 103–119, at 115: John Erskine, Earl of Mar, 'Description of the Designe for a New

Royall Palace for the King of Great Britain at London', 1726, line 247.

17 Falda, plates 7 and 17. The Villa Mattei is now the Villa Celimontana.

18 Richard Hewlings, 'Ripon's Forum Populi', *Architectural History*, 24 (1981), 39–52.

19 Rowe, 69.

20 *Dunham Massey* (London: The National Trust, 1995), 40.

21 Harris 1994, 2.

22 Pope 1713.

23 Switzer 1715, ii.

24 Ibid., xxviii.

25 Switzer 1718, vol. 3, 110.

26 Compare the small palisaded grove shown on the Rocque plan of Chiswick to be in the angle between the forecourt and this visto, and the *bosquet* at the Villa Ludovisi in Falda, plate 12.

27 Falda, plate 7. At the Villa Medici there was a gap between the upper and lower halves of the hedge, forming an open grove in effect.

28 James, 2nd edn (1728), 58.

29 Castell, 89.

30 Ibid., 116–17.

31 Myers, 24–5, 28.

32 Vanbrugh, vol. 4, Vanbrugh to the Duchess of Marlborough, 11 June 1709.

33 James, 13.

34 Dryden, xiv; the original by Philostratus the Younger is in the 'Prooemium' to his *Imagines*.

35 Alexander Pope, 'To Mr Jervas', 1715, lines 20 and 23–32, in Dryden, 2nd edn (1716), preface (no pagination).

36 Pope 1956, vol. 1, 377; Pope to Charles Jervas, 29 November 1716.

37 For Pope's 'literary pictorialism', see Brownell, chapter two.

38 Alexander Pope, *The Iliad of Homer* (two vols., London: Bernard Lintot, 1716), vol. 2, 5.

39 Pope 1956, vol. 1, 515: Pope to Martha Blount, 5 July 1718.

40 Pope 1731, lines 57–64.

41 Jonathan Swift, 'Horace, Lib. 2. Sat. 6. Part of it Imitated', 1714, in *Miscellanies: The Third Volume* (London: Benjamin Motte, 1732), 169, lines 1–8.

42 Pope 1956, vol. 2, 37: Pope to John Caryll, 3 March 1719/20.

43 Batey, 68–9.

44 Pope 1956, vol. 2, 109: Pope to Francis Atterbury, 19 March 1722.

45 Spence, anecdotes 603, 610 and 611.

46 Dryden, 12, 19, 39, 43 51 and 173.

47 Pope 1956, vol. 2, 264: Pope to the Earl of Oxford, October 1724.

48 Pope 1956, vol. 2, 240: Pope to Martha Blount, 22 June 1724.

49 Jacques 2005, based on entries in the manor court book for Twickenham.

50 Pope 1956, vol. 2, 256–7: Pope to William Broome, 12 September 1724.

51 Pope 1956, vol. 2, 372: Pope to the Earl of Oxford, 22 March 1725/6 (more likely to be Marble Hill rather than Pope's own garden at Twickenham).

52 Green, 214–15; appendix IV.

53 Ibid., 142–3.

54 Berkshire RO, D/EX/258/9: Agreement between the Earl of Cadogan and Stephen Switzer of Newbury, Berkshire, 1718.

55 Bedfordshire RO, X800/1–8.

56 Kent RO, U269 E21.

57 Pope 1956, vol. 2, 309: Pope to the Earl of Strafford, 1725.

58 Eburne, 199–201.

59 Sir George Clutton and Colin MacKay, 'Old Thorndon Hall, Essex: A History and Reconstruction of its Park and Garden', *Garden History Society*, *Occasional Paper No. 2*, 1970, 27–40, at 28. Some authors identify Bourginion as Hubert-François Bourguignon, known as Gravelot, well known as a book illustrator in London, 1732–45.

60 Langley 1728, i.

61 *London Journal*, 1 May 1731.

62 Thurley, 34.

63 De Saussure, 143.

64 James, 15.

65 Ibid., 20.

66 James 1728, advertisement.

67 Ibid., 34 and 58, and plate 5A.

68 Ibid., 18–19 and 40.

69 Ibid., plate 5A.

70 Ibid., 18–19.

71 Woodbridge, 268, noted this similarity. The original composition of the lines of Pope's *Epistle* was probably a decade earlier.

72 Pope 1731, lines 47–56.

73 Joseph Spence, *An Essay on Pope's Odyssey* (Oxford: S. Wilmot, 1727), vol. 2, 132–3; Bridgeman and Richmond Gardens fits the description better than Pope and his garden, as proposed by Brownell, pp. 126–34.

74 Langley 1728, xi.

75 Walpole, vol. 4, 53.

76 Willis 1977 reproduces the vast majority and provides a catalogue.

77 Hussey 1967, 95, citing Lord Perceval to Daniel Dering, 14 August 1724.

78 James, 117 and fig 4 on plate G referring to p. 117.

79 James, 2nd edn (1728), 145 and plate 3H.

80 Switzer 1715, xiii–xiv.

81 Jonathan Marsden, 'The Garden at Erddig', *Journal of Garden History*, 11/3 (July–September 1991), 140–7, at 141.

82 Staffordshire RO, D1287/3/8c: John Bridgeman, account book, 1716–19 and 1732–47.

83 Stukeley, 44.

84 Switzer 1715, xxvi.

85 Ibid., xiii–xv.

86 Switzer 1718, vol. 3, vii–viii.

87 Catherine E. Parsons, 'Horseheath Hall and its Owners', *Proceedings of the Cambridgeshire Antiquarian Society*, 41 (1948), 1–50, at 29.

88 MSGD, a4, fol. 64.

89 Taigel and Williamson, 83–9.

90 East Riding Archives and Local Studies Service, DDX 31/173: Thomas Pattison, 'Londesborough Hall and Gardens' (map), 1738.

91 Bradley 1731, 565–7.

92 Hussey 1967, 143; the Duncombe Park terrace remains today.

93 Switzer 1718, vol. 2, 154 and 163–4, and plate 26, fig. 4, opp. 186.

94 Ibid., 175–6.

95 Scott, appendix C.

96 BL, Add. MS 47,030, fols 147–9; Lord Perceval to Daniel Dering, 9 August 1724.

97 Avray Tipping, 'Wentworth Woodhouse, Yorkshire – II', *Country Life*, 27 September 1921, 476–83, at 478.

98 Harris 1964, plate 30; 'Ewston diagonall walk towards the south front', *c*.1725.

99 James, 77.

100 Switzer 1729, vol. 1, plate 3, opp. 130.

101 Bradley 1731, 164.

102 Hussey 1967, 73.

103 Vertue, 55.

104 Markham, 148 and 238.

105 Pope 1956, vol. 2, 14: Pope to Lord Bathurst, 13 September 1719.

106 Langley 1728, v.

107 Ibid., viii.

108 Ibid., vi.

109 Miller, article on 'Gardens'.

110 Vertue, 54.

111 Gervase Jackson-Stops, 'Broadlands, Hampshire – III', *Country Life*, 18 December 1980, 2334–7, at 2336.

112 Miller, article on 'Cedrus Libani'.

113 Switzer 1715, xi.

114 Langley 1728, 203; this gave a list of statues suitable 'For open Lawns and large Centers'.

115 Langley 1728, viii and x, and plate III.

116 Langley 1728, plate IX.

117 Falda, plate 13: 'Veduta del Giardino dell'Eccellentis^{mo} Signor Prencipe Ludovisi'.

118 Gibbs, plate 138.

119 Malins and Glin, 18, quoting *The Dublin Journal*, 15–19 December 1730.

120 Markham, 99, 147 and 250.

121 Miller, articles on 'Gardens' and 'Parterre'.

122 Mavis Batey, 'An Early Naturalistic Garden', *Country Life*, 22 December 1977, 1912–14, plate 5.

123 Switzer 1718, vol. 3, 55–9; Switzer 1718, 2nd edn (1742), vol. 3, 'A Farther account...', plate 39, shows a 'lawn' that was no more than a small plain parterre 250 feet deep; the accompanying text can be dated by internal evidence to about 1730.

124 Markham, 250.

125 Switzer 1718, vol. 3, 272–3.

126 Pope 1731, lines 115–18.

127 London and Wise, vol. 2, 744.

128 James 1712, 51.

129 Switzer 1718, vol. 2, 212–18.

130 Willis 1977, plate 98.

131 Langley 1726, 101–2.

132 Langley 1728, xii, and plate VI.

133 Switzer 1718, vol. 2, 218–21.

134 Langley 1728, x–xi.

135 Ibid., xiii, and plate XI.

136 Markham, 148, 239 and 243.

137 Harris 1994: compare catalogue nos 96 and 98 with no. 29.

138 James, 47.

139 Fairchild, 40–1.

140 Laird 1999, 30, citing Richard Bradley, *The Weekly Miscellany for the Improvement of Husbandry, Trade, Arts and Sciences*, London, 26 September 1727.

141 Langley 1728, part 5, 181–3.

142 Pope 1956, vol. 2, 237: Pope to Martha Blount, *c.*1722.

143 Miller, article on 'Wildernesses'.

144 Langley 1728, part 5, 186.

145 Spence, anecdote 609.

146 Northamptonshire RO, Boughton MSS, Steward's correspondence, W1: William Sutton to John Booth for the Duke of Montagu, 20 January 1723/4.

147 Langley 1728, xii.

148 Ibid., vi.

149 Christopher K. Currie, Martin Locock and Lesley Howes, 'Fishpond Wood Cascade, The Gnoll, West Glamorgan', *Archaeologia Cambrensis*, 126 (1994), 236–71.

150 Evelyn 1955, vol. 1, for May 1546; Fiennes, 222.

151 Cooper, vol. 2, 393.

152 Ridgway and Williams, chapters five, seven and eight.

153 Gibbs, plates 77(d) and 79(b).

154 Fougeroux, 84: Gibbs, plate LXVII, may be related.

155 Gibbs, xix, and plates LXXII, LXXIII, LXXIV and LXXXIV.

156 Ibid., plates LXXV and LXXVI.

157 Switzer 1729, 404, and plate XXXVI.

158 Switzer 1729, title page, 403, and plate 33.

159 Bradley 1731, 168.

160 TNA, AO 1/2453/165.

8 ICHNOGRAPHIA RUSTICA

1 Switzer 1718, 2nd edn (1742), vol. 3, 'A farther account of rural and extensive gardening'; the accompanying text can be dated by internal evidence to about 1730.

2 Switzer 1733–4, vol. 1, June 1733, 1–35.

3 Switzer 1715, xvii.

4 NRS, GD/18/4404/1: Sir John Clerk, 'The Country Seat', a poem, 1727.

5 Switzer 1715, xxvi.

6 Switzer 1718, vol. 3, 88.

7 Ibid., vol. 2, plate 36, opposite 95, and plate 37, opposite 115, and vol. 3, 86–91.

8 Switzer 1715, 346–7.

9 Switzer 1718, vol. 3, 47.

10 Ibid., 107.

11 Ibid., 46–7.

12 Michael Charlesworth, 'Thomas Wentworth's Monument: The Achievement of Peace', in Patrick Eyres (ed.), *The Georgian Landscape of Wentworth Castle, New Arcadian Journal*, 57/8 (2005), 31–63, at 49.

13 Scott, 23: letter from John Hanbury, 17 August 1732.

14 Switzer 1727, Dedication.

15 Ibid., Chapter LXXX.

16 Switzer 1718, 2nd edn (1742), vol. 3, plate in 'A farther account...'; comparing the 1742 plate with the 1727 text makes it clear that these were intended to be together.

17 Hertford, vol. 1, 171.

18 Pope 1956, vol. 2, 503: Pope to Jonathan Swift, 28 June 1728.

19 Luxborough, 22–3: Lady Luxborough to William Shenstone, 28 April 1748.

20 Switzer 1727, Dedication and Chapter LXXX.

21 Switzer 1718, 2nd edn (1742), vol. 3, Appendix: internal evidence dates its writing to about 1730.

22 Luxborough, 170: Lady Luxborough to William Shenstone, 12 December 1749.

23 Pope 1731, lines 99–100, 105–8, 167–8.

24 Ibid., lines 167–190.

25 Alexander Pope, *An Epistle to the Right Honourable Allen Lord Bathurst*, 1733, lines 223–6.

26 Switzer 1718, 2nd edn (1742), 'Prooemial Essay', 11.

27 Miller, article on 'Avenues'.

28 Baker and Baker, 161.

29 Hussey 1967, 93.

30 Switzer 1718, vol. 2, 204.

31 Ibid., vol. 2, 202.

32 Harris 1979, plate 195a: John Setterington (attrib.), views of Ebberston Hall, *c.*1745.

33 Harris 1964: plate 1; 'East Anthony', 1727.

34 Hussey 1967, 80.

35 Jackson-Stops, plate 18.

36 Hussey 1967, 121.

37 Langley 1728, plates XIX–XXII.

38 Michael Cousins, 'Ditchley Park – a Follower

39 Milles, fol. 271.

40 Gibbs, xix.

41 James, 76–7.

42 Whistler, 76.

43 Mark Girouard, 'Ambrose Phillips of Garendon', *Architectural History*, 8 (1965), 25–31.

44 Delany, vol. 1, 421.

45 Langley 1728, plate XVI.

46 MSGD A4, fol. 37; the place is as yet unidentified.

47 MSGD A3, fol. 7.

48 Miller, article on 'Avenues'.

49 Langley 1728, xiv.

50 Campbell 1725, 9.

51 John Barnatt and Tom Williamson, *Chatsworth: A Landscape History* (Macclesfield: Windgather Press, 2005), 96 and 98.

52 Barrington, 127.

53 Timothy Mowl, 'Rococo and Later Landscaping at Longleat', *Garden History*, 23/1 (Summer 1995), 56–66, at 60.

54 Jacques 1998, 8.

55 Rowe, 70.

56 Markham, 88.

57 YCBA: Robert Tracey, 'Iter Boreale', 1732, fol. 23.

58 Macky, vol. 1, 23.

59 Kate Felus, 'Boats and Boating in the Designed Landscape, 1720–1820', *Garden History*, 34/1 (Summer 2006), 22–46, at 26–7 and 35.

60 Badeslade and Rocque, plate 84–5.

61 M. A. Newman, 'Fountains Abbey and Studley Royal Estate: An Archaeological Survey', unpublished report for the National Trust, 1996, 244.

62 Hussey 1967, 155; quoting Sir William Robinson to Lord Carlisle, 1731. See Palladio, Book 3, 66–7 and plates III and IV – these are designs for timber-frame buildings, illustrating that 'Palladian' bridges were not necessarily of the Wilton type.

63 Rigaud and Baron describes this bridge as Palladian; also it is shown as a timber frame on Bickham 1753, plate m, 'A view in the Elysian Fields, from the Spring of Helicon'.

64 Switzer 1718, 2nd edn (1742), vol. 3, Prooemial Essay, 13.

65 Eburne, figure 1: Thomas Badeslade, 'A Map of the Mannor of Houghton', 1720.

66 Historical Manuscripts Commission, *The Manuscripts of the Earl of Carlisle, Preserved at Castle Howard*, No. 42, 15th Report, Appendix VI (1897), 143–4, 85: Sir Thomas Robinson to Lord Carlisle, 9 December 1731 and 23 December 1734.

POSTSCRIPT

1 Spence, anecdote 1060.

2 Ibid., anecdote 1121.

3 Laird 1999, 54–9.

4 Jackson-Stops, fig. 34.

5 As is being done by Christopher Dingwall.

6 Ruairí Ó Baoill, 'Lisburn Castle Gardens, Lisburn: 17th-century Formal Garden and Site of Manor House' (Belfast: Archaeological Development Services, 2003).

7 Delany, vol. 3, 517: Mrs Delany to Mrs Dewes, 19 December 1758.

8 Martin, 8, and Fig. 3.

9 Nicholas Luccketti, 'Archaeological Excavations at Bacon's Castle, Surry County, Virginia', in Kelso and Most, 23–42.

10 Martin, 104, and fig. 53.

11 Ibid., 19–20, and fig. 10.

12 Ibid., 38–40, 42–53.

13 Stoney, 56–7, and 123.

14 Elise Pinkney (ed.), *The Letterbook of Eliza Lucas Pinkney, 1739–1762* (2nd edn, Columbia, SC: University of South Carolina Press, 1997), 61.

15 Martin, 18–19, 25–6, 66–7 and 74–7, and plates 36–40.

16 Stoney, 64–5.

17 Ex inf. Barbara Doyle of the Middleton Place Foundation, 27 May 1996.

18 Taigel and Williamson, 15–16.

Glossary

John Evelyn provided an 'Advertisement' (a glossary) and a 'Table' (or index) in the 1679 edition of *Sylva*. Otherwise meanings must be deduced from usage in the major garden books and writings of the time, although Philip Miller's *The Gardener's Dictionary*, issued from 1724, provides more solid ground. The terminology of garden-making has altered in some respects since the seventeenth century. To compound matters, certain terms are sometimes misused by modern writers: for example, 'claire-voie' instead of 'grate'. The terms that are defined below include those that might be unfamiliar, those that have shifted in meaning, and those used in contexts that are unusual today. Italics indicate a word borrowed from French or other foreign languages. Words taken unaltered from architectural usage are not included.

Ah, Ah
See *Claire-voie*; later extended into 'the ha-ha', for which see Fossee.

Alley, ally, *allée*
A walkway, for example a subsidiary walk running between the beds of knots, down an arbour or within the quarters of groves or kitchen gardens.

Amphitheatre
Ground shaped into the form of a theatre, or other geometric earthwork, including terracing for the display of plants, as in an orangery.

Anfilade
See *Enfilade*.

Anse de panier
See Baskethandle.

Arbour, Arbor-work
Trees and/or climbers trained over trellis to make a small room, such as a bower. A tunnel arbour or cradle walk was an arbour continued in length, sometimes for a considerable distance. See Bower.

Arcade, arches in a palisade
A palisade pierced with arches, providing the effect of an architectural arcade. See Palisade.

Avenue
The principal walk to the front of a house. The word came to apply to any planted riding or visto in the park, superseding 'Walk'; see also Double walk and Counter-walk.

Aviary
A cage or small building fronted by wirework for keeping songbirds. See Volery.

Banquette
A hedge kept at three or four feet in height, allowing walkers to see over it.

Bas court
Court before the house; later the court for offices, etc., to the side of the forecourt.

Baskethandle
The termination of a garden in the shape of a half-oval or half-circle; in French, *anse de panier*.

Bason, basin
An ornamental pond, usually wharfed (revetted) with timber or edged in masonry, and often receiving the water from a fountain or *jet d'eau*; larger basons could be circular, octangular or rectangular, and have apsed ends; very large expanses could be termed 'lakes'. See also Canal and Reservoir.

Bastion
Terrace in the form of a part-circle, often where two straights met.

Belvedere
A tower built for prospect.

Berceau
French term for a cradle, in gardens being plants bent over to form an arbour. See Arbour.

Best garden
See Great garden.

Bollard
Knee-high stone blocks intended to discourage wheeled traffic from leaving a carriageway.

Border, bordure, bordar
Perimeter strip for a garden area, which may take several forms – for example, a *plate-bande* around the in-work of a parterre; a strip of grass with clipped greens; a strip of sand for setting out the tubs around an orangery; or a bed for feeding wall fruit around a walled garden.

Bosquet, boscage
French term for a small wood. See Grove.

Bower
A small arbour – for example, a half-circle to cover a seat. See Arbour.

Bowling green
Area of grass kept short for the game of bowls. The word was sometimes used generically for a plat of finely kept grass, as with *boulingrin* in France.

Breast wall
Wall retaining higher ground on one side.

Broad walk
Path wide enough for several to walk abreast.

Broderie
See Embroidery.

Buffet d'eau
An artificial waterfall.

Cabinet
Turret or summer-house at a node of arbour-work; later, the unroofed nodes within a wilderness, often with a seat and grass-work.

Canal
An artificial watercourse; in a garden, a straight but narrow length of ornamental water.

Carpet walk
Grass walk.

Carriage circle, oval, ring or sweep
Loop of carriageway for turning a carriage within a court.

Carved iron
A term for *repoussé* ironwork. *Repoussé* is a technique for modelling ironwork by hammering to create decorative detail such as foliage.

Cascade
Fall of water by steps; hence sometimes 'staircase cascade'.

Case
Wooden container for an evergreen.

Causeway
Roadway for carriages, surfaced and drained, and often slightly elevated.

Chaise riding
Roadway prepared for chaises, and taking a route around the park for the best views. See *Enfilade*.

Cherry garden
A garden where the chief pleasure was fruit trees in blossom; the term was subsumed into Fruit garden.

Cheval de frize (plural **Chevaux de frize**)
A bank protected by many projecting wooden spikes. The name derives from their use as an obstacle to cavalry.

Circle
Any circular feature, such as a circular walk or a circle of grass.

Claire-voie
A section of garden wall lowered to the ground with a ditch outside, allowing unimpeded views.

Clipped greens
Yew obelisks, globe silver hollies and other species and forms of evergreens trained to geometric shapes; the term 'topiary' did not generally supersede 'clipped greens' till around 1830.

Close walk
A narrow walk with the canopy closed overhead.

Clump, plump
A wood composed of a small number of trees, as found in old parks; a small round or square plantation.

Column
A freestanding Classical column usually supporting a statue or urn, and often placed to be an eyecatcher.

Compartment
A component part of a parterre; together with others making an entire design; in Renaissance gardens generally one of four squares. See also 'parterre of *compartiments*' and 'grove opened in *compartiments*'.

Conservatory
See Greenhouse, and Reservoir.

Coppice, copse, coppy
A wood that is cut down to the ground in rotation, producing fuel and poles.

Coronary garden
Anciently, a garden used to grow flowers for wreaths and garlands (*coronarius* in Latin), but latterly more generally for ornamental flowers.

Counter-walk
A subsidiary walk in a double avenue flanking a middle avenue or alley; separated in a parterre by a *plate bande isolée* or counter-border, in a grove by rows of detached trees.

Cradle walk
See Arbour.

Cross-walk
A walk at right angles to the principal axis.

Crypta
An artificial passage underground.

Cutwork
A grass plat carved into shapes by removal of turf and filling with sand; borders divided by alleys.

Decoy
An arrangement of water channels designed for attracting and then netting wildfowl.

Dédale
A French term for a labyrinth, recalling Daedalus who devised the labyrinth of King Minos of Knossos; see Labyrinth.

Demesne
Land held directly by the lord of the manor.

Demi-lune
See Half-moon.

Disposition
The distribution or layout of areas within a garden.

Ditch
Excavation for defence. In a garden, a ditch generally lay below a terrace wall, and could be wet or dry; the dry version was alternatively known as a 'ha-ha'.

Double walk, double avenue
Four lines of trees or clipped shrubs, forming three alleys, a middle one and two, usually narrower, counter-walks.

Dove-house, dovecot, doocot, pigeon-house
A building for housing and breeding pigeons.

Drying ground
An area for drying laundry.

Dummy avenue
The term used in this book for avenues planted merely to give the appearance of the principal approach to a house.

Dwarf
A fruit tree grafted onto dwarfing rootstock, low enough to be picked without ladders.

Edging
A low barrier, either quick or dead, preventing soil contaminating a path or sand strip.

Embroidery, embroidery, imbroidery, *broderie*
Low box hedges in an embroidery pattern of grotesques, branch-work, foliage, flourishings, etc., against a contrasting background of sand, and sometimes with red smith's dust or black earth for enhancement.

Enamel
In gardens, adornment by flowers of various colours.

Enfilade
In gardens and parks, a route displaying a sequence of views; an alternative term to Chaise riding.

Espalier
Trees trained into a thin hedge, either free-standing on a frame or against a wall. A popular means of training fruit trees around kitchen garden quarters.

Esplanade
An area for taking walks.

Etoile
See Star.

Evergreens
Evergreen trees and shrubs, such as yew, holly, pine, fir, *alaternus*; hence 'Evergreen Grove'.

Exotics
Rare and choice foreign plants.

Fence
Means of defence against livestock; could be a brick wall, hedge or wooden post and rail.

Ferme ornée
Literally, an ornamented farm; though seemingly a French term, it was invented in England to describe layouts with extended garden arms and belts running through and around farmland.

Figure
A representation in wood, metal or stone of a person or deity, otherwise a statue, in a garden usually atop a pedestal; also a device in embroidery. See Embroidery.

Floor
A unit of volume in earthmoving, being one pole square and a foot deep (40 square poles make a rood, and four roods an acre).

Florist
Grower of flowers for their rarity and beauty.

Flower pot
In the orangery, an ornamental pot of glazed ceramic or lead containing plants.

Forecourt
Court before a house, sometimes separated into inner and outer courts.

Fortifications
Mock-military motifs used in forming the boundaries of a garden.

Fossee, fosse, foss, *fossé*
A dry ditch faced with a terrace wall towards the garden, allowing uninterrupted views; an alternative term to ha-ha.

Fountain
A bason with sculpted centrepiece, either the Renaissance form with a bowl, or figures with jets.

Fret
The pattern of a knot.

Fruit garden
A walled garden devoted to the cultivation of fruit and having ornamental qualities.

Garden-house
See Summer-house.

Gateway
An opening between gate piers.

Gazon coupé
See Cutwork.

General plan, general scheme
A drawn plan showing the intended disposition of a scheme.

Glacis
In gardens, a gentle grassed slope or bank below a terrace.

Glade
Visto through a wilderness of tall trees.

Glass case
See Hothouse.

Goose-foot
See *Patte d'oie.*

Graff
A Dutch term for a trench serving as a fortification; a dry ditch or fossee.

Grand court
See Great court.

Grand garden
See Great garden.

Grand walk
See Great walk.

Grass plat or plot
Level area of grass, often in a parterre or a wilderness room; an alternative term to 'plain parterre' or the garden 'lawn'.

Grate, *grille*
Palisade of wood or iron allowing partial views through.

Great avenue
Avenue of uncommonly large dimensions.

Great court, grand court
A forecourt large enough to accommodate many coaches.

Great garden, grand garden
The principal garden under the windows of a mansion.

Great terrace
The terrace running past a house's garden front.

Great walk, grand walk
The principal axial walk, or any other walk providing the main lines of a garden.

Greenhouse
House for the protection against frosts of evergreens, such as oranges, citrons and myrtles, and increasingly tender exotics; some heating was generally provided by stoves and/or flues.

Greens
Evergreen plants, either yews, hollies, phillyreas, etc., for the parterre; or the more tender contents of the greenhouse.

Grille
See Grate.

Grotto, grott
A natural cave, or room of rustic architecture decorated with grotesque-work of shells and minerals.

Ground-work
The rarely used Englished term for 'parterre'. See Parterre.

Grove
In gardens, a general term for plantations; if it included underwood, 'grove' was also an alternative term to 'wilderness'.

Grove in quincunx
Natural woodland with a random arrangement of trees where the underwood was grazed, shaded or cleared out; its garden form was lines of trees planted in quincunx or quadrate formation with no underwood or palisades.

Grove opened in *compartiments*
An arrangement of alleys flanked by trees set in low hedges, over which views are obtained of the *compartiments* within, embellished with grass cutwork, flowering shrubs, bulb planting or other ornaments.

Ha-ha, haw-haw
A ditch that caused an expression of surprise on discovery; from the French *ah!-ah!*. Superseded by 'fossee', but in modern times it has gained popularity again. See Fossee.

Half-moon, half-circle, half-oval, half-round, *demi-lune*
Rows of trees in a semicircle, often to form an avenue termination.

Hall
Open space within a grove, larger than a cabinet, often containing a parterre or bowling green.

Head
The upper end of steps or a parterre; a dam to a pool.

Headed plant
Round-headed clipped green.

Hot bed
A raised bed filled with rotting manure and covered with glass, providing moist heat for the cultivation of melons and other succulent vegetables.

Hothouse, glass case, stove
A building specially designed for the care of tender exotics, heated by stoves and the use of glass to simulate at least sub-tropical conditions.

Ichnography, *ichnographia*
The drawing-up of general plans.

Inner court
A court mainly enclosed by a principal façade and its connecting wings.

Inward plantation
A grove within the walled garden enclosure.

In-work
The design enclosed by a parterre's *plate-bande.*

Iron fence
See Palisade.

Iron-work
Gates, palisades, balconies or other structures wrought from iron. See Carved iron.

***Jet d'eau*, jetteau, jetto, getto**
A spout of water from a nozzle.

Kitchen garden, kitching garden, kitchen ground
A garden devoted principally to the cultivation of produce for the kitchen; in the early eighteenth century it was adapted to become both a fruit and kitchen garden, which over time became known simply as the 'kitchen garden'.

Knot, knott
An intricate pattern of beds or interlacing lines of evergreen shrubs. The term became archaic with the introduction of 'parterre'.

Labyrinth
The huge complex of burial chambers by Crocodopolis in Lower Egypt; in gardens, applied to any asymmetrical arrangement of paths in a wilderness causing loss of orientation. See Maze.

Lattice-work
See Trellis-work.

Lawn, laune
A great plain of fine grass in the park; an area of grass over which there is an open view. In the late 1710s the term began to be applied to large plain parterres within pleasure gardens.

Lodge
A lodging for the keeper of a park or a gate.

Mall, *maille*
An alley flanked by boards down which the game of pall-mall was played with balls and mallets.

Maze
A pattern designed as a puzzle in meanders, circles, windings and intricate turnings; originally in gravel and grass, and from the seventeenth century in gravel between double-sided palisades; often synonymous with 'labyrinth'.

Meander
A winding shape, especially of close walks.

Melon ground
An area devoted to the cultivation of succulent vegetables in hot beds.

Menagerie
An area of cages for keeping exotic wildlife, usually birds.

Mount
Earth mounded up into an artificial hillock, usually for prospect; or a raised terrace at the end of the garden.

Obelisk
A structure in imitation of obelisks from Egyptian and Roman Antiquity, usually supported on a pedestal; sometimes the word refers to clipped yews.

Offices
Outhouses, such as brewhouse and laundry, often arranged in one block to provide symmetry with a stable block.

Open knot
A knot garden in a pattern of beds.

Open grove
See Grove opened in *compartiments*.

Open walk
A walk without an overarching canopy.

Orangery, orangerie
An area for setting out orange trees and other evergreens in the warmer months, sometimes laid out in a parterre with grass-work and fountains.

Orchard, ortchard
An area for standard fruit trees, generally outside the garden enclosure.

Ornament
A general term for figures, fountains, arbours, etc., ornamenting a garden.

Outer court
A courtyard where visitors alighted, and often where the stables and offices were situated.

Outward plantation
A plantation outside the walled enclosure of the garden, in contradistinction to 'wildernesses' and other 'inward' plantations.

Outwork, out-worke
Works outside the main walled enclosure, hence a peripheral garden area, or a military-style enlargement of a forecourt.

Pale, paling
The fence around a deer park.

Palisade, *palissado*
An impassable barrier, either a clipped hedge as in a wilderness, one trained on poles, or an open pale of wooden slats or iron bars.

Parade
A place where troops assemble for parade; at country houses, an area of clear ground outside the gates for the assembly of coaches and riding parties.

Park, imparkment
A area enclosed and maintained for deer, or with the appearance or reputation of such; until 1701 all parks technically required a licence from the monarch, which gave them special legal status.

Parterre, parterr, partir
A level division of ground laid out in an ornamental design of paths, borders, grass, statuary, fountains, etc.

***Parterre à l'Angloise*, parterre after the English manner**
A parterre with in-work of grass or cutwork in grass.

Parterre d'orangerie
See Orangery.

Parterre fleuriste
See Parterre of cutwork for flowers.

Parterre of *compartiments*
A parterre including quarters of both *broderie* and cutwork in grass, often divided by internal beds or strips of grass, and necessarily symmetrical about both axes.

Parterre of cutwork for flowers
A pattern of beds for flowers with sand paths between, an elaborated version of the open knot. In French, *parterre de pièces coupée pour les fleur* or *parterre fleuriste*

Parterre of embroidery, *parterre de broderie*
A parterre with in-work of embroidery. See Embroidery.

Path
A way to get around a garden area. In a parterre, a narrow alley between beds, sometimes just a strip of gravel, sand or crushed brick two feet wide separating a border and adjacent grass-work.

***Patte d'oie*, goose-foot**
An arrangement of radiating alleys or avenues.

Perron
A platform reached by paired flights of steps.

Perspective
In gardens, a painting in oil or fresco to give the illusion of further space.

Physic garden
A garden devoted to the cultivation of plants used in medicine.

Pier, peer
Upright to the side of a gateway on which to hang a gate, or at the junction of two walls, often topped by a ball finial, urn or heraldic sculpture.

Pigeon-house
See Dove-house.

Pitching
Pavement composed of stones laid so that they form a rigid whole.

Plain parterre
A parterre of grass, perhaps embellished with statues but with minimal gravel paths and no *plates-bandes*.

Plashing, pleaching
Weaving the boughs of a tree after first making cuts, for example to make a bower or in the laying of a quick hedge.

Plat, plot
An area set aside for a garden or other use; see also Grass plat.

Plate-bande
The peripheral beds of a parterre, standardised in England to be slightly mounded in the centre, with clipped greens down the middle, flowers on the sides and a box edge around. See Border.

Plat forme, platform
A drawn layout of a house or garden.

Platoon, plattoon, poletoon
A small detached arrangement of trees, or clump, part of an arrangement of several platoons devised to frame a visto.

Pleaching
See Plashing.

Pleasure garden, garden of pleasure
A garden laid out principally for pleasure, in contradistinction to areas for physic or the kitchen; the term 'garden' became associated with places of public resort, for example, Vauxhall Gardens in London.

Plinth
Stone set at near ground level for setting out tubs or flower pots.

Plump
See Clump.

Pole hedge
A free-standing *espalier* hedge. See *Espalier*.

Pollard
Tree cut periodically above the grazing level for fuel and poles.

Pond
An artificial body of water, such as a millpond, fishpond or stewpond; in the garden, a general term for ornamental pieces of water, such as basons. See Stew.

Privy garden
The private garden of a monarch, from which all but the closest family members and most intimate friends were excluded.

Prolated
Extended or enlarged.

Prospect
A broad view; a term frequently found in describing a painting or engraving of a country house, with the direction indicated by cardinal points – for example, a 'north prospect' was from the north looking south.

Pyramid
A structure imitating Classical pyramids. The word was also applied to trained trees and shrubs of that shape.

Quarters
Subdivisions of a garden area, not necessarily one fourth of them.

Quincunx
Several rows of tall trees planted 'like the cinque-points of a die'; in France, planted quadrate (foursquare). Generally understood to be a grove without palisades or underwood, and laid as turf underneath.

Rail
A horizontal bar intended to discourage visitors from the interiors of knot gardens, or horseriders from grass; the horizontal members of an iron fence.

Relief, *relievo*
The three-dimensional effect given by a bed or border with a raised centre, or by groves.

Reservoir, reserver
A pond at a high level for supplying *jets* and fountains via pipes, or else cascades; alternatively, 'conservatory'.

Ride, riding
A track for hunting through a forest, or intended for horseriding exercise around a park.

Rural garden, rural gardening
A garden in an unaffected style appropriate to a country life, with an emphasis on turf and woods.

Rural planting, rural manner
As found in Nature – planting in a promiscuous manner.

St Andrew's cross
Diagonal walks in a cross.

Screw-walk, snail mount
A spiral walk up a mount.

Scrollwork
An in-work bed in scrolls and straights.
See In-work.

Seat
A place to sit and admire the view; sometimes
a wooden bench with a high back, sometimes
under cover, and sometimes within a small
building; also used in the sense of a nobleman's
seat of power, a country house.

Serpentine
A winding shape, of a walk or pond.

Sharawadgi
A kind of beauty resulting from laying out in an
irregular manner.

Side terrace
A low terrace flanking the side of a parterre.

Situation, scituation
The location of a house with respect to views,
soil, water supply, etc.

Snail mount
See Screw-walk.

Solitude, solitary recess
A place of retirement for contemplation.

Star, *étoile*
The intersection of alleys or rides, so making a
multi-pointed star.

Stew
Pond for keeping fish.

Stove
See Hothouse.

Summer-house, garden-house
A small building for escaping the heat of the
summer.

Sunk fence
A means of defence sunk below ground level.
It could be post-and-rail in a ditch, or a wall on
the garden side, making a ha-ha.

Sweep
The semicircular advance of a pool edge or
garden boundary, usually on axis. See also
Carriage circle.

Term
A stone post marking a property's boundary,
rising into a bust of Terminus, the Roman god
who protected it; by Renaissance times the bust
could be of any person or god.

Terrace, terrass, tarras
A walk raised above nearby ground by a breast
wall or *glacis* slope; sometimes terraces were one
above another.

Topiarie work, *ars topiarius*
Arbours and hedges trained by clipping; a
topiarius being an ornamental gardener in
ancient Rome. See Clipped green.

Trayle, trail
A wreath or spray of leaves or tendrils
represented in embroidery; an alternative
English term to *broderie*. See Embroidery.

Trellis-work, *treillage*, lattice-work
Architectural structures of timbers and laths
designed to support vegetation.

Undertaker
A tradesman whose business was to undertake
work by contract.

Urn
Garden ornament in stone or metal in the form
of Antique urns with sealed lids made for the
ashes of the dead.

Vase
Garden ornament usually in the form of a vessel
with flared lip and open top, often in lead, but
may take a variety of forms, including that of
an urn.

***Verso* walk**
An endless loop within a wilderness.

Vineyard
A place for growing vines over wooden frames.
The word was sometimes applied to soft fruit,
such as currants and raspberries, grown in a
similar manner.

Visto, vista
A view to the far distance, often framed by
planting.

Viviary
An enclosure for keeping wild animals
(sometimes merely a warren); displaced by the
term 'menagerie'.

Volery, *volière*
Aviaries large enough for birds to fly within.

Walk, walke
Line of communication on foot, often lined with
rows of trees to either side to provide a visto,
always so in parks; the term was superseded by
'avenue' in the park. See Close walk and Open
walk.

Water-work
A general term for canal, bason, leat, reservoir,
fountain and other water-works.

Wilderness
An alternative term to 'grove', a plantation used
for recreation, but of variable form through
time. In the early seventeenth century it could
be a coppice, and later would have palisades
flanking a geometric arrangement of alleys with
undergrowth between. In the reign of George
I it included meandering walks through the
quarters, and palisades reduced to low hedges.

Wood-work
The formation of a wood or grove by the art of
planting and other works.

Yews
In gardens, yew trees clipped into pyramids
of between four and seven feet in height. See
Clipped greens.

Bibliography

Place of publication is London, unless stated otherwise.

Addison
Joseph Addison, *The Spectator*, no. 414, 25 June 1712

Amherst
Hon. Alicia Amherst, *A History of Gardening in England*, Bernard Quaritch, 1895

Atkyns
Sir Robert Atkyns, *The Ancient and Present State of Glostershire*, W. Bowyer, 1712

Aubrey 1718–19
John Aubrey, *The Natural History and Antiquities of Surrey*, ed. Richard Rawlinson, five vols, Edmund Curll

Aubrey 1847
John Aubrey, *The Natural History of Wiltshire*, ed. John Britton, Wiltshire Topographical Society

Aubrey 1898
John Aubrey, *Brief Lives Chiefly of Contemporaries Set Down by John Aubrey between the Years 1669 and 1696*, ed. Revd Andrew Clark, Oxford: Clarendon Press

Aubrey 1982
John Aubrey, *Monumenta Britannica: Or a Miscellany of British Antiquities*, ed. John Fowles, Boston, MA: Little Brown

Austen
Ralph Austen, *A Treatise of Fruit-Trees*, Oxford: Thomas Robinson, 1653

Bacon
Francis Bacon, Viscount St Albans, 'On Gardens', in *The Essayes or Counsels, Civill and Morall, of Francis Lo. Verulam Viscount St. Albans. Newly Enlarged*, Essay XLVI, 266–79, John Haviland, 1625

Badeslade and Rocque
Thomas Badeslade and John Rocque, *Vitruvius Britannicus*, vol. 4, two vols, published for the authors, 1739

Bailey
Bruce A. Bailey, *Northamptonshire in the Early Eighteenth Century: The Drawings of Peter Tillemans and Others*, Northampton: Northamptonshire Record Society, 1996

Baker and Baker
C. H. Collins Baker and Muriel I. Baker, *The Life and Circumstances of James Brydges, 1st Duke of Chandos, Patron of the Liberal Arts*, Oxford: Clarendon Press, 1949

Barrington
Hon. Daines Barrington, 'On the Progress of Gardening', *Archaeologia*, 7 (1785), 113–30

Batey
Mavis Batey, *Alexander Pope: The Poet and the Landscape*, Barn Elms, 1999

Batey and Lambert
Mavis Batey and David Lambert, *The English Garden Tour: A View into the Past*, John Murray, 1990

Bezemer Sellers
Vanessa Bezemer Sellers, *Courtly Gardens in Holland 1600–1650: The House of Orange and the Hortus Batavus*, Amsterdam: Architectura and Natura Press, 2001

Blith
Walter Blith, *The English Improver Improved*, John Wright, 1649; third impression, much augmented, 1653

Blomfield
Reginald Blomfield, *The Formal Garden in England*, Macmillan, 1892

Bradley 1725
Richard Bradley, *A Survey of the Ancient Husbandry and Gardening Collected from Cato, Varro Columella, and others...*, B. Motte

Bradley 1731
Richard Bradley, *New Improvements of Planting and Gardening, both Philosophical and Practical*, 6th edn, J. and J. Knapton et al.

Britton
John Britton, *Architectural Antiquities of Great Britain*, vol. 2, Longmans, 1809

Browne
Thomas Browne, *Hydriotaphia, Urne-buriall, or, A Discourse of the Sepulchrall Urnes Lately found in Norfolk. Together with The Garden of Cyrus, or The Quincunciall, Lozenge, or Net-work Plantations of the Ancients, Artificially, Naturally, Mystically Considered*, Henry Broome, 1658

Brownell
Morris Brownell, *Alexander Pope and the Arts of Georgian England*, Oxford: Oxford University Press, 1978

Camden
William Camden, *Britannia*, ed. Edmund Gibson; F. Collins, 1695

Campbell, 1715
Colen Campbell, *Vitruvius Britannicus, or the British Architect*, vol. 1, published for the author

Campbell, 1717
Colen Campbell, *Vitruvius Britannicus, or the British Architect*, vol. 2, published for the author

Campbell, 1725
Colen Campbell, *The Third Volume of Vitruvius Britannicus, or the British Architect*, published for the author

Cantor and Squires
Leonard Cantor and Anthony Squires, *The Historic Parks and Gardens of Leicestershire and Rutland*, Newtown Linford: Kairos Press, 1997

Castell
Robert Castell, *The Villas of the Ancients Illustrated*, published for the author, 1728

Chauncy
Sir Henry Chauncy, *The Historical Antiquities of Hertfordshire*, Ben Griffin and others, 1700

Chesterfield
Letters of Philip, Second Earl of Chesterfield, to Several Celebrated Individuals, E. Lloyd and Son, 1829 edn

Colvin
H. M. Colvin (general edn), *The History of the King's Works* (six vols), Her Majesty's Stationery Office, 1963–82

Conan 1999
Michel Conan (ed.), *Perspectives on Garden Histories*, Dumbarton Oaks Colloquium 21, Washington, D.C.: Dumbarton Oaks

Conan 2005
Michel Conan (ed.), *Baroque Garden Cultures: Emulation, Sublimation, Subversion*, Dumbarton Oaks Colloquium 25, Washington, D.C.: Dumbarton Oaks

Cook
Moses Cook, *The Manner of Raising, Ordering, and Improving Forrest-trees: Also, How to Plant, Make and Keep Woods, Walks, Avenues, Lawns, Hedges, etc.*, Peter Parker, 1676

Cooper
Anthony Ashley Cooper, third Earl of Shaftesbury, *Characteristicks of Men, Manners, Opinions and Times*, three vols, John Danby, 1747

Defoe
Daniel Defoe, *A Tour thro' the Whole Island of Great Britain...*, three vols, G. Strahan et al., 1724, 1725 and 1727

De Jong
Erik de Jong, *Nature and Art: Dutch Garden and Landscape Architecture, 1650–1740*, Philadelphia, PA: University of Pennsylvania Press, 2000

Delany
Mary Delany, *The Autobiography and Correspondence of Mary Granville, Mrs Delany*, ed. The Right Honourable Lady Llanover, three vols, Richard Bentley, 1861

De Saussure
César-François de Saussure, *A Foreign View of England in the Reigns of George I and George II*, trans. Madame van Muyden, John Murray, 1902

Dezallier d'Argenville
Antoine-Joseph Dezallier d'Argenville, *La Théorie et pratique du jardinage*, Paris, 1709; 2nd edn, 1713 (authorship given as 'L.S.A.J.D.A.'); 3rd edn, 1722 (authorship given as Jean-Baptiste Alexander le Blond)

Dickinson
H. W. Dickinson, *Sir Samuel Morland: Diplomat and Inventor, 1625–1695*, Newcomen Society, 1970

Dryden
John Dryden, *The Art of Painting by C. A. du Fresnoy with Remarks*, W. Rogers, 1695; 2nd edn, William Taylor, 1716

Dugdale
William Dugdale, *Antiquities of Warwickshire Illustrated*, Thomas Warren, 1656

Dunbar
John Dunbar, 'The Building Activities of the Duke and Duchess of Lauderdale 1670–82', *Archaeological Journal*, vol. 132:1 (1975), 202–30

Eburne
Andrew Eburne, 'Bridgeman and the Gardens of the Robinocracy', *Garden History*, 31/2 (Winter 2003), 193–208

Edwards
Ifor Edwards, *Davies Brothers, Gatesmiths: 18th century Wrought Ironwork in Wales*, Cardiff: Welsh Arts Council, 1977

Evelyn 1658
Nicolas de Bonnefons, *The French Gardiner*, trans. John Evelyn; John Crooke

Evelyn 1660
Antoine Legendre, *The Manner of Ordering Fruit Trees*, trans John Evelyn, Humphrey Moseley

Evelyn 1664
John Evelyn, *Sylva, or a Discourse of Forest-Trees, and the Propagation of Timber…to which is Annexed Pomona…also kalendarium hortense*, John Martyn and James Allestry, 2nd edn, 1670; 3rd edn, 1679; 4th edn, 1706

Evelyn 1693
Jean-Baptiste de la Quintinie, *The Compleat Gard'ner*, trans. John Evelyn; Matthew Gillyflower and James Partridge

Evelyn 1955
John Evelyn, *The Diary of John Evelyn*, six vols, ed. E. S. de Beer, Oxford: Oxford University Press

Evelyn 2001
John Evelyn, *Elysium Britannicum, or The Royal Gardens*, ed. John E. Ingram, Philadelphia: University of Pennsylvania Press

Fairchild
Thomas Fairchild, *The City Gardener*, T. Woodward and J. Peele, 1722

Falda
Giovanni Battista Falda, *Li Giardini di Roma*, Rome: Giovanni Giacomo de Rossi, 1683

Felton 1785
Samuel Felton, *Miscellanies on Ancient and Modern Gardening; and on the Scenery of Nature*, published for the author

Felton 1829
Samuel Felton, *Gleanings on Gardens, Chiefly Respecting those of the Ancient Style in England*, Lowe and Harvey, 1829

Fiennes
Celia Fiennes, *The Journeys of Celia Fiennes*, ed. Christopher Morris, Cresset Press, 1947

Finch
Pearl Finch, *History of Burley-on-the-Hill, Rutland*, two vols, John Bale, 1901

Fougeroux
Pierre-Jacques Fougeroux, 'Voiage d'Angleterre d'hollande et de flandre fair en l'année 1728', National Art Library, Victoria and Albert Museum, London, MS 86NN2

Friedman
Ann Friedman, 'What John Locke saw at Versailles', *Journal of Garden History*, 9/4 (October–December 1989), 177–98

Gautier
Pierre and Jean Gautier, *Divers ouvrages de balustrades, cloisons, paneaux et d'autres ornemens pour les serruriers faits et inventez par Pierre Gautier Maistre Serrurier du Roy dans son arsenal des galères a Marseille…*, Paris: Louis Crépy, 1685

Gibbs
James Gibbs, *Book of Architecture*, William Bowyer, 1728

Gibson
John Gibson, 'A Short Account of Several Gardens near London…Upon a View of Them in December 1691', *Archaeologia*, 12 (1796), 181–92

Goody
Jack Goody, *The Culture of Flowers*, Cambridge: Cambridge University Press, 1993

Green
David Green, *Gardener to Queen Anne: Henry Wise (1653–1738) and the Formal Garden*, Oxford: Oxford University Press, 1956

Gunnis
Rupert Gunnis, *A Biographical Dictionary of Sculptors in Britain, 1660–1851*, ed. Ingrid Roscoe et al., London and New Haven, CT: Yale University Press, 2009

Gunther
R. T. Gunther, *The Architecture of Sir Roger Pratt*, Oxford: Oxford University Press, 1928

Hadfield
Miles Hadfield, *Gardening in Britain*, Hutchinson, 1960

Hanmer
Sir Thomas Hanmer, *The Garden Book of Sir Thomas Hanmer*, 1659, ed. E. S. Rohde, Gerald Howe, 1933

Harper
Revd William Harper, *The Antiquity, Innocence, and Pleasure of Gardening in a Sermon…at a Meeting of Gardeners and Florists*, William Harper, 1732

Harris 1719
John Harris, *History of Kent*, D. Midwinter, 1719

Harris 1964
John Harris (ed.), 'The Prideaux Collection of Topographical Drawings', special volume of *Architectural History*, 7 (1964)

Harris 1979
John Harris, *The Artist and the Country House: A History of Country House and Garden View Painting in Britain, 1540–1870*, Sotheby, Parke, Burnet

Harris 1982
John Harris, *William Talman: Maverick Architect*, George Allen and Unwin

Harris 1986
John Harris, 'The Artinatural Style', in *The Rococo in England: A Symposium*, ed. Charles Hind, Victoria and Albert Museum, 8–20

Harris 1994
John Harris, *The Palladian Revival; Lord Burlington, his Villa and Garden at Chiswick*, New Haven, CT, and London: Yale University Press, 1994

Harris 1995
John Harris, *The Artist and the Country House from the Fifteenth Century till the Present Day*, Sotheby's Institute, 1995

Harris and Hunter
Frances Harris and Michael Hunter (eds), *John Evelyn and his Milieu*, The British Library, 2003

Harvey 1972
John Harvey, *Early Gardening Catalogues*, Chichester: Phillimore and Co.

Harvey 1974
John Harvey, *Early Nurserymen*, Chichester: Phillimore and Co.

Harwood et al.
Edward Harwood, Tom Williamson, Michael Leslie and John Dixon Hunt, 'Whither Garden History?', *Studies in the History of Gardens and Designed Landscapes*, 27/2 (April–June 2007), 91–112

Hazlehurst 1966
Franklin Hamilton Hazlehurst, *Jacques Boyceau and the French Formal Garden*, Athens, GA: University of Georgia Press

Hazlehurst 1980
Franklin Hamilton Hazlehurst, *Gardens of Illusion: The Genius of André le Nostre*, Nashville, TN: Vanderbilt University Press

Hertford
Frances Seymour, Countess of Hertford, *Correspondence between Frances, Countess of Hartford [sic] (afterwards Duchess of Somerset) and Henrietta Louisa, Countess of Pomfret, Between the years 1738 and 1741*, three vols, Richard Phillips, 1805

Hunt
John Dixon Hunt, *Garden and Grove: The Italian Renaissance Garden in the English Imagination, 1600–1750*, J. M. Dent, 1986

Hunt and De Jong
John Dixon Hunt and Erik de Jong, 'The Anglo-Dutch Garden in the Age of William and Mary', in *Journal of Garden History*, 8/1 and 8/2 (April–September 1988; published as single volume)

Hunt and Willis
John Dixon Hunt and Peter Willis, *The Genius of the Place: The English Landscape Garden 1620–1820*, Paul Elek, 1975; 2nd edn, Cambridge, MA: MIT Press, 1988

Hussey 1927
Christopher Hussey, *The Picturesque: Studies in a Point of View*, G. P. Putnam's Sons

Hussey 1967
Christopher Hussey, *English Gardens and Landscapes, 1700–1750*, Country Life

Hyde
Elizabeth Hyde, *Cultivated Power: Flowers, Culture, and Politics in the Reign of Louis XIV* (Penn Studies in Landscape Architecture), Philadelphia, PA: University of Pennsylvania Press, 2005

Jackson-Stops
Gervase Jackson-Stops, *An English Arcadia, 1660–1990: Designs for Gardens and Garden Buildings in the Care of the National Trust*, Washington, D.C.: American Institute of Architects Press, 1991

Jacques 1989
David Jacques, '"The Chief Ornament" of Gray's Inn: The Walks from Bacon to Brown', *Garden History*, 17/1 (Spring 1989), 41–65

Jacques 1995
David Jacques, 'The History of the Privy Garden', in Thurley, 23–42

Jacques 1997
David Jacques (ed.), 'The Techniques and Uses of Garden Archaeology', special issue of *Journal of Garden History*, 17/1 (January–March 1997)

Jacques 1998
David Jacques, 'George London's Last Masterwork', in Katherine Myers (ed.), *The Gardens of Canons* (Proceedings of a Study Day held at Canons, 1997), London Historic Parks and Gardens Trust, 3–13

Jacques 1999
David Jacques, 'The Grand Manner: Changing Style in Garden Design, 1660–1735', PhD thesis, Courtauld Institute, University of London, 1999

Jacques 2001
David Jacques, 'Garden Design in the Mid-Seventeenth Century', *Architectural History*, 44 (2001), 365–76

Jacques 2005
David Jacques, 'Design History at Marble Hill', unpublished report for English Heritage

Jacques and Rock
David Jacques and Tim Rock, 'Pierre-Jacques Fougeroux: A Frenchman's Commentary on English Gardens of the 1720s', in Martin Calder (ed.), *Experiencing the Garden in the Eighteenth Century*, Bern: Peter Land AG, 2006, 213–35

Jacques and Van der Horst
David Jacques and Arend Jan van der Horst (eds), *The Gardens of William and Mary*, Christopher Helm, 1988

James
[Antoine-Joseph Dezallier d'Argenville], *The Theory and Practice of Gardening*, trans. John James; Bernard Lintot, 1712; 2nd edn, 1728

Jeffery
Sally Jeffery, 'John James and George London at Herriard', *Architectural History*, 28 (1985), 40–70

Jekyll 1904
Gertrude Jekyll, *Some English Gardens*, Longmans

Jekyll 1918
Gertrude Jekyll, *Garden Ornament*, Country Life

Johnson
George Johnson, *A History of English Gardening, Chronological, Biographical, Literary, and Critical*, Baldwin and Cradock, 1829

Kelso and Most
William M. Kelso and Rachel Most, *Earth Patterns: Essays in Landscape Archaeology*, Charlotte, VA: University Press of Virginia, 1990

Kimball
Fiske Kimball, *The Creation of the Rococo*,
Philadelphia, PA: Philadelphia Museum of Art,
1943

Knyff and Kip
Leonard Knyff and Johannes Kip, *Britannia illustrata*, David Mortier, 1707

Lablaude
Pierre-André Lablaude, *The Gardens of Versailles*,
Zwemmer, 1995

Laird 1999
Mark Laird, *The Flowering of the Landscape Garden:
English Pleasure Grounds 1720–1800*, Philadelphia,
PA: University of Pennsylvania Press

Laird 2015
Mark Laird, *A Natural History of Gardening
1650–1800*, New Haven, CT, and London: Yale
University Press

Laird and Harvey
Mark Laird and John Harvey, '"A Cloth of
Tissue of Divers Colours": The English Flower
Border, 1660–1735', *Garden History*, 21/2 (Winter
1993), 158–205

Lamb and Bowe
Keith Lamb and Patrick Bowe, *A History of
Gardening in Ireland*, Dublin: National Botanic
Gardens, 1995

Langley 1726
Batty Langley, *Practical Geometry Applied to the Arts
of Building, Surveying, Gardening, &c.*, printed for
W. and J. Innys, et al.

Langley 1728
Batty Langley, *New Principles of Gardening:
Or, the Laying Out and Planting Parterres, Groves,
Wildernesses, Labyrinths, Avenues, Parks, &c. After
a more Grand and Rural Manner, than has been done
before…*, A. Bettesworth, et al.

Laurence
Revd John Laurence, *Gardening Improv'd:
Containing I. The Clergyman's Recreation…II. The
Gentleman's Recreation…III. The Lady's Recreation*,
W. Taylor, 1718

Lawson
William Lawson, *A New Orchard and Garden…*,
R. Jackson, 1618

Leith-Ross
Prudence Leith-Ross, *The John Tradescants:
Gardeners to the Rose and Lily Queen*, John Owen,
1984

Liger
Louis Liger, *Le Jardinier fleuriste et historiographe*,
Paris: Damien Beugnié, 1704

Loggan
David Loggan, *Oxonia Illustrata*, Oxford: The
University, 1675

London and Wise
George London and Henry Wise, *The Retir'd
Gard'ner*, two vols, Jacob Tonson, 1706

Longstaffe-Gowan
The London Square: Gardens in the Midst of Town,
New Haven, CT, and London: Yale University
Press, 2012

Loudon
John Claudius Loudon, *Encyclopaedia of Gardening*,
Longman, Hurst, Rees, Orme, and Brown, 1822

Luxborough
Henrietta, Lady Luxborough, *Letters Written by the
Late Right Honourable (Henrietta) Lady Luxborough to
William Shenstone Esq.*, J. Dodsley, 1775

Lysons
Daniel and Samuel Lysons, *Magna Britannia*,
Cadell and Davies, 1813

Macky
John Macky, *A Journey through England*, two vols;
vol. 1, 2nd edn, John Hooke etc., 1722, vol. 2,
2nd edn, John Pemberton, 1724

Magalotti
Count Lorenzo Magalotti, *Travels of Cosmo the
Third, Grand Duke of Tuscany, through England…
1669*, J. Mawman, 1821

Malins
Edward Malins, *English Landscaping and Literature,
1660–1840*, Oxford: Oxford University Press,
1966

Malins and Glin
Edward Malins and The Knight of Glin, *Lost
Demesnes: Irish Landscape Gardening 1660–1845*,
Barrie and Jenkins, 1976

Markham
Sarah Markham, *John Loveday of Caversham 1711–
1789: The Life and Tours of an Eighteenth-Century
Onlooker*, Salisbury: Michael Russell, 1984

Marot
Daniel Marot, *Oeuvres du Sr D. Marot, architect de
Guillaume III, roy de la Grande Bretagne*, The Hague:
Chez Pierre Husson, 1703

Martin
Peter Martin, *The Pleasure Gardens of Virginia*,
Princetown, NJ: Princetown University Press,
1991

Matthews
W. H. Matthews, *Mazes and Labyrinths: A
General Account of their History and Developments*,
Longmans, 1922

Miller
Philip Miller, *The Gardener's Dictionary*, 3rd edn,
Philip Miller, 1737

Milles
Jeremiah Milles, 'Travels in England and Wales,
1735–43', British Library, Add. MS 15,776

Mollet 1651
André Mollet, *Le Jardin de plaisir, contenant plusiers
desseins de jardinage…*, Stockholm: Henry Kayser

Mollet 1670
Andrew Mollet, *The Garden of Pleasure Containing
Several Draughts of Gardens…*, John Martyn and
Henry Herringham

Molyneux
The London Letters of Samuel Molyneux, 1712–13, ed.
Ann Saunders, London Topographical Society,
2011

Morris
Robert Morris, *An Essay in Defence of Ancient
Architecture…*, D. Browne et al., 1728

Morton
John Morton, *The Natural History of
Northamptonshire*, R. Knaplock and R. Wilkin, 1712

Murray
Cieran Murray, *Sharawadgi: The Romantic Return to Nature*, Bethesda, MD: International Scholars Publications, 1998

Myers
Katherine Myers, 'Visual Fields: Theories of Perception and the Landscape Garden', in Martin Calder (ed.), *Experiencing the Garden in the Eighteenth Century*, Bern: Peter Lang, 2005, pp. 13–35.

North 1713
Roger North, *A Discourse of Fish and Fishponds*, E. Curll

North 1981
Roger North, 'Cursory Notes of Building Occasioned by the Repair, or Rather Metamorfosis, of an Old House in the Country', in Howard Colvin and John Newman (eds), *Of Building: Roger North's Writings on Architecture*, Oxford: Oxford University Press, 1–103

Ogilby and Morgan
John Ogilby and William Morgan, *A Large and Accurate Map of the City of London*, William Morgan et al., 1677

O'Halloran
Sally O'Halloran, 'The Serviceable Ghost: The Forgotten Role of the Gardener in England from 1630 to 1730', PhD thesis, University of Sheffield, 2013

Palladio
Andrea Palladio, *The Four Books of Architecture*, trans. Isaac Ware; Isaac Ware, 1738

Parkinson
John Parkinson, *Paradisi in sole: paradisus terrestris*, Humfrey Lownes and Robert Young, 1629

Pattison
Paul Pattison (ed.), *There by Design: Field Archaeology in Parks and Gardens*, British Archaeological Report 267, Swindon: RCHME, 1998

Pepys
Samuel Pepys, *The Diary of Samuel Pepys*, ed. Robert Latham and William Matthews, eleven vols, Bell and Hyman, 1970–83

Percival
Sir John Percival, 'A Journey Thrô Severall Countys of England', 1701, in *The English Travels of Sir John Percival and William Byrd II: The Percival Diary of 1701*, ed. Mark R Wenger, Columbia, MO: University of Missouri Press, 1989

Pevsner
Nikolaus Pevsner, 'The Genesis of the Picturesque', *Architectural Review*, 96 (November 1944), 139–46

Plot 1677
Robert Plot, *The Natural History of Oxford-shire*, Oxford: The University

Plot 1686
Robert Plot, *The Natural History of Staffordshire*, Oxford: The University

Pope 1713
Alexander Pope, 'An Essay on Verdant Sculpture', *The Guardian*, 29 September 1713

Pope 1731
Alexander Pope, *An Epistle to the Right Honourable Richard Earl of Burlington*, L. Gilliver

Pope 1956
Alexander Pope, *The Correspondence of Alexander Pope*, ed. George W. Sherburn, five vols, Oxford: Oxford University Press

Ray
John Ray, *Philosophical Letters*, W. Derham, 1718

RCHME 1975
Royal Commission on the Historical Monuments of England, *An Inventory of Archaeological Sites in North-East Northamptonshire*

RCHME 1979
Royal Commission on the Historical Monuments of England *An Inventory of the Historical Monuments in the County of Northampton*, vol. 2, *Archaeological Sites in Central Northamptonshire*

Rea
John Rea, *Flora: seu, De Florum Cultura; or, a Complete Florilege*, Richard Marriott, 1665

Reid
John Reid, *The Scots Gard'ner*, Edinburgh, David Lindsay and partners, 1683

Repton 1803
Humphry Repton, *Observations on the Theory and Practice of Landscape Gardening*, J. Taylor

Repton 1806
Humphry Repton, *An Enquiry into the Changes of Taste in Landscape Gardening*, J. Taylor

Repton 1816
Humphry Repton, *Fragments on the Theory and Practice of Landscape Gardening*, J. Taylor

Ridgway and Williams
Christopher Ridgway and Robert Williams (eds), *Sir John Vanbrugh and Landscape Architecture in Baroque England 1690–1730*, Stroud: Sutton, 2000

Rigaud and Baron
Jacques Rigaud and Bernard Baron, *Fifteen Perspective Views, and a Large Plan of the Gardens, at Stowe in Buckinghamshire, Belonging to the Right Hon. The Lord Viscount Cobham, laid out by Mr. Bridgeman…*, Sarah Bridgeman, 1740; 2nd edn, 1746

Roberts
Jane Roberts, *Royal Landscape: The Gardens and Parks of Windsor*, New Haven, CT, and London: Yale University Press, 1997

Robinson
John Martin Robinson, *The English Country Estate*, Century Hutchinson, 1988

Røstvig
Maren-Sophie Røstvig, *The Happy Man: Studies in the Metamorphosis of a Classical Ideal*, two vols: vol. 1 (1600–1700), Akademisk Forlag, 1954; vol. 2 (1700–60), Oslo: Oslo University Press, 1958

Rowe
Anne Rowe, *Garden Making and the Freman Family: A Memoir of Hamels 1713–1733*, Hertfordshire Record Publications, 17 (2001)

Scott
Simon Scott, *The Follies of Boughton Park Revisited*, Northampton: Scott Publications, 2011

Serle
John Serle, *A Plan of Mr Pope's Garden as it was Left at His Death*, R. Dodsley, 1745

Sladen
Teresa Sladen, 'The Garden at Kirby Hall 1570–1700' in *Journal of Garden History*, 4, No. 2 (1984), pp. 139–56

Sloane
Hans Sloane, *Voyage to the islands Madera, Barbados, Nieves, S. Christophers, and Jamaica*, two vols, London: B.M. for the Author, 1707–25

Smith
John Smith, *England's Improvement Reviv'd in a Treatise of all Manner of Husbandry and Trade by Land and Sea*, printed by Thomas Newcomb for the author, 1670

Spence
Joseph Spence, *Observations, Anecdotes, and Characters of Books and Men Collected from Conversation*, ed. James M. Osborn, two vols, Oxford: Oxford University Press, 1966

Stoney
Samuel Gaillard Stoney, *Plantations of the Carolina Low Country*, Charleston, NC: Carolina Art Association, 1938

Stukeley
William Stukeley, *Itinerarium curiosum, or an Account of the Antiquitys and Remarkable Curiositys in Nature and Art*, published for the author, 1724

Switzer 1715
Stephen Switzer, *The Nobleman, Gentleman, and Gardener's Recreation: Or, an Introduction to Gardening, Planting, Agriculture, and the other Business and Pleasures of a Country Life*, B. Barker

Switzer 1718
Stephen Switzer, *Ichnographia Rustica: or, the Nobleman, Gentleman, and Gardener's Recreation*, three vols, D. Browne et al.; 2nd edn, J. and J. Fox, 1742

Switzer 1727
Stephen Switzer, *The Practical Kitchen Gardener, Or, A New and Entire System of Directions for his Employment in the Melonry, Kitchen-Garden, and Potagery*, Thomas Woodward

Switzer 1729
Stephen Switzer, *An Introduction to a General System of Hydrostaticks and Hydraulicks, Philosophical and Practical*, two vols., T. Astley

Switzer 1733–4
Stephen Switzer, *The Practical Husbandman and Planter: or, Observations on the Ancient and Modern Husbandry, Planting, Gardening, &c.*, two vols, published by the author

Taigel and Williamson
Anthea Taigel and Tom Williamson, 'Some Early Geometric Gardens in Norfolk', *Journal of Garden History*, 11/1 and 11/2 (January and June 1991), published as a single volume.

Temple
William Temple, 'Upon the Gardens of Epicurus; or, of Gardening, in the Year 1685', in *Miscellanea, The Second Part, In Four Essays*, William Miller, 1692

Thompson
E. M. Thompson (ed.), *Correspondence of the Family Hatton*, Camden Society, new series, 23 (1878)

Thurley
Simon Thurley (ed.), *The King's Privy Garden at Hampton Court Palace 1689–1995*, Apollo, 1995

Triggs
Inigo H. Triggs, *Formal Gardens in England and Scotland*, B. T. Batsford, 1902

Vanbrugh
The Complete Works of Sir John Vanbrugh, vol. 4, *The Letters*, ed. Geoffrey Webb, Nonesuch Press, 1928

Vertue
George Vertue, 'A Description of Easton-Neston in Northamptonshire', 1734, appended to Brian Fairfax, *A Catalogue of the Curious Collection of Pictures of George Villiers Duke of Buckingham*, ed. Horace Walpole, W. Bathoe, 1758, 53–66

Walpole
Horace Walpole, *Anecdotes of Painting in England*, four vols, 2nd edn, Strawberry Hill, 1782

Ware
Isaac Ware, *The Plans, Elevations, and Sections of Houghton in Norfolk…*, published for the author, 1735

Wasson
Ellis Wasson, *Born to Rule: British Political Elites*, Stroud: Sutton Publishing, 2000

Whistler
Laurence Whistler, *The Imagination of Sir John Vanbrugh and his Fellow Artists*, Arts and Technics, 1954

Williamson
Tom Williamson, *The Archaeology of the Landscape Park: Garden Design in Norfolk, England, c.1680–1840*, British Archaeological Reports, British Series 268, Oxford: Archaeopress, 1988

Willis 1974
Peter Willis (ed.), *Furor Hortensis: Essays on the history of the English Landscape Garden in memory of H. F. Clark*, Edinburgh: Elysium Press

Willis 1977
Peter Willis, *Charles Bridgeman and the English Landscape Garden*, Zwemmer, 1977; 2nd edn, 2002

Willis 1993
Peter Willis, 'Charles Bridgeman and the English Landscape Garden: New Documents and Attributions', in John Bold and Edward Chaney (eds), *English Architecture Public and Private: Essays for Kerry Downes*, Hambledon Press, 247–64

Woodbridge
Kenneth Woodbridge, *Princely Gardens: The Origins and Developments of the French Formal Style*, Thames and Hudson, 1986

Worlidge
John Worlidge, *Systema Horti-culturae; Or, The Art of Gardening*, Thomas Burrel and William Hensman, 1677

Worsley
Giles Worsley, *Classical Architecture in Britain: The Heroic Age*, New Haven, CT, and London: Yale University Press, 1995

Woudstra 1997
Jan Woudstra, 'British Gardens by Daniel Marot (1661–1752), Architect to the King of England', *Proceedings of the Huguenot Society*, 26, no. 5 (1997), 553–63

Woudstra 2003
Jan Woudstra, 'The Planting of the Pleasure Garden of Squerryes Court, Westerham, Kent, in 1718', *Garden History*, 31/1 (Spring 2003), 34–47

Illustration List

16 Leonard Knyff, print study of Hampton Court from the south, 1702. BM P & D, 1961,0408.1. © Trustees of the British Museum.

17 Thomas Kirkland, detail from 'Melbourn Hall and Gardens', an incomplete print study, c.1722. Melbourne House, P2/9. Photo: the author, reproduced by kind permission of Lord Ralph Kerr.

18 Jan van der Vaardt (attrib.), *Bifrons Park, Kent*, c.1695–1705. YCBA, B1977.14.83. © Yale Center for British Art, Paul Mellon Collection.

19 John Drapentier, 'Balls', c.1685, in Chauncy, plate opp. p. 265. Reproduced by kind permission of John Harris.

20 Leonard Knyff (*delin.*) & Johannes Kip (*sculpt.*), 'Althrop, in the County of Northampton', 1697, in Knyff & Kip, plate 27. GAC, 00467. © Crown copyright: UK Government Art Collection.

21 Edmund Prideaux, *Mount Edgecumb in Devon*, c.1727. © and reproduced by kind permission of Elisabeth Prideaux-Brune.

22 William Stukeley, plan of Lord Hertford's House at Marlborough, 1723. BL Maps K.Top.43.36.b. © The British Library Board.

23 Anon., *Arlington House*, etching, sometime 1674–1702. BM P&D, G, 5.190. © Trustees of the British Museum.

24 Hendrick Danckerts (attrib.), sketch of Charles II walking in St James's Park, c.1670. Westminster Archives, F132-2 (61). © and reproduced by permission of Westminster City Council.

25 Anon., *Plan of Duck Island in St James's Park from a drawing made in 1734*, 1807. Westminster Archives, Gardner Box, No. 4. © and reproduced by permission of Westminster City Council.

26 John Aubrey, map of the Deepdene, 1673. Bodleian Library, Aubrey MS 4, ff. 49–50. Photo: the author, reproduced by permission of the Bodleian Library.

27 Reconstruction of the garden at Albury Place as made in 1667, in Jacques 1978, p. 37. © The author.

28 Golden holly (*Ilex acquifolium* 'Aureamarginata') at Hampton Court, 2013. © and reproduced by kind permission of Terry Gough.

29 Leonard Knyff (*delin.*) & Johannes Kip (*sculpt.*), 'Stansted, in the County of Sussex', c.1700, in Knyff & Kip, plate 36. RIBA 10029. © RIBApix.

30 John Evelyn, *Hunc Villæ nostræ et Viridarij Spectatissimi prospectum … in Agro Deptfordiæ* (viz Sayes Court), 1653. BL, Add. MS 78628 A. © The British Library Board.

31 John Drapentier, 'Bedwell Parke', c.1685, in Chauncy, opp. p. 276. Reproduced by kind permission of John Harris.

32 Michael Burghers, 'S.S.E Prospect of Ingestre Hall, and the Beautiful Church Newly Erected at his Sole Charge', in Plot 1686, tab. XXVI. Photo: the author.

33 Israël Silvestre, Château Neuf at St Germain-en-Laye, France, c.1675. By courtesy of Fabian Sylvestre.

34 Reconstruction of Wotton House in 1651, in Jacques 1978, p. 36. © The author.

35 Lorenzo Magalotti, pen and wash view of Wilton House, 1669. BL, Add. MS 33,767B, fo. 23–4. © The British Library Board.

36 G. Williamson (*delin.*) & James Smith (*sculpt.*), 'The Seat of the Honble. Collonel Williamson in Oakingham, Berkshire', in Badeslade and Rocque, plate 92-3. Photo: the author.

37 John Aubrey, 'A Draught of Sr John Danvers Garden at Chelsey…', 1691. Bodleian Library, Aubrey MS 2, fo.59. Photo: the author, reproduced by permission of the Bodleian Library.

38 Anon., 'ye ground-plott of ye Old House' (i.e. Burley-on-the-Hill), c.1690. Finch I, after p.6. © The British Library Board.

39 Abraham Walter, 'The manor of Albury in Surry', 1701. Syon House, SyAcc3. Collection of the Duke of Northumberland, Alnwick Castle.

40 Jonas Moore, section of 'A Mapp or Description of the Manor' (viz. Woburn Abbey), 1661. Bedfordshire Record Office, X1/33/1; R1/282. By kind permission of the Duke of Bedford and the Trustees of the Bedford Estates.

41 Frederick Hendrik van Hove, an idea for a round garden, in Worlidge, p. 17. © Royal Horticultural Society, Lindley Library.

42 Anon., Sir Roger Pratt's house at Ryston, c.1680. Photo: the author, reproduced by kind permission of Mrs Susan Pratt.

43 John Evelyn, 'The house of Geo: Evelyn Esqr: taken in perspective from the top of the Grotto by Jo: Evelyn 1653' (viz. Wotton House). BL, Add. MS 78610 G. © The British Library Board.

44 Anon., Thorpe Hall, Peterborough, c.1770. Northamptonshire Record Office, Map 1969. © Northamptonshire County Council.

45 Leonard Knyff (*delin.*) & Johannes Kip (*sculpt.*), 'Eaton Hall on the River Dee near the Citty of Chester', by 1700, in Knyff & Kip, plate 62. Photo: the author.

46 Leonard Knyff (*delin.*) & Johannes Kip (*sculpt.*), 'Dawly in the County of Middlesex', in Knyff & Kip, plate 48. Photo: the author.

47 Anon., 'Hortus Botanicus: The Phisick Garden in Oxon', in Loggan, plate 3. Reproduced by kind permission of John Harris.

48 Walter Stonehouse, plans of open knots for Darfield rectory, 1640. Magdalen College Archives, MSS 329. Photo: John Gibbons Studios, reproduced by permission of the President and Fellows of Magdalen College, Oxford.

49 Leonard Knyff (*delin.*) & Johannes Kip (*sculpt.*), 'Esher Place in ye County of Surry', in Knyff & Kip, plate 72. GAC 10133. © Crown copyright: UK Government Art Collection.

50 Leonard Knyff (*delin.*) & Johannes Kip (*sculpt.*), 'Grimsthorpe in the County of Lincoln', *c.*1703, in Knyff & Kip, plate 20. Photo: the author.

51 Michael Burghers, 'S.E. Prospect of Madeley Manor Taken from the Garden Side', in Plot 1686, tab. XVI. Photo: the author.

52 John Fisher, *Survey & Ground Plot of the Royal Palace of White Hall*, 1680, but published in 1747. MoL, image ID: 139393. © the Museum of London.

53 John Ogilby and William Morgan, detail of Essex House, the Strand. Photo: the author.

54 Frederick Hendrik van Hove (*sculpt.*), plate showing parterre and palisade, in Worlidge, opp. 19. © the Royal Horticultural Society, Lindley Library.

55 John Drapentier, 'Hamells', *c.*1685, in Chauncy, plate opp. p. 227. Reproduced by kind permission of John Harris.

56 King Charles Gate, Euston Hall, 2013. Photo: the author.

57 Jan Siberechts, the south front of Longleat House, 1678. GAC 04959. © Crown copyright: UK Government Art Collection.

58 Jan Siberechts, Bayhall Manor, Kent, *c.*1680. YCBA, B1994.18.4. © Yale Center for British Art, Paul Mellon Collection.

59 Michael Burghers, the gateway at Statfold Hall, in Plot 1686, tab. I. Photo: the author.

60 Sutton Nicholls, *Southampton or Bloomsbury Square*, *c.*1725. BM P&D, 1880,1113.4405. © Trustees of the British Museum.

61 Sutton Nicholls, *Sohoe or King's Square*, 1728. BM P&D 1880,1113.4463. © Trustees of the British Museum.

62 Reconstruction of Wimbledon Manor as it was in 1649, 2013. © The author.

63 André Mollet, design for a parterre with eagle heads, in Mollet 1651, planche 11. Photo: the author.

64 Hendrick Danckerts, a panorama of St James's Park, *c.*1670. BM P&D, 1853,0409.78. © Trustees of the British Museum.

65 Hendrick Danckerts, Hampton Court Palace from the canal, *c.*1667. RCIN 402842. Royal Collection Trust/ © Her Majesty Queen Elizabeth II 2014.

66a and b André Mollet, the west and east ends of the Royal Garden, St James's, in Mollet 1670, plate 25. © Royal Horticultural Society, Lindley Library.

67 Robert Thacker (*delin.*) & Francis Place (*sculpt.*), 'Prospectus Orientalis', in *Vivarium Grenovicanum*, 1676. BM P&D, 1865,0610.950. © Trustees of the British Museum.

68 André Le Nostre, a scheme for Greenwich Park, *c.*1662. Institut de France, Ms 1605, 61. © Bridgeman Art Library, image BLT 174226.

69 Anon., the so-called 'Pepys Plan' of Greenwich Park, *c.*1675–80. PL, 2972/268a-269a. © The Pepys Library, Magdalene College, Cambridge.

70 Francis Place, the north slopes of Windsor Castle, 1680s. YCBA, B1975.3.1228. © Yale Center for British Art, Paul Mellon Collection.

71 Leonard Knyff (*delin.*) & Johannes Kip (*sculpt.*), 'St James's House', *c.*1700, in Knyff & Kip, plate 2. Photo: the author.

72 Edmund Prideaux, sketch of Stowe House, Kilkhampton, 1716. © and reproduced by kind permission of Elisabeth Prideaux-Brune.

73 Moses Cook, plan of the parterre at Cassiobury House, in Cook, fig 47. Photo: the author, reproduced by kind permission of Peter Goodchild.

74 Edmund Prideaux, 'Back front of Ewston & orangerie towards yᵉ West', *c.*1725. © and reproduced by kind permission of Elisabeth Prideaux-Brune.

75 Jacob Knyff, *The Durdans*, 1679. Photo: the author, reproduced by kind permission of Charles Berkeley and The Berkeley & Spetchley Estates.

76 Henry Winstanley, 'Wimbledon as it is Seen from the Great Walke of Trees in the Principle garden', 1678. BM P&D, 1881,0611.353. © Trustees of the British Museum.

77 Hendrik Danckerts, *Ham House, Surrey*, *c.*1672. © Bridgeman Art Library, Image number: USB 393106.

78 Leonard Knyff (*delin.*) & Johannes Kip (*sculpt.*), 'Cashiobury', *c.*1700, in Knyff & Kip, plate 28. GAC 12899. © Crown copyright: UK Government Art Collection.

79 Anon., printed plan entitled *Badminton the Duke of Beaufort his House*, published between 1682 and 1699. © and reproduced by kind permission of the Duke of Beaufort.

80 Leonard Knyff (*delin.*) & Johannes Kip (*sculpt.*), 'Burlington House in Pickadilly', *c.*1700, in Knyff & Kip, plate 29. GAC 6901. © Crown copyright: UK Government Art Collection.

81 John Slezer, 'The house and garden at HAM', *c.*1671. V&A, E385-1951. © V&A.

82 Hendrick Danckerts, The deer park at Badminton House from the east avenue, *c.*1669. BM P&D, 1948,1126.11. © Trustees of the British Museum.

83 John Rocque, plan of Windsor Little Park, 1738, in Badeslade & Rocque, plate 38-9. Photo: the author.

84 Moses Cook, planting arrangements, in Cook, figs 16–25. Photo: the author, reproduced by kind permission of Peter Goodchild.

85 Anon., Moseley Wood, Cookridge, 1694, reproduced in Ralph Thoresby, *Ducatus Leodiensis*, 1715, following dedication. Photo: the author, reproduced by kind permission of Peter Goodchild.

86 Leonard Knyff (*delin.*) & Johannes Kip (*sculpt.*), 'Wrest House & Park', *c.*1703, in Knyff & Kip, plate 19. GAC 00457. © Crown copyright: UK Government Art Collection.

87 James Simon (*delin.*), *The North Prospect of Mountague House*, 1714, in David Mortier (publisher), *Nouveau Theatre de Grand Bretagne*, 1724. GAC 00479. © Crown copyright: UK Government Art Collection.

88 Leonard Knyff (*delin.*) & Johannes Kip (*sculpt.*), 'Ragly', *c.*1700, in Knyff & Kip, plate 71. Photo: the author.

89 Leonard Knyff (*delin.*) & Johannes Kip (*sculpt.*), 'Hutton Hall', *c.*1700, in Knyff & Kip, plate 59. Photo: the author.

90 William Talman, plan showing Hampton Court and its parks, sometime 1694–8. RIBA Drawings Collection, B4/1. © RIBApix.

91 John Haynes, 'An Accurate Survey of … Burghley … before Mr Brown's Alterations', 1755. CCA, DR1985:0414. © and reproduced by permission of the Collection Centre Canadien d'Architecture, Montréal.

92 Robert Thacker, Longleat House from the rising ground east of the garden, *c.*1694. © and reproduced by permission of the Marquess of Bath, Longleat House, Warminster, Wiltshire, Great Britain.

93 George London (attrib.), design for a cutwork parterre at Longleat House, *c.*1695. Photo: the author, reproduced by kind permission of John Harris.

94 George London, design for gardens at Herriard House, 1699. Hampshire Archives and Local Studies, 44M69/P1/61. © Hampshire County Council: Jervoise of Herriard Collection.

95 Leonard Knyff (*delin.*) & Johannes Kip (*sculpt.*), 'Chatsworth House', 1699, in Knyff & Kip, plate 17. Photo: the author.

96 William Talman (attrib.), general plan for Castle Howard, *c.*1699. V&A, E.434-1951. © V&A.

97 Anon., Chelsea Hospital from the Thames, *c.*1710. Bodleian Library, Gough Maps 17, fo. 32r. Photo: the author, reproduced by permission of the Bodleian Library.

98 Robert Skyring, 'A Map of Leavens Garding', *c.*1750. Photo: Chris Crowder, reproduced by kind permission of Hal Bagot, Esq.

99 Philip Buffle (or Bouffler), plan for a parterre at Stonyhurst, *c.*1705. Dorset History Centre, D/WLC/P85 Item 2. © Dorset County Council.

100 London and Wise, plan for a parterre at Stonyhurst, *c.*1705. Dorset History Centre, D/WLC/P85 Item 1. © Dorset County Council.

101 Kees J. van Nieukerken, reconstruction of the palace and gardens at Het Loo as at 1689, 2012. By kind permission of Kees J. van Nieukerken.

102 Leonard Knyff (*delin.*) & Johannes Kip (*sculpt.*), 'Bredby in Darby Shire', *c.*1700, in Knyff & Kip, plate 26. GAC 11821. © Crown copyright: UK Government Art Collection.

103 Gabriel Delahaye, 'Plan de la maison et jardins de Boughton …', 1712. Bodleian Library, Gough Drawings a4, fo. 84. Photo: the author, reproduced by permission of the Bodleian Library.

104 Leonard Knyff (*delin.*) & Johannes Kip (*sculpt.*), 'Badminton in the County of Gloucester', 1699, in Knyff & Kip, plate 11. Photo: the author.

105 Leonard Knyff (*delin.*) & Johannes Kip (*sculpt.*), 'Wansted House in Essex' (from the east), *c.*1713. Essex Record Office, I/Mp 388/1/34. © and reproduced by courtesy of the Essex Record Office.

106 Michael Burghers, 'W. & by S. Prospect of Trentham Hall taken from yᵉ Hill near yᵉ Cistern', in Plot 1686, tab.XXIII. Photo: the author.

107 Leonard Knyff (*delin.*) & Johannes Kip (*sculpt.*), 'Fair Lawn in yᵉ County of Kent', *c.*1700, in Knyff & Kip, plate 49. Photo: the author.

108 Jan Siberechts, *Wollaton Hall and Park*, 1697. YCBA, B1973.1.52. © Yale Center for British Art, Paul Mellon Collection.

109 William Lansdowne (*delin.*) and John Clark and John Pine (*sculpt.*), south-east aspect of Risby Hall, *c.*1720. The Hepworth Gallery, Wakefield, Gott Collection, A1.91 6/99. © The Hepworth Gallery.

110 Royal Commission on Historical Monuments, drawing of earthworks at the 'Falls' at Harrington in 1974–5, in RCHME 1979, fig. 74. © Historic England.

111 Leonard Knyff (*delin.*) & Johannes Kip (*sculpt.*), 'New Parke in Surry', *c.*1700, in Knyff & Kip, plate 33. Photo: the author.

112 Thomas Badeslade, 'North West Prospect of Belvoir Castle', 1731, in Badeslade & Rocque, plate 47-8. Photo: the author.

113 Jacques Rigaud (*delin.*) & Sᵗ Torres (*sculpt.*), *A Prospect of St James's Park*, 1752. BM P&D, 1877,0609.1849. © Trustees of the British Museum.

114 Michael Burghers, 'N.N. West Prospect of Aqualate House', in Plot 1686, tab.XX. Photo: the author.

115 One of the twelve panels of the Tijou screen at Hampton Court, 2013. © and reproduced by permission of Historic Royal Palaces.

116 White Gates at Cholmondeley Hall, 2012. Photo: the author.

117 Thomas Smith, Badminton House from the north, *c.*1710. © and reproduced by kind permission of the Duke of Beaufort.

118 Johannes Kip, 'Fairford', *c.*1708, in Atkyns, before p. 430. Photo: the author.

119 Leonard Knyff, *The South East Prospect of Hampton Court in Herefordshire*, 1699. YCBA, B1981.25.389. © Yale Center for British Art, Paul Mellon Collection.

120 Anon., Denham Place from the west, *c*.1705. YCBA, B1976.7.116. © Yale Center for British Art, Paul Mellon Collection.

121 Thomas Badeslade (*delin*.), & Toms (*sculpt*.), 'Shardeloes in Buckinghamshire', *c*.1730, in Badeslade & Rocque, plate 100-1. Photo: the author.

122 Leonard Knyff (*delin*.) & Johannes Kip (*sculpt*.), 'The House att Chelsey, one of the Seats of . . . The Duke of Beaufort', *c*.1700, in Knyff & Kip, plate 13. Reproduced by kind permission of John Harris.

123 Anon., Pierrepont House, Nottingham, *c*.1705. YCBA, B1976.7.125. © Yale Center for British Art, Paul Mellon Collection.

124 Anon., print sketch of Lullingstone Castle, *c*.1700. YCBA, B1975.2.843. © Yale Center for British Art, Paul Mellon Collection.

125 Nicholas Hawksmoor (attrib.), general plan for the rebuilding of Hampton Court palace, 1689. Soane Museum, volume 110/4. © 2013 The Trustees of Sir John Soane's Museum.

126 Daniel Marot, design for the Great Garden, Hampton Court, 1689. YCBA, B1977.14.6212. © Yale Center for British Art, Paul Mellon Collection.

127 Daniel Marot, 'Jardin en Bosquet d'Espalliers de diferentes figures', in Marot, plate 18. Cooper Hewitt 1988-4-30. © Scala Archives/ Cooper-Hewitt.

128 Sutton Nicholls, etching of the Hampton Court Privy Garden, *c*.1696. PL 2972/213. © Pepys Library, Magdalen College, Cambridge.

129 Anon., 'Design for Kensington Gardens' (the so-called 'Sandby Plan'), *c*.1720. BL, Add. MS 42,572C. © The British Library Board.

130 George Russell, 'A Map of Cobham Deer Parke and the Paddock', 1718. Rochester-upon-Medway Local Studies Centre, U565/P3. © and reproduced by permission of Medway Council.

131 Sir Christopher Wren, a design for the Maastricht Garden at Windsor Castle, 1698. Codrington Library, Wren V, 16. © and reproduced by permission of All Souls College, Oxford.

132 Sir Christopher Wren, 'Plan of the Palace, Gardens, Canals, and Decorations', 1697. Codrington Library, Wren, V, 3. © and reproduced by permission of All Souls College, Oxford.

133 Daphne Ford, 'plan of the Privy and Mount Gardens as they were in 1680', in Thurley, figure 37. Crown Copyright/ Historic Royal Palaces.

134 Daphne Ford, 'reconstruction of the Privy and Mount Gardens as they were in 1695', in Thurley, figure 41. Crown Copyright/ Historic Royal Palaces.

135 Daphne Ford, 'reconstruction of the extended Privy Garden as it was in 1702', in Thurley, figure 47. Crown Copyright/ Historic Royal Palaces.

136 Henry Hulsbergh (*sculpt*.), 'Plan of Woodstock Park . . .', *c*.1717, in Campbell 1725, plate 71-2. Photo: the author.

137 Nicholas Hawksmoor (attrib.), general plan for the parkland at Blenheim Palace, 1705. Bodleian Library, MS. Top Oxon a. 37* fo.1. Photo: the author, reproduced by permission of the Bodleian Library.

138 Reconstruction of the gardens at Kimbolton Castle in 1728, 2013. © The author.

139 William Stukeley, 'The Cascade at Chatsworth', 1725. Bodleian Library, MS Top Gen. d.14, fo. 18r. Photo: the author, reproduced by permission of the Bodleian Library.

140 Jan Griffier the Younger, *The Grange, Hurstbourne Priors*, 1748. © English Heritage Trust, Image ref. E870079.

141 Sir Godfrey Kneller, *Henry Wise*, sometime 1702 to 1723. RCIN 405636. Royal Collection Trust/ © Her Majesty Queen Elizabeth II 2014.

142 London & Wise (attrib.), design for the Great Parterre or Fountain Garden at Hampton Court, *c*.1707. TNA, WORK 32/311. © and reproduced by permission of The National Archives.

143 London & Wise (attrib.), a design for the Maastricht Garden at Windsor Castle, 1712. Soane Museum, vol.111/45. © 2013 The Trustees of Sir John Soane's Museum.

144 London & Wise (attrib.), a design for a parterre at Cliveden House, *c*.1706. Ginge Manor, Cliveden Album, fo. 12. Photo: John Gibbons Studio, reproduced by permission of the Viscount Astor of Hever Castle.

145 Charles Bridgeman (attrib.), 'An Accurate Plan of Winds[r] Parks & Part of the Forrest', *c*.1712. RCIN 929579. Royal Collection Trust/ © Her Majesty Queen Elizabeth II 2013.

146 London & Wise (attrib.), a design for the gardens at Melbourne Hall, *c*.1710. Melbourne House P2/8. Photo: the author, reproduced by kind permission of Lord Ralph Kerr.

147 London & Wise (attrib.), plan of the Newdigate House gardens, Nottingham, in London and Wise, inside rear cover. Photo: the author.

148 James Lightbody (*delin*.) and John Harris (*sculpt*.), *The South West Prospect of his Grace y[e] Duke of Marlboroughs House in S[t] James Park*, *c*.1715. BM P & D 1880,1113.2271. © Trustees of the British Museum.

149a and b Leonard Knyff (*delin*.) & Johannes Kip (*sculpt*.), 'Wansted House in Essex' (from the south), *c*.1713. Essex Record Office, I/Mp 388/1/33. © and reproduced by courtesy of the Essex Record Office.

181 Anon., sketch plan of the boundaries of Wray Wood, Castle Howard, c.1705. V&A, E.432-1951. © V&A.

182 William Stukeley, 'The Duchesses Bastion' at Grimsthorpe Castle, 1736. Bodleian Library, MS Top. Gen. d.14, fo. 38v. Photo: the author, reproduced by permission of the Bodleian Library.

183 J. Clark (sculpt.), 'The Plan of an Octangular Kitchen Garden', in Switzer 1727, pp 368-9. Photo: the author.

184 Leonard Knyff (delin.) & Johannes Kip (sculpt.), 'Wansted House in Essex' (from the west), c.1713. Essex Record Office, I/Mp 388/1/35. © and reproduced by courtesy of the Essex Record Office.

185 Charles Bridgeman (attrib.), 'A Plan of the Lodge, the Gardens, the Park, and other Grounds at Richmond', c.1726. Reproduced by kind permission of John Harris.

186 Leonard Knyff (delin.) & Johannes Kip (sculpt.), 'Long Leate', c.1700, in Knyff & Kip, plate 40. Photo: the author.

187 Anon., estate survey of Wotton House, Surrey, 1739. Surrey History Centre, 329/15/1. © and reproduced by permission of the Surrey History Centre.

188 John Wood (delin.) and Henry Hulsbergh (sculpt.), The Plan of Bramham Park in the County of York, c.1725. BL, King's Maps, K.Top.45.16. © The British Library Board.

189 T. Willson (delin.) and T. Bowles (sculpt.), 'The South Prospect of Bullstrod House & Garden', c.1725, in Badeslade & Rocque, plate 43-4. Photo: the author.

190 John Richardson, Jr, A Survey of the Estates in the Parishes of Beaconsfield…, 1763. By kind permission of the Beaconsfield & District Historical Society.

191 John Rocque, 'A Plan of the Gardens & View of yᵉ Buildings…at Echa', 1737, in Badeslade & Rocque, plate 110-1. Photo: the author.

192 Peter Tillemans (attrib.), view of the Garden and main Parterre of Winchendon House from the east, c.1720. YCBA, B1981.25.2804. © Yale Center for British Art, Paul Mellon Collection.

193 Thomas Badeslade (delin.) and Johannes Kip (sculpt.), 'Chevening', 1719, in Harris 1719, I, 74. © Kent Library and History Centre.

194 Charles Bridgeman (delin.) and Henry Hulsbergh (sculpt.), 'Plan of the Gardens and Plantations of Eastbury in Dorsetshire', in Campbell 1725, plate 15. Photo: the author.

195 Sutton Nicholls (attrib.), 'Grovenor Square', c.1735. BM P&D, 1880,1113.4567. © Trustees of the British Museum.

196 Batty Langley (delin.) and Thomas Bowles (sculpt.), 'A Garden that Lies Irregularly to the Grand House', in Langley 1728, part VI, plate XI. Photo: the author.

197 Ralph Fowler, an estate map of Castle Howard, 1727. Castle Howard Archive ref. P1/4. © and reproduced by kind permission of the Hon. Simon Howard.

198 Colen Campbell (delin.) and Henry Hulsbergh (sculpt.), 'Plan of the Garden and Plantations of Narford…', Campbell 1725, plate 95. Photo: the author.

199 Pieter Andreas Rysbrack, The Gardens at Chiswick House from the West, c.1729. English Heritage Trust image J950300. © and reproduced by permission of English Heritage Trust.

200 Alexander Pope (attrib.), design for gardens at Marble Hill,1724. Norfolk Record Office, MC 184/10/3. © Norfolk County Council.

201 Robert Castell (delin.) and Peter Fourdrinier (sculpt.), imaginary reconstruction of Pliny's villa in Tuscany, 1728, in Castell, plate between pp. 126 & 127. Reproduced by kind permission of John Harris.

202 John Serle, 'A Plan of Mʳ Pope's Garden as it was left at his Death', in Serle, plan. Reproduced by kind permission of John Harris.

203 Anon., 'The Plan of the House Garden & Inclosures of Marblehill…', c.1752. Norfolk RO, MC 184/10/1. © Norfolk County Council.

204 Colen Campbell (delin.) and Henry Hulsbergh (sculpt.), 'Plan of the Park, Gardens and Plantations of Caversham', c.1719, in Campbell 1725, plate 97. Photo: the author.

205 Colen Campbell (delin.) and Henry Hulsbergh (sculpt.), 'Wilton in Wiltshire', in Campbell 1725, plate 57-60. Photo: the author.

206 Thomas Badeslade (delin.) and John Harris (sculpt.), 'The West Prospect of Knole', c.1715, in Harris 1719, I, 278. © Kent Library and History Centre.

207 Charles Bridgeman (attrib.), plan for the wilderness at Houghton Hall, c.1717. Bodleian Library, Gough Drawings a4, fo. 57. Photo: the author, reproduced by permission of the Bodleian Library.

208 John Rocque, 'Plan and elevations of South Dalton, 1737, in Badeslade & Rocque, plate 90-1. Photo: the author.

209 Batty Langley, 'a beautiful Garden at Twickenham', in Langley 1728, VI, plate IX. Photo: the author.

210 John Rocque, 'Plan of yᵉ Royal Palace and Gardens of Kensington', 1736. BM P & D, 1881,0312.99. © Trustees of the British Museum.

211 John Rocque, 'Plan of the House Gardens Park and Hermitage of their Majesty's at Richmond', 1736, in Badeslade & Rocque, pl. 9-10. Photo: the author.

212 Henry Fletcher (sculpt.), 'A Hedge cut with Pilasters' and other designs, in James 1728, plate 3ʳᵈ **, after p. 59. Photo: the author, reproduced by courtesy of Peter Goodchild.

213 Henry Fletcher (*sculpt.*), 'The general disposition of a Garden of about four Acres', in James 1728, plate 5th A, after p. 34. Photo: the author, reproduced by courtesy of Peter Goodchild.

214 Sir James Thornhill, 'old Master Charles Bridgeman', *c.*1721. © Bridgeman Art Library, image no: CH 698691.

215 Jacques Rigaud (*delin.*) and Bernard Baron (*sculpt.*), 'View of the Parterre from the Portico', 1734, in Rigaud & Baron, plate 16. BM P & D 1917,1208.1244. © Trustees of the British Museum.

216 Charles Bridgeman (attrib.), bird's-eye view of Stowe House from the south-west, *c.*1723. Bodleian Library, Gough Drawings a4, fo. 46. Photo: the author, reproduced by permission of the Bodleian Library.

217 Charles Bridgeman or Thomas Badeslade (attrib.), Boughton House from the west, *c.*1729. Buccleuch Collection, BH-I-304_B. Reproduced by kind permission of the Duke of Buccleuch & Queensberry KBE.

218 Charles Bridgeman (attrib.), general plan for outward plantations at Rousham House, *c.*1718. Bodleian Library, Gough Drawings a4, fo. 63. Photo: the author, reproduced by permission of the Bodleian Library.

219 Charles Bridgeman (attrib.), general plan for outward plantations at Hackwood House, *c.*1725. Bodleian Library, Gough Drawings a4, fo. 34. Photo: the author, reproduced by permission of the Bodleian Library.

220 Henry Fletcher (*sculpt.*), 'An Amphitheatre at the End of a piece of Water' and other designs, in James 1728, plate 3rd H, after p. 146. Photo: the author, reproduced by courtesy of Peter Goodchild.

221 Charles Bridgeman (attrib.), design for an amphitheatre and circular pool at Claremont, *c.*1724. Soane Museum, Drawer 62.I.2. © 2013 The Trustees of Sir John Soane's Museum.

222 Jacques Rigaud (*delin.*) and Bernard Baron (*sculpt.*), 'View of the Queen's Theatre from the Rotunda', 1734, in Rigaud & Baron, plate 8. BM P&D, 1871,0812.1576. © Trustees of the British Museum.

223 Thomas Badeslade (*delin.*) and William Henry Toms (*sculpt.*), *The West Prospect of Erthig in Denbighshire*, 1740. NLW, Top. C6 C011. © National Library of Wales.

224 Charles Bridgeman (attrib.), general plan for gardens and plantations at Sacombe House, *c.*1715. Bodleian Library, Gough Drawings a4, fo. 64. Photo: the author, reproduced by permission of the Bodleian Library.

225 Edmund Prideaux, 'Raynham South Front', 1725. © and reproduced by kind permission of Elisabeth Prideaux-Brune.

226 Batty Langley, 'a Fruit-Garden, in a more delightful and advantageous manner than has been practised by any', in Langley 1728, part II, plate II, after p. 110. Photo: the author.

227 Colen Campbell (delin.) and Henry Hulsbergh (sculpt.), 'Plan of the Garden and Plantations of Clare Mont', *c.*1717, in Campbell 1725, plate 67-8. Photo: the author.

228 Terrace at Duncombe Park, 2013. By courtesy of Dr Jan Woudstra.

229 Stephen Switzer (*delin.*) and J. Clark (*sculpt.*), 'The Profile of a side Terrass Walk & Fossee', in Switzer 1718, II, plate after p.150. Photo: the author.

230 Thomas Badeslade (*delin.*) and John Harris (*sculpt.*), *Boughton Within Two-Miles of Northampton*, 1732. © and reproduced by kind permission of Simon Scott of Spectacle Lodge, Boughton Park.

231 Batty Langley, 'Design of a small Garden situated in a *Park*', in Langley 1728, part VI, plate XII. Photo: the author.

232 George Bickham, view of Shotover House from the east, 1750. Bodleian Library, Gough Maps 26, fo. 71. Photo: the author, reproduced by permission of the Bodleian Library.

233 Edmund Prideaux, 'Ewston Front next the Garden on the South', *c.*1725. © and reproduced by kind permission of Elisabeth Prideaux-Brune.

234 Thomas Badeslade (*delin.*) and William Henry Toms (*sculpt.*), *The West Prospect of Chirk Castle*, *c.*1735. NLW, PFC 2/M E2 (E6). © the National Library of Wales.

235 Thomas Badeslade (*delin.*) and John Harris (*sculpt.*), 'The North or Garden front of Belton House extending 150 feet', in Badeslade & Rocque, plate 88-9. Photo: the author.

236 John Donowell, print study for Cliveden House, 1750s. BM P&D, 1962,0714.26. © Trustees of the British Museum.

237 Charles Bridgeman (attrib.), 'Down Hall', 1720. Bodleian, Gough Maps 46, fo. 262. Photo: the author, reproduced by permission of the Bodleian Library.

238 Stephen Switzer, 'A Plann of some Groves in Quincunx &c. with two Mazes or Labyrinths', in Switzer 1718, II, 218 & plate 34. Photo: the author.

239 Jacques Rigaud, the grove at Chiswick House, *c.*1733. Chatsworth Photo Library, WC 160. © Devonshire Collection, Chatsworth, and reproduced by permission of Chatsworth Settlement Trustees.

240 Thomas Badeslade (*delin.*) and John Harris (*sculpt.*), *Hammels in the County of Hertford...*, 1722. Herts Archives and Local Studies, CV/BRAU/46. © Hertfordshire County Council.

241 Batty Langley, 'An Improvement of the Labyrinth at Versailles', in Langley 1728, part VI, plate VIII. Photo: the author.

242 Thomas Holmes, survey plan of the estate at Gobions, *c.*1725. Glos Record Office, D/1245.FF75. © Gloucestershire County Council.

243 Colen Campbell (*delin.*) and Henry Hulsbergh (*sculpt.*), 'Plan of the Garden and Plantations of Lowther Hall...', 1717, in Campbell 1725, plate 76. Photo: the author.

244 Charles Bridgeman (attrib.), general plan of Lumley Castle, *c.*1729. Collection of the Earl of Scarbrough, Sandbeck. Also by courtesy of Peter Goodchild.

245 Pieter Andreas Rysbrack, *A View of the Orange Tree Garden*, *c.*1729. Chatsworth Photo Library, PA 335a. © Devonshire Collection, Chatsworth, and reproduced by permission of Chatsworth Settlement Trustees.

246 Bartholomew Rocque, 'A Plan of the Garden, & House...at Weybridge', 1737. Badeslade & Rocque, plate 67-8. Photo: the author.

247 Anon., engraving of 1748 from drawing by John Wootton of Castle Hill, *c.*1733. *The Universal Magazine of Knowledge and Pleasure*, IV (May 1749), before p. 193. © and reproduced by permission of the Bodleian Library.

248 Anon., plan of the gardens at Worksop Manor, 1720s. Arundel Castle archives MS. H2/47. © The Duke of Norfolk.

249 William Stukeley (attrib.), 'The antient manner of Temples in Groves', *c.*1730. Bodleian, Gough Maps 229, fo. 322. Photo: the author, reproduced by permission of the Bodleian Library.

250 Balthasar Nebot, view through the topiary arcades, 1738. Buckinghamshire County Museum collection, AYBCM: 1955.153. (no.?). © and reproduced by permission of the Buckinghamshire County Museum.

251 Adam François Van Der Meulen (*delin.*) and Adriaan Frans Boudewyns (*sculpt.*), 'Veuë du Chasteau de Fontainebleau du costé du Jardin', *c.*1680. BM P&D, 1869,0410.1923. © Trustees of the British Museum.

252 J. Gravelot (*delin.*) and Claude Dubosc (*sculpt.*), *View of the Hermitage in the Royal Garden at Richmond*, *c.*1735. BM P&D, 1876,0708.2441. © Trustees of the British Museum.

253 Trist and Watney Norton, 'Plan of the Heythrop Park Estate', 1870. BL Maps 137 b.1(10). © The British Library Board.

254 Stephen Switzer (*delin.*) and Michael van der Gucht (*sculpt.*), 'The Manor of Paston Divided and Planted into Rural Gardens', in Switzer 1718, II, before 115, & III, 84. Photo: the author.

255 Stephen Switzer (*delin.*) and Michael van der Gucht (*sculpt.*), 'Plan of a Forest or Rural Garden', in Switzer 1718, III, 46-7. Photo: the author.

256 Edward Linnell, estate plan of Farnborough Hall, by 1772, redrawn by Jennifer Meir. Warwickshire Record Office, Z403. Courtesy of Jennifer Meir.

257 Anon., *A General Plan of the Woods, Park and Gardens of Stowe...*, in Rigaud & Baron, title plan. RIBA 38396. © RIBApix.

258 Bernard Lens III, a scene in Bushy Park, *c.*1720. YCBA, B1977.14.5690. © Yale Center for British Art, Paul Mellon Collection.

259 Thomas Robins (*delin.*), *The North East View of* KING ALFRED'S HALL, Cirencester Park, 1763, and engraved by another. BM P & D, 1955,0425.45. © Trustees of the British Museum.

260 Thomas Badeslade (*delin.*) and John Harris (*sculpt.*), *A Prospect of Stainborough and Wentworth Castle*, 1730, in Badeslade & Rocque, plate 55-6. Photo: the author.

261 Stephen Switzer (*delin.*) and J. Clark (*sculpt.*), 'The Plan of a Kitchen Garden on Three Levels with a Canal at the Bottom', in Switzer 1727, chap. LXXVII. Reproduced by kind permission of John Harris.

262 John Rocque, map of Middlesex, 1754. Photo: the author.

263 William Hogarth (*pinxit*), *A Rake's Progress No. 2*, engraved in 1735. BM P&D, 1868,0822.1529. © Trustees of the British Museum.

264 Matthew Brettingham, engraving of Kent's design of about 1733 for the Triumphal Arch at Holkham, 1748. Holkham House. © Viscount Coke & the Trustees of the Holkham Estate.

265 Anon., survey of Gisburn Park, Yorkshire, 1735. © Yorkshire Archaeological Society, MS 918.

266 Sieur Bourguignon, *A General Plan of the Park & Garden at Gisbourn*, 1735. © Yorkshire Archaeological Society, MS 918.

267 Nicholas Hawksmoor (attrib.), general plan for the parkland at Blenheim Palace, *c.*1705. Bodleian Library, MS Top Oxon a.37*, fol. 1. Photo: the author, reproduced by permission of the Bodleian Library.

268 Edward Grantham, survey of the Ditchley House estate, 1726. Oxfordshire History Centre, DIL.I/i/2b. © The Oxfordshire History Centre.

269 Jacques Rigaud (*delin.*) and Bernard Baron (*sculpt.*), *View from the Portico of the House to the Park*, 1734, in Rigaud & Baron, plate 5. BM P&D, 1871,0812.1574. © Trustees of the British Museum.

270 Stephen Switzer, 'View of the New House, Offices and Park at Nostel, Yorkshire, with yᵉ Improvements made and to be made in yᵉ [severall] Plantations in yᵉ Park', *c.*1735. National Trust, image no: 48186. © National Trust Images.

271 Belvedere at Claremont from the bowling green, 2012. © The author.

272 Carrmire Gate and Pyramid Gate at Castle Howard, 2012. © The author.

273 Anon., *Holkham in the County of Norfolk, the seat of the Rᵗ Honᵇˡᵉ Thoˢ Earl of Leicester*, *c.*1754-9. Holkham Estates, M.68. Holkham House. © Viscount Coke & the Trustees of the Holkham Estate.

274 Anthony Walker, *A View of the Banqueting House and Round Temple at Studley*, 1758. BL Map Library K Top XLV.27.3.c. © The British Library Board.

275 Anon., 'Plan of Garrendon', 1777. Photo: the author, reproduced by kind permission of Squire de Lisle.

276 Anon., map of the park at Foremark Hall, c.1738. Derbyshire Record Office, D5054/26/1. © Derbyshire County Council.

277 Batty Langley (*delin.*) and T. Bowles (*sculpt.*), 'An Elegant, Large, Open Large Cabinet, or Lawn, in a Thicket on yᵉ Top of a Hill, with a Temple of View in its Center', in Langley 1728, part VI, plate XVI. Photo: the author.

278 Pieter Andreas Rysbrack, aerial view of Tottenham from the north-west, 1753. By kind permission of the Trustees of the Savernake Estate.

279 James Mynde (*sculpt.*), *A View of the West Front of the Hall at Kelmarsh...*, c.1740. Photo: the author.

280 John Wootton (attrib.), 'Bridgman's Design for Badminton', c.1733. Badminton House. © and reproduced by kind permission of the Duke of Beaufort.

281 Anon., estate survey of Ston Easton, c.1740. Somerset Heritage Centre, DD/HI/A/265. © Somerset Archives and Local Studies Service.

282 Charles Bridgeman (attrib.), general plan for plantations in Lodge Park, c.1729. Bodleian Library, Gough Drawings a4, fo. 68. Photo: the author, reproduced by permission of the Bodleian Library.

283 Peter Fourdrinier (*sculpt.*), *The Geometrical Plan of the Park and Plantations of Rookby, in the County of York*, 1741. BL, King's Maps K.Top.45.26. © The British Library Board.

284 Batty Langley (*delin.*) and T. Bowles (*sculpt.*). 'Part of a Park Exhibiting their Manner of Planting after a more Grand Manner than has been done Before', in Langley 1728, VI, plate XIII. Photo: the author.

285 Thomas Smith (*delin.*) and François Vivares (*sculpt.*), *A South West View of Chatsworth*, 1744. GAC 2324. © Crown copyright: UK Government Art Collection.

286 John Ladd, estate map of Longleat, 1747. Longleat House. © Marquess of Bath.

287 John Rocque, *The Plan of the House Gardens Park & Plantations of* WANSTEAD..., 1735. Essex Record Office, I/Mo 388/1/2A. © Essex County Council.

288 Thomas Brown, *A Plan of the Manor and Parish of Woburn*, 1738. Bedfordshire Record Office, R1/237. By kind permission of the Duke of Bedford, and the Trustees of the Bedford Estates.

289 Isaac Ware, 'Geometrical Plan of the Garden, Park, and Plantation of Houghton, from Plans, Elevations, and Sections...of Houghton in Norfolk', in Ware. Norfolk Record Office, BL/WA/1/11. © Norfolk County Council.

290 William and J. Ballard, *A Map of the Hundreds of Huxlow, Polbrook & Navisford*, 1737. Buccleuch Collection, BH-I-123_C. By kind permission of the Duke of Buccleuch & Queensberry KBE.

291 John Rocque, 'Plan du Jardin & Vue des Maisons de Chiswick...', 1736, in Badeslade & Rocque, plate 82–3. Reproduced by kind permission of John Harris.

292 John Donowell, *A View of the Garden of the Earl of Burlington, at Chiswick; Taken from the Top of the Flight of Steps Leading to yᵉ Grand Gallery in yᵉ back Front*, 1752. MoL, image ID: 415882. © The Museum of London.

293 Anon., 'A Draught of Stamp Brookbanks Esqʳ Gardens at Hackney', c.1735. Bodleian Library, Gough Maps 17, fo. 21B. Photo: the author, reproduced by permission of the Bodleian Library.

294 Anon., *A Plan of Weald Hall in Essex, the seat of Samuel Smith Esqʳ*, 1738. Essex Record Office, D/DTw P1. © Essex County Council.

295 Thomas Reading, *A Map of the Demesne Land...of Powerscourt*, 1740. Irish Architectural Archive, 89/62.

296 Augustine Stoney, 'Crowfield Hall, South Carolina', in Stoney, p.123. Photo: the author.

297 Augustine Stoney, 'Middleton Place, South Carolina', in Stoney, p.177. Photo: the author.

298 Thomas Vivares (*sculpt.*), 'South East View of Wimbourn Sᵗ Giles', c.1760. By courtesy of Suzannah Fleming.

299 Francis Adams Comstock, *Owlpen Manor*, c.1924. Photo: Brooke Roberts Studio, reproduced by kind permission of Sir Nicholas Mander.

General Index

Place names are generally those used at the time for the place in question. County names in the British Isles are added in brackets in the short forms of the historic counties pre-1888.

A

Index of People